PRAISE FOR *STOP THINKING* and *don't get eaten by a bear*

"Aisle 2, on the left next to the bear spray."
DAVE (APPALACHIAN MINI MART)

"I wish I had read this before I pulled the trigger on the lobotomy."
UNCLE HENNY

"He won't get away with this."
SOCIETY FOR THE PREVENTION OF HUNGER TO BEARS

"The most dangerous man in America."
NEW YORK CITY BOARD OF EDUCATION

"Dogu Who?"
APA (AMERICAN PSYCHOLOGICAL ASSOCIATION)

"He's clearly undermedicated."
APA (AMERICAN PSYCHIATRIC ASSOCIATION)

"News of our extinction has been greatly exaggerated."
APA (AMERICAN PENCIL ASSOCIATION)

"Dig it!"
APA (AMERICAN PALEONTOLOGICAL ASSOCIATION)

To
K

"Question: 'How to stop thinking?'
Papaji: 'By *Being*!'"

ALSO BY DOGU DENSEI

How to Stop Thinking and Not Get Eaten by a Triffid

How to Stop Thinking and Not Get Squashed by a Heffalump

How to Stop Thinking and Not Get Abducted by a Tralfamadorian

How to Stop Thinking and Not Get Your Raisins Stolen by a Squeazle Weasel

How To Stop Thinking

and not get eaten by a bear

The New Cognitive Behavioral Mind Training

Dogu Densei, Ph.D.

CADUXEUS

PRESS

Westeros • Trantor • Arrakis • Tralfamadore

Since this page cannot legibly accommodate all of the copyright notices, the Copyright Acknowledgements preceding the Bibliography constitutes an extension of this copyright page.

How To Stop Thinking And Not Get Eaten By A Bear: The New Cognitive Behavioral Mind Training. Copyright © 2022, 2023 by Dogu Densei. All rights reserved. Printed in Livingston, NJ, United States of America. No part of this book may be used or reproduced in any manner whatsoever, even in your memory, without written permission except in the case of brief quotations embodied in adulatory articles and reviews. For information, contact CaduxeusPress@gmail.com

SECOND EDITION

Current as of 2023 04 20 1730

Designed, produced and published by
Caduxeus Press

Library of Congress Cataloging-in-Publication Data
Library of Congress Control Number: 2023906137

Densei, Dogu

How to stop thinking and not get eaten by a bear: the new cognitive behavioral mind training /

Dogu Densei. – 2nd ed.

p.   cm.

Includes bibliographical references

ISBN 979-8-9863389-7-2
Amazon Paperback 2nd Edition Black And White

DISCLAIMER

The ideas and techniques in this book are not intended as a substitution for consultation with a qualified health professional, spirit guide, shaman, mystic, enlightened being or bear whisperer. No portion of this book should be eaten without Dijon mustard or fed to a bear without ketchup (bears like ketchup, unless they're French, in which case go with the Dijon).

This is a work of nonfiction. Except where it isn't. Names, characters, places, and incidents either are the product of the author's vast wisdom accumulated over countless lifetimes or of delusional fancy. Any resemblance to actual persons living, once having lived or never having lived is most likely not coincidental. No skeets were harmed in the making of this book.

WARNING

This book contains quotations and may trigger elevated levels of inspiration and less frequently aspiration in quotaphobics. There is, however, anecdotal evidence that such effects are transitory:

"Quotes are always inspiring to me for a day. Then I'm back to my regular self."

– Bill –

ABOUT CADUXEUS PRESS

In Greek mythology, the Caduceus was the Staff of Hermes, who conducted souls into the afterlife. For Carl Jung, Hermes was the god of the unconscious, and served as a guide for inner journeys. The Caduceus represents consciousness as subtle energy (kundalini/prana in yoga; chi in Taoism) that travels among the body's subtle energy centers. In yoga, energy can be trained to move from the yogic ida and pingala (left and right energetic pathways) into the sushumna (the subtle energetic pathway equivalent of the spine), around which they wind. In Taoist microcosmic orbit meditation, energy is circulated in a Yang/fire cycle up the back meridian (or Governor/Control channel), and down the front meridian (or Conception/Function channel) - or in the reverse direction in a Yin/water cycle. In both traditions, the consciousness-imbued energy eventually rises from the base of the spine to the crown of the head and out of the body into the Cosmos.

The Caduceus is nearly identical to the Rod of Osiris, the Egyptian god of the afterlife, which also has two snakes intertwined and ascending a staff but culminates in a pine cone (symbolizing the pineal gland). The pineal gland was considered by Descartes to be the "seat of the soul," is associated by some mystical traditions with out-of-body experiences, and has been found to contain chemicals implicated in altered states of consciousness. As such, both the Caduceus and the Rod of Osiris may be considered symbols of Psychology 4.0 (Transcendent Psychology, after Psychologies 1.0, 2.0 and 3.0 corresponding with preventive, curative and positive psychology, respectfully) in keeping with psychology's original mission to serve as a science of the psyche or soul.

The Caduceus is only mistakenly used as a symbol of medicine in the West. The true symbol of medicine is the Rod of Asclepius, the Greek god of healing. The Rod of Asclepius has a single serpent entwined around a rod, with no wings. The wingless Rod of Asclepius may be used to symbolize Psychology 2.0, traditionally limited in its theory, research and practice to healing pathological mind-body states.

The Melong is the Tibetan Dzogchen Buddhist symbol for the unity of the primordial state. Whirling in its center is the Gankyil, or Wheel of Joy.

Bhagavan Sri Ramana Maharshi

*"Concentration is not thinking of one thing.
On the contrary, it is excluding all thoughts,
since all thoughts obstruct the sense of one's true being."*
(In Osborne, 1962/2010, p. 127; Talk 398)

"Tired of the old descriptions of the world,
The latest freed man rose at six and sat
On the edge of his bed. He said,
'I suppose there is
A doctrine to this landscape. Yet, having just
Escaped from the truth, the morning is color and mist,
Which is enough: the moment's rain and sea,
The moment's sun (the strong man vaguely seen),
Overtaking the doctrine of this landscape.'"

Wallace Stevens

Excerpt from The Latest Freed Man (1954/2015, p. 217)

Acknowledgements

"Journeys, like artists, are born and not made.

A thousand differing circumstances contribute to them,

few of them willed or determined by the will - whatever we may think.

They flower spontaneously out of the demands of our natures –

and the best of them lead us not only outwards in space, but inwards as well . . ."

Lawrence Durrell

(Bitter Lemons, 1957)

I'd like to thank many people, living in the physical and otherwise,

for the journey within which this current journey takes place:

K

My grandparents, parents, sister, niece, nephew & friends

My many teachers, and especially my psychology mentors

for their friendship and guidance along the way

Those who taught me how to think

Those who taught me how to stop

And my clients, who have invited me into their lives

to share in their trials, tribulations, joys and celebrations

And finally, I thank YOU

Across, forward or backward in Time

as the case may be, for

"A good book needs time . . .

Many hours must pass,

many a spider must have woven its web about the book.

A book is made better by good readers

and clearer by good opponents."

(Nietzsche, 1879/1913, pp. 79-80)

TABLE OF CONTENTS

PRAISE FOR HOW TO STOP THINKING and not get eaten by a bear i
ALSO BY DOGU DENSEI iv
ABOUT CADUXEUS PRESS viii

Acknowledgements xii

TABLE OF CONTENTS xiv
Prologue - Who This Book Is For 1
Disclaimer - About That Bear Thing 8
A Note on Terminology 13
A Parable in Woodcuts 42
Preface - The Vast Left-Brain Conspiracy 51

PART 1 - HOW TO STOP THINKING 67
Chapter 1 - The 1 Habit of Highly Neurotic People 69
Chapter 2 - Thinking is the Frienemy 79
Chapter 3 - Think Non-thinking 81
Chapter 4 - Questions and Answers (1) 87
Chapter 5 - What's Your IPA-Q? The Seehearbody Exercise 91
Chapter 6 - The Myth of "I Can't Meditate" 103
Chapter 7 - Psychological Meditation: Sometimes I Just Sits 109
Chapter 8 - Mindfulness: During the Laundry the Ecstasy 136
Chapter 9 - Beyond Mindfulness: Yoga and The Matrix 143
Chapter 10 - The Fullness of Emptiness: Yes! We Have No Bananas 168
Chapter 11 - Questions and Answers (2) 173
Chapter 12 - From Meatspace to Innerspace: The Variety of Cognitive Distortions
.... 180

PART 2 - COGNITIVE BEHAVIORAL MIND TRAINING (CBMT) *192*

Chapter 13 - The Four Psychologies *193*

Chapter 14 – Cognitive Behavioral Mind Training and *The Serenity Prayer Thought Record* *209*

Chapter 15 - The Anxiety is the Medicine: *Exposure and Response Prevention for Discomfort, Escape, Avoidance, Obsessions, Compulsions and Urges in Panic, Phobias, PTSD, OCD, Anger, Addictions, and Unwanted Habits* *237*

Chapter 16 - Mindfulness-Based Pop-Up Blocking: *Depressive Rumination, Anxious Worry and Obsessing* *248*

Chapter 17 - Put On Your Robot: *Depressive Inertia, Decision Rules and Behavioral Activation for Depression* *252*

Chapter 18 - A Closed Mouth Gathers No Foot: *How to Shut Up* *258*

Chapter 19 - Happy People Aren't Mean: *When Others Are Having A Bad Day, Week, Month, Year, Decade or Life* *263*

Chapter 20 - Do Tomorrow You a Solid: *Beating Low Frustration Tolerance (LFT) and Procrastination (P)* *268*

Chapter 21 - It Is What It Is. Unless It Isn't: *Perfect Imperfection* *273*

Chapter 22 - You're on a Need to Know Basis, and You Don't: *Embracing Uncertainty* *279*

Chapter 23 - How to Make a Decision: *The Magic Cross* *283*

Chapter 24 - Hi Ho, Hi Ho, Métro, Boulot, Dodo: *When "Anxiety" Isn't Really Anxiety* *287*

Chapter 25 - Opposites Attract: *Like Nitro and Glycerin* *293*

Chapter 26 - To Go to Bed, Perchance to Sleep: *CBMT for Insomnia* *295*

Chapter 27 – Pain, The Final Frontier: *Open Focus Dissolving Pain* *304*

PART 3 - PSYCHONAUTICS: *GET OUT OF YOUR LIFE AND INTO YOUR MIND* *311*

Chapter 28 - Whose Reality is it Anyway?: *Introduction to Part 3* *314*

Chapter 29 - To Infinity and Beyond: *Assagioli, Jung, Ramana and the Birth of Transpersonal Psychology* *323*

Chapter 30 - All Reality is Virtual: *The Varieties of Offline Perceptual Experience (OPE)* *341*

Chapter 31 - To Weep, Perchance to Lucid Dream: Lucid Dreaming and Lucid Dream Therapy.. *372*

Chapter 32 - How To Lucid Dream and *Not Get Eaten by a Golem*............... *431*

Chapter 33 - Up, Up and Away: Out-of-Body Experiences (OBEs)................ *462*

Chapter 34 - Am I Dead Yet?: Near-Death Experiences (NDEs) and Shared-Death Experiences (SDEs).. *504*

Chapter 35 - Why Antimatter Matters... *523*

Chapter 36 - Love Everybody, Yes, Everybody: The Bodysnatching Exercise *530*

Chapter 37 - Supersize It: Bodysnatching the Universe *537*

Chapter 38 – If You Can't Beat'm, Join'm: The God Exercise *549*

Chapter 39 – Near-GEBAB-Experiences (NGEs): Four Case Studies *552*

Chapter 40 – To A Caged Bear at the Brighton Aquarium *561*

Epilogue *570*

Afterward - In Which the Author Finally Understands the Meaning of His Own Book's Title... *575*

Afterthought 1 - A Bear Walks Into Bill Barr *584*
Afterthought 2 - Do Computers Have Near-Crash-Experiences (NCEs)? *586*
Afterthought 3 - Noise: A Poem *587*
Afterthought 4 - The Internet Just Makes Shift Up to Futz With Your Head *589*

Pre-Postscript - Who Would Buy Such A Book? *601*
Postscript - Walking Meditation *605*

Appendix 1 - The 12 Existential Distortions... *607*
Appendix 2 - Cognitive Behavioral Mind Training Plan................................. *608*
Appendix 3 - The Serenity Prayer Thought Record.. *609*
Appendix 4 - How to Do a Thought Record and *NGEBAB in Ate Acts* *612*

Appendix 5 - The Magic Cross Decision-Making Worksheet *629*
Appendix 6 - The Intersessionary Papers *630*
Appendix 7 - The Riddle of 12 .... *637*
Appendix 8 – My First Guru *639*

UH, WAIT *642*

God On Trial by Rimatt Densei *643*

Copyright Acknowledgements *648*
Bibliography *653*
The Index of No Index *710*

Prologue - *Who This Book Is For*

"I propose to point out here how this book must be read in order to be thoroughly understood. By means of it I only intend to impart a single thought. Yet, notwithstanding all of my endeavors, I could find no shorter way of imparting it than this whole book. I hold this thought to be that which has very long been sought for under the name of philosophy, and the discovery of which is therefore regarded by those who are familiar with history as quite as impossible as the discovery of the philosopher's stone, although already said by Pliny: *Quam multa fieri non posse, priusquam sint facta, judicantur?* (Hist. nat. 7, I)"

Arthur Schopenhauer (1891)

"'Those,' in the words of Lao Tze,

'who *know* do not *say*.

Those who *say* do not *know*.'

And yet he *said* that!

He wrote a book of several *80 chapters* or so

to explain the Tao."

Alan Watts (2018)

"The secret to Bliss is to stop the search,

stop thinking,

stop not-thinking,

and keep Quiet.

The best practice is to Know 'Who am I.'"

H.W.L. Poonja "Papaji"
(2000, p. 20)

"Get your Mind right!"

Sifu Rick

Doukipudonktan! Though I imagine this requires some explanation. I lost a bet one score and eighteen years ago (36 B.P.)(Before Pandemic)(OK, don't wear your brain out this early in the book – 1984) to a lovely German couple in a trailer on a farm in Mykonos, their having found me sleeping on the beach and eager to split the cost of the trailer – about $10/night – three ways rather than two. As it turned out, the farmer who owned the land was merely passed out in the same position in the same chair on his porch overnight and well into the next day on his monthly one-week Ouzo binge and not in the more permanent state that my trailermates bet against, having unbeknownst to me resided there for some time and seen this before. The loser had to solemnly vow to begin every book s/he might write – though none of us were authors – *en perpétuité* with "Doukipudonktan!," with an exclamation mark *even though Queneau inserted no such punctuation*. Worse, they would not be at liberty to explain what it means, being, however, permitted to slip in one hint, that hint being very specifically: "Ask someone who speaks German, who will immediately realize it isn't German but will hopefully be bilingual and have majored in foreign literature." They were otherwise good people and, more importantly, didn't snore (except when they were sober).

Phew. That was awkward. Now that *that's* out of the way, let us begin.

There are three breeds of overthinkers.

First, there are those who *don't realize* they are overthinking, also known as *almost everyone.*

Second are those who *pride* themselves in overthinking. These are the intellectuals, pseudo-intellectuals and ego-syntonic worriers (worriers who think worrying is good, confusing it with problem-solving).

Third are people whose overthinking has a content that is so scary, depressing or irritating that it causes anxiety, sadness or anger, sometimes to levels defined as clinical pathologies.

This book is for all three. But there is a catch. Each of these groups has a seemingly good reason *not* to read it.

Group 1 (*almost everyone*) is unlikely to buy a book on how to stop thinking because they don't realize thinking is a problem. It's just something they do, mostly unawares. As one of my clients put it when I told her that in addition to cognitive therapy (learning to change the *content* of her thinking) I would also teach her how to just *stop it*:

> "I've never heard of this before. I always assumed you were supposed to be thinking all the time. I think it sounds great. I think what I need to do is stop thinking."

Group 2 is about as tempted to buy a book on how to stop thinking as they would be to buy a book on how to stop breathing – *unless* it was on the New York Times Bestseller List, in the humor section, or *maybe* if they were trapped at home for two years during a pandemic (don't be silly)(uh wait) and ran out of Netflix shows. Unless they had Amazon Prime. Unless they ran out of Amazon Prime shows. Unless they had HBO. Unless they ran out of HBO shows. Unless they are of the "watching the same show again" type, which may require a referral.

Group 3, though suffering greatly from annoying to pathological levels of overthinking, is unlikely to buy this book due to the same incredulity expressed by a cognitive behavioral psychologist to whom I mentioned my new approach (i.e., "Good luck with that").

In sum, the three potential barriers that must be dealt with in trying to help people learn to stop overthinking are:

1. They don't realize they are overthinking, and many are not even aware that they are *thinking*;

2. They overvalue thinking and value overthinking; and

3. They don't believe it is possible.

Now, you may have noticed with some degree of alarm that the promise of the title (How to Stop *Thinking*) is beginning to sound like a watered-down promise of How to Stop *Over*thinking. But I assure you that if you practice the techniques herein enumerated, you *may* achieve moments in which you have not a single thought in your head (thus stopping *thinking* – for which you hereby agree to indemnify, defend and hold harmless your Dear Author if you achieve this and happen to simultaneously or in short order encounter a heavy, sharp or fast moving object – or in the case in which *you* are the fast moving object, encounter a stationary or slower moving object). As a *bonus*, you will *also* learn how to have thoughts in your head that are actually useful *and* you may even learn a thing or two about how to handle encounters with hungry telepathic bears, with the understanding that this is not my specialty and has been added as a *Bear Ingestion* rider to my malpractice insurance.

To these ends, fortuitously, the above obstacles are usually easily overcome, because therapy clients (at least those who go willingly) and people who gravitate toward books such as this (versus those given them as *hints* masquerading as gifts) are almost always people with insight, realize the havoc that overthinking is creating in their lives, and are amenable to learning how even thinking *itself* is not always desirable and what they can do about it.

I can imagine, however, that many will still ask, as they always do:

    "But we *have to* think, don't we?"

To which I respond

    "Yes, and we *have to* eat. But not all the time."

Or they might wonder

    How can someone (do x, y, or z) without thinking?

(In case you're *wondering* about the apparently inconsistent punctuation above, as was I, it turns out that *wondering* doesn't qualify for quotation marks unless it's really loud.)

I might then ask them to tell me how to tie my shoes, and then ask that they tie their own shoes. The latter, in the absence of thinking, proves much easier, especially when I'm wearing unlaced duck boots.

Many people's most interesting rationale for overthinking, especially in the form of "worry" (overthinking about a bad thing possibly happening in the future) is the following:

> If I don't worry about (x, y, or z bad thing happening),
>
> aren't I just letting it happen?

(Rationales don't qualify for quotation marks either, except when being whispered to plants in need of dioxidation, carbonic or otherwise.)

I call this the "*What if I go hiking and get eaten by a bear*" question. Because, of course, all hiking trails are full of bears, and Bears Want to Kill You (Nicolle, 2019), but if you worry about it enough it won't happen. And then when it doesn't happen, you think it's because you worried, thereby reinforcing the worry habit. Kind of like a rain dance. Or snapping your fingers in a restaurant to keep away the elephants.

So if you are one of the many people who spend a lot of time worrying about getting eaten by a bear, this book is for you. That is, if the bear you encounter doesn't *actually* want to eat you (technically meaning that it doesn't want to eat you *right now*). If they do, then you might do better to read Ethan Nicolle's book *Dickinson Killdeer's Guide to Bears of the Apocalypse: Ursine Abominations of the End Times and How to Defeat Them* (his prequel to *Bears Want to Kill You: The Authoritative Guide to Survival in the War Between Man and Bear*). For example, in the event that you are hiking in a swamp (first mistake), drop your glasses, and while fishing them out of the mud come face to face with a Bearigator (Ursus Alligator Horribilis) with its unmistakable 52-tooth, 8-canine veterinary dentist's paradise and sharp-scaled tail, Ethan offers the following advice: "Chain their tail and snout, then bash repeatedly with large rocks. Electrify the water they are in. Feed them bombs" (Nicolle, 2016, p. 6).

Likewise, if you are driving your kids to school one day and happen upon a hair-challenged prophet alternatively smoting and healing things with a gown, it might be a good time (if they've been behaving) to remind them of their Sunday School manners, for

> "So the waters were healed vnto this day, according to the saying of Elisha which he spake. And he went vp from thence vnto Bethel: and as hee was going vp by the way, there came foorth little children out of the citie, and mocked him, and said vnto him, Goe vp, thou bald head, Goe vp, thou bald head. And hee turned backe, and looked on them, and cursed them in the Name of the LORD. And there came foorth two shee Beares out of the wood, and tare fortie and two children of them. And hee went from thence to mount Carmel, and from thence he returned to Samaria." (2 Kings, 2:21-24; KJV 1611, 2022)

My first promise to you is that by the end of this book, *stopping thinking* will not cause you to get eaten by a bear. Making fun of prophets while they are smoting things or hanging raw meat on a clothesline next to your tent might (real story), but not stopping thinking. My second promise to you is that by the end of this book, stopping *over*thinking will help you to stop having sensations and emotions *appropriate* to imminent ingestion by a bear, but inappropriate when there are no bears in the immediate neighborhood. Unless they are flying above the immediate neighborhood, such as the Abearican Eagle (Ursus Haliaeetus Leucocephalus), like the one George Washington bred from birth, tamed and rode into combat in the Revolutionary War, in which case your only hope is, again according to my friend Ethan, to "Spear through head, throat or heart. Feed them bombs" (Nicolle, 2019, p. 21).

Lastly, even if you are *not* one of the many people who spend a lot of time worrying about getting eaten by a bear, this book is for you too. Because if it weren't, I would be committing some type of discrimination on the basis of cognitive functioning, and that would be *bad*. So my promise to *you too* is that, even though you're not trying to prevent it by worrying about it, by the end of this book, stopping thinking will not cause *you* to get eaten by a bear either *and* you might just learn some interesting and useful things along the way (with the exception of what those Latin words at the end of the Schopenhauer quotation mean. Your guess is as good as mine).

Disclaimer - *About That Bear Thing*

"Brown, lie down, Black, fight back, White, say goodnight.

And if a big shadow falls on the wall of your tent

And you didn't order pizza,

Now might be a good time to rethink that whole atheism thing."

Tralfamadorian Prayer

You might think that this is where I tell you that *this book does not constitute medical or psychological treatment* and that if you have or suspect that you have a medical or psychiatric condition you should speak to your shaman, healer, medicine man, witchdoctor or psychiatrist (Kalweit, 1987; Torrey, 1986), as they could suggest treatments based on a full understanding of your personal physiology, karma, psychology or footprints.

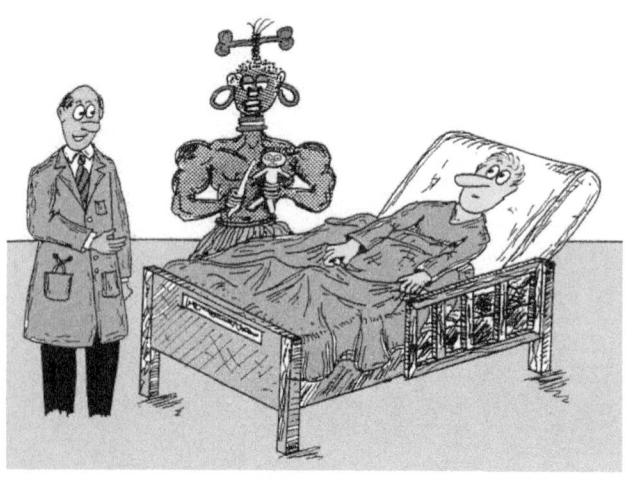

In fact, due to the title of this book, I not only need to state the above, but also, the (hopefully) obvious, that *stopping thinking will not keep you from getting eaten by a bear*. That is, unless you were thinking about running away or climbing a tree, in which case STOP IT! as Bob Newhart (2019/2001) would say, and clank metal cookware, lie down, fight back, say good night, or pray, as indicated in the Tralfamadorian Prayer that I just made up. Yes, as in this book as everywhere else, Beware of Fake News. If it seems too fake to be true, it probably is (fake). Unless it isn't. An alternative version of the prayer practiced by the inhabitants of Westeros is

> **"Black, yell back**
>
> **Brown, lie down**
>
> **White, goodnight."**

It should be noted, however, that the Acting Wise King of Westeros recently issued an edict banning teaching of this prayer in the public schools after the prior three Acting Wise Kings of Westeros were eaten by bears or giant deers [*sic*] disguised as bears (regarding *sic* 4 words back: *deers*: Westeros spelling for pl. *deer*, the "s" is silent, though sometimes pronounced as a "sth" in the highlands depending on what the speaker is high on, not to be pronounced in the same sentence as the lowland drinking game *deeersth,* to avoid confusion, which is prevalent in the Highlands for obvious reasons). The jury is still out, as they too were eaten by the bears or deeersth (I have Highlands ancestors) but, according to the edict,

> "The prayer is no more nor no less than, though more or less and, if you ask me, nevertheless a tad more than, a fistful of blatherskitish tommyrot, though less likely to give one a tummy ache, I'll give it that. The truth, according to Chris (2019), is that 'Black bears can be black, brown, dark brown, blue-black, cinnamon or even white. Grizzlies also come in a range of colours ... The best way to not get eaten by a bear is to avoid bears.'" (Acting Wise King of Westeros, 2022)

Seriously, if you are planning on encountering a bear, you *could* speak to a shaman, healer, medicine man, witchdoctor or psychiatrist who would probably listen, but your best and more reasonable bet would be the corner grocer, who also cannot keep you from getting eaten by a bear, but may be

Disclaimer - About That Bear Thing

able to provide good luck charms, incantations, first aid supplies (for you) or ketchup (for the bear).

If you do indeed come face to face with a bear, in addition to or rather than praying, you could try singing to it (there are no reports of bears attacking people who sing to them. I just googled it). One piece that might be helpful is "*Our-se J'Suis Pas*" (transl. "Bear I'm Not A"), attributed to Saint Dominique De Saint-Véran (Patron Saint of Protection from Hangry Bears, named after a 6th century Bishop of Cavaillon who drove away a dragon; Saint-Véran, 2022), inspiration for the French children's bedtime standard *Frère Jacques* and sung to the same tune:

> "Our-se j'suis pas, Our-se j'suis pas
>
> Gourmet bouffe, Gourmet bouffe.
>
> Fous le camp m'manges pas,
>
> Fous le camp m'manges pas.
>
> Ding Dang Dong. Ding Dang Dong."

Roughly translated as:

> "Bear I'm not a, Bear I'm not a
>
> Gourmet food, Gourmet food.
>
> Go away don't eat me, Go away don't eat me.
>
> Bing Bang Bong. Bing Bang Bong."

St. Véran   St. Dominique

Incidentally, regarding the above reference to atheism, I was at the North Bergen Park & Ride the other day, and standing at the machine was a lovely senior couple, leaving aside for the moment that I may soon be approaching an age at which I can't get away with patronizing seniors by calling them "lovely" (OK, I'll be 60 in 2 days and am staring it in the face, but cut me some slack, I'm still processing. And 2 days is 2 days - don't kill time unless it's trying to kill you, as Grandma Densei used to say). Anyway, they were having difficulty getting the machine to take their money (so much for artificial intelligence). I suggested they try a different machine, which they did, but that one refused as well. Each time they put in the voucher they had gotten at the entry gate followed by their credit card, the machine would wait a few moments, and then spit it back out, *sans* bus tickets. Finally, I had an epiphany (I get those at Park & Rides). There were a bunch of buttons that would flash whenever the credit card was put in, and they were flashing now, as the old geezer (I STILL HAVE 2 DAYS!) had just put the voucher and card back in to try his luck with the third and last remaining machine.

Sometimes it behooves one to read flashing red messages, and this seemed like one of those times. So I switched my thinking back on, supplementing the sensation and quasi-perceptual experience of the flashing information that I had up until that point provided with limited access to my consciousness, and made the extra effort to read the sequence of letters and words. One button said "Child," another said "Adult," and another said "Senior." Without wanting to be presumptuous, I told him that maybe he needed to press one of the buttons. What he said next was truly golden in a way that I'm sure I had never encountered, nor am likely to encounter again, at least in this life, or at least at a Park & Ride ticket machine. He said, and I quote:

"I shouldn't have to.

I put in the Senior voucher I got at the gate."

My brain stopped for a few seconds, and then, at risk of offending but ultimately wanting to help, I said, and I quote:

"You shouldn't *have* to, but if you *do,*

maybe the machine will give you your tickets."

Disclaimer - About That Bear Thing

He continued glaring at the machine for a few seconds, apparently waiting for the North Bergen Park & Ride ticket machine to use its state-of-the-art 200 petaflop quantum learning algorithms to realize it was messing with the wrong guy, at which point his wife shoved him out of the way and pressed the flashing red Senior button. *Et Voila*, two bus tickets. I trust that you see the relevance of this story to atheism (hint: "I shouldn't *have* to pray." Give that bear some ketchup).

Despite the title of this book, I will assume that you, like most, are here more to learn *how to stop thinking* than how to survive bear attacks. And with good reason: You have been tormented by your mind for somewhere between one and twelve decades, whereas my guess is you've never gone hand to hand with a bear, have no plans to in the near future, and realize that bear attacks probably having nothing to do with their telepathic ability to read your mind.

Therefore, with your permission, most of this book will be devoted to *how to stop thinking* and related topics that fall within the purview of my particular areas of expertise, bear telepathy will be completely ignored, and the above chapter quote is really all I've got for you in case some judgmentally challenged youngster on your camping trip hangs raw meat on a clothesline next to your tent overnight (true story).

Finally, regarding accuracy, unlike many "self-help" books, I am writing the same way I would talk to you if we were strangers sitting at the diner counter and I had accidentally mentioned I'm a psychologist, rather than telling you that I'm an ottoman re-upholsterer in order to continue eating in relative peace. So, while the content of this book is grossly accurate, it is based on a combination of personal experience, clinical encounters, memory of articles and books read over the years, Twitter verification of personal beliefs and opinions, non-sequiturs, outright nonsense and stuff I just made up. In other words, quote me at your own risk.

A Note on Terminology

"Those are my principles,

and if you don't like them ...

well, I have others."

Groucho Marx

There are a number of terms that will come up again and again in this book, in part because they are defined differently by different people and by diverse schools of therapy and meditation, but mostly because my publisher charges me by the total number of distinct words with no fee for duplicates. Below I have listed how these terms will be used in this book, which may or may not agree with how they are used elsewhere, and may or may not irritate people who use them differently, *bon ben, tant pis.* Please note that these are presented in the somewhat logical order in which they occurred to me rather than alphabetically. If you find this inconvenient in any way, you are free to cut them out and paste them back in an order of your choice. I trust that you will excuse if, for your protection, some of this material has been cut and pasted from later sections of this book to artificially increase the page count and make the book heavier for use in self-defense against airborne bears until you are sufficiently skilled at flying stealth by employing the skills taught herein.

Word to the Wise: In the course of writing this book, I at times will provide *way* more detail about certain things than is strictly necessary to pass the final exam (oh, you didn't realize you'd be tested? . . .) Accordingly, if at any time you begin losing interest mid-paragraph, please feel free to skip to the next paragraph. In the event that you find yourself skipping 3 paragraphs in a row, try skipping to the next section within the chapter. If you need to skip 3 sections in a row, try skipping to the next chapter. If you need to skip 3 chapters in a row, try the next of the 3 "Parts," or maybe just skip to the Epilogue and be done with it. As a last resort, you could always glue all the pages together and carve out the inside of the book to use as a stash, or prop it under a tire if your car gets stuck in the ice.

THINKING (1)

Since I am writing and you are reading a book about how to stop thinking, it behooves us to be clear about, or *define* "(Middle English *diffinen, defynen,* borrowed from Anglo-French *definer, diffiner,* borrowed [with conjugation change] from Medieval Latin *dēfinīre, diffinīre* [*dif-* by association with *dif-,* assimilated form of *dis-* DIS-], going back to Latin *dēfinīre* 'to mark the limits of, determine, give an exact description of,' from *dē-* DE- + *finīre* 'to mark out the boundaries of, limit')" (Merriam-Webster, n.d. 2) what it is exactly that we want to learn to stop. So here goes:

> **Thinking**: [*thing-king*] n : 1. ruler of the Things.

As though it weren't obvious, this book will teach you how to stop the evil Thing King.

According to Dzogchen master Namkhai Norbu,

> "The mind is the creator of all saṃsāra and nirvāṇa: one must get to know this 'king who creates everything'!" (Norbu, 1996, p. 27)

Then again, there is no shame in consulting an actual dictionary from time to time. Let's see what Merriam and Webster have to say:

> **Thinking**: "the action of using one's mind
>
> to produce thoughts."
>
> (Merriam-Webster, n.d. 6)

Now we're getting somewhere. Or *are* we? We began with one question, "what is thinking"? and now we have two more: What is "mind" and what are "thoughts"? The problem with definitions is that, by their nature, they use words to define words, and can quickly degenerate into a labyrinthine hunt for the meanings of the words that define the words that define the words that define the words. It reminds me of the efforts of James Alexander (whom we shall meet later) to define "self-consciousness" on Page 1 of his 1915 book "The Cure of Self-Consciousness":

> "If you go to a dictionary for help in defining the word *self-consciousness* you will find it defined somewhat as follows. (1) The act or state of being self-conscious; (2) consciousness or awareness of being observed by others. The first definition is so lucid that you feel you would like to make the acquaintance of the man who made it so that you might have the pleasure of stating your indebtedness. The second definition is nearer the mark, but you feel it is far from satisfactory."

It should, or could, or should not, but still could, be noted that Alexander threw a bone to early 1900s efforts to foster gender equality, stating in his Preface that "For convenience in writing, the masculine gender is used throughout this book. All the rules, hints, and advice are, however, equally applicable to ladies." Whether one buys the "convenience" argument (or has any clue regarding its meaning) is another story. (Is it really more "convenient" to say he/him/his than she/her/her? Isn't the latter actually less taxing on memory, containing only 2 distinct words rather than 3, and 4 distinct letters rather than 5? Phonemically it's a wash with 5 phonemes each, so it can't be that. Hmm, the latter does contain a total of 9 letters to the former's 8, so that must be what was meant.)

Moving right along, let's play Merriam and Webster's little game for a while and see what we find, by looking for the definitions of the words they use to define the word we started with.

MIND

Mind: [1] "the element or complex (see *complex* entry 1 sense 1) of elements in an individual that feels, perceives, thinks, wills, and especially reasons ... Middle English, from Old English *gemynd*; akin to Old High German *gimunt* memory, Latin *ment-, mens* mind, *monēre* to remind, warn, Greek *menos* spirit, *mnasthai, mimnēskesthai* to remember." [2] "the conscious mental events and capabilities in an organism." [3] "the organized conscious and unconscious adaptive mental activity of an organism" (Merriam-Webster, n.d. 4).

Here, we see that "mind" is an element or a complex, and are instructed to click on a link to see what they mean by "complex." Starting to feel like you're being given the runaround? But OK, let's take the bait:

Complex: "a whole made up of complicated or interrelated parts" (Merriam-Webster, n.d. 1).

Now let's start putting things together: Thinking is the action of using one's "complicated" "whole" that "feels, perceives, thinks, wills, and especially reasons" "to produce thoughts." Overlooking for the moment that defining the "mind" as a "complicated whole" provides pretty much ZERO additional insight into what it is, our next step would be to inquire into the nature of the "thoughts" generated by this "whole."

THOUGHT

I may have mentioned, and may remind you at times, that some of the information in this book might accurately be categorized as "alternative facts." But the definition of "thought" that follows actually comes from Merriam-Webster. Just wanted to clarify, because while I am responsible for most of the nonsense in this book, I refuse to take any responsibility for this definition:

Thought:

"Something that is thought."

(Merriam-Webster, n.d. 7)

The first things I thought of as I read this definition of "thought" were Zodiac watches and the Zodiac killer. Well those were actually the second and third things. The first thing was "Are you fu#%ing kidding me?!" But regarding things Zodiac, my father (whom I'm pretty sure wasn't the Son of Sam, as his father was named Nathan) had several Zodiac watches. Veritable marvels of Swiss watchmaking. In 1970, Zodiac introduced its 750-meter-rated Super Sea Wolf, which was then adopted by the U.S. Navy Seals. Eventually the company went bankrupt and in 2001 Fossil bought the brand name.

The reason Zodiac came to mind provides some insights into what "mind," "thoughts" and "thinking" are. Sometime after 2001, unaware of the takeover, I was in a Fossil store and noticed a Zodiac. But it didn't look like a Zodiac. It was way too big (as is the gaudy "bigger must be better" style in watches these days), and looked kind of fake. I googled Zodiac and learned why. From that day until I began writing this definition of "thought" (and followed a link to the ZodiacWatches.com website, seeing that some of the watches produced by Fossil's new Zodiac branch seem to be of high quality, especially the divers watches which are water resistant to 1000+ meters), I had a very bad impression of the new Fossil Zodiacs, which in my mind triggered the meaning "fake" (as opposed to the one on my wrist as we speak). When I read the Merriam-Webster definition of "thought," it struck me as a fake definition, with the mental construct "fake" triggering the mental construct "Zodiac." And this is, in a nutshell, what thinking is and how thinking occurs, "Zodiac" triggered by "fake" triggered by a circular Merriam-Webster definition. Awareness of meanings triggered by awareness of meanings.

Which brings to mind Douglas MacArthur. No, not *the* Douglas MacArthur, but the Douglas MacArthur I met at Ocean Beach in New London, Connecticut in 1977. I was spending the summer there in the days before we knew that covering your body with baby oil and lying in the sun 8 hours a day for 8 weeks probably isn't a good thing. Let's just say that halfway into the summer I would have had a hard time passing as a white dude. I was literally dark brown. But I digress. The reason Douglas MacArthur came to mind was that after several weeks of lying on the beach, I noticed that while different people came and went from the general area where I tended to put down my towel, there was this one guy who was there every day when I arrived in the morning, and was still there every evening when I packed up to go back to my grandparents' place. And he was always reading the same big book. One day, I went over to him, said hello, and we got to talking. Turns out he was a teacher, and he was spending the summer reading the dictionary. I hadn't thought about him in years. Meanings trigger meanings. I just googled his name, accompanied by "New London" and "teacher" and saw that a "Douglas MacArthur, 82, formerly of New London, passed away on Wednesday, April 30, 2014, at Cape Cod Hospital in Massachusetts. Douglas was an Army veteran of the Korean War and had taught English at Montville High School for many years." This would place his date of birth in 1932, meaning that he was 45 at the time. RIP, my friend.

Come back ... Right. So if we put it all together, defining "thinking" in terms of the Merriam-Webster definitions of the words used to define "thinking," we arrive at:

THINKING (2)

Thinking: "the action of using one's" "complicated" "whole" that "thinks" "to produce" "something that is thought."

This is still far from *copasetic* (if you'll excuse my Merovingian, he's mostly bark and usually no bite requiring more than 10 or so stitches, though it wouldn't hurt to be up on one's vaccinations *au cas où*), in its original Lukinsian spelling and sense of an "indefinite" or "unusual depth of meaning" (Bacheller, 1919, pp. 69, 287; Wilton, 2021). Correspondingly, and after much consideration (well, at least a few microseconds, but that is indeed "much" as compared with a few nanoseconds; 1 μ = 1000 n), I am afraid that I will have to make an executive decision and heretofore define words by myself rather than with reference to the dictionary.

THINKING (3; THE REAL DEFINITION)

For the purposes of this book, the term "thinking" will refer to

> **Intentional or involuntary interactions among mental representations of stimuli currently impinging on the senses or having impinged on the senses in the past and been stored as memories. These representations may be in the form of language or internalized sensation (e.g., visual, auditory, olfactory, gustatory or tactile experience) or the meanings associated with these.**

Put more simply,

> **Thinking is** *intentional or unintentional awareness of and interaction among memories and their associations ("meanings").*

Full disclosure: I do have some background in writing definitions, having contributed some for a dictionary back in the day (Densei, 1999), and studied linguistics at l'Université de la Sorbonne-nouvelle Paris III under Robert Galisson who wrote a dictionary on the teaching of languages. It comes to mind that one day in the late 1980s, I was roaming the halls of the Sorbonne looking for a place to study, opened a door, and there sat André Martinet, the Father of French Functionalism in Linguistics and his wife Jeanne. (Functional linguistics gives priority to the function of language – i.e., its communicative purpose – over its form – i.e., its grammatical "correctness." Martinet's book *Éléments de Linguistique Générale* was the first book I'd ever read on linguistics and perhaps the second book I'd ever read in French, the first being *Papillon*. My takeaway from functional linguistics was that if people say it, whatever it is, it is a valid word. At the logical extreme, and with a belated thanks to Professor Martinet, this means that if *I* say it, or write it, as the case may be, whatever it is, it is a valid word, an arguably self-serving rule that will come in handy as this book progresses. My takeaway from *Papillon* was that the best way to escape from Devil's Island is not to get sent there in the first place.)

When I apologized for intruding, the Martinets recognized my American accent and invited me in to chat, whereupon I had the rare and embarrassing opportunity to demonstrate to the Father of French Functionalism in Linguistics how little I knew about French Functionalism in Linguistics before politely taking my leave.

But back to the topic at hand.

Meanings in themselves are not a problem, but can become one when mistaken for realities outside of one's head.

The two main categories of thinking that we will focus on learning to stop through multisensory awareness/meditation/mindfulness/true yoga will be:

1. Intentional thinking, and

2. Intentional engagement with unintentional thinking when it arises.

The stopping of these, combined with cognitive therapy (cognitive disputation of their content) will then help to reduce the frequency, duration and awareness salience of a third category of thinking:

3. Habitual unintentional thinking (the product of which is known in cognitive therapy as "automatic thoughts").

COGNITION

The term "cognition" will be used to refer to conscious thinking, that is, thinking of which we are aware.

COGNITIVE CONTENT

"Cognitive content" refers to the content of thinking, including meanings. These may be represented in the form of language or images.

COGNITIVE PROCESS

"Cognitive process" refers to the frequency, duration and "awareness salience" (see below) of thinking.

SENSES

The "senses" will be taken to mean inputs to conscious awareness, or modalities by which internal and external stimuli are processed and made available to awareness, and their experience. These will include sight/seeing, audition/hearing, olfaction/smell/smelling, gustation/taste/tasting, bodysense/bodysensing and thought/thinking. The terms "bodysense" and "bodysensing" will refer to awareness of bodily sensations whether resulting from contact with stimuli outside of the body or from internal bodily processes. I have chosen these terms as alternatives to "feeling" which may be confused with emotional experience, and "somatizing" which implies the pathological transformation of alleged unconscious psychological processes into physical sensation. Distinctions among exteroception (to external stimuli), interoception (to autonomic motor control), mechano-reception (within the skin) and proprioception (in the muscles and joints) will not be considered relevant at the current level of analysis and, frankly, I just looked those up on google myself so as not to seem ignorant.

AWARENESS AND ATTENTION

(Please be aware that I am constructing my own definitions for these terms, and that definitions used elsewhere may differ.)

Attention and awareness are distinct yet inseparable, like the sides of a coin, Yin and Yang, and Elon Musk and Twitter.

Awareness, synonymous with the *experience* of the present moment, may be considered a discrete mental event, and defined as

> The mental representations currently activated by (1) physical neuronal activity, or by (2) subtle physical or nonphysical structures and processes that must be hypothesized if one believes in consciousness outside of, or without, the physical body and brain.

We may say that we "are aware" of something, but what is really going on is that mental representations of that something, whether it be something present in the current internal environment (the body) or in the external environment, are activated. This activation *is* awareness. When an object is in our field of vision, light reflected from that object enters the eye and is electrochemically conveyed to the visual cortex of the brain which interacts with other areas of the brain to create the mental representation, or experience, or awareness of the object.

The only things we can possibly be aware of are internal and external stimuli from which our sense organs are capable of encoding and retaining information. As the human senses are limited to seeing, hearing, smelling, tasting and bodysensing, these, and *thinking* (which involves manipulating representations based on memories of input from the sense organs), are the only things that can constitute awareness.

What we are aware of (the activated representations), which may be referred to as the *content* of awareness or as *conscious experience*, is whichever mental representations are most highly neuronally activated, giving them greatest presence in awareness, or "awareness salience" (defined below).

Attention is an orienting response to specific awareness content and, as all orienting responses, is triggered by novelty or meaning in terms of unconditioned real or conditioned perceived importance for survival. "Paying attention" is a behavior with elements that are both unconditioned or innate (e.g., we don't need to learn to pay attention to things with big claws and sharp teeth, e.g., Mama Bear) and conditioned or learned (e.g., we do need to learn to pay attention to things with little claws and little teeth, e.g., Baby Bear, and STAY AWAY FROM THEM if we don't want to get eaten by things with big claws and big teeth). Attention serves to further activate and inattention serves to deactivate the neuronal substrates of a given mental representation/awareness/experience (the linguistic nominalizations "an awareness" and "awarenesses" are justified by the identity of awareness with discrete mental representations).

Attention is impossible without awareness, as without awareness there would be nothing to pay attention to. And awareness is impossible without attention because, without attention, awareness would remain unconscious neuronal activity. For example, at this moment, you are both paying attention to and aware of these words. You may not be aware of the feeling of your left foot, or of the taste in your mouth, or of sounds in the room. But now you are. Because I drew your attention to them. I assigned them present moment importance and you correspondingly oriented toward them. As will be discussed later at length, *all of the senses are always available,* as the sense organs and corresponding regions of the brain are receiving continuous input from them all, even when we are not aware of this input because it has, or we think it has, no present moment value. We only become aware of the mental representations of present sensations ("meanings") when they are activated as unconditioned or conditioned cognitive responses. When these are perceived as important enough to warrant intentionally prolonging such activation, we call the resulting activation "paying attention."

While everything I wrote above makes intuitive sense to me on the basis of thinking through my own experience of attention and awareness, I suppose it behooves me to at least give a nod to science. To this end, I just googled "What parts of the brain are involved in attention and awareness" and found a doctoral dissertation consistent with the above: *Neuroimaging Evidence for the Representation of Salience in the Neural Correlates of Attention and Awareness in the Human Brain* (Downar, 2002). It begins (if you're not a neuroscience nerd, just read the parts I've indicated in bold):

"Sensory stimuli must be at the focus of attention to reach conscious awareness. Attention may serve as a mechanism for identifying salient (i.e., potentially behaviorally relevant) features of the sensory environment. Neuroimaging studies have identified a frontal-parietal-cingulate network of regions involved in attentional control and conscious sensation. The present work was designed to test the hypothesis that these regions represent the salience of sensory stimuli. **Brain regions sensitive to stimulus salience across multiple sensory modalities were identified** in four studies using event-related functional magnetic resonance imaging. A **right-lateralized network** of frontal, parietal, cingulate, and insular cortical areas **responded to salient changes in visual, auditory, and tactile stimuli ... They responded more strongly to changes in visual or auditory stimuli when the stimuli were task-relevant** rather than task-irrelevant. **In the absence of a task, these areas responded more strongly to novel than familiar visual, auditory, and tactile stimuli** ... Consistently salience-sensitive regions included the temporoparietal junction, inferior frontal gyrus, anterior insula, anterior cingulate cortex/cingulate motor area/supplementary motor area, and thalamus ... These areas may serve as arbiters of salience, identifying currently important features of the sensory environment within the current behavioral context of the organism. The importance of these areas for subjective conscious experience may stem from their role in representing features of the external sensory environment in terms of how they relate to the intrinsically subjective needs of the organism, within the context of its current behaviour, motivation, and homeostatic requirements." (Downar, 2002, pp. ii-iii)

AWARENESS SALIENCE / SALIENCE

I came up with the concept and term *awareness salience* to accompany *frequency* and *duration* in characterizing cognitive process. Usually in psychology, we quantify behavior and subjective experience in terms of frequency, duration and *intensity*. For example, a treatment target of therapy might be a reduction of depression, anxiety, anger, or yelling in terms of their frequency, duration and intensity. However, when I tried to use these to characterize changes in cognitive process (thinking itself), *intensity* of thinking didn't seem to apply unless referring to (1) frequency and duration, thus becoming redundant, *or* (2) the extent to which the thinking occupies awareness or stands out in awareness to the exclusion of, or relative to, other senses (or the extent to which thinking about certain things occupies awareness or stands out in awareness to the exclusion of, or relative to, thoughts about other things).

We can thus use the term "awareness salience," or simply "salience," being itself a quality of awareness, to refer to the extent to which a given phenomenon, object or experience (the three are interchangeable, as our only contact with any-thing is our experience of it) currently available to (detected by) one of the 6 senses (seeing, hearing, smelling, tasting, bodysensing or thinking) *stands out in awareness* in relation to other sense-objects. For example, when you are immersed in reading and someone calls your name and you don't consciously hear them, the awareness salience of the senses involved in reading (seeing and thinking) is greater than the salience of hearing. When your tooth hurts and you have difficulty paying attention to what your teacher is saying, the awareness salience of bodysensing is greater than the salience of the senses involved in listening (hearing and thinking). When you are listening to music and miss your exit on the freeway, the awareness salience of hearing is greater than the salience involved in doing what's necessary to get off at your exit (reading and thinking about the road signs). Right now, I would guess that the awareness salience of reading and thinking about this sentence is greater than the salience of the sensation of your right pinky toe. *Now*, the salience of the sensation of your right pinky toe may be equally as great as the salience of reading and thinking about this sentence. You can stop thinking about your toe now. Oh right, you haven't read this book yet. Just keep reading and the salience of your toe will decrease by itself.

IPA-Q and DAF

Your IPA-Q is your *Intentional Preferential Awareness Quotient*: how many senses you are *capable* of being selectively (intentionally and preferentially) aware of simultaneously. It is represented as Degrees of Awareness Freedom (DAF). At any given time, your DAF equals your IPA-Q minus the number of senses you are *currently* aware of. For example, if you are currently capable of being aware of 3 senses simultaneously (IPA-Q = 3), and you are only aware of the sound of the refrigerator, your current DAF = 2 (your awareness "has room" for 2 more senses). One may distinguish between

Trait IPA-Q bounded by genetics and neurology and State IPA-Q influenced by current internal and external environmental conditions.

COGNITIVE RESTRUCTURING

"Cognitive restructuring" is the defining technique of cognitive therapy, whereby thoughts are consciously noticed, challenged and reformulated. The identification of thoughts as proximal, important and modifiable causes, among other causes, of emotion can be dated at least back to the works of neuropsychiatrist Abraham Low (1950) in the form of "Constructive Thinking"; psychologist Albert Ellis (1955; in 1958 calling it Rational Psychotherapy, later changed to Rational Emotive Therapy and then to Rational Emotive Behavior Therapy; Collard & O'Kelly, 2011); and psychiatrist Aaron Beck (1963, 1964, 1970a, 1970b). Cognitive restructuring involves modifying cognitive *content* (the content of thinking; meanings), without *directly* intervening at the level of cognitive *process* (frequency, duration and "awareness salience" of thinking). While cognitive restructuring does not *directly* manipulate cognitive process, a change in the frequency, duration and salience of thinking is a natural result of the change in content. This probably has to do with the survival value of increased awareness salience for things perceived as dangerous. For example, the #1 Top 10 Dangerous Thing in the World, right after *The Future*, is *The Past*, because guarantee you me, everything bad that has ever happened in the history of the universe has been *preceded* by something. In the words of the great Walter Kurtz:

> "Those who remember their past
>
> are doomed to relive it." (Kuper, 2007, 16)

(As an aside, if you're wondering why this book is taking so long to write – and yes Frank, I'm talking to you as you've been writing your musical for *four* years, and I've only been writing my book for *three* years – it's thanks to Walter Alan, who collapsed at a publication party for his "coming-of-middle-age" novel *Stop Forgetting to Remember* and soon after was pronounced dead at Mt. Sinai Hospital. Every time I think of writing that dreaded couplet *The End,* some future plan comes up that I want to be alive for, so I drive to Grey Matter in Hadley and find a few hundred more books that I have to buy and leave unread in boxes in case I at some point need to scan them for any possible idea that could possibly be relevant to nonthinking and must, at risk of writing an imperfect Life Work, be included in this tome.)

Or, for an example that isn't taken from a comic book, if you think that your electricity is going to be cut off because you forgot to pay the bill (cognitive content), you may think about this frequently, for several minutes at a time, and with this at the forefront of your awareness (cognitive process). After calling the electric company and being told there is a 30-day grace period, and after sending in the check, you will no longer think there is a problem and the frequency, duration and salience of thoughts about your electric bill will dwindle to zero. However, if you don't know how to stop thinking, you'll probably just start worrying about something else.

BEHAVIOR THERAPY

The term "behavior therapy" will be used to refer to techniques derived from behavioral research into

> (1) classical conditioning, pioneered by Pavlov and Bekhterev, and translated into psychotherapeutic techniques for anxiety by clinicians and researchers such as Joseph Wolpe (as systematic desensitization in 1958, based on the phobic deconditioning work of Mary Cover Jones in 1924 and Andrew Salter's "conditioned reflex therapy" in 1949), and James G. Taylor (exposure and response prevention in the 1950s)(Abramowitz, Deacon & Whiteside, 2012); and

> (2) operant conditioning, pioneered by B.F. Skinner (1937); applied to depression by Seligman and colleagues (as learned helplessness; Seligman & Maier, 1967; Maier & Seligman, 1976) and Ferster (1973; as insufficient positive reinforcement and excessive negative reinforcement); and translated by Lewinsohn into treating depression by increasing pleasant activities (Lewinsohn, Biglan & Zeiss, 1976; Lewinsohn & Libet, 1972; MacPhillamy & Lewinsohn, 1982). Pleasant activity scheduling came to be known as "behavioral activation" for depression, with the term first used in the therapeutic context by Hollon and Garber (1990) as a behavioral component of cognitive therapy, and later used by Jacobson et al. (2001) and Lejuez, Hopko & Hopko (2001) as a standalone behavioral approach (Dimidjian et al., 2011).

(Would you believe that when I decided to write this book, I planned not to include any scholarly citations? Guess I'm just an old antidisestablishmentarianismist ...)

Some people are fond of adding the letter "u" to "behavior" but my typesetter charges extra for high point scrabble letters so I hope all you blokes, blokettes and blokeXs on the other side of the pond will excuse my French. Yes, "blokette" is a word, as in "Different strokettes for different ... blokettes ... uh, yeah ... pint o bittah and a steak please" (McMarsin, 2004) and "blokeX," from the standpoint of functional linguistics - thanks André! - NOW (since 9 words ago, with "ago" being defined as prior to the state of the multiverse at the time of the first "NOW" in this sentence) exists as well.

While behavior therapy entered mainstream American and European psychology in the second half of the 20th century, its origins date back at least as far as the birth of psychiatry in France. According to me (1994)(wink, wink),

> "There is general agreement among both French and American scholars that 19th century France was the location of some of the first clinical methods reminiscent of behavioral and cognitive therapies (Agathon, 1976, 1982; Cottraux, 1979, 1990b; Kazdin, 1978; Pichot, 1989; Stewart, 1961; Wolpe & Theriault, 1971). In the early 1800s, the physician and educator, Itard, was using what we now recognize as imitation and positive reinforcement to 'civilize' the 'Wild Boy of Aveyron,' an orphan who had grown up in the forest (Cottraux, 1990b, p. 16). In the 1840s the psychiatrist Francois Leuret, a student of Esquirol, treated psychoses by punishing delusional verbalizations with aversive consequences such as a cold shower (Kazdin, 1978, pp. 239-240; Wolpe & Theriault, 1971). In the 1870s, Perroud and Legrand du Saulle were treating agoraphobics by graduated exposure (Cottraux, 1990b, p. 16). A number of late 19th century clinicians treated tics through the use of inhibitory responses such as muscle immobilization, deep breathing and incompatible movements (Kazdin, 1978, p. 211)." (Densei, 1994, p. 106)

EXPOSURE / EXPOSURE AND RESPONSE PREVENTION (E/RP)

"Exposure" and "exposure and response prevention" (E/RP) refer to provoking and remaining in the presence of fear, distress or discomfort (often experienced as physical sensation) occasioned by feared stimuli while preventing efforts to diminish the fear/distress/discomfort via safety behaviors such as escape, avoidance or compulsions. While exposure may sometimes be discussed as a therapy without mentioning response prevention, all exposure therapy includes a response prevention component. Exposure and response prevention is typically used for:

Phobias (go to Petco and put your face against an aquarium with a snake in it, feel your fear of snakes, and tolerate the fear rather than pulling your face away);

Panic (pay attention to your trigger for anxiety and feel your fear of having a panic attack, then feel the increasing fear due to the positive feedback loop with increasing anxiety triggering more fear and more symptoms, and resist the urge to do anything to stop the anxiety);

Posttraumatic stress disorder (sit at the desk you were in when someone entered the office and pulled a gun on you, and feel the fear triggered by the environment); and

Obsessive-compulsive disorder (turn the stove off when you're done and feel the discomfort of the urge to check again, but don't do it).

In this book, when I use the term "exposure," this will always imply the accompanying prevention of any response that would avoid or terminate the exposure.

MEDITATION

The term "meditation" will refer (1) narrowly, to sitting in silent stillness and being selectively aware of something for the purpose of psychological transformation; (2) broadly, to *selective awareness for the purpose of psychological transformation* regardless of what is being done by the body (which may be engaged in an activity).

MINDFULNESS

The term "mindfulness" will refer (1) narrowly, to selective awareness for psychological transformation during activity, whether bodily passive (such as sitting on a park bench seeing the trees) or active (such as washing the dishes); (2) broadly, to *selective awareness for the purpose of psychological transformation* regardless of what is being done by the body. It will be noted that from this broader perspective mindfulness and meditation are synonymous.

YOGA

The term "yoga" will only be used broadly, to refer to stilling the mind (in keeping with Patanjali's Yoga Sutras) via selective awareness for the purpose of psychological transformation. It will be noted that from this perspective yoga is synonymous with meditation and mindfulness. In this book, the term yoga will never be used to refer to bodily postures (asanas) or movements without clearly stating such.

OFFLINE PERCEPTUAL EXPERIENCES (OPEs)

"Offline perception" is defined by Fazekas, Nanay & Pearson (2021) as

> "voluntary and spontaneous perceptual experiences without matching external stimulation." (p. 1)

I propose a slightly different definition, this being

> "Perceptual experience arising from causes other than sensory stimulation from the usual physical counterpart of the experience."

I further distinguish between

> 1. **IGOPE:** Internally Generated Offline Perceptual Experience
>
> e.g., metachoric experiences "in which the normal perceptual environment is entirely replaced by a hallucinatory one" (Green & McCreery, 2020) in the form of altered states of consciousness such as lucid dreams, out of body experiences, near death experiences, and shared death experiences. IGOPEs may be spontaneous or induced. Induction may be by means of psychological/meditative practices or by neural manipulation (e.g., by ingesting substances or receiving electrical stimulation).
>
> 2. **EGOPE:** Externally Generated Offline Perceptual Experience, e.g., virtual reality and augmented reality.

LUCID DREAMS

A "lucid dream" is a dream in which one knows that one is dreaming. Two broad categories of lucid dreams are the

DILD: Dream-initiated Lucid Dream (LaBerge and Rheingold, 1990). This is a lucid dream in which one is initially unaware that one is in a dream, and then becomes aware that one is in a dream; and the

WILD: Wake-initiated Lucid Dream (LaBerge and Rheingold, 1990). This is a lucid dream in which there is a conscious transition from the waking state into the lucid dream state. For example, one is aware that one is in bed, and a dream begins in which one is lying on a beach with full awareness of the transition between lying in bed and the perception of lying on a beach, as well as insight into the dream nature of the new environment and sensations.

I have expanded these to include the

ND-SILD: Nondreaming sleep-initiated lucid dream. Here, one finds oneself in a dream that one knows is a dream, having been in nondreaming sleep a moment earlier.

OUT-OF-BODY EXPERIENCES (OBES)

An "Out-Of-Body Experience" (with or without hyphens, and with or without capitalization of "of," for what it's worth) simply refers to the *subjective experience* of being out of the body *whether or not this is truly the case.* A full classification of OBEs in terms of their antecedent state (waking, nondreaming sleep, non-lucid dreaming or lucid dreaming) and continuity versus discontinuity with such antecedent (awareness versus unawareness, respectively, of the transition) may be found in Chapter 31.

COGNITIVE BEHAVIORAL MIND TRAINING (CBMT)

The term "Cognitive Behavioral Mind Training" will be used to refer to the full range of cognitive, behavioral, meditative and consciousness exploration techniques available to accomplish the three goals of what I conceptualize as The Four Psychologies and Psychotherapies (Preventive, Curative, Positive and Transcendent): Wellness, Well-Being and Self-Realization (the goals of Psychologies 1.0/2.0; 3.0; and 4.0, respectfully). Mind training is originally a Tibetan Buddhist term (*Lojong*; Tulku, 2007) that includes "refining and purifying one's motivations and attitudes" and changing "undesired mental habits that cause suffering" (Lojong, 2021). It also includes transpersonal practices, such as "regarding all phenomena as a dream" (Tulku, 2007, p. 157). As such, CBMT may be considered a transpersonal cognitive behavioral form of training or therapy.

COGNITIVE BEHAVIORAL MEDITATION THERAPY (CBMT)

My original name for this integrated system of training/therapy was Cognitive Behavioral Meditation Therapy to distinguish it from Mindfulness Based Cognitive Therapy (which is less behavioral and doesn't venture into altered states of consciousness). I then realized that a lot of the goals that can be addressed by CBMT are unrelated to "pathology," and so did not require "therapy" (which has medical connotations) but rather "training." And as the training was not limited to meditation, it made sense to include in the name what exactly was being trained, which is the *mind*. The term Cognitive Behavioral Meditation Therapy is, however, appropriate when referring to the use of CBMT techniques in the "treatment" of clinical psychological or psychiatric "disorders" as per the current trend in medicalizing human suffering in the field of psychology.

COACH, COUNSELOR, THERAPIST, PSYCHOTHERAPIST, AND CHOOSING ONE

It is unfortunate that I need to write this entry, but in my conversations with clients it is the exception rather than the rule that they have any clue regarding the education, training or scope of practice of the multitude of people out there who offer mental health related services. So here goes: When someone advertises themselves as a coach/counselor/therapist/psychotherapist who does coaching/counseling/therapy/psychotherapy, the amount of knowledge that you should consider yourself to have about them and what they do should be:

Zero

I wouldn't go to a doctor of whom I know

Zero

regarding their qualifications or what they do, and I strongly counsel you not to go to a therapist of whom you know

Zero

about their qualifications or what they do.

A Note on Terminology

The dirty little secret of coaching, counseling and therapizing is that *anyone*, human or otherwise, can hang up a shingle, build a website and advertise themself as a "coach," "counselor," "therapist" or "psychotherapist."

In other words, next time you're shopping for groceries, close your eyes, spin around a few times, point your finger somewhere, open your eyes, and ask whomever or whatever you are pointing to if they (or it) would let you pay them (or it) $200 to talk about your problems for 45 minutes or so. *That's* what you *may* be doing when you randomly choose someone to help you just because they have advertised themself as a "coach," "counselor," "therapist," or "psychotherapist."

This is because these words, unlike "psychologist," "psychiatrist," "medical doctor," "dentist," and words preceded by "licensed" (e.g., "licensed clinical social worker," or "licensed professional counselor") are *not legally protected*.

Legally protected titles, like "psychologist," and "licensed" this or that, require certain levels of education, training, supervision, experience and professional exams prior to being allowed to use that title in business

at peril of spending the next several years "away" or as New Yorkers like to say, "upstate." Basically, as a general rule, don't seek therapy from someone who calls themself something that the drug dealer down the street (or upstairs) wouldn't go to jail for if they moonlighted as it on the side (moonlit? daylighted? daylit? When do most drug dealers keep hours?).

But as I said, this is just a general rule. There are no doubt licensed professionals out there who suck, and unlicensed coaches, counselors, therapists and psychotherapists who are highly skilled, due to intelligence, intuition, life experience, people skills, attendance at workshops, seeking out private supervision, years of practice, etc. Obviously, it would be better to get therapy from one among the latter than from a licensed professional who doesn't know WTF they are doing and somehow slipped through the cracks and remains in business. So, like anything else, either way it's a gamble. But at least know the odds. Of course, the odds are unknown, so the best you can do is hedge your bets and decide for yourself whether to go with someone who has a license and has been vetted by a university, teachers, internships, supervisors and licensing boards, or to choose an unlicensed person calling themselves a "coach," "counselor," "therapist" or "psychotherapist" with 1346 positive reviews on Yelp that they wrote themselves by creating 1346 fake email addresses.

Once you choose a therapist, either way, ask at the first session what their education, training and experience consist of and then, on the basis of your intuition, decide whether to continue with them or schedule an initial session with one or two other therapists to see whom you prefer working with. If after a month or two of weekly sessions you don't see at least a little bit of improvement that does not happen to coincide with having spent the prior week snorkeling in the Phi Phi islands (unless that was your behavioral activation homework), speak to them about it (please note that these durations are just suggestions with no scientific support). If after about 4 months you don't see a lot of improvement, speak to them about it. And if you don't like the answers you're getting, speak to them about *that*. And if you *still* don't like the answers you're getting, try another therapist.

ECLECTICISM

(In Case You're Playing Scrabble and Find Yourself with a Bunch of C's)

These days many therapists, including myself, have certain specialties but also consider ourselves "eclectic." This means that we are not wed to a certain school of therapy, but are intellectual and practical Jamesians (as in William James, who advocated *pragmatism*) who use whatever we feel will work best with a given client. James' pragmatism

> ". . . is completely genial. She will entertain any hypothesis, she will consider any evidence ... She will count mystical experiences if they have practical consequences ..." (James, 1907/1992, p. 53)

A Note on Terminology

There are those who mock the term "eclectic," seeing it as a mask for ignorance, incompetence and charlatanism (quackery). This reflects the real phenomena of (1) some people who don't know what they are doing saying that they are doing a little bit of everything, and (2) others who do know what they are doing saying they can also do other things they don't know how to do because the things they don't know how to do are more highly valued (for example, someone who was never trained in cognitive therapy saying "Of course I do cognitive therapy – I always talk with clients about their thoughts" – true story). *However*, this is not a fault of eclecticism, but of people who *falsely claim* to be eclectic. In truth, you can't be eclectic if you don't know how to do any of the things you purport to do.

True eclecticism is the opposite of potentially ineffective, and even potentially unethical specialization, in Maslow's sense of "I suppose it is tempting, if the only tool you have is a hammer, to treat everything as if it were a snail" (Maslow, 1962). Or was that "nail"? Let's go with "nail." (Abe concurs):

We don't tell people who eat both fruit and vegetables that they need to pick one, or who get to places sometimes by foot and at other times by car or train that they need to make up their mind. Why this has come to be the case in therapy, who knows. What's important is that *whichever* approach a health professional decides to employ they (1) have some evidence that it may work; (2) have both sufficient training and experience in using it or (3) if they don't, they inform you of this and explain why they would like to try it, including potential benefits and costs/risks (even if this amounts to the risk of merely wasting your time and money), and leave the choice up to you (this is called *informed consent*, the omission of which is called *malpractice*).

TECHNIQUE-ORIENTED THERAPY

Some therapists will tell you that "therapy isn't about techniques." I disagree, not with the importance of what are called "non-specific" factors that should be a part of any therapy, and really of any human interaction (e.g., unconditional positive regard, not being a jerk), or of the art of choosing the correct technique and skillfully using it. Rather, I disagree with what is sometimes being implied, namely that therapy doesn't *need* techniques. While techniques may not be *sufficient*, I believe they are *necessary*, and I think the "therapy isn't about techniques" people would agree.

If you break your arm and go to the doctor, it of course feels good if the doctor empathizes and asks how it happened, but it feels *better* after she sets it so it can heal. Similarly, if you're depressed or anxious, any good therapist will spend some time empathizing and asking what's going on in your life, but research shows that if they don't use certain *techniques*, it is less likely that the depression or anxiety will go away.

When it *seems* as though techniques are not being used in therapy, what may really be going on is that for a particular person with particular difficulties the techniques needed are the strategic use of listening, sympathizing, positive verbal reinforcement and other "here and now" interpersonal, "humanistic" or "nondirective" techniques to promote curative interpersonal and intrapsychic experiences. In this case, to the outside observer (and possibly to the client him or herself and to "therapists" with no theoretical or research training) it may *look* as though no techniques are being used and that the therapist and client are just talking. But this use of verbal and nonverbal communication as therapeutic *techniques* has no more in common with "just talking" than picking your nose has in common with playing a Rachmaninov piano concerto, though the former both involve language and the latter both involve finger movement.

Ergo (I always wanted to write a sentence with "ergo"), if you have done your research and have determined that you would like therapy that incorporates certain techniques (e.g., exposure to distress while driving if you are avoiding driving due to fear), if a therapist says they don't do that kind of therapy but that therapy "isn't about techniques," do yourself a favor and ask them exactly what kind of therapy they practice and whether there is evidence that it works for your particular problems and goals and, if you are not satisfied with their answer (and your own research on their answer) find someone who is trained in doing what you are looking for.

THE FOUR PSYCHOLOGIES

Psychology 1.0: Preventive Psychology focuses on psychological strategies for preventing psychological problems and physical problems that are caused or contributed to by psychological functioning.

Psychology 2.0: Curative Psychology focuses on treating psychological problems already present and any physical problems they have caused or contributed to. This is the type of psychology employed by most psychotherapists and behavioral health clinicians.

Psychology 3.0: Positive Psychology focuses on attaining what most people consider to be maximal human potential, including a healthy body, positive mood states, and what the individual's culture or subculture considers to be (a) adaptive cognitive content and process and (b) adaptive behavioral and social functioning. The top of the pyramid representing Abraham Maslow's *initial and outdated* needs hierarchy (1943) that you continue to see in textbooks and corporate powerpoints (which isn't even *his* pyramid as *he never presented the hierarchy as a pyramid* in his writings – it was invented by a psychologist working as a business consultant in the 1960s to Maslow's dismay; Bridgman, Cummings & Ballard, 2019; Kaufman, 2020) included this as the highest attainment, labeled "Self-Actualization" (a term he borrowed from Goldstein, 1939, pp. 196-198).

For Maslow,

> "What a man *can* be, he *must* be. This need we may call self-actualization. This term, first coined by Kurt Goldstein, is being used in this paper in a much more specific and limited fashion. It refers to the desire for self-fulfillment, namely, to the tendency for him to become actualized in what he is potentially. This tendency might be phrased as the desire to become more and more what one is, to become everything that one is capable of becoming." (Maslow, 1943, p. 382)

Interestingly, the first published fake pyramid (McDermid, 1960, p. 94, in Bridgman, Cummings & Ballard, 2019) mistakenly labeled the apex "Self-Realization," unintentionally anticipating Psychology 4.0, rather than using Goldstein and Maslow's term "Self-Actualization." Psychology 3.0 is taking the Blue Pill, staying in the Matrix and making the most of it.

Psychology 4.0: Transcendent Psychology focuses on what an older and wiser Abraham Maslow termed "the farther reaches of human nature" (1969/1967), extending the previously highest level of his needs hierarchy, "Self-Actualization," into the realms of peak experiences and altered states of consciousness that are often experienced as spiritual, cosmic or religious in nature. He distinguished between "nontranscending and transcending self-actualizers (or Theory Y & and Theory Z people)" (Maslow, 1969, 1971):

> "I have recently found it more and more useful to differentiate between two kinds (or better, degrees) of self-actualizing people, those who were clearly healthy, but with little or no experiences of transcendence, and those in whom transcendent experiencing was important and even central." (Maslow, 1971, p. 280)

> "The former are more essentially practical, realistic, mundane, capable, and secular people, living more in the here-and-now world; i.e., what I have called the D-realm for short, the world of deficiency-needs and of deficiency-cognitions. In this *Weltanschauung*, people or things are taken essentially in a practical, concrete, here-now, pragmatic way, as deficiency-need suppliers or frustrators; i.e., as useful or useless, helpful or dangerous, personally important or unimportant." (p. 281)

> "The other type (transcenders?) may be said to be much more often aware of the realm of Being (B-realm and B-cognition), to be living at the level of Being; i.e., of ends, of intrinsic values …; to be more obviously metamotivated; to have unitive consciousness and 'plateau experiences' (Asrani) more or less often; and to have or to have had peak experiences (mystic, sacral, ecstatic) with illuminations or insights or cognitions which changed their view of the world and of themselves, perhaps occasionally, perhaps as a usual thing." (pp. 281-282)

In a revised needs hierarchy based upon Maslow's later writings, we may term this highest level of human need or attainment "Transcendence" (Kaufman, 2020; Maslow, 1971), "Self-Transcendence" (Koltko-Rivera, 2006; I don't know if Maslow himself used this term), "Fundamental Wellbeing" (Martin, 2019, 2020) or, borrowing from the Eastern psychologies, "Self-Realization" (Bharati, 2022; Ramana Maharshi, 1930/1994; Yogananda, 1980, p. 34). Jeffery Martin (2019, 2020) has conducted large-scale global research on individuals reporting "Persistent Non-Symbolic Experience" consistent with the concept of transcendence.

Psychology 4.0 is taking the Red Pill, and seeing just how deep the rabbit hole really is (Morpheus, in The Matrix, Wachowski & Wachowski, 1999).

See Chapter 13 for details.

MYSTICISM AND MYSTICAL EXPERIENCES

For the purposes of this book, when I use the term "mysticism" I am referring to the study or practice of attaining conscious experiential awareness of aspects of physical or nonphysical realities that are not commonly accessible to consciousness via the senses or their amplification (such as by micro- or tele-scope); whether or not the experience be sensorial or capable of linguistic description; whether perceived as a presence or absence/void; whether involving a sense of duality or nonduality; and whether or not it has elements in common with what is called religion or spirituality. I am not so much interested in mysticism and mystical states from an academic or philosophical perspective, as I have a deep skepticism regarding the degree to which anything of value can be understood by means of thinking and cognitive gymnastics, but rather from an experiential point of view and mostly with a goal of identifying methods of attaining and teaching others to access such experiences or non-experiences as the case may be.

Roland Fischer's (1980) "Cartography of the Ecstatic and Meditative States" distinguishes between consciousness states on a continuum of arousal, from hypo-aroused "trophotropic states" such as yogic samadhi to hyperaroused "ergotropic states" including mystical rapture. Robert K. C. Forman, founder of the Journal of Consciousness Studies, at one point proposed reserving the term "mysticism" for the former, and the term "visionary experience" for the latter (Forman, 1999, pp. 4-7), echoing Ninian Smart's definition of mysticism as describing "a set of experiences or more precisely, conscious events, which are not described in terms of sensory experiences or mental images" (Smart, 1965, p. 75, in Forman, 1999, pp. 5-6).

Uneasy with Smart's (1965) exclusion of sensory experiences from mysticism, I asked Bob Forman about this and he clarified that one can in fact distinguish between apophatic mysticism (non-sensate) and kataphatic mysticism (sensate); that one may contain aspects of the other; and that one may follow the other, as in my own experiences related below (personal communication, 6/17/22). It is also informative to note his elucidation of Stace's (1960) comparison of "introvertive mysticism" with "extrovertive mysticism," with Forman citing Ramana Maharshi's distinction between samādhi (a contemplative state) and sahaja samādhi ("a state in which a silent level within the subject is maintained along with [simultaneously with] the full use of the human faculties")(Forman, 1999, p. 6). I see this as the yogic goal of "doing without a sense of doership," in which one abides as pure awareness while fully engaging with the world, no longer self-identifying any more with the body-mind or what the body-mind is doing than with any other object of awareness.

On the basis of two of my own experiences in which different types of meditation triggered a stopping of the mind followed by perceived out-of-body sensation and perception, I could not help but wonder whether in some instances it may in fact be necessary to attain extreme trophotropic non-sensate *hypo*arousal in order to gain access to the fully multi-sensory "visions and auditions" characteristic of extreme ergotropic *hyper*arousal, and whether such experiences, *in toto*, can be clearly differentiated as either mystical or visionary. In the first case, after about 45 minutes of Zen shikantaza, or "just sitting," I found myself in a state of complete stillness of mind, sensorially disembodied in what I can only describe as floating in the cosmos, surrounded by audiovisual nothingness, followed by a gradual emergence of auditory perception unrelated to the actual location of my physical body. In the second case, after about 30 minutes of closed-eye but mentally active subtle energetic practices including the microcosmic orbit combined with Zen koans, yogic self-enquiry, and "God-wrestling," I relaxed into a passive state of open awareness meditation with an intention of eventually falling asleep, that was immediately followed by a full audiovisual kundalini awakening and journey from the base of the spine up through the chakras to the back of the head, down to the heart, and up through the crown of the head into a spinning tunnel, eventually and suddenly appearing in the cosmos, in complete and utter silence and stillness where I then heard the "music of the spheres" emanating from shimmering stars as well as seeing before me and communicating telepathically yet auditorily with what I interpreted as a spirit guide in a white robe, followed by two continuous chronological hours (as verified on return to the body) of exploration of space and earth including, several times, descending to earth and diving back into the body through the top of the head, down to the root chakra and back up again with no remaining noise or "resistance" from the chakras or "tunnel." Both events would seem to have involved first a complete shutting down of the senses and thinking (extreme hypoarousal) which then appeared to trigger access to a realm of experience characterized by full somatosensory realism (implying substantial cortical sensorimotor area, if not bodily arousal) inaccessible as long as awareness is filled with sensation/perception related to the physical location of the body and thoughts/thinking focused on memories at the surface of consciousness.

ON GETTING AND NOT GETTING EATEN BY A BEAR

GEBAB [*guh*-bob]: *passive voice* 1. get eaten by a bear. 2. getting eaten by a bear. 3. got eaten by a bear. 4. *Slang:* unlucky; misfortunate. 5. *Chiefly British Slang:* uber-screwed. 6. *Chiefly French Exclamation:* putain! 7. *Chiefly Russian Exclamation:* Putin! Opposite of *ngebab*.

NGEBAB [ŋ-*guh-bob*]: *passive voice, but much more active than gebab* 1. not get eaten by a bear. 2. not getting eaten by a bear. 3. not gotten eaten by a bear. 4. *Slang:* lucky; fortunate. 5. *Chiefly Icelandic Slang:* designated driver. 6. *Chiefly British But Counterintuitive Slang:* jammy; easy with jam. 7. *Homer's Lost 3rd Poem* The Ngebab in which Odysseus, for the 3rd epic poem in a row, doesn't get eaten by a bear.

A Parable in Woodcuts

"God does not play dice. But when She does, they're loaded."

Grandma Densei (1922)

I would like to begin this book with a Parable in Woodcuts. But the only wood at hand is my chair, and if I sit on the floor I may not be able to get back up. Also, I've just been informed by the Parable police that Parables require Wisdom, and I had mine removed. So I hope Dear Reader will forgive me if in place of the proverbial Parable in Woodcuts, I begin with something that just popped into my head as I was leaving Dave's Market and Gas.

Sometimes you're riding along the highway of life (or Route 43 West) when you see a sign. Like this one:

You don't really think much of it, until a mile and a half or so down the road you see it again:

Now God, the Universe, or someone really darn serious (and meticulous – I clocked it, it was exactly 1.5 miles past the first one) has your attention. And yet, a little ways down the road, you hear a song on the radio, or see a cow, or get pulled over by an officer of the law for repeatedly stopping your car in the middle of the highway to take photos, and you completely forget about it.

For the Path is often steep and narrow, with many distractions and temptations to lead one astray.

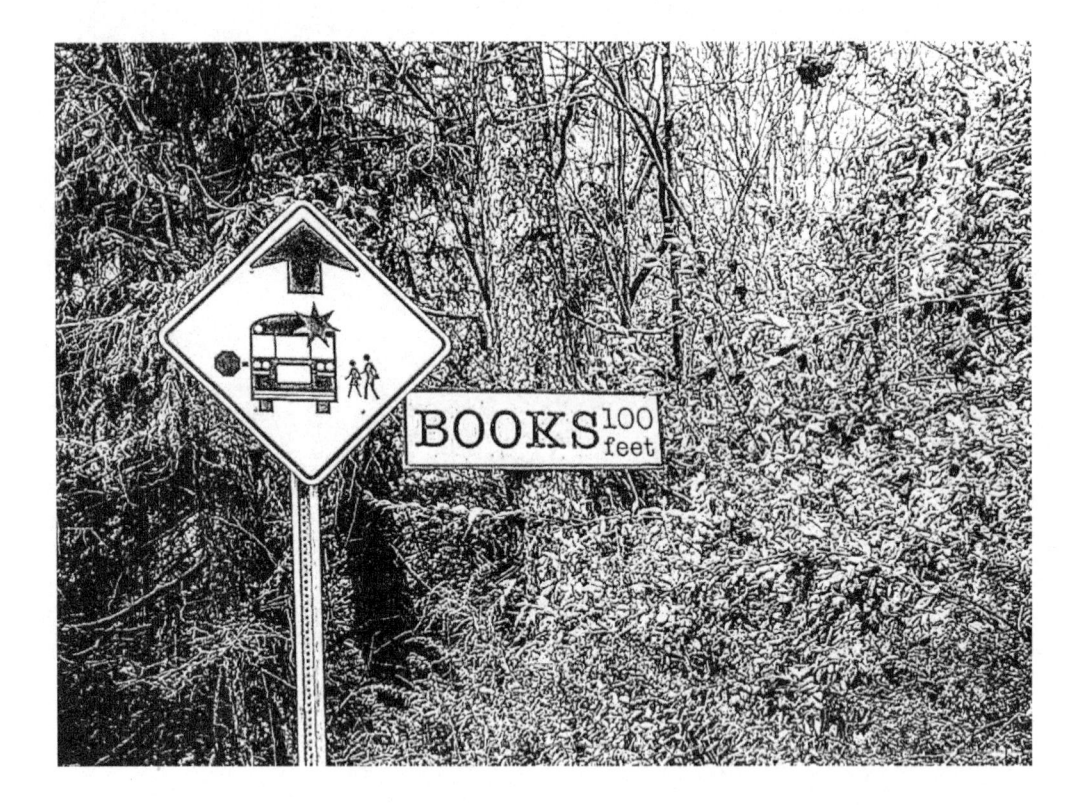

Luckily, God, the Universe, or someone really darn serious is persistent, and in however many feet 1 mile minus 100 feet is, you see *another* sign, along with a warning to look up for falling buses, and just beyond that, a red barn (use your imagination – woodcuts are usually, like the woodcut classic, *God's Man,* black and white) that turns out to be, you guessed it, a bookstore. And whadya know, today is your lucky day, it's open weekends and today is Sunday.

But then you see another cow or have to speed up and take evasive maneuvers to avoid another wreckless driving ticket (though you still don't see why you should be getting a ticket for *not* getting into a wreck), and you find yourself once again lost.

However, God, the Universe, or someone really darn serious is just not willing to let you fail at your true purpose in life (to buy so many books that there is nowhere to put them all and people don't compliment you anymore on your beautiful hardwood floors because, first of all, you don't have hardwood floors, and there therefore can't logically be a second of all). So they send you another sign coming from the opposite direction that puts you back on course:

Now, I wish this parable had a happy ending, but alas, sometimes God, the Universe, or someone who really *seemed* darn serious works in mysterious ways (or is taking a nap).

The moral of the story is: Man plans; God, the Universe, or someone who really should be more accurate regarding their opening hours laughs (or takes a lot of naps). Then again, had these signs *not* appeared at *precisely* this point on your ride, leading you on a wild book chase, who knows what might have happened. For example, maybe you would have gotten out of the car to pee in the woods (safer than rest stops these days) and gotten eaten by a bear. Then again, maybe since you *were* led on this wild book chase, later when you *do* stop to pee in the woods you will *then* get eaten by a bear who wouldn't have been there yet had you not wasted time following signs, thereby giving them a head start.

Either way, I hope that you have enjoyed this little Parable in Woodcuts, *sans* Woodcuts, and will continue on to the main body of the treatise where you will learn many *other* useful things that will hopefully guide you on your path toward, or away from, the proverbial bookstore that said it was open on weekends but was in fact closed.

Preface - *The Vast Left-Brain Conspiracy*

"Eventually, all that one has learnt will have to be forgotten."
Ramana Maharshi

". . . a no entender entendiendo,

toda ciencia transcendiendo."

San Juan De La Cruz

". . . to understand unknowing,

rising beyond all science."

St. John of the Cross

"'Say whatever you choose *about* the object,

and whatever you might say *is not* it.'

Or, in other words: 'Whatever you might *say* the object 'is,'

well it *is not.*'"

Alfred Korzybski

(1933/1993, p. 35)

> "Everything you experience is born out of thought,
>
> so everything you experience, or <u>can</u> experience,
>
> is an illusion."
>
> U.G. Krishnamurti (1988, p. 111)
>
> (NOT Jiddu Krishnamurti)

Several months ago, after over 20 years of practicing therapy and 15 years of meditating fairly consistently in various traditions, I was summarizing one psychologically useful form of meditation to someone as "coming back from thinking." They looked confused and said they spent all of their time thinking and had no idea that there was any other way to be. This surprised me, because I tended to consider "thinking all the time" to be a "problem" seen in therapy.

In an ethnopsychiatric article I once read, a case was made that if one uses a normative definition of pathology, then in a village in which everyone has leprosy, everyone is normal and therefore healthy.

Overthinking is a modern-day psychological leprosy.

Most of us, most of the time, do not distinguish between the world outside of our heads and our internal representations of it. They blend into one another, seamlessly, innocently, becoming our world as best we can know it using the equipment provided, namely, the human senses, and the memory-based meanings programmed into our brain by our interactions with the physical and social environment.

Unfortunately, not only are our internal representations fantasies, mediated by our senses, but the meanings assigned to these, through the filter of social learning, are fantasies as well. Paradoxically, "meaning" distances us from what it purports to mean. The moment we say something "means" something, we are distancing ourselves from its true meaning as simply *what it is*; we are saying that it means something *other* than what it is. In truth, it should be rather obvious that

Nothing really means anything other than itself.

What does a chair "mean"? It doesn't mean anything. It's a *chair*. While meaning isn't meaningless, it does point in the direction of a reduction in meaning. It's oxymoronic. To say that A means B is ridiculous. A means A. So why not just say A and forget about "meaning"?

> "'Whatever you say a thing *is*, it *is not*.' This rejection of the 'law of identity' ('everything is identical with itself') may be Korzybski's most controversial formulation."

> (Pula, in Korzybski, 1933/1993, p. xvii, not quoting Korzybski but paraphrasing him, despite internet fake news assigning the quotation to Korzybski, some of whose original formulations were: "'Say whatever you choose *about* the object, and whatever you might say *is not* it.' Or, in other words: 'Whatever you might *say* the object 'is,' well it *is not*'" [p. 35]; "The chunk of nature, the specially shaped accumulation of materials, which we call a pencil, 'is' fundamentally and *absolutely un-speakable*, simply because whatever we may *say* about it, *is not it*. We may write with this something, but we cannot write with its name or the *descriptions* of this something. So the object is *not words*" [p. 226]; "So we see clearly that outside of our skins there is something going on, which *we call* the world, or a pencil, or anything, which is *independent* of our words and which is *not* words" [p. 227]).

Here's Big Al himself:

In effect, thinking, which is a game of meanings, often represented by words, is *fantasizing about fantasies* (cognitive interpretations of sensory impressions of objects), leaving us at least twice removed from reality. This is an important point that bears repeating:

A thought is a fantasy about a fantasy.

Though I haven't read it yet, I suspect that this is touched upon in the book *The Case Against Reality* (Hoffman, 2019), which was worth buying for the title alone (I keep it behind me as I do teletherapy, within view of the webcam, as a subliminal teaching).

It behooves us, however, before hastily discarding thoughts on the basis of their status as fantasies, to heed Ramana Maharshi's caution that

"Illusion itself is illusory."

(Talk 446; 24 January, 1938)

After the conversation recounted above, I began paying more attention in therapy to how many clients have as a primary complaint that they "think all the time," "can't keep their mind still," "have racing thoughts," "can't stop worrying," etc. These are naturally things that therapists hear several times daily when clients spontaneously mention them. However, when I began systematically asking clients about this (even those who did not initially conceptualize their problems in terms of overthinking), it turned out to be pretty much everyone. And when I probed further, it became clear that many of the rest were overthinking without realizing it.

Despite having taught clients meditation for the same 15 years that I've been meditating regularly (I'm a firm believer that in order to teach someone something, you don't necessarily need to be an expert, you merely need to be one step ahead of them – this does not, of course, make you the ideal teacher, but at least you can get them started), I simply hadn't been aware of the full extent to which many of us live in our heads and can't stop the movies. It doesn't help that the main way we try to silence the noise *inside* is by distracting ourselves by watching or listening to louder noise *outside*, which is then internalized as memory, providing more fuel for more thinking.

We often think that the solution to overthinking

is to distract ourselves from thinking,

not realizing that *thinking is the distraction.*

Luckily, we can learn to *come back* from the distraction of thinking to what it is distracting us from: *a clear mind.*

Even one of the bestselling self-help books of all time, Dale Carnegie's (1948/1990) *How to Stop Worrying and Start Living*, with all due respect to Mr. Carnegie and his "over six million" buyers, has at least some of it wrong. He tells the story of a man who had lost two children and noticed that the first few hours of mental peace that he had in months came when he built a toy boat with his one remaining child, a four-year-old son. The man shared this insight:

> "I realized that those three hours spent building that boat were the first hours of mental relaxation and peace that I had had in months . . . I realized that it is difficult to worry while you are busy doing something that requires planning and thinking. In my case, building the boat had knocked worry right out of the ring. So I resolved to keep busy.
>
> The following night, I went from room to room in the house, compiling a list of jobs that ought to be done . . . Astonishing as it seems, in the course of two weeks I had made a list of 242 items that needed attention . . . During the last two years I have completed most of them. Besides, I have filled my life with stimulating activities . . ." (p. 58)

Mr. Carnegie concluded:

> "No time for worry! That is exactly what Winston Churchill said when he was working eighteen hours a day at the height of the war. When he was asked if he worried about his tremendous responsibilities, he said: 'I'm too busy. I have no time for worry.'" (pp. 58-59)

He tells a similar tale of Charles Kettering, former vice-president of General Motors, who after retirement decided to invent an automobile self-starter but was "so poor that he had to use the hayloft of a barn as a laboratory."

Whereas his wife was "so worried I couldn't sleep," she said that "Mr. Kettering wasn't. He was too absorbed in his work to worry" (p. 59).

He then cites the field of psychiatry:

> "Any psychiatrist will tell you that work – keeping busy – is one of the best anesthetics ever known for sick nerves . . ." (p. 60)

But not to neglect poetry:

> "As Tennyson declared when he lost his most intimate friend, Arthur Hallam: 'I must lose myself in action, lest I wither in despair.'" (p. 61)

And Heaven forbid he should neglect the insights of the Miseducational Establishment, which as we know, has solved all of the world's problems by teaching us such valuable things:

> "James L. Mursell, professor of education, Teacher's College, Columbia, puts it very well when he says: 'Worry is most apt to ride you ragged not when you are in action, but when the day's work is done . . . The remedy for worry is to get completely occupied doing something constructive.'" (pp. 61-62)

Finally, to nail down his case, he interviews the Mom in the street, justifiably worried about her son who enlisted in the armed forces the day after Pearl Harbour:

> "When I asked her how she overcame her worry, she replied: 'I got busy.'" (p. 62)

She "dismissed her maid," did all her own housework, and when that wasn't enough, she

> "took a job as a saleswoman in a large department store . . . That did it . . . and when night came, I could think of nothing except getting off my aching feet. As soon as I ate dinner, I fell into bed, and instantly became unconscious. I had neither the time nor the energy to worry." (p. 62)

Well, thank you Mr. Carnegie. If we want to stop thinking, all we need to do is keep busy, ideally so busy that we wind up unconscious.

Now, Dale was on to something, though not entirely what he thought he was on to. Because most of us never needed a book to tell us that keeping busy could take our mind off things *temporarily*. Neither did the many people Carnegie read about or spoke to (in fact, *he* learned it from *them*, and then sold them a book on what they already knew). We *all* know that *doing* trumps *thinking*. Just like we know that if we want to feel less socially awkward at a party, all we need to do is get sh#tfaced. *But just because something seems to work doesn't mean it's a good solution.* If we solve one problem in an unwise manner, we often create other problems. And this is exactly what happens if we blindly follow Carnegie's advice (which we unfortunately do, more often than not).

Do you know who excel at Mr. Carnegie's method? People with obsessive compulsive disorder (OCD). As a remedy for thinking virtually non-stop about something distressful (obsessing), the person with OCD will accidentally stumble upon the "just keep busy" principle, and because this does indeed distract from thinking, the behavior will then be repeated as frequently as the thought, becoming a compulsion. But OCD is only the extreme of the "just keep busy" continuum of this bad advice on how to stop thinking. Most of us, at one time or another, in order to avoid thinking about or dealing with something unpleasant, will get the busy bug. This may take the form of binge-watching TV, workaholism, excessive attention to decorating the house, all-day video gaming, and any number of activities taken to excess. While Carnegie was ahead of his time and there are no doubt things of great value in his book (as 6 million people can't be wrong, unless of course they happen to be *human* people), a case can be made that Mr. Carnegie taught us how to stop obsessing by teaching us how to compulse.

But now let's take a look at what Carnegie got *right*. On the basis of his observations, Carnegie formulates a psychological principle:

> "Why does such a simple thing as keeping busy help to drive out anxiety? Because of a law – one of the most fundamental laws ever revealed by psychology. And that law is: that it is utterly impossible for any human mind, no matter how brilliant, to think of more than one thing at any given time." (p. 59)

Here he has struck upon two important things. First, it will be noticed that a number of Carnegie's examples of the virtues of "keeping busy" as an antidote for "worry" involve people who are grieving. This suggests that he was confounding *depressive rumination* with *anxious worry*. Some of his informants were not experiencing (1) the heightened arousal of anxiety accompanied by an excessive frequency, duration and salience (cognitive process) of *danger* thoughts (cognitive content), but rather suffered from (2) the lower arousal of depression accompanied by an excessive frequency, duration and salience (cognitive process) of *loss* thoughts (cognitive content). Rather than discovering the antidote for anxious worry, he stumbled upon the therapeutic utility of *behavioral activation* (do more fun or productive stuff) for depression, thus lifting the depression and its associated rumination.

Herein lies the importance of what the medical profession calls *differential diagnosis*. The same *symptom* (here, excessive cognitive process) can be a part of different *syndromes* (collections of symptoms). Mistaking a symptom for syndrome used to be mostly limited to medical students self-diagnosing themselves with diseases due to the presence of one or another of the individual symptoms (termed "medical student syndrome" – like learning that a symptom of ulcerative colitis is stomach pain, and then assuming that stomach pain means you have ulcerative colitis). Today, thanks to the internet, we have all become medical students, performing Google diagnostics on our various aches and pains and learning that they can be symptoms of terrible diseases. Carnegie correctly identified excessive thinking as a problem, found that many people successfully stop thinking by keeping busy, and formulated this into a psychological principle that pointed in the right direction but failed to distinguish between different causes of overthinking that require different remedies. A differential diagnostic approach reveals that (1) when overthinking is a symptom of behavioral *deactivation* and *depression*, keeping busy can lift the depression and with it the depressive rumination, but that (2) when overthinking is a symptom of behavioral *overactivation* and *anxiety*, making oneself busier merely adds to the overactivation and, in the long run, can increase both the anxiety and the associated worry.

Second, the therapeutic utility that he applies to our inability to simultaneously *think* about multiple *thoughts* anticipates the thesis of the current book regarding our inability to simultaneously *be aware* of multiple *senses*, and growing recognition of meditation and mindfulness as remedies for overthinking and its associated psychological disorders.

As Carnegie was not a psychologist and was writing in the 1940s when psychotherapy itself mostly involved dream analysis, he must be recognized for his insights into the causal role of overthinking in human misery and forgiven for overgeneralizing his "keeping busy" solution. This especially as even today, 70 years later, psychology still has little to say about overthinking as a problem or what to do about it. For a long time I myself, though speaking daily with clients about the problematic nature of their thinking, assumed along with most psychologists that the main problem is *what* people think, less so *how* they think, and certainly not *that* they think. I had drunk Western Psychology's Kool Aid. Luckily, I became wary of the party line as the years progressed, until the Eastern Psychologies, which I had dabbled in since my teens, provided the antidote.

In cognitive behavioral therapy, my own specialty and that which is currently favored by the medical and psychological establishments, the cognitive component addresses the *content* of thoughts (i.e., the meaning: rational versus irrational, helpful versus unhelpful) and not the thought *process*. As you may remember from earlier in the book, I have come to define cognitive *process* as the *frequency, duration and salience* of thinking, with salience itself referring to the extent to which thinking is at the forefront of *awareness* in relation to the other senses, i.e., sight, hearing, smell, taste and bodysense. Cognitive process may be considered problematic when the frequency, duration and salience of thinking in general, or of thinking with certain content, is unhelpful in achieving one's goals.

In the martial art Tai Chi, the foot supporting more weight is said to be more Yang and the foot supporting less weight is said to be more Yin. Similarly, relative awareness of the 6 sense modalities, understood as "awareness inputs" or "potential foci of awareness" (seeing, hearing, smelling, tasting, bodysensing and thinking) may also be conceptualized in terms of Yin and Yang. Right now, I am aware of (1) subvocalizing (subtly moving my vocal cords) and (2) seeing the words as I feel myself type them; (3) feeling discomfort in my right forearm which rests un-ergonomically on the edge of the too-high round wooden table; and (4) hearing the sound of the refrigerator. However, most of this time I am more aware of the subvocalization, sight and typing of the words than I am of the arm discomfort or refrigerator sound. In the Tai Chi "bow and arrow" stance, the forward foot supports 65% of the weight and the rear foot supports 35% of the weight. As I type and subvocalize, tactile sensations from fingers on the keyboard, movements of the throat and vocal cords, and visual awareness of the words, at this moment at least, occupy about 65% percent of awareness to the refrigerator's 35% (it's a really loud fridge). Here, the sensory salience of the activities of generating language and typing (albeit subjectively) is 65% (thus "yang") and the sensory salience of the fridge sound is 35% (thus "yin"). When we worry, the sensory salience of "worry awareness," so to speak, is very high, I'd guess over 50%, and when we obsess, salience of the obsessive content might be as high as 75%, in either case cutting significantly into the amount of awareness left for other thoughts or senses.

As cognitive process seems, at least to me, obviously as important as cognitive content, it is surprising that more emphasis is not given to it in the fields of psychology and psychotherapy. Granted, in obsessive compulsive spectrum problems, the process of repetitive thinking, i.e., obsessing, is a defining characteristic, and in "Generalized Anxiety Disorder," characterized by excessive worrying, this worry is a blend of negative content and excessive frequency, duration and salience. But even cognitive restructuring for obsessing and worrying has traditionally focused on challenging content to alter process (as well as the necessary behavioral component, exposure and response prevention, for OCD). One seeming exception is the scheduling of "worry time," with an instruction to put off worry until a specific time, e.g., 7 pm tomorrow, but this pretty much amounts to telling yourself "stop thinking" when it isn't worry time, without telling you how exactly to do that. So, although "worry time" (I prefer to assign "*problem solving* time") is effective in stopping *intentional* overthinking, it does nothing to address automatic overthinking. Although proponents of the CBT strategy "thought stopping" (with and without snapping a rubber band on your wrist as you internally yell "STOP!") may beg to differ, in my experience telling oneself to stop thinking without instruction on what to do instead is like telling oneself not to think of a pink elephant or, in research psychology, of a white bear (Wegner, 1994). Good luck with that. This said, before reading any further, maybe take a day or two to do this experiment: When you notice yourself overthinking, scream inside your head (silently but really loudly), "STOP!" with or without snapping a rubber band that you will wear around your wrist for that purpose. If it works, I stand corrected, at least as concerns you personally.

Welcome back! (which I will take to mean that "STOP!" didn't work). Anyway, over the last 50 years, at an accelerating pace, techniques to alter cognitive *process* (frequency, duration and salience of thinking) have entered the therapy world in the form of techniques inspired by Buddhism and Hinduism, validating the Tibetan teacher Chogyam Trungpa's prediction that "Buddhism will come to the West as a psychology" (Goleman, 2004, p. 72). The most common meditative technique taught in healthcare is "mindfulness," defined by Jon Kabat Zinn as "paying attention in a particular way: on purpose, in the present moment, and nonjudgmentally" (2005, p. 4). Mindfulness is often taught by therapists as some variant of Kabat-Zinn's 12-week Mindfulness Based Stress Reduction (MBSR) program, which he originated in 1979 and emphasizes is neither Buddhist nor a therapy. One MBSR-derived therapy is Mindfulness-Based Cognitive Therapy (Segal, Williams & Teasdale 2002) in which unhelpful cognitive *content* is addressed by instruction in weighing the evidence for and against its validity (known in cognitive therapy as *cognitive disputation* or *cognitive restructuring*), and the cognitive *process* of overthinking is targeted by mindfulness training (which I see as amounting to selective awareness training, a position with which I believe they disagree).

Another technique used in healthcare is Herbert Benson's (1975) Relaxation Response (RR), modified by Benson from Maharishi Mahesh Yogi's Hindu-based Transcendental Meditation (TM) practice, with RR borrowing TM's mantra meditation technique divorced from its original Hindu Sanskrit content and lacking its puja ceremony invoking Maharishi's Master Guru Dev Shankaracharya Swami Brahmananda Saraswati. More recently RR has been reconceptualized to refer to the physiological mind-body *state* triggered by diverse practices, such as meditation, yoga or tai chi, rather than to any particular *technique*, and may therefore be less focused on cognitive process than when if favored mantra meditation.

Perhaps because meditation in Buddhism and Hinduism is an "exoteric" (outside or public) practice, whereas meditation in Judaism, Christianity and Islam is more "esoteric" (internal or hidden), most public meditation instruction either adheres to or is inspired by the Buddhist or Hindu tradition. However, as every major religious tradition has its own forms of meditation (e.g., Jewish Hitbodedut, Christian Centering Prayer, Sufi Murāqabah), a case could be made for capitalizing upon the strength of one's religious or spiritual beliefs and learning an "entheosyntonic" (Densei & Lam, 2010) approach to meditation. Here, a form is chosen that is consistent (syntonic) with one's own inner (en) theological (theo) beliefs or lack thereof.

Given all the books out there on meditation in religious, spiritual and therapeutic traditions, all including components addressing overthinking, why another one? Why this one? Over the past 40 or so years I have read or perused hundreds if not thousands of books on Eastern, Western, ancient, modern, scientific, religious, spiritual and mystical consciousness practices involving attention, concentration, awareness, meditation, mindfulness and other mental phenomena. In the past 15 years I've read hundreds of research articles on meditation and skimmed through countless more. I've been to lectures, workshops, conferences and retreats. While most of these were interesting and useful, and some were life changing, when all is said and done, I am in utter awe at

so many people (including myself) making such a fuss

about something so simple.

You might notice that the title of this book is not just "How to Stop Thinking" but also includes content on how to not get eaten by a bear and cognitive behavioral mind training. And if you take a look at the Table of Contents, you will also see a section on consciousness exploration. This is because if I wrote a book limited to "How to Stop Thinking," it wouldn't be a book, it would be a book chapter. Or a paragraph, or word, or blank page. Nobody would buy it, so nobody would read it, and you would be right back where you started, confronted with the big mess of your mind and the bigger mess of books and trainings telling you how to clean it up. Kind of like using mud as laundry detergent. As Ramana Maharshi said,

> "A day will dawn when you will yourself laugh at your past efforts. That which will be on the day you laugh is also here and now." (Talk 146, 26th January, 1936; Ramana Maharshi, 2006)

So this book is an attempt at honesty, parsimony, Occam's razor, etc., to explain something simple in the simplest way possible.

And after simply explaining how to stop thinking, as a bonus I will simply explain cognitive behavioral psychological techniques that you can use to treat problems such as low mood/depression, stress/anxiety/panic/phobias, worry/obsessing/OCD, insomnia, and pain, because these too have solutions far less wordy than the way they are usually taught. And, if you order now, you will receive several chapters on some far-out stuff that really isn't any more far out than our very existence that we take for granted every waking second. And regarding the bear thing, as far as I know, make a lot of noise, preferably with pots and pans that you just happen to have in your day bag; brown lie down, black fight back, white say goodnight *and have the wisdom to know the difference.* Whatever you do, don't run or climb a tree; and if there is a WARNING: BEAR SIGHTINGS sign in front of the campsite pay station, *for God's sake* (actually for your own sake; God's doing just fine, last I heard), pull over and google "airbnb" which has a pretty good track record for guests not getting eaten by bears.

Pondering the common practice, in psychology, psychotherapy, meditation, mindfulness, religion and spirituality of specialization and "branding," I'll pass on to you a piece of advice given to me by Chögyal Namkhai Norbu Rinpoche, a Tibetan Dzogchen Master known in the West for his books on dream yoga. When I met him in Hong Kong a few years back, I told him about my various practices and asked for some pointers. He looked me in the eye, remained silent for a few moments, and then said, quite firmly, just one word: "*Integration.*" Now, when a reincarnated lama tells you something, it might be a mistake to take it at face value. So I did my research and found in his 2000 book *The Crystal and the Way of Light: Sutra, Tantra and Dzogchen*, that

> "The existence of duality is nothing but an illusion, and when this illusion is undone the primordial inseparability of the individual and the universe is fully discovered and the functions of that inseparability manifest; that is to say, through the *integration* of the internal and the external ying, the Body of Light manifests . . ." (Norbu, 2000, pp. 157-158; italics added)

Elsewhere in the same book, he writes:

> "So the path is not something strictly different from the fruit; the process of self-liberation becomes ever deeper, until the deluded consciousness that was unaware of the Base which was always our own nature disappears: this is what is called the Fruit. The Tibetan word *sewa*, which means 'to *integrate*' or 'to mix', is used here because one *integrates* each and every experience of ordinary life in the state of contemplation. Since in Dzogchen there is nothing to

change – no special clothes to wear and nothing that may be seen from the outside – there is no way to know whether or not someone is practicing. In fact, the practice does not depend at all on outward forms; its principle is that everything in one's relative situation may be brought into practice and *integrated* with the state of contemplation. This means, though, that our contemplation must of course be precise, because otherwise there would be nothing with which to *integrate* the experiences and actions of ordinary life." (Norbu, 2000, p. 150; italics added)

For Norbu,

"The pure State of Enlightenment is our own mind as well, not some sort of dazzling light coming from the outside. If we recognize our primordial State of pure presence, pure from the beginning, albeit temporarily obscured, and we stay present in this recognition without getting distracted, then all the impurities dissolve: this is the essence of the path. Now the nature of the primordial State as total purity manifests, and recognizing it for what it is we become its owner forever. It is this decisive knowing, this pure presence of the true original condition, that is called nirvāṇa. Enlightenment too, therefore, is our own mind, purified. (Norbu, 1996, p. 29)

Ultimately, integration means realizing Unity in multiplicity, that "It is One Event" (Nisargadatta, 1999/1973, p. 138), and realizing that the duality of *Unity's Pulse* (Densei, 2008) is the single Unity ItSelf, that the Yin and Yang, apparently two, are the one Yin Yang.

Returning to the phenomenon of "branding" and the common practices in psychology of (1) seemingly competing to make simple things sound complex in one's own trademarked jargon (intellectual bullying via mystification), and (2) making people jump through expensive hoops before "certifying" them to make simple things sound complex to others down the chain, here's something I once read: An elder in one of the Wisdom traditions was asked why there were so many doctrines and rituals to learn and what's with the funny hats. He responded that the reason they make things so complicated is that if people knew how simple it is, they wouldn't be interested.

Still, I have a feeling that if people knew how simple it is to learn *How To Stop Thinking* they *would* be interested. I guess we'll have to wait and see.

INTERMISSION

PART 1 - HOW TO STOP THINKING

"We now begin our study of the mind from within . . .
The first fact, for us, then, as psychologists,
is that thinking of some sort goes on."

William James

(1890/1950, p. 224)

"**Q:** But thoughts arise, inevitably.

How does one deal with thoughts that arise?

Papaji: I will tell you how to deal with them.

I think you can devote an amount of time equal to a finger snap.

That is all the time I need to stop your thoughts.

What is a thought?

What is mind?

There is no difference between thought and mind.

Thought arises from mind and mind is merely a bundle of thoughts.

Without thoughts there is no mind.

What is mind?

'I' is mind.

Mind is past, it is clinging to past, present and future.

It is clinging to time, clinging to objects.

This is called mind.

Now, where does the mind arise from?

When the 'I' rises, mind rises, senses rise, the world rises.

Now, find out where the 'I' rises from

and then tell me if you are not quiet."

H.W.L. Poonja, "Papaji"

(in Greenwald, Who Are You?)

Chapter 1 - *The 1 Habit of Highly Neurotic People*

"'Some people,'

remarked Mary Poppins . . .

'think a great deal too much.'"

P.L. Travers

(1935/1997, p. 86)

"When you stop thinking,

you are no longer imagining things that are not true."

H.W.L. Poonja "Papaji" (n.d.)

"Which of you by taking thought

can add one cubit unto his stature?"

First Century Carpenter

(Matthew, 6:27, KJV)

"Take it easy"

Jackson Brown & Glen Frey (1972)

Chapter 1 - The 1 Habit of Highly Neurotic People

First, let's be clear: We are all highly neurotic. At least anyone who has gotten to the point of writing or reading a book, and that is, for present purposes, me and you. But since I wouldn't want to be called neurotic, and I'm sure you wouldn't either, *let's agree to agree* and understand the word in a neutral, purely descriptive sense, meaning that our moment-to-moment experience is at least in part related to the firing of *neurons* in our brains. There is, of course, the possibility that our experience has nothing to do with neuronal firing, as in the Eastern traditions in which the Mind has a body rather than the body having a mind (and in which the Mind has a mind as well, with both your body and mind being *objects* of Your awareness, and thus not having anything to do with You Who *Am* the Subject), or in the Christian framework in which we are in the world but not of it, or in the Teilhardian sense of our identity as "a spiritual being having a human experience." But let's not go there for the moment (as there is no further need, for we just did).

And the one habit of highly neurotic people such as ourselves is (drumroll . . .)

(1) Overthinking

I assume that this needs no explanation, as some of us do it all the time, and all of us do it some of the time. Then again, we are aware of only a small portion of what we do, and understand even less. And since this is a book, and books are intended to increase knowledge (even books with a goal of decreasing thinking and thereby decreasing knowledge, but we will address such paradoxes in later pages, if we remember), this assumption, as most assumptions, is not to be trusted and is merely an example of the above habit in action. All this to say that maybe I should explain the 1 habit for those fish who don't yet know they are in water.

By "overthinking," I am referring to

(1) excessive thinking in general (i.e., too much time spent thinking as compared with awareness of the other senses); and

(2) excessive thinking about certain things as compared with thinking about other things.

THE VARIETIES OF OVERTHUNK EXPERIENCE

Overthinking can take many forms, some relatively innocuous and others that can make spending time with yourself a living hell. Some common forms are:

(1) **Garden variety overthinking:** This is an emotionally neutral habit of "thinking all the time." It may involve some mild obsessive-process or Obsessive-Compulsive Disorder (OCD) neurology. It can probably be corrected by a disciplined practice of meditation/mindfulness;

(2) **Worry:** This can be caused by and exacerbate anxiety (though at times it can also, paradoxically, focus attention and temporarily reduce anxiety, possibly functioning as a cognitive compulsion). It may be related to a high baseline level of nervous system activation combined with OCD neurology. It can most likely benefit from a combination of cognitive restructuring, problem solving and meditation/mindfulness;

(3) **Depressive rumination:** This is overthinking caused by depressive neurology, which is related to OCD neurology. It can benefit from treatment of the depression by techniques including behavioral activation and cognitive restructuring; sometimes medication (especially if severe); and meditation/mindfulness. Exposure and response prevention (purposely thinking about the thought content for extended lengths of time) should *not* be used for overthinking associated with depression; and

(4) **OCD "Pure O" and the "O" component of OCD:** This is overthinking likely caused by OCD neurology. It may respond to cognitive restructuring, exposure and response prevention and meditation/mindfulness, but often benefits most from medication.

HOW MUCH SHOULD WE THINK?

In case you are having difficulty determining what amount of thinking is excessive or unnecessary, let's look at this together. First, let's simplify our terms, noting that if it is *unnecessary* it is *excessive*. Now we just have to figure out how much thinking is necessary. How about . . . NONE. Wait, come back. Indeed, "none" is not one of our more popular answers, except at those triennial Zen Master conferences in Kiyoto. How about . . . SOME. We good? Ok, agreed.

But *which* some? How about the *some* that is actually *helpful* in some way. But helpful how? Take your choice: helpful to accomplishing your goals, increasing the happiness and well-being of you and those you care about, promoting the peace and happiness of all beings, preventing blockage of your goals, preventing the misery and suffering of you and those you care about, preventing war and famine, preparing for alien invasion, the list is kind of endless. Since "helpful in accomplishing your goals" pretty much covers the rest, let's go with that and write it in bold:

Necessary thinking is thinking that is helpful in accomplishing your goals.

Correspondingly,

Unnecessary thinking is thinking that is *not* helpful in accomplishing your goals.

So really, *this* is the thinking you probably would do well to stop. Still, we need to identify precisely which thinking is helpful and which is not helpful in accomplishing your goals. While this depends in part on what your goals are, there are certain types of thinking that are usually helpful and certain types that are usually unhelpful:

Usually *helpful:*

> (1) **Rational Analysis of the Past:** Mentally reviewing a past event and identifying factors that led to its turning out in a constructive or unconstructive way (e.g., how many beers did I drink before forgetting how many beers I drank and waking up on a park bench; which words was I using to describe that politician right before Twitter froze my account);
>
> (2) **Problem Solving for the Present:** Thinking about how to do what we are doing right now (e.g., what to use to open something that has a little picture of scissors and a dotted line when we have no scissors handy; how long we can reheat the hot and sour soup in a non-microwaveable bowl without blowing up the kitchen and waking up the baby); and
>
> (3) **Planning for the Foreseeable Future:** Thinking about what to do about something we are planning for in the future that needs to be figured out in advance (e.g., how many people we need to reserve for in order for them to give us a reservation and how long we should wait after getting there before telling them the rest of the party can't make it; where to buy a house in Vancouver that will still be above water with access to a 7-11 in ten years when the glaciers melt).

Usually *unhelpful* (unless you are method acting and need to cry to get the part):

> (1) **Obsessive Rumination about the Past:** Thinking over and over about something bad that happened in the past (e.g., the look on your friend's face when you spilled red wine on his white shirt at Tzack's wedding – sorry Friedy; the look on that woman's face when you dropped a Bloody Mary on her white gown on your first night working as a cocktail waiter – sorry, I never got your name);

(2) **Freaking Out in the Present:** Whatever one is thinking simultaneously with screaming, flailing one's arms, stomping one's feet and frothing at the mouth when the occasion arises (use your imagination); and

(3) **Worrying about the Future:** Thinking over and over about something bad that might happen in the future (e.g., I might get fired, not find another job, have to sell the house, and end up living in a box on a street without a Dunkin Donuts; I might not get fired and have to stay in this job working 60 hour weeks for the next 40 years with no time to go to Dunkin Donuts). In the words of Lord Dewar (14 March 1860 – 14 June 1917; the fourth son of John Dewar, Sr., the distiller and founder of John Dewar & Sons; Solicitor General for Scotland, 1909-1910):

"Worry is interest paid on trouble before it is due."

(Alexander, 1928, p. 175)

If we analyze these, three patterns emerge and none have to do with "being in the present moment," "being here now" (R.I.P. Ram Dass) or any such spaciotemporal advice. In fact, thinking about the past and future can be helpful, and thinking about the present can be unhelpful. The real distinction between helpful and unhelpful thinking is that:

Helpful thinking is rational, time limited and focuses on possible change.

Unhelpful thinking is irrational, repetitive and focuses on the unchangeable or unreal.

Our ways of thinking can therefore be evaluated along three dimensions for retention or elimination.

Content: Rational versus Irrational

Serenity (Regarding Rational Content): Changeable versus Unchangeable

Process: Time Limited versus Repetitive

Each of these dimensions may benefit most from a specific approach, or a combination of approaches, to maximize the helpful and minimize the unhelpful thinking at play:

Cognitive Content: Irrational thinking may be addressed using the cognitive therapy technique of cognitive restructuring (also known as cognitive disputation), in which (1) the negative irrational thought is identified; (2) evidence supporting the thought is generated; (3) evidence challenging the thought is generated; and (4) a rational alternative thought is generated that takes into account the evidence for and against the original thought and is so true you would bet your life on it. These can be thought of using the analogy of a trial, in which the thought being evaluated has a defense attorney (presenting evidence for its truth/innocence); a prosecuting attorney (presenting evidence for its guilt or falsehood); and a jury (that weighs the evidence presented by the two attorneys and announces a verdict).

For example, if the thought is "I'm gonna get fired," the supporting evidence might be "My boss didn't say hello when I passed her in the hall," and "I think she actually grimaced at me." The contrary evidence might be "My boss is my favorite aunt and she had two root canals this morning." An alternative thought might therefore be "My boss probably won't fire me. She probably didn't talk to me because she can't move her mouth, and even if she could move her mouth she would probably just thank me for shoveling her driveway last week." A useful tool for cognitive restructuring is the "thought record," the most common of which are the ones presented in publications by Aaron and Judith Beck; David Burns; and Dennis Greenberger and Christine Padesky. I have altered the traditional thought record to incorporate elements that I find important. My Serenity Prayer Thought Record can be found in the Appendix, as well as an example of how to use it.

Serenity (Regarding Rational Content): Change what you can, Accept what you can't, Know the difference (Serenity Prayer Short Form).

Cognitive Process: Repetitive thinking can be dealt with by, you guessed it, Stopping Thinking. Coming right up in Chapter 3.

Interestingly (at least to me) and sacrilege to some less meditation-oriented CBT colleagues, is that in theory, if you get really, *really* good at stopping thinking, you don't need to learn to think rationally. You can just stop thinking. However, in practice, I find it most useful to teach people how to do all three: *challenge* catastrophic or repetitive negative thoughts; *accept* any remaining negative but unchangeable content; and *stop thinking* by returning to the other senses (seeing, hearing, smelling, tasting, or bodysensing, as explained in Chapter 3). This three-step procedure can be remembered as:

Challenge. Serenity. Come Back.

Or alternatively, for those who are so sick of thinking that they don't even want to engage in thinking their way out of thinking, as just

Come Back.

In this latter case, the whole sequence of Challenge, Serenity, Come Back may only be necessary if you find yourself not *staying* back for an acceptable amount of time.

I mention these two alternatives because (1) some people prefer challenging thoughts to stopping thinking, (2) others prefer stopping thinking to engaging in even more thinking as is required by cognitive disputation, and (3) still others prefer and try one but it isn't sufficient without the other.

If whichever one tries first, stopping thinking or challenging thoughts, doesn't work by itself,

Cognitive disputation and mindfulness can be used as a "*one-two punch*" to stop thinking,

thereby addressing both cognitive content (via challenging and acceptance) and process (via coming back to non-thinking). This is especially useful if one is being assailed by negative thoughts that are emotionally charged. If you hear a loud noise at night and fear that someone has broken in, it will probably be futile to simply instruct yourself to "Come back, see the room." However, after considering for several moments the evidence for and against a home invasion (e.g., there was one in town last year, but the alarm is on and the dog didn't bark), "Come back, see the room" is likely to orient the mind away from thoughts of danger and keep it there with fewer subsequent intrusions by the latter.

In sum, the **Challenge. Serenity. Come Back.** procedure involves:

(1) *Challenging* a given irrational thought when it arises on various occasions. Most people tend to cycle through a limited number of negative automatic thoughts, e.g., "I'm going to fail the test," "I'll get fired," or themes, e.g., "I'm a failure" or "Nobody cares about me." These latter may be related to early

childhood ways of processing information about and coping with unmet needs such as safety; autonomy; self-control; free expression of needs; and spontaneity. When these become generalized expectations for and ways of interpreting similar situations, they are known as schemas. Just as certain situations can act as triggers for certain automatic thoughts, they can also trigger schema activation whereby situations in adulthood are interpreted and emoted to in ways similar to how they were experienced in childhood (Arntz & Jacob, 2013; Young, Klosko & Weishmaar, 2007). If certain automatic thoughts persist despite challenging them regularly, there may be schemas in play and treatment with schema therapy may be helpful.

(2) *Accepting* any remaining negative content (not as necessarily "good," but as being a possibly unchangeable Reality).

As a result, the negative thought will eventually arise less often and in a milder form, making non-thinking easier. And finally,

(3) *Coming back* to senses other than thinking (explained in Chapter 3).

Once the mind is clear, you can then either remain in a meditative state of multisensory nonthinking and nondoing, or attend to and fill awareness with senses (possibly including thoughts) involved in activities more enjoyable and useful than directing and watching mental horror movies about your life. For example, you could read the entire 11-volume, 13,549-page set of Will Durant's *The Story of Civilization* (written between 1935 and 1975 with some volumes co-authored with his wife Ariel), as did my friend's father when he emigrated from Italy, speaking no English, in order to learn how to communicate with anglophones (whom he apparently thought spent their days chatting about ancient history).

In my experience, even hardcore *mushins* (Japanese for "no-minds") who want to practice non-thinking and have an aversion to cognitive disputation usually find that in order to stop the thought from re-appearing it does help to do some cognitive disputation and acceptance (in Buddhist lingo, "equanimity"). Acceptance can be turbo charged by *committing* to action in accordance with one's *values* with regard to what *can* be changed, as pointed out in Acceptance and Commitment Therapy (ACT; Hayes, Strosahl & Wilson, 2016) and by learning to surf the squiggly line between the Yin and the Yang of acceptance and change as in Dialectical Behavior Therapy (DBT; Linehan, 2015; McKay, Wood, & Brantley, 2007).

Chapter 1 - The 1 Habit of Highly Neurotic People

Chapter 2 - *Thinking is the Frienemy*

"Now, tell me, is the air seen as 'square' in the square box, really square or not?

If so, it should not be round when 'poured' into a round box.

If not, then there should be no 'square' of air in the square box.

You say that you do not know where the 'meaning' of all this really 'lies,'

(but) the 'meaning' being so, where do you want it to 'lie'?

Ananda, if you want the air to be neither square nor round, *just throw the box away.*"

Buddha's Surangama Sutra

(Trans. Charles Luk, 1966/1999, p. 67; italics added)

Even though the goal of this book is to teach you how to stop thinking, it goes without saying, I hope, that its purpose is not to completely eradicate cognition.

As explained in Chapter 1, thinking can be either helpful or unhelpful, and it would be silly to stop doing something that is consistent with our goals. Rather, the intent here is to provide you with the ability to bring thinking under the same control that you have over the movements of your physical body. Just as you keep your legs still when you don't need to walk or kick someone, and your hands still when you don't need to drink coffee or rewind Game of Thrones to try to figure out how Bronn tackled Jaime just in time to escape Drogon's breath of fire, wouldn't it be nice to be able to keep the mind still when its services aren't needed? (that's rhetorical).

In Chapter 1, we learned (literally "we," as I'm making this up as I go along) that certain types of thinking are friendly and others more akin to White

Chapter 2 - Thinking is the Frienemy

Walkers. If there ever was a frienemy, *thinking* is it. Friendly thoughts are rational (content), time limited (process), and focus on that which can be changed (content). Enemy thoughts are irrational (content), repetitive (process) and dwell on the unchangeable (content). The analogy to the physical body holds here as well, especially as relates to motor tics and what are known as quasi-volitional body focused repetitive behaviors (BFRBs) such as nail biting, skin picking, hair pulling, teeth clenching and cheek biting. Parts of the body that are otherwise useful tools here develop habits of moving in ways that cause discomfort and sometimes constitute medical conditions.

It is useful to think of irrational and repetitive thoughts as similar to the above bodily movements. At some point they were learned, and now they need to be unlearned. They have become habits that need to be broken. One strategy for deconditioning tics and BFRBs is behavior modification, in which the undesired behavior is replaced by an incompatible behavior. For example, if one's habit is nail biting, you can bring awareness to the location of the hands and, when they are not in use for incompatible useful activities such as typing and hailing cabs, keep them folded in the lap or down at the sides. If the habit is cheek biting or teeth clenching, the incompatible habit of flattening the tongue between the teeth or whistling can be developed, depending on where you are, whom you're with and whether you can hold a tune. A similar strategy, involving reinforcement of a behavior incompatible with thinking, will be learned in Chapter 3 (the suspense builds!).

Finally, remember, we are no longer bound by the false dichotomies of Western Psychology to make false choices such as thinking inside or outside the box. As a great psychologist reminded us 2500 years ago, when we Westerners were using our busy minds to invent catapults and ice cream, we now know that we have the option to just

Throw away the box.

Chapter 3 - *Think Non-thinking*

"... [M]an will be better off if he quits monkeying with his mind

and just lets it alone."

James Thurber

(1937/2021)

"When Priest Yaoshan was sitting in meditation a monk asked,
'What do you think about, sitting in steadfast composure?'
Yaoshan said, 'I think not thinking.'
The monk said, 'How do you think not thinking?'
Yaoshan said, 'Non-thinking.'"

Zen Master John Daido Loori (2000)

"The mind and the world are opposites,

and vision arises where they meet.

When your mind doesn't stir inside,

the world doesn't arise outside.

When the world and the mind are both transparent,

this is true vision.

And such understanding is true understanding."

Bodhidharma's Wake-Up Sermon

(In Red Pine, 1989, p. 51)

"You see the objects on forgetting your own Self.

If you keep hold of your Self, you will not see the objective world."

Ramana Maharshi

(1955/2006, Talk 6)

"Throw out the garbage."

Socrates

(In Dan Millman, The Way of the Peaceful Warrior, 1980/2000, p. 118)

And here we are. As a guy in my motorcycle trail braking class said when he saw on the syllabus that we were going to learn to knee-drag around turns, "That moment has come!" This is why you bought, rented, stole or are loitering in the bookstore reading this book, right? So I'll tell you exactly what I tell my clients, for the price of whatever you paid for this book, which is probably less than the cost of a therapy session:

THE 10 LAWS OF NON-THINKING

1. During every waking moment of your day, such as right now, as well as during dreaming sleep (and nondreaming sleep, if you are a Tibetan dream yogi) *you are having an experience.*

2. Your experience is bound by the inputs to human awareness: *seeing, hearing smelling, tasting, bodysensing and thinking* (all 6 referred to as "the senses").

These can be visualized by imagining what I now call the "Awareness Clock." Around 2005 I began using it with clients and calling it the "Wheel of Attention," but then in 2013 I was at a meeting where Dan Siegel mentioned his "Wheel of Awareness," later including it in his book "Awareness" (2018). As I had similarly shifted the emphasis of my instruction from a more active attention to a more passive awareness, I changed my wheel to a clock to avoid confusion as our teachings differ.

AWARENESS CLOCK STUCK AT THINKING O'CLOCK

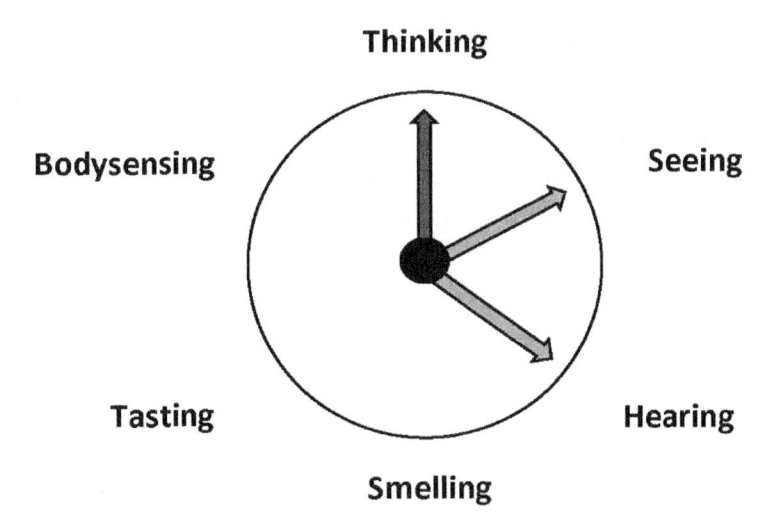

Thinking — *Seeing* — *Hearing* — *Smelling* — *Tasting* — *Bodysensing*

3. *All of the senses are American Automobile Association.* Hmm, that doesn't sound right. The mnemonic was AAA. Oh yeah, *All Always Available*. All of the senses are All Always Available (that's the problem with mnemonics).

4. *We can only be fully aware of about 2 plus or minus 1 senses at a time* for 1 to 3 degrees of (simultaneous) awareness freedom (DAF). Let's err on the optimistic side and call it 3.

5. *There is a vast left-brain conspiracy.* Due to the ignorance of our programmers (parents, teachers, etc., who themselves were victims of the same) and in the name of "education," "socialization," "enculturation" or some other such nonsense (or as our friends across the pond and those whom they colonized say, *"rubbish"*), we were misundereducated such that *one of these three degrees of freedom was locked on Thinking*, causing us to suffer for decades until discovering books such as the one I'm writing while waiting for the spaghetti to boil.

Chapter 3 - Think Non-thinking

Think about it: We were imprisoned moment by moment, step by step, inch by inch, minute after minute, hour after hour, day after day, week after week, month after month, year after year for over a decade in drab buildings; sitting for hours on end in decidedly unergonomic chairs; rewarded or punished on the basis of how much useless information we could cram into our heads and spit back, and for how long we could resist looking at interesting things, like clouds and squirrels, outside in the Free Zone; and in all that time not 2 minutes was devoted to teaching us how to control our mind. Instead one of our 3 precious degrees of awareness freedom became locked on *thinking*, the frienemy.

6. So at any given moment, *we are usually either purposely or automatically thinking*, and aware of thinking and whichever two of the other senses are momentarily more important than the remaining three.

7. Now for the $64 question: If you can only be aware of 3 senses, and you don't want to be aware of thinking, *what do you have to do?* (reminder, the 6 senses are seeing, hearing, smelling, tasting, bodysensing and thinking).

8. Come on, you can figure it out, I know you can. If you can't, that's ok too, but try again before continuing to #9.

9. BINGO! *Be aware of 3 other senses.* Usually this will involve Seeing, Hearing and Bodysensing. A useful mnemonic is See Hear Body, or ***Seehearbody*** (pronounced seeHEARbody, like Mr. Peabody, the smartest being in existence, who created the WABAC Time Machine).

AWARENESS CLOCK RESET

TO NON-THINKING O'CLOCK

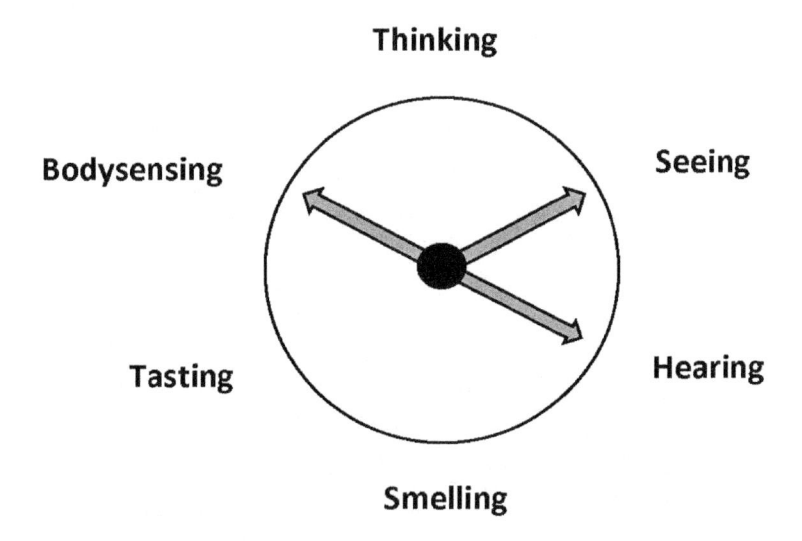

Thinking

Bodysensing

Seeing

Tasting

Hearing

Smelling

10. Throw out the garbage.

Chapter 3 - Think Non-thinking

Chapter 4 - *Questions and Answers (1)*

"But aren't ten too many to remember?"

Chapter 4 - Questions and Answers (1)

> "Walking meditation means to enjoy walking without any intention to arrive.
>
> We don't need to arrive anywhere.
>
> We just walk.
>
> We enjoy walking.
>
> That means walking is already stopping,
>
> and that needs some training."
>
> **Thich Nhat Hanh (2021, Resting in the River)**

Q: Huh?

A: Excellent question, "Don't Know Mind" say the Zen Masters. And Proverbs, 4:7: "*The beginning of wisdom is this: Get wisdom.*" And as U.G. Krishnamurti (NOT Jiddu Krishnamurti) says, "... freedom exists not in finding answers, but in the dissolution of all questions" (1988, p. 92).

Q: Say what?

A: I'm not really sure you need this book as you seem to be doing pretty well on your own, but as Mr. Huxley says, you pays your money and you takes your choice.

It all boils down to this: *Be aware of 3 other senses (Seehearbody)*. Alternatively, you can read every book on mindfulness out there, download all the apps, go to seaside mindfulness workshops, eat vegetarian food, drink ayurvedic tea at woodsy mindfulness retreats, and fly round and round the world to $5000 "mindfulness teacher certification training" programs. You can even take one of those 30-minute Saturday afternoon certificate programs out on the Harvard quad, and then you can call yourself Harvard Trained! – I'll sign your Staples certification certificate if you'll sign mine. You could then fly down to Florida and take a tour of the Kennedy Space Center and sit with someone with an I.D. badge in the cafeteria and talk to her about meditation. Then you could put on your CV that you taught at

NASA. And if you have some cash to burn, you could fly to Dharmsala and take a selfie with the Dalai Lama, and you can show it on a big powerpoint slide at conferences where you're invited to teach people to be aware of their breaths because you're Harvard trained and have taught meditation to astronauts (well, she could have been an astronaut, who knows). OR, you could just . . . *Be aware of 3 other senses (Seehearbody).*

Q: O . . . K . . . But I'm always aware of 3 senses, I mean, I'm seeing you, hearing you, I'm kind of feeling a headache coming on – are you sure you're a therapist?, but I can't stop thinking. I don't get it.

A: You *think* you're always aware of 3 senses, and you are, or you were, or you were and you are, but you're not really aware *simultaneously* of 3 senses other than thinking, except when you get really desperate and binge-watch Amazon Prime while shoving junk food into your mouth. THEN you are aware of seeing, hearing and tasting. And since that's 3 senses, there is no more awareness left for thinking (about anything other than the show, which most likely alternates with taste for a total of 3 senses at any given moment, seeing-hearing-tasting or seeing-hearing-thinking about what's going on in the show). Which would be a great plan, in a kind of unhealthy zombiac tempting heart disease sort of way, if you could spend all of your time binge watching TV eating junk food. But sooner or later you run out of cheese doodles, or have to get up to use the bathroom or go to sleep or school or work or the rec dispensary or pick up the kids at day care or something, and then KABOOM, the thoughts return with a vengeance to reclaim their begrudgingly abandoned degree of freedom AND you have a stomach ache possibly simultaneous with the munchies.

Q: Why do you hate thinking so much, Dude, or *think* you hate thinking, 'cause you seem to be doing a whole lot of thinking for a dude who hates thinking.

A: That sounded like a statement, but I'll answer it anyway. I don't hate thinking any more than I hate moving my hands or legs and yes, I move my hands, legs and mind quite frequently *when it is useful to do so.* But if hands or legs were as wild and uncontrollable as thinking, doing one thing when we want them to do something else or to just be *still,* if our hands were moving as though they were packing snowballs when we were driving our cars and our legs were moving like they were punting footballs when we were sitting in

Chapter 4 - Questions and Answers (1)

the barbershop getting a haircut, I'd be writing a book on How To Stop Moving Your Hands and Legs.

Q: Yeah, I guess. So how do I stop?

A: I just told you. But I'll go into more detail in the next chapter.

Chapter 5 - What's Your IPA-Q?
The Seehearbody Exercise

"The most merciful thing in the world,

I think,

is the inability of the human mind

to correlate all its contents."

H.P. Lovecraft

The Call of the Cthulhu (1928)

Chapter 5 - What's Your IPA-Q? The Seehearbody Exercise

The Call of Cthulhu
by H.P. Lovecraft

"The ring of worshipers moved in endless bacchanale between the ring of bodies and the ring of fire."

"Of such great powers or beings there may be conceivably a survival . . . a survival of a hugely remote period when . . . consciousness was manifested, perhaps, in shapes and forms long since withdrawn before the tide of advancing humanity . . . forms of which poetry and legend alone have caught a flying memory and called them gods, monsters, mythical beings of all sorts and kinds. . . ."
—*Algernon Blackwood.*

1. The Horror in Clay.

THE most merciful thing in the world, I think, is the inability of the human mind to correlate all its contents. We live on a placid island of ignorance in the midst of black seas of infinity, and it was not meant that we should voyage far. The sciences, each straining in its own direction, have hitherto harmed us little; but some day the piecing together of dissociated knowledge will open up such terrifying vistas of reality, and of our frightful position therein, that we shall either go mad from the revelation or flee from the deadly light into the peace and safety of a new dark age.

Theosophists have guessed at the awesome grandeur of the cosmic cycle wherein our world and human race form transient incidents. They have hinted at strange survivals in terms which would freeze the blood if not masked by a bland optimism.

Found among the papers of the late Francis Wayland Thurston, of Boston.

Now, bear with me here. No, not a real bear, just a figure of speech. If it was (were?) a real bear (or possibly worse yet, a real cthulhu), I might (mert?) have alerted you in a manner more akin to NOW! BEAR WITH ME! HERE! OVER HERE! HELP! OVER HERE I SAID! WHY ARE YOU ALL RUNNING THAT WAY?! Or is it "bare" with me. No, that would be inappropriate. Unless you're reading this in the tub, in which case, carry on. Bayer with me? (Did my childhood friend Joel's father really invent aspirin? He did work at that Bayer plant a few miles away in Whippany. Hold on. Just checked. "By 1899, Bayer had created acetylsalicylic acid and named the drug 'Aspirin'" – which turned out to be a good move. "Take two acetylsalicylic acid compounds and call me in the morning" just doesn't have the same ring to it. Well, I met Joel in 1975, which would have been 76 years after the invention of Aspirin. I suppose if his father went to work for Bayer after college at age 22, say, and invented Aspirin during his first year there, that would have made him 98 in 1975. Adults do look older when we're children, but he hardly looked 98. Joel was 13 when I met him, so that means his father would have been 85 when he was born. Possible, but on second thought maybe it was his great grandfather who invented Aspirin. I'll have to check and get back to you on this. Or not.)

Moving right along, if you are reading this in the 1980s or any time prior to the extinction of the Pencils, please take out a number 2 pencil (how many times you've heard that phrase is, in fact, an accurate indicator of your age). If you are reading this in the 2020s, turn off your phone and place it somewhere outside of your field of vision. You can do it. Unless you are reading this on your phone, in which case keep it in your field of vision. Unless you are listening to this as an audiobook. 1980s people, if you have an eraser and pencil sharpener, please place them on your desk.

Item 1: Who was George Hodgson?

Item 2: Where was Captain Cook on August 25, 1769 and what does it have to do with George?

Item 3: According to *The Compleat English Brewer*, published in 1767, how many bushels to the hogshead was October ale traditionally brewed at and what was the upper limit before it became too "heady"?

Oops, wrong book.

Chapter 5 - What's Your IPA-Q? The Seehearbody Exercise

If you're still trying to figure out the answers to the above, either *be aware of 3 other senses* or learn more about craft beers at Zythophile.co.uk. I would highly recommend the Clown Shoes American Monastic.

THE IPA-Q TEST

Your IPA-Q is your *Intentional Preferential Awareness Quotient*: how many senses you are capable of being selectively (intentionally and preferentially) aware of simultaneously. It is represented as Degrees of Awareness Freedom (DAF).

You will benefit most from this exercise if you remain in the same place and in the same position, standing, sitting, reclining or lying down for the entire 3 minutes. If you are strap-hanging, that's OK too, just be careful of looking toward people who might think you're staring at them.

Warning: Do not take the IPQ-Q Test while in any situation requiring awareness of potential dangers, such as operating a vehicle or piece of machinery with sharp blades, like a helicopter or chainsaw, or while walking, or flying, in an area where other people are operating vehicles or machinery with sharp blades.

INSTRUCTION 1

Sitting, reclining or standing right where you are, **SEE what is in your visual field.** Don't "pay attention" to it, don't "concentrate" on it, don't "focus" on it (though from a hypnotic perspective, I've just conversationally programmed you to do all three, but I really don't want you to, so please don't). These are all tight, authoritarian words that have gotten the world in the mess it's in. So just *see*. Passively *see*. Be aware of *seeing*. Your eyes are open and you *see*, without any effort, trying or striving. (If you are vision impaired, just see whatever you see or consider seeing to be.)

To illustrate, right now, alternate for about 5 seconds each among simply *seeing* what's in front of you, then *paying attention* to it, then *concentrating* on it, then *focusing* on it, then just *seeing* it again, and repeat the sequence one or two more times. I think you'll notice a difference between the relaxation and passivity of *just seeing* and the tightness and activity of the others. Another way to avoid the effort trap is rather than seeing something small or defined as an object or shape, you could be aware of your entire visual field, what's in front of you, as well as what's in your peripheral vision to the right and left, above and below, with a soft focus. If you wear glasses or contacts, it could even help to remove them so things are a little blurry, preventing focusing on anything in particular (as long as your eyes don't automatically try to focus to compensate for the blurriness and give you a headache, in which case take some acetylsalicylic acid, invented by my friend's great grandfather, by the way, and call me in the morning. Oh yeah, I'm not *that* kind of doctor). Alternatively, if you don't wear glasses, you could borrow a pair from someone who does (being sure to take pandemic precautions if reading this during the End of Days. Uh oh, did I just practice ophthalmology without a license?).

Now, set a timer (such as on your phone) for 1 minute and *just see* and *be aware* of seeing. If at any moment you realize that seeing has *RE-appeared*, meaning that it had disappeared (like knowing you've been asleep because you've awoken), turn off the alarm. Test Over. **Your score is ZERO, less than 1 degree of awareness freedom.** Now, please, *don't worry about this*, we've all been there, and all are currently there at times. I was probably there myself earlier in this paragraph. However, at the moment, you are not capable of being aware of 1 sense continuously for 1 minute. If the condition persists, turn in your driver's license and be really, *really* careful doing anything other than lying in bed watching TV eating cheese doodles. Careful not to bite your tongue. Whatever you do, if you are chewing bubblegum, don't walk, and if you are walking make sure someone is spotting you.

If the alarm rings and you've been continuously aware of seeing for 1 minute, Congratulations, You Did It, go to Instruction 2.

INSTRUCTION 2

Set the timer for 1 minute. **While continuing to *SEE* what is in front of you, *HEAR*** whatever sounds are available to hearing, near or far, pleasant or aversive, internal or external. Don't "pay attention" to them, don't "concentrate" on them, don't "focus" on any sound in particular (#BanEducation), just *hear* the full cacophony, the refrigerator, someone at the next table talking really loudly so strangers in the whole diner will know how smart they are and validate their existence, car noises in the distance, your tinnitus, just *hear* this organic free jazz, and *see* simultaneously and continuously.

Chapter 5 - What's Your IPA-Q? The Seehearbody Exercise

If at any moment you realize that seeing OR hearing has *RE-appeared*, meaning that it had disappeared, turn off the alarm. Test Over. **Your score: 1 degree of awareness freedom (because you completed the 1 minute in Instruction 1).** *You're getting there.* You are capable of being aware of 1 sense continuously for 1 minute. However, if you do choose to chew bubblegum and walk at the same time, make sure to wear knee and elbow guards, and stop both chewing and walking before sending an important text to your boss.

If the alarm rings and you've been continuously aware of both seeing and hearing for 1 minute, without either of them re-appearing, Congratulations, You Go Girl, Bob's Your Uncle, go to Instruction 3.

INSTRUCTION 3

Set the timer for 1 minute. **While continuing to *SEE* and *HEAR* what is available to your eyes and ears**, *be aware of your **BODYSENSE***, the feeling of your body in space. Be aware of the overall physical sensation of having a body, internal sensations such as tingling, lightness, heaviness, aches, pains or, not to discriminate against readers in the not-so-distant future, neurosocket itching; the feeling of bodily contact with external objects such as clothing, shoes or, for our backward time-traveling readers, chain mail, brass knuckles or spears; sensations of contact with objects supporting the body such as the chair, bed, rock or ground; and any sensations arising from contact with the air in the room or prairie, the heat from lamps, fireplaces, volcanos or distant suns, or for our future readers, the coolness of the air con in your houseboat in the Arizona ocean.

Again, don't "pay attention," don't "concentrate," don't "focus" on any sensation in particular (#FreeTheChildren), just be aware of the overall *seeing, hearing and bodysensing simultaneously and continuously.*

If at any moment you realize that seeing OR hearing OR bodysensing has *RE-appeared*, meaning that it had disappeared, turn off the alarm. Test Over. **Your score: 2 degrees of awareness freedom (from completing the 1 minute in Instruction 1 and the 1 minute in Instruction 2)**. Give that (wo)man a chocolate cigar.

If the alarm rings and you've been continuously aware of seeing, hearing and bodysensing for 1 minute, without any of them re-appearing,

Congratulations, Tickety Boo, Polka Dots and Moonbeams, You're the New Normal, go to Instruction 4.

INSTRUCTION 4

Set the timer for 1 minute. **While continuing to *SEE, HEAR* and *BODYSENSE*, be aware of any *TASTE* in your mouth.**

Again, don't "pay attention," don't "concentrate," don't "focus" on any taste in particular (#TurnOnTuneInDropOut), just be aware of the overall *seeing, hearing, bodysensing and tasting simultaneously and continuously.*

If at any moment you realize that seeing OR hearing OR bodysensing OR taste has *RE-appeared*, meaning that it had disappeared, turn off the alarm. Test Over. **Your score: 3 degrees of awareness freedom (from completing the 1 minute in Instruction 1, the 1 minute in Instruction 2, and the 1 minute in Instruction 3).** Congratulations! Give me some of whatever you're vaping.

However, if the alarm rings and you've been continuously aware of seeing, hearing, bodysensing and tasting for 1 minute, without any of them re-appearing, **you have a score of 4+.** You are not men, you are Devo. You are way too skilled at this for the average bear. Keep an eye out for my upcoming book "How to Tell if You're an Android." Be a good fellow(ette)(X) and activate the time machine function of your FTL transporter and beam yourself here to finish writing this book for me while I go to DD and buy some munchkins. Strike that, I still have some in the car from Sunday. Continue as you were. Be right back.

PAT ON THE BACK

If you got a sucky score on the above exercise, don't fret. I just did it myself and, being all inside my head at the moment, which isn't a bad place to be when trying to write a book (that's called *rationalization*), I actually got a score of 0. Luckily, I have a problem with authority, so I didn't turn in my driver's license. Instead, I continued on and then got a score of 1. Persisting, I eventually got a score of 2 and then 3. But a score of 4 was beyond me, and when I tried to add a 5th sense (imagining a pink elephant), senses kept re-appearing like there was no tomorrow (which there never really is, as it has a nasty habit of becoming "today"). I also realized that when doing this exercise, it is quite easy *not* to notice when a sense re-appears, meaning it had disappeared, because at the moment that it re-appears, especially if it had only disappeared momentarily, there is an illusion of continuity, like with movies projected through reels (google it) that consist of single frames that look like they're moving when they appear on the screen one after another really fast. I know, it sounds like science fiction, but it was actually invented decades just preceding the extinction of the Pencils, like the electric car, and then erased from the history books (those paper things at your grandma's house).

Unless you're already a seasoned meditator, it is likely that you will be tricked by the illusion of continuity to overestimate your score. That's OK, as even if you base your initial individualized How To Stop Thinking program on an inflated score, I'll teach you a simple technique to titrate (vary the dosage) down to a more accurate one. Also to keep in mind is that the Seehearbody Degree of Awareness Freedom (SDAF), also known (starting now) as the Intentional Preferential Awareness Quotient (IPA-Q) is probably more of a state (frequently changing) than a trait (unchanging, immutable, eternal) and, perhaps most importantly, that it is just a bunch of words that crossed my mind at a MacDonald's drive through (psychologists love making up stuff, naming it, preferably referring to it by its initials, and then gloating as the culture *reifies* it (refers to something abstract as though it's real) and turns it into a *dryad* (a tree nymph)(but see also Ebel, 1974).

YOUR IPA-Q

Most of us, most of the time, will score a 2 or 3 on the Seehearbody exercise, meaning that we can fairly comfortably be aware of 2 or 3 senses simultaneously and continuously for 1 or more minutes. Anyone with less than a 2 has smaller fish to fry than reading this book, or possibly any book, and anybody with a 4+ should probably just read the instruction manual that came with their neurodrive wetware to learn how to set their awareness parameters.

But for us Twobies and Threebies writing and reading this book, since we have been programmed by the Public Miseducational System (PMS) via various forms of coercive conditioning to be almost continuously aware of thinking as one of our 2 or 3 degrees of awareness freedom (remember when your parents or teachers had hissy fits in which they pulled out their hair while yelling "Why can't you just pay attention?!," "Focus!," "Can't you listen for once?!," "Concentrate!"), that means that there are only 1 or 2 degrees of freedom, respectively, available for awareness of other senses to occur simultaneously with thinking. For example, when a person with a Seehearbody score of 2 is driving, they will be thinking and simultaneously (or quickly alternating between) seeing the road and hearing road noises. They will probably not be aware of the feeling of their hands on the steering wheel or their feet on the accelerator unless specifically asked, but steering wheels and accelerators take this into account and have low sensitivity and so are sufficiently forgiving that we usually make it home each day without having to replace an airbag. After leaving Manhattan, they will exit the New Jersey end of the Lincoln Tunnel with no memory of having driven through it, but we made it through alive so what's the big deal?

The big deal (Debby Downer Alert, but you did buy a self-help book) is that some of us spend our nearly 500 yearly journeys through the Lincoln Tunnel making ourselves depressed, anxious, or enraged by ruminating on depressing pasts, worrying about catastrophic futures, or ranting in our minds about some theistically doomed incestuous excretory organ who cut in front of us on line to the tunnel. In other words, we allot one of our 2 or 3 degrees of awareness freedom to automatic or intentional (or automatic intentional) THINKING about things that have nothing to do with getting safely to work or back home and which add insult to injury by making us *miserable*. And the Lincoln tunnel is of course just a metaphor for every waking moment of every day.

How is this knowledge helpful in learning how to stop thinking? First, it demonstrates the truth of Law 4 of The 10 Laws of Non-thinking (*We can only be fully aware of about 2 plus or minus 1 senses at a time* for 1 to 3 degrees of simultaneous awareness freedom), without me having to do actual research and then trying to publish it and have a journal editor sit on the manuscript for **TWO YEARS** failing even to inform me of what's going on until a whole year later when I send him a really polite email (you don't want to piss off an editor) telling him that I'm just *wondering* when I *might* expect a decision regarding my manuscript, and then receive an email saying that no reviewers have been identified with an expertise in How to Stop Thinking (surprise, surprise) and that I am of course free to withdraw the article and submit it elsewhere. Second, it allows us to individualize your How To Stop Thinking program and tweak the general *be aware of 3 other senses* rule to your current **IPA-Q** using the guidelines below.

INDIVIDUALIZING YOUR
HOW TO STOP THINKING PROGRAM

Your IPA-Q will be most relevant to the practice of mindfulness (see Chapter 8), but may also help when starting a sitting meditation practice (see Chapter 7). Attempting to be simultaneously aware of more senses than your score or your score plus 1 may be tiring, and attempting to be aware of a number of senses less than your score will allow thoughts to arise frequently, as is their current habit. In the latter case, you will, by returning from the thoughts to the other senses, be getting valuable practice in stopping thinking. However, in the process, you'll continue to suffer from the effects of the overthinking such as ineffectiveness in doing something that requires awareness (as at work) or that requires a lack of awareness (as in bed) (unless you work in bed, in which case, STOP IT). Meditation, as you will see in the next chapter, purposely begins with awareness of only 1 sense (e.g., the feeling of the breath, or the internalized sound of a mantra) in order to be below most individuals' IPA-Q and therefore leave 1 or 2 degrees of awareness freedom unused (in the case of IPA-Qs of 2 or 3, respectively), allowing thoughts to enter awareness frequently enough to obtain training in returning from them.

As a general rule, when learning to stop thinking,

If your DAF is 0, such that you have difficulty being continuously aware of 1 sense for 1 minute, practice being aware of 1 sense other than thinking (e.g., seeing).

If your DAF is 1, such that you can be continuously aware of 1 sense for 1 minute, practice being aware of 2 senses other than thinking (e.g., seeing and hearing).

If your DAF is 2, such that you can be continuously aware of 2 senses for 1 minute, practice being aware of 3 senses other than thinking (e.g., seeing, hearing and bodysensing).

If your DAF is 3, such that you can be continuously aware of 3 senses for 1 minute, practice being aware of 3 or 4 senses other than thinking, noting that 3 is usually sufficient to stop thinking and 4 can get tiring (e.g., seeing, hearing, bodysensing and, if 4, tasting).

If your DAF is 4, my hunch is that either you have fallen victim to the illusion of continuity discussed above or, if not, please remember to beam us your people's cures for cancer and aging and the blueprints of your antigravity, perpetual motion, worm hole transport and time displacement devices.

A Note on Titration (Dosing)

How can you know whether you inadvertently misoverestimated or misunderestimated your score by mistaking a re-appearing sense for a continuous one (or concluding that a sense re-appeared when it was in fact present the entire time)? Easy. When you practice being simultaneously aware of the number of senses specified above, if senses keep re-appearing, then you have probably overestimated your score and should subtract a sense. If, on the other hand, when you practice being simultaneously aware of the number of senses specified above, thinking remains fairly continuous, then you have probably underestimated your score and should add a sense.

USING THE SEAHEARBODY EXERCISE
AS A MEDITATION AND MINDFULNESS PRACTICE

The Seahearbody technique can be used to stop thinking anytime, anywhere, whether in the midst of activity, sitting still, or lying in bed trying to fall asleep. While it does not need to be coordinated in any way with the breath, and does not require mentally voicing instructions, these can be helpful in the beginning, as follows:

1. Begin by breathing normally through your nose (or through your mouth if your nose is stuffy).

2. On the first inhale and exhale, mentally say "See" and be aware of whatever is in your visual field.

3. On the next inhale and exhale, mentally say "Hear" and, in addition to seeing, be aware of whatever sounds are in your environment.

4. On the next inhale and exhale, mentally say "Body" and, in addition to seeing and hearing, be aware of your whole bodysense, or the feeling of the air entering and leaving your nose.

Chapter 5 - What's Your IPA-Q? The Seehearbody Exercise

5. On the next inhale and exhale, and as you continue to breathe in and out, do not mentally repeat See, Hear or Body. Just continue being aware of all three senses, seeing, hearing and the bodysensing at the same time.

6. Whenever you notice that you are not aware of one or more of the senses because of thinking, return to awareness of all three of the senses, repeating 1 through 5 if necessary.

WARNING: *Do Not Practice The Seehearbody Exercise in any situation in which it is important to be aware of your surroundings to avoid danger* (e.g., driving, crossing a street, cutting down a tree or figuring out where to hide from a bear). *I mean it.* In 2006, when I was receiving training in Ericksonian hypnosis, I was practicing a sequential monosensing exercise and suddenly heard a car honking at me. It seems that I had approached a crosswalk and most likely seen the little red "don't walk" man, but must have been attending uniquely to *seeing* and did not process its *meaning* ("how not to die today") or hear the oncoming cars.

Chapter 6 - *The Myth of "I Can't Meditate"*

"Generally then if you would make any thing a habit, do it;

if you would not make it a habit, do not do it,

but accustom yourself to do something else in place of it."

Epictetus

(The Discourses, Book 2, Chapter 18; Long, 1890, p. 159)

The most common thing I hear from people with whom I am for whatever reason discussing meditation is

"I can't meditate, I think too much."

This has always struck me as the equivalent of

"I can't take a Tylenol, my head hurts too much."

It's a *faulty conclusion* based on a *faulty premise*, the premise being an inaccurate understanding of what meditation is and why people do it.

Those who think "I can't meditate, I think too much" would be correct if meditation were defined as having a "still mind" or "not thinking." Just as hypothetical people who think "I can't take a Tylenol, my head hurts too much" would be right if taking a Tylenol required not having a headache. But the truth of the matter is that we take Tylenol (or whatever) *because* we have a headache, and we meditate *because* we can't stop thinking. If effects were necessarily conditions for their causes, we would be in big trouble, both logically and pragmatically. There would, of course, be some upsides, like getting things done before starting them, or driving away with things before having to pay for them, but wait a minute, that's called "credit card debt."

Chapter 6 - The Myth of "I Can't Meditate"

Ok, bad counter-example. Or starting life with wisdom and ending it with an orgasm, to steal from Woody Allen, but he stole it from Sean Morey (1980) who stole it from Mark Twain anyway:

> "Life would be infinitely happier if we could only be born at the age of eighty and gradually approach eighteen." (Twain, in Phelps, 1939)

In any event, from a Yin-Yang and Zen perspective, causes and effects occur simultaneously, and are really the same thing, because one can't exist without the other. However, for our purposes, in the *realm* of sequential time, let's stick with "causes precede effects," with the understanding that "we meditate in order to learn how to stop thinking" rather than "meditation requires the stopping of thinking."

"But," the curious reader who pays attention to the stories below the chapter headings may ask, "didn't Priest Yaoshan tell the monk that when meditating he thinks not thinking by non-thinking?"

Yes, Grasshopper, he did indeed. Just as when lying in bed after the Tylenol has taken effect you feel no headache by feeling non-headache. *But first you had to take the Tylenol. And before you took it, and for a while as it began to take effect, you had a headache.* While Yaoshan isn't here to correct me if I'm wrong, I would bet the rest of yesterday's egg McMuffin that he did not always have a still mind, that he began meditating when his mind was like ours (monkey mind or wild horse mind, as they say), and that on some days his mind was busy for some time before it settled down into thinking non-thinking.

So are you ready to realize that you are, at this very moment, capable of being a *perfect* meditator? Ok then. Here's how it works:

(1) MEDITATION *DOES NOT MEAN* KEEPING THE MIND STILL (which is impossible) **OR NOT THINKING** (which is impossible for extended periods). Wanna know when your mind will be still without any thinking? *After you get eaten by a bear.* By contrast:

(2) Meditation means:

>   (a) **Setting an *intention* to be continuously aware of something** for however short or long this happens to be; and

(b) **Whenever you realize you're not aware of it** (because you're human or a Dollar Store android), **become aware of it again (*COME BACK*).**

That's it (with the caveat that in some forms of meditation the intention is to be aware of the continuous flow of whatever arises in awareness, without fixating on any one thing).

So if I tell you to sit and meditate for 10 hours, using the feeling of the breath as it enters and leaves your nose as the object of awareness, and you are aware of it for 5 seconds, then zoom off into thinking without even realizing it for the next 9 hours 59 minutes and 50 seconds, then realize you haven't been aware of your breath and become aware of it again for the remaining 5 seconds until the 10 hour timer rings, how would you rate your 10 hour meditation session on a scale of 1 to 10?

Just in case you didn't rate it yet, let's do this together. You were aware of your breath for 10 seconds and you were thinking for 9 hours, 59 minutes and 50 seconds. Would you give your meditation session a score of 0, meaning it was not good at all? Would you give it a 5 as a mediocre meditation session? After you rate it, continue to the next paragraph for my take on it.

According to the above definition of meditation . . . *You've been perfectly meditating for 10 hours.* Even though you only spent 10 seconds aware of your breath and possibly non-thinking, and you spent 9 hours 59 minutes and 50 seconds thinking, *you perfectly meditated for 10 hours.*

But How Is This Possible???

Very good question. Because, *you followed the instructions.* You (1) set an intention to be continuously aware of something for however long or short it happened to be, and (2) when you realized you weren't aware of it, you *came back* (returned to awareness of it). To belabor a point, because this misunderstanding is probably the single biggest barrier to people beginning or continuing to practice meditation:

Chapter 6 - The Myth of "I Can't Meditate"

Meditation *does not mean* keeping the mind still or not thinking.

Meditation means setting an *intention* to be continuously aware of something, and whenever you realize you're not aware of it, COME BACK, be aware of it again.

That's it (again, with the caveat that in some forms of meditation the intention is to be aware of the continuous flow of whatever arises in awareness, without fixating on any one thing).

Imagine that you live in a 500 square foot studio apartment and a friend asks you to take care of her 2-year-old black Labrador Boris for a few weeks while she's on vacation, and Boris has spent his whole life on a farm with free rein of the pastures, never having seen a leash. Now imagine that you don't hang up on her. When you put a leash on Boris and begin walking with him down the street, how long do you think he will walk next to you for? Right. About 2 seconds, until he sees a squirrel, and he's off. So what do you do? You pull him back. Now he stays next to you for about 4 seconds until he sees a butterfly. And he's off again. Walking Boris has now become Training Boris to Heel. Over the course of the next week, Boris spends a little more time walking next to you each day, with the operative term being "a little." By the end of the week he might, if you're lucky, walk next to you for about 10 seconds before pulling away to try and chase something.

Now, if I were to ask you at the end of the week how training Boris is going, what would you say? Are you failing because Boris isn't walking next to you the whole time? Are you failing because Boris still spends most of his time pulling you rather than you walking him? The correct answer is no. You're doing fine. Training a dog to heel doesn't mean the dog is walking next to you the whole time, or that it isn't pulling away. If that were the case, we wouldn't call it "training a dog to heel," we'd call it "walking a dog that has been trained to heel." What training a dog to heel really involves is putting the leash on with an intention of having the dog walk next to you, and when it pulls away you pull it back. If each time Boris pulls away you pull him back, you are a perfect dog trainer. If it turns out that Boris is too stupid to learn to walk next to you (or so smart that he lets you think he's stupid so you'll give up and just let him pull you around and maybe even refuse to take him next time so his owner will have to find a friend with a farm) that's not your problem. You still performed perfectly as a dog trainer. Likewise, when you meditate, if each time you realize your mind has wandered away from your breath you become aware once again of your breath, you are a perfect meditator, even if it only stays put for a few seconds before starting to think again.

Another analogy is that of an airplane flying overhead. If you are walking and hear an airplane, you may look up for a moment, but probably won't continue looking at it as you walk, trying to count the windows, wondering where each person behind each window lives and what they do for a living. You'll simply hear it, maybe look at it for a moment and then continue walking. Does the fact that you hear the airplane and see it mean that you are "bad at walking?" Of course not. You're doing exactly what's necessary for walking, and if you become momentarily aware of hearing and seeing the plane you just as soon *come back* to awareness of walking. Being a good walker doesn't mean you stay continuously aware only of walking and don't become aware of things other than walking. It just means that among the myriad things that will enter and leave your awareness, you *favor* the awareness of walking (a shout out to my transcendental Cousin Paul for turning me on to "favoring" awareness of certain things when meditating as opposed to "paying attention" to them).

Chapter 6 - The Myth of "I Can't Meditate"

Meditation, understood as *returning* to the object of awareness rather than as *staying* with the object of awareness, is not only easy to do perfectly, it is also relatively effortless. If I were to give you a transparent plastic shoe box, place a penny in the middle of the bottom of the box and place an ant on it with the instruction: "Bring this to work, and make sure the ant stays on the penny," you probably wouldn't do it because it sounds kind of crazy. However, if you did do it, you probably wouldn't get much work done that day (no, you are not allowed to cup something over the penny, and NO, you may not harm the ant in any way). This is the predicament of people who think *"meditation means keeping the mind still and not thinking."*

On the other hand, if I were to instruct you to bring the ant on the coin in the box to work, and to just go about your work day and *kind of* keep an eye on the box and whenever you happened to notice that the ant was off the penny to just pick it up and put it back on, you still probably wouldn't do it. But, if you did, you wouldn't find this too difficult. You'd put the box somewhere nearby, do your work, look over at the box every once in a while, notice that the ant had moved, pick it up and put it back on the penny, and go back to your work until you noticed the ant had moved off the penny again or until they wheeled you away in a straitjacket. This is the correct view of meditation as *"just come back"* (with this instruction being more relevant to "concentrative" meditation than to "open awareness" meditation, but even in open awareness traditions, some concentrative practice is often combined with open awareness, such as breath counting to 10 prior to Zen *shikantaza* or "just sitting").

Chapter 7 - Psychological Meditation:
Sometimes I Just Sits

Vicar's Wife (sympathizingly). "NOW THAT YOU CAN'T GET ABOUT, AND ARE NOT ABLE TO READ, HOW DO YOU MANAGE TO OCCUPY THE TIME?"

Old Man. "WELL, MUM, SOMETIMES I SITS AND THINKS; AND THEN AGAIN I JUST SITS."

William Gunning King

(*Punch*, October 24, 1906, p. 297)

Chapter 7 - Psychological Meditation: Sometimes I Just Sits

FIRSTLY, *contrary to the Internet,* it was not Pooh Bear who first distinguished between sitting and thinking and just sitting, purportedly saying:

"Sometimes I sits and thinks and sometimes I just sits."

This partly because bears never just sits, being always on the lookout for people to eat, but also because Winnie the Pooh was written in 1926 and the above cartoon was published in 1906, and because those words just do not appear in any Pooh book. Even the Punch cartoon was repeating something apparently first said by a Maine fisherman in 1905:

"A bond salesman just back from Maine

says he asked an old fisherman in a snow-bound hamlet

what he did with himself evenings.

The reply was:

'Oh, sometimes I sit and think, and then again I just sit.'"

(Boston Record, 1905)

Then in 1911, a novel entitled "A Saga of the 'Sunbeam'" about yachting included the following passage, repeating the 1906 usage of the third-person "I":

"There is some reading done, a deal of sleeping and much eating, but for the most part it rather resembles the days of a bucolic old gentleman who was asked, since he was past bucolic activities, what he did with his time. 'Sometimes,' he said, 'I sits and thinks, and other times I just sits.'" (Hutchinson, 1911, p. 16)

In 2006, the lyricism of the second "sometimes" seems to have been added in a misattribution to Winnie the Pooh of the formulation:

"Sometimes I sit and think,

and sometimes I just sit." (Le Beau, 2006)

The combination of the second "sometimes" and the third person "I" was then provided by a Reverend David Huber (2009), attributing to baseball player Satchel Paige the expression in question:

> "Sometimes I sits and thinks,
>
> and sometimes I just sits."

Whether it was Satchel Paige who said this or the Reverend who heard, mis-heard, heard of, mis-heard of or simply mis-remembered Satchel Paige saying it, is beyond the scope of my, and likely your, interest, and frankly I'm getting tired of sitsing. As an aside, while Winnie the Pooh most definitely did not say

> "Sometimes I sits and thinks,
>
> and sometimes I just sits,"

Pooh did have a lot to say about thinking, which I won't repeat here because I'm running out of copyright permission coupons.

SECONDLY, in what may now seem a non-sequitur, though I assure you that this is a mere appearance occasioned by my having begun the chapter with a non-sequitur cum non-praecedunt, the true praecedunt being the beginning of the preceding chapter, the second most common thing I hear when I ask people if they meditate, after the first most common thing I hear when I ask people if they meditate ("I can't meditate") is:

> "I have an app."

To which, with all due respect to apps, and despite their obvious usefulness for things such as stealing all of your personal information and selling it to people who will one day steal all of your money, I inform them, nicely, in small case, and without exclamation marks, except this once:

YOU DON'T NEED AN APP TO MEDITATE!!!

People have meditated without apps other than their nose for *thousands*, and possibly *millions* of years *in this galaxy alone*, let alone on Tralfamadore in the Small Magellanic Cloud (Be right back – My Pseudointellectual Reference to Slaughterhouse Five Alarm just went off and the neighbors of myself or some unfortunate soul actually named Dogu Densei will soon be on their way with torches and pitchforks).

Chapter 7 - Psychological Meditation: Sometimes I Just Sits

But before they get here (for if they merely get *there*, as unfortunate as that may likely be for Dogu, my own ability to continue writing is unlikely to be perturbed) it is worthwhile noting that the Small Magellanic Cloud (NASA, 2013) is known as a "star nursery" and actually looks like it is birthing an infant:

Please note that this image is NOT photoshopped, at least not to my *knowledge*. It is on the NASA website, and governments don't lie. Well at least not usually about what galaxies look like, I mean, what would their *angle* be? OK, I *know* you think it's a fake photo, and I don't want your distrust to interfere with our author-reader *rapport,* so here, look, it really is

an official NASA photo:
https://www.nasa.gov/mission_pages/spitzer/multimedia/pia16884.html

Uh oh. While proofreading 2 years after writing the foregoing I clicked that link which did load a NASA webpage but with the message: "404 The cosmic object you are looking for has disappeared beyond the event horizon." But I assure you that that is where I originally found the photo. Guess I'll have to do a little investigating. No problem, I'll just enter "Small Magellanic Cloud" into the Search box on the NASA webpage and see what I find. Well, these show the baby's face from a different angle:

https://apod.nasa.gov/apod/ap101017.html

https://apod.nasa.gov/apod/ap080918.html

Chapter 7 - Psychological Meditation: Sometimes I Just Sits

AHA! Found it:

(https://www.jpl.nasa.gov/images/pia16884-taken-under-the-wing-of-the-small-magellanic-cloud)

Apologies accepted. But I'd like to hear you say it out loud: "Dogu did not photoshop the Small Magellanic Cloud and add a baby's face." And yet, the description of the photo on the NASA webpage should win some kind of award:

> "The tip of the 'wing' of the Small Magellanic Cloud galaxy is dazzling in this new view from NASA's Great Observatories. The Small Magellanic Cloud, or SMC, is a small galaxy about 200,000 light-years away that orbits our own Milky Way spiral galaxy. The colors represent wavelengths of light across a broad spectrum. X-rays from NASA's Chandra X-ray Observatory are shown in purple;

visible-light from NASA's Hubble Space Telescope is colored red, green and blue; and infrared observations from NASA's Spitzer Space Telescope are also represented in red. The spiral galaxy seen in the lower corner is actually behind this nebula. Other distant galaxies located hundreds of millions of light-years or more away can be seen sprinkled around the edge of the image. The SMC is one of the Milky Way's closest galactic neighbors. Even though it is a small, or so-called dwarf galaxy, the SMC is so bright that it is visible to the unaided eye from the Southern Hemisphere and near the equator. Many navigators, including Ferdinand Magellan who lends his name to the SMC, used it to help find their way across the oceans. Modern astronomers are also interested in studying the SMC (and its cousin, the Large Magellanic Cloud), but for very different reasons. Because the SMC is so close and bright, it offers an opportunity to study phenomena that are difficult to examine in more distant galaxies. New Chandra data of the SMC have provided one such discovery: the first detection of X-ray emission from young stars, with masses similar to our sun, outside our Milky Way galaxy. NASA's Jet Propulsion Laboratory, Pasadena, Calif., manages the Spitzer Space Telescope mission for NASA's Science Mission Directorate, Washington. Science operations are conducted at the Spitzer Science Center at the California Institute of Technology in Pasadena. Data are archived at the Infrared Science Archive housed at the Infrared Processing and Analysis Center at Caltech. Caltech manages JPL for NASA. For more information about Spitzer, visit http://spitzer.caltech.edu and http://www.nasa.gov/spitzer" (NASA, 2022)

What's obviously missing from this description is any mention of THE GINORMOUS BABY'S HEAD FLOATING IN THE CLOUD. Talk about avoiding the elephant in the room.

Now where were we? Oh, right, you want to use an app to meditate. If you insist on using an app to meditate, that's your prerogative, it's still a free world on some isolated patches of land or maybe under the ocean somewhere, but another option is to just *put down the damn phone for 2 minutes and give the hackers who are monitoring your every move a break. Hackers are people too.*

Chapter 7 - Psychological Meditation: Sometimes I Just Sits

Seriously though, many of my clients swear by their meditation apps, many people were first introduced to meditation by an app, and in that sense they provide a great service to humanity. I would, however, suggest that if you use an app to meditate, it could be interesting to try simple non-electronic breath awareness from time to time and see if you like it.

While meditation, mindfulness and yoga are really the same thing (see Chapter 9), I have relegated, delegated and otherwise -elegated them to different chapters in keeping with the common ignorance that they are fundamentally (as opposed to merely surfacely) different. This, for two reasons. First, even if ultimately everything is "One," until we are "there yet," it is useful to use "expedient means" to start us on our way. Second, since these words that we come across on a daily basis are often misrepresented and misunderstood, it could be useful to present them each in detail.

Since there are many definitions of meditation out there, and any one of them can be picked apart and criticized for omissions, commissions and redundancies, I will propose a starting point, that will in turn be picked apart and criticized for omissions, commissions and redundancies by others, and which I will develop further elsewhere in this book, providing further fodder for those of the critical persuasion:

Meditation is Selective Awareness
for Psychological Purposes.

Regardless of the type of meditation that one is doing, one is being *selectively aware* of *one or more of the senses* (seeing, hearing, smelling, tasting, bodysensing or thinking). This holds as well for open awareness meditation in which one is selectively aware of information from whichever sense happens to be most salient at a given moment. But if meditation was just selective awareness, then everyone would by definition be meditating all the time, because we are all selectively aware during every waking moment, and such a broad definition would remove the need for "meditation" as a word and concept, not necessarily a bad thing but, in the *realm* of words and concepts, such as in *books* such as this, and when *communicating* to other humanoids (or mushrooms, which have recently been found to communicate with word-like units of meaning; Adamatzky, 2022; you can listen to a mushroom conversation here: https://youtu.be/tjIG0wTVIBo) words and concepts can be useful. Thus, the addition of "for psychological purposes" in the definition. People meditate for a reason, and this reason involves the psychological effects of meditation, whether to still the mind, trigger physical relaxation, attain altered states of consciousness, become "enlightened" or reduce physical or mental health issues related to conditioned emotional and physical responses to cognitive content (thoughts) and process (thinking).

In the following basic meditation exercise (breath awareness), selective awareness is given to the physical sensation of the air as it enters and leaves the nose, and the psychological purpose will be to reduce intentional initiation of thinking and intentional engagement with automatic (unintentional) thinking. This basic form of meditation has been referred to as "concentrative" meditation, because it resembles concentrating on one thing (the breath) as opposed to other things (thoughts). Concentrative meditation is often contrasted with "open awareness" meditation, in which one does not concentrate on any one source of information (e.g., sensory information from a given sense organ, or a thought or image). I believe that this is a useful, but false dichotomy, as even open awareness meditation involves selectively attending to whatever sensory information appears in awareness rather than to whatever one would be aware of if one was not doing open awareness meditation. I also prefer not to associate the word "concentration" with meditation, due to what I, at least, and maybe others, perceive as it's effortful connotations of constriction, tightness and self-control. An alternative to the label "concentrative meditation" might be "selective object awareness," as compared with "selective subject awareness" and "selective pure awareness." These types of meditation are addressed further in Chapter 9.

You will notice that contrary to the instructions in Chapter 3 to *be aware of 3 of the other senses*, the meditation exercise below reduces *Seehearbody* to just *body*, and specifies awareness of only one sense, the bodysense, in the form of awareness of the sensation of the breath in the nose. This is because one purpose of time spent in sitting meditation is to create a situation in which thoughts are likely to arise with more vigor (in terms of frequency, duration and salience) than usual, in order to provide ample opportunity to train the mind to function a certain way at other times.

It's kind of like skeet shooting (without the kickback). When you go skeet shooting and you yell "PULL!," the skeet is released so you can practice your aim by shooting at it. (For those unfamiliar with skeets, they belong to the species Clayadiscia Inanimata and feel no pain when shot.) The more you yell "PULL!," the more practice you get (as long as they actually release a skeet and aren't just having fun listening to you yell "PULL!," and as long as you aren't a deputy sheriff in Longmire shooting skeets with your batscheisse crazy father who is both very disappointed in you and homicidal). If no skeets are released, skeet shooting is not very fruitful, though it may delay their extinction. The same is true in meditation. As above, so below. As it is in skeet shooting, it is in meditation. You can't practice stopping thinking unless thinking arises. If you were to be aware of 3 other senses continuously in meditation, thinking would not arise as frequently, and you would not get as much practice in *coming back.* By only filling *one* of your three degrees of awareness freedom (with bodysensing), information from the other 5 senses (seeing, hearing, smelling, tasting, thinking) will naturally enter awareness as the brain is programmed to detect changes in sensory information for purposes of survival. As thinking is the most habitual awareness input, it will be the most likely sense to distract you from selective awareness of the breath, possibly combined with seeing, hearing, smelling or tasting which will compete for the third remaining awareness slot.

BREATH AWARENESS MEDITATION INSTRUCTIONS

Any amount of time set aside for meditation will help you accomplish the goal of learning to *stop thinking* (as the Zensters say, "One second of Zazen is one second of enlightenment)(I just hypnotized you again). It's no different from developing any other skill. The more time on task, the faster the skill will develop. If you wanted to learn to improve your aim in darts, even 2 minutes per day would increase your accuracy, though you might want to wait a while before buying rounds each time you don't hit the bullseye. (For those unfamiliar with bullseyes, they are circles drawn on things and, like skeets, feel no pain when hit.) As you will see, even 2 minutes of meditation will eventually give you access to a state of consciousness (SoC; Tart, 1969) that you don't ordinarily experience.

In terms of "dosage" for stress or anxiety, the rule of thumb, corresponding with the Transcendental Meditation and Relaxation Response research, appears to be 20 minutes twice per day. Research has indicated certain physiological changes that build up to and level off at the 20-minute point.

However, experimentation will reveal distinct effects after other durations. A 45- or 60-minute sit can produce powerful experiences that don't tend to happen within the first 20 minutes. The most important thing is to meditate for a duration that you find enjoyable (so you won't give up and look for a hobby easier than *sitting and doing nothing*) and that does not interfere with other important daily activities. I'm reminded of a Zen retreat some years back. At lunch, my job was to dry the dishes after a fellow retreatant had washed them. At one point he said "this is so boring." I asked him how his morning had gone, while he was *staring at the wall* for 3 hours. "Oh, that was fine," he responded. Guess some people just don't like washing dishes.

Time will sometimes expand and sometimes contract during meditation. As Einstein famously said:

> "When you sit with a nice girl for two hours you think it's only a minute, but when you sit on a hot stove for a minute you think it's two hours. That's relativity." (QuoteInvestigator.com, 2014)

Depending on whether there is something you need to do after meditating, you might find it useful to set a timer or alarm. If you do, turn it around (or turn you around) so you won't be tempted to look at the time. If you are setting the alarm on a digital clock, you might add a minute, especially if you have set it for only a few minutes, in the event that it is already at the end of the minute shown.

(1) ***Sit comfortably.*** You don't need to sit any particular way. You can sit on the couch, or the chair, or the bed or the floor, wherever you feel the most comfortable. You can sit as comfortably as you would if you were about to watch your favorite show on TV. Your back does not need to be straight. Your head does not need to be suspended from the ceiling. Your chin does not need to be pulled in. Your eyes do not to be staring down at 45 degrees or staring upwards to trigger alpha waves. Your legs do not need to be crossed in ways that will require knee surgery in 10 or 20 years. Your tongue does not need to be touching the roof of your mouth behind your teeth. Your arms do not need to be extended with your fingers touching each other in mudras. The main purpose of all the fancy yogic stuff is mainly to keep you from falling asleep. To this end, if your goal is to meditate rather than sleep, I would merely recommend that you not lie down, that you not lean your head back against the chair or couch, and that you not believe my

doctor's nurse if he tells you "decaf is your friend." Because decaf is most certainly not my friend. Friends don't let friends fall asleep at work.

However, if you *want* to sit cross-legged on the floor in a lotus position because you've been doing it for a while and it's comfortable, or because you studied with the Zen Master who taught "pain is the flavor of Zazen" rather than "We are not in the business of creating crippled monks," or because that's your tradition and you like it, or because you're 8 years old and your body is still malleable enough to adapt to such unnatural ways of bending, go for it.

The instructions you will often hear regarding what to do with the body when meditating are not (or *maybe* are not) without merit. They may facilitate energy flow and alertness, and may trigger subtle energetic processes such as the movement of chi or kundalini and resulting consciousness states. (As you will see later in the book, I'm not joking. I may be wrong and misinterpreting experience for realities beyond the experience, but I'm serious about the chi and kundalini). However, to get started, let's keep it simple and *just sit comfortably*. Even Patanjali's Yoga Sutras (the "Bible" of Yoga) specifies a meditation posture that is "steady and comfortable."

If you can find a quiet place to meditate, that's nice. But if you can't, that's nice too. You can meditate at home, or on a train. In the sun, or soaking rain. (Where's Dr. Seuss when you need him?) Meditation is about *what you do and don't do with your mind*, and has nothing to do with what is going on around you. You can keep your eyes open, half open or shut. Totally up to you. And you can experiment with how you sit, where you sit, and what your body and eyes are doing to see what is most rewarding. There is no right answer, other than that there is no right answer.

(2) Breathe normally and bring awareness to the feeling of the air as it enters and leaves your nose.

Just breathe the same way you would breathe if you were watching TV. Forget everything about breathing that you learned on YouTube. You don't need to breathe deeply. You don't need to breathe slowly. You don't need to do alternate nostril breathing. There is an entire yogic science of breath control called *pranayama* (if interested, see B.K.S. Iyengar's book *Light on Pranayama*) and while pranayama is used in some forms of meditation, just as chocolate is used in some forms of cakes, cakes don't require chocolate,

chocolate is not a defining characteristic of cakes, and meditation does not require pranayama.

Unless it is really hot out or your body temperature is abnormally low, the air will feel cool on the inhale (as the air outside of the body is generally cooler than the inside of the body). For,

> "Outside of a dog, a book is man's best friend. Inside of a dog, it's too dark to read." (with apologies to Jim Brewer or Groucho Marx; QuoteInvestigator.com, 2010)

The feeling of the exhale may not be as easy to detect, but just be aware of any sensation at all in your nose as you breathe out, such as a slight rush of air against the inside of the nostrils or between the bottom of the nose and the upper lip. Another possibility is being aware of the feeling of the stomach as it rises and falls as you breathe. If you have health anxiety and awareness of the breath makes you anxious, you can substitute awareness of a word or mantra of your choosing, repeating it slowly in your mind, without synchronizing it with the breath. If you do choose something other than the feeling of the air as your object of awareness, substitute it for "the air" in the following instructions.

(3) *Set an intention to be aware of the feeling of the air, for as long or as short as awareness of it remains*, as it enters and leaves the nose. Don't *pay attention* to it, don't *focus* on it, don't *concentrate* on it, just *be aware* of it. The nose bone's connected to the ... brain bone, and you don't need to *do* anything (e.g., pay attention, focus, concentrate, sniff, snort) to be aware of stimulation to the nose nerves by the air. Just be aware of what's already happening, the feeling of the air as it enters and leaves your nose. At the same time, *realize that it's impossible* to be continuously aware of it, or anything, as sooner or later, and usually sooner (likely within seconds), other objects of awareness will appear, without our even realizing, such as *thinking*.

(4) *Whenever you realize that you are no longer aware of the feeling of the air, come back to awareness of it.* When you realize that you have been thinking and are no longer aware of the feeling of the air, just remember that this is not a problem, it is just the brain doing what it has been overtrained to do (think), and return to breath awareness. Remember, *meditation does not mean stilling the mind, or not thinking*. It means setting an intention to be aware of something, and when you realize you are not aware of it anymore, becoming aware of it again. That's it. You are not responsible for automatic thinking. That's why it's called automatic. But when you realize you have been thinking, you have a choice. You can either continue thinking or return to breath awareness. If, when you realize you are not aware of the breath and have been thinking, you return to awareness of the feeling of the air, you are deciding to continue meditating. If you decide to keep thinking, you are not meditating badly, you have simply decided to momentarily stop meditating, and that's OK. We all do it at times. I did it myself this morning. I was meditating and had an idea for this book, and knowing that I do have a tendency to forget things if I don't write them down, I got up, wrote it down, and then sat down again and continued meditating.

(5) **After the alarm sounds, sit for about 1 minute with your eyes open, readjusting to your usual waking state of consciousness.** There is a whole field of study on "emerging" from the meditative state. Some suggest that after meditating, before standing up, one should sit for a time with eyes open, and that not doing so could lead to negative emotions later in the day. I would suggest, as in all *safe* things, that you experiment and see what works for you. (By the way, you know how they say "moderation in all things"? If you think about it for a second – "moderation in *all* things" – you'll realize that this is nonsense).

If after meditating in this manner several times you notice that you are still thinking during almost the entire sit, it could be useful to increase the number of sensory modalities that you are selectively aware of. You could begin with a few sits in which you are selectively and simultaneously aware of 2 senses, e.g., both the breath and seeing (if with eyes closed, seeing the back of the eyelids), returning to both breath and seeing whenever you notice that thinking has arisen. If you are still thinking most of the time during awareness of breath and seeing, you could increase awareness to 3 senses, such as breath, seeing and hearing whatever sounds are in the environment, returning to simultaneous awareness of breath, seeing and hearing whenever you notice thoughts have arisen.

Regarding the wealth of meditative traditions out there with their various techniques, remember that you don't *need* to do any of them to learn to stop your mind. All you really need to do is train yourself to *be aware of 2 plus or minus 1 other sense*. If you do choose to meditate in a religious or spiritual tradition, that's great, but realize that not all practices that are called "meditation" will actually train you to gain the same control over your mind that you have over your arms and legs. A good indicator as to whether a given technique will train you to stop involuntary thinking is whether it involves *coming back* from random thinking to one or more of the senses (which in some traditions could mean coming back to awareness of a single thought such as a mantra).

IF YOU PREFER MEDITATION IN A RELIGIOUS TRADITION

Some people will prefer to learn to stop thinking using a nonsectarian technique such as Seahearbody, whereas others may favor a more nonsecular approach. If you are not sure of the difference between nonsectarian and nonsecular, or used to know the difference but have forgotten, or know the difference but don't know which is which, you are in good company (Well, at least in some kind of company). Oh, you thought I was going to remind you of the difference? Actually, I've already re-forgotten Well, we've gotten this far without remembering, so how 'bout if we ever really need to know, we'll look it up

While most Westerners are introduced to meditation in the form of an Eastern religious teaching, meditation has been a part of Western religious traditions for thousands of years. In the Jewish Talmud, meditation is both a prerequisite and postrequisite for prayer. It is stated that:

> "We learned in the mishna that the early generations of pious men would wait one hour in order to achieve the solemn frame of mind appropriate for prayer . . . And Rabbi Yehoshua ben Levi said: One who prays must also wait one hour after his prayer . . . The sages taught in a *baraita* with regard to waiting before and after prayer: The early generations of pious men would wait one hour, pray one hour, then wait one hour again." (Berakhot, 32b, 20, 24; composed in Babylon c.450 – c.550 C.E.)

And

> "One may only stand and begin to pray from an approach of gravity and submission. There is a tradition that the early generations of pious men would wait one hour, in order to reach the solemn frame of mind appropriate for prayer, and then pray, so that they would focus their hearts toward their Father in Heaven." (Mishnah Berakhot 5; Composed in Talmudic Israel c.190 - c.230 CE)

For those preferring to cultivate non-thinking in the context of a religious practice, use of a *mantra* is a common technique. A mantra is a word that you can set an intention to be aware of and return to via selective awareness. Religious meditation uses a mantra to still the mind while permeating consciousness with a devotional atmosphere, as preparation for direct communion with God. This potential opening of a direct line with the (Wo)Man upstairs may explain why meditation is not typically taught by religious institutions, who benefit from serving as the middleman. It would be kind of like retailers handing out the business cards of their wholesalers. However, such cynicism may be unfounded, as there may be a simpler explanation, i.e., ignorance, or a more selfless motivation such as to protect people from the very real risk of experiencing visions and interpreting these for themselves in less than helpful ways.

Here are some approaches to religious meditation that make use of mantras:

Jewish Meditation

From the standpoint of orthodox Judaism, meditation in some of the Eastern traditions constitutes idolatry. My suspicion regarding the attraction of the Eastern forms of meditation for Jews, however, has less to do with an inclination to idolatry than to our never having heard of meditation in Hebrew school and then learning about it through the popular culture (which also never heard of Jewish meditation). In *reality* (don't knock it 'til you've tried it), Jewish meditation *may* predate some of the more popular Eastern meditative traditions.

Here I will defer to Orthodox Rabbi and physicist Aryeh Kaplan (who too had an issue with the miseducational system, having been expelled for acting out and growing up as a "street kid" in the Bronx, later catching up by earning higher degrees in physics and directing MagnetoHydrodynamics research for the National Bureau of Standards). I am quoting Rabbi Kaplan at length from his book *Jewish Meditation: A Practical Guide* (1985), as I find that Jewish meditation is the least known among the religious meditative traditions. However, even with the wealth of information contained in the following citations, reference to the originals will be helpful, as will consulting the works of (or studying personally with) Rabbi DovBer Pinson (e.g., 2004; *Meditation and Judaism: Exploring the Jewish Meditative Paths,* 2004) and Rabbi David Cooper (e.g., 2000; *The Handbook of Jewish Meditation*

Practices: A Guide for Enriching the Sabbath and Other Days of Your Life), among other scholars and teachers of Jewish meditation.

As an aside, Rabbi Pinson was very helpful when my father transitioned. When I visited his Yeshiva in Dumbo, the building housing the room functioning as the Yeshiva had some floors and walls that either hadn't been totally constructed yet or were well on their way to demolition. But the arrows on the walls helped with navigation over and around the cement slabs serving as hallways, and eventually one came to the door which, when opened, surprisingly didn't house the Oracle's kitchen.

Rabbi Kaplan writes:

> "The mantra can serve as a means of clearing the mind of mundane thought, leaving it open to other, transcendental experiences. This can be true no matter how nonmystical the mantra is. Indeed, in certain types of clinical meditation, a nonsense word can be used as the mantra." (1985, p. 55)

(This reference to clinical use of a "nonsense word" may be referring to Herbert Benson's "Relaxation Response," itself inspired by Transcendental Meditation.) Kaplan continues:

Chapter 7 - Psychological Meditation: Sometimes I Just Sits

"Nevertheless, if the mantra has spiritual power in its own right, it not only clears the mind of mundane thought, but also puts the meditator into a special spiritual space . . ." (p. 55)

". . . There appear to be references to mantra meditation even in the Bible. On the basis of philological analysis, it seems that the Hebrew verb hagah denotes a kind of meditation in which a word or sound is repeated over and over." (p. 55)

". . . The earliest unambiguous reference to a mantra type of meditation is found in Heykhaloth Rabbatai, the primary text of Merkavah mysticism, dating from Talmudic times . . ." (p. 56)

". . . It is significant that in the Heykhaloth, the mantra is seen not as an end in itself, but rather as the first step in the discipline of the chariot. The mantra was used to bring the initiate into a state of consciousness from which he could travel from chamber to chamber in the supernal worlds." (p. 56)

". . . This concept is even more graphically illustrated in a technique used by Rabbi Joseph Caro (1488-1575) and his followers. Instead of using a biblical verse, this technique made use of a selection from the Mishnah, the earliest portion of the Talmud, completed around 200 C.E." (p. 56)

". . . It is significant that there may be an allusion to this technique in the Talmud itself. The Talmud speaks of reviewing a mishnah and says, 'Repeating one's mishnah one hundred times is not the same as repeating it one hundred and one times.' There may be an allusion in this teaching that even in Talmudic times, the Mishnah was used as a type of mantra." (p. 57)

". . . There is also evidence that the Ari (Rabbi Isaac Luria) made use of a similar technique with the Zohar." (p. 57)

Rabbi Kaplan recommends beginning with the mantra *Ribbono shel Olam* (Master of the Universe), if preferred in its Chasidic pronunciation, Ribboinoi shel Oylawm, as taught by Rabbi Nachman of Bratslav who was known for emphasizing the use of *hitbodeduth* meditation, which is "an unstructured, spontaneous and individualized form of prayer and meditation through which one would establish a close, personal relationship with God and ultimately see the Divinity inherent in all being." (Hitbodedut, 2022)

According to Kaplan,

> "... In relatively modern times, a practical form of mantra meditation was prescribed by the noted Chasidic leader Rabbi Nachman of Bratslav (1772-1811). Of all the Chasidic masters, none spoke of hitbodeduth meditation more often than he. As we shall see, his main technique consisted in engaging in conversations with God. Nevertheless, Rabbi Nachman said that if a person does not know what to say, he should simply repeat the phrase Ribbono shel Olam, which is Hebrew for "Master of the Universe." From the description of the technique, it seems obvious that Rabbi Nachman was prescribing the use of this phrase as a mantra to bring a person into a higher state of consciousness." (p. 57)

> "... Some, for the sake of authenticity, prefer the Chasidic pronunciation, Ribboinoi shel Oylawm. In any case, it is an ideal phrase for anyone who wants to engage in an authentic Jewish mantra meditation. Not only was it prescribed by one of the great Chasidic masters, but the phrase itself was used as an introduction to prayer as far back as early Talmudic times. The expression Ribbono shel Olam was used as early as the first century B.C.E. by Simeon ben Shetach, and according to the Talmud, it was also in use in biblical times." (pp. 57-58)

> "... In general, the preparations for meditation are straightforward and simple." (p. 58)

> "... the place is not important, as long as it is an environment where you will not be interrupted." (p. 59)

> "... During meditation, sit with the eyes lightly closed, totally relaxed. Your hands can rest comfortably on the table or on your lap. Your fingers should not be clasped or intertwined, as the Kabbalists teach that this should be avoided. Rather, if your hands are together, one should rest lightly on the other. Before beginning a meditation, settle yourself in the

Chapter 7 - Psychological Meditation: Sometimes I Just Sits

place. This means sitting quietly in the place where you will be meditating, fitting into it and making yourself at ease. During this period, try to relax completely, clearing your mind of all extraneous concerns. Some people find it helpful to hum a relaxing melody during these preparatory moments. This period should last between five and ten minutes." (pp. 59-60)

". . . Let us assume that you are using Rabbi Nachman's mantra, Ribbono shel Olam, Repeat the phrase over and over, slowly, in a very soft voice. The meditative norm is that it should be said in the softest voice that you can comfortably pronounce. You can either whisper it or vocalize it softly, whichever is more comfortable to you.

There are no firm standards regarding this in Jewish meditation. Some people find it easier to whisper the mantra. It is also permissible to mouth it without voicing it at all. It is not recommended, however, that it merely be thought in the mind, at least for beginners. If the mantra is repeated mentally, without at least mouthing it, it can be interrupted by extraneous thoughts. Therefore, one should not place too much emphasis on how the mantra is said, as long as it is said for the designated time. This usually consists of a period between twenty minutes and a half hour, as mentioned earlier." (p. 60)

". . . At first, during meditation, you may allow the mind to wander freely or concentrate on the images you see in your mind's eye. However, as you become more advanced, you should begin to allow the words of the mantra to fill the mind completely, blanking out all sensation. This involves keeping all other thoughts out of the consciousness. All of your attention should be focused on the words of the mantra, leaving no room for any other thought." (pp. 61-62)

". . . After the meditation is over, remain in place for approximately five minutes, allowing the mind to absorb the effects of the meditation. You also need some time to "come back down" before returning to your daily routine. Again, you may wish to hum a soft melody during this period. It should be a time of intimate closeness with the Divine.

You may wish to use the moments following a meditation to have a short conversation with God. As mentioned earlier, Rabbi Nachman saw mantra meditation primarily as a means of preparing for such a divine conversation, which he saw as a higher type of meditation. In any case, one can feel very close to God after a meditation, and it is a good time to express that closeness. Whereas Eastern schools see mantra meditation as an end in itself, Jewish sources seem to indicate that it is more of a preparation for a deeper spiritual experience. Some sources state that after meditating, one should smell fragrant spices or perfumes, so as to reinvolve oneself in the physical world. It is also prescribed that some light food be eaten shortly afterward, since through the blessing, the food can elevate the entire body.

Of course, meditating on the phrase Ribbono shel Olam, "Master of the Universe," has great value in its own right, and some people may be content to make it a lifetime practice. Others, however, may want to use it as a way to learn meditative techniques and recognize higher states of consciousness, and then go on to what are considered more advanced methods." (pp. 62-63)

In sum, Kaplan's meditation instructions prescribe first finding an environment without interruptions; lightly closing the eyes and relaxing; resting the hands on the table or lap and, if they are together, with one hand on top of the other and without intertwining the fingers; and spending 5-10 minutes "settling in" and relaxing prior to using the mantra.

You then begin the meditation, repeating the mantra as softly as possible for 20 to 30 minutes, by vocalizing it, whispering it or even just mouthing it without sound. He counsels beginners against merely imagining the word in the mind which would leave the mind vulnerable to extraneous thoughts. Initially one can let the mind wander as the mantra is repeated, but at more advanced levels one should focus uniquely on the mantra to the exclusion of other thoughts. When the mantra meditation is finished, one is to remain seated for about 5 minutes for "intimate closeness with the divine" and possibly conversing with God, for which Rabbi Nachman considered the mantra meditation a preparation. One can then reacclimate to the physical world by "smelling fragrant spices" or eating light food which elevates the body when the food is blessed.

Chapter 7 - Psychological Meditation: Sometimes I Just Sits

While Rabbi Kaplan suggests that this use of meditation in Judaism as preparation for "deeper spiritual experience" stands in contrast to Eastern schools of meditation which see meditation as an "end in itself" (Kaplan, 1985, pp. 57-63), I don't personally find this to be the case. Buddhism and Hinduism, for example, have as their goals enlightenment and union with God, respectively.

Christian Contemplative Prayer

There is a long history in Christianity of using prayer to silence the mind in the service of communion with Jesus and God. A modern form of contemplative prayer is known as Centering Prayer. Here is some history:

> "Centering Prayer was developed as a response to the Vatican II invitation to revive the contemplative teachings of early Christianity and present them in updated formats. In this way, the method of Centering Prayer is drawn from the ancient practices of the Christian contemplative heritage, notably the traditional monastic practice of Lectio Divina and the practices described in the anonymous fourteenth century classic *The Cloud of Unknowing* and in the writings of Christian mystics such as John Cassian, Francis de Sales, Teresa of Avila, John of the Cross, Therese of Lisieux, and Thomas Merton. Most importantly, Centering Prayer is based on the wisdom saying of Jesus in the Sermon on the Mount:
>
>> '...when you pray, go to your inner room, close the door and pray to your Father in secret. And your Father, who sees in secret, will repay you.' (Matthew 6.6; *New American Bible*)
>
> In the 1970s, answering the call of Vatican II, three Trappist monks at St. Joseph's Abbey in Spencer, Massachusetts, Fathers William Meninger, Basil Pennington and Thomas Keating, looked to these ancient sources to develop a simple method of silent prayer for contemporary people. The prayer came to be known as Centering Prayer in reference to Thomas Merton's description of contemplative prayer as prayer that is 'centered entirely on the presence of God.' The monks offered Centering Prayer workshops and retreats to both clergy members and laypeople. Interest in the prayer spread, and shortly after the first intensive Centering Prayer retreat in 1983, the organization Contemplative Outreach was

formed to support the growing network of Centering Prayer practitioners.

Today Centering Prayer is practiced by people all around the world, creating local and global networks of Christians in communion with Christ and each other and contributing to the renewal of the contemplative dimension of Christianity." (ContemplativeOutreach.org)

Centering prayer is described as

". . . a method of silent prayer that prepares us to receive the gift of contemplative prayer, prayer in which we experience God's presence within us, closer than breathing, closer than thinking, closer than consciousness itself. This method of prayer is both a relationship with God and a discipline to foster that relationship.

Centering Prayer is not meant to replace other kinds of prayer. Rather, it adds depth of meaning to all prayer and facilitates the movement from more active modes of prayer — verbal, mental or affective prayer — into a receptive prayer of resting in God. Centering Prayer emphasizes prayer as a personal relationship with God and as a movement beyond conversation with Christ to communion with Him.

The source of Centering Prayer, as in all methods leading to contemplative prayer, is the Indwelling Trinity: Father, Son, and Holy Spirit. The focus of Centering Prayer is the deepening of our relationship with the living Christ. The effects of Centering Prayer are ecclesial, as the prayer tends to build communities of faith and bond the members together in mutual friendship and love." (CenteringPrayer.com)

Thomas Keeting's instructions for contemplative prayer are as follows:

1. Choose a sacred word as the symbol of your intention to consent to God's presence and action within.

2. Sitting comfortably and with eyes closed, settle briefly and silently introduce the sacred word as the symbol of your consent to God's presence and action within us.

3. When you become aware of thoughts return ever-so-gently to the sacred word.

4. At the end of the prayer period, remain in silence with eyes closed for a couple of minutes."

(Pennington, 2001, p. 65)

The sacred word or phrase chosen is of course a personal matter. One possibility is the mantra that St. Francis of Assisi used: "My God and My All."

Mantra Meditation in Other Religious Traditions

Eknath Easwaren's (1977/2009) book *The Mantram Handbook: A Practical Guide to Choosing Your Mantram and Calming Your Mind* is a valuable resource for mantra meditation in the Jewish, Hindu, Buddhist, Christian and Muslim traditions. Easwaren counsels:

> "I wouldn't suggest making up your own mantram.... Choose a mantram of proven power, one which has enabled many men and women before you to realize for themselves the unity of life. The roots of such a mantram are far deeper than we can know when we first begin to use it, and this is what enables it to grow in our consciousness.... All of the mantrams which I recommend are mantrams of proven power, bequeathed to us by the great spiritual teachers of many traditions." (2009, pp. 28-29)

Some religious mantras identified by Easwaren include:

Judaism:

Barukh attah Adonai; Ribono shel olam.

Hinduism:

Rama; Om Sri Ram jai Ram jai jai Ram; Krishna; Hare Rama Hare Rama, Rama Rama Hare Hare, Hare Krishna Hare Krishna, Krishna Krishna Hare Hare (simplified to Hare Rama, Hare Krishna; itself simplified to Rama); Om namah Shivaya.

Buddhism:

Namu Amidabutsu; Om mani padme hum.

Christianity:

Lord Jesus Christ Son of God, have mercy on us; Lord Jesus Christ; Lord have mercy; Hail Mary; Jesus; Ave Maria; My God and my all (St. Francis of Assisi's mantra).

Islam:

Bismillah ir-Rahman ir Rahim; Allah; Allahu akbar.

Impersonal:

Om / Aum.

Easwaren provides examples of how mantra meditation can be helpful in keeping the mind steady; overcoming likes and dislikes; avoiding cycles of excitement and depression; harnessing fear, anger and greed; and transitioning at the moment of death. He says that

> "Over a period of many years, if you have been practicing all the other spiritual disciplines which strengthen your will and deepen your concentration, the taproot of the mantram will extend fathoms deep, where it works to unify your consciousness – resolving old conflicts, solving problems you may not even be aware of, and transforming negative emotions into spiritual energy.
>
> Finally, when this mantram root reaches the bedrock of consciousness, you become established in the mantram. It has become an integral part of your being, permeating your consciousness from the surface level down to the very depths. Then it is no longer necessary to repeat the mantram; it goes on repeating itself, echoing continuously at the very deepest levels of the mind. This is what Saint Paul means when he exhorts us to 'pray without ceasing.'" (2009/1977, p. 181)

Easwaren also suggests "passage meditation," in which a simple inspirational passage is memorized and used as a mantra.

> "Then, with your eyes gently closed, go through the words of the passage in your mind as slowly as you can. Do not follow any association of ideas, but keep to the words of the memorized piece. When distractions come, do not resist them, but give more and

more of your attention to the passage. The secret here is that we become what we meditate on; sustained concentration on the inspirational passage drives it deep into our consciousness.

This method has become known as passage meditation, and it is a perfect way to begin the day. It is good to have your meditation as early as is convenient for you, while the morning is still and cool and before the noise and bustle of the day begins. Devote half an hour each morning to the practice of meditation; do not increase this half-hour period, but if you want to meditate more, have half an hour in the evening also." (2009/1977, p. 161)

His book *Passage Meditation* (2016/1978) treats the topic at length, and proposes beginning with the Peace Prayer of St. Francis of Assisi due to its universal appeal:

> "Lord, make me an instrument of your peace:
> where there is hatred, let me sow love;
> where there is injury, pardon;
> where there is doubt, faith;
> where there is despair, hope;
> where there is darkness, light;
> where there is sadness, joy.
>
> O divine Master, grant that I may not so much seek
> to be consoled as to console,
> to be understood as to understand,
> to be loved as to love.
> For it is in giving that we receive,
> it is in pardoning that we are pardoned,
> and it is in dying that we are born to eternal life.
> Amen." (Loyola Press, 2019)

Passages he cites from other traditions include Lao Tzu's The Best; The Song of David: Psalm 23; The Rig Veda: United in Heart. He advises saying the passage word by word, as slowly as possible, in accordance with the saying that:

> "A mind that is fast is sick
>
> A mind that is slow is sound
>
> A mind that is still is divine."

(Meher Baba, in Easwaren, 1978/2016, p. 5)

WHICHEVER FORM OF MEDITATION YOU CHOOSE . . .

Ultimately, whether you opt to train yourself to stop thinking via selective awareness of non-thinking or via selective awareness of a mantra or passage, religious or otherwise, it all amounts to:

A nose by any other name is still a nose,

and, from a psychological meditational perspective,

Selective awareness by any other name is still selective awareness.

Whichever you choose as an anchor for selective awareness, "three other senses," a mantra or a passage, the approach (and possibly the result) is the same: greater and greater control of *cognitive process*, and with it increased freedom to use your mind efficiently for what you *want* to use it for, whether secular/nonsectarian or nonsecular/sectarian (look them up if you want, or get a taste of Chapter 15 by resisting the urge and continuing reading).

Chapter 8 - *Mindfulness: During the Laundry the Ecstasy*

"The sea is high again today, with a thrilling flush of wind. In the midst of winter you can feel the invention of Spring. A sky of hot nude pearl until midday, crickets in sheltered places, and now the wind unpacking the great planes, ransacking the great planes."

Lawrence Durrell

(1957, Justine)

If "meditation" may be broadly defined as "selective awareness for psychological purposes," and meditation and mindfulness are to be falsely distinguished from one another in order to fall in line with the status quo, additional specifications must be added to their definitions. To this (somewhat nefarious) end, I would propose the following definitions of meditation and mindfulness:

Meditation is Selective Awareness in *Stillness* for Psychological Purposes

Mindfulness is Selective Awareness in *Activity* for Psychological Purposes

In other words, meditation is *mindful inactivity*, whereas mindfulness is *meditation in-activity*

Mindfulness fully capitalizes on Chapter 3's Ten Laws of Non-thinking, as activity typically involves multiple senses.

You would think that, as most activities are multisensory, often involving several senses other than thinking, we would naturally stop thinking when engaged in them. That we are fully capable of being neurotic while engaged in multisensory endeavors is a tribute to our skill at accomplishing important, overlearned tasks mindlessly, that is, in unconscious autopilot mode. The common example is, without actually doing it, to narrate the movements involved in tying your shoes. When I just tried this myself, I accomplished it only by narrating the internally visualized imaginal performance of the action in real time with my imaginal body through multisensory memory of the image of shoes, shoelaces, fingers, hands and arms; and imaginal movement accompanied by imaginal sensations of my arms, hands and fingers as they tied the imaginal shoelaces. While narration is possible, it is tedious (at least for me), whereas the real act of tying shoelaces coordinates seeing and bodysensing so automatically that they may, for the purposes of information processing, be occupying only 1 degree of awareness freedom, leaving 2 open, 1 which is usually hijacked by thinking with 1 left (thus the ability to carry on a conversation involving speaking/hearing and thinking while tying one's shoes).

To return to the Lincoln Tunnel example, or even to driving in general, the behavior of driving is so overlearned for many of us that, although theoretically it is important to keep your eyes on the road and your hands upon the wheel, we often mindlessly continue doing whatever we are doing with the wheel and accelerator and attend to a multitude of other things. We zone out into awareness of the sound of our music, the taste of the coffee and whatever thoughts we are thinking, with confidence that when a car cuts us off the novelty of its intrusion into our visual field will shock us out of awareness of non-survival-related thoughts, sounds and tastes and prompt us to respond by braking or swerving or doing some other politically and preferably legally correct thing that doesn't violate our probation.

All this to say that you would think that the multisensory awareness involved in daily activities would preclude overthinking. And indeed it does, to some extent (thus the common dalecarnegian strategy of keeping busy to stop ruminating or worrying). However, due to overlearning and our adaptive ability to function on automatic pilot, there usually seems to be sufficient room for overthinking during most daily tasks. And this is where mindfulness comes in. Wherever we are, whatever we are doing, we can stop thinking by returning to three senses other than thinking. Naturally, it makes sense for these to be the three senses that are most important to the task at hand. If thinking about Thing A happens to be the task at hand, and the distraction is thinking about Thing B (for example, the Thing King) that is irrelevant to the task at hand, then we return to the desired Thing A thinking content and two senses other than thinking. If thinking about something in

Chapter 8 - Mindfulness: During the Laundry the Ecstasy

the future happening somewhere else is the task at hand (e.g., whether the next exit will be from the left or right lane), it is incumbent upon us to be mindful of this "there-then" thought by coming back to it from our here-now awareness of the song on the car radio, defying common "Be Here Now" and "Present Moment" wisdom, if we want to remain alive as we approach the here and now of the there and then.

MINDFULNESS MEDITATION INSTRUCTIONS

Whereas "meditation" typically refers to sitting meditation and is done for a specific amount of time once or twice per day, mindfulness meditation can be practiced every waking moment, simply by being aware of the senses involved in what we are doing in the moment and coming back to awareness of these when distracted by thoughts of things unrelated to what we are currently doing. Certain activities have become favored for use in mindfulness meditation, such as mindful walking and mindful eating, but as Thich Nhat Hanh's book "Present Moment Wonderful Moment: Mindfulness Verses for Daily Living" illustrates, any activity whatsoever can be used as an opportunity to practice mindfulness. Some examples he gives are washing your hands and getting dressed.

Doing something mindfully just means being selectively aware of your experience of the various senses, ideally 3, when doing the activity. For example, when you are washing a dish, see the dish, hear the running water, be aware of what your hands feel at the moment. And when you realize that you are not aware of one or more of these because you have drifted into thinking, return to the multisensory awareness. See the dish, hear the running water, be aware of how the hands feel. If you are walking, see whatever is in front of you, hear the sounds in your environment, feel the bodysense including the movement of the body as it walks and the feeling of the feet as they step down or lift up.

To develop your multisensory awareness as the antidote to overthinking, you could take a (or "an" if you are so inclined) habitual activity and practice it in slow motion, being aware of every micro-movement and every sensation involved. You could do this while washing the dishes, folding the laundry, walking down your hallway, brushing your teeth, getting into your car, getting out of your car, using the TV remote, getting something from the refrigerator, getting and drinking a glass of water, etc. This exercise will be especially revelatory for practitioners of Tai Chi, who will suddenly, and experientially, realize that *every movement is Tai Chi.*

(1) Begin doing whatever task you have decided to practice with, and ***set an intention to be continuously and simultaneously aware (for however long or short the continuity and simultaneity last) of the 3 non-thinking senses that appear most salient.*** For example, if you are folding the laundry, be aware of seeing the laundry, hearing the sounds in the environment, and how your hands feel as you fold the laundry. If you are eating, at the point that food is in your mouth, be aware of seeing whatever is in front of you, and the feeling and taste of the food in your mouth.

(2) ***Whenever you realize that you are no longer aware of one or more of the 3 senses, come back to awareness of it/them.***

There is a story I tell my clients that makes me out to be much more domestic than I actually am because it involves laundry; much cooler than I actually am because it involves a motorcycle; and much more enlightened than I already am because it involves a slight glimpse of the Big E. Circa 2007 I was passing a Dunkin Donuts and there was a Harley Davidson motorcycle out front with a sign that said Police Raffle. I figured what the heck, I've always wanted a motorcycle. So I bought a ticket or two, and for the next few months anxiously awaited the drawing. I eventually mostly forgot about it, remembering from time to time, and one day realized that the raffle must have taken place. So when I got home (this was before "smartphones") I went online and saw that I hadn't won. I was pretty bummed out for about a minute or so, thinking how great it would be to have a motorcycle. Then the lightbulb went on, the AHA! moment when I suddenly realized: I could just *buy* a motorcycle. I told my friend Tony about it, and he said "why don't you buy a Triumph?" Couldn't argue with that, so I went on ebay, found a 1998 Triumph Thunderbird 900, won the bid at about $2800, took the Motorcycle Safety Course where they told us not to buy anything too powerful for starters (too late), and I was good to go.

I learned a number of valuable lessons that year and fairly fast. First, if you are going to wear so much body armor that you can barely move, summer might not be the best time to ride. Luckily when I was about to keel over from dehydration one day, I found a house with a garden hose within reach (luckily, I happened to know the owner and figured they wouldn't mind my trespassing under the circumstances). Second, even the biggest, toughest guys

Chapter 8 - Mindfulness: During the Laundry the Ecstasy

with the most leather, chains and tats stay the hell away from certain highways, because tough doesn't mean insane, and most do, in fact, aim to live to ride another day.

But the most valuable lesson I learned from my motorcycle was about mindfulness. And it happened not while I was riding, but while folding the laundry. It was late morning on a gorgeous sunny day, I had by then decided to lose most of the body armor, and I was eager to get out and ride. Then I saw that there was a laundry basket that needed folding. My initial inclination was to do it later, but I decided to challenge my usual need for immediate gratification and low frustration tolerance and *do the right thing*. I proceeded to place the laundry basket on the bed and start folding the laundry as fast as I could, so I could just get outside and ride already. Then I remembered Thich Nhat Hanh's book *Present Moment Wonderful Moment* and realized that rather than rushing to finish folding the laundry, I should rather be thinking something like "Folding the laundry, I know that I am folding the laundry, Present Moment, Wonderful Moment." I decided this was an opportunity to test it out, and see if there was really any good reason to spend more time folding laundry and less time riding the motorcycle.

Soon after starting, I stopped folding for a moment, took a breath, noticed my agitation and urge to stay on speedy laundry folding autopilot, and said to myself "later I will be outside in the sun, right now I am inside folding laundry, I can enjoy both" or something like that. Then I let myself just see the laundry in the basket and slowly moved one hand to lift a sock, be aware of how it felt, be aware of the movement of my other hand as I looked for the sock it matched, lift that sock and be aware of how it felt, and then wrap the socks into a ball, each movement slow and with full awareness of sight, physical sensation and movement.

Suddenly, as I continued to fold the laundry in this manner, I experienced what I can only describe as an "opening" in awareness. It wasn't that I was seeing anything that wasn't there, but it was as though there was a continuity between me and the room and a vaster space. It was a feeling of utter well-being, kind of like when you're sitting on a beach watching the sunset, standing on top of a mountain you just climbed looking out over the range, or finally sitting on a hospital bed hooked up to an IV drip that contains a painkiller after several hours of thinking you could just tough out a kidney stone.

The Buddhist teacher Jack Kornfield wrote a book entitled *After the Ecstasy the Laundry* (2000) in which he reminds us that meditative insights are not a get out of jail free card, and that we still need to learn to navigate life in the world. A compilation of sayings by the Lubovitcher Rebbe, Rabbi Menachem Mendel Schneerson, *Bringing Heaven Down to Earth*, has a similar theme (Freeman, 1977). However, I have always felt that the flip side of Jack's title (which is the crux of his teachings) is "During the Laundry, the Ecstasy," in the Thich Nhat Hahnian sense of "Doing the laundry, I know that I am doing the laundry, Present Moment, Wonderful Moment."

What I learned from folding the laundry that day was that the most mundane, or worldly tasks can themselves be pathways to ecstasy. It all depends on how we approach them. Since that time, I have experienced meditation-induced altered states, lucid dreams and out-of-body experiences, some literally cosmic, but "laundry day" stands out in my mind as the best example of how the most extraordinarily joyful state may very well be that simple sense of being, accessible to each of us at every moment, wherever we are, whatever we are doing, if we would just bring our awareness to our senses, which are American Automobile Association – I mean, *All Always Available*. Darn mnemonics . . .

POSTSCRIPT

Today, several days after finishing this chapter, I was doing my morning meditation practice, and at a certain point my mind began racing with ideas for the chapter in which I recount my cap gun experience at age 12, after having my hand cut open by a flying beer bottle at age 11, followed by the thought of what I would like to say to those responsible for both, followed by realizing I would need to add a note about this to the chapter on how to shut up, pretty much deciding throughout to put meditation on hold for the moment as I developed these ideas, then worrying I would forget them and having the urge to get up and type them, then realizing I'm meditating and this is exactly what meditating is for, to learn to resist such urges, then thinking I already know how to resist the urges but sometimes it's useful not to resist them for higher purposes, then remembering that I'm writing a book on How To Stop Thinking things like "what if I forget what I'm thinking," followed by OK, enough of this, you're probably not going to forget, and if you do, you'll remember later, at which point I returned to where I was in my morning sequence of practices.

Chapter 8 - Mindfulness: During the Laundry the Ecstasy

After I finished doing these for a couple of minutes and sat in silence, I realized that I was experiencing the exact feeling that I wrote about above, triggered by laundry awareness, and which I experience each morning as I sit with my eyes open at the end of my meditation practice. I have come to think of it as "the current," a term used by Ramana Maharshi to describe what I believe, correctly or incorrectly, to be this state. And I realized that this sense of peace has become fairly frequent, and capable of being called upon at will by a certain shift of awareness first to object awareness mode (what is commonly called "mindfulness"), and then to the "witness" or subject awareness mode (yogic *pratyahara*, withdrawing the senses from their objects), landing me somewhere between object awareness mode and pure awareness (the True I or Self that is aware of the false I, or ego, that thinks it is a body-mind).

It is fascinating that the state brought about by, this morning, 30 minutes of asana (yogic poses), pranayama (breath work), kundalini practice, Zen koans, atma-vichara (jnana yogic – the yoga of knowledge – self-enquiry), and loving kindness meditation, should lead to the exact same state as that which can occur in the midst of daily activities, such as folding the laundry. I have also experienced this standing in the back of a bus and standing on a subway platform, after less than a minute of just shifting awareness by first *being aware of other senses* (as I did when folding the laundry) or *being aware of who is aware* (as I recall having done on the bus and in the subway). This same state has on occasion appeared spontaneously, as when I was crossing 42nd Street at 5th Avenue one day after an afternoon Iyengar *pranayama* workshop. Truly wonderful, as you will hear the Zen masters say again and again, referring to nothing obviously happening or special. Now, if only we could feel this way all the time, but alas, such thinking is notorious for preventing the very thing we are seeking ...

Chapter 9 - *Beyond Mindfulness: Yoga and The Matrix*

"When he reaches a certain stage
and becomes fit for enlightenment,
the same God whom he was worshipping
comes as Guru and leads him onward.
That Guru comes only to tell him,
'That God is within yourself.
Dive within and realize'.
God, Guru and the Self are the same."

Bhagavan Sri Ramana Maharshi

(in Mudaliar, 1965)

"Nobody can be told what the Matrix is.
You have to see it for yourself."

Morpheus

(in The Matrix, Wachowski & Wachowski, 1999)

Chapter 9 - Beyond Mindfulness: Yoga and The Matrix

[Cartoon: A cat sitting cross-legged in meditation pose, with a thought bubble reading "I THINK, THEREFORE I AM." Signed SEIDEN.]

First of all, I would like to thank Ramanasramam and Warner Brothers Entertainment for supporting this book by waiving the licensing fee for quoting Bhagavan Sri Ramana Maharshi and Morpheus, respectively. This was very kind, and lends an air of good *karma* to this chapter on yoga, which gave us the term, and which I do believe was the inspiration for The Matrix (Australian yoga teacher Celia Roberts has written that the premise of The Matrix, "that there is something more than meets the eye," is a concept from the ancient Hindu text Yoga Vasistha which, as I write this, I recall as being one of Bhagavan Sri Ramana Maharshi's favorite texts)(Roberts, 2021).

Yoga, meditation and mindfulness all involve (1) techniques to still the mind, and (2) states of consciousness characterized by or arising from a still mind.

According to the Kathopanishad (composed sometime between the 5th and 1st centuries BCE),

>"When the senses are stilled,
>
>When the mind is at rest,
>
>When the intellect wavers not –
>
>then, say the wise, is reached the highest stage.

This steady control of the senses and mind

has been defined as Yoga.

He who attains it is free from delusion.'"

(In Iyengar, 1979, p. 20)

I have in front of me 6 translations of Patanjali's Yoga Sutras, and will begin by providing their 6 translations of his definition of Yoga in Sutra 1.2, written in Sanskrit as something to the effect of

***Yoga cittavrtti nirodhah,* or**

Yogas citta vrtti nirodhah.

These 6 translations, and there are probably as many translations as there are translators, are:

1. "Yoga is controlling the activities of mind (chitta)." (Purohit, 1938/1975, p. 25)
2. "Yoga is the control of thoughts waves of the mind." (Prabhavananda & Isherwood, 1952/1981, p. 150)
3. "The restraint of the modifications of the mind-stuff is Yoga." (Satchidananda, 1978/1999, p. 3)
4. "Yoga is the complete settling of the activity of mind." (Egenes, 2010, p. 11)
5. "Yoga is the cessation of movements of the consciousness." (Iyengar, 1966/1996, p. 46)
6. "We become whole by stopping how the mind turns." (Roach & McNally, 2005)

I have placed these in the order of the extent to which they emphasize yoga as an *activity* as opposed to a *state* (activity itself might of course be considered a state, as merely another organization of phenomena in the phenomenal multiverse, and thus the seemingly diverse translations). It will be noted that the first 3 translations emphasize a *volitional* aspect of yoga (*controlling, control,* and *restraint*, each which refer to both an action and the effect achieved so long as the action continues), progressing in translations 4 and 5 to *complete settling* and *cessation*, the end states of an activity. The final definition, by Geshe Michael Roach, includes a result of such *stopping,* which is not contained in the definition of yoga but is rather the etymological origin of the word itself:

> "The Sanskrit noun योग yoga is derived from the root yuj (युज्) 'to attach, join, harness, yoke' ... Yoga is a cognate of the English word 'yoke' ... According to Mikel Burley, the first use of the root of the word 'yoga' is in hymn 5.81.1 of the Rigveda, a dedication to the rising Sun-god, where it has been interpreted as 'yoke' or 'control' ... Pāṇini (4th c. BCE) wrote that the term yoga can be derived from either of two roots: yujir yoga (to yoke) or yuj samādhau ('to concentrate') ... In the context of the Yoga Sutras, the root yuj samādhau (to concentrate) is considered the correct etymology by traditional commentators ... In accordance with Pāṇini, Vyasa (who wrote the first commentary on the Yoga Sutras) ... says that yoga means samadhi (concentration) ... In the Yoga Sutras (2.1), kriyāyoga is yoga's 'practical' aspect: the 'union with the supreme' in the performance of everyday duties ... A person who practices yoga, or follows the yoga philosophy with a high level of commitment, is called a yogi; a female yogi may also be known as a yogini." (Yoga, 2022)

As an aside, it is interesting how among all of the writings and lectures and teachings that one may be exposed to, it is sometimes a single word or phrase that sticks. For example, Namkhai Norbu's single-word answer to my question of how to proceed in my practice: *"Integration!"* (the penetrating stare may have been operative). Or the words of the old monk I happened to cross paths with on the mountain, after I bowed: "We are all on this path together." Regarding Geshe Roach, the one thing that has stuck with me from the evening I received instruction from him at a massively attended talk he held in Hong Kong was "Relax your eyelids."

While most people associate yoga with postures and movements of the body (*asanas*), the body is only a tool used in the service of yoga. According to B.K.S. Iyengar:

> "Without firm foundations a house cannot stand. Without the practice of the principles of yama [self-purification by discipline] and niyama [universal moral commandments], which lay down firm foundations for building character, there cannot be an integrated

personality. Practice of asanas without the backing of yama and niyama is mere acrobatics." (Iyengar, 1979, p. 57)

I would propose, similarly, that even if a person can do every physical asana (body posture) perfectly, if they are not working on stilling their mind, they are doing calisthenics, not yoga. Not that there's anything wrong with calisthenics. It just isn't yoga (unless done with the intent of stilling the mind via *selective awareness for psychological purposes*, in which case it, or anything thus practiced, such as smelling a flower or cleaning a window, becomes meditation, mindfulness and yoga).

In other words, when the *intention* is to still the mind, one is practicing yoga whatever one is doing with the body. Baking and stealing bread may both be perfect yoga if done to still, or with a still mind.

The beginning practice of meditation and mindfulness involves the intention of stilling the mind, and the later fruit of meditation and mindfulness is a still mind or the ability to still the mind at will. However, in both the beginning and later stages of practice, one can be perfectly practicing meditation and mindfulness regardless of how much of the "meditation" or "mindfulness" time is spent thinking.

Meditation, mindfulness and yoga are, at a general level, identical. They are all techniques to increase awareness and still the mind, and they all refer as well to the resulting state of consciousness. The term "meditation" is typically used to refer to awareness in silent stillness, and the term "mindfulness" is typically used to refer to awareness in the midst of activity. In other words,

Meditation is mindful inactivity, and mindfulness is meditation in-activity.

As the above will hopefully clarify, any activity, including inactivity, and any inactivity, including activity, constitutes yoga, meditation and mindfulness if it is done in a psychological context of full, still, silent awareness (and make no mistake, silent awareness may be experienced in the midst of noisy activity, because awareness is silent by nature. Silent awareness may even be done while one is oneself talking or otherwise making loud noises, if the identity is with the awareness and not with the activity or the sound being made, in which case one is "doing without a sense of doership"). As Bhagavan Sri Ramana Maharshi teaches,

> ... be fixed in the Self and act according to nature without the thought of doership. Then the results of action will not affect you. That is courage and heroism." (Ramana, 1966/2006, Talk 58, July 4, 1935, p. 66)

And

> "Surrender once for all and be done with the desire. So long as the sense of doership is retained there is the desire; that is also personality. If this goes the Self is found to shine forth pure. The sense of doership is bondage and not the actions themselves. 'Be still and know that I am God.' Here stillness is total surrender without a vestige of individuality. Stillness will prevail and there will be no agitation of the mind. Agitation of mind is the cause of desire, the sense of doership and personality. If that is stopped there is quiet. There 'Knowing' means 'Being.' It is not the relative knowledge involving the triads, knowledge, subject and object . . . 'I am that I am.' *I am* is God – not thinking, 'I am God.' Realize *I am* and do not think *I am*. 'Know I am God' – it is said, and not 'Think I am God.'" (Ramana, 1955/2006, Talk 354, February 8, 1937 p. 335)

Most of us who have been meditating for a while have at one time or another fallen into the trap of equating meditation with the arbitrary spiritual or religious trappings in which we first encountered it, be they Buddhist, Hindu/Yogic, Taoist, Jewish Kabbalistic, Christian Contemplative, Sufi Islamic, etc. (but usually Buddhist or Hindu Yogic, as meditation is a component of their common "exoteric" practice, rather than embedded in esoteric or secret teachings as in Western traditions).

But meditation is like sugar. If someone comes up to you and hands you a chocolate cake and says "this is sugar," and someone else comes up to you and hands you cotton candy and says "this is sugar," and someone else comes up to you and hands you a pineapple and says "this is sugar," you would probably roll your eyes and say to them something to the tune of "No, that's a chocolate cake, that's cotton candy, and that's a pineapple." Similarly, Zen Buddhist meditation, Hindu Kundalini meditation, Taoist Microcosmic Orbit meditation, Jewish Kabbalistic meditation, Christian contemplative meditation, Sufi Islamic meditation and Western Mystery Tradition pathworking meditation are *forms* of meditation but not "meditation" itself. They are Buddhist, Hindu, Taoist, Jewish, Christian, Sufi and Western Mystery Tradition practices that have meditation as a component and use it as an ingredient in their own spiritual and religious recipes.

This is not in any way to knock religion, spirituality or religious or spiritual meditation. I have studied, practiced and benefited in various ways from each of the above systems. I personally believe in a number of religious and spiritual teachings and at times engage in various religious and spiritually-related practices. But the most important thing that I have learned from the multitude of meditational systems is what they have in common.

If you wanted to learn to read, and the only local place to learn to read was in a Zen center, Hindu temple, church or synagogue that used their own religious texts to teach you to read, it would make sense to go there to learn to read, but it would be incorrect to identify the skill and benefits of reading with that particular religion, or to adopt the philosophies and practices of that religion out of a belief that these constitute "true" reading. The same goes for meditation in the above traditions, unless of course you are sincerely interested in practicing these, which can be a beautiful thing.

SOME DEFINITIONS OF MEDITATION

There are numerous definitions of meditation and scholarly articles enumerating these. Rather than enter that maze, I believe that it is a form of respect to the entirety of the meditative systems to define meditation as that which they have in common.

All systems of meditation aim at what is defined by Patanjali as Yoga itself: Stopping thinking and thoughts (translations vary, but this is the gist – except when the word "meditation" is used to refer to what would be more correctly termed "contemplation" which involves cognitive content). It may come as a surprise that you can do true yoga anywhere, anytime, without even moving your body. No downward dog required.

If stilling the mind is the common aim of yoga, meditation and mindfulness, the common method boils down to the definition that I provided earlier:

Meditation is Selective Awareness

for Psychological Transformation

This definition contains a cognitive behavior (selection), a non-activity (awareness), and a motivation/goal/outcome of the practice (psychological transformation).

Why define meditation as involving *awareness* rather than *attention* as is more common in *the biz*? And isn't "selective awareness" really the same thing as "attention"? Point well taken. But in order to pay attention to something, you first must be aware of it. Therefore, awareness precedes attention. To then pay attention to something you are already aware of would further require *doing* something. And aren't we already *doing* enough? From the moment we wake up to the moment we go to sleep, we are *doing, doing, doing*. That's why wise teachers such as Ram Dass (who was a Harvard psychologist before he got too inquisitive and started studying things that upset *the man*) instruct us to *Be Here Now*. They don't say *Do There Then*, but *Be Here Now*. "Paying attention," "concentrating," and "focusing" can easily degenerate into just more egoic doing, which is part of the problem. Active/passive awareness of what already is, is the meditational solution. Since Awareness is closer to Being than attention – unless you are Being Attention, which is then the same as awareness which is Being Awareness – and since one of the goals of meditation is to learn to Just Be, awareness wins this round.

Of course, *selecting* what to be aware of and what *not* to be aware of is also a form of doing (B.F. Skinner referred to such behavior, directly experienced only by the individual emitting it, as a "*private event*"; 1953/2014, p. 257). But at least *awareness itself*, prior to the "cognitive behavior" of selection, is given primacy in the definition (as the noun, only then adjectivally modified by "selective"), honoring its place as the key to consciousness and thus to experience. Awareness is at once (1) our interface with reality, the psychological space within which arises what we perceive as reality and, (2) according to Eastern teachings, the Self of not only the individual, but also of the world and of God. In addition, "selective awareness" has a lighter feel than "paying attention," at least for those of us (sorry in advance to again belabor a point, but it's an important one) still recovering from years of being told to "pay attention to," "focus on" or "concentrate on" this or that boring and ultimately useless thing, rather than to what our innate curiosity and creativity naturally gravitated toward (i.e., events in the Free Zone outside the classroom windows).

Another possible definition (of IPA-Q fame) would expand the notion of selectivity into intention and preference:

Meditation is Intentional Preferential Awareness (IPA)

for Psychological Transformation

I again have to thank my cousin Paul, a Transcendental Meditation (TM) teacher and the first person I ever saw meditate, probably sometime back in the 1970s when I was a teen. I came in from a backyard family reunion to get something from upstairs, and there was Paul sitting cross-legged on the bed. But what I should thank him for, which I briefly mentioned earlier, is more recently suggesting that when I teach meditation to clients, rather than instructing them to "pay attention" to their breath, I counsel them to "favor" their breath. This evolved into shifting my emphasis, both in practicing and teaching meditation, from attention to awareness. I'm sure this is something taken for granted by many more experienced meditators than myself across traditions, and that I have probably read hundreds of times in writings ancient and modern without grasping its significance, but that pointer by Paul finally effected the shift. Thanks Cousin!

You can experience for yourself the flavor of *awareness* as compared with attention, focus or concentration very easily. Your eyes are currently open and receiving visual information, thanks to light, from your environment. You are seeing what is in front of you without expending any effort, because your eyes are open. You do not need to "pay attention" to it, or "focus" on it, or "concentrate" on it to be aware of it. You really don't have to do anything to be aware of what is right here and impinging sensorially on a sense organ other than to be "selectively aware" of it as opposed to being lost in thoughts or selectively aware of information impinging on other senses.

Meditation is fundamentally a non-doing, in order to experience what is being obscured by too much doing. The song *Alice in Wonderland* is *à propos*:

"How do you get to Wonderland?

Over the hill or underland, or just behind the tree? . . .

Where is the land beyond the eye that people cannot see . . .

Chapter 9 - Beyond Mindfulness: Yoga and The Matrix

> Where do stars go, where is the crescent moon?
>
> They must be somewhere in the sunny afternoon."
>
> (Bob Hilliard, 1951)

Indeed, sometimes what we are seeking is "beyond the eye," and yet "just behind the tree." Other times, things are right where we left them, such as the stars and crescent moon that are in our direct line of vision, but which we can't see because we are blinded by the Sun. Ultimately, the goal of meditation is not to find something that we lack, but to find what has always been right here, outshone by our constant selective awareness of thinking and sensory stimuli.

The "selective" aspect of this definition of meditation refers to the unavoidable and paradoxical necessity of *doing to undo* ("doing without a sense of doership" in Hindu lingo), *thinking to stop thinking* ("thinking non-thinking" in Zen Buddhist terms). Selective awareness *does* involve thinking and doing (switching from intentional or automatic selective awareness of one thing to another thing). However, these are transformational modalities of thinking and doing that are necessary for the meditational goal of gaining the ability to bring thinking and non-thinking, and the "doing" of thinking and non-thinking, under voluntary control.

I have included the goal "psychological transformation" as part of the definition so that the definition would preclude selective awareness of things and purposes unrelated to what is generally considered meditation. Being selectively aware of the senses involved in planting a flower with no goal whatsoever other than to plant a flower would certainly be experienced as "meditative," but I would not consider it "meditation" unless it is accompanied (or was accompanied in the past, with a current continuous meditative state as a fruition) at some level of consciousness by a motivation for psychological transformation.

Similarly, smoking a cigarette is very "meditative" without being "meditation." In fact, the meditative elements of smoking may be even more important than the nicotine in maintaining the behavior. What does smoking involve? Selective awareness of breathing, the sight of fire and smoke, the smell of burning tobacco, the taste of tobacco, the sensation of breathing, and the awareness of the repetitive movements of the hand, lips and diaphragm. Add to this the relative absence of thought, as awareness has been driven to so many sensory modalities that little cognitive availability remains for awareness of thinking. Finally, as for example during a smoking break at work, the behavior is often positively reinforced by the pleasure of standing outside looking out at space and negatively reinforced by the removal of boredom or stress caused by the tasks that are being avoided. While the addictive properties of nicotine account for the withdrawal symptoms that occur when one stops smoking, and smoking is to that extent maintained by negative reinforcement (the removal of the discomfort caused by not smoking), it is possible that meditative components of smoking play an important role as well. This may be why one of the most effective ways to stop smoking includes mindfulness techniques. I like to teach my smoking clients behavioral techniques as well, such as taking "nonsmoking breaks" at the same times and for the same durations as they used to take smoking breaks. After all, why should you have to stop taking breaks and chilling out with your coworkers several times each a.m. and p.m. just because you've stopped smoking?

The present definition of meditation breaks down to some extent in as much as being selectively aware of doing something evil, even if accompanied in some twisted way by a motivation for psychological transformation (e.g., to study one's own reactions to do doing something evil) cannot be excluded on purely semantic grounds. However, everyone knows that in *this* universe purposely committing evil is not meditation, and it would seem clumsy to specifically include such exceptions in the definition (e.g., "Selective Awareness of Non-Evil Things for Psychological Transformation).

The psychological outcomes that people typically have for meditation correspond with the three goals of my Four Psychologies:

> **Goal of Psychology 1.0, Preventive Psychology:** Wellness (Preventing disease).
>
> **Goal of Psychology 2.0, Curative Psychology:** Wellness (Curing disease).
>
> **Goals of Psychology 3.0, Positive Psychology:** Well-Being / Self-Actualization.

Goals of Psychology 4.0, Transcendent, Transformational, Transpersonal Psychology: Self-realization / Cosmic Consciousness / Enlightenment / Being ItSelf

It should, however, be noted that for a given individual, even if meditation or mindfulness are undertaken as a Psychology 2.0 practice with a goal of simply feeling less anxious, other results may ensue whether or not they were known about, desired or intended. As Styron (2005) points out,

> ". . . the fact that mindfulness practice turns out to have application for all kinds of mental disorders that the clinician encounters in the psychotherapy office is wonderfully fortuitous. To conclude that such application is the primary purpose of mindfulness practice, however, would be very wide off the mark. It would be like using rocket fuel to kindle a campfire and subsequently concluding that such use was fundamental." (p. 263)

And it should not be assumed that people seeking relaxation through meditation will necessarily be pleased when as a bonus they gain insight into the workings of their mind and the world. I have had more than one client whose main reason for seeking therapy was that they had expanded their consciousness through the use of hallucinogens, and as a result of increased self-knowledge could no longer continue living in their previous ignorant, irresponsible bliss. Suddenly, they found themselves aware of and facing certain realities of themselves and the people and things around them that threw their prior unexamined lives into question. Their treatment goal was to be the way they used to be (ignorant). As I didn't see any way of accomplishing this, I presented to them an alternative goal of helping them to realize that the only way is up, that they are stardust, they are golden, and that they *haven't* got to get themselves back to the Garden . . .

TYPES OF MEDITATION

There exist various taxonomies of meditation. Perhaps the most common and broadest distinction is that between "concentrative" and "open awareness" meditation. A given meditational system may employ each of these for specific purposes, sometimes in sequence, such as Zen which may begin a sit with breath counting (concentrative meditation) to still the mind, similar to swabbing alcohol on the skin prior to administering an injection, followed by "just sitting," relinquishing control of the mind and just being aware of what arises as seeing, hearing, smelling, tasting, bodysensing and thinking. "Mindfulness" is sometimes considered to be an integration of the two.

I distinguish four main types of meditation from a psychological point of view, one leading naturally to the next over time as the brain or mind begins to abide more and more in the meditative state both when intentionally induced and as a new default mode of consciousness during everyday activities. A definition of the "path" of meditation, pointing to its beginning, middle and end, that takes all four into account is:

The Path of Meditation is the psychological transition

from Object Awareness to Subject Awareness

to Being Awareness or Pure Awareness,

to Self-Enquiry into the nature of Being or Pure Awareness.

In order of departure from the problem (involuntary object awareness of thinking, that is, awareness of thinking which is itself an object) to proximity of the solution (involuntary awareness of Being ItSelf and inquiry into its nature), these include:

(1) Selective awareness of an object of the senses or of the mind (e.g., the feeling of the breath, circulation of the chi energy around the microcosmic orbit, movement of the kundalini energy through the chakras, the mental sound of a mantra, a prayer, a thought), or of some combination of objects of the senses and mind (e.g., seeing, hearing and movement when walking, known as walking meditation or mindfulness of walking; seeing, hearing and feeling when washing the dishes; feeling the breath while engaging in breath counting; or any combination of sense impressions during any activity whatsoever). This is the dualistic type of meditation that one is doing when practicing "mindfulness" *of* a specific thing. Both concentrative and open awareness sitting meditation are also of this type when they are *more* focused on the object(s) arising in awareness than on the abiding awareness itself. Open Focus meditation as taught by Les and Susan Fehmi may be a transitional meditative technique in-between object awareness and subject awareness. Here,

> "'Objectless imagery' – the multisensory experience and awareness of space, nothingness, or absence – almost always elicits large amplitude and prolonged periods of phase-synchronous alpha activity ... Space is unique among the contents of attention because space, silence, and timelessness cannot be concentrated on or grasped as a separate experience." (Fehmi & Robbins, 2007, p. 36)

(2) Selective awareness of the subject. This is awareness of awareness itself, still in a dualistic sense of "I" as the subject being aware of "my" awareness as an object. This seems a transitional meditational practice aiming at the third type of meditation. Subject Awareness as transitional to Being or Pure Awareness can be found in practices including Zen Buddhist meditation (Shikantaza, Just Sitting), Tibetan Buddhist meditation (Self-Liberation Through Seeing With Naked Awareness), and Nondual Hindu meditation (Advaita Vedanta). Adyashanti's "True Meditation" seems to be of this type.

(3) Being awareness or pure awareness. Here there is a merging of subject awareness and object awareness, with a disappearance of any psychological or sensed boundary between subject and object. The entire multisensory experience is perceived as oneself in the sense of One-Self. From a materialistic neurological point of view, this is the nature of all experience, which is the brain's own representation of information gathered by the senses and memory. However, *experiencing* subject and object as unity is different from understanding this intellectually and constitutes a distinct psychological state. As Bodhidharma put it:

> "When the world and the mind are both transparent, this is true vision." (Red Pine, 1989, p. 51)

And as Grandma Densei (1922) put it:

> "Silence is not the absence of sound.
>
> Silence is a state of mind,
>
> A tuning in to, resonance or synchrony
>
> With a fundamental frequency
>
> Of Nature, the Universe or Being."

(4) *Self-enquiry* into the nature of Who or What is aware, or What is this awareness in (1), (2) and (3) above. This is known in India as "*atma-vichara*," popularized in recent times by the Hindu sage Ramana Maharshi (1879-1950), published as "Who Am I" (in the original 1902 version, which is more concise, and in an expanded 1931 version).

It is important to understand that although most of Ramana Maharshi's recorded teachings contain a lot of philosophical, spiritual and religious content, this was in response to the state of mind of the individuals who came to him for guidance, and their formulation of questions in philosophical, spiritual and religious terms. He would usually begin by meeting them where they were, so to speak, gradually leading them back from their conceptual jungles to his purely psychological technique of enquiring into the root of the experience of "I," emphasizing that no spiritual or religious practices are necessary. He was famous for his use of what came to be known as his "*brahmastra*" or cosmic sword, sooner or later asking his questioners, regardless of their questions, something to the extent of "Who wants to know," as in the following:

> Questioner: "From where did the knower and his misperceptions come?"
>
> Ramana: "Who is asking the question?"
>
> Questioner: "I am."
>
> Ramana: "Find out that 'I' and all your doubts will be solved. Just as in a dream a false knowledge, knower and known, rise up, in the waking state the same process operates. In both states in knowing this 'I' you know everything and nothing remains to be known. In deep sleep, knower, knowledge and known are absent. In the same way, at the time of experiencing the real 'I' they will not exist. Whatever you see happening in the waking state happens only to the knower, and since the knower is unreal, nothing in fact ever happens."
> (Madhavatirtha, 1981, pp. 154-155, in Godman, 1985, p. 191)

Ramana's technique, in brief, is as follows (my summary, not direct quotations of Ramana): When aware of any experience (i.e., seeing, hearing, smelling, tasting, bodysensing or thinking/imagining) ask yourself (or wonder nonverbally) "Who is having this experience?" The answer will naturally be "I am." Then ask yourself or wonder nonverbally, "But Who

Am I?" Kind of like if you had amnesia and you were trying to remember who you really are. This might also be likened to trying to remember a word that is on the tip of your tongue, or what you just walked into the room to get. But don't ask in a repetitive mantra-like way. You don't continuously repeat "what was that word, what was that word?" or "why did I come in here? why did I come in here?" Rather, you in a way clear your mind with an intention of remembering, somewhat confident from past experience that the remembering/realization will eventually arise of itself, not as something new, but as something that was already there but hidden from conscious awareness.

The "I" in "Who Am I" is the false self, being that perceived as an *object* of awareness, an idea/image/sensation of what one *thinks of* as the self, as contrasted with the *pure experience* of Self considered to be the True Self. "I see the wall" has 3 elements: a subject, contact, and an object. The seer, seeing and seen. If I see the wall, I am not the wall. I am the subject, aware of an object. We all know this. But we rarely if ever take this to its logical conclusion. If I am aware of my thoughts, emotions, sensations, and body, these are objects of which "I" am the aware subject, meaning that "I" can't be "them." In other words, contrary to popular belief, "I" am not the body, of which I am aware, as a separate thing, nor am "I" the content or processes of the mind, of which I am aware, as separate things. To the extent that I distinguish between the body and an "I" that is aware of the body, the body can't be me, and the same goes for the mind.

But if "I" am not the body or mind, Who Am I? What Am I? What is this experienced "I" that has sensory and cognitive experiences of the world, body and mind? What is its source? This is Self-Enquiry, "'I' Diving," "the backward step," "turning the light around," the Greek "Gnothi Seauton" (know thyself), and the answer cannot be found intellectually. We can only humble ourselves by sincerely asking the question, with the determination of a drowning person seeking the surface of the water, sincerely wondering about Who or What we really are. According to U.G. Krishnamurti (NOT Jiddu Krishnamurti),

> "It is clear to me that to find out for yourself
>
> you must be absolutely helpless with nowhere to turn."
>
> (1988, p. 90)

Once you get the hang of it, it is not necessary to do each step of the procedure (e.g., "Who sees?" "I see." "Who Am I?"). Instead, for example, you can merely be aware of the sense of sight and wonder "Who is this I that sees?" or "What is this I that sees?" Or even, using Ramana's cosmic sword, "Who" or "What" is this 'I' that wants to know, or "Who asks?"

Ram Dass (Richard Alpert, perhaps the first Western psychologist to devote his life to the practice and teaching of meditation) proposes this technique:

> "You sit down quietly and you say, 'Who am I?' and then the way I do it is I put the 'I,' the thought of the 'I' right in the middle of my head, right here, and I say, 'I am not this body.' Then I experience my body as object to the 'I' in the middle of my head. I see it. I feel it. I sense it as an object. Then I say, 'I am not my five organs of action,' and then I experience my arms as objects, my legs as objects, my tongue as an object, my anal sphincter as object, and my genitals as objects. Each of them are experienced as 'that' and here 'I' am in the middle of my head. Then I say, 'I am not my senses.'
>
> Now, you have been in a room where there is a clock ticking and you start to read something, and you get so turned on by what you're reading, you don't hear the clock tick. Everybody is in that situation, and when you finish reading, then the clock is ticking again. Now actually, all the time you were there, the clock was ticking, your ear was hearing the clock tick, but you weren't *attending* to your ear hearing the clock tick. It was involuntary. In other words, there is a place between the three and the two. There's a place between your attention and your ear hearing the clock tick, so what you do is you don't turn off, but you observe your hearing, like when I'm talking, watch your ear hearing me talk. Watch your eyes seeing, watch your nose smelling; note your mouth tasting; note your skin feeling. Do it all from a place right in the middle, the 'I' thought. Then 'I' am not my five internal organs, and you go through digestion, erection, excretion, respiration, perspiration, and circulation, and then you're ready for the clincher, the exquisite one. You got all that? You're finished with your body; now where are you? You're in the middle of this 'I' thought, in the middle of the head that you own, and you say, 'I am not this thought.'

So then it becomes 'Well, where am I?'... 'I am here; I am here.' Any thought you can think of, you're not that one.

If you can do that, and it takes quite a while, I mean really, a long time, you come to a place where you go behind your senses, and behind your thinking mind. When you are able to do that, you go through a doorway and you enter into what in Zen is called *Satori*, in Hindu is called *Samadhi*, and the beginning of what is known as *Satchitananda*. When you have gone through these stages within that, you come to a place where you are synonymous with that very fine energy, that is an identity with consciousness. Now you've got to understand that the identity, that energy, that very, very, fine energy, is an identity with consciousness – that the universe is consciousness; it is not self-consciousness, but it is consciousness." (Ram Dass, 2021a)

The former Catholic nun, Bernadette Roberts, recounts in her book *The Experience of No-Self: A Contemplative Journey* that when she camped for 5 months in the High Sierras

> "One of the great mysteries
>
> that I hoped to solve in this mountain solitude
>
> was the answer to my question:
>
> what is it that sees this Oneness everywhere?"
>
> (Roberts, 1982, p. 33)

As though in answer (from the past), Christian mystic William Law, in Chapter 2 of *The Spirit of Prayer*, entitled *Discovering the true Way of turning to God, and of finding the Kingdom of Heaven, the Riches of Eternity in our Souls*, wrote in 1749 (and I will retain his formatting):

> "But there is a *Root*, or *Depth* in Thee, from whence all these Faculties come forth, as
>
> Lines from a *Centre*, or as Branches from the Body of the Tree. This Depth is called the
>
> *Centre*, the *Fund* or *Bottom* of the Soul. This Depth is the *Unity*, the *Eternity*, I had

almost said, the *Infinity* of thy Soul; for it is so infinite, that nothing can satisfy it, or give

it any Rest, but the infinity of God."

Ramana Maharshi devoted the last 50+ years of his life to teaching all who approached him the method that he had discovered, at age 16, for opening the "doors of perception" and realizing this ground of being. He said "The only enquiry leading to Self-realisation is seeking the source of the 'I' with in-turned mind and without uttering the word 'I'" (Verse 29 of Ulladu Narpadu, 40 Verses on Reality; in Osborne, 1997, p. 80).

Seeking the source of the "I" is seeking the source of seeking itself and of the impulse, at this moment, to seek. It is to ask, or more precisely to nonverbally wonder, "What is the Matrix?" (Wachowski & Wachowski, 1999).

Eventually, enquiring as to the source of something that we don't understand (the ego) causes another thing that we don't understand (awakening) to happen, making us aware of still another thing that we don't understand (the True Self) but which rings Truer than our prior experience, Truer than true.

In Christian terminology,

> "Ask, and it shall be given you;
> seek, and ye shall find;
> knock, and it shall be opened unto you:
> For every one that asketh receiveth;
> and he that seeketh findeth;
> and to him that knocketh it shall be opened."
> (Matthew, 7:7-8)

Similarly, in Talk 197 from *Talks with Ramana Maharshi*, he tells a questioner:

> "You need not eliminate the wrong 'I'. How can 'I' eliminate itself? All that you need do is to find out its origin and abide there. Your efforts can extend only thus far. Then the Beyond will take care of itself. You are helpless there. No effort can reach it." (Ramana Maharshi, 1955/2006)

Zen Buddhism has a form of meditation, known as koan practice, in which one deeply inquires into such paradoxes as "Who is seeing?," "Who is hearing?," etc., progressing to enquiring still further into "Who Am I?," "What is This?," "What is the Object Corresponding with I?" (These were my own koans. My Zen Master then turned me on to Nisargadatta, and I then found Ramana and realized that the deeper you go into all of these systems the more you realize they are saying the same thing and that this could be distilled from their particular spiritual and religious content.) Herbert Benson psychologized Transcendental, or Hindu mantra, meditation; Jon Kabat Zinn psychologized Buddhist mindfulness meditation, and it may be useful for someone to psychologize Self-Enquiry in both the Hindu and Buddhist, and possibly other traditions as well. I have recently been reading books by Toni Packer, who I believe has done just this with her path of "Meditative Inquiry" (Packer, 2002, 2007). Toni's meditative inquiry appears to integrate the third and fourth types of meditation above. There is a sense, both from her writings and from discussions among teachers and students in her tradition at a silent retreat that I attended, of a "meditative" aspect pointing to being *in* the moment, being *with* the moment (which Toni sometimes refers to as "awaring"), and even *being* the moment itself, along with all that arises within and without. During the retreat, self-inquiring into what exactly I was doing when meditating, there came to mind what seems to be a useful and parsimonious working definition of meditation:

Meditation is *Being With*.

When one practices *Being With*, eventually the dualistic "with" drops out, and one is then simply Being. But there is also an "inquiry" component of questioning or wondering about the essential nature of what is arising and simply *What Is*. In "The Work of This Moment" (1990/2007) Toni states that

> "Truth is not found by striving for attainment of a goal in the future, but it has to do with questioning, wondering and seeing *what is* this instant" (p. 24); and

> "This work of deeply wondering about everything that is going on – wondering who and what one actually is, and whether there may actually be something beyond the endless struggles of daily life – can never be the result of any imposed outward pressure. Pressure only

results in more pressure. A free spirit of inquiry isn't the result of anything. It is there, spontaneously, when we are not dominated by systems of inner and outer control. Let me give an example. When one needs to listen to a strange sound, doesn't one naturally stop making noise? One cannot listen carefully as long as one is talking, thinking, or moving about inattentively. The need to listen carefully creates its own stillness. When one actually realizes how inattentive one is and begins to wonder about what is actually going on inside and out, doesn't one *have* to look and listen quietly?" (p. 60)

Here then is a combination, possibly an integration, of both being (seeing) and doing (questioning, wondering). However, even such "doing" is itself then seen and inquired into, for example the "doing" of "wanting":

"The moment one sits still and attends for brief instants at a time, doesn't the thought of wanting something, and of getting something arise? It happens. We have been conditioned that way from earliest childhood on and have seen it in others ever since we can remember. 'Do something. Be somebody. Get someplace.' Or 'Be quiet. Stop fiddling. Don't do this. Don't think. Don't want this or that. Just be in the moment.'

Can there be awareness of this running stream of thoughts, commands, reactions, desires, goals, without judgment, without reacting for or against? As long as I am wrapped up in what I want or should not want, wanting itself does not come into awareness. The wanting is just running its habitual course. What *is* wanting? Can we see?

Do you see the difference between wanting something, and the actual process of wanting as it manifests throughout the mind and body? I always come back to the question: Is one wondering how the mind actually functions from moment to moment, and if so, can one begin to attend quietly, in all simplicity?" (Packer, 1990/2007, p. 16)

The four types of meditation need not be practiced in any particular sequence, but what Ramana found is that some people had difficulty jumping right into Self-Enquiry. Therefore, some may find it easier to master one before attempting the next. This is because when one's current habit is to be lost in awareness of thinking (as an object of awareness), it may be easiest to transition to awareness of a different *object,* the only remaining ones being sensory objects (that which is seen, heard, smelled, tasted, or physically felt), rather than trying to jump right into subject awareness or pure awareness or self-enquiry. Once one has developed a facility with returning from thoughts to sense objects, it is then easier to practice *pratyahara*, withdrawal of the senses from their objects, which is the fifth limb of the eight branches of Yoga (*ashtanga*). When awareness is withdrawn from objects, it naturally is pulled toward the subject itself, the I that is aware, resulting in the second form of meditation above (selective awareness of the subject). From there, one can loosen the boundary between subject and object, experiencing the unity of all experiences present in awareness, and awareness itself, as "I," and finally inquire into what this I is, or from whence arises this I. This makes one aware of whatever subtle I-I duality may remain, even in Being Awareness or Pure Awareness. Voicing "I," wondering "Who" is voicing "I," can trigger abidance in what the Christian mystics refer to as the Cloud of Unknowing, and what Zen refers to as "Don't Know" Mind.

Said another way, once one's default mode is multisensory awareness rather than thinking, it is easier to spot the subject, the "I" that is aware of the senses. This "I" may at first be mistaken to be the mind or body. Finally aware of this false "I," one can realize the totality of the senses, mind, body and awareness of these, and of itself, as one thing, one "I," and then wonder what this "I" really is, what is its source. For example when the word "I" is voiced in the mind, from whence does the sound arise before it is mentally voiced? And when the impulse to mentally voice it arises, from whence does this impulse arise? This ultimate meditative practices of Being Awareness or Pure Awareness and Self-Enquiry consists of abiding in "I"-ness, inquiring into the source of this "I"-ness, and continuously abiding in this silent enquiry, this inquiring "don't know" mind.

Ramana Maharshi explains the superiority of Self-Enquiry to meditation on objects as follows:

> "Reality is simply the loss of the ego. Destroy the ego by seeking its identity. Because the ego is no entity it will automatically vanish and reality will shine forth by itself. This is the direct method. Whereas all other methods are done only retaining the ego. In those paths there arise so many doubts and the eternal question remains to be

tackled finally. But in this method the final question is the only one and it is raised from the very beginning. No sadhanas [spiritual practices] are necessary for engaging in this quest. There is no greater mystery than this – *viz.*, ourselves being the reality we seek to gain reality. We think that there is something hiding our reality and that it must be destroyed before the reality is gained. It is ridiculous. A day will dawn when you will yourself laugh at your past efforts. That which will be on the day you laugh is also here and now." (Talk 146, 26th January, 1936; Ramana Maharshi, 1955/2006)

At the beginning, the "selective" quality of meditation involves a certain amount of thinking and volition, in order to remember to "do" meditation when one realizes that one is currently mindlessly aware of the habitual contents of awareness (and that one is in whatever emotional state these are triggering, e.g., low mood, anxiety, anger, mental dullness, etc.).

However, over time, the meditative state itself becomes one's default mode of awareness, and then thinking itself requires selective awareness of the content of thought. Rather than constantly and mindlessly swinging our legs when sitting and then purposely stilling them in order to stand up and walk, we have learned to keep them still when sitting, and then purposely move them in order to stand up and walk. *So can it be with the mind.*

We are all performing the "selective" aspect of meditation all of our waking (and for some of us, lucid dreaming, and even lucid non-dreaming sleep) hours. Only, all of us are sometimes and some of us are almost always choosing as objects things that are useless at best (repetitive TV news stories, repetitive TV news stories) and often harmful (obsessive worry/anger thoughts, the taste of junk food, the feeling of inhaling a cigarette, repetitive TV news stories . . .). Often, we are selectively aware without being intentionally aware, as when we realize we have been worrying, without having intended to worry.

In sum, meditation is merely doing what we already spend our lives doing (being selectively aware of stuff) but with a goal of psychological transformation. The "stuff" we are selectively aware of in meditation may be (among myriad other mundane, spiritual and religious possibilities):

(1) objects (e.g., the feeling of the air entering and leaving the nose during sitting breath awareness meditation, or selective awareness in silent stillness;

the sight of the sink, the sound of the water, the feel of the silverware when washing dishes during mindfulness, or selective awareness in activity);

(2) the subject itself, the "I" (awareness of awareness, the simple sense of being);

(3) the total unitive experience of subject, object, and awareness of these as One-Self with no boundaries; or

(4) the sense that there is something beyond the "I" awareness, a "ground of being," and verbally or nonverbally wondering what That Is (Self-Enquiry).

It should be noted that while I am listing these 4 forms of awareness as a logical sequence and calling them 4 types of meditation, I am not advocating each as necessarily useful for everyone, claiming that 4 >3>2>1 for everyone, or proposing that these are superior to other types of meditation. To this point, I recently had a very eye-opening exchange with Bob Dattola, a teacher in Toni Packer's tradition. I was mentioning to him that when I meditate and notice thinking, I "come back" from thinking to awareness of the senses. He pointed out that he sees this as the complete opposite of "coming back from thinking." He proposed that when thinking is noticed, *this* is when the "I" (of thinking) has disappeared, and by supposedly "coming back" from thinking one is merely adding new thinking (in the form of judgment of one object of awareness being better than another and what should be done about it, i.e., "*come back*"). He also felt that practicing self-inquiry is again adding thinking. For example, in self-inquiry, one might begin with noticing that "I see the flower," then wonder "Who sees the flower?," have a sense of an "I" seeing the flower and then wonder "Who Am I?" Bob challenged whether there needs to be an "I" that "sees" the flower, or whether there is simply the experience of "flower." Despite the fact that in a matter of seconds Bob basically blew up the entire premise for one of the basic techniques offered in this book to stop thinking (*come back* to the senses), I believe his insights are worth thinking about, or not thinking about, as the case may be, as we simply *Be With* whichever arises.

> *"First there is a mountain, then there is no mountain, then there is."*
>
> **Donovan Phillips Leitch (1967)**

Chapter 10 - *The Fullness of Emptiness:* Yes! We Have No Bananas

"Sadhakas [seekers] rarely understand the difference between this temporary stilling of the mind [*manolaya*] and permanent destruction of thoughts [*manonasa*]. In *manolaya* there is temporary subsidence of thought-waves, and though this temporary period may even last for a thousand years, thoughts, which are thus temporarily stilled, rise up as soon as the *manolaya* ceases. One must therefore watch one's spiritual progress carefully. One must not allow oneself to be overtaken by such spells of stillness of thought. The moment one experiences this, one must revive consciousness and enquire within as to who it is who experiences this stillness. While not allowing any thoughts to intrude, one must not, at the same time, be overtaken by this deep sleep [*yoga nidra*] or self-hypnotism. Though this is a sign of progress toward the goal, yet it is also the point where the divergence between the road to liberation and *yoga nidra* takes place. The easy way, the direct way, the shortest cut to salvation is the enquiry method. By such enquiry, you will drive the thought force deeper till it reaches its source and merges within.

It is then that you will have the response from within and find that you rest there, destroying all thoughts, once and for all."

Ramana Maharshi

(in Swarnagiri, 1981, pp. 25-27; cited in Godman, 1985 pp. 63-64)

"The trouble with quietism is that it cheats itself in its rationalization and manipulation of reality. It makes a cult out of 'sitting still,' as if this in itself had a magic power to solve all problems and bring man into contact with God. But in actual fact it is simply an evasion. It is a lack of honesty and seriousness, a trifling with grace and a flight from God. So much for 'pure quietism.' But does such a thing really exist in our day?

Absolute quietism is not exactly an ever-present danger in the world of our time. To be an out-and-out quietist, one would have to make heroic efforts to keep still and such efforts are beyond the power of most of us. However, there is a temptation to a kind of pseudo-quietism which afflicts those who have read books about mysticism without quite understanding them. And this leads them to a deliberately negative spiritual life which is nothing but a cessation of prayer, for no other reason than that one imagines that by ceasing to be active one automatically enters into contemplation. Actually this leads one into a mere void without any interior, spiritual life, in which distractions and emotional drives gradually assert themselves at the expense of all mature, balanced activity of the mind and heart. To persist in this blank state could be very harmful spiritually, morally and mentally."

Thomas Merton

(Contemplative Prayer, 1969/2019, pp. 114-115)

"Hey, Marianna
You gotta piana
Yes, banana, no
No, yes, no bananas today
We gotta no bananas.
Yes, we gotta no bananas today."

Silver & Conn (1923)

Chapter 10 - The Fullness of Emptiness: Yes! We Have No Bananas

"Nothin' from nothin' leaves nothin'.

"Billy Preston & Bruce Fisher (1974)

So here you are, almost finished with Part 1, entitled *How to Stop Thinking*, in a book entitled *How to Stop Thinking*. You've learned perhaps the greatest thing you'll ever learn other than, of course, "just to love and be loved in return" (Cole & ahbez, 1948). Maybe you've practiced it (stopping thinking, but hopefully loving and being loved in return as well), and perhaps you've had some moments of non-thinking and thought "Wow! This is Great!," and then realized that this too is a thought and come back to 3 other senses. And now I hit you with this: a chapter on the potential *downside*.

Well, consider yourself lucky. The only people who need to learn about potential *downsides* are those on the path to *upsides*.

So what are all those quotes up there talking about? This isn't really a book on spirituality or religion, and yet here's that Hindu yogi Ramana Maharshi again, this time accompanied by Trappist monk Thomas Merton (with a splash of Billy Preston to get the juices flowing). Nevertheless, whichever way you slice it, a mind made still by non-thinking is in a very powerful psychological state of pure potential, with awareness freed up for things we usually aren't aware of to rush in, including:

> **From a mainstream psychological point of view:** Assagioli's Lower and Middle Unconscious (Freud's Unconscious and Preconscious);

> **From a transpersonal psychological point of view:** Assagioli's Higher Unconscious or Superconscious, and Jung's Collective Unconscious;

> **From a Hindu non-dual point of view:** Self-Realization; and

> **From an Abrahamic religious point of view:** God.

In other words, just because we empty the mind does not mean it is likely to stay empty. Emptiness rather invites fullness, and may even be considered identical with fullness as each contains, and therefore IS the other (in a "Yes, we gotta no bananas today" sort of way). This is the central theme of the Buddhist Heart Sutra, a treatise on Form and Emptiness (Shunyata):

> "Form is no other than Shunyata,
>
> Shunyata is no other than form.
>
> Form is exactly Shunyata, Shunyata exactly form.
>
> Feeling, thought, volition and consciousness
>
> are likewise like this." (Zen Studies Society, 2021)

If using meditation to relax is like using rocket fuel to light a campfire, to run with Styron's (2005) metaphor, the same might be said of using selective awareness to stop thinking. By gaining control of your thought process you can certainly benefit in ways corresponding with the wellness goal of Psychologies 1.0/2.0 (Preventive/Curative) and the well-being goal of Psychology 3.0 (Positive). But whether you're interested or not, you may eventually find yourself having subjective experiences more akin to phenomena in the realms of Psychology 4.0 (Transcendent), spirituality or religion.

According to Shunryu Suzuki,

> "In the beginner's mind there are many possibilities,
>
> but in the expert's there are few." (1970/2006, p. 1)

Now we can see why: The expert's mind is cluttered with thoughts, whereas the beginner's mind is empty and waiting.

If you want to learn to stop thinking for purely preventive, curative or positive psychological purposes, the question is whether some of the more transcendent possibilities might present themselves to your non-thinking mind uninvited. The above statements of Ramana Maharshi and Thomas Merton suggest that they may not. It seems that the real risk is for the state of non-thinking to remain just that: non-thinking, *without progressing further* to identity with the True Self (in systems which equate the True Self with the Godhead) or communion with God (in the dualistic religions). But if your goal is precisely for the state of non-thinking to stop right there and not pass Go and not collect $157 (cutbacks), you probably have nothing to worry about as you won't be approaching the endeavor (or non-endeavor) with the type of devotion conducive to such Identity or communion. In any event, if you do happen to meet the Buddha on the road, you can always kill him

(Kopp, 1972), and if God did show you her face, and you survived, would it really be so bad?

More likely than finding God when you have no desire to, is the possibility of becoming aware of negative unconscious and preconscious memories that you would rather continue repressing. Depending upon how you interpret these, this could lead to distress. This distress can be dealt with by first regarding the negative experience as just that, an *experience* of thoughts, emotions and physical sensations as *objects*, and returning to non-thinking via selective sensory awareness. If the distress persists, the Cognitive Behavioral Mind Training (CBMT) tools in Part 2 of this book can be used.

There is also the possibility that abidance in non-thinking could trigger what Stanislav and Christina Grof term a *spiritual emergency* (Grof & Groff, 1989):

> "Feelings of oneness with the entire universe. Visions and images of distant times and places. Sensations of vibrant currents of energy coursing through the body, accompanied by spasms and violent trembling. Visions of deities, demigods, and demons. Vivid flashes of brilliant light and rainbow colors. Fears of impending insanity, even death." (p. 3)

Realistically though, non-thinking, in the sense of keeping the mind still when it doesn't need to move just as you keep your arms, legs and mouth still when they don't need to move, is way more likely to help than harm. On the off chance that non-thinking by itself causes high levels of distress that don't decrease either by continuing or stopping the practice, it would be wise to seek personalized advice from a health care professional or meditation instructor.

Chapter 11 - *Questions and Answers (2)*

"It is necessary to practice meditation

frequently and regularly

until the condition induced

becomes habitual and permanent

throughout the day.

Therefore meditate."

Ramana Maharshi

(in Brunton, Conscious Immortality, 1983)

"You asked how to stop thinking;

this is how!"

H.W.L. Poonja "Papaji"

(2000, p. 388)

Chapter 11 - Questions and Answers (2)

Q: I've tried to meditate a few times, but I can't push away the thoughts.

A: You don't have to push away the thoughts. Since American Automobile Association (*all of your senses are always available*), the only way to stop being aware of one is by being aware of a sufficient number of others, with sufficient saliency, to occupy your degrees of awareness freedom at that particular moment. Right now, there are certain sounds wherever you happen to be (that you are now aware of, and may not have been aware of several seconds ago). As your ears are open, once you become aware of hearing one or more of these, you cannot make yourself stop. You can't "push them away." However, sooner or later while reading these pages, you will notice that certain sounds that have been there all along re-appear, meaning that you had up until that moment again stopped being aware of them. So rather than trying to push thoughts away (which will only make you think about them more), merely turn away from them by being aware of other senses, such as the feeling of the air as it enters and leave the nose. Whenever you realize you are not aware of it anymore, become aware of it again. Once again: *The instruction is not to keep your mind still or to not think, as both are impossible on demand.* Rather, be continuously aware of what you decided to be aware of, realizing that this too is impossible for any extended length of time. Then when you aren't aware of it anymore because your awareness has gravitated toward thinking, no problem, be happy you're alive and have a working brain, and then become aware once again of the feeling of the breath.

Q: I get dizzy from the deep breathing.

A: Then STOP IT (Newhart, 2019/2001). There is no need to do deep breathing, fast breathing, alternative nostril breathing or any other special type of breathing. These all have their place in the yogic science of Pranayama, which you may learn elsewhere, just as you may learn elsewhere to play the bagpipe (which *does* require deep breathing). For our purpose, which is to learn how to stop thinking, all you need to do is be aware of senses other than thinking. One that is often useful is the physical sensation of the breath, which is always available. But for the purposes of practicing awareness, you already know how to breathe and don't need to breathe any differently than you usually would. So when you sit down to meditate, just sit and breathe as comfortably and normally as you would if you were sitting on a couch at a friend's house and they told you "I'll be right back, just wait here for a few minutes."

Q: When I try to meditate for more than a few minutes, I get antsy and can't sit still.

A: Meditation should be, mostly, an enjoyable experience, so don't force it. After determining how long you are sitting still before feeling agitated, settle on that amount of time for a while, maybe twice a day for a month. This will accomplish a number of important goals: (1) Any amount of meditation is training you in how to stop thinking, and 2 minutes is a very respectable amount of time to practice something. If you were to practice shooting hoops for 2 minutes twice per day, you would get better and better at it. If you were to read and listen to a course on how to speak French twice per day for 2 minutes, you would eventually be able to understand the Merovingian in the Matrix (be careful what you wish for); (2) Doing something twice per day for any amount of time develops it as a habit, and the most important parts of the habit are merely deciding to do it and starting to do it. You can then expand the duration after the habit has been established; (3) Two of the best predictors of whether we continue doing something is how rewarding we find it and how convenient it is. A 2-minute practice is likely to be both rewarding and convenient. Two minutes may not seem like a lot, but clients often say, after having done 2 minutes of meditation for the first time, things like "That's the most relaxed I've felt all day."

Q: But I really want to be able to stop thinking, and I'm willing to sit longer even though it makes me feel agitated.

A: I would still recommend starting with what you experience as relaxing and then gradually increasing your meditation time, but if you prefer to meditate for longer, and up to about the 20 minutes twice per day that appears to be a therapeutic dosage, you could do it in the spirit of behavioral exposure therapy. Here, you (1) do something that you have an aversive reaction to but that you have decided is ultimately good for you (such as driving over a bridge or taking an elevator if you are agoraphobic), (2) be aware of the discomfort and tolerate it, and realize it has nothing to do with you any more than the color of the wall. Both the color of the wall and your own discomfort are *phenomena in the phenomenal universe.* Nothing to do with you, in the sense of "you" or "I" as pure awareness. If you are aware of it, it is an object and you are the subject. "Agitated" is the object of awareness. You are the subject, aware of the object. You *are* (in the sense of *identity*) not agitated, *you* are *aware* (or *Awareness*) of agitation. You can begin with (1) *object awareness* of negative aspects of the experience such as discomfort, the thought "this is uncomfortable," the physical sensations of hyperactivity or agitation and the mental and physical urge to get up; followed by (2) *subject awareness* of the "I" that is aware of the discomfort, but which itself is without thought, feelings or sensations, as IT is aware (or Awareness) of these and therefore is not itself these.

Q: I have to leave early for work in the morning, so could I do a few minutes in the morning and then meditate for longer in the evening?

A: Certainly. How do you get to work?

Q: I take the train.

A: You could even meditate on the train.

Q: But it's so noisy, aren't you supposed to meditate somewhere quiet?

A: What's happening outside of you doesn't really matter. And if you have any concerns about safety, you could do open or half-open-eyed meditation and make sure nothing valuable is at risk of disappearing. You can practice meditation on the train by coming back from awareness of noise to awareness of your breath just as you come back from thoughts. Or you could practice mindfulness by being aware of visual movement and noise as two senses, coming back to them when you notice that one or both has disappeared due to thinking. As I've mentioned, two of the most powerful meditative experiences I've ever had were in the New York transit system, 10 to 15 years ago, one while waiting for a subway train and the other while standing in the back of a bus. In both cases, I was practicing open multisensory awareness when suddenly there was a sense of profound peace, as though everything was still and time had stopped, despite awareness of continuing movement.

Q: Some of the things that you wrote about, especially in Chapter 9 seem pretty far out. I'm religious and I don't believe in Buddhism, Hinduism or mysticism. Can I meditate without buying in to all of that?

A: Yes, and pretty much all of the teachers whom I've quoted would say the same. And if you are religious, you might even benefit from exploring meditative teachings in your own tradition. Although I quote Buddhism, Hinduism and mystical writings from other religions such as Judaism, Christianity and Sufism, what I am really teaching here is Psychological Meditation, or Meditation in the Psychological Tradition as a psychological technique to realize a psychological state. There is nothing in "*Be aware of senses other than thinking*" that conflicts with any religion. As we've seen, the ancient Jews used to meditate, in the sense of clearing their minds, for one hour prior to and for one hour after prayer in order to better absorb the prayer's essence without interference from prior or subsequent thoughts (known in psychology as proactive and retroactive interference, or the tendency of immediate prior or later experience to inhibit learning).

Q: I keep telling myself to remember to practice mindfulness and then I forget.

A: You could get an interval timer such as the Gym Boss, clip it to your belt or put it in your pocket, and set it to vibrate every 15 minutes to remind you to come back to your senses. Or set your phone to vibrate every however many minutes to remind you. Even in Thich Nhat Hahn's monasteries, where monks and nuns who have left their families to dedicate themselves to a mindfulness tradition live, a bell is rung every 15 minutes to remind them to be aware of their breath. Alternatively, as Thich Nhat Hanh teaches, you could choose certain things that happen every day as reminders to practice multisensory awareness, such as standing up, sitting down, walking, or looking at the time.

Q: How long will it take until I stop thinking?

A: That depends on things such as genetics, diet, exercise, air quality, access to healthcare, and how much time you spend driving on U.S. Route 1 in Florida.

Q: I mean, how long will it take until I can stop thinking whenever I want?

A: There will probably always be times when you want to stop thinking and you can't, but these will gradually become fewer and farther between the more you train yourself in selective awareness. The goal is not to never think, just as if you had a tendency to shake your legs all the time when sitting the goal would not be to never move your legs but just to learn to

Chapter 11 - Questions and Answers (2)

move them when useful and not move them when not useful. What we are trying to do is alter your default frequency, duration and salience of thinking. In a sense, your brain needs to be deprogrammed after decades of miseducation by the individuals, institutions and media that over-brainfed you and continue to over-brainfeed you. We want to replace your default cognitive process of overthinking with a cognitive process characterized by an increased ratio of *sensory awareness to thinking awareness* (SA2TA), a new ratio that is more conducive to your peace of mind and physical well-being.

Q: Is it possible to spend too much time practicing meditation and mindfulness?

A: As long as you *define* these correctly, both as simply referring to *selective awareness*, they can be practiced as often and for as long as you like. It is both possible, and helpful, to be continuously selectively aware of what you have determined to be *useful* sensory information from the moment you awaken until the moment you fall asleep, and even during dreams (in which case, as you will be aware that they are dreams, they will be what are known as *lucid* dreams). Advanced meditators are eventually able as well to maintain awareness during nondreaming sleep, with this experience known in Buddhism as "the clear light" (Varela, 1997). Being aware of the senses most relevant to what you are doing at a given moment (some combination of seeing, hearing, smelling, tasting, bodysensing, and thinking) can only be helpful. On the other hand, if you were to detach yourself from daily responsibilities in order to sit silently for 6 hours per day, and practice walking meditation in the backyard for 4 hours a day, this could conceivably cause some problems for you, and you would do well to accept as constructive any criticisms from family members, employers, work colleagues, or repo agents. Even in monasteries more time is spent on daily living tasks (cooking, cleaning, cutting wood, building) than on sitting in silent meditation.

Q: I think my spouse could benefit from learning to stop thinking. Should I tell them to read this book?

A: No, just leave it lying around. If they're interested, they'll sneak a peek.

Q: If a stranger asks me what this book is about right when we're getting off the bus, what should I tell her?

A: Tell her to watch her step.

Chapter 12 - *From Meatspace to Innerspace: The Variety of Cognitive Distortions*

"It is normal to think about immortality, and abnormal not to do so or not to bother about it. If everybody eats salt, then that is the normal thing to do, and it is abnormal not to.

. . . If a person does not 'believe' in salt, it is up to the doctor to tell him [them] that salt is necessary for physiological health. Equally, it seems to me that the doctor of the soul should not go along with the fashionable stupidities but should remind his [their] patient what the normal structural elements of the psyche are. For reasons of psychic hygiene, it would be better not to forget these original and universal ideas; and wherever they have disappeared, from neglect or intellectual bigotry, we should reconstruct them as quickly as we can regardless of 'philosophical' proofs for or against (which are impossible anyway)."

Carl Jung, 1938 (in Jung, 1950/1977, p. 4)

"Do not confuse or limit existence and reality

with its expressions in matter, space, and time.

Reality, like matter itself, is ultimately

transtemporal and *transspatial*."

Edward Bruce Bynum (2012, p. 2)

A clear view of reality is as fleeting as a clear view of the sun by a fish that has succeeded in momentarily jumping up from the sea.

But whereas fish must jump *up* to perceive higher realities, humans must dive *down*. Deep down into our own consciousness. Eventually, glimpses of Truth occur, and though brief, few and far between, leave an indelible mark on one's memory and perspective that can be called upon at will for the rest of one's lifetime when the going gets tough.

In traditional cognitive therapy, automatic thoughts (thoughts that come to mind uninvited) are evaluated for the presence of ways of making sense of reality that may trigger negative emotions and make them more frequent, intense or of longer duration. These are correspondingly pathologized as "cognitive distortions," though their very existence is due to the fact that, when used skillfully, they are, for the most part, necessary in order for any of us to make any sense of the world or function at all in our daily lives (for example, everything we do is based on fortune telling, i.e., what our best guess is about the result. We sit down in a chair trusting that it will hold our weight). For this reason, cognitive therapy does not aim at eliminating cognitive distortions per se, but at learning to evaluate evidence for and against the specific cognitive content in question in order to adjust one's thinking to correspond with reality (or a more helpful fantasy). Cognitive therapy is not about changing thinking from negative to positive, but from irrational (unsupported or weakly supported by evidence) to rational (more strongly supported by evidence), or from unhelpful to helpful.

Alfred Korzybski, in *Science and Sanity: An Introduction to Non-Aristotelian Systems and General Semantics*, states that

> "A general theory of sanity leads to a general theory of psychotherapy, including all such existing medical schools, as they all deal with disturbances of the *semantic reactions* (psycho-logical responses to words and other stimuli in connection with their *meanings*)." (1933/1993, pp. 8-9)

As "some words will be repeated so often" that he abbreviates them (which isn't true, as it is then not the words that are repeated but rather the abbreviations), he refers throughout the text to "semantic reactions, both singular and plural" as "*s.r* or (*s.r*)" (Ibid., p. 15) regarding which:

Chapter 12 - From Meatspace to Innerspace: The Variety of Cognitive Distortions

> "The present investigation discloses that the *s.r* may assume very diversified forms, one of which is the production of very powerful psychophysiological blockages. These, when once we understand their mechanism, can be eliminated by proper education and training in appropriate *s.r* ." (Ibid., p. 18)

It is no wonder that Albert Ellis, one of the Fathers of cognitive therapy, was a big fan of his fellow "Al," to the point that

> "Ellis credits Alfred Korzybski, his book, *Science and Sanity*, and general semantics for starting him on the philosophical path for founding rational therapy." (Albert Ellis, 2022)

While various lists of distortions have been proposed by researchers and practitioners (e.g., Burns, 2020), I tend to group them into the following 9 categories:

1. Negativizing / De-positivizing / Minimizing (e.g., Catastrophizing negatives; Minimizing positives)

2. Overgeneralizing (e.g., "All-or-nothing thinking"; Assuming one or more of the parts equals the whole)

3. Assuming unknowns (e.g., "jumping to conclusions"; "mind reading"; "fortune telling")

4. Personalizing (e.g., blaming yourself)

5. Otherizing (e.g., blaming others)

6. Idealized Comparisons / "Shouldism" (e.g., "Should/ought/must" statements regarding the self, others, the world, the past or the future)

7. Emotional State-Dependent Thinking (e.g., "Emotional reasoning"; assuming that an emotional state reflects a corresponding external reality; believing that anxiety/fear means there is real danger, sadness means there was a real loss, or anger means there is a real aggression)

8. Idiosyncratic Causal Reasoning (e.g., "Magical thinking")

9. Labeling (Objectifying someone or something into a word, concept or stereotype)

Even a brief perusal of the above will make clear that although they are known in psychology as cognitive "distortions" and treated in therapy as an enemy of sorts, they pretty much sum up the way we usually think and usually get the job done. Just as negative emotions themselves are normal and are only pathological when their frequency, intensity or duration are excessive to the extent that they interfere with our quality of life, most of these cognitive heuristics, or shortcuts to understanding reality, are generally adaptive. It is when their frequency, duration or awareness salience become excessive that they pose a problem. For example, if we react with fear upon realizing we've almost stepped on a snake, and we establish some distance before looking back to see what kind of snake it was, we are negativizing, overgeneralizing, assuming unknowns, and emotional-state dependent thinking. AND, we may have just kept ourselves from being poisoned. Whereas, if we react with irritation when someone asks us for money in the Home Depot parking lot so he can buy gas for the truck he's been sleeping in since being kicked out of his house, we are negativizing, assuming unknowns (e.g., that he is lying), possibly otherizing (e.g., blaming him for his situation) and possibly making idealized comparisons (e.g., people shouldn't ask for money in parking lots). AND, we may be turning a blind eye to someone who is suffering and whom we could easily help by giving him a few bucks which we might not miss anyway.

As an aside, idiosyncratic magical thinking (a belief for which one has little evidence and which other people don't believe – like thinking that if you step on a crack something bad will happen to your family) must be distinguished from what I call "entheosyntonic" (Densei & Lam, 2010) beliefs, thought content consistent (syntonic) with one's conception of God and spiritual or religious beliefs (en: inside; theos: God; entheos: full of God, inspired). Encouraging a client to challenge magical beliefs about danger to his family from aliens if he misinterprets their signals regarding what to take out of the refrigerator would be considered good therapy, whereas encouraging a client to challenge magical beliefs about dangers to her soul if she doesn't behave in accordance with her own mainstream orthodox religious beliefs, which are not causing her distress, would be considered malpractice.

Chapter 12 - From Meatspace to Innerspace: The Variety of Cognitive Distortions

While the above ways of thinking, taken to extremes, may be self-defeating, there is another entire category of thinking that can cause as much, or more distress in the face of inevitable types of suffering that we all have or will experience at one time or another in our lives. I refer to beliefs about the nature of human existence itself, its meaning and its impermanence.

Without getting into philosophical terminology (which despite having doctorates in "philosophy," even most PhDs, including myself, are not very familiar with) I would like here to present the terms:

Epistemology (inquiry into the nature of knowledge);

Axiology (inquiry into the nature of value, or what is important to us); and

Ontology (inquiry into the nature of being or reality).

It seems to me that traditional cognitive therapy does a good job of addressing problems of epistemology, in terms of leading us to critically examine the basis for our thoughts and beliefs.

Some other therapeutic orientations focus more on axiology, and use it in a curative Psychology 2.0 manner, for example Viktor Frankl's logotherapy (logo means "meaning") and Stephen Hayes' Acceptance and Commitment Therapy (with its emphasis on "value orientation").

The axiological component of any therapy kicks in when the therapist assists the client in gaining insight into what is meaningful to them and increasing the presence in their life of things that they find valuable. However, when this is not being done "curatively" to address a "medical necessity" in the form of a psychiatric disorder as defined by the International Classifications of Diseases (ICD) or the Diagnostic and Statistical Manual of Mental Disorders (DSM – what a horrid name, sure to eventually join the dustbin of history along with the American Psychiatric Association's original name, the *Association of Medical Superintendents of American Institutions for the Insane*, AMSAII), insurance won't cover it, which places purely axiological therapy, which may be more akin to "life coaching" than to psychotherapy, out of the financial reach of many.

I do suspect that any good therapist helps their clients find meaning simultaneously with leading them toward other forms of insight or teaching them specific therapy skills. I may of course be wrong. Even behavior therapy includes the technique of "behavioral activation" which boils down to "do more fun or productive things," at least some of which, I would hope, are perceived as fun or productive because they are in some way meaningful (personally, when teaching behavioral activation, I instruct clients to generate activities that they would find fun, productive *or meaningful*).

On the other hand, what clearly appears to be missing from cognitive behavior therapy, and perhaps many schools of therapy, is inquiry into the nature of being or reality. This might sound "far out," but beliefs about the nature of being and reality can be a cause of profound suffering. The most obvious example is whether we believe in immortality, the persistence of consciousness (or, in some religions, transference of the soul to another physical body) after death, and what happens after we and our loved ones die. The psychiatrist Carl Jung considered the belief in immortality to be as important for psychological well-being as salt is for physical wellness, and if a client came to him without a belief in immortality he considered it his duty to treat this as seriously as he would a sodium deficiency.

Think about it (said the author of the book on how to stop thinking): How would you feel if you believed you would never see your loved ones again after you and they die, versus how you would feel if you believed you would see them again? How would you feel when you age and experience sickness and pain if you believed all you had to look forward to in your future was more of the same, versus how you would feel if you knew that "this too shall pass," and that rather than passing into nothingness, you would outlive this sick and painful body. These are of course rhetorical questions, and I will consider myself to have made my point: Ontological beliefs regarding the nature of being and reality are the gateway to psychological well-being.

Now, you might say "well of course, I wish I believed in immortality, that I would outlive my body and continue to enjoy the company of my loved ones after we die, but I can't just make myself believe something that I don't." The Father of Psychology, William James, begs to differ. In *The Will to Believe,* James (1912) presents reasons for choosing to believe in something despite lack of proof (the implication being that this is possible). One of his rationales is that sometimes we do not have access to evidence for a belief until we assume its truth and act accordingly. It's a catch-22. Without evidence we won't believe, but we won't obtain the evidence until we believe.

Chapter 12 - From Meatspace to Innerspace: The Variety of Cognitive Distortions

I would argue that every single thing we do is based on prediction rather than proof, on faith gathered from knowledge of our own or others' past experience rather than on current realities. In other words,

Every act is a faith-based act,

not necessarily grounded in faith in God but involving faith that the future will repeat the past. I get up from my chair because I believe, based on prior experience, that if I stand up my legs will support me and I won't fall down. I get a drink of water from the tap because I have *faith* (at least in this part of Massachusetts) that the water is potable, on the basis of not being sick despite drinking it yesterday and today, and that there wasn't some accident within the past few hours involving the reservoir or pipes.

Personally I, and many people, *believe* in the persistence of consciousness after the physical body ceases to function not because we've undergone religious indoctrination but because (1) the evidence for it (out of body experiences and near death experiences, both which I've personally experienced and both which have been reported by countless people throughout history) grossly outweighs the evidence against it (for which there is none – first, you can't prove a negative; second, absence of evidence is not evidence of absence; and third, nobody has ever come back from the dead to tell us they don't exist); and (2) the alternative is unacceptable, both cognitively and emotionally.

And with that, let's take a look at my Twelve Existential Distortions and see if my claim that they are, in fact, distortions, makes any sense to you, for "It is astonishing what havoc is wrought in psychology by admitting at the outset apparently innocent propositions, that nevertheless contain a flaw" (James, 1890/1950, p. 224).

Dogu's Twelve Existential Distortions

1. I am this body

2 I am this mind

3. Others are their bodies

4. Others are their minds

5. I am mortal

6. Others are mortal

7. The universe is physical

8. Time is unidirectional

9. Space is unidimensional

10. Cause and effect only operate in physical spacetime

11. Events are random and without a higher purpose

12. Things are as they seem

Interestingly, it turns out that each of these assumptions is consistent with a model of reality called "scientific materialism," more commonly known as "science" though it is really nothing of the sort. Rather, these are merely temporohistorically delimited (spacetime bound)(particular to human thought at a given time and place in history) best-guesses as to the nature of "life, the universe and everything" (Adams, 1982). Mistaking the best guesses of science for Reality is known as "scientism" (Wellmuth, 1944), which

> "... goes beyond the actual findings of science to deny that other approaches to knowledge are valid and other truths true." (Smith, 1976, pp. 16-17)

Scientism at any given point in time will insist that the current state of science is the ultimate truth.

> "History has taught us that unless a theory or practice is acceptable from the standpoint of the spatiotemporally dominant arbiters of political, ontological, epistemological or theological (P.O.E.T.-ical) 'truth' regarding power, existence, knowledge or God, respectively, it risks marginalization and persecution. The birth of scientific psychology in the late 19th to early 20th century corresponded with an ideology of scientific materialism characterized by (a) objectivism (the use of empirical methods to test empirical facts and arrive at third-person verifiable results); (b) reductionism (redefinition of the unfamiliar/poorly understood in terms of the more familiar/understood); (c) the 'closure principle' (that even if non-physical phenomena exist, they remain causally closed-off from the physical universe); and (d) physicalism (' ... that the universe consists

Chapter 12 - From Meatspace to Innerspace: The Variety of Cognitive Distortions

solely of configurations of matter and energy within space and time')
(Wallace, 2007, pp. 30-33)." (Densei & Lam, 2010)

Scientism is a caricature of science created by small minds, including the small minds of many scientists themselves. By contrast, the great minds such as Philip Warren Anderson, who won the Nobel Prize in Physics in 1977, see right through it. Anderson was a fierce critic of reductionism. In an article in *Science* entitled "More is Different" (1972), he asserted that:

> ". . . at each new level of complexity entirely new properties appear, and the understanding of the new behaviors requires research which I think is as fundamental in its nature as any other. That is, it seems to me that one may array the sciences roughly linearly in a hierarchy, according to the idea: The elementary entities of science X obey the laws of science Y . . . But this hierarchy does not imply that science X is 'just applied Y.' At each stage entirely new laws, concepts, and generalizations are necessary, requiring inspiration and creativity to just as great a degree as in the previous one. Psychology is not applied biology, nor is biology applied chemistry." (p. 393)

One of the most liberating moments of my life was when I decided to say "I don't know" more often.

"I don't know" is what drives science, whereas "I know" drives scientism.

Simply put, scientism is dogma masquerading as truth, often by using scientific-looking things, such as numbers, formulas and criteria, in pseudoscientific, or bogus ways. You know, like school Individualized Miseducational Plans (IMPs):

> "By the end of the quarter, Johnny will light Jimmy's hair on fire $\sum_{k=0}^{n} \binom{n}{k} x^k a^{n-k}$ percent less frequently on days when the sun shines with a $a_0 + \sum_{n=1}^{\infty} \left(a_n \cos\frac{n\pi x}{L} + b_n \sin\frac{n\pi x}{L} \right)$ percent greater intensity on the school parking lot $(1\frac{nx}{1!} + \frac{n(n-1)x^2}{2!})$ minutes through sunrise (where n, k, x, a, L, & b = whatever, ∞ = something that seems really big when it flies right above your face when you're trying to sleep, like a waterbug, and 0 = something really small, like the treatment utility of assessment [Hayes, Nelson & Jarrett, 1987] when

it fetishizes quantification) than it shone on August 3rd, 1994 at 2:20 p.m. at Latitude: 7.7367 Longitude: 98.7700 on the snorkel that Jimbo left on top of the 48-quart beer cooler next to the 12-inch high blue bong on the trampoline of the red- and white-sailed Nacra Formula-16 catamaran next to the guy passed out in the sand in front of the Monkey Beach Bar on Phi Phi Island."

In Transpersonal Cognitive Therapy (TCT), one would put the culturally or subculturally received beliefs that I have labeled *Existential Distortions* through the same evidentiary procedures as any other thoughts, weighing the evidence for and against, coming up with interpretations that one believes are warranted by the evidence, and then choosing courses of action or acceptance based on one's conclusions.

As Western culture takes these ontological statements as assumptions and premises for the interpretation of all aspects of one's own and others' lives, one is very unlikely ever to have come across evidence either for or against these in miseducational contexts. For this reason, their evaluation is usually done as a "sadhana" or spiritual path, on the basis of books on the perennial philosophy (the world's wisdom traditions; Aldous Huxley, 1945), mysticism, spirituality, consciousness exploration or quantum physics.

If this is of interest, the first thing to do would be, for each existential distortion, consider how your sense of well-being would be better or worse if it were true and if it were false (See Appendix 1). Then choose the distortions which, if true, would cause the most suffering and if false would cause the greatest well-being. Finally, begin your own wisdom quest, seeking out information wherever you can find it regarding the truth or falsehood of these unexamined assumptions that you may be living by and allowing to block your path to fulfillment.

Chapter 12 - From Meatspace to Innerspace: The Variety of Cognitive Distortions

ALDOUS HUXLEY
(In: A Case For ESP, PK and PSI. Life Magazine. 11 January, 1954)

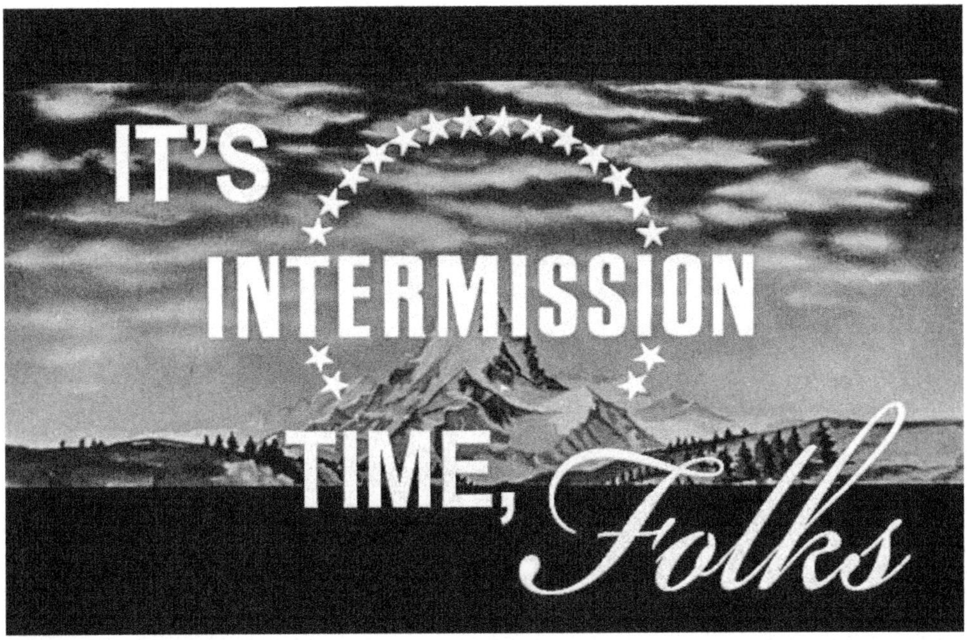
IT'S
INTERMISSION
TIME, Folks

PART 2 - COGNITIVE BEHAVIORAL MIND TRAINING (CBMT)

"The forms or conditions of Time and Space, as Kant will tell you, are nothing in themselves, – only our way of looking at things. A mind that is stretched by a new experience can never go back to its old dimensions. You are right, I think, however, in recognizing the category of Space as being quite as applicable to minds as to the outer world. Every man of reflection is vaguely conscious of an imperfectly-defined circle which is drawn about his intellect. He has a perfectly clear sense that the fragments of his intellectual circle include curves of many other minds of which he is cognizant. He often recognizes these as manifestly concentric with his own, but of less radius. On the other hand, when we find a portion of an arc outside our own, we say it *intersects* ours, but are very slow to confess or to see that it *circumscribes* it. **Every now and then a man's mind is stretched by a new idea or sensation, and never shrinks back to its former dimensions.** After looking at the Alps, I felt that my mind had been stretched beyond the limits of its elasticity, and fitted so loosely on my old ideas of space that I had to spread these to fit it."

Oliver Wendell Holmes, Sr.

(1858, p. 502; bolding added)

Chapter 13 - *The Four Psychologies*

"The purpose of thinking

is to learn to stop thinking."

Grandma Densei (1922)

The fields of psychology and psychotherapy have naturally evolved over time. Edna Hiedbreder (1933) distinguished 7 psychologies:

(1) Titchener and Structuralism;

(2) William James;

(3) Functionalism;

(4) Behaviorism;

(5) Dynamic Psychology;

(6) Gestalt Psychology; and

(7) Freud and Psychoanalysis.

Abraham Maslow (1962) specified 3 "forces" in psychology as being:

(1) Psychoanalysis;

(2) Behaviorism; and

(3) Humanism.

However, in a lecture in 1967, Maslow explained that

"this third psychology is giving rise to a fourth, 'transhumanistic psychology' dealing with transcendent experiences and transcendent values" (Maslow, 1969/1967), and in his journal on August 25, 1968, in preparation for his Presidential Address to the American Psychological Association, Maslow noted:

> "Let me call behavioristic psychology the first psychology, Freudian psychology the 2nd, and humanistic psychology the 3rd. And then what I think of as a real possibility, what I am fascinated with, is the psychology of transcendence & of ends, the transhuman or transpersonal (really should be 'transcendent'[)] psychology = the 4th psychology." (Maslow, 1979, Vol. 2, p. 1059; Maslow, 1982, p. 267; Cited in Koltko-Rivera, 2006, p. 306)

Psychologist Scott Barry Kaufman relates how going through Maslow's last notebook entries before he transitioned on June 8, 1970, he discovered that Maslow was even working on a new book with a chapter

> "proposing the need for a fifth force in psychology – *transhumanism* – that would transcend human interests and focus on species-transcending values." (Maslow, 1969-1970 in Kaufman, 2020)

This gives us, according to Maslow,

> (1) Behavioristic Psychology;
>
> (2) Freudian Psychology;
>
> (3) Humanistic Psychology;
>
> (4) Transpersonal / Transcendent Psychology; and
>
> (5) Transhuman Psychology.

In addition to the proposal of transpersonal psychology as the elusive Fourth Force (Chinen, 1996; Hastings, 1999; Maslow, 1969/1967, 1979, 1982), multiculturalism (Pedersen, 1990) has been floated at times as well as has, I believe, cognitive or brain science.

Within psychoanalysis itself, four psychologies have been distinguished (Pine, 1988; drive, ego, object relations and self) and, in cognitive behavior therapy, three waves are identified. These include

> (1) the "first wave" (behavior therapy, operating at the level of classical and operant conditioning);
>
> (2) the "second wave" (cognitive therapy, focusing on the cognitive *content* of language-based conscious cognition); and
>
> (3) the "third wave of cognitive and behavioral therapies" (Hayes, 2004) "based on contextual concepts focused more on the person's relationship to thought and emotion than on their content." (Hayes & Hoffman, 2017, p. 245)

Hayes and Hoffman (2017) include as third wave CBT such topics and practices as:

> "... mindfulness, emotions, acceptance, the relationship, values, goals, and meta-cognition. New models and intervention approaches included acceptance and commitment therapy, dialectical behavior therapy, mindfulness-based cognitive therapy, functional analytic psychotherapy, meta-cognitive therapy, and several others." (p. 245)

There may even be room in Third Wave CBT for spirituality, whether or not defined behavior analytically. For example, Hayes (1984) quotes Arthur Deikman who wrote the 1982 book *The Observing Self: Mysticism and Psychotherapy*:

> "'By dis-identifying with automatic sequences (of thoughts) we lessen their impact and provide free space in which to choose an appropriate response . . . By identifying with the observing self, we can make a more realistic assessment . . . permitting more effective and creative behavior' (Deikman, 1982, p. 108). Despite the mentalistic language, the point is fairly clear. Control by self-rules can be weakened by viewing them from the point of view of you-as-perspective, and perhaps more creative (presumably contingency-shaped) behavior can then emerge . . ." (Hayes, 1984, p. 106-107)

Hayes' "you as perspective" may be as close as Western psychological *theory* can get to verbally describing and intellectually conceptualizing the referents of religious, spiritual or mystical terms such as "oneness," "unity," "cosmic consciousness," "ground of being," "true Self," and "God." And in Hayes' (2004) Acceptance and Commitment Therapy, there is a technique inspired by the work of Roberto Assagioli, one of the founders of Transpersonal Psychology:

> "The observer exercise (a variant of the self-identification exercise developed by Assagioli, 1971, pp. 211-217) is a key eyes-closed ACT exercise designed to promote experiential contact with this transcendent sense of self." (Hayes, 2004, p. 654)

Thus, from a theoretical perspective and from this one practical example, techniques aimed at provoking the ultimate transpersonal realization (according to some) of "I" as "Pure Awareness" would seem to fall within the Third Wave of cognitive behavior therapy. However, I doubt that mainstream cognitive behavior therapy will ever be "all in" with goals such as Self-Realization and the cognitive, or non-cognitive shift that it may entail. This is because, and here is what I see as the value of my Four Psychologies, CBT is, for institutional reasons (mainstream miseducational contingencies of reinforcement, mainstream economic contingencies of reinforcement, mainstream health care organization related contingencies of reinforcement) squarely situated in my Psychology 2.0, Curative Psychology. Most people pay for therapy using their insurance policy, and insurance policies will reimburse for *"medical" treatment* of a *"medical disease."* At present, Buddhic Ignorance (being un-enlightened) and the "three poisons" of "greed, anger and ignorance" (to use but one transpersonal definition of suboptimal human functioning) have not yet entered into the Diagnostic and Statistical Manual of Mental Disorders (DSM) or International Classification of Diseases (ICD) (where you will find a code for whatever you are getting therapy for, or the closest "disorder" or "disease" that applies). But grok you me, if they thought they could make money off it, the American Psychiatric Association would quickly vote these into the DSM as full-fledged mental disorders. To this point, the 1st Edition of the DSM in 1952 was a 130-page pamphlet just thick enough to level the leg of a wobbly bar stool or scoop up a spider from your kitchen counter to bring it outside where it could live out its life in freedom evading birds, frogs and parasitic wasps. *Par contre*, the current DSM-V-TR has 1142 pages and could not possibly fit under a spider, though if utilized to its maximum potential could be depaginated (torn up) and save a multitude of household insects and vermin. The "transdiagnostic" trend in assessment and therapy (e.g., Barlow et al, 2011) is one attempt at reeling back the kaleidoscopic proliferation of overlapping diagnostic syndromes responsible for the current global deforestation maintaining publication of larger and larger editions of the DSM and placing humanity and most other earthbound life forms at an ever-increasing risk of asphyxiation.

MY OLD FOUR PSYCHOLOGIES

In 2010, I attempted to categorize approaches to psychology at a broad level, inclusive of anomalous states of consciousness I had experienced through meditation practice (and others I'd read about) in a practical manner that might help people. I came up with an initial taxonomy (now revised) of four psychologies and psychotherapies. Here is the original (un-revised) formulation:

> 1. **Negative, curative, or deficit focused psychology**, focusing mainly on problems and pathology (e.g., psychoanalysis, behavior therapy and cognitive therapy);
>
> 2. **Positive, or growth-focused psychology**, concerned with human potential and self-actualization in the ordinary sense (e.g., existential/humanistic psychology);

3. **Transpersonal, or transcendence-focused psychology**, with its sight set on the "farther reaches of human nature" (Maslow, 1971) and "ultimate states" (Sutich, 1969); and

4. **The "Integral Approach,"** or "the endeavor to honor and embrace every legitimate aspect of human consciousness" (Wilber, 2000a, p. 2).

(in Densei & Lam, 2010)

I later realized that Ken Wilber's Integral Psychology was really all-encompassing, containing the others, and that I had left out the psychology that precedes Curative Psychology, namely, Preventive Psychology that ideally would make Curative Psychology unnecessary (fun fact: in the old days, if you were a doctor and a patient got sick, you had already failed in your care for him or her, as your main job was to help people not get sick. Health insurance companies have now caught up with the ancient Greek "prevention is better than cure" approach, and realize that they make more money if you don't get sick than if you do – which latter involves first paying staff to deny your claims, then reluctantly authorizing some initial tests that hopefully won't find what's wrong, then refusing to authorize better more expensive tests for fear they will find what's wrong until you and your doctor insist, and then having to authorize and pay for treatment).

So I removed Integral Psychology, which logically should not be on a list of things that it contains, added Preventive Psychology as the first psychology, and added Transcendent Psychology as the fourth. The Four Psychologies, together, may be considered my own humble attempt at clarifying the components of an Integral Psychology/Psychotherapy. Thus:

THE NEW-OLD FOUR PSYCHOLOGIES

Psychology 1.0: *Preventive Psychology* focuses on psychological strategies for preventing psychological problems and physical problems that are caused or contributed to by psychological functioning.

Psychology 2.0: *Curative Psychology* focuses on treating psychological problems already present and any physical problems they have caused or contributed to. This is the type of psychology employed by most psychotherapists and behavioral health clinicians, at least when providing services for which in- or out-of-network claims will be submitted to healthcare insurance companies.

Psychology 3.0: *Positive Psychology* focuses on attaining what most people consider to be maximal human potential, including a healthy body, positive mood states, and what the individual's culture or subculture considers to be (a) adaptive cognitive content and process and (b) adaptive behavioral and social functioning. The top of the pyramid representing Abraham Maslow's *initial and outdated* needs hierarchy (1943) that you continue to see in textbooks and corporate powerpoints (which isn't even *his* pyramid as *he never presented the hierarchy as a pyramid* in his writings – it was invented by a psychologist working as a business consultant in the 1960s to Maslow's dismay; Bridgman, Cummings & Ballard, 2019; Kaufman, 2020) included this as the highest attainment, labeled "Self-Actualization." This is a term that Maslow borrowed from Kurt Goldstein:

> "We can say, an organism is governed by the tendency to actualize, as much as possible, its individual capacities, its 'nature,' in the world. This nature is what we call the psycho-somatic constitution, and as far as considered during a certain phase, it is the individual pattern, the 'character' which the respective constitution has attained in the course of experience. This tendency to actualize its nature, to *actualize 'itself,' is the basic drive, the only drive by which the life of the organism is determined.*" (Goldstein, 1939, p. 196)

> "The tendency of normal life is toward activity and progress. For the sick, the only form of self-actualization which remains is the existent state. That, however, is not the tendency of the normal ... *Normal behavior corresponds to a continual change of tension, of such a kind that over and over again that state of tension is reached which enables and impels the organism to actualize itself in further activities, according to its nature.*" (p. 197)

> "Thus, experiences with patients teach us that we have *to assume only one drive, the drive of self-actualization* and that the goal of the drive is not a discharge of tension. Under various conditions, various actions come into the foreground; and while they thereby seem to be directed toward different goals, they give the impression of independently existing drives. In reality, however, these various actions occur in accordance with the various capacities which belong

to the nature of the organism, and occur in accordance with those instrumental processes which are then necessary prerequisites of the self-actualization of the organism." (pp. 197-198)

For Maslow,

> "What a man *can* be, he *must* be. This need we may call self-actualization. This term, first coined by Kurt Goldstein, is being used in this paper in a much more specific and limited fashion. It refers to the desire for self-fulfillment, namely, to the tendency for him to become actualized in what he is potentially. This tendency might be phrased as the desire to become more and more what one is, to become everything that one is capable of becoming." (Maslow, 1943, p. 382)

Interestingly, the first published fake pyramid (McDermid, 1960, p. 94, in Bridgman, Cummings & Ballard, 2019) mistakenly labeled the apex "Self-Realization," unintentionally anticipating Psychology 4.0, rather than using Goldstein and Maslow's term "Self-Actualization." Psychology 3.0 is taking the Blue Pill, staying in the Matrix and making the most of it.

Psychology 4.0: *Transcendent Psychology* focuses on what an older and wiser Abraham Maslow termed "the farther reaches of human nature" (1969/1967), extending the previously highest level of his needs hierarchy, "Self-Actualization," into the realms of peak experiences and altered states of consciousness that are often experienced as spiritual, cosmic or religious in nature. He distinguished between "nontranscending and transcending self-actualizers (or Theory Y & and Theory Z people)" (Maslow, 1969, 1971):

> "I have recently found it more and more useful to differentiate between two kinds (or better, degrees) of self-actualizing people, those who were clearly healthy, but with little or no experiences of transcendence, and those in whom transcendent experiencing was important and even central." (Maslow, 1971, p. 280)

> "The former are more essentially practical, realistic, mundane, capable, and secular people, living more in the here-and-now world; i.e., what I have called the D-realm for short, the world of deficiency-needs and of deficiency-cognitions. In this *Weltanschauung*, people or things are taken essentially in a practical, concrete, here-now, pragmatic way, as deficiency-need suppliers or frustrators; i.e., as

useful or useless, helpful or dangerous, personally important or unimportant." (p. 281)

"The other type (transcenders?) may be said to be much more often aware of the realm of Being (B-realm and B-cognition), to be living at the level of Being; i.e., of ends, of intrinsic values ...; to be more obviously metamotivated; to have unitive consciousness and 'plateau experiences' (Asrani) more or less often; and to have or to have had peak experiences (mystic, sacral, ecstatic) with illuminations or insights or cognitions which changed their view of the world and of themselves, perhaps occasionally, perhaps as a usual thing." (pp. 281-282)

In a revised needs hierarchy based upon Maslow's later writings, we may term this highest level of human need or attainment "Transcendence" (Kaufman, 2020; Maslow, 1971), "Self-Transcendence" (Koltko-Rivera, 2006; I don't know if Maslow himself used this term), "Fundamental Wellbeing" (Martin, 2019, 2020) or, borrowing from the Eastern psychologies, "Self-Realization" (Bharati, 2022; Ramana Maharshi, 1930/1994; Yogananda, 1980, p. 34). Jeffery Martin (2019, 2020) has conducted large-scale global research on individuals reporting "Persistent Non-Symbolic Experience" consistent with the concept of transcendence.

"Self-Realization," can be understood as "realizing" the "Self." "Realize" is variously defined as: "to bring into concrete existence: accomplish"; "to cause to seem real: make appear real"; or "to conceive vividly as real: be fully aware of" (Merriam-Webster, n.d. 5). The word "Self," with a capital "S," is distinguished in religious and spiritual writings from the word "self" with a lower case "s," with the capitalized version referring to the "true" Self, who or what we "really" are (our "true nature"), as opposed to the "little" self that we *think* we are (e.g., the body, mind, or social identity). As such, "Self-Realization" may be defined as *full awareness of our true nature.* This of course begs the question of what our "true nature" is, but there seems to be a general consensus in writings on religion, spirituality and mysticism that this involves full knowledge of or identify with God or the Cosmos.

For Paramahansa Yogananda,

"Self-realization is the knowing – in body, mind, and soul – that we are one with the omnipresence of God; that we do not have to pray that it come to us, that we are not merely near it at all times, but that God's omnipresence is our omnipresence; that we are just as much a part of Him now as we ever will be. All we have to do is improve our knowing." (Yogananda, 1980, p. 34)

For Bhagavan Sri Ramana Maharshi,

"There is a picture presented to you on a screen. That screen is *asti*, omnipresent, and the light that shows the pictures is *bhati* and *priyam*, lustre and love. The pictures with names and forms come and go. If one is not deluded by them and discards them, the canvas screen, which has been there all through, remains as it is. We see pictures on the screen with the help of a small light in an atmosphere of darkness; if that darkness is dispelled by a big light, can the pictures be visible? The whole place becomes luminous and lustrous. If, in the same way, you see the world with the small light called mind, you find it full of different colours. But if you see it with the big light known as Self-Realisation (*atma-jnana*), you will find that it is one continuous universal light and nothing else." (Ramana Maharshi, in Nagamma, 1970/1985, p. 254)

"*Jnana* is given neither from the outside nor from another person. It can be realised by each and everyone in his own Heart. The *jnana-Guru* of everyone is only the supreme Self that is always revealing its own truth in every Heart through the existence-consciousness 'I am, I am.' The granting of being-consciousness by him is initiation into *jnana*. The grace of the Guru is only this Self-awareness that is one's own true nature. It is the being-consciousness by which he is unceasingly revealing his existence. This divine *upadesa* [teaching] is always going on naturally in everyone. As this *upadesa* alone is what reveals the natural attainment of the Self through one's own experience, the mature ones need at no time seek the help of external beings for *jnana-upadesa*. The *upadesa* obtained from outsiders in forms such as sounds, gestures and thoughts are all only mental concepts. Since the meaning of the word *upadesa* (*upa* + *desa*) is only 'abiding in the Self' or 'abiding as the Self,' and since this is one's own real nature, so long as one is seeking Self from outside, Self-realisation cannot be attained. Since you are yourself the reality that is shining in the Heart as being-consciousness, abide always as a *sthita prajna* [one who is established in wisdom] having thus realised your own true nature. This firm abidance in the experience of the Self is described in the *Upanishads* by such terms as 'the import of the *mahavakyas*,' 'Supreme silence,' 'Being still,' 'Quiescence of mind,' and 'Realisation of one's true nature.'" (Ramana Maharshi, in Natanananda, 2002, pp. 38-39)

Psychology 4.0 is taking the Red Pill, and seeing just how deep the rabbit hole really is (Morpheus, in The Matrix, Wachowski & Wachowski, 1999).

Wellness is the goal of Psychologies 1.0 and 2.0, Preventive and Curative Psychology, respectively.

Well-Being is the goal of Psychology 3.0, Positive Psychology.

Self-Realization or Transcendence is the goal Psychology 4.0, Transcendent, Transformational, Transpersonal Psychology, paralleling the ultimate goal in a variety of meditational systems.

The cool thing about my taxonomy, if I do say so myself, is that rather than being a historical sequence with no other rhyme or reason (well, mine doesn't rhyme either, so strike that), it is a conceptual functional hierarchy. In other words, "Psychoanalysis, Behaviorism, Humanism, Transpersonalism" and "behavior therapy, cognitive therapy, contextualism" make quasi-sense historically, but they are otherwise theoretically "orthogonal" (independent). *Par contre* as the Yellow Vests say, "Preventive, Curative, Positive, Transcendent" reflects a logical hierarchy of prevention and remediation of problems, cultivation of well-being, and exploration of desirable states transcending traditional conceptions of well-being. In other words:

"From Wellness to Well-Being and Beyond."

This isn't to disparage or discard the other ways of slicing the psychological pie. In fact, these other classifications can be folded into the New Old 4 Psychologies. There are surely preventive, curative, positive and transcendent applications of psychoanalytic/psychodynamic, behavioral, humanistic, transpersonal, multicultural and neuroscientific psychologies. For example, the cognitive-behavioral technique of prospective memory training (learning how to remember to do something in the future, for example by making a list of things to notice each day and then logging your successes; LaBerge, 1990, pp. 76-77) can help you to

Psy 1.0 *prevent* heart disease by remembering to exercise several times per week,

Psy 2.0 *treat* your diabetes by remembering to bring healthy food to work rather than going to Dunkin' Donuts for lunch,

Psy 3.0 *perform optimally* at work by remembering to take breaks to meditate or micronap, and

Psy 4.0 *induce a beneficial altered state of consciousness* (ASC) so you can consciously hang out with transitioned loved ones in a lucid dream by remembering to ask yourself "Is This A Dream?" at which point you will become self-aware.

Integrating my Psychologies 2.0, 3.0 and 4.0 (50 years ago, in a time travel or quantum plagiarism sort of way, though that would probably put me on the wrong end of it), Maslow suggested that

> "Specially noteworthy for research purposes as well as therapy purposes is to pick out of the special kinds of transcendence, the transcendence of fear into the state of not-fearing or of courage (these are not quite the same thing) ... Also useful would be Bucke's [1923] use of cosmic consciousness. This is a special phenomenological state in which the person somehow perceives the whole cosmos or at least the unity and integration of it and everything in it, including his Self. He then feels as if he belongs by right in the cosmos. He becomes one of the family rather than an orphan. He comes inside rather than being outside looking in. He feels simultaneously small because of the vastness of the universe, but also an important being because he is there in it by absolute right. He is part of the universe rather than a stranger to it or an intruder in it. The sense of belongingness can be very strongly reported here, as contrasting with the sense of ostracism, isolation, aloneness, of rejection, of not having any roots, of belonging no place in particular. After such a perception, apparently one can feel permanently this sense of belonging, of having a place, of being there by right, etc." (Maslow, 1971, p. 277; the reference to Bucke may be found in the present volume as Bucke, 2009/1901)

A VERY BRIEF AND LAZY OVERVIEW OF PSYCHOLOGY 4.0: TRANSCENDENT PSYCHOLOGY

A glimpse into the breadth of Psychology 4.0 is provided by the Table of Contents of the Textbook of Transpersonal Psychiatry and Psychology (Scotton, Chinen, and Battista 1996)(After all, why reinvent the wheel . . .):

Foreword / Ken Wilber

1. Introduction and Definition of Transpersonal Psychiatry / Bruce W. Scotton

2. The Emergence of Transpersonal Psychiatry / Allan B. Chinen

3. William James and Transpersonal Psychiatry / Eugene Taylor

4. Freud's Influence on Transpersonal Psychology / Mark Epstein

5. The Contribution of C. G. Jung to Transpersonal Psychiatry / Bruce W. Scotton

6. Abraham Maslow and Roberto Assagioli: Pioneers of Transpersonal Psychology / John R. Battista

7. The Worldview of Ken Wilber / Roger Walsh and Frances Vaughan

8. The Consciousness Research of Stanislav Grof / Richard Yensen and Donna Dryer

9. Consciousness, Information Theory, and Transpersonal Psychiatry / John R. Battista

10. Shamanism and Healing / Roger Walsh

11. The Contribution of Hinduism and Yoga to Transpersonal Psychiatry / Bruce W. Scotton and J. Fred Hiatt

12. The Contribution of Buddhism to Transpersonal Psychiatry / Bruce W. Scotton.

13. Kabbalah and Transpersonal Psychiatry / Zalman M. Schachter-Shalomi

Chapter 13 - The Four Psychologies

14. Transpersonal Psychology: Roots in Christian Mysticism / Dwight H. Judy

15. Native North American Healers / Donald F. Sandner

16. Aging and Adult Spiritual Development: A Transpersonal View of the Life Cycle Through Fairy Tales / Allan B. Chinen

17. Meditation Research: The State of the Art / Roger Walsh

18. Psychedelics and Transpersonal Psychiatry / Gary Bravo and Charles Grob

19. Parapsychology and Transpersonal Psychology / Charles T. Tart

20. Contemporary Physics and Transpersonal Psychiatry / John R. Battista

21. The Contribution of Anthropology to Transpersonal Psychiatry / Larry G. Peters

22. Western Analytical Philosophy and Transpersonal Epistemology / Allan B. Chinen

23. Diagnosis: A Transpersonal Clinical Approach to Religious and Spiritual Problems / David Lukoff, Francis G. Lu and Robert Turner

24. Offensive Spirituality and Spiritual Defenses / John R. Battista.

25. The Phenomenology and Treatment of Kundalini / Bruce W. Scotton

26. Transpersonal Psychotherapy With Psychotic Disorders and Spiritual Emergencies With Psychotic Features / David Lukoff

27. Transpersonal Techniques and Psychotherapy / Seymour Boorstein

28. Transpersonal Psychotherapy With Religious Persons / Dwight H. Judy

29. The Near-Death Experience as a Transpersonal Crisis / Bruce Greyson

30. Treating Former Members of Cults / Arthur J. Deikman

31. Psychopharmacology and Transpersonal Psychology / Bruce S. Victor

32. Psychedelic Psychotherapy / Gary Bravo and Charles Grob

33. Clinical Aspects of Meditation / Sylvia Boorstein

34. Guided-Imagery Therapy / William W. Foote

35. Breathwork: Theory and Technique / Kathryn J. Lee and Patricia L. Speier

36. Past-Life Therapy / Ronald W. Jue

37. Transpersonal Psychiatry in Psychiatry Residency Training Programs / Francis G. Lu.

38. Toward a Psychology of Human and Ecological Survival: Psychological Approaches to Contemporary Global Threats / Roger Walsh

39. Integration and Conclusion / Bruce W. Scotton, Allan B. Chinen and John R. Battista

40. An Annotated Guide to the Transpersonal Literature / John R. Battista.

While most psychologists have never even heard of transpersonal psychology, no less most of the topics in the above book, I think that it is rather obvious that these are of a psychological nature. The fact that they go beyond what most people think of as psychology merely means that they go beyond what most psychologists think of as psychology, which is a shame. This was my rationale for distinguishing between Psychologies 3.0: Positive Psychology and 4.0: Transcendent / Transformational / Transpersonal Psychology, corresponding with (a) Maslow's revision of his Needs Hierarchy to add transcendence above the previous apex of Self-Actualization, and (b) his proposal of Transpersonal Psychology as a Fourth Force beyond Humanistic Psychology (at least in terms of chronological mainstream American scientific recognition). It will be noted that in terms of actual *history*, Roberto Assagioli proposed his transpersonal theory and practice of psychosynthesis in the early 1900s:

"In 1907 he began a doctoral dissertation and finished it at the age of 21, entitled 'La Psicosintesi' [Psychosynthesis]. Here he also presented a vision of a holistic approach to psychology with a focus on human growth and human experiences with spiritual dimensions. This approach aimed at living a more complete life, and as he himself puts it, 'To live as well as possible, and look at oneself with a smile.'" (Kenneth Sørensen, 2019)

It therefore turns out that what every Psychology 101 student has memorized as the Four Forces in psychology (psychoanalysis, behaviorism, humanism and whatever the flavor of the decade is) is chronologically inaccurate. A historically-informed list would better read: Psychoanalysis, Transpersonal Psychology, Behaviorism, Humanistic Psychology. So for the two or three of you history of psychology wonks who are still with me (while most of our other friends have already skipped to less academic portions of the book, or to other books on the shelf, such as *Think And Grow Anxious*), you can remember the above when there's a lull in conversation during the break at your next CE credit workshop.

Chapter 14 – *Cognitive Behavioral Mind Training* and *The Serenity Prayer Thought Record*

"Language is a virus."

Laurie Anderson (1986)

"A map is not the territory it represents, but, if correct, it has a similar structure to the territory, which accounts for its usefulness. If the map could be ideally correct, it would include, in a reduced scale, the map of the map; the map of the map, of the map; and so on, endlessly, a fact first noticed by Royce."

Alfred Korzybski

(1933/1993, p. 58)

Thinking is a silent epidemic. If language is a virus, thinking is the delivery mechanism. Meaning distances us from meaning.

**To say what something "means"
is to say that it means something other than itself,
which is absurd.**

Clearly, the map is not the territory of anything other than the map itself.

You can't go snorkeling in a map of Phi Phi Island, and if you tried you would hit your head on the floor and miss out on coming face to face with some of the most beautiful fish you'll ever see. Just remember to put on suntan lotion (when in Phi Phi, not when in the map) so you won't get sun

Chapter 14 – Cognitive Behavioral Mind Training and The Serenity Prayer Thought Record

poisoning and spend the rest of the afternoon shivering back in Phuket (for example).

Similarly, you can't eat a picture of an apple (unless it's drawn in cookie dough on top of a seven-layer cake, but the CDC cautions against this unless you're wearing a mask, for which case the mask has special little holes that let in oxygen but not large toxic particles such as cookie dough. But since you would have to take the mask off anyway to eat it the CDC advice is kind of useless here. Probably politically motivated). But I digress.

Thinking is fantasizing about fantasies

(thoughts, which are merely dreams constructed of past memories, organized into dreams about predicted futures).

Often the biggest problem is thinking there's a problem.

(Rant over).

Moods are part of the mind-body's "Trouble Detection System" (TDS; Densei, 2022). Sadness signals perceived loss; anxiety, fear and anger signal perceived danger. When TDS signals happen in the absence of actual loss and danger, they are unhelpful and, if excessive in frequency, duration or intensity (FDI), can constitute an "emotional disorder." Treating unhelpful emotional TDS-FDI involves finding out why it is happening (what are its "controlling variables") and changing these. As emotions may be affected by chains of causation including interactions among situations, thoughts, physiology and behaviors, any of these may be targeted to produce emotional change. Different types of therapy target either one or some combination of these, but any good treatment chooses targets which it considers causal, important and controllable (Haynes & O'Brian, 1990, p. 654). For example, psychiatry (psychopharmacology) targets brain chemicals; neurofeedback targets brainwaves; psychoanalysis targets unconscious meanings; cognitive therapy targets conscious thought; and behavior therapy targets behaviors (which can include thoughts as "cognitive behaviors") and contingencies of reinforcement. Some proponents of cognitive therapy point out that cognitive therapy targets behaviors too, and consider behavioral activation and exposure and response prevention to be cognitive therapy techniques. My personal opinion is that at the point at which one says that "Cognitive Therapy" as a distinct modality (versus which techniques cognitive therapists may or may not happen to use in their practice, which I am sure varies widely) includes the behavior therapies, and is open to including whatever therapy techniques work, what's the use of even having the terms "cognitive therapy" or "behavior therapy"? For this reason, when I use the term "cognitive therapy" in this book, I am referring *uniquely* to its core component known as cognitive restructuring or cognitive disputation. As somewhat of a history of psychology purist, I will continue to consider behavioral activation as a behavior therapy and not as cognitive therapy, and exposure and response prevention as a behavior therapy and not as a cognitive therapy. This is *not* to deny the cognitive elements in the practice of the behavior therapies (e.g., helping the client to identify automatic thoughts that may be posing barriers to using the behavioral techniques, such as "I didn't do my exposure homework because when I got to the bridge I was afraid that in the middle of it I would panic, lose control of the car, crash through the guard rail and fall into the canyon"). Clearly, cognitive restructuring is necessary to get clients to use behavioral techniques that pretty much amount to "Do exactly the things you don't feel like doing or are afraid to do." But, again according to me, the fact that cognitive disputation is often necessary in order to get clients to use behavioral techniques does not mean that these behavioral techniques are actually cognitive therapy techniques.

Rant over.

Usually we think that things make us sad/depressed, stressed/anxious or irritated/angry. We think "X makes me so depressed," "Y makes me so anxious," and "Z makes me so angry." However, throughout history this intuitive model of causality has been challenged. Almost 2000 years ago, Epictetus (2007) wrote:

> "It is not things that disturb us,
>
> but our interpretation of their significance."

Shakespeare (Hamlet Act 2, scene 2; Shakespeare, Circa 1600) proposed, similarly:

> ". . . for there is nothing either good or
>
> bad, but thinking makes it so."

Chapter 14 – Cognitive Behavioral Mind Training and The Serenity Prayer Thought Record

And B.F. Skinner (of all people) said in The Steep and Thorny Way to a Science of Behavior (1975, p. 43):

> "Reality may be merely an inference and,
>
> according to some authorities, a bad one.
>
> What is important may not be the physical world
>
> on the far side of the skin
>
> but what that world means to us on this side."

B.F. SKINNER
(Photograph By Steven Stone)

In the mid-20th century, psychologist Albert Ellis, inspired by Epictetus, developed what he called Rational Psychotherapy (later renaming it Rational Emotive Therapy and finally Rational Emotive Behavior Therapy), and psychiatrist Aaron Beck, on the basis of his observations of depressive ways of thinking, developed Cognitive Therapy. Both models put forth that emotions are caused, to a great extent, not by events themselves, however negative, but by ways of thinking about the events, and both include therapeutic techniques aimed at changing thought content to reduce the strength of negative emotions. The thought content challenged can be either the facts of events themselves, or their "awfulness" even if objectively negative (the latter being Ellis' "elegant solution").

Around the same time, behavioral techniques for emotional distress were emerging out of research into Pavlov's classical and Skinner's operant conditioning. Some techniques developed included desensitizing people to conditioned fear responses through purposely exposing oneself to the feared stimulus rather than avoiding it (which Wolpe originated as systematic desensitization, in which exposure was paired with relaxation, but which is more commonly practiced as exposure therapy in the absence of relaxation techniques – imaginal exposure therapy, in-vivo exposure therapy or types of exposure that few know about, active-imaginal exposure therapy [Rentz et al., 2003] and lucid dream exposure therapy [Densei & Lam, 2010]).

A forerunner of both Ellis and Beck, who began integrating cognitive and behavioral techniques into a self-help program in the 1930s, was neuropsychiatrist Abraham Low, who wrote in his 1950 book *Mental Health Through Will Training* that

> "The psychoneurotic individual is considered a person who for some reason developed disturbing symptoms leading to ill-controlled behavior. The symptoms are in the nature of threatening sensations, 'intolerable' feelings, 'uncontrollable' impulses and obsessive 'unbearable' thoughts. The very vocabulary with its frenzied emphasis on the 'killing' headache, the dizziness that 'drives me frantic,' the fatigue that 'is beyond human endurance' is ominously expressive of defeatism. The first step in the psychotherapeutic management of these 'chronic' patients must be to convince them that *the sensation can be endured, the impulse controlled, the obsession checked.*" (p. 19)

Chapter 14 – Cognitive Behavioral Mind Training and The Serenity Prayer Thought Record

The language here brings to mind Albert Ellis' later emphasis on teaching clients to de-catastrophize how they think about their symptoms, and Ellis (1962) does reference Low, as well as the behavior therapy technique of exposure. Low may in fact have been an early pioneer in training clients in selective sensory awareness reminiscent of current mindfulness interventions (Low, 1950, pp. 116-117). As an aside, back in the 90s, I went to one of Ellis' big birthday bashes, and the raffle prize was an enormous framed photograph of him sitting naked on the toilet. Can't say Al, who claimed to have once been shy, didn't practice what he preached!

Given REBT's and Cognitive Therapy's attention to the role of thoughts in causing negative emotion (and Ellis' fondness for "elegant" solutions), it is surprising that it wasn't until decades after the development of these schools of therapy that they began to give lip service to the elegant solution of *simply learning to reduce thinking* using meditative and yogic techniques that have been tried and proven for millennia.

It would be unfair to say that the field of psychotherapy has completely ignored the "cognitive process" issue. Interestingly, it was the behaviorists and not the cognitivists who experimented with the technique they called "Thought Stopping" in which you yell "Stop!" in your head, sometimes accompanied by snapping a rubber band worn around the wrist for such occasions. And a perusal of scholarly journals will reveal that:

> "The idea that thought control is important for good psychological adjustment is an old one (Bain [*sic*], 1928; Coué, 1922), and has been accepted generally in psychology. In fact, the process of psychotherapy itself is based on the assumption that overt behavior is influenced by covert changes. Until recently, the most common ways of manipulating private events were through persuasion (e.g., Ellis, 1962), verbal conditioning (Krasner, 1958), or by redirecting attentional responses to absorbing events which elicit competing cognitive activities (Bandura, 1969).
>
> In light of current evidence, we have found it possible to manipulate thoughts by more direct means. Three specific types of procedures have been utilized for that purpose: the Premack Principle, as adapted by Homme (1965); the 'covert conditioning' techniques developed by Cautela (1967, 1970a, 1970b, 1971, 1973); and the Thought Stopping procedure itself. The first two classes of

techniques are employed primarily for increasing the probability of a particular response which may be antagonistic to the maladaptive thought. Thought Stopping, on the other hand, is used to decrease the response itself." (Cautela & Wisocki, 1977)

More recently, there has been research on therapeutically using behavior analysis to identify contingencies of reinforcement maintaining overthinking in the form of negative rumination, transdiagnostically implicated in a multitude of clinical disorders, and treating this with a multimodal behavioral intervention that

> "encourages a guided discovery to the *process* of thinking, rather than a 'changing thoughts' approach." (Watkins, 2016, Rumination-Focused Cognitive-Behavioral Therapy for Depression, p. 47; italics added)

It will be noted that the above reference to Alexander Bain (1928) is **WRONG** and the authors must be referring rather to James Alexander who was the real author of *Thought Control in Everyday Life* (1928). It's interesting that just about every psychologist who writes about the history of "thought stopping" attributes authorship of this book to Alexander Bain whom I know for a fact *didn't* write it. While there are many alternative facts in the present book, this is a *factual* fact. What tipped me off was when about 2 seconds into my online investigation of the matter (gone are the days when I had to travel all the way to a library in France to research the history of behavior therapy), I learned that Alexander Bain lived from 1818 to 1903, and would have been unlikely to be coming up with new ideas in 1928. Upon realizing this, I did what you're really supposed to do rather than cite someone on the basis of other people's citations: Lay eyes on the original source material. And when I found the book *Thought Control in Everyday Life* online (now on my shelf) it was evident that the author was James Alexander.

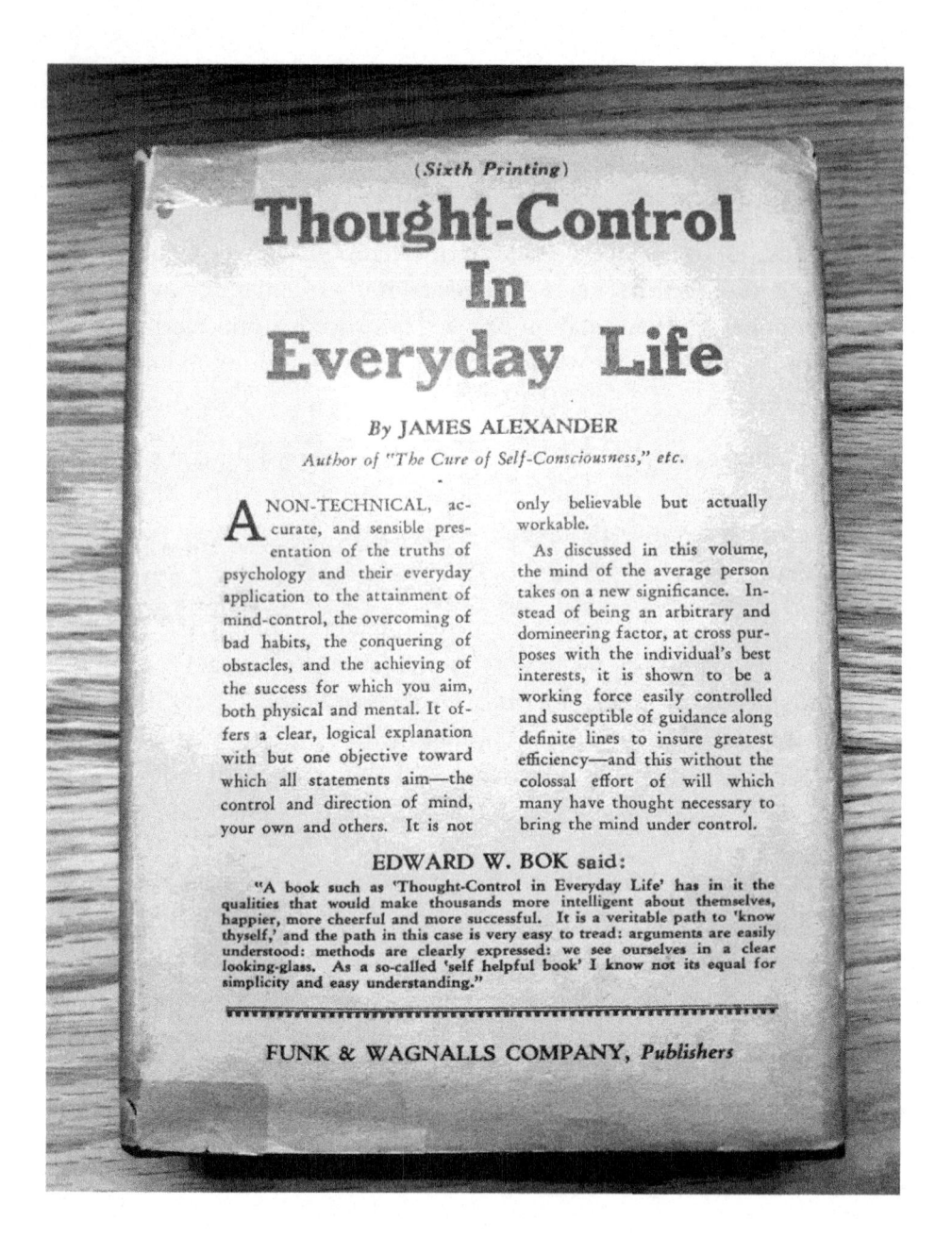

Chapter 14 – Cognitive Behavioral Mind Training and The Serenity Prayer Thought Record

> **(Sixth Printing)**
>
> # Thought-Control In Everyday Life
>
> ### By JAMES ALEXANDER
> *Author of "The Cure of Self-Consciousness," etc.*
>
> A NON-TECHNICAL, accurate, and sensible presentation of the truths of psychology and their everyday application to the attainment of mind-control, the overcoming of bad habits, the conquering of obstacles, and the achieving of the success for which you aim, both physical and mental. It offers a clear, logical explanation with but one objective toward which all statements aim—the control and direction of mind, your own and others. It is not only believable but actually workable.
>
> As discussed in this volume, the mind of the average person takes on a new significance. Instead of being an arbitrary and domineering factor, at cross purposes with the individual's best interests, it is shown to be a working force easily controlled and susceptible of guidance along definite lines to insure greatest efficiency—and this without the colossal effort of will which many have thought necessary to bring the mind under control.
>
> **EDWARD W. BOK said:**
>
> "A book such as 'Thought-Control in Everyday Life' has in it the qualities that would make thousands more intelligent about themselves, happier, more cheerful and more successful. It is a veritable path to 'know thyself,' and the path in this case is very easy to tread: arguments are easily understood: methods are clearly expressed: we see ourselves in a clear looking-glass. As a so-called 'self helpful book' I know not its equal for simplicity and easy understanding."
>
> **FUNK & WAGNALLS COMPANY,** *Publishers*

James Alexander had previously written: The Cure for Self-Consciousness (1915) and probably other books as well which are near impossible to locate *as he has apparently been scrubbed from the internet.* But I just ordered it from AbeBooks.com, so maybe the dustjacket will, like his newer book, mention his older books (on the cover of *Thought Control in Everyday Life* is written "Author of 'The Cure of Self-Consciousness,' etc.," which "etcetera" now requires some literary archeology). (Since writing the above I received the book, which I quoted in the Glossary, and it unfortunately provided no further information re: that "etcetera.")

I suppose it wouldn't hurt after all that fuss to present some of Alexander's actual thoughts here, for what they are worth and as a show of respect to one of those giants on whose shoulders we stand in our quest to stop thinking. The first thing that becomes apparent upon reading "Thought Control in Everyday Life" is that the book is more a forerunner of cognitive therapy (changing thought *content* in order to reduce negative emotions) than it is about changing cognitive *process* or the logical extreme of the latter, stopping thinking, which is the task at hand. Alexander echoes the Buddha (without anywhere mentioning him) when he writes:

> "The world for each of us is *our* world. It is what we *think* it is. If we were denied the power to think – to have thoughts and to reflect upon them – the world (our respective worlds) would cease to exist for us, and since the world is our world and what we think it is, it follows that our world is constantly changing. For thoughts enter the mind, from moment to moment, in a constant stream, thereby affecting and changing the character of our world. Smith's world, for example, was a different world after meeting his secretary." (Alexander, 1928, p. 2)

As I see it, Alexander's writings are more in line with those of Napoleon Hill (of 1937 *Think and Grow Rich* fame, who in 1928 published *The Laws of Success*), while being less focused than Hill on acquiring wealth and more on promoting emotional well-being:

> "Thoughts can fill us with hope or plunge us into despair; can fill us with inspiration or crush all initiative; can make us persevere against any odds, or raise up difficulties to bar our every step.
>
> Let me bring this close to you. Your thoughts can make you or unmake you. Your thoughts can do this, nay are doing this. Will you not have a say in the matter? Will you not see to it that only good thoughts, brave thoughts, inspiring thoughts, hopeful thoughts, cheerful thoughts, shall form your world?

Chapter 14 – Cognitive Behavioral Mind Training and The Serenity Prayer Thought Record

> You can do this. This book will show you how to do it. It will teach you how to cast out of your world every thought that tends to rob you of your peace of mind and your hope of success." (Alexander, 1928, p. 5)

Alexander discusses the relevance of thought control to worry/fear/phobias; depression; anger; obsessions; habit formation; ill health; and sleep, among other applications. As in cognitive therapy, his focus is on how to change thoughts to change emotions. In the process, he even anticipates the behavior therapy technique of imaginal exposure for phobias and obsessions:

> "Any one who suspects that he is developing a phobia, or any one troubled by an obsessing idea, should try to recall the original cause. Here is what I advise him to do. Write down your recollection of the cause – the original happening – just as though you were sending an account of it to some person or doctor, for instance. Never mind how bare the details may be at the first writing. Dwell on the details and try to add to them. Keep going over the account, for a few days, with a critical attitude of mind, until you feel you have made as full a confession as possible of the cause or origin of the phobia, or obsessing idea. *The mere writing, which is really a liberating or opening up of the mind, may itself effect a cure. Where it does not, you should say, with the full details before you: 'I am very silly to let this affect me. There is no reason why it should do so. I am not going to allow it to do so any more.'* This method is the basis of all mental treatment for such cases. Where the phobia or obsession is deeply seated, a qualified practitioner should be consulted." (Alexander, 1928, pp. 188-189; italics added)

Along with modern cognitive behavior therapists, Alexander is telling the phobic/obsessional reader to *do the opposite* of what they might otherwise be inclined to do (try to escape or avoid thinking about the phobic or obsessional content) and rather to purposely think about it for prolonged periods. His cognitive therapy is a little on the light side, as he doesn't have the reader systematically generate evidence for and against the thoughts supporting the implied anxiety/fear, satisfied that the reader will see that they are just being "silly." But given that I've had clients whose prior 21st century therapists and psychiatrists haven't done or suggested exposure therapy for phobias or OCD, I think we can give our 1928 friend a pass.

While the great majority of Alexander's book is on changing thinking rather than stopping it, he does have a section entitled "How to Forget":

> "To forget a thought, don't concentrate on it; don't repeat it over and over again in your mind; don't take any interest in it; don't link it up with other thoughts; don't let it appeal to your understanding. The most troublesome thought you can think cannot stand all those 'don'ts' hurled at its head. It has to retire to oblivion." (p. 115)

> "Let me repeat them in a simpler, handier form. Give the thought you wish to forget no attention (that is, do not dwell on it); give it no repetition (that is do not allow it to repeat itself over and over in your mind); substitute for the disturbing thought some opposing thought, and do it *instantly*." (p. 116)

> "Apply this method in your daily life whenever a disturbing thought enters your mind. Give it no rest, no opportunity to settle down. Go on immediately to fill your mind with new thoughts – pleasant thoughts, stimulating thoughts – and the disturbing thought, unless of a disruptive emotional character, will soon be forgotten." (p. 117)

Here he is suggesting two techniques to stop thinking certain thoughts: (1) Don't think about them; and (2) Think about something else. The first sounds like "Don't think of a white bear," which, in a famous experiment by Harvard psychologist Daniel Wegner, actually increased the frequency with which participants thought about a white bear (Wegner, 1987; see also Wegner, 1994, *White Bears and Other Unwanted Thoughts: Suppression, Obsession, and the Psychology of Mental Control*). Alexander's second strategy, known in behavior modification as "reinforcement of an incompatible behavior," was prescient but limited as it offers only more thinking as a remedy for overthinking without applying the underlying principle ("reinforcement of an incompatible behavior") in ways that don't involve more thinking (i.e., attending to multiple senses simultaneously). But again, he was writing in 1928 and probably hadn't been exposed to meditation, mindfulness or the Seahearbody technique, and he was on the right track.

Chapter 14 – Cognitive Behavioral Mind Training and The Serenity Prayer Thought Record

Maybe the reason that everyone erroneously cites Alexander Bain for the book by James Alexander is that they both have Alexander in their names and Alexander Bain is famous for his associationist theories of the thought process. Bain

> ". . . was a Scottish philosopher and educationalist in the British school of empiricism and a prominent and innovative figure in the fields of psychology, linguistics, logic, moral philosophy and education reform. He founded Mind, the first ever journal of psychology and analytical philosophy, and was the leading figure in establishing and applying the scientific method to psychology." (Alexander Bain, 2022)

In 1855, Bain wrote *The Senses and the Intellect*, and Dacey (2022) explains that Bain theorized that thinking occurs on the basis of

> " ... three fundamental principles of association: similarity, contiguity, and contrast. Contiguity is the basic principle of memory and learning, while similarity is the basic principle of reasoning, judgment, and imagination. Nonetheless, the three are interdependent in complex ways. For instance, similarity is required for contiguity to be possible: Similarity is required for us to recognize that this sequence is similar enough to a former sequence for them to both strengthen the same association by contiguity. The principle of contrast has a more complex role. On the one hand, it is fundamental to the stream of consciousness in the first place. We would not recognize changes in consciousness as changes without this principle. As such, we cannot be conscious of anything as something without recognizing that there is something else it is not: If red were the only color, we would simply not be conscious of color. The other principles would be impossible. Nonetheless, it can also drive sequences, but only when properly scaffolded by similarity or contiguity. Similarity is necessary for association by contrast because contrast is always within a kind, and similarity is necessary for recognition of that original kind; he notes, 'we oppose a long road to a short road, we do not oppose a long road to a loud sound.'" (Bain, 1868, pg. 567 is the citation for the quotation in the final sentence here. The longer quotation is Dacey's summary of Bain's theory)

Truth of the matter is that without the widespread mistaken attribution of James Alexander's book to Alexander Bain, I wouldn't have stumbled upon the writings of Bain himself. Guess alternative facts and fake news aren't all bad.

Joe Wolpe (1958), the father of modern behavior therapy, states that Thought Stopping found its way into the Behavior Therapy literature with the work of Taylor in 1955. I fondly remember corresponding with Dr. Wolpe in the days before the internet, sending a paper that I had written for the Journal of Behavior Therapy and Experimental Psychiatry back and forth by snail mail. He would edit it by hand and I would retype it on a *typewriter* and send it back, only for him to once again edit it by hand and send it back for me to again retype and resubmit. One of these exchanges involved a certain page disappearing from my manuscript each time he would send it back. After 2 or 3 back and forths in which I reinserted the page before sending my edits of the other material back to him, I realized that the page that kept disappearing contained one of my quotations of Melinée Agathon, arguably the "Mother of behavior therapy in France," in which she had told me when I interviewed her for the historical article at issue that Wolpe was "her God." When I deleted that quotation from the page in question, it reappeared in the material he sent back to me. Those were the days! So here, as a tribute to Joe, I will quote a section of his book "Psychotherapy by Reciprocal Inhibition" regarding the theme of the present treatise:

> "In certain patients a great deal of anxiety is due to insistent trains of thought that are disturbing out of all proportion to the realities involved. For example, a person may think constantly of the consequences of his business collapsing even though there is no objective threat of this. It is clearly not unreasonable that thoughts of this kind should generate anxiety; but the very persistence of a useless thought is itself unadaptive. The desirability of suppressing such thoughts was pointed out by Dollard and Miller (1950, pp. 445-59), but no method was given other than suggesting that the patient be told to keep his thoughts on the tasks of the day – which very few patients can do merely in obedience to a prescription.
>
> Not long ago a surprisingly simple method for freeing patients from useless thoughts was devised by J. G. Taylor (1955) of the University

Chapter 14 – Cognitive Behavioral Mind Training and The Serenity Prayer Thought Record

of Cape Town. The patient is asked to shut his eyes and to verbalize a typical unadaptive thought sequence. Suddenly the therapist shouts, 'Stop!' All this is repeated several times, and attention is drawn to the fact that the thoughts actually do stop each time. The patient is then told that he himself can stop his thoughts equally successfully by saying 'stop' subvocally. The thoughts of course soon return, but after repeated stopping, they return less readily and become progressively easier to stop. With assiduous practice some patients become largely or entirely free from these futile thoughts within a week or so.

For patients on whom this procedure fails I have adopted a modification that usually has the desired effect. A buzzer activated by pressure on a telegraph key is placed on the desk between us. The patient is told to try to keep his mind on pleasant thoughts, about the objects around him or anything else. If, however, any disturbing thought intrudes, he is at once to depress the knob on the telegraph key. Upon the buzzer sounding I instantly shout, 'Stop!' Usually during the first two or three minutes, the patient may depress the key between 10 and 20 times per minute, and then the frequency progressively declines so that toward the end of the 15 minutes allowed for this procedure, he depresses it perhaps once every two minutes. Evidently, a habit of inhibiting disturbing thoughts has begun to be built up. The patient is enjoined to go on trying at all times to exclude useless thoughts from his mind. This is generally highly successful except in the case of chronic, well-defined obsessional ideas, and even with these, worth-while amelioration is sometimes obtained.

Like the correcting of misconceptions this method is not directly therapeutic in the sense of detaching neurotic responses from stimuli. But its lowering of the general level of anxiety both alleviates the patient's suffering and makes for easier therapeutic reciprocal inhibition of the anxieties aroused by specific stimuli. Of course, there may be cases whose neurosis consists basically of a habit of thinking disturbing thoughts. One case treated by Taylor was apparently of this character, for a long-standing chronic anxiety state with insomnia was very largely overcome by this method in four interviews. This person has maintained her improvement for two years ." (Wolpe, 1958, pp. 200-201)

Unfortunately, as noted above, three decades later we learned that thought stopping doesn't really work. I suspect that the subjects in Taylor's study experienced a reduction in unwanted thoughts due to the first part of the procedure (purposely thinking the unwanted thought, i.e., exposure therapy). And I wager that the reduction in telegraph key-presses by Dr. Wolpe's patients may have been due more to not wanting him to yell at them than to a reduction in intrusive thoughts supposedly indicated by pressing the key. Thus, he may have been punishing and reducing honest reporting rather than the symptom itself.

Interestingly, in a review of thought stopping, in which O'Neill and Whittal (2002) concluded that

> "The work of Wegner, Salkovskis, and Purdon has demonstrated that thought suppression increases the frequency of the target thought(s)" (p. 805),

they proposed an alternative technique with better results:

> "As part of recent developments in cognitive treatments for OCD, Maureen Whittal and Peter McLean have described a process coined 'come and go.' Clients are encouraged to *experience the intrusive unwanted thought and not try to control it* (i.e., do not try to ignore, suppress, distract or anything else that will serve to get rid of the thought). Rather, clients are instructed to practice this 'come-and-go' strategy and their usual style of thought control on alternate days and predict their anxiety and the frequency of intrusive unwanted thoughts on each of the days. Clients invariably predict that letting thoughts come and go will result in higher levels of anxiety and more frequent intrusive thoughts. They are often surprised that letting go of their efforts at thought control (i.e., letting thoughts come and go) lessens the anxiety and typically lowers the frequency of the target thought(s)." (O'Neill & Whittal, 2002, p. 806; italics added)

This "come-and-go" technique sounds suspiciously like exposure therapy practiced spontaneously and passively whenever an obsession arises (as opposed to more intensive exposure in which one purposely thinks a disturbing thought for an extended period of time, or purposely continues to

Chapter 14 – Cognitive Behavioral Mind Training and The Serenity Prayer Thought Record

think it when it arises). It sounds even more suspiciously like mindful open-awareness, just letting whatever comes to mind be there without trying to either keep it there or make it leave.

While the subtitle of this book is "The New Cognitive Behavioral Mind Training," cognitive, behavioral and meditative techniques are anything but new. I am merely defining and combining them in some new ways that I have found make sense in light of my own life experience and readings, and which have proven helpful for my clients. Scholars agree that cognitive and behavioral interventions were already being practiced in 19th century France. For example, graduated exposure was being used for agoraphobia in the 1870s – see my 1994 article in the Journal of Behavior Therapy and Experimental Psychiatry on the history of behavior therapy in France (that's the one that Wolpe and I sent back and forth). And meditative approaches to reducing thinking have been around for millennia. In a review of similarities between Buddhist teachings and Western psychotherapy, de Silva (2000) notes that The Buddhist Vitakkasanthaana Sutta of the Majjhima Nikaaya (composed between the 3rd century BCE and 2nd century CE) and its commentary, the Papa ncasuudanii, propose 5 techniques to stop unwanted thoughts, with instructions to progress to the next technique if the preceding one(s) fail. These include:

1. switch to an opposite and incompatible thought;

2. ponder on harmful consequences;

3. ignore the cognition and distract oneself;

4. reflect on removal of causes; and,

5. control with forceful effort.

de Silva (2000) further notes that in the Satipatthana Sutta, the Discourse on the Foundations of Mindfulness (composed around 20 BCE), a sixth method is proposed involving concentrating on the unwanted thought rather than trying to eliminate it (which is akin to exposure therapy).

Regarding the word "training" in Cognitive Behavioral Mind Training, I find it to be just as accurate and, in some cases, more accurate than the term "therapy." The latter is just a fancy word for training used in the context of "healing" (Greek: therapeia). And while healing is the bread and butter of my Psychology 2.0, the techniques employed by Psychologies 1.0, 3.0 and 4.0 are more akin to training modalities without the medical connotations.

Really, the term "training" is equally appropriate for Psychology 2.0, at least in the cognitive behavioral model. Despite the health professions' pathologization of just about anything that can possibly go wrong in your day as a "psychiatric disorder" (otherwise how would we get paid for helping you with it as your health insurance holds the purse strings), the truth is that negative emotions, and even excessive and really uncomfortable negative emotions, are normal and need more to be simply changed than "healed." Teaching people techniques to alter normal but unhelpful cognitive and behavioral content and process, in the service of effecting emotional change, is clearly a form of "training" (recap: cognitive content is *what* you think, and cognitive process is the *frequency, duration and salience* of thinking; behavioral content is *what* you do, and behavioral process is the *frequency, duration and intensity* of what you do). However, one doesn't bite the hand that feeds one, and so no matter how normal your psychological experience, if you are using insurance to pay for "therapy," you will indeed receive a medical psychiatric diagnosis even if you're actually fine and the people who really need therapy (usually your family or hostile colleagues) don't think they have a problem. But it's really a win-win-win-win-win situation: you get your training (I mean "therapy") and learn how to change what you can and accept what you can't, the insurance company gets your premium, the therapist gets the insurance company's reimbursement, your family gets to stay crazy, your colleagues get to stay hostile, and life goes on.

In the chapters that follow, I will teach you a number of really easy techniques (easy to understand but, like anything, requiring some effort on your part), drawn from the fields of cognitive therapy, behavior therapy, meditation, and consciousness studies. Although names of psychiatric disorders are thrown around (e.g., depression, panic disorder, OCD), please note that the techniques helpful for any of these in their full clinical forms are equally useful for much milder manifestations, such as single symptoms (e.g., low mood or worry) which, when not occurring in the context of a clinical disorder (e.g., Major Depression or Generalized Anxiety Disorder) are actually not even symptoms (which would imply that a syndrome, or disorder, is present) but are merely negative experiences amenable to change.

Chapter 14 – Cognitive Behavioral Mind Training and The Serenity Prayer Thought Record

A final note on any appearance (such as the name of this book) that I am proposing a "new" therapy. The reason that I am giving a name to what I am offering clients (eclectically combining cognitive restructuring, behavior therapy, and meditation) is because there do in fact exist a number of therapies that do the same, to a limited extent. However, they do so in their own idiosyncratic systematic ways (as do I), emphasizing certain techniques and minimizing or not including others. I am calling this approach Cognitive Behavioral Mind Training (CBMT) primarily to distinguish it from these other systems that have chosen their own emphases and modalities.

For example, Mindfulness Based Cognitive Therapy will not teach you exposure and response prevention for obsessions and compulsions; Mindfulness Based Stress Reduction will not teach you how to use sleep restriction for insomnia; Beck's Cognitive Therapy will never teach you lucid dream exposure for nightmares or how to leave your body to visit The Park where one has the experience, whether real or not, of being in the place where people are said to go after they die to be greeted by their loved ones; and Rational Emotive Behavior Therapy will never teach you to be aware of the One Who Is Aware. In a way, distinguishing CBMT from the others is as much to protect them from association with where CBMT is willing to go (*From Wellness, to Well-Being and Beyond*, *way* beyond Mainstream Psychology's "consensual reality") than to compete with them in any way or claim any sort of "betterness" or "newness." If anything, CBMT (get it? See, Be Empty! Or better yet, as the Zensters would say, See! Be! Empty!, serendipitously corresponding to the types of meditation discussed earlier, Object Awareness, Subject Awareness, and Pure Awareness) capitalizes on the oldness of the techniques it employs, and that they have stood the test of time.

A summary of the types of techniques employed by CBMT is listed below. Appendix 2 provides a CBMT Treatment Plan illustrating correspondences among specific techniques and a number of common psychological challenges. It should be noted that it is usually important to approach problems by using a combination of modalities.

COGNITIVE RESTRUCTURING

Excessive levels of the negative emotions (sadness, anxiety, fear and anger), the thought patterns both triggering and resulting from them, and emotionally-triggered medical problems and insomnia can usually benefit from cognitive restructuring. This involves changing cognitive *content* by challenging thoughts via comparison of evidence that supports them with evidence that doesn't, and replacing the negative irrational thoughts with rational alternative interpretations of the situation. The thoughts that are challenged can involve "automatic thoughts" that arise in consciousness in response to an internal or external stimulus (e.g., a pain or an event in the environment), or "underlying" beliefs or "schemas" that act as a lens through which we perceive and interpret events (Beck, Rush, Shaw & Emery, 1979; Young & Klosko, 2003). For example, if someone doesn't say hello to you at work, you might have the automatic thought "I hate when she ignores me." The content of this automatic thought may, however, be influenced by the underlying belief that "nobody likes me." Someone without this underlying schema might have the same (anti-)social (non-)event of someone not saying hello to them, but might instead think "She seems really preoccupied. I hope she's OK."

It is important to distinguish between cognitive restructuring, which replaces irrational negative content with rational content, from "positive thinking," which replaces negative content (whether rational or irrational) with positive content (whether rational or irrational). The use of positive thinking in psychology dates back at least as far as Emile Coué's book "*La Maîtrise de Soi-Même par l'Autosuggestion Consciente* (1920; *Self-Mastery Through Conscious Autosuggestion*). Coué was a French psychologist and pharmacist who discovered the placebo effect and devised a system of self-improvement in which he prescribes the mantra "Tous les jours à tous points de vue je vais de mieux en mieux" ("Every Day in Every Way I Am Getting Better and Better") which, of course, is utter hogwash for most of us (cognitive skills begin declining at age 24; Thompson, Blair & Henrey, 2014; and body-wide DNA damage over time causes an increasing unreliability of cell regeneration, experienced as physiological *aging*), but at least positive, self-affirming hogwash. He influenced such authors as the minister Norman Vincent Peale (1952; *The Power of Positive Thinking*), electrical repairman José Silva (1977; The Silva Mind Control Method, now the Silva Method), and cosmetic surgeon Maxwell Maltz (1960; *Psycho-Cybernetics*), the latter who noted the importance of rational thinking in a chapter entitled "*The Power of Rational Thinking*":

> "Many of my patients are plainly disappointed when I prescribe something as simple as using their God-given power of reason as a

Chapter 14 – Cognitive Behavioral Mind Training and The Serenity Prayer Thought Record

method of changing negative beliefs and behavior. To some, it seems incredibly naive and un-scientific. Yet, it does have one advantage—it works. And as we shall see later, it is based upon sound scientific findings. There is a widely accepted fallacy that rational, logical, conscious thinking has no power over unconscious processes or mechanisms, and that to change negative beliefs, feelings or behavior, it is necessary to dig down and dredge up material from the 'unconscious.' Your automatic mechanism, or what the Freudians call the 'unconscious,' is absolutely impersonal. It operates as a machine and has no 'will' of its own. It always tries to react appropriately to your current beliefs and interpretations concerning environment [sic]. It always seeks to give you appropriate feelings, and to accomplish the goals which you consciously determine upon. It works only upon the data which you feed it in the form of ideas, beliefs, interpretations, opinions. It is conscious thinking which is the 'control knob' of your unconscious machine. It was by conscious thought, though perhaps irrational and unrealistic, that the unconscious machine developed its negative and inappropriate reaction patterns, and it is by conscious rational thought that the automatic reaction patterns can be changed." (pp. 64-65)

Maltz goes on to cite a 1954 book by physician John A. Schindler (*How to Live 365 Days A Year*) whose "method of treatment was what he called 'conscious thought control'" (Maltz, 1960, p. 74) and, incidentally predated Albert Ellis' 1955 article which is commonly seen as inaugurating the field of Cognitive Therapy (though it is unclear whether Schindler's approach involved systematic rational disputation of irrational thoughts – positive thinking may also be considered "conscious thought control" despite running counter to the theory and practice of rational disputation). Schindler (1954) writes that

> "... regardless of the omissions and commissions of the past, a person has to start in the present to acquire some maturity so that the future may be better than the past. The present and the future depend on learning new habits and new ways of looking at old problems. There simply isn't any future in digging continually into the past . . .
> The starting point in the treatment of E.I.I. [emotionally induced illness] becomes simple and clear when one realizes that the

underlying emotional problem has the same common denominator in every patient. This common denominator is that the patient has forgotten how, or probably never learned how, to control his present thinking to produce enjoyment . . .

My method of therapy places the patient on the enjoyment principle by a conditioned reflex through conscious thought control, by substituting equanimity, courage, determination and cheerfulness, whenever anxiety, apprehension, and so on, begin to make their appearances. This substitution is done by conscious thought control until habit can eventually take over. Such substitution is what people with emotional stasis are doing habitually all the time." (p. 205)

While positive thinking certainly feels better, momentarily, than negative thinking, it suffers from the problem of non-credibility. If you really believe a certain negative thought, you are not going to stop believing it just because you try to think its opposite.

If you have been out of work for 8 months and suffer from thinking "I am a loser for not contributing to the family's well-being" (an *automatic thought* to the extent that it arises seemingly automatically in response to the situation), you are not going to be convinced by positive thinking in the form of "Every day in every way I am getting better and better, in fact I'm actually a winner and bringing in lots of bacon." This is where Ellis' Rational Emotive Behavior Therapy and Beck's cognitive therapy come into play. Rather than saying "I'm not a loser I'm a winner," you critically evaluate the evidence that you are a loser and the evidence that you aren't a loser. This is called *cognitive disputation*. This can involve exploring the meaning of the term "loser" itself (including whether it is even a valid concept with any relevance to a human being); what the criteria of "loser" are; the extent to which you have these qualities; and the extent to which you don't have these qualities.

Another useful technique is the *downward arrow*, or as I prefer to call it in therapy because it is immediately understood by my clients, *down the rabbit hole*. Here, after writing down all of your automatic thoughts, you pick one or two that bother you the most (the "hot" thoughts) and ask yourself the Rabbit Hole Question (RHQ): If the hot thoughts were true, what would it mean for or about you, others, the world or the future? In sum, why would it be *bad*? For example, assuming it is true that you are unemployed and haven't made money for 8 months, what does this mean to you and why is it

Chapter 14 – Cognitive Behavioral Mind Training and The Serenity Prayer Thought Record

bad. Maybe it means to you that you will use up all your savings to pay your expenses. Then you ask yourself the **RHQ** regarding this. To which you might reply that it means you will run out of money in 6 months. Then you again ask yourself the **RHQ**, and respond that you will have to sell the house, etc., discovering that you further fear you won't be able to afford a place to live, will end up homeless and without food and will die in a stranger's doorway in the winter. Having followed the rabbit hole to its logical conclusion, you then look at both the list of automatic thoughts and rabbit hole thoughts, and ask yourself which are the most bothersome. These then become new *hot* thoughts to work with. You then begin the cognitive restructuring, or cognitive disputation component of the therapy, and generate any evidence that the hot thoughts are true, evidence that they might not be true, and alternative ways of thinking about the situation based on the evidence.

One alternative interpretation of the situation might be: "I'm not in the best situation but I wouldn't think of someone else in my situation as a 'loser' so I guess I'm not one either; I don't have a job right now but I'm looking, my wife is working so we're getting by, she's pretty happy that I'm taking care of the house and the kids and cooking dinner, and one way or another I'll eventually get a job." Clearly, this is not as positive as "Every day in every way I'm getting better and better, in fact I'm a winner and making lots of money" but, more importantly, it's *believable*, and is not as "terrible" as being a "loser." After explicitly challenging automatic irrational negative thoughts for a while, what happens is that the rational, less negative alternatives begin showing up more in consciousness, eventually replacing the irrational thoughts. In time, the rational alternatives themselves become automatic thoughts that arise in response to situations, reducing whatever component of your unhappiness or distress was due to the irrational negative thinking addressed.

A standard tool for cognitive restructuring/disputation is the Thought Record, presented in Appendix 3 in the form of my Serenity Prayer Thought Record. An example of how to use it without getting eaten by a bear is presented in Appendix 4.

The Serenity Prayer Thought Record shares the main themes of traditional cognitive therapy thought records, but includes columns that are not included on most other thought records, these being:

1. The downward arrow technique ("down the rabbit hole"), and

2. A column that allows, after arriving at a more rational but not necessarily desirable assessment of the situation, to apply the Serenity Prayer in order to determine what can be done and what can be accepted.

Instructions for completing the thought record are written on it. One clarification would perhaps be useful. Often when generating the Automatic Thoughts column, clients report their first AT as a question, such as "Why Me?," "How could she do that?" or, in extreme cases "Why can't he just pick up his damn socks for Pete's sake?" As columns 3, 5, 6, 7 and 8 can't be completed using questions as material (e.g., If "Why Me?" is true, why is that BAD?; or If "Why can't he just pick up his damn socks" is true, what does it mean about me, others, the world or the future?), it is helpful to convert the questions into the statement representing the implicit answer to the question that is giving it an emotional charge. In other words, convert the question into the answer that you don't like such that, just as examples:

> "Why me" could mean to you "I'm a loser";
>
> "How could she do that?" could mean to you "She's ignoring my feelings"; and
>
> "Why can't he just pick up his damn socks for Pete's sake" could mean "If he doesn't pick up his socks, our dog Pete will eat them."

Having now converted the automatic thought into a statement, it will be possible to identify Rabbit Hole Thoughts (e.g., "If it's true that Pete will eat the socks, it will be bad because he won't be hungry for dinner").

The basic structure of this 8-column thought record is 4 columns for *The Problem* and 4 columns for *The Solution*. To paraphrase *The Buddha's* Four Noble Truths, there is Suffering, the Causes of Suffering, the End of Suffering and the Path to End Suffering (ever notice how everyone spells Buddah differently. He's kind of like Hannuka, which attempted spelling just got me scolded by the Google Bot:

> "Hannuka does not appear to be spelled correctly.
>
> Suggestions: Hanukkah Hanuka Hank hank Hakka Hanukkahs."

Chapter 14 – Cognitive Behavioral Mind Training and The Serenity Prayer Thought Record

Come back ... In the Serenity Prayer Thought Record, the reason you're doing it at all is that you are *suffering* (from low mood, anxiety, anger, etc.); which to some extent is *caused* by how (and that) you're thinking; there is a hoped-for *end* to the thinking: and doing the thought record is part of the *path* to STOP IT (Newhart, 2019/2001).

The Problem is that Situations trigger Automatic Thoughts, which then spin out of control in a falling domino-like fashion (downward arrow, rabbit hole, turtles all the way down, or whatever metaphor you prefer), and gravitate toward worst case scenarios resulting in negative emotions.

The Solution is to evaluate the evidence that supports these negative thoughts and evidence that doesn't support them, arrive at a more rational interpretation of the situation based on the evidence, and then decide what you can do about it and what you can accept about it if it can't be completely resolved.

Until we learn to think in this way, we can spend years, decades or even a lifetime living in the first 4 columns, bouncing between our negative thoughts and negative emotions. When we're depressed, anxious, fearful or angry, it seems that

> **"Every silver lining**
>
> **Has a cloud."**
>
> Grandma Densei (1922)

Negative thoughts become conditioned cognitive responses to situations, negative emotions become conditioned emotional responses to negative thoughts, negative emotions then trigger further negative thoughts through a neuropsychological process called "state dependent cognition," and negative thoughts and emotions create further negative situations which we then think and feel negatively about.

Once we begin to use negative situations, thoughts and emotions as triggers for cognitive disputation, eventually this becomes a habit, alternative rational interpretations begin to become conditioned to the trigger situations, and the rational interpretations begin popping up as automatic thoughts rather than their negative predecessors. These rational automatic thoughts, as they trigger more positive emotions, begin to improve our emotional responses to situations and eventually our general emotional state.

MEDITATION AND MINDFULNESS

Excessive levels of the negative emotions (sadness, anxiety, fear and anger), to the extent that they are triggered by overthinking, can benefit from meditation and mindfulness (changing cognitive *process*, stopping thinking or reducing the ratio of the awareness salience of thinking to that of the sum of the awareness saliences of the other senses). Meditation and mindfulness have the additional benefit of calming the nervous system and improving attention and concentration. They can also decrease the amplitude of high frequency brainwaves characteristic of primary insomnia (excessive Beta and Gamma wave activation of 14-45 hz; Perlis et al., 2001)

BEHAVIORAL ACTIVATION (BA)

(Do More Fun Stuff)

Low mood and depression can benefit from increasing the frequency and duration of potentially pleasant, productive and meaningful activities. The word *potentially* here is important, as these activities may be neither pleasant nor productive when one is depressed, which is part of the reason they are commonly avoided or escaped from. The other part of the reason is *state dependent cognition* – thinking about doing the activity occurs in the presence of the emotional state of depression – causing the thought/prediction to be subject to the cognitive distortion of *emotional reasoning*, e.g., "thinking about it I feel depressed, so it must be an unenjoyable thing to do." Here, one misattributes the pre-existing depressive state to the incidental cognitive content. Behavioral activation involves doing these activities *anyway*, even if, due to the depression, they are not pleasant or productive at first.

> "The expanded BA model is based on a conceptualization of depression that emphasizes the relationship between activity and mood and the role of contextual changes associated with decreased access to reinforcers that may serve an antidepressant function. The model highlights the centrality of patterns of avoidance and withdrawal (e.g., of interpersonal situations, occupational or daily-life routine demands, distressing thoughts or feelings, and so forth). Because contacting potential antidepressant reinforcers is often

initially punishing, avoidance of contact minimizes distress in the short-term but is associated with greater long-term difficulty, both by reducing opportunities to contact potentially antidepressant environmental reinforcers and by creating or exacerbating new problems secondary to the decreased activity. Increased activation is presented as a strategy to break this cycle. In general, BA seeks to identify and promote engagement with activities and contexts that are reinforcing and consistent with an individual's long-term goals. Specific behaviorally focused activation strategies include self-monitoring, structuring and scheduling daily activities, rating the degree of pleasure and accomplishment experienced during engagement in specific daily activities, exploring alternative behaviors related to achieving participant goals, and using role-playing to address specific behavioral deficits. In addition, the expanded BA model includes an increased focus on the assessment and treatment of avoidance behaviors, the establishment or maintenance of regularized routines, and behavioral strategies for targeting rumination, including an emphasis on the function of ruminative thinking and on **moving attention away from the content of ruminative thoughts toward direct, immediate experience.**" (Dimidjian et al., 2006, p. 660; bolding added, indicating a mindfulness component of this expanded behavioral activation protocol)

In a randomized trial of treatments for severe depression, an expanded behavioral activation protocol performed as well as antidepressant medication, and both performed better than cognitive therapy (which intervened at the levels of "situation-specific negative thinking and cognitive distortions" and "underlying dysfunctional beliefs or cognitions" and included its own less comprehensive behavioral activation component)(Dimidjian et al., 2006, p. 660). However, a 24-month follow-up study (Dobson et al., 2008) found that among treatment responders from the Dimidjian et al. study (2006) there were minimal and nonsignificant differences between those who had been treated with cognitive therapy (including its own BA component) and those treated with the expanded BA treatment condition and that both were at least as effective as antidepressant medication. Cognitive therapy emphasizes the importance of behavioral activation when patients are most depressed, such as early in treatment (Beck, Rush, Shaw & Emery, 1979).

EXPOSURE AND RESPONSE PREVENTION (E/RP)

Any problem involving an urge to do something to escape or avoid discomfort (or the expected trigger of the discomfort) – or an urge to *not* do something expected to cause discomfort – can benefit from intentionally increasing the discomfort and preventing responses aimed at escape, until the brain learns that the stimulus isn't actually dangerous. Problems that involve such urges to escape or avoid include phobias; panic disorder, which is really a fear of fear itself and thus a *phobophobia*; obsessions and compulsions; and anger, which involves an urge to act to terminate the environmental conditions that triggered the anger sequence of angry thought, emotion, urge to attack verbally or physically, decision as to whether to do so, and behavior. Fear of flying is an interesting example, as it is in most cases not truly a fear of flying but rather a fear of panicking when flying. That is, one is not excessively concerned about crashing, one is afraid of feeling afraid. "Urge surfing," which involves feeling the physical discomfort or the urge to perform unhelpful body-related behaviors such as hair pulling, or the physical discomfort and urge that tempt one to use a substance to which one is addicted, and not doing it, is another name for exposure and response prevention.

SLEEP CONSOLIDATION

Insomnia due to a learned habit of interrupted sleep can benefit from spending less time in bed until the brain readjusts to a pattern of more continuous sleep, then gradually increasing the time in bed to the amount necessary to obtain a sufficient amount of sleep to feel rested. Cognitive Behavior Therapy for Insomnia (CBT-I) integrates sleep consolidation with cognitive restructuring for worry, which can overactivate the body and brain and thus impact sleep, into a single therapy.

DISSOLVING PAIN

While chronic pain is ideally treated multimodally, potentially including some type of movement therapy, possibly medication and with surgery as a last resort, there is an awareness-based approach developed by Les Fehmi, Ph.D., a pioneer in the field of neurofeedback and alpha neurosynchrony, that can significantly reduce pain (Fehmi & Fehmi, 2021; Fehmi & Robbins,

2010). This is a mindfulness-based exposure approach in that it brings full awareness to the pain, followed by bringing full awareness to the area around the pain. Much as with the neurophysiology involved in scratching around an itch, it is possible that attention-triggered activation of currently non-pain-emitting neurons corresponding with the physical area surrounding the area with the pain interferes with the pain signals of the neurons currently creating the pain sensation.

Chapter 15 - *The Anxiety is the Medicine:* Exposure and Response Prevention for Discomfort, Escape, Avoidance, Obsessions, Compulsions and Urges in Panic, Phobias, PTSD, OCD, Anger, Addictions, and Unwanted Habits

You go back, Jack, do it again

Fagen & Becker (1972)

"Whether you are with a teacher

or by yourself,

the real teacher is always yourself

and your experience."

Tulku Urgyen Rinpoche

(As It Is, Volume 2)

Chapter 15 - The Anxiety is the Medicine: Exposure and Response Prevention for Discomfort, Escape, Avoidance, Obsessions, Compulsions and Urges in Panic, Phobias, PTSD, OCD, Anger, Addictions, and Unwanted Habits

The two main techniques used in behavior therapy are Behavioral Activation (for depression) and E/RP for anxiety disorders, OCD and breaking habits.

The technique of Exposure and Response Prevention (E/RP) is perhaps what best distinguishes behavior therapy from other forms of therapy. It is at once the most counterintuitive therapy for certain types of problems and one of the best supported by the research. Whether a psychotherapist uses E/RP (with or without other potentially helpful modalities) for Panic, Phobias, PTSD, OCD, Anger, Addictions, and Unwanted Habits may be the best indication of whether they know what the f#@% they are doing.

If with no knowledge of psychology you had to guess what the behavior therapy for a given problem is, you could figure it out pretty easily:

Think of what you want to do,

and do the opposite

(as long as it's safe and legal).

Behavioral Activation can be summed up as: *Do it* because you don't feel like it (if it would be fun, productive or meaningful and if you would do it if you were feeling great), or Just Do It (Nike Therapy).

E/RP can be summed up as:

Do it because you're afraid of doing it

(as long as it *isn't actually dangerous* – don't feel the fear and pick up the rattlesnake anyway), and

Don't do it even though you have a strong urge to do it

(unless *not* doing it is actually dangerous – don't feel the urge to swerve and *not* swerve when about to be hit by a truck). With these caveats, the title of Susan Jeffer's (1987) book is really all you need: *Feel the Fear and Do It Anyway.*

As to whom to trust regarding *whether something is or isn't actually dangerous*, all I can propose is to be suspicious of people whose first and last names both begin with the same letter *and* have equal numbers of letters. I say this on the basis of a recent interview with George Gorman, New York

State Parks Regional Director for Long Island who, when asked if it was safe to swim given that three people have been bitten by sharks within the past two days, offered the following:

> "I, I don't want to feel like the *Mayor* of *Amity* from *Jaws*. The *waters are safe*. There *have* been some . . . shark bites. The experts have been saying that these shark bites *are really* because the sharks *are feeding* on bait fish, bunker fish. They, eeeee, *accidentally* will bite a foot, a toe . . ." (Gorman, 2022)

Thanks, George. That inspires confidence. To some people. Like Andriana.Marine on *TikTok* who reassures us that

> "The sharks don't get the *credit* for swimming *past* people on a daily basis and *not* thinking that they're food. I mean, you're more likely to be bitten by a New Yorker than a shark." (Andriana.Marine, 2022)

While she may have a point, until we've gone a few days without "accidental" shark bites, I think I'll stick with leisure activities that allow my feet and toes to stay attached to my body, where they seem quite happy.

Exposure therapy is similar to logotherapist Viktor Frankl's "paradoxical intention," in which one purposely increases a symptom that one has an ultimate goal of decreasing (Frankl, 1984; Originally published in 1946).

While it sounds counterintuitive to go to therapy to feel *worse*, it really isn't any different than lots of things we do that function along the lines of "no pain, no gain" or "no pain, more pain" such as:

> Exercising,
>
> Getting up early for work,
>
> Eating four fruits a day,
>
> Cleaning the bathroom,
>
> Going to sleep early for work,
>
> Not eating the whole 25-piece munchkin box by yourself driving up to Massachusetts,
>
> Going to work,

Chapter 15 - The Anxiety is the Medicine: Exposure and Response Prevention for Discomfort, Escape, Avoidance, Obsessions, Compulsions and Urges in Panic, Phobias, PTSD, OCD, Anger, Addictions, and Unwanted Habits

and I'm sure you could think of a few more.

The history of E/RP, with all due respect to Wikipedia, does not date back to the 1950s but can be traced back at least as far as 1870s France when Perroud and Legrand du Saulle were treating agoraphobics by graduated exposure (Cottraux, 1990b, p. 16). Even prior to exposure therapy's entry into mainstream research psychology in the 50s (e.g., Wolpe's 1958 systematic desensitization), in 1937 the neuropsychiatrist Abraham Low founded Recovery Inc. (now called Recovery International) and devised cognitive behavioral practices to help people conquer emotional distress including panic attacks. Some history is provided by Ferrigno (2018) who writes that "Low went beyond the popular school of 'positive thinking' with his 'constructive thinking' technique." Here is an excerpt from Recovery Inc.'s 1950 book *Mental Health Through Will Training*:

> "Annette (panel leader): The subject for today's panel is 'The Vicious Cycle of Panic' . . . I remember the first panic I experienced. Shortly before I went to the hospital I awoke at night with a numbness in my arm. I looked in the mirror and it seemed to me I saw a slight swelling in the side of my nose. Looking on the swelling in the nose I became more painfully aware of the numbness in the arm. **Suddenly I was gripped with fear** . . . I felt as though I couldn't get my breath, as if each breath was the last. While my aunt called the doctor I began to tremble . . . the doctor arrived and after examining me carefully said he could not find anything wrong . . . **After that I dreaded the thought of numbness.** I was always in fear of it. I developed the vicious cycle. If I only thought of the numbness it was there. And each time I thought I was going to die. Then I went to the hospital and came in contact with Recovery and attended the physician's classes. There I learned that **sensations are distressing but not dangerous.** It took me a long time to understand that fully. I remember once I had a slight numbness and kept repeating, a sensation is not dangerous; it is not dangerous. I repeated that again and again but finally I got sore and decided it didn't help. Then I thought what else can I do? I started out again chanting it isn't dangerous, it isn't dangerous and I did not work myself up to a vicious cycle. One night I awoke with a sensation that I felt in every muscle of my body, something like you feel when the elevator drops slightly. I got tense and weak and **felt like waking my husband** to ask

him for a glass of water. But I remembered my recovery training and *knew that if I gave way to the impulse to awaken him that meant I was helpless and needed help.* And that meant I was on the way to establish a vicious cycle. I knew if I was to control the vicious cycle *I must not act on the impulse.* It was difficult to restrain myself. *So I lay quietly*, but then I got mad because there my husband slept peacefully while I was so uncomfortable. I was provoked at the idea that I had to curb my desire to call for help. Suddenly I remembered the doctor had told us the best way to calm down is to do something absolutely unemotional, something that has definitely nothing to do with excitement and temper, something that is utterly objective. So I said to myself, 'I am going now to view this sensation objectively and without fear. *I shall look at my sensation as I would look at an object.*' I asked, 'Where is that sensation? Where do I feel it most? In my arms, or in my stomach or legs? Just exactly what kind of sensation is it? Could I describe it? *I had by now become objective, indeed. And then something extraordinary happened. When I set out to look at the sensation and to describe it it was gone the very moment I started to look at it*, and I fell asleep. In the morning I felt refreshed and proud of my accomplishment. Has anyone else got an example?" (Low, 1950, pp. 116-117; italics and bolding added)

A woman named Gertrude then goes on to report a similar experience with palpitations, and similarly "remembered the doctor asked us to do nothing about sensations, that they were *distressing but not dangerous*" (p. 118).

I have italicized and bolded portions of the above to point out several key features of the use of the cognitive, behavioral and meditational components of exposure therapy for anxiety, *IN 1950*, before the alleged origins of cognitive therapy, behavior therapy or the mindfulness therapies in the works of their alleged founders, which involve relating in a certain way to (1) the anxiety itself, (2) unhelpful urges to avoid stimuli which trigger it and (3) unhelpful urges to do things to reduce it. We see that there was an initial awareness of numbness and swelling, with associated fear (it is unclear why Annette was so terrified by numbness and swelling – possibly due to a belief that it was very dangerous, or possibly due to unrelated overactivation of the nervous system which was then misattributed to the numbness and swelling). As numbness was now associated with fear, and the mental representation of numbness was naturally associated with actual numbness, Annette became

Chapter 15 - The Anxiety is the Medicine: Exposure and Response Prevention for Discomfort, Escape, Avoidance, Obsessions, Compulsions and Urges in Panic, Phobias, PTSD, OCD, Anger, Addictions, and Unwanted Habits

fearful of the mere thought of numbness. Then she learned in Dr. Low's Recovery group that *"sensations are distressing but not dangerous,"* a form of therapeutic rational disputation or cognitive restructuring years before Ellis or Beck formulated their respective therapies (Ellis does cite Low in his own writings, and one of my professors once invited a member of Recovery to come speak to our CBT oriented doctoral program). She then felt like waking her husband, an urge to do something to reduce the fear. However, she had learned that doing something to reduce the fear (a safety behavior) would reinforce the thought that she was helpless and needed help, and she followed the instruction not to act on the impulse to escape the discomfort (response prevention). She then practiced *non-thinking* by using the Meditation 1.0 technique of *object awareness*, shifting her awareness to the mere sensation of discomfort (mindfulness of bodysense), at which point *it disappeared.*

Abraham Low's (1950, and likely earlier) Recovery Inc. teachings thus contain the modern cognitive behavioral components of cognitive restructuring ("*sensations are distressing but not dangerous*"), exposure (she "lay quietly" and allowed the sensations to continue), response prevention ("I must not act on the impulse" to escape/avoid discomfort), and meditation/mindfulness (selective awareness of the senses). It also anticipated the Open Focus Dissolving Pain technique of Les Fehmi (Fehmi & Robbins, 2010) and Shinzen Young's (2011) sensory mindfulness approach to pain management. Recovery International continues to this day to function as a self-help alternative to psychotherapy, with 500 client-led meetings per week in the U.S., Canada, Ireland and Puerto Rico.

Often in the creation of an anxiety disorder, there is an "establishing event" (in the above narrative, Annette's numbness and swelling, which was likely initially related to the reason for her hospital stay or resulting medical treatment and not caused by anxiety). This is the event that creates the association between certain internal or external environmental events and the anxiety response, followed by the cognitive representation of the events as "dangerous." The event may indeed have been dangerous the first time it happened (e.g., almost choking on a chicken bone), acting as an unconditioned stimulus for fear, with associated internal and external environmental stimuli (including memories in the form of thoughts or images of the event) becoming conditioned stimuli for fear. In the future, objects and experiences associated with the establishing event (e.g., sensations in the throat, hard food substances, and even, through stimulus generalization, chicken eggs, meals in general or thoughts of an upcoming meal) may themselves trigger anxiety and be avoided or escaped from in order to reduce perceived danger of choking, perceived danger of anxiety, or merely the discomfort occasioned by the anxiety/fear (through negative reinforcement, in which a behavior that reduces discomfort becomes more frequent in the future). This same combination of events could lead to a phobia (e.g., fear of eating things with bones); panic disorder with agoraphobia (*fear of fear itself* occurring in certain environments, and avoiding these environments, e.g., fear of having a panic attack when eating, and possibly of associated social embarrassment, and *avoidance* of or escape from social situations involving eating); or posttraumatic stress disorder (with symptoms such as mental re-experiencing of the event, avoidance of associated stimuli, negative thoughts and distressful emotions, heightened nervous system arousal, and possibly depersonalization or derealization). Such establishing events could also feed into OCD process, with obsessing about choking and compulsions aimed at reducing risks of choking.

E/RP involves instructing you, if you feel comfortable with such an approach, to *intentionally and temporarily* make worse exactly the same problem that you want to get rid of. You seek out conditions which trigger your discomfort and *expose* yourself to the discomfort (exposure is always to the discomfort and not to the environmental trigger, a common misunderstanding), then *preventing* the response you would usually do to escape the discomfort. More informally, in the course of your daily life, you would notice the discomfort triggered by the thought of doing something, and rather than avoiding doing it you would do it and allow yourself to feel the discomfort, again without trying to escape from it.

For example, if you are having panic attacks in subways and have conveniently found buses that get you where you need to go, albeit in twice the time (Panic Disorder with Agoraphobia), we have you take the subway more; alternatively (and theoretically, as I've never seen this) if you are having panic attacks in buses and have conveniently found subways that get you where you need to go, albeit in twice the time, we have you take the bus more. If you are afraid of social situations (Social Phobia), we have you socialize more; if you were robbed at gunpoint in the mall parking lot and you're afraid to go to malls (possibly PTSD), we have you imagine it in detail in real time, and (if safe) spend more time in mall parking lots.

Chapter 15 - The Anxiety is the Medicine: Exposure and Response Prevention for Discomfort, Escape, Avoidance, Obsessions, Compulsions and Urges in Panic, Phobias, PTSD, OCD, Anger, Addictions, and Unwanted Habits

If you are afraid of germs and would rather hold it in all day than use a public toilet (Contamination OCD with avoidance), we have you use public toilets even when you don't have a need to; if you check the stove several times each hour after dinner and before going to sleep to make sure you or someone else didn't leave it on (OCD with checking), we have you check it less frequently, perhaps once after dinner and once before sleep. You are then instructed to at other times be aware of the fearful thought and anxiety without reducing these by checking.

If you keep thinking "what if I'm really a serial killer and am going to go crazy and kill someone (OCD Pure O – much more common of a problem than you might think), first we make sure that even though you are having thoughts of killing people you have no intent and that the thoughts are "ego-dystonic" (you find them foreign to your true preferences and distressing rather than acceptable or pleasurable). Because the fact is, real serial killers don't sit around wondering and worrying "what if I'm a serial killer?" They're too busy planning their next murder. Once we are confident you're not a sociopath, we would have you purposely think for several minutes several times a day about all the scenarios in which you might kill people and imagine killing them in all the gory detail.

If you get angry whenever someone suggests that you could have done something differently, with your permission we might use this as a trigger to purposely try and get you angry in the session by having you do things, then suggesting to you other ways you could have done them. Or you might be instructed to tell your spouse to let you know even more frequently what you could have done differently. These verbal provocations are known as "anger barbs," with the interventions termed "barb exposure" (Tafrate & Kassinove, 1998). The goal is to get you more comfortable with just feeling anger without reacting. While E/RP is effective for reducing the anger response, this would best be done under the supervision of a therapist in order to make sure that there is nothing else going on psychologically that could increase the risk that exposure to angry thoughts and anger could lead to acting on these. If you tend to get really, really angry, on a regular basis, and act on it verbally or physically, you might meet diagnostic criteria for Intermittent Explosive Disorder (notice that I didn't say you might "have" Intermittent Explosive Disorder, which would buy into considering it a real thing, disease, entity, dryad/tree nymph, [Ebel, 1974], rather than a social construction by mental health professionals). However, and unfortunately, milder forms of excessive anger are not set on par with excessive sadness, anxiety or fear as a diagnostic category (Kassinove, 1995) – i.e., the DSMs and ICDs have no diagnostic category for "Anger Disorders" (possibly as this would classify so many powerful people at so many levels of government and industry as mentally ill that the whole sh#@ show would collapse).

But back to E/RP. If you are addicted to smoking (nicotine addiction), we could have you keep a cigarette in your shirt pocket at all times, like Kirk Douglas and his father did and, whenever you have the urge to smoke, take it out, look at it, and say "Who's stronger, you - me? I stronger" (Douglas, 2003; a combination of E/RP and cognitive restructuring).

If you have trichotillomania and pull hair out of small patches on your scalp, or pick at your skin, bite your nails or bite your cheeks, we have you feel the discomfort of the physical sensations accompanying the urge and just continue feeling them without enacting the behavior.

As you can see, although these appear to be diverse problems, the E/RP solution is the same: (1) trigger the discomfort if it's not already there, (2) feel the discomfort and (3) don't do what you usually do, or don't refrain from doing what you usually refrain from doing in order to reduce the discomfort.

Exposure therapy for obsessive thoughts involves setting aside time to purposely think about them, rather than trying to stop them. This will naturally increase your anxiety in the short-term, and requires a commitment to tolerate this increased discomfort in exchange for the future reduction in the frequency, duration and salience of the thoughts and a corresponding future decrease in anxiety. It can be useful to purposely think about them long enough to realize that they are only thoughts and not reality, and long enough to realize that you can tolerate the anxiety rather than *needing* to escape from it (here we are adding some cognitive restructuring). It is not necessary to do the exposure until the anxiety completely diminishes. And importantly, if you don't get yourself to do it when you planned to do it, or if you relapse into the unhelpful behaviors you want to stop, *don't give up.* Just because you didn't succeed this time doesn't mean you won't succeed next time, or the time after that, or one out of every 2 times, or even just once in a while. You may fail on one or more, or even on many or most occasions, but it doesn't make you a failure. It makes you someone who is determined

Chapter 15 - The Anxiety is the Medicine: Exposure and Response Prevention for Discomfort, Escape, Avoidance, Obsessions, Compulsions and Urges in Panic, Phobias, PTSD, OCD, Anger, Addictions, and Unwanted Habits

and trying. So keep trying. As they say, One Day at a Time. Look forward not back (except when backing up).

E/RP can be used for overthinking involving thoughts with anxious or angry content, **but should NOT be used for depressive thoughts**. This is because E/RP proceeds from an insight, at some level, that the anxiety and anger are in fact overreactions, and that at the present moment the activation of the nervous system to a level appropriate to fighting or fleeing isn't necessary. When we expose ourselves to the feared situations and thoughts in the absence of any catastrophic outcomes, the brain eventually realizes that there is no imminent danger, and the fight or flight response shuts down. By contrast, when depressed, sad thoughts merely further one's sense of hopelessness and helplessness and increase the depth of the sadness. For sadness and depression, the psychological treatments that work are modifying the cognitive content via cognitive restructuring, modifying the cognitive process via meditation and mindfulness training, and behavioral activation (spending more time doing pleasurable, productive or meaningful activities). For severe depression, medication can be an important supplement to psychological treatment.

While exposure therapy may appear similar to mindfulness, in that one remains aware of the aversive stimulus, there is a crucial difference: Mindfulness consists of being aware of what is already happening, without purposely making it happen or increasing it. Mindfulness for depressive rumination, anxious worry or obsessing is simply being fully aware of it when it occurs and not trying to increase it, decrease it or stop it. Exposure therapy, on the other hand, in addition to being aware of the targets when they spontaneously occur, often involves *purposely* triggering the aversive thoughts, emotions and sensations and *then* being aware of these without trying to reduce them, and even purposely trying to increase them in order to further be aware of them. One exposure technique is interoceptive exposure, in which one purposely hyperventilates or spins in a chair in order to induce shortness of breath, dizziness or tingling sensations in order to *purposely* trigger a panic attack. The components of the panic attack can then be observed for what they are: an uncomfortable combination of thoughts, emotions and sensations that are *not dangerous.* Due to the actual absence of danger, the brain eventually realizes that these experiences are not dangerous by using its implicit *3B or Bed Bath and Beyond rule,*

No Blood, no Broken Bones, no problem,

if we just let them *be*. We replace the thought that they are dangerous and *need* to be stopped, with the rational alternative interpretation that it would be *nice* if they were to stop and that's why we're doing exposure, because it is a research-proven technique to stop them.

Ideally, E/RP should be part of a combined treatment that also includes (1) cognitive restructuring (challenging the thought that there are rational reasons for doing or avoiding what you think you need to do or avoid, by comparing evidence that supports the need to do it and evidence that does not support the need to do it); (2) meditation and mindfulness to train the mind to come back from thinking at will, but *not practiced during the E/RP* as that would defeat the goal of increasing exposure to the scary thoughts and discomfort; and (3) relaxation techniques practiced regularly in order to reduce baseline default sympathetic nervous system arousal but *not practiced during E/RP* for the same reason as above.

Chapter 16 - Mindfulness-Based Pop-Up Blocking: Depressive Rumination, Anxious Worry and Obsessing

"Get back, get back.

Get back."

Lenon & McCartney (1970)

If you've ever had a dog, or had a meal in the house of people with dogs, you may have noticed that some dogs beg at the table for food and some don't. The ones that beg do so because people have fed them at the table. The ones that don't beg are the ones that people have not fed when they have begged in the past. Well,

Thoughts are like begging dogs

(with no insult intended to dogs).

And what are the Golden Rules of being a dog person? (besides loving dogs and not letting them poop on your neighbor's lawn):

(1) **Let sleeping dogs lie (don't purposely think unless necessary), and**

(2) **Don't feed them when they beg (don't engage with a thought just because it has arisen).**

If you invite a dog to eat by holding out food, they will get in the habit of coming to the table to beg for food. If you engage with them by giving them food when they beg, they will continue begging.

Every time that you purposely think, you are reinforcing the general habit of thinking. And every time you engage with an automatic thought that just popped up by itself, you are reinforcing the popping up of thoughts. Dogs need to be fed and people need to think. But if you don't want your dog to beg and disrupt your meal, and you don't want your thoughts to pop up and disrupt your life, feed your dog at a time that is appropriate for the dog and convenient for you, and think at a time that is most productive for that purpose. In short, make your mind a "good dog." Alternatively, make your mind a normal cat for, as a "cat person" recently informed me, cats don't beg. They learn your schedule and wait patiently. (Never having had a pet cat, I'll take his word for it.)

How much would you pay for a button that could turn off rumination, worry and obsessing at will? A lot, right? Negative repetitive thoughts are like website pop-ups. You probably don't click on pop-ups, and instead X them away. And yet, we usually go about our day engaging with whatever thought pops up in our mind, however irrelevant to what we are currently doing and often irrelevant to anything we ever do.

For many people, repetitive thoughts are like pop-ups of a YouTube video that somehow recorded something in our life that makes us feel really bad. If multiple times per day you heard a notification from your phone and when you looked to see what it was you saw a 5 minute pop-up video of your argument with your friend yesterday, or you getting fired next week, or the headache that you had this morning turning out to be a brain tumor, or failing tomorrow's test, or actually getting sick from seeing the word "sick" online and not washing down the computer screen with alcohol, would you hold your phone in front of your face and watch the video to the end? And if you did, when the notification sounded 30 minutes later and you saw the same pop-up video starting, would you again watch the whole thing? Of course not. But isn't this exactly what we do when a negative thought or image pops up in our head and we focus on it and chew on it for minutes or hours at a time?

So what to do? Do the same thing you would do if your phone notification sounded again and you picked it up and saw the video starting. Put the phone down and go back to whatever you were doing. In mindfulness terms, *come back* to awareness of 3 other senses (which could include thinking, if you were engaged in thinking of something useful) most relevant to what you were doing before the thought popped up. Maybe the thought or image stays put and won't budge, but even so, you can still assign the majority of your awareness to three senses other than thinking (or 2 senses other than thinking and the thinking sense focused on the more helpful thoughts) just as if the pop-up video wouldn't let you turn it off you could still put the phone down and continue your activity.

Of course, rumination, worry and obsessing may have content that is important and could benefit from some thinking, but *don't engage with it when it pops up.* If you do, you are teaching the dog to beg, reinforcing the mind's habit of random thinking. If the thought is important, assign a later time when you will purposely think about it in a strategic and time-limited way, say in 5 minutes, or from 7:00 to 7:15 that evening. This is sometimes called assigning "worry time," but I prefer to conceptualize this as "problem solving" time, as it would be silly to purposely spend time worrying (unless the worry is really an obsession, in which case "worry time" is actually E/RP) whereas problem solving can be very useful.

In addition to training the mind to "come back" from depressive rumination, anxious worry and obsessing, cognitive restructuring (challenging negative irrational content of the thoughts and replacing these with more rational, even if not 100% rational or positive content) may be helpful. As previously suggested,

> **Cognitive restructuring and coming back to the senses can be used as a *"one-two punch"* to weaken the habit of negative overthinking.**

You can do whichever you prefer first and see if it works alone. If you prefer to begin with cognitive restructuring, when the thought pops up, challenge it. What is the evidence it's literally true? What is the evidence it might not be literally true? What is a more rational statement that you would bet a large sum of money on? Once you have removed any irrational content from the thought, now you can *come back* and *just be aware of 3 other senses* involved in what you are doing or, if you are doing nothing, just see what is in front of your eyes, hear the ambient sound, be aware of the feeling of your body in space. If you're not a big fan of debating, you could begin with coming back from the thought and *just be aware of 3 other senses.* If the thought tends to recur, then challenge it each time prior to coming back to your senses and, over time, as the frequency, duration and salience of the thought decrease, you could return to just coming back from it without challenging it, taking more of a "been there, done that" attitude toward engaging with it.

Chapter 17 - *Put On Your Robot:* *Depressive Inertia, Decision Rules and Behavioral Activation for Depression*

"The secret is just to say 'Yes!'

and jump off from here."

Shunryu Suzuki

(in Lesser, 2013, p. 255)

"We don't think our way to right action, we act our way to right thinking."

Probably Not Bill W.

("It comes from the Hebrew Concept of Knowledge and it has also been taken from the Greek Concept of Knowledge. Who ever took these two concepts and put them together forming the quote is still a mystery to me ... The Greek Concept of Knowledge is that we think our way in to right action. The Hebrew Concept of Knowledge is that we act our way in to right thinking"; 1Cor13, SoberRecovery.com, 2008)

"'And then we must go,' said the robot, in all seriousness, 'to a party.'"

Douglas Adams

(1982, p. 85; Life, The Universe, and Everything)

> "A body in motion tends to stay in motion.
>
> A body at rest tends to stay at rest."
>
> **My Client's Father Larry**

After Exposure and Response Prevention, Behavioral Activation is the next most paradoxical intervention in behavior therapy. Or, as Groucho Marx once didn't say:

> "Outside of a dog, Behavioral Activation is a man's best friend.
>
> Inside of a dog, there isn't much to do."

If you were to come to me with depression, here's what I would tell you:

(1) When we are feeling pretty good, or not too bad, we often do or don't do things on the basis of the following *decision rule*:

> **What do I feel like doing?**

This rule works, because when we are feeling pretty good, or not too bad, our minds are clear enough to actually generate a list of things that would be potentially fun, productive or meaningful, and if we don't feel like doing one thing, we likely do feel like doing something else.

(2) When we are depressed, the above rule not only doesn't work, it digs us deeper into the hole. This is because when we are depressed, the answer to "What do I feel like doing?" is: "Nothing," or maybe taking a nap, to the extent that that qualifies as "Something" and wasn't covered under "Nothing." So if we ask and answer the question in this way (which, if you've ever been depressed, you don't need me to tell you, but I will anyway), we won't do anything. We will just spend more time isolating ourselves, saying "no" when people ask us to go out, possibly wasting our vacation days by taking sick days, maybe not even getting dressed in the morning, and at (almost) worst sleeping much of the day, going on disability, and having way too much time on our hands for the nothing that we have now made our primary activity.

But there is a solution . . .

Chapter 17 - Put On Your Robot: Depressive Inertia, Decision Rules and Behavioral Activation for Depression

(3) *Throw away the box!* Oops, wrong rule for wrong problem. Let's try again: *Use a new decision rule!*

If you want to spiral up rather than spiral down, one of the most powerful research-based behavioral techniques around (and you *can* quote me on this) is: *Behavioral Activation.* If you're in the biz (on either side of the fake Persian rug) you may know this by a different name, such as "pleasant activity scheduling." I like to refer to it simply as:

Do More Fun Stuff.

Technically, do more *fun or productive or meaningful* stuff, so you can insert a silent "or productive or meaningful" into the above.

However, if you're depressed and we leave it at that, I assure you that when we review your homework at next week's session you will tell me the following: "I tried to do more fun stuff, but I didn't feel like it." This is where the new decision rule comes in, which is:

If I were feeling great, what would I do?

In other words, rather than doing what you feel like doing (nothing), you do what you would do if you felt great (most likely something other than nothing. Unless you are a yogi, in which case you would do nothing, not in the sense of not doing anything, but rather in the sense of *doing* nothing, which technically would amount to doing something, just without a sense of *doership*).

To which we immediately run into the following problem: you don't feel like doing it, and you're pretty sure that even if it used to feel great it won't feel great now, because you're *depressed.* Which may very well be true, but is irrelevant to whether you should do it, because even if you get minimal enjoyment out of doing it at first, you will experience that much more enjoyment than if you didn't do it and stayed in bed binge watching 11,398 hours of General Hospital (474 days 22 hours) and eating 22,796 bags of cheese doodles (at a conservative estimate of 2 bags/hour)(Disclaimer: this isn't a plug either for or against cheese doodles or the chemical in them that makes your hands turn orange – if you want your hands to turn orange without needing multiple organ replacements, carrots would probably be a healthier alternative. Unless you are allergic to constipation, hypercarotinemia, or vitamin A toxicity, in which case you could instead tape pennies to your hands, especially if you are a fan of copper-induced brown ring-shaped markings in your eyes [Kayser-Fleischer rings] or yellowing of the eyes and skin [jaundice]).

But I digress. Think of it like putting jumper cables on your car's battery after leaving the lights on overnight. The battery won't start your car, but it isn't completely dead either. So you put on the cables and connect the other ends to the battery of another car or to one of those souped-up USB chargers. But the battery is not going to regain its charge right away. Even though the engine will immediately start, you will need to run it for a while (either idling or driving – the armchair mechanics on google disagree) to recharge the battery. It's the same with behavioral activation. Even when you get yourself to do an activity that was fun or productive in the past when you felt better, it will likely not be as fun or productive at present. That's normal and that's OK. You are still reaping the benefits of the activation, and if you stick at it you will notice that, over time, the depression will lift (though it will help to integrate this technique with cognitive restructuring, meditation and mindfulness and, if it is a severe depression, possibly with a prescription medication or a prescribed over-the-counter supplement such as SAM-E).

(4) This is where your robot comes in. You do have a robot, right? Of course you do, because you *are* the robot. What I mean is this: Despite your depression, you are perfectly capable of operating your legs, arms and vocal cords (and if you are not, due to other illness or injury, there are still fun or productive things you could add to your day, though it might take some creativity on your part, or a talk with a friend, family member or therapist who could offer some suggestions). What you need to do, then is *just say yes*, and

Put on your robot.

Once having determined what fun or productive thing you would do *if you felt great*, you observe (mindfulness/exposure) the thought "but I don't feel like it" and you respectfully tell it to go to hell (cognitive restructuring). You remind yourself (cognitive restructuring) that you are going to do what is good for you, not what you *feel like* doing (response prevention), and then you *just say yes, put on your robot* (cognitive restructuring) and do it (behavioral activation). You operate your legs, arms and the rest of your body to *make them do* whatever you have decided to do *to accomplish your*

Chapter 17 - Put On Your Robot: Depressive Inertia, Decision Rules and Behavioral Activation for Depression

own goals, including beating depression by being aware of but not obeying dictatorial depressive hopeless/helpless thoughts.

Another little trick I share with my clients is a solution for what I call "*depressive inertia,*" the tendency, when depressed, to continue whatever you are already doing. Inertia is defined as:

> "a property of matter by which it remains at rest or in uniform motion in the same straight line unless acted upon by some external force." (Merriam Webster, n.d. 3)

As depression is a state of de-activation, we are likely to gravitate toward a state of rest, such as by sitting or lying down, as frequently as possible. This means that decisions when depressed are at a high risk of being made when sitting or lying down, in which case *depressive inertia* will favor a tendency to do things which can be done sitting or lying down rather than other things that we might feel like doing *if we were feeling great* (and the depressive inertia will thus short-circuit enactment of decisions arrived at by use of the new decision rule). A simple solution when depressed is therefore:

Don't make decisions sitting or lying down.

Alternatively,

Stand up before deciding whether to stay seated.

For example, imagine you are sitting on the couch, feeling depressed, kind of thinking you should go for a run. You know not to ask yourself "What do I feel like doing?," as the answer will be to continue sitting on the couch. So you ask yourself "What would I do if I felt great?" and you answer "I would go for a run." OK, well you're halfway there. The problem is, you will likely then think "but I don't feel like it," because your depressive inertia makes it easier to stay seated. If, however, you stand up and ask yourself what you would do if you felt great, and answer that you would go for a run, the fact that you are already standing makes it psychologically easier to stay standing, *put on your robot,* put on your robot's sneakers and go for the run.

This principle works well as a remedy for spending the morning in bed. If upon waking you ask yourself what you feel like doing, or even if you ask yourself what you would do if you felt great, you risk staying in bed. Therefore, you should, as Shunryu Suzuki instructed:

JUMP OUT OF BED!

Or, in accordance with my own advice to *utilize* (as Milton Erickson might say) and capitalize upon the principle of inertia:

Stand up before deciding whether to stay in bed.

In other words, put on your robot before its thinking comes online.

If you were one of my webcam therapy clients, at this point I might say to you:

"So, you know what your homework is?"

And you might respond like one of my clients did last week:

"Yes. Treat my body like a robot, treat my thoughts like they're lies, exposure and response prevention, and what would I do if I was feeling great."

I couldn't have put it better myself.

Chapter 18 - *A Closed Mouth Gathers No Foot:* How to Shut Up

"A sharp tongue can cut your own throat."

Portuguese Metalcore Band

More than a Thousand (2010)

"An eye for an eye

a tooth for a tooth

will only make the world

full of rich eye doctors and dentists."

Grandma Densei (1922)

"Silence is true wisdom's best reply."

(Attributed all over the Internet to Euripides, but apparently absent from his writings. It appears that someone decided to self-publish Euripides' play Hippolytus and sell it for $9.99 [Nine Ninety-Nine Euripides, 2017] and made up the subtitle "Silence is True Wisdom's Best Reply" [which they have every right to do, never claiming that it was said by Euripides]. This was then picked up by human and nonhuman bots, disseminating fake news about Euripides that will probably be what he is remembered for. The actual text of Hippolytus, which doesn't contain the phrase in question, is free [Free Euripides, 2021])

"Q: What is K.M.S.?

A: Keep Mouth Shut, the golden rule."

(I kid you not, that was my fortune cookie this evening after writing this chapter, 2/9/19, but I'm sure that it will eventually be attributed to Agamemnon or someone online. Which will be a dead giveaway as Agamemnon was a mythological figure)

When was the last time you got really angry and said something to someone that was so brilliant that you wrote it down so you wouldn't forget, and later felt so proud of that you bragged about it at work?

The thing about anger is that it makes us stupid. It turns off the part of our brain that thinks all the smart stuff, and makes us say things that create such a mess that we then spend days, years or lifetimes walking around in those white moon suits spraying the fallout with that special fallout spray. It temporarily takes (on average) about 30 to 40 points off of our I.Q. (don't quote me on that). As a reference point, if you have an average to above average I.Q., as do most of us who are writing and reading this book (somewhat lower for those who are eating it), anger will bring you from your I.Q. of about 100-120 down to about 60-90, in other words, to about the scholastic equivalent of a 3rd grader at the low end to a max of about the smartest of the most intellectually challenged 25th percentile of the population (again, no quotes, please, as these facts are potentially *alternative* and could change after I've had my morning coffee). But you get the point (unless you're angry).

I'm a big fan of parsimony and elegant solutions (known in the biz as K.I.S.S.), and the elegant solution to not messing up your life by saying things you'll later regret when you're angry, according to 29 meta-analyses of over 500,000 double blinded clinical trials published in 498 peer reviewed journals edited by Nobel Laureates is:

Shut up.

How do you shut up? By *Not Talking*.

Chapter 18 - A Closed Mouth Gathers No Foot: How to Shut Up

How do you not talk? By *Shutting Your Mouth* (can you believe you actually paid to have me tell you this? Welcome to Cognitive Behavior Therapy). The sad thing is, you *do* need me to say it, and I too need to keep remembering it, in order to do it.

Of course, we are all *capable* of closing our mouths, and we do it pretty often, sometimes even when we are eating or when we're hiking and find ourselves in a gnat cloud.

So why don't we just keep our mouths closed when we are angry? Because we've suddenly been transported back to 3rd grade and our brain won't be fully developed for another 16 to 17 years (please remember the *no quote* rule).

In order to remediate this problem, it is helpful to look at the full sequence of events occurring from the time that someone says or does something that pisses us off to the time that we say something that makes us the bad guy:

Sequence of Events Leading to Losing Our $#!t

(1) They *say or do* something,

(2) We *think* WTF,

(3) We *feel* anger,

(4) We *think* of saying something hurtful,

(5) We have an *urge* to say it,

(6) We *think* it's a good idea to obey the urge,

(7) We *say* what we think,

(8) *Effects happen* that we could have foreseen if our frontal cortex were still online,

(9) *We're sorry*, but

(10) *The damage is done*, we have no friends left, we're single again, we have to look for a new job, we're in jail, etc.

So how do we use this knowledge to keep our mouth shut? By choosing an entry point with access to an important, causal and modifiable *target variable* in the above causal sequence and intervening in some way.

POTENTIAL TARGET VARIABLES

Event 1 involving ***The World*** can be prevented or interrupted by *leaving civilization and living off the land* if you know how to tell the difference between nutritious and poisonous plants and can distinguish between bears you can escape from by "bopping them in the nose" (black bears; advice from a campground brochure) versus those that this will antagonize but which might cut you a break if you play dead (grizzlies). If we are not endowed with such knowledge, we could instead buy a houseboat, but then we would get angry at the waves, or become the hermit down the street who nobody's ever actually seen and pay someone through the mail slot to deliver food to the back porch. But being *that guy* is highly overrated and it's hard to wipe the eggs off your windows the day after Halloween which just becomes a new Event 1. We can also prevent or minimize Event 1 by making nicer friends or spending less time interacting with annoying relatives or colleagues. Finally, we can re-evaluate and respect our own personal boundaries, and respectfully tell people when they have crossed these. Most likely, however, is that as long as you are a passenger on Spaceship Earth, and even if you are eventually a passenger on interplanetary or interstellar vehicles or relocate to a different planet or star system, there will always be people (or aliens, but then technically *you* will be the alien) and events that do not behave the way you prefer. And so preventing, avoiding or escaping Event 1 is not really a sustainable option. In behavior analytic lingo, it is causal and important, but often not modifiable.

Events 2, 4 and 6 involving ***Thoughts*** can be prevented or interrupted by being aware of the cognitive content or meanings (mindfulness); heeding the advice of the wise old bumper sticker: *Don't believe everything you think*; evaluating the evidence for and against the truth of what we are thinking (cognitive restructuring); *being aware of 3 other senses* (stopping thinking); and realizing that a thought is just something happening, a phenomenon in the phenomenal world, like the color of the wall, and has nothing to do with you, *because if you are aware of it, it isn't you, it is the object and you are the subject, pure awareness, still, joyful, eternal.*

Event 3 regarding ***Emotions or Feelings*** can be prevented or interrupted by being aware of the anger (mindfulness) as a *physical sensation*, observing where in the body we feel it, and its shape, intensity and movement. We can further reduce it by realizing (cognitive restructuring) that anger is like fire. If

Chapter 18 - A Closed Mouth Gathers No Foot: How to Shut Up

someone lit our hair on fire our first response would be to put out the fire rather than teach them a lesson, after which there will be ample time to educate them (if we still want to) after the fire is out and our I.Q. has returned to normal or above. Finally, we can be aware that an emotion is just something happening, a phenomenon in the phenomenal world, like the color of the wall, and has nothing to do with you, *because if you are aware of it, it isn't you, it is the object and you are the subject, pure awareness, still, joyful, eternal.*

Event 5 involving **Urges** can be prevented or interrupted by being aware of the urge as a *physical sensation* (mindfulness), realizing that a physical sensation is just something happening, a phenomenon in the phenomenal world, like the color of the wall, and has nothing to do with you, *because if you are aware of it, it isn't you, it is the object and you are the subject, pure awareness, still, joyful, eternal.*

Event 7 involving **Opening Your Big Mouth** can be prevented or interrupted if, you guessed it, you would just **Shut Up.**

Event 8 can be prevented by addressing Events 1 through 7.

Event 9 should be repeated until the cows come home.

Event 10 Is What It Is, Isn't What It Isn't, Shift Happens, better luck next time, you have the right to an attorney, and if you cannot afford an attorney, one will be anointed.

Chapter 19 - *Happy People Aren't Mean: When Others Are Having A Bad Day, Week, Month, Year, Decade or Life*

Realtor: "A neighbor knocked on my door and wanted me to come down and shoot a bear outside the building. I have a 9 mm. A 9 mm leaves a small hole going in and a big hole going out."

> **Me**: "Guess if I see a bear with a band-aid on one side and a bandage on the other I'll know it was him."

Realtor: "I wouldn't shoot a bear."

> **Me**: "You wouldn't?"

Realtor: "Not only would I not shoot a bear, I wouldn't shoot a bear on Main Street."

Dinner Conversation with My Realtor (3/4/19)

Chapter 19 - Happy People Aren't Mean: When Others Are Having A Bad Day, Week, Month, Year, Decade or Life

DISTANT REALMS

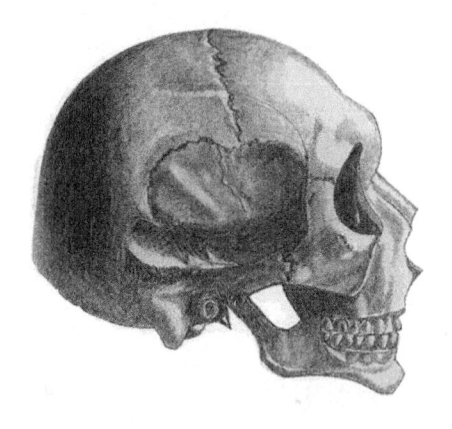

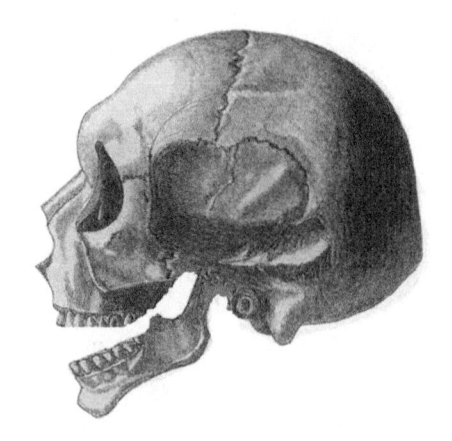

"What do you mean, 'How are you?' How the hell do I look!?"

SEIDEN

My realtor is a happy guy. And happy people aren't mean. Even to bears.

Those acquainted with antiquated psychobabble will no doubt be familiar with the myth that "*depression is anger turned inward.*" While this is delusional hogwash (let's not forget that Freud was a cocaine fiend), it does contain, when turned inside out and re-thunk, like playing a Beatles record backward and becoming enlightened to the fate of Paul, the insight that

Meanness is Misery Turned Outward.

That's right, when people are mean to you, it's because they're miserable. How do I know this? I don't, really, but it seems to follow from my, and perhaps your, observation that *Happy People Aren't Mean*. For example, none of us are angels and all of us have probably said something outright mean at some point in our lives, last Tuesday for example. Can you remember ever saying something mean to someone when you were feeling happy?

Now, you might protest that most of the people who are mean to you seem pretty happy. They're the cool kids or the popular people at work, and they often have more power or money than you. So what don't they have to be happy about?

That is a reasonable question. Give me a moment.

OK, it doesn't take into account how they became part of the "in" group, and how they gained their power and money in the first place. Call me cynical, but my guess, given their combination of meanness and social standing/money/power, is that they are *sociopaths.* I am not saying that all people who appear charming, rich and powerful are sociopaths, just the ones who are mean. We can cut the other ones a break, as they seem to be aiming for the win-win, so it might not hurt to play along.

I am also not saying that all people who are mean are sociopaths. Just the ones who get rich and powerful despite their meanness, suggesting that they are skilled at being nice when they need to be and mean when they don't, which is pretty much the definition of sociopathy (social pathology).

How does knowing that happy people aren't mean and that mean people are miserable help you deal with them? First of all, it takes you off the hook. Mean people will try to make you feel that there is something wrong with *you,* or that *you* have done something wrong (known as *gaslighting,* after the Alfred Hitchcock film *Gaslight*), which they can only accomplish if you believe them. They are trying to make *you* feel bad. By remembering that you actually felt good before they tried to brainwash you, and that *they* are the ones who feel so bad that they are using their sick trick of trying to make you feel bad so they can then feel they are better than you, you can turn the tables on them (in your mind, which is all that really matters).

If they really thought they were better than you, why would they be expending so much energy trying to make you think you are worse than them in order to feel better themselves? Because they *don't really think they are better than you.* Your happiness is getting on their nerves, and they will do whatever they can to take it away. Because you have something they don't have. You may not have their power, you may not have their money, but you seem *too happy* and that pisses them off because they are, in fact, miserable.

Chapter 19 - Happy People Aren't Mean: When Others Are Having A Bad Day, Week, Month, Year, Decade or Life

What to do about it? If you can see through their meanness to their pathetic misery, or even to their sociopathy (which is a serious psychiatric disorder) maybe you can find it in yourself to feel badly for them. Here are some suggestions:

Plan A: Compassion. Loving Kindness. Turn the Other Cheek. Easier said done. Hint: First Remove the Beam Out of Your Own Eye.

Plan B: Give them a good bop in the nose. Wait, that was plan B for what to do if the black bear attacks, or when your wimpy F14 Tomcat co-pilot pushes the eject button after you just lost an engine at 1544 miles per hour, even though you *told* him that you can take it in with just the one engine and if he pushes the eject button you'll break his nose (which my realtor did to his fellow fighter pilot right after recovering from the broken arm and leg he got when he landed on the ocean).

Another little trick you can use is to challenge your own belief (cognitive restructuring) that what they are saying or implying (that there is something wrong with you) is true. Because ultimately, they are getting to you not because of what *they* believe (or pretend to believe) about you, but because of what *you* believe about you. If the pain in the ass in the next cubicle said something to you like "How can you be so stupid. Don't you know that Emperor Zorthan of Star System Thromdal B expressly forbade us to place page numbers in the bottom margin," you probably wouldn't take it personally because you would know they were nuts or getting a little too friendly with the budtender (which are not necessarily mutually exclusive, though neither are they necessarily correlated).

But what about people in your life whom you love, who you know (or are pretty sure) aren't sociopaths, but are mean to you from time to time. I would suggest time travel. Right now they are saying something mean, but chances are earlier in the day, or yesterday, or last week, you had a really good time together. So time travel. Even though they said something mean just now, superimpose your memory of a fun time together over this moment. After all, it's just arbitrary that now is now. Yesterday, now was tomorrow, and tomorrow, now will be yesterday. And until you open the box, the cat is both alive and dead (in your mind, where it doesn't matter, since there's actually no cat). So why react to "now" rather than to yesterday or tomorrow or to the live-dead cat? It's just a silly habit that can be changed, like all habits.

To sum up, when someone is mean to you, remember:

(1) Happy people aren't mean;

(2) Meanness is misery turned outward;

(3) It's better to be happy-you than to be pathetic-mean-them;

(4) Sociopathy is a serious psychiatric disorder, we can have compassion for those less fortunate than ourselves, and if we are ourselves sociopaths then we can at least commiserate;

(5) Even if they are not sociopaths, at the moment they are behaving like sociopaths (introducing pathology into a social relationship), and we can have compassion for their temporary insanity;

(6) Time travel; and

(7) If all else fails, give them a good bop to the nose and hope they have been possessed by a black bear rather than a brown bear or polar bear, in which latter 2 cases you're pretty much screwed.

Chapter 20 - *Do Tomorrow You a Solid:* Beating Low Frustration Tolerance (LFT) and Procrastination (P)

"If you're going to do something tonight
that you'll be sorry for tomorrow morning,
sleep late."

Henny Youngman

"Imagine your face
there in their place
standing outside their snowshoes."

Uncle Dealy Stan Densei

One thing that Freud got right was the pleasure principle. He no doubt got lots of things right (hard not to, given how much he wrote, like an aardvark given enough time will, by chance, eventually type Alice's Adventures in Wonderland, if he has one of those special aardvark keyboards. Fun fact: The aardvark is the only non-extinct species of the order Tubulidentata - "tubes for teeth" - and it is in many countries illegal to extract their teeth to use as straws). Unfortunately, the things he got wrong have caused so much wasted time, money and energy on the part of therapists and suffering clients that it's hard to see past them.

This is, however, just a thought, a bias, so be careful about believing it. I have not read the research on psychoanalysis as compared to, for example, cognitive behavior therapy, which is empirically supported for depression, anxiety and other common problems that people go to therapists for. I'm merely stating an opinion, as I would in conversation, but you would do better to take it with a grain of salt and research it yourself, if interested.

One thing Freud did get right, to continue from where the mental hyperlink took us astray, and nobody can possibly make a case otherwise, is that people behave to increase pleasure and decrease pain, and when they don't, it is because the pain they are willing to suffer is outweighed by a higher pleasure, or good, that they seek (or a higher pain, or bad, that they fear).

The Buddha based his entire system upon this, which he called the Second Noble Truth. The First Noble Truth is that Shift Happens. The second is that Shift Has Causes, which he identified as the Three Poisons: Greed, Anger, and Delusion.

> **Greed is wanting what we don't have (so we chase what we think will bring us pleasure);**
>
> **Anger is not wanting what we do have or expect to have (so we smash what we think is bringing us pain or will bring us pain);**
>
> **Delusion is confusion or ignorance, which in cognitive therapy we refer to as *irrational thinking*.**

Albert Ellis pointed to how we sabotage ourselves and our goals due to Low Frustration Tolerance (LFT). Here, we have a goal, but (think we) cannot tolerate the hard work, or sacrificed pleasure, that are required to achieve it. We are stuck in the short view, calculating a cost/benefit ratio biased by the cognitive distortion known as "emotional reasoning" in which our emotion *right now* (aversion to working on the means) shapes our decision regarding whether to work on it to accomplish the desired end.

Unfortunately, the perceived cost is supercharged by present emotion, whereas the benefit remains just a thought in some distant, hypothetical, star system. It's like when George Bush Senior ("Now, I'm President of the United States and I'm not going to eat any more broccoli") compared pork rinds with tobasco sauce (his favorite) to broccoli and imprisoned the latter in the White House dungeon.

Chapter 20 - Do Tomorrow You a Solid: Beating Low Frustration Tolerance (LFT) and Procrastination (P)

When we are depressed and give in to LFT by making decisions on the basis of emotions rather than thought, we often exaggerate the difficulty of the thing we are avoiding. For example, the "hard work" may be merely bending down to pick up a scrap of paper lying on the floor that we've passed over and over on our way from the bed to the fridge and from the fridge to the bed thinking "I really should pick that up and throw it away. Nah, I'll do it later."

In behavioral terms, procrastination often involves the following sequence of events: Thinking of something that would be useful to do, having negative thoughts about doing it (e.g., thinking that it will be difficult, unenjoyable, a waste of time, imperfect or scary), having negative emotions triggered by the thoughts (e.g., low mood, anxiety, anger), thinking of something else we would rather do, deciding to do the other thing, and feeling a reduction in the negative mood. This behavioral avoidance is then negatively reinforced (becomes more likely in the future) due to the reduction in the negative mood and often positively reinforced by a better experience of doing what we decided to do instead. The solution involves combining cognitive restructuring; exposure and response prevention; and behavioral activation. Namely,

> 1. **Cognitive Restructuring**: Challenge the thoughts leading to not wanting to do the activity;
>
> 2. **Exposure**: Feel the negative emotions or sensations (some variety of low mood/lethargy, anxiety, or anger);
>
> 3. **Response Prevention**: Decide not to do the alternative activity or non-activity;
>
> 4. **Behavioral Activation**: Do the task even though you don't want to.

In short,

Challenge. Feel. Do.

We've also seen a behavioral technique for accomplishing things that we don't feel like doing, that is, **Put On Your Robot** in the chapter on Behavioral Activation. Another technique is . . . you guessed it:

Time Travel.

Well, maybe you didn't guess it, but I'm sure you were getting close. Or not. Specifically, you need to make friends with your doppelganger, namely:

Tomorrow You,

who from your perspective is naturally "Tomorrow Me," though, from where I'm sitting, it's very clearly "Tomorrow You."

Tomorrow Me is, God willing, who I will be tomorrow. Whatever I choose to do today, tomorrow (next week, next year, next decade) will be here before I know it. That's just how time, space and consciousness work. And Tomorrow Me will live in a body and world created by Today Me.

When I succumb to LFT, Today Me is basically saying to Tomorrow Me: I don't care about you. Let that sink in. Whenever I decide to do what I feel like doing right now, or to not do what I don't feel like doing right now, ignoring the consequences for *me, myself,* I am telling Tomorrow Me: I don't care about you. Which is pretty sad and, in a way, the logical extreme of either selfishness or selflessness, I can't quite figure out which. I'm being *so* selfish or *so* selfless that I'm valuing *my own* current wants over *my own* future well-being. This would appear to be Buddha's greed, anger and delusion all rolled up in one. Greedy for current pleasure, averse to current sacrifice and oblivious to the absurdity of it all.

But what if, as Adyashanti counsels, we were to treat ourselves like we were someone whom we actually cared about? Then, perhaps we would do what would make Tomorrow Me happy. As they say, *"hoy por tí, mañana por yo."*

What I am here proposing as the *Tomorrow Me Solution* (TMS)(if you call a mental health clinic, it might be better not to ask for this by its initials, unless you want your head surrounded by giant magnets) can be applied to any number of things you are doing or not doing that are negatively impacting Tomorrow Me's quality of life. Some common ones are: staying up late doing things you enjoy, trading an extra hour or two of entertainment tonight for 16 or more hours of sleep deprived misery tomorrow; increasing rather than decreasing your credit card debt each month while decreasing rather than increasing your savings; smoking; drinking; gambling; eating junk food; watching CNN and FOX, the list is endless.

Chapter 20 - Do Tomorrow You a Solid: Beating Low Frustration Tolerance (LFT) and Procrastination (P)

You could make this easier by doing the following: When you are at the decision point (you know, that moment when you say to yourself "I really shouldn't do this, I'll be sorry" quickly followed by "screw it, I'm doing it," such as punching holes in the walls at Fred's MRCC house parties, which I can assure Fred I never personally engaged in - I'm broken-bone averse - but which my mother did ask me about when, as a realtor, she was showing it to clients – probably around the time that Myron Bolitar appeared in her backyard and saved her from Art Teacher and Ascot Bite), stop and do this exercise for about 30 seconds:

(1) Imagine being Tomorrow You (Next Week You, Next Month You, Next Year You, etc.), sitting, standing or lying down right where you are at the decision point, and imagine thinking and feeling what you will be thinking or feeling at that moment about the decision you're about to make if you decided to give in to the LFT.

(2) Now do the same, but imagining thinking and feeling what you will be thinking or feeling at that moment about the decision you're about to make if you decided NOT to give in to the LFT.

If you decide to give in on a given occasion, that's OK, don't beat yourself up over it, what's done is done, "One Day At A Time" and so on. Tomorrow's another day (except for North Pole polar bears, arctic foxes, ringed seals, black legged kittiwakes, northern fulmars, snow buntings, unidentified shrimps and amphipods and sea anemones for whom tomorrow is sometimes a distant month; WorldAtlas.com, 2022), and you can learn from the consequences of your choices, now that you are more AWARE of what's really going on. Just try to keep Tomorrow You in mind a little more often, and eventually it will become a win-win for both of you.

Chapter 21 - *It Is What It Is. Unless It Isn't:* Perfect Imperfection

"We should find perfection in imperfection."

Zen Master Shunryu Suzuki

(Zen Mind Beginner's Mind, 2003/1970, p. 103)

"One day I sat thinking, almost in despair;

a hand fell on my shoulder and a voice said reassuringly:

cheer up, things could get worse.

So I cheered up and, sure enough,

things got worse."

James Haggerty

(Eighth White House Press Secretary, 1953-1961)

"It is not imperfect or unkind reality which makes millions of humans miserable, but their unthinking addiction to Irrational Idea No. 9: *The idea that people and things should be different from the way they are and that it is catastrophic if perfect solutions to the grim realities of life are not immediately found.* This idea is idiotic for several reasons . . ."

Ellis & Harper

A Guide to Rational Living (1962, p. 162)

Chapter 21 - It Is What It Is. Unless It Isn't: Perfect Imperfection

I remember one day as a kid, sitting at the piano, getting really frustrated that I couldn't play something correctly. Kind of like how I started to feel trying to remember how to spell "eighth" above. After investigating why in the world it has a "gh" in the middle, I learned that

> "Spelling substitution of -gh- for a "hard H" sound was a Middle English scribal habit, especially before -t-. In some late Old English examples, the middle consonant was represented by a yogh." (Fight, 2022, cited in Eighth, 2022)

Leaving aside for the moment that no self-respecting anglophone would ever even think of pronouncing "eight" with a "hard H" (ay-HHHH-th?), and without further hyperlinking from the initial intent of this chapter to find out what a "yogh" is, gratuitously adding a "g" and an "h" to the middle of words that have neither a "g" nor an "h" sound strikes me more as compounding a problem than arriving at a solution. In short, if a 60-year-old pseudointellectual after writing nearly 200 pages of a marginally intelligible book without major orthographic catastrophes can't remember how to spell a word, it really has no business continuing to exist and torture generations of his fellow pre-senile citizens, not to mention innocent schoolchildren and Tralfamadorians trying to learn English to blend in.

Now, one might think that we could resolve the issue by merely deciding, collectively, to change the spelling of "eight" to something more sensible, like "ayt." However, and unfortunately, "eight" is just the tip of the iceberg. It turns out that the real problem is the unholy alliance between the letters "g" and "h" that plagues the English language by infiltrating countless words that contain neither or just one of their sounds. For example, in the present volume alone, the combination "gh" appears, at last count, 1982 times (including, with some overlap, 986 times for "ugh," 976 times for "igh," 929 times for "ough," 62 times for "eigh," and 7 times for "aigh") with 3 times for "agh" (not counting this one) which we'll give a pass as all three instances involve "spaghetti" which at least has a "g" sound in it and tastes good. As this issue is beyond the scope of the present exposition, I will leave it to you, Dear Readers, to lobby your local representatives to #FixEnglish and, in the glorious tradition of "spelling reform" (Spelling Reform, 2022), bring it in line with more humane modes of communication such as Esperanto and Serbo-Croation (Phonemic Orthography, 2022).

But getting back to piano day. I probably started banging on the keys, and my father came and sat next to me, assessed the situation (not difficult, as he'd been in the kitchen suffering through my massacre of the piece more than I), and said "If you always want everything to be perfect, you're never going to be happy." Funny the things you remember.

As a psychologist, I've often had occasion to pass on this wisdom to clients. But I add a twist that I must have picked up in my Eastern readings and practices, that of Perfect Imperfection. By this is meant that even if something is not "perfect" (perfectly what you *want* it to be), it is nevertheless perfectly what it *is*. If there is a scratch on your watch, or a scar on your body, or a blemish on your reputation, it may not be what you would *prefer* or what most people would think of as *perfect*, but it is nevertheless perfectly what it is, perfectly imperfect.

Accordingly, in my office I have a wooden sign saying "It Is What It Is" that I picked up at American's oldest continuously operating Farmer's Market in Lancaster, Pa. Well, it's only open Tuesdays, Fridays, and Saturdays, but on those days it *is* open continuously from 6 to 4, or from 6 to 2, depending on which website you look at.

Case in point: Say, for example, you want to help your 8-year-old granddaughter Gussie Myrna write an essay about computers. She's crying because she doesn't know what to write and you figure what could it hurt if you helped out a little. Or maybe she's crying because your kid named her Gussie Myrna and the nurse at the hospital wasn't brave enough to change it to something else on the birth certificate. Regardless, she needs help with the essay, her parents don't have their own copy of the 1968 World Book Encyclopedia so they aren't in a position to help her, and as the real purpose of "schools" is to babysit rather than to teach anyone anything it doesn't really matter whether she writes the essay or you do, and you write faster which will give her more time to clean the horse stable so you can binge watch another 6 episodes of *Shameless*. As you don't know anything about computers and still use a flip phone, you walk over to the shelf, pull out volume 4, or Ci to Cz of your trusty 1968 World Book Encyclopedia, take a mechanical pencil out of your pocket protector, grab a pencil sharpener, put back the pencil sharpener (as mechanical pencils don't need to be sharpened, silly), locate an eraser, piece of paper and slide-rule (one must always be prepared) in your briefcase, and start copying:

Chapter 21 - It Is What It Is. Unless It Isn't: Perfect Imperfection

COMPUTER

COMPUTER is a machine that handles information with amazing speed. It works with such information as names and addresses, book titles, lists of items sold in stores, mathematical problems, and weather forecasts. A computer handles information in the form of numbers. It solves problems dealing with words by changing them into problems dealing with numbers. The fastest computers can do millions of arithmetic problems in a few seconds.

Businessmen use computers for bookkeeping and accounting. A computer keeps track of sales, customer payments, and the amount of stock in warehouses. It figures out employees' wages and prints their paychecks. Many banks have computers to record the amount of money deposited or withdrawn by each customer. Engi-

"Computer [no, not 'a computer,' just 'computer,' according to the 1968 Internet 1.0] is a machine that handles information with amazing speed. It works with such information as names and addresses, book titles, lists of items sold in stores, mathematical problems, and weather forecasts ... Special machines are used to put information and instructions into a computer [don't ask me why here they used an 'a']. One of the most important of these machines is similar to a tape recorder. It records information in the form of tiny magnetic spots on a plastic tape. This machine 'reads' the tape and sends information to the computer in the form of electric signals. A piece of magnetic tape about an inch long could hold the names, addresses, and telephone numbers of 15 persons ... Computers of the Future will be used more and more to give immediate answers to problems ... Each 'customer' will communicate directly with the computer by telephone or by means of a keyboard machine similar to a typewriter. The computer will handle many questions at the same time. It will give each questioner a spoken reply, a typed answer, or information projected onto a screen similar to that of a television set." (Linick, 1969, p. 740)

The next afternoon you get a call from the school saying they would like you to come in for a meeting. Hmm, wonder what *that's* about.

I once had a client who saw my sign and said he hated when people say "It Is What It Is." We figured out that he saw it as invalidating, meaning that something he thought was important didn't matter to the person he was talking to such as, in this case, his psychologist. This became a teaching moment (I could have just turned the sign around, but the damage was done), and we played out possible meanings and intentions.

"It Is What It Is" could certainly be said in a mean spirited or oblivious way by a non-empathetic person who may be correct but knows or doesn't know the effect of saying such to the other. It could also be said by someone who equates "it" with what they *think* "it" is, rather than what it really is, and "is" with how they *think* it will remain even though their interlocutor hopes or has evidence to the contrary.

In the end, the concept itself is blameless even if used insensitively, maliciously or untruthfully. Used correctly, it embodies the Acceptance phase of suffering, that comes after any initial shock, anger and depression, in whichever order and however intense these may be experienced after a negative event.

When things aren't going our way, it can be helpful to stop and just be aware of what is going on, step back mentally, and observe it from the outside as simply What Is. However undesired, or even terrible as it may be (no, I'm not going to go all Ellis on you, and say something like "so, you lost 4 fingers, it could have been worse, you could have lost 5"), be aware of its Perfect Imperfection. We can allow ourself to rage against it, cry out at it, but from time to time we can just stop and be aware of it, and be aware of the I that is aware, the awareness itself, the still, silent space, within which the rage, the cry, arises – and vanishes.

The 5 Laws of Imperfection

Everything IS perfectly what it IS.

If it IS imperfect, it IS perfectly imperfect.

Nothing IS good or bad but thinking makes it so (Shakespeare).

Perfection IS not good, and imperfection IS not bad. They just ARE.

So don't even think of sending your food back to the kitchen.

(Sign on wall at the Grub-Is-Us Eatery and Watering Hole, Westeros)

Chapter 22 - *You're on a Need to Know Basis, and You Don't: Embracing Uncertainty*

> "If God had wanted Man to know the future,
> She would have given him crystal balls."
>
> **Grandma Densei (1922)**

Reader Advisory: Word has it that Roger Zelazny's entire Hugo-winning novel *Lord of Light*, a sci-fi version of Hesse's Siddhartha (itself a fictional biography of the Buddha), was mostly a set-up for the moment when a character with epilepsy, known as "the Shan," was hit by a fit (get it?). Similarly, the present chapter, possibly even this whole book, *may* have been birthed by a need for an appropriate venue for the above quip by Grandma Densei. This is, of course, mere conjecture.

Many of us are risk-averse, preferring the devil we know to the devil we don't. So we stay in dead end jobs or never venture far from the beliefs we were raised with, and take the road most traveled, missing out on what could have been.

While there is wisdom in "better safe than sorry," an irrationally conservative appraisal of what is necessary to keep us safe can eventually end in sorrow over missed opportunities.

In actuality, we are flying by the seat of our pants during every waking moment. We never know what the next moment could bring. We shift our

Chapter 22 - You're on a Need to Know Basis, and You Don't: Embracing Uncertainty

weight to get out of a chair, not even considering that at any moment the chair leg could crack and we could fall over and break our back. We eat granola for breakfast without an inkling that a hard clump is about to break a tooth. We drive to work mostly oblivious to the possibility of being hit by a truck. We stroll through the mall without a thought of a bomb exploding the next second.

And yet, from time to time some of us find ourselves refusing to make certain decisions without assurance of absolute certainty. We know we hate our job but keep putting off looking for a new one because we don't know whether the next one might be worse. We've been single for years, and want to be in a relationship, but refuse to start dating because we don't know how many people we'll have to date before we meet "the one," or whether we'll ever even meet them after all of that effort. Someone we love behaves in a way that drives us crazy, without realizing it, but we don't say anything because we're afraid of how they might react.

The solutions here are:

(1) **Mindfulness**: Be aware of your goal and of the uncertainty that keeps you from pursuing it;

(2) **Cognitive Disputation/Restructuring**: Challenge the thought "I can't do anything until I know for sure what will happen," and evaluate the evidence available to you currently regarding the likelihood of favorable and unfavorable outcomes; and

(3) **Behavioral Activation**: Make a decision and act on it, by *putting on your robot* and *giving Tomorrow You a gift*.

UNCERTAINTY IN OBSESSIVE COMPULSIVE DISORDER

Uncertainty of an extreme nature, and resulting paralysis, escape or avoidance is the cornerstone of obsessive-compulsive disorder (OCD) with compulsions or without compulsions (OCD Pure O), in which one is perpetually asking oneself "but *what if* X," or "how can I know *for certain* that Y."

OCD is a magnet for one's greatest fears. The brain becomes like a spinning clothes dryer, vortex or whirlpool that sucks in fearful thoughts and spins them round and round.

If one's current greatest fear is getting a scratch on the car that one saved up for over the past 5 years, one might go check the garage every hour to make sure nobody went in and knocked something into it causing a scratch. If one's greatest fear is of harm coming to one's dog, one might obsess about "What if I really hate animals and am going to lose it and poison my dog." If one's greatest fear is losing respect at work, one might obsess on "How can I know I won't make a programming mistake that shuts down the network for hours and loses our clients millions of dollars." If one's greatest fear is that one is of the opposite sexual orientation from what one wants to be and is really lying to oneself and one's partner, one might obsess about "How can I know I'm really gay/straight?"

The rule of thumb here is that when someone actually has OCD and is obsessed with "What if I'm really X," or "What if I do X," not only are they not X, but they are the last person who would ever be or do X. When someone is deathly afraid that they will murder their dog, it is because their dog's safety and well-being is their greatest concern, injury to their dog is their greatest fear, and they are the LAST person who would ever harm their dog.

In OCD, the cognitive error is the belief that "thinking about X means I want to do X." OCD is an extreme case of overvalued ideation, when in fact the truth is the opposite. Thinking about X really means that the thought of X triggers extreme fear. The reason I'm thinking so much about X is because doing X is the farthest thing from what I really want, which is the opposite of X. This being so, the *thought* of it is supercharged with fear. My brain, which is programmed to be hypervigilant to danger and to *mental representations of danger*, in order to help alert me to danger to keep me alive, then gets caught in a positive feedback loop. I think about the thing that scares me (e.g., killing my dog), this triggers fear, the fear supercharges the thought that triggered it (e.g., killing my dog), which then continues to arise, with thought triggering fear triggering thought in a vicious cycle.

The solutions are:

(1) **Cognitive Disputation**: Realize that rather than the thoughts meaning you are likely to do the thing you're afraid of doing, they really just mean you're afraid of it because it goes against what you really value, and that *you are the last person who would actually do it.* People who kill dogs don't spend their days being tormented about "what if I don't really love dogs, what if I really

Chapter 22 - You're on a Need to Know Basis, and You Don't: Embracing Uncertainty

hate dogs and I'm gonna lose it and kill Sherwood." They're spending their days meticulously plotting how they are going to get away with killing their neighbor's dog without getting caught. It can also be helpful to respond to the "what if" thought with the phrase "*what if nothing*," as some of my clients with OCD find helpful, or imagine that your thought is someone saying to you "what if what I'm about to tell you is a lie?" In which case you might respond, as one of my clients recently suggested, "Shut up you weirdo."

(2) **Exposure and Response Prevention (E/RP):** Set aside a few minutes a few times a day and during those periods think over and over about all the ways you could kill your dog, or about whatever your obsession is, in all its gory details until it becomes boring or ridiculous. Prevent yourself from distracting yourself from these thoughts in any way.

(3) **Mindfulness:** Just be aware of the obsession when it arises, and then come back to 3 other senses (but not during E/RP, during which time it is important to let the obsession continue).

WARNING AND DISCLAIMER: The above applies to thoughts of causing harm when you find such thoughts *distressing* and consider the thought of acting on them to be *repugnant.* If you *enjoy* the repetitive thoughts of causing harm and *want* to carry them out, *please disregard the above and seek professional help* from a licensed mental health professional to sort things out and avoid the risk of doing something that you will later regret.

Chapter 23 - *How to Make a Decision:* The Magic Cross

"You don't have to floss all your teeth.

Just floss the teeth you want to keep."

Phil McCavity, D.D.S.

I was thinking of naming this chapter "How to weigh your options by conducting a cost-benefit analysis." But I wouldn't read a chapter with that title. Would you?

Over the years, my clients and I have developed a decidedly pseudoscientific way of making decisions, but since it's [*sic*](for the record, I disagree English's disposal of *it's* possessive apostrophe and will re-insert it at whim). positive outcome rate is only incrementally lower than the Rosencrantz Method, I will reproduce it here in case you have a decision to make and don't have any spare change. But first, regarding "its" versus "it's":

> "*Its* is just as possessive as *cat's*, but it doesn't have an apostrophe. Why not? **Because the printers and grammarians** [of the nineteenth century - Alex B.] **never thought the matter through** [emphasis mine - Alex B.]. They applied their rule to nouns and forgot about pronouns, thus creating an exception (along with *the food is hers, ours, yours, theirs*) without realizing it. And even if they had noticed, they wouldn't have done anything about it, for *it's* was already taken, as it were, as the abbreviation of *it is*." (Crystal, 2006, pp. 134-135)

Nice try, it's unfortunate that *nineteenth century printers and grammarians* dropped the ball but, as they say, they being I, not my aquarium not my seamonkeys. I'll stick with It's possessive *It's* except when my grammariaconformitis starts acting up.

Chapter 23 - How to Make a Decision: The Magic Cross

Rant over and back to our Magic Cross:

1. Take a piece of paper and make a big cross on it, dividing the paper into 4 equal-size quadrants.

2. At the top of the vertical line, write "Option 1" followed by that decision (for example, flossing my teeth tonight).

3. Just above the intersection of the lines in the middle of the page, write "Option 2" followed by that decision (for example, not flossing my teeth tonight).

4. At the top of the top left quadrant, write "A. Potential Advantages."

5. At the top of the top right quadrant, write "B. Potential Disadvantages."

6. At the top of the bottom left quadrant, write "C. Potential Advantages."

7. At the top of the bottom right quadrant, write "D. Potential Disadvantages."

8. In the top left quadrant, write down up (remember to put your seat back forward first) to 10 potential advantages of Option 1, and then next to each one write down how good it would be on a scale from 0 to 100 with 100 being intergalactic peace (unless you're an intergalactic arms dealer or mercenary, in which case consider 100 to be intergalactic war).

9. In the top right quadrant, write down up to 10 potential disadvantages of Option 1, and then next to each one write down how bad it would be on a scale from 0 to 100 with 100 being accidentally stepping in a bear trap in the Home Depot parking lot.

10. In the bottom left quadrant, write down up to 10 potential advantages of Option 2, and then next to each one write down how good it would be on a scale from 0 to 100.

11. In the bottom right quadrant, write down up to 10 potential disadvantages of Option 2, and then next to each one write down how bad it would be on a scale from 0 to 100.

12. Calculate the average or mean score for each quadrant (add the scores and divide by the number of scores you added), write it in the quadrant and circle it.

13. Subtract the mean score of the top right quadrant from the mean score of the top left quadrant and write the difference as A-B = Score for Option 1. If B is greater than A, the difference will be negative.

14. Subtract the mean score of the bottom right quadrant from the mean score of the bottom left quadrant and write the difference as C-D = Score for Option 2. If D is greater than C, the difference will be negative.

15. According to the Magic Cross, you are leaning toward the option with the biggest difference (with the biggest difference being the larger number resulting from the subtraction of a right quadrant from a left. For example, a difference of positive 2 is bigger than a difference of negative 10).

Please note that you should consider the result of this exercise only as *food for thought.* It would most likely be *highly* unwise to make an important decision based on this exercise alone, as the result depends on factors not considered, such as the truth or reasonableness of each of the advantages and disadvantages generated (as they are all, after all, guilty of the cognitive distortion "Fortune Telling"), as well as the likely temporal fluctuations in one's weighting of them. However, this exercise may be useful in informing a decision when combined with other strategies such as researching the matter at hand or discussing the options with friends, family members or professionals whose opinions or knowledge may be relevant.

You can also use this method for evaluating more than two options. This merely requires you to fold a piece of paper in half, quarters or eighths and draw a magic cross in each section, and if there are an odd number of options you can tear off the final section and make a paper airplane.

If the Magic Cross gives you an answer you don't like, find a coin (no, not the two headed one you use to trick your kids into thinking it's just bad luck that they keep having to clean the horse stable), and try the Rosencrantz method (Hint: Even if it's a real coin, *pick heads because no coin that you are likely to have in your pocket actually has a side with a tail on it*). If the coin toss gives you the same answer as the Magic Cross, the Universe may be trying to tell you something. Then again it may just be futzing with your head. If you still tend to want to do the opposite, and the potential negative outcomes are not catastrophic, maybe cut yourself a break, just do what you feel like doing this time, and live to fight another day.

Chapter 23 - How to Make a Decision: The Magic Cross

A Magic Cross Decision-Making Worksheet (slightly different in format) is provided in Appendix 5 for reference.

Chapter 24 - *Hi Ho, Hi Ho, Métro, Boulot, Dodo:* When "Anxiety" Isn't Really Anxiety

"Métro, boulot, bistro, mégots, dodo, zéro."

("Metro, work, bistro, cigarette butts, sleep, zero.")

Pierre Béarn

(1951, Transl: Google Translate)

"My keyboard must be broken.

I keep hitting the escape key, but I'm still at work."

Author Unknown

(By us, that is. Someone somewhere probably knows her)

I once had a client who said that he was very anxious, especially at work, but we couldn't find much that he was worried about other than the anxiety itself and its effect on his performance. When we did find some worries here or there and try to pin the anxiety on these, it just wasn't convincing. The fact that he was now worried about the anxiety, causing a "secondary" anxiety in the form of a positive feedback loop, or panic attack, did not clarify why he was so anxious in the first place.

Since both anxiety and work performance were at issue, initially, this brought to mind the Yerkes-Dodson Law (Yerkes & Dodson, 1908), which states that as nervous system activation increases, performance also increases, but only up to a point, and then drops off at a different rate for different types of tasks.

ORIGINAL YERKES-DODSON LAW (1908)

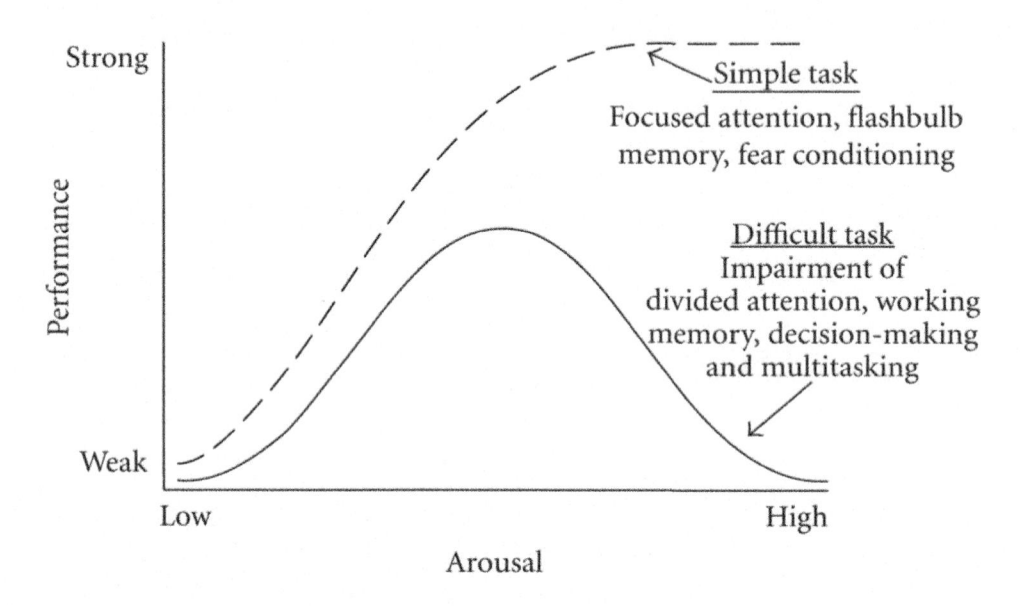

[Graph showing Performance (Weak to Strong) vs Arousal (Low to High). Dashed curve labeled "Simple task — Focused attention, flashbulb memory, fear conditioning" rises and plateaus. Solid curve labeled "Difficult task — Impairment of divided attention, working memory, decision-making and multitasking" forms an inverted U.]

The Yerkes-Dodson Law *did* explain why he was having difficulty performing to his potential (due to the effect of the heightened arousal characterizing anxiety) but still didn't address the onset of the anxiety itself. Since he also reported boredom at work, I then I considered the Flow Diagram of Mihaly Csikszentmihalyi (1975):

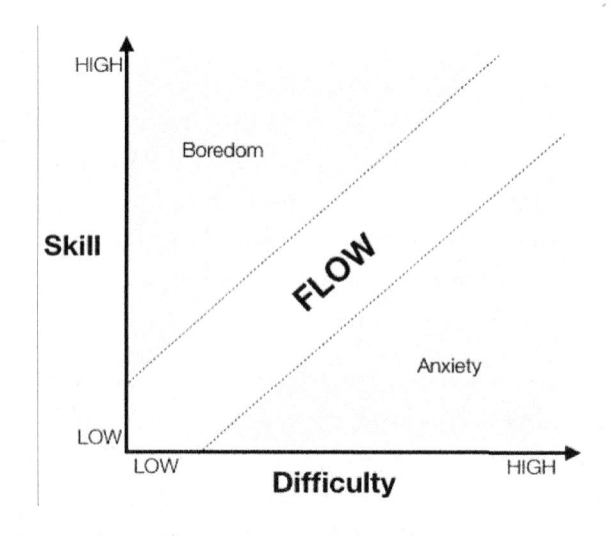

[Diagram showing Skill (LOW to HIGH) vs Difficulty (LOW to HIGH), with regions labeled "Boredom" (upper left), "FLOW" (diagonal middle), and "Anxiety" (lower right).]

Here, anxiety results when one is confronted with a task that is too challenging for one's current skill level, but my client felt competent to do his work. The Flow Diagram did explain his boredom (as many of his work tasks were not intellectually challenging for him), but it still did not address the origin of the anxiety.

Finally, I began suspecting that the problem was much simpler: He was a strong, energetic guy with way too much energy to sit still at a desk all day. Maybe what he perceived as "anxiety" was just a healthy, if above average, energy level that was being underutilized. I have tried to represent this admittedly seat-of-the-pants theory in the diagram below.

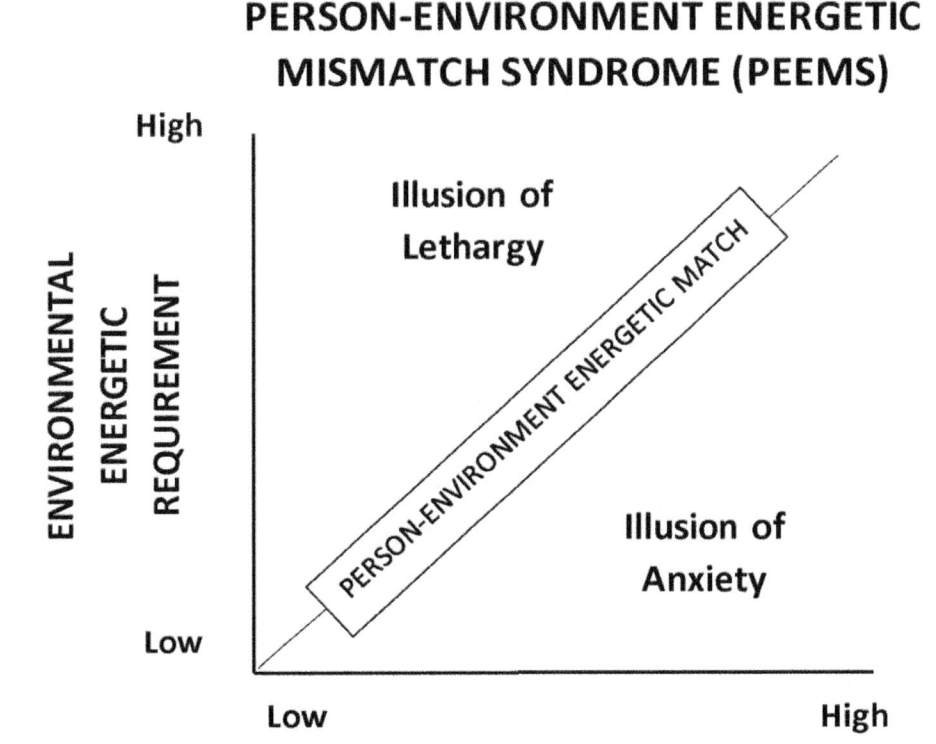

PERSON-ENVIRONMENT ENERGETIC MISMATCH SYNDROME (PEEMS)

(Graph: ENVIRONMENTAL ENERGETIC REQUIREMENT on y-axis from Low to High; PERSONAL ENERGETIC SETPOINT on x-axis from Low to High. A diagonal line labeled "PERSON-ENVIRONMENT ENERGETIC MATCH" runs from low-low to high-high. Above the line: "Illusion of Lethargy". Below the line: "Illusion of Anxiety".)

What seemed to be going on was that he and his job were in a state of *energetic mismatch* and he was suffering from the Person-Environment Energy Mismatch Syndrome (PEEMS). (Yup, just made it up.) In the course of the workday, he experienced this excess energy, or drive to expend energy that he had no current outlet for, as uncomfortable. This is naturally how

Chapter 24 - Hi Ho, Hi Ho, Métro, Boulot, Dodo: When "Anxiety" Isn't Really Anxiety

unsatisfied drives are subjectively experienced, in order to prompt us to fulfill them.

However, rather than interpret this energetic mismatch and resulting drive to expend more energy as just that, a mismatch, he (and I, at first) interpreted the discomfort as "anxiety." This misattribution of a healthy high energy level as anxiety was the beginning of the sequence that led to his panic attacks. The sequence was as follows:

> (1) He had a healthy high nervous system activation setpoint (he was an energetic guy).
>
> (2) He worked in an environment that did not require much physical energy expenditure.
>
> (3) The sensation of excess energy and drive to expend this energy was uncomfortable.
>
> (4) This discomfort was perceived as anxiety.
>
> (5) The excess energy interfered with performance (Yerkes-Dodson Law).
>
> (6) Worry about (illusory) anxiety led to nervous system activation becoming a trigger for worry and anxiety.
>
> (7) Anxiety triggered by anxiety creates the positive feedback loop known as "panic," further interfering with performance.
>
> (8) Worry about performance increased anxiety, with another positive feedback loop between increased anxiety and decreased performance.

Ultimately, we settled on a treatment plan that involved meditation to decrease baseline nervous system activation, cognitive disputation involving reframing the excess energy as healthy even though uncomfortable, and exposure and response prevention to address avoidance and escape from environments that had developed into triggers for panic attacks (due to having been in these environments when he experienced the initial PEEMS symptoms).

Ideally, if you are genetically blessed with high energy, you would seek a job that involves a good amount of physical activity. Alternatively, you could increase physical activity in the context of your current job, for example by using a standing desk or office exercise equipment (such as pedals placed under the desk to use when sitting and working). High energy people sometimes prefer tai chi and hatha yoga, which are forms of moving meditation, to sitting meditation, and research indicates that they have similar effects on lowering nervous system overactivation.

Perhaps most importantly, however, is to challenge the belief that there is something "wrong" with you for feeling agitated (and don't believe it if someone tells you you have a psychiatric disorder called **PEEMS** which you and I know is a bogus diagnosis I just made up), or that the excess energy means that you are anxious and that there must be some problem that is making you anxious. Otherwise, you will scan your environment and memory for problems and, guess what? You'll find some! Then you will scapegoat these, misattribute your anxiety to them, and start thinking that they are bigger problems than they are. As a result, you will start worrying about them, and eventually will be authentically anxious and not just highly energized. I call this "The Myth of *About"* or *somatic scapegoating* in which:

> (1) for purely physiological/neurological reasons (e.g., sleep deprivation; neurotransmitters; caffeine/alcohol/sugar; hunger; hormonal activity; brainwave frequency/amplitude) we experience an uncomfortable sensation or mental state of underactivation or overactivation;

> (2) we then seek a "reason" for the state, such as that we are tired/bored/sad (in the case of underactivation) or anxious/fearful/angry (in the case of overactivation) and scan our memories or physical/social environment;

> (3) we find a likely suspect (something or someone that isn't *exactly* as we – in our infinite Godly right to personally decide how *everything* and *everyone* should be – want them to be, and there's never a shortage of candidates);

> (4) we formulate a misattribution (choose our scapegoat) for the state, such as "X is tiring me out," "Y is really boring," "I'm so sad about what happened with Z," "XX is making me extremely anxious," "I'm too scared to go to YY," "I just can't stand it when ZZ does XYZ," etc.; and finally

Chapter 24 - Hi Ho, Hi Ho, Métro, Boulot, Dodo: When "Anxiety" Isn't Really Anxiety

(5) we behave accordingly (in a tired, bored, sad, anxious, fearful or angry manner).

In the case in question of "anxiety" at work, rather than follow that very unhelpful path, cognitive restructuring would involve generating evidence that there is something wrong with you (e.g., you feel anxious at work), generating evidence that there isn't anything wrong with you (e.g., your energy level is simply mismatched with a desk job), and then coming up with an alternative way of seeing things that takes all of the evidence into account. Your eventual rational alternative to "I'm so anxious there must be something wrong with me" might look something like this:

> "I am genetically programmed to have a lot of energy.
>
> Often, I have more energy than needed to do my work.
>
> I interpret this as anxiety.
>
> Then I scan my mind for problems, find some, and think they were making me anxious even though they aren't.
>
> Then I start worrying about them, and make myself anxious.
>
> Then I think there is something wrong with me and I feel depressed.
>
> Knowing what is really happening, I need to remind myself that excess energy isn't anxiety, and that the real problem is that there is a mismatch between my high energy level and the low amount of energy required of me at work. I can then work on addressing this by using techniques such as meditation, hatha yoga or tai chi to lower my baseline activation level; change to a more physical job; or find a way to expend more energy at work (or during breaks, or after work)."

Chapter 25 - *Opposites Attract: Like Nitro and Glycerin*

"Think on these things."

Jiddu Krishnamurti

(1970 Retitling of 1964 book "This Matter of Culture")

I don't actually have anything to write in this chapter. I just remembered that a client was telling me how he and his estranged wife "had always been very different, but I guess opposites attract." To which I spontaneously responded "yeah, like nitro and glycerin" and he burst out laughing. So I guess it was good one. He was dying of cancer at the time and had a few more months to live. Just to put our own problems in perspective, and remember to laugh. RIP, old friend.

Well, as they say, that was Zen, this is Tao. Two days after writing the above, I woke up with some actual things to write in this chapter. Not about opposites in relationships, but about opposites in general. Because, you see,

Opposites make the world go 'round

(when they aren't blowing it up).

Literally, physically, organically, psychologically and spiritually.

On the physical level, it's all about things holding together. How? (If you're a physicist, biologist or someone who paid attention in elementary school science, please skip to another chapter):

Chapter 25 - Opposites Attract: Like Nitro and Glycerin

Yin and Yang. Protons and electrons. Positive and Negative. Big and Small. Gravity. Spin. From **atoms** (very tiny solar systems), to **planets** (rocks we're stuck to), to **moons** (rocks stuck to the rocks we're stuck to), to suns (stars that rocks we're stuck to are stuck to), to stars (great balls of fire that rocks we're stuck to aren't stuck to), to **galaxies** (groups of great balls of fire that great balls of fire that rocks we're stuck to are stuck to are stuck to) to **galaxy groups** to **galaxy clusters** to **galaxy superclusters** to **universes** to **universe groups** to **universe clusters** to **universe super clusters** to **God** (it's turtles all the way up, but it has to end somewhere), opposites attract and spin around one another (unless they're nitro and glycerine, in which case they blow up the house).

On the organic level, reproduction. One plus one equals three. Be born, grow up, shorten down, die. Rinse. Repeat. (if you believe in reincarnation).

On the psychological level, when the going gets tough, the tough get going. On vacation. Vacating space to vacate the mind. Making money to spend it. Métro, boulot, dodo, Juan-les-Pins. Fill up, empty. Fill up, empty.

Spiritually, identify with the body, world and universe. Reject the body, world and universe. Become the body, world and universe. First the mountain is a mountain. Then the mountain isn't a mountain. Then the mountain is a mountain.

"Now I'm done.

Or just begun."

Grandma Densei (1922)

Chapter 26 - *To Go to Bed, Perchance to Sleep: CBMT for Insomnia*

"Sleep is the best meditation."

The Dalai Lama

"If you think you are too small to make a difference,

try sleeping with a mosquito."

(Ibid.)

The body, including the brain, requires a certain duration of sleep of a certain quality in order to function optimally (do any of you authors out there sometimes look at a sentence you wrote and ask yourself why you don't just write like a normal person, e.g., "People need sleep," or "The body and brain need sleep"?). As this varies among individuals, the best way to know whether you have a sleep problem is to ask yourself whether you are generally feeling awake and alert during the day and, *if not*, whether you are sleeping 7 to 9 hours per night. As a general rule, if you wake up bright-eyed and bushy-tailed and feel awake and alert as you go about your day, you are actually a rabbit dreaming of being a human and need about 11.4 hours of sleep per day (Jonathan, n.d.). In this case it doesn't matter how many hours you sleep, how fast you fall asleep, how many times you awaken in the night or what time you wake up in the morning: *you don't have a sleep problem* (though you may want to have that tail checked out). I say this because people sometimes come to me seeking treatment for insomnia because they wake up in the middle of the night craving carrots or because they sleep fewer hours than they think they should. However, they then tell me that they feel fine during the day without fatigue or drowsiness. In this case, they are merely a pregnant rabbit OR a human with a sleep pattern that works for them but is different from what works for most other people (and a potential Vitamin A deficiency).

Interestingly, while most of us have grown up thinking that "normal" sleep consists of 8 interrupted hours of unconsciousness per night, A. Roger Ekirch, a historian of sleep (yes, that exists), discovered and reported in his 2005 book "At Day's Close: Night in Times Past" that, until about the late 1700s or early 1800s, nighttime included both a "first sleep" and a "second sleep" (also termed "dead sleep" and "morning sleep," no doubt related to the first several hours of sleep involving deep, slow brainwave, unconscious sleep, as compared with the faster brainwave REM dreaming sleep that occurs for increasing periods of time as the sleep cycle progresses). The time in-between these was sometimes called "the Watching," or "quiet wakefulness" which may be akin to a meditative state, a human birthright that we have been deprived of due to the modern, dysfunctional practice of an unnaturally condensed sleep pattern.

In our long-lost segmented sleep cycle, we typically retired at sunset and slept until around 2 a.m., woke up and engaged in one or another activity for one or two hours, and then slept again until around 6 a.m. However, in the 1800s, when artificial starlight delivered by gas lamps began tricking our brain into thinking that it was still daytime after the sun went down (likely by reducing the brain's darkness-stimulated production of the melatonin that makes us sleepy), we stayed up later (many of us working for the industrial revolutionists in whose interest it was to prolong our definition of the workday). The gap between the "first sleep" and "second sleep" gradually decreased, possibly due to sleep deprivation occasioned by decreasing sleep opportunity (time in bed) caused by staying up too late. In the 1900s, artificial starlight delivered by electricity put the nail in the coffin of healthy bi-phasic sleep, and I'll be right back after I brew another pot of vanilla macadamia nut coffee.

Hi again. To continue where we left off. The natural human segmented sleep cycle has been supported by research conducted by Wehr (1991), in which 7 individuals were permitted to move about in natural or artificial lighting for up to 10 hours per day and then stay in a dark bedroom for up to

16 hours per night. This continued for 4 weeks. Results indicated that when permitted this prolonged period of darkness, the participants slept several hours, were then awake for 1 to 3 hours, and then slept several more hours (supporting Ekirch's historical findings of natural sleep being bimodal). The mean amount of time from their first falling asleep until their final awakening was 11.75 hours, with their sleep duration ranging from 7.54 to 9.18 hours. This represented an increase from their sleep duration of 7.05 to 7.47 hours when their time in the dark bedroom had previously been limited to 8 hours. In addition, there was an increase in overall melatonin production by the brain when permitted to experience an amount of darkness more akin to that experienced by humans prior to the advent of artificial lighting. Moral of the story: Plan A: We should really be allowing about 12 hours between bedtime and wakeup time, and getting about 7.5 to 9 hours of sleep divided into 2 periods, waking up in-between and doing something or other for 1 to 3 hours. Plan B: Caffeine. But seriously, what am I supposed to do with those study results? Are you or anyone you know with a 9-5 job and a 1-hour commute really going to go to bed at 7 pm, wake up at 11 pm to go to the gym, come home and go back to sleep at 2 am and sleep until 7 am? The main benefit of that study, as I see it, is that at least we now know why we're never quite as awake and alert as we would like to be, and have a comeback when our doctors tell us to lay off the caffeine.

HOW TO KNOW WHETHER AND WHY YOU HAVE A SLEEP PROBLEM

Ignoring the above study results for purposes of living in the real world, if (a) you are not feeling awake, alert and refreshed during the day, and (b) you are not sleeping 7 to 9 hours per night most nights (especially on the nights preceding not feeling awake, alert and refreshed), this would suggest that the daytime fatigue may be due to sleep of inadequate duration or quality. As it could also, however, be due to a medical condition, it would be advisable to consult with a physician to rule out issues such as thyroid or blood sugar dysregulation, or sleep apnea in which breathing stops, sometimes many times per hour. One sign of potential sleep apnea is snoring. Both snoring and stopping breathing are more than likely noticeable by one's sleeping partner (or neighbors if the walls are thin). If sleep apnea is suspected, speak to your doctor about getting a "sleep study."

Chapter 26 - To Go to Bed, Perchance to Sleep: CBMT for Insomnia

Insomnia that is not due to a medical condition can take a variety of forms and can have a variety of psychological causes that are treatable.

Some common types of insomnia are sleep-onset insomnia (difficulty falling asleep initially), middle insomnia (difficulty staying asleep and falling back asleep after awakenings) and terminal insomnia (don't worry, it's not fatal – it just refers to waking up too early and not being able to fall back asleep at all).

Perhaps the most common type of insomnia these days is not really insomnia (involuntary sleep deprivation), but rather *voluntary* sleep deprivation (what the heck: VSDD – Voluntary Sleep Deprivation Disorder) in which you know you need to get to sleep at a certain time in order to feel good tomorrow, but you stay up playing with your phone, surfing the web, playing video games, watching TV or reading, usually because your daytime activities are so crushingly boring that you feel you deserve to enjoy yourself at night. Which you do. The only problem is that the next day you are both crushingly bored *and* completely exhausted and useless, with impaired mood, concentration and performance. Time for a career change? . . .

Aside from voluntary sleep deprivation, enemies of sleep include:

(a) Overthinking when in bed (which increases the power of fast brainwaves, whereas sleep requires an increase in the power of slow brainwaves);

(b) Not adhering to "sleep hygiene" guidelines, including not ingesting caffeine less than about 6 hours before bedtime; not looking at blue light from a smartphone, computer screen or digital TV less than an hour or so before bedtime (it tricks your brain into thinking the sun is up, and reduces the production of melatonin); and some others.

Whatever the initial cause of the insomnia, once the schedule, duration and quality of sleep have settled into a dysfunctional pattern, the pattern tends to continue, and the brain begins to associate the bed with being awake rather than being asleep. At this point, you may benefit from a psychological treatment called "Cognitive Behavior Therapy for Insomnia (CBT-I)." CBT-I involves changing some daytime, pre-sleep, nighttime, and early morning habits, as well as learning to challenge negative thinking during the hours that you want to be asleep. Some practitioners such as myself supplement CBT-I with various techniques to gain control over the cognitive *process* of overthinking, such as *learning to stop thinking* through selective awareness training also known as meditation and mindfulness. As mentioned earlier, this goes beyond traditional cognitive therapy, which focuses on cognitive *content.*

COGNITIVE BEHAVIORAL MIND TRAINING FOR INSOMNIA

After ruling out medical causes for daytime fatigue, the following techniques may help to improve sleep:

(1) **Behavioral Component:** Prior to concluding that you need to use the rigorous CBT for Insomnia (CBT-I) protocol, set a consistent sleep routine, allowing for 8 hours of sleep per night, going to bed at the same time each night and waking up at the same time each morning. Your immediate response will be that this either isn't possible or that you don't want to do it. Fine, don't do it, and continue getting rotten sleep and being tired all the time. Or . . . humor me and try a 7-day experiment in which you do what I just said (yes, even on the weekend – it's just one weekend, deal with it) and see in 7 days how you feel. Then decide whether to continue or not. If you don't continue, at least you will know that it is a choice and not a life sentence.

If at any time in the night, you can't fall asleep within about 20 minutes, get out of bed, keep the lights low and don't look directly at anything that emits blue light (including your phone, tablet, computer or TV, unless you have an old tube TV, in which case maybe it doesn't emit blue light, but you can find that out by googling it as easily as I) as blue light reduces melatonin production, alters your sleep cycle and leads to daytime fatigue. Yes, there are glasses, filters and apps that reduce the amount of blue light getting into your eyes from these devices, but they don't eliminate all of it, and even bright light that is not blue will interfere with sleep physiology. So, ideally, keep the lights low, read a book made of paper with the minimal light necessary to read, pay some bills, clean the kitchen (ideally by candle light or with a light dimmer), write some poetry using paper and pen, etc. Then stay out of bed either for 30 minutes or until you feel sleepy (the experts disagree on which is better – I tell people to stay out of bed for 30 minutes). Either way, what will happen is that you may be *more* tired the next day (because remember, you are still waking up at your pre-chosen time), but the following night (as long as you *don't take naps*), by the time your pre-chosen bedtime arrives you may be more tired than usual (due to what we call built up "sleep pressure" from not sleeping enough the prior night) and you should sleep more soundly than usual. Continue this routine for 7 days, and see if your sleep improves (when combined with the below cognitive and meditational strategies). If not, you may benefit from seeking out a provider of CBT-I, possibly supplemented by use of the CBT-I Coach app designed in collaboration with the US Department of Veterans Affairs (VA).

(2) **Cognitive Content Component:** As the initiation of sleep requires increased power of slow brainwaves, anything that keeps the fast brainwaves dominant will interfere with sleep. One thing that stimulates fast brainwaves is *thinking*, and especially *scary thinking*. It is very difficult to fall asleep if the content of your thoughts involves danger of some sort, which stimulates the body's fight or flight response (sleeping people are notoriously bad at fighting and fleeing). Now, if there is a *real* danger, by all means continue to think about it and figure out how to neutralize it. Some examples are if you smell smoke, see fire, hear a rattlesnake, or see the shadow of a bear on the wall of your tent because some degenerate on your camping trip hung raw meat from your clothesline. However, in the absence of these, you would do well to *challenge* any automatic thoughts about problems using *cognitive restructuring*. Notice the negative thought, generate the evidence that supports it, the evidence that contradicts it, and then come up with a more rational alternative. In addition, if you are not thinking something necessarily negative or irrational but rather are thinking about a real problem or goal, you should challenge the thought that *right now* you need to figure it out. Some things you don't need to figure out while lying in bed are all the things you have to do tomorrow at work, what to say to so and so when you see them tomorrow, where you will go on your next vacation, and how to pay the bills. Really, the things you don't need to figure out while lying in bed include: *anything*.

(3) **Cognitive Process (Meditational) Component:** Which brings us to the most *elegant* solution to problems involving thinking: *Stop It* (Newhart, 2019/2001).

Once you have used the traditional cognitive therapy tool of cognitive restructuring to challenge any scary thoughts (e.g., that the noises you hear are people trying to break in), and dispute the thought that bedtime and the middle of the night are good times to problem solve (unless you are taking an intentional 3 hour break in the middle of two four and a half hour periods of bimodal sleep), you are ready to meditate yourself to sleep by being *selectively aware* of senses other than thinking. Research shows that the combination of CBT for Insomnia and meditation produces superior results to CBT-I alone (Vanhuffel, Rey, Lambert, Da Fonseca & Bat-Pitault, 2018). One possibility is to simply practice breath awareness, breathing normally (not abnormally slowly or deeply) and being aware of the feeling of the air as it enters and leaves your nose. If after a few minutes you're still awake, you could add one or two more senses, such as being aware of the light behind your eyelids at the same time as being aware of your breath and any sounds in the room. If after a few minutes you're still awake, then it's time to use the ultimate psychological sleep aide, the nuclear option, so to speak: the *Body Scan.*

When I first learned the body scan as a meditation/mindfulness technique, not as a sleep-aide, and began teaching it to clients, I found it a real challenge to remember the script, so I would read it out loud. Over time, I realized that psychotherapy, meditation and mindfulness are not rocket sciences. Sure, we begin with some techniques we learned in grad school or on the cushion, but every therapy client or meditation student is different, with a personality that responds to this and doesn't respond to that, with problems that the thing that worked for the last client or student either works for or doesn't, and so the TRUTH is that we're all just kind of winging it, making stuff up, seeing if it works, and if it does we continue using it as a part of your individualized treatment/training and if it doesn't we throw it away and try something else. All this to say that eventually I stopped trying to memorize other people's body scan scripts and made up my own. To paraphrase and conflate some teachings of my old Zen Master, RIP, "Eventually you stop reading and start thinking. Then you stop that too." My advice is to read it, practice it once as you read it, and then without reading it again just use whatever you remember of it to help fall asleep. Eventually, you can shorten it or lengthen it as you like, removing or adding whatever you want. If you want, you could record it and listen when you want to fall asleep, or have someone read it to you.

THE WHAM BAM BODY SCAN

This script will move your awareness from the left side of your body to the right, then move up the right side, then cross to the left side, them move up the left side, then cross to the right side, then move up the right side, etc. The movement may be remembered as: Left to right; Up; Right to left; Up; Repeat. Sometimes awareness will move from front to back, or from lower to higher, rather than from left to right. When I say "feel ___" or "be aware of the feeling of ___," this means "without touching or moving any part of your body, just passively be aware of the sensation of X part of your body." For example, right now, feel your pinky toe, not with your hand, but just without touching or moving your left pinky toe be aware of the sensation of your left pinky toe. That is what I mean by "Be aware of the feeling of your left pinky toe." Many people do not have experience being aware of body parts without touching them or moving them, so at first you may not feel anything in a certain body part. That's OK. It comes with practice. For the moment, just be aware of whatever you feel there, or aware of the absence of any feeling there.

Awareness of each body part mentioned will last for the duration of one in-breath and one out-breath. For example, breathe in and out through your nose, and on both the in breath and the out breath be aware of the feeling of your left pinky toe. Then on the next in and out breath, be aware of the feeling of your left fourth toe. This is how we will progress from one body part to the next, being aware of each body part for the duration of one breath in and one breath out.

So here is the Body Scan:

Breathing in and out normally through your nose (or, if your nose is stuffed, through your mouth), be aware of each of the below, in sequence, for one in-breath and one out-breath:

Left pinky toe, left fourth toe, left third toe, left second (index?) toe, left big toe

Right big toe, right index toe (what the heck), right third toe, right fourth (ring?) toe, right pinky toe

Right side of the right foot, top of the right foot, left side of the right foot

Right side of the left foot, top of the left foot, left side of the left foot

Left ankle, right ankle, right lower leg, left lower leg, left knee, right knee

Right upper leg, left upper leg, left hip, right hip

Stomach, lower back, upper back, chest

Left hand pinky, left ring finger, left third finger, left index finger, left thumb

Right thumb, right index finger, right middle finger, right ring finger, right pinky

Right side of the right hand, top of the right hand, left side of the right hand

Right side of the left hand, top of the left hand, left side of the left hand

Left wrist, right wrist, right lower arm, left lower arm, left elbow, right elbow

Right upper arm, left upper arm, left shoulder, right shoulder, front of the neck, back of the neck

Back of the head, top of the head, forehead, nose, mouth, chin.

If you are still awake, repeat the entire body scan again until you fall asleep. People fall asleep at various times during the body scan, some at the beginning, some in the middle, some at the end, and some after two, three or more repetitions. These days when it's time to fall asleep but my mind is wide awake, once I initiate the scan it's rare that I'm awake past the 4th or 5th toe. If you are still awake after about 20 minutes, get out of bed and do something for 30 minutes that doesn't involve blue light unless you have blue light filters or glasses.

If after trying all of the above cognitive, behavioral and meditative techniques you still have difficulty sleeping, you might benefit from working with a professional on individualizing your insomnia treatment plan. There are times that medication is an important and effective intervention. One example would be when the sleep cycle is disrupted and has shifted from nighttime to daytime for any variety of reasons such as shift work or not wanting to deal with people. In this case, a physician or psychiatrist may prescribe a medication such as Trazodone (both an antidepressant and a sedative) to knock you out for as many nights as it takes to recalibrate the sleep cycle. Any medication such as this should only be taken when prescribed by a medical provider, who has assessed the likelihood of both its effectiveness and possible side effects given your personal health history as well as possible interactions with other medicines you may be taking.

Chapter 27 – *Pain, The Final Frontier: Open Focus Dissolving Pain*

"Sous le pont Mirabeau coule la Seine
Et nos amours
Faut-il qu'il m'en souvienne
La joie venait toujours après la peine

Vienne la nuit sonne l'heure
Les jours s'en vont je demeure."

"'Neath Mirabeau bridge flows the Seine
And our love
Must I recall how then
After pain always the joy again

Night come bells toll eventide
The days retire I abide."

Guillaume Apollinaire

(From Le Pont Mirabeau, 1912; my translation)

Pain is different from other targets of psychological treatment, both in terms of assessment and evaluating the progress of therapy. Whereas people don't always know whether their subjective experience constitutes "depression," "anxiety," "obsessive-compulsive disorder" or "panic disorder," everyone knows when they're in pain. And while people may stay in therapy for years with a therapist with grass for brains and think they must be getting better because they've been in therapy for years, well, let's just say that if you're going to take a weekend certificate course and then advertise yourself as a "psychotherapist," don't put "pain management" on your website.

Psychological and meditational therapy for pain by themselves rarely completely eliminate the pain. Ideally, these are components of a multimodal intervention, involving some combination of approaches such as physical therapy, chemical pain antagonists, acupuncture, tai chi, yoga, neurofeedback or possibly medical procedures. However cognitive behavioral therapies and meditation can significantly reduce the pain experience. Within the space of several minutes, I have seen the Dissolving Pain technique reduce perceived pain from somewhere between 5 and 10 (out of 10) to somewhere between zero and 2 for the amount of time that it was practiced.

Psychological pain reduction techniques involve cognitive content (challenging the meaning of the pain), cognitive process (reducing the frequency and duration of time spent giving preferential awareness to the pain and it's perceived consequences) and the use of attention and awareness to strategically activate and deactivate regions of the nervous system currently processing and not processing pain signals. This latter approach has been systematized as the "Dissolving Pain" technique (Fehmi & Robbins, 2010).

In the Dissolving Pain technique, you first become fully aware of the sensation of pain in a certain region of the body. You then imagine the painless space around the area of the pain, and you imagine dissolving the pain into this surrounding space. You repeat this process as many times as necessary for the pain to dissipate. I have used this technique both in acute care facilities and in private practice with people experiencing mild to severe pain, and it is very rare that it does not work, despite my wondering each time I use it whether it will work, since it frankly sounds a little nutty. One elderly gentleman in an acute care facility I worked with called it "magic," and an outpatient clinic client whose life had come to a standstill due to chronic back pain returned to his hobby of building and restoring large pieces of furniture after learning how to "dissolve" the pain.

I have developed my own theory of why it works, and it is important to understand that this is so far beyond the realm of gross oversimplification that I probably should just keep it to myself. Just like I shouldn't eat ice cream before bed. I did have, however, the opportunity to discuss it over cigars and cognac with Dr. Fehmi in his backyard one afternoon a few years back (he transitioned recently, RIP, a great loss to those who were blessed to know him and to the field of psychology), and he agreed that it didn't sound like complete nonsense. Or maybe he was just being polite. So here it is, for what it's worth: Sensations from each part of the body are conducted along nerve fibers to the spinal cord and then to the brain, where they are processed by the thalamus and then sent to the somatosensory cortex, a strip of the brain running across the top of the head from left to right. Sensation and pain from one side of the body are perceived by the opposite side of the somatosensory cortex. The exact location of the brain corresponding with each body part has been mapped in what is called the "cortical homunculus." You may have seen his picture. He's the guy with the enormous hands and the big mouth (which is why paper cuts hurt so much and you curse when you accidently bite your tongue. Be especially careful licking envelopes).

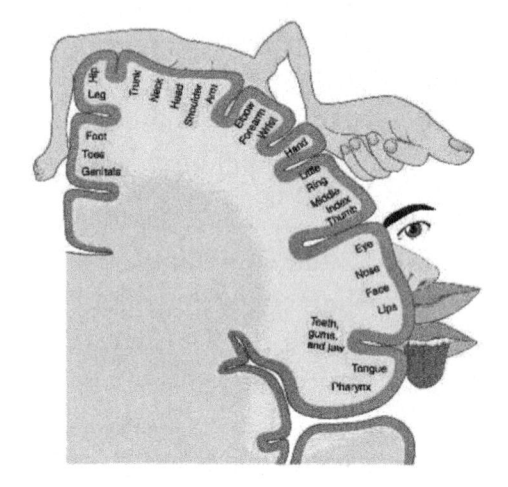

Illustration from Anatomy
& Physiology, Connexions Web site
http://cnx.org/content/col11496/1.6/
Jun 19, 2013. Creative Commons License.

By Mpj29 - Own work, CC BY-SA 4.0
https://commons.wikimedia.org/
w/index.php?curid=54045144

When you feel pain in a part of your body, this is because the entire nervous pathway from the area of the pain to the somatosensory cortex has been activated. Now, using a mosquito bite metaphor, what do you want to do when you feel an itch. Of course. You want to scratch it and the area around it. Why? Here's where my theory comes in. When you activate the sensory receptors around it *that don't itch*, you disrupt the signal being conveyed from that region of the body. Jumping from the itch metaphor to your experience of pain, when you imagine or *become aware of* the space around the pain that isn't sending pain signals, this activates the neural pathway to the non-pain-signal-receiving areas in the somatosensory cortex that surround the area receiving the pain signal. By following the Dissolving Pain instruction "*can you imagine the pain dissolving into the space around it,*" you are bringing awareness to the non-painful region around it (which incidentally increases blood flow to that area) and thereby activating neutral neural pathways around the neural pathway that is lit up with pain. You are, in effect, "scratching the pain."

My most interesting experience with pain occurred when I lived in Hong Kong where, in my carnivore days, I ate a lot of roast pork. Karma's a witch (not that there's anything wrong with witches – just trying to keep my French under control), and I eventually experienced a gout attack. I didn't really know what gout was at the time and so I just wondered why my toe was getting bigger and bigger and redder and redder and more and more painful. I of course swiftly googled it and identified it as gout, learned that it was caused by just about anything you could possibly eat or drink, and decided to treat myself by eliminating meat from my diet and replacing it with tofu. It wasn't until much later that I learned that in Hong Kong everyone knows that gout is caused by tofu (though more recently this has been contradicted by research).

So for the next month, because naturally I didn't think I needed to see a doctor since I had Google, I learned what it was like to live with a knife stuck in my foot. And I learned to walk very, very slowly, which can be problematic when you need to take 3 subway lines to work, each which includes a substantial walk between connections, and are living in the fastest city on the planet, where "stroll" would be a four-letter word if Chinese had letters. Luckily, I was by that time a regular practitioner of meditation and mindfulness, and I used my health situation to justify (at least to me) becoming the slowest walker in the history of Hong Kong. And I have to say, the sense of peace brought about by mindful walking at a snail's pace across Hong Kong to and from work each day vastly outweighed the suffering from the pain which was, happily, reduced to a minimum by walking very carefully.

This continued for several weeks as I slowly debated whether to just go see a doctor and get proper treatment. It might have continued even longer, when

Chapter 27 – Pain, The Final Frontier: Open Focus Dissolving Pain

one night I tried to get out of bed and couldn't put my foot on the floor as the pain was just unbearable. I then realized that the pain was unbearable even just keeping my foot on the bed. So I did the third thing any sane person would do. I started speaking to the pain in ways that I had seen in some sappy book on lovingkindness. I told the pain "thank you, I know you are just trying to help me, but I understand now, I need to see a doctor. I love you, please stop." I then did the second thing any sane person would do, and googled "how to reduce unbearable pain," and was instructed to "take 5 Advil" which I swiftly did (Do NOT try the 5 Advil solution without consulting with a physician). I then got back in bed and did the first thing any sane person would have done one month earlier, locating a doctor and leaving a voice mail that I needed an appointment ASAP the next morning. Finally, I remained in bed practicing acceptance of the pain realizing there was nothing more I could do until tomorrow. And this is when things got interesting. Although the pain remained just as intense as it had been all along, it somehow stopped having anything to do with me. It was there, and it was painful, but it didn't bother me. For the first time, I understood experientially the difference I had read about in the literature between pain and suffering. Was I in pain? Yeah, 100%, the worst I'd ever experienced. Was I suffering? No, not after accepting it.

The skeptic in me says "of course you weren't suffering as much, you just took 5 Advil," which is a valid point. But the Advil didn't work right away. For a while the pain was still there simultaneous with a meditative sense of peace. Maybe the meditative perspective I was taking with regard to the pain was, as research now suggests (Kaliman et al., 2014), turning off the inflammatory mechanism at the genomic level, and this, combined with the Advil, was creating some sort of paradoxical state of simultaneous pain and no pain. Or maybe the pain just wanted to be loved. Who knows. But the next morning when I woke up, I couldn't believe what I saw and felt: My foot was fine. No swelling, no pain. That weekend I even went to a yoga class and stood on my toes. No offence to Advil, but it really didn't seem possible that 5 Advil had cured the gout to the point that the next day when the doctor looked at my foot she said it looked fine. Possible? Sure. She gave me a prescription for a strong NSAID in case it recurred, which it did several times until I changed my diet, but never did I experience a cure as sudden and complete as that which had followed sending love to the pain, accepting the pain and taking 5 Advil (Don't ask me why I didn't just use that formula again – maybe because it seemed so crazy). Would I do the whole thing again if I had a choice? Hell no. Do I wish it hadn't happened? Not at all: It prompted me (for the most part) to stop eating animals (for a while) and get more disciplined about meditation and mindfulness. I guess the pain served its purpose, and its services were no longer needed (knock on wood). Possibly for dietary reasons (or because I drink massive amounts of coffee, which reduces uric acid levels) the gout went away and hasn't returned in years. Fingers crossed.

INTERMISSION

PART 3 - PSYCHONAUTICS: *GET OUT OF YOUR LIFE AND INTO YOUR MIND*

"The duty of science is

(1) to be very daring—boundlessly audacious—in forming hypotheses;

(2) to be very cautious—inexorably cautious—in affirmation.

I think I am acting in conformity with these equally important principles when, on the one hand, I recommend that you do not neglect the study of metapsychical phenomena:

because it seems to me that the future of psychology is linked with discovery in that realm; and, on the other hand, I urge those who devote their efforts to this study to cultivate prudence and patience."

Charles Richet

(1906; French physician, 1913 Nobel Laureate)

"... I am about to ask the modern scientific individual to regard seriously, in order to learn from, a class of literature that has long been rejected. This type of literature, I must warn in advance, has even been labeled with that nasty epithet of the rationalist era, 'mystic' - as though man's reason has any greater goal than to penetrate the clouded *mysteries* of human existence. That epithet, however, should not stop our turning to such a source for information and insights of an objective and productive kind; especially since this kind of material will eventually contribute significantly to the modern, rational attempt to build a science of man."

Ira Progoff

(1957, pp. 1-2, The Cloud of Unknowing)

"If there is a higher form of consciousness obtainable by man than that which he can for the most part claim at present, it is probable - nay certain - that it is evolving and will evolve slowly, and with many a slip and hesitant pause by the way ... What could be more marvellous than the first revealment of the sense of sight, what more inconceivable to those who had not experienced it, and what more certain than that the first use of this faculty must have been fraught with delusion and error? *Yet there may be an inner vision which again transcends sight, even as far as sight transcends touch.*"

Edward Carpenter

(1892, p. 153; in Bucke, 2009/1901, p. 242; italics added)

How To Stop Thinking and Not Get Eaten By A Bear

I.D.

"I just l-o-v-e the way you've evolved"

Chapter 28 - *Whose Reality is it Anyway?: Introduction to Part 3*

"I look crazy but I'm not.

And the funny thing is

that other people don't look crazy

but they are."

eden abhez, author of the song Nature Boy, theme song for The Boy with Green Hair. eden, who inspired the Hippie movement, spelled his name with lower-case letters, claiming that "only the words God and Infinity were worthy of capitalization." (eden ahbez, n.d.)

"In engaging in shamanic practice, one moves between what I term an Ordinary State of Consciousness (OSC) and a Shamanic State of Consciousness (SSC) . . . The myth of the SSC is ordinary reality; and the myth of the OSC is nonordinary reality."

Anthropologist Michael Harner

(1990, pp. xix - xx)

Psychonautics: "The exploration of the psyche by means of techniques such as meditation, prayer, lucid dreaming, brainwave enhancement, sensory deprivation, and the use of hallucinogens or entheogens."

Psychonaut: "'Sailor of the mind' or 'navigator of the psyche'"; "individuals who seek to investigate their mind using intentionally induced altered states of consciousness. The aim of this investigation may be either spiritual in nature (as in mysticism or shamanism) or of a more mundane nature (as in scientific drug experiments designed to study the effects of hallucinogens such as LSD, mescaline, or cannabis)."

Psychiatrist Jan Dirk Blom

(2009, p. 434, cited in Wikipedia: Psychonautics)

The final chapters of this book treat of states of consciousness other than what we consider the ordinary waking state. While "other than the ordinary waking state" might seem to refer to states in which one is asleep or in which the ordinary waking state is altered by a drug or brain injury, this is not necessarily the case. Firstly, there are varieties of "waking" experience, along such continua as (but not limited to):

Sensory alteration: such as sober, buzzed, drunk/high, hallucinating;

Arousal: such as calm, aroused, hypomanic, manic;

Mood: such as ecstatic, happy, sad, depressed; irritated, angry, enraged; anxious, fearful, panicked;

Reality Testing: such as rational, irrational, delusional;

Positivity: such as optimistic, pessimistic, nihilistic; and

Cognitive Process: such as cognitive flexibility, stubbornness, obsessiveness.

Similarly, there are varieties of "sleeping" experience, such as

Nondreaming sleep: which is self-explanatory;

Chapter 28 - Whose Reality is it Anyway?: Introduction to Part 3

Nonlucid dreaming: in which one doesn't realize one is dreaming; and

Lucid dreaming: in which one realizes one is dreaming.

However, even these distinctions limit the broad categories of consciousness to waking, nondreaming sleep and dreaming sleep. They do not address the issue of the extent to which any of these states of consciousness represent a *reality* beyond themselves, that is, a reality of which they, as sensory experiences, are a reflection. Not only does this taxonomy of waking/sleeping/dreaming fail to answer the question as to whether a "vision" of the afterlife in a near death experience is "just" a dream or a glimpse of a veiled reality; it doesn't even admit of the question itself.

For this reason, I have developed a taxonomy of 10 consciousness states to encompass what I see as the relevant variables in any discussion of the varieties of waking, dreaming, and dreamless sleep. As the main bone of contention in reports of altered states is whether these are merely hallucinations or glimpses of real things, beings or events beyond our ordinary con-sensual – "with senses" – reality, I have therefore distinguished these states by the truth or falsehood of their perceived content, or their "referential reality of experience." By "referential reality of experience" I mean the extent to which an experience corresponds with a reality external to itself, of which it is a representation or reflection in consciousness.

When an experience has a referential reality, regardless of the state of consciousness in which it occurs, it is represented in the taxonomy as *True*. When an experience does not have a referential reality, it is represented in the taxonomy as *False*. If one has insight into whether the experience has a referential reality, regardless of the state of consciousness in which it occurs, the experience is labeled as *lucid*. If one has no insight into whether the experience has a referential reality, the experience is labeled as *nonlucid*.

The proposed hierarchy of these states ranges from least conscious of reality (1. Nonlucid Dreamless Sleep), which would constitute what the spiritual systems call "ignorance," to most conscious of reality (10. Lucid Waking True), which the spiritual systems call "enlightenment." It is not a typo in the chart that Lucid Dreamless Sleep is numbered higher than (representing a higher level of consciousness of reality than) Lucid Dreaming False and Lucid Waking False (as will be discussed below). This is because realizing, while asleep, the true nature of the state of sleep itself, would seem less encumbered than realizing the true state of either dreaming or waking but continuing to generate – albeit without believing – imaginary content.

10-State Taxonomy of Sleeping, Dreaming and Waking Consciousness

Insight Into Referential Versus Nonreferential Reality → State of Consciousness and Truth or Falsehood of Perceived Content ↓	Without Insight (Nonlucid)	With Insight (Lucid)
Dreamless Sleep (No Content)	1. Nonlucid Dreamless Sleep	8. Lucid Dreamless Sleep
Dreaming False	2. Nonlucid Dreaming False	6. Lucid Dreaming False
Waking False	3. Nonlucid Waking False	7. Lucid Waking False
Dreaming True	4. Nonlucid Dreaming True	9. Lucid Dreaming True
Waking True	5. Nonlucid Waking True	10. Lucid Waking True

As an example of how the categories work, imagine that a person on LSD is hallucinating a unicorn sitting across from her at breakfast, and realizes that this is a hallucination. This would be categorized as Lucid Waking False because she has insight into the lack of referential reality (there is not really a unicorn there) for the waking experience.

If, however, she were to believe there really was a unicorn there, this would be a state of Nonlucid Waking False (lack of insight into the absence of a referential reality for waking experience). Nonlucid Waking False is the definition of delusion or psychosis.

Now, imagine that she lived in a universe in which there really were unicorns that one only sees when on LSD, but she didn't know this and thought she was just hallucinating. Then she would be in a state of Nonlucid Waking True (lack of insight into the referential reality of the waking experience).

Chapter 28 - Whose Reality is it Anyway?: Introduction to Part 3

Finally, if she lived in such a universe in which real unicorns can only be perceived on LSD, and she knows this and knows the unicorn sipping coffee across the table is real, she is in a state of Lucid Waking True (insight into the referential reality of the waking experience).

Some examples of each of the 10 varieties of lucidity, from ignorance to enlightenment are:

>*1. Nonlucid Dreamless Sleep:* This is the sleep that we all experience during which we are not dreaming and have no awareness of being asleep.

>*2. Nonlucid Dreaming False:* This is a dream that is merely a hallucination, having no correspondence with an external reality, but which one thinks corresponds with an external reality. An example is dreaming about being back in first grade with a different teacher and thinking you are really there.

>**3. Nonlucid Waking False:* This is the state in which one is awake but the consensual waking environment is in fact a dream and one doesn't realize this. This is how certain spiritual traditions such as Buddhism and Hinduism consider the consensual reality of most people, which these traditions call Samsara, Ignorance or Delusion. An example is my experience while writing this sentence that I am actually here writing this sentence if I am not really here (for example if this is a dream), and your experience while reading this sentence that you are actually here reading this sentence if you really are not here reading this sentence. In other words, what we take to be reality when we are awake if the Buddhists and Hindus are right that this too is a dream and we don't realize it.

>**4. Nonlucid Dreaming True:* This is a dream in which one is psychologically or energetically in a truly existent environment other than that which the sleeping physical body is in, doesn't realize it is a dream, but is accurate in the belief that the environment is real. An example would be dreaming that you are in heaven with a transitioned family member, not realizing you are in a dream but correctly thinking that you are in heaven with her or him.

>**5. Nonlucid Waking True:* This is a state in which one is awake and perceives something that is real but does not believe it to be real. For

example, seeing a statue of Jesus shed a tear and thinking that it isn't really Jesus shedding a tear if in fact it is. This may also correspond with reports in the literature of people who are enlightened without realizing it. It may also correspond with the experience of each one of us at every moment, if we are, as is sometimes said, all already enlightened without being aware of it.

6. Lucid Dreaming False: This is a dream that is merely a hallucination, having no correspondence with an external reality, and in which one realizes one is in a dream experiencing a hallucination. An example would be the above dream about being back in first grade with a different teacher but realizing it is a dream and doesn't correspond with present reality.

*7. Lucid Waking False: This is the state in which one is awake with awareness limited to the consensual waking environment, but in which this environment is in fact a dream and one recognizes it as such. It is the waking equivalent of Lucid Dreaming False, in which one is aware that one is having a hallucinatory dream. This is consistent with the teachings of spiritual traditions such as Buddhism and Hinduism in which the world of consensual reality is a dream. It is not yet Enlightenment, as even though one knows that the illusion is an illusion, one does not yet know the truth. An example would be the experience of a person reading this sentence and realizing that it is just a dream sentence in the dream of waking life.

8. Lucid Dreamless Sleep: This is a state in which one is asleep and not dreaming and is aware of the sleep state. In the advanced Tibetan Buddhist teachings known as Vajrayana, this is called the "clear light of sleep" (Varela, 2015, p. 40).

*9. Lucid Dreaming True: This is a dream in which one is psychologically or energetically in a truly existent environment other than that which the sleeping physical body is in, realizes it is a dream, *and is aware* that the environment is real. An example would be dreaming that you are in heaven with your transitioned father, realizing you are in a dream and correctly thinking that you are in heaven with him.

10. Lucid Waking True: This is a state in which one is awake and aware of the true nature of reality. This is the state known as Enlightenment, as was said of the Buddha and of jnanis (individuals considered to be self-realized) such as Bhagavan Sri Ramana Maharshi.

In reading the above, you may have noticed that certain of the above states, which are preceded by asterisks (Nonlucid Waking False, Nonlucid Dreaming True, Nonlucid Waking True, Lucid Waking False and Lucid Dreaming True), assume the existence of a transcendent reality of which we are not usually (or not at all) experientially aware. I don't consider Lucid Waking True as necessarily implying a reality beyond that of which one is aware, as it is of course possible that the reality that we are usually aware of is indeed the one and only true reality and that insight into this constitutes lucidity and enlightenment. Finally, the proposed hierarchy elevates lucidity to a status above the truth of the perceived content, for example placing Lucid Dreaming False closer to enlightenment than Nonlucid Dreaming True. This is because it would seem that awareness that one is in a dream in which everything is a product of the imagination is a higher state of consciousness than experiencing the true nature of reality in a dream but failing to realize it as such. Similarly, Lucid Dreamless Sleep is considered a higher state than Lucid Dreaming False, Lucid Waking False and Nonlucid Waking whether false or true.

The reason I present this taxonomy as an introduction to this section is because the following four chapters will focus on:

(1) **transpersonal psychology**, which assumes transcendent realities;

(2) **lucid dreaming (LD), out of body experiences (OBEs), near death experiences (NDEs) and shared death experiences (SDEs)**, each of which may be interpreted either as a dream or hallucination with no referential reality, or as an experience of a referential reality that is usually veiled from consciousness; and

(3) **antimatter** which is neither here nor there.

When reading accounts of LDs, OBEs, NDEs and SDEs, the above taxonomy may be helpful in identifying a given writer/experiencer's personal ontological premises (beliefs regarding the nature of being), as well as the distance from ignorance that their inner journeys have taken them on the path from ignorance to enlightenment if this latter itself has any referential reality.

The Taxonomy can also be helpful to clinicians for differential diagnosis of syndromes involving similar symptoms but which are nonetheless psychiatrically unrelated. As a case in point, psychologists and psychiatrists who have not done their homework often fail to differentiate obsessions in OCD from psychotic delusions with or without risk of harm to self or others. I say this from experiences reported by clients I've seen who definitely have OCD and are definitely not psychotic or dangerous. An example may be found in "Harm" OCD (Obsessive Compulsive Disorder with obsessions about harming oneself or others). Here someone may be tormented by the recurring thought that they "might" kill their roommate, for example by pouring ammonia in the milk carton before going to bed, and might forget they've done it until they find their roommate dead after their morning corn flakes. A clinician familiar with OCD will assess whether there is intent to harm and hear something like "of course not, I would never hurt anyone, the thoughts terrify me, but how can I know if maybe I really do want to hurt him and don't realize it?" The therapist well trained, or "well experienced," in treating patients with OCD will pick up on the "what if" nature of the thoughts and know immediately that this is OCD Pure O and not psychosis or homicidality. This clinician will know that the reason for the obsession is that this is currently the thing the client most fears, and therefore is the last thing this client would ever do. By contrast, a clinician ignorant of the subtleties of OCD will hear the same thing, conclude that the client has homicidal ideation and plan with possible intent (as the client thinks there is a possibility that he wants to kill his roommate and thinks he might do it), and have him hospitalized (and in some states will also alert the police who may confiscate any firearms possessed by the client), despite the FACT that they are the least likely people to harm others. Whereas the first clinician knows that this client would be the safest person to hire as a babysitter (as not only would he never purposely harm anyone, but he is also likely very conscientious due to the OCD), the second clinician considers him a clear and present danger.

Here, the knowledgeable clinician is *correctly* seeing the client's mental state as Nonlucid Waking False (as lacking insight into the absence of referential reality of the experience – not realizing that he is not homicidal) whereas the diagnostically challenged clinician is *incorrectly* interpreting the client's mental state as Lucid Waking True (as having insight into the referential reality of the experience – "realizing" he is actually homicidal)(despite the fact that he is not).

I hope that this taxonomy will be received in the spirit that it is intended: not as a declaration of some kind of "Truth" about "reality" or "enlightenment," but as an organization of subjective phenomena in the form of a heuristic capable of generating hypotheses to be tested, possibly using (altered)-state-specific scientific methodologies (Tart, 1972).

Chapter 29 - *To Infinity and Beyond: Assagioli, Jung, Ramana and the Birth of Transpersonal Psychology*

"I do not doubt that it would be easier for fate to take away your suffering than it would for me. But you will see for yourself that much has been gained if we succeed in turning your hysterical misery into common unhappiness."

Sigmund Freud

(1895, in Freud & Breuer, 1895/2004, p. 306)

". . . I would like to add that psychosynthesis as I conceive it, should not only be a method of treatment of physical and psychological ills, but ought also to develop as a method of education and of self-education, as it represents not only an ideal of health and harmony, but also of dynamic development and growth of personality ... May it thus contribute to the preparation of a healthier, better and happier humanity."

Roberto Assagioli

(1927, pp. 19-28)

"Shh! Just gather everyone up for a staff meeting, and be happy."

Woody

(Toy Story; Lasseter, 1995)

Chapter 29 - To Infinity and Beyond: Assagioli, Jung, Ramana and the Birth of Transpersonal Psychology

DOCTOR, DOCTOR!

"Psychologists used to all be Freudians. Now they're all Buddhas."

By contrast with Freud's gloom and doom theories rooted in the unconscious and his ultimate therapeutic goal of "turning your hysterical misery into common unhappiness" (Freud, 1895, in Freud & Breuer, 1895/2004, p. 306), his younger contemporary Carl Jung anticipated Abraham Maslow's later interest in the "farthest reaches of human nature." Jung was influenced by Roberto Assagioli (1933) in whose theory the "higher unconscious" or "superconscious" extends upward from Freud's unconscious.

In 1927, Assagioli developed his science of Psychosynthesis as a positive alternative to Freud's psychoanalysis. According to Assagioli,

> *"Psychosynthesis*, as its name indicates, is founded upon the principle of organisation around a central point, of ordered hierarchy, of synthesis.

While descriptive, experimental and behavioral psychology, as well as psychoanalysis, are directed towards the analytical and objective study of psychological phenomena as such, and consider mental life as a mechanism ruled by fixed laws, psychosynthesis *starts from the living centre of the human being, from the self,* and studies all psychological facts in their vital relationship with that centre . . .

. . . Thus psychosynthesis is based upon the study and the actions of the *self.*

Now the question arises: What is, or rather, *who* is the self in us?

The answer may at first appear easy and simple, yet it proves very difficult. The *ego,* the reality of which we seem to be the most sure, strangely eludes and baffles us when we try to grasp it.

I will not enter now into the complications of this question, but will state only that, for all practical purposes, we may, and we must, distinguish between two kinds of selves: the *personal self* and the *individual* or *spiritual Self,* and to these correspond two kinds of synthesis: *psychological* or *personal synthesis,* and *individual* or *psycho-spiritual synthesis.*

The *personal* or *psychological self* is the conscious self of the normal human being . . .

The question of the *individual* or *spiritual Self* is a more difficult and obscure one, but it has been somewhat elucidated by modern studies of the *superconscious* psychological activities which are going on in the human soul . . .

. . . These and other studies, as well as the direct records and testimonials of many individuals, oblige every unbiassed [*sic*] person to admit that there is in us a higher kind of psychological activity, which habitually transcends the everyday consciousness, but which can make a connection with this on more or less frequent occasions.

From these higher levels come the inspiration of the great artists and prophets, the illuminations of the mystics, the flashes of intuition, the great decisions which lead to heroic deeds. This higher inner life must have, as our normal one, a center from which it manifests and which directs and controls it: this center is the *individual* or *spiritual Self.*

As has already been said, in many persons the spiritual or superconscious Self remains for all practical purposes latent, and as if non-existent – but there are many others in which it begins to make itself felt, to try to influence the personal self. This fact creates at first a new complication: the existing synthesis is disturbed and the personal self ignorantly resents this disturbance.

There is thus a definite repression of the higher impulses which is quite similar to that of the lower ones, discovered by psychoanalysis. This is a key which explains many facts: for instance why certain persons show such a marked hostility toward spiritual subjects. Yet we must not blame nor judge these persons: hostility is better than indifference and at any time the resistance may be overcome, the personality flooded by the light of the spirit and the whole attitude reversed. What happened to Paul can and does happen, on a lesser scale, to many persons . . .

. . . The practical use of psychosynthesis is a delicate art. It implies:

. . . When the spiritual synthesis is needed, the use of all the means liable to bring about this awakening, the birth of the new spiritual self in the personality, which may be aptly called *epigenesis*, that is, birth from above. These means are on the whole the same that have been more or less spontaneously used by religious souls or recommended by spiritual teachers:

The study of the experiences of those who have successfully achieved the *epigenesis;* regular and graded exercises of concentration, meditation and 'silence'; the development of true intuition and of the power of discriminating between the promptings of the higher Self and the impulses or suggestions from the subconscious; the development of a willing obedience to the higher intimations; an active and intelligent cooperation with the process of assimilating the spiritual elements in the personality.

But in the case of patients, who generally have a particular sensitiveness and special difficulties to overcome, the use of those means must be wisely advised and regulated by the doctor, in order to suit the psychological type and the possibilities of each patient, to avoid the danger of excesses and exaltation, to prevent as much as possible the reactions and complications which easily occur in such cases.

. . . I would like to add that psychosynthesis as I conceive it, should not only be a method of treatment of physical and psychological ills, but ought also to develop as a method of education and of self-education, as it represents not only an ideal of health and harmony, but also of dynamic development and growth of personality.

When it will be generally known and practiced, it may even be extended to social life: it may become a method of eliminating misunderstandings and unnecessary conflicts between individuals and groups, and point out the principles and methods of a wider, more harmonious and real human synthesis.

May it thus contribute to the preparation of a healthier, better and happier humanity." (Assagioli, 1927, pp. 19-28)

Assagioli wrote in 1933:

"We must get rid of the various attachments, fear, attractions, and repulsions to individuals, things and places which bind us in so many ways and hamper our inner development and outer adjustments, and which retard our spiritual growth. All this field [sic] has been dealt with extensively in psychoanalysis and similar lines of psychological research, and if we eliminate the exaggerations, the undue generalizations and the materialistic trends which make the Freudian psychoanalysis an unsafe and dangerous method, we shall find much that is useful and illuminating. The higher aspects can be found in Dr. Jung's books and in the good presentation of these matters made by Dr. B. Hinkle in her book *The Recreating of the Individual*. It would be well worth while to select from these studies and methods those which are the most applicable to the Yoga and the New Age." (Assagioli, 1933)

As an aside, I often teach my clients a formula for happiness that I haven't quite perfected, and keep changing, but it goes something like this:

Happiness [0..100] = 100 – Attachment to Preferences [0..100]

Chapter 29 - To Infinity and Beyond: Assagioli, Jung, Ramana and the Birth of Transpersonal Psychology

This, at least, is my take on the Buddha's three causes of suffering: greed, anger and confusion, understood as

1. **Attachment to wanting** things to be the way we want them to be;

2. **Attachment to not wanting** things to be the way we don't want them to be; and

3. **Ignorance** of the problematic nature of 1 and 2.

The emphasis here is on the problem posed by attachment to wanting/not wanting, rather than to wanting/not wanting per se. Wanting and non-wanting themselves serve useful functions (such as wanting food if we're hungry, not wanting the approaching bear to make us into food if it's hungry, etc.). To these ends, we are programmed to "want" and "not want" in the form of discomfort/urges which prompt approach or avoidance behavior when the want is unsatisfied or the non-want seems a real possibility. Where discomfort ends and suffering begins is when we elevate a want into a perceived need, and catastrophize its remaining or becoming unmet. If the perceived result is loss, we emote and behave on a continuum from sadness to despair; if danger, we emote and behave on a "fight" continuum from annoyance to rage (if we think we can destroy the source) or on a "flight" continuum from concern to panic (if we think the source is more likely to destroy us).

The ultimate remedy for the irrational escalation of wants into needs is acceptance (not signifying approval, but rather acknowledgement of the current reality, which can set the stage for effective problem solving) or equanimity (seeing everything as six of one, half dozen of another). Whether to aspire to complete equanimity is a personal choice, and one that probably wouldn't be functional in our present human state.

ROBERTO ASSAGIOLI AND RAMANA MAHARSHI

Roberto Assagioli, along with William James before him, had a lot to say about things that would only become part of the human potential and New Age movements much later. Interestingly, Assagioli's 1965 book Psychosynthesis contains an exercise *that is identical to the Self-Enquiry procedure of Ramana Maharshi* and that I have specified in Chapter 9 as the 3rd and highest form of meditation (Self-awareness) after object awareness and subject awareness. Assagioli calls this the "Exercise in Dis-Identification":

> "The first step is to affirm with conviction and to become *aware* of the fact: 'I *have* a body, but I *am not* my body' . . .
>
> . . . The first step is comparatively easy; but the second step is much less so. It is the realization: 'I *have* an emotional life, but *I am not* my emotions or my feelings' . . .
>
> . . . The third step consists in realizing: 'I *have* an intellect, but *I am not* that intellect' . . . This indicates that *we are not our thoughts* . . . We get ample proof of *not being* our thoughts when we try to control and direct them . . . If the mind is rebellious and undisciplined it means that the *'I'* is *not* the mind . . .
>
> . . . These facts give us evidence that the body, the feelings and the mind are *instruments* of experience, perception and action – instruments that are changeable and impermanent, but which can be dominated, disciplined, deliberately used by the *'I',* while the nature of the *'I'* is something entirely different . . .
>
> . . . The 'I' is simple, unchanging, constant and *self*-conscious. The experience of the 'I' can be formulated as follows: 'I am I, *a centre of pure consciousness.'* To state this with conviction does not mean one has yet reached the *experience* of the 'I', but it is the way which leads to it. And it is the key to, and the beginning of, the mastery of our psychological processes." (Assagioli, 1965, 116-120)

He goes on to say that

> "When one has practiced the exercise for some time, it can be modified by a swift dynamic use of the first three stages of dis-identification, leading to a deeper consideration of the fourth stage of self-identification, coupled with an inner dialogue along the following lines:
>
> 'What am I then? What remains after discarding from my self-identity the physical, emotional and mental contents of my personality, of my ego? It is the essence of myself – a center of pure self-consciousness and self-realization. It is the permanent factor in

Chapter 29 - To Infinity and Beyond: Assagioli, Jung, Ramana and the Birth of Transpersonal Psychology

the ever varying flow of my personal life. It is that which gives me the sense of being, of permanence, of inner security. I recognize and affirm myself as a center of pure self-consciousness. I realize that this center not only has a static self-awareness but also a dynamic power; it is capable of observing, mastering, directing and using all the psychological processes and the physical body. I am a center of awareness and of power." (Assagioli, 1965, 116-120)

Now compare Assagioli's Dis-Identification exercise with Ramana Maharshi's introduction to his Self-Enquiry meditation instructions in Nan Yar or Nan ar, which is usually translated as Who Am I but literally corresponds with I Am Who (I [Nan] Am Who [Yar/ar]). The original instructions were answers to questions posed to Ramana by Sri Sivaprakasam Pillai in 1901 when Ramana was observing silence and wrote his answers in the sand, on a slate or on scraps of paper. Pillai did not publish these from his notebooks until over 20 years later, and various editions then appeared, based on his notebooks, with different numbers of questions and answers. In 1927, Ramana himself wrote his instructions in essay form. The following is Michael James' translation from the Tamil:

"**Who am I?** The *sthūla dēha* [the 'gross' or physical body], which is [formed] by *sapta dhātus* [seven constituents, namely chyle, blood, flesh, fat, bone, marrow and semen], is not I. The five *jñānēndriyas* [sense organs], namely ears, skin, eyes, tongue and nose, which individually [and respectively] know the five *viṣayas* ['domains' or kinds of sensory phenomena], namely sound, touch [texture and other qualities perceived by touch], form [shape, colour and other qualities perceived by sight], taste and smell, are also not I. The five *karmēndriyas* [organs of action], namely mouth, feet [or legs], hands [or arms], anus and genitals, which [respectively] do the five actions, namely speaking, going [moving or walking], giving, discharge of faeces and enjoying [sexual pleasure], are also not I. The *pañca vāyus* [the five 'winds', 'vital airs' or metabolic processes], beginning with *prāṇa* [breath], which do the five [metabolic] functions, beginning with respiration, are also not I. The mind, which thinks, is also not I. All *viṣayas* [phenomena] and all actions ceasing [as in sleep], the ignorance [namely the absence of awareness of any phenomena that then remains and] that is combined only with *viṣaya-vāsanās* [dispositions, propensities, tendencies, inclinations, impulses or desires to experience phenomena] is also not I. Eliminating everything mentioned above as not I, not I, the **awareness** that stands isolated [or separated] **alone is I. The nature of** [such] **awareness is** *sat-cit-ānanda* [being-consciousness-bliss]."

(Ramana Maharshi, Undated, in James, 2021a)

The final two sentences in Pillai's original, preceded by his questions, are translated by Dr. T. M. P. Mahadevan as:

"If I am none of these, then who am I? After negating all of the above-mentioned as 'not this', 'not this', that Awareness which alone remains – that I am.

What is the nature of Awareness? The nature of Awareness is existence-consciousness-bliss."

(Ramana Maharshi, 1901/1982)

Michael James, who translated the essay version above, explains the importance of the concept of Neti Neti (Not This, Not This) as a precursor to Self-Enquiry with its goal of Self-Realization:

"When Bhagavan rewrote the original question and answer version of *Nāṉ Ār?* as the present essay, he highlighted the first question, 'நானார்?' (*nāṉ ār?*), which means 'I [am] who?', and his first two answers, 'அறிவே நான்' (*aṟivē nāṉ*), which means 'awareness alone is I', and 'அறிவின் சொரூபம் சச்சிதானந்தம்' (*aṟiviṉ sorūpam sat-cit-ānandam*), which means 'the nature of [such] awareness is being-consciousness-bliss', in bold type. The reason he did so is that the rest of the second paragraph, in which this question and two answers are contained, consists of ideas that were not actually a part of the answers that he gave to Sivaprakasam Pillai.

Before its publication, a draft of the original question and answer version was shown to Bhagavan for his approval, and when he read it he noticed that Sivaprakasam Pillai had expanded his original answer to the first question, adding a detailed list of things that we mistake ourself to be, but that in fact we are not. On seeing this, he remarked that he had not answered in such a detailed manner, but then

Chapter 29 - To Infinity and Beyond: Assagioli, Jung, Ramana and the Birth of Transpersonal Psychology

explained that, because Sivaprakasam Pillai was familiar with *nēti nēti*, he had added such detail thinking that it would help him to understand his answer more clearly.

The term *nēti nēti* refers to the rational process of self-analysis described in the ancient texts of *vēdānta*, a process that involves the analytical elimination or rejection of everything that is not 'I'. *Nēti* is a compound of two Sanskrit words, *na*, which means 'not', and *iti*, which is a quotative marker and therefore serves a similar function to quotation marks in English, so *nēti nēti* literally means 'not', 'not', but implies 'not this, not this'. The ancient texts of *vēdānta* use these words *nēti nēti* when explaining why all the adjuncts that we mistake to be ourself, such as the body, senses, life-force, mind and ignorance-enveloped *viṣaya-vāsanās* (propensities, inclinations or desires to experience phenomena), are not 'I'.

The rational and analytical process which is thus described in the ancient texts of *vēdānta* as *nēti nēti* or 'not this, not this' is essentially the same as the logical analysis of our experience of ourself that Sri Bhagavan taught us (which is described in chapter two of *Happiness and the Art of Being*). If we did not first critically analyse our experience of ourself in such a manner, we would not be able to understand either the reason why we should seek true self-knowledge, or what exactly we should investigate in order to know our real nature.

However, though Bhagavan taught us how we should critically analyse our experience of ourself in our three states of awareness, namely waking, dream and sleep, in order to understand that we are nothing other than our fundamental self-awareness, 'I am', which is the only thing that we experience in all these three states, and though this process of self-analysis is essentially the same as the process that is described in the ancient texts of *vēdānta* as *nēti nēti*, he would not himself have said, '**மேற்சொல்லிய யாவும் நானல்ல, நானல்ல வென்று நேதிசெய்து தனித்து நிற்கும் அறிவே நான்**' (*mēl solliya yāvum nāṉ alla, nāṉ alla v-eṉḏru nēti-seydu taṉittu niṟkum aṟivē nāṉ*), 'Eliminating everything mentioned above as not I, not I, the **awareness** that stands isolated [or separated] **alone is I**', as Sivaprakasam Pillai wrote when he expanded his first answer, 'அறிவே நான்' (*aṟivē nāṉ*), 'awareness alone is I'.

In this expanded sentence the adverbial participle that I translated as 'eliminating' is 'நேதிசெய்து' (*nēti-seydu*), which is a compound that literally means 'doing *nēti*', so qualifying 'அறிவு' (*aṟivu*), 'awareness', by adding the relative clause 'மேற்சொல்லிய யாவும் நானல்ல, நானல்ல வென்று நேதிசெய்து தனித்து நிற்கும்' (*mēl solliya yāvum nāṉ alla, nāṉ alla v-eṉḏru nēti-seydu taṉittu niṟkum*), 'that stands isolated [or separated] eliminating [or doing *nēti* of] everything mentioned above as not I, not I', is potentially misleading, because it could create the impression that simply by thinking '*nēti nēti*' or 'this is not I, this is not I' we can separate our fundamental self-awareness from everything with which we now confuse it. In fact, many scholars who attempt to explain the ancient texts of *vēdānta*, which often describe this analytical process of *nēti nēti* or negation of all that is not our real nature, interpret it to be the actual means by which we can attain self-knowledge. However, the sages who first taught the rational process of self-analysis called *nēti nēti* did not intend it to be understood as the actual practice of self-investigation (*ātma-vicāra*) but only as the means to gain the understanding required in order for us to be able to investigate what we actually are.

So long as we assume that we are really this physical body, thinking mind or any other phenomenon or object of perception, we will imagine that we can know ourself by attending to such things, and hence we will not be able to understand what is really meant by terms such as *ātma-vicāra*, self-investigation, self-examination, self-scrutiny, self-enquiry, self-attention, self-attentiveness or self-remembrance. Only when we understand that we are nothing other than our fundamental self-awareness — our adjunct-free awareness of our own existence, which we experience just as 'I am', not as 'I am this' — will we be able to understand what actually is the 'self' or 'I' that we should investigate, scrutinise or attend to.

Chapter 29 - To Infinity and Beyond: Assagioli, Jung, Ramana and the Birth of Transpersonal Psychology

Once we have understood that we are not actually this physical body, thinking mind or any other object known by us, we should not continue thinking, 'this body is not I', 'this mind is not I', and so on, but should withdraw our attention from all such things, and focus it wholly and exclusively upon our simple self-awareness, 'I am'. We cannot know our real nature by thinking of anything that is not 'I', but only by investigating, scrutinising or attending keenly to what is actually 'I' (what we really are), namely our fundamental self-awareness. Unless we withdraw our attention entirely from all other things, we will not be able to focus it wholly and exclusively on ourself, and unless we focus it wholly on ourself, we will not be aware of ourself as we actually are.

This is why in verse 16 of *Upadēśa Undiyār* Bhagavan emphasises the need for us to cease being aware of any phenomena in order to be aware of ourself as we actually are, namely as pure awareness, which is our own 'ஒளி உரு' (*oḷi-uru*) or 'form of light' ..." (James, 2021b)

FREUD'S BASEMENT AND ASSAGIOLI'S PENTHOUSE

We see here the similarity between what scientific psychology could have become and what true meditation has always been. Psychology could have regained the heights of our human birthright, as passed down through the millennia in the Upanishads and crystallized into a single meditative technique taught day after day by Ramana Maharshi for 50 years to all who came to him at Arunachala, had Roberto Assagioli's theory and practice of contacting the higher unconscious, or superconscious, virtually identical to that of the ancients, won out over those of Freud which are mired in the deepest, darkest depths of the lower unconscious. As Assagioli said in an interview, regarding the difference between psychoanalysis and psychosynthesis:

"We pay far more attention to the higher unconscious and to the development of the transpersonal self. In one of his letters, Freud said, 'I am interested only in the basement of the human being.' Psychosynthesis is interested in the whole building. We try to build an elevator which will allow a person access to every level of his personality. After all, a building with only a basement is very limited.

We want to open up the terrace where you can sunbathe or look at the stars." (Assagioli, in Keen, 1974)

These differences are illustrated by a comparison of Freud's and Assagioli's views of the psyche as illustrated by Freud's "Iceberg" and Assagioli's "Egg Diagram,"

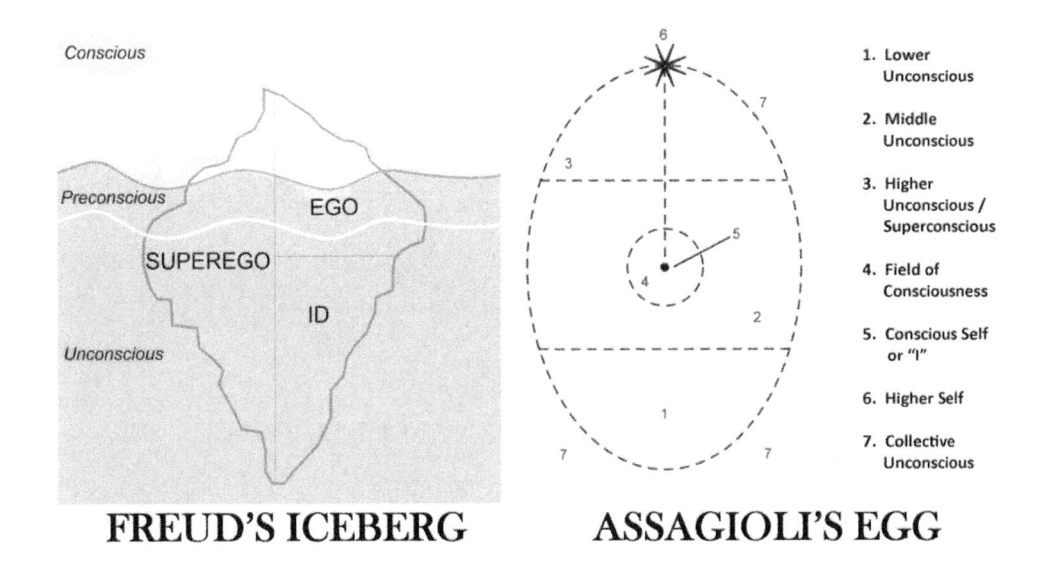

FREUD'S ICEBERG　　**ASSAGIOLI'S EGG**

1. Lower Unconscious
2. Middle Unconscious
3. Higher Unconscious / Superconscious
4. Field of Consciousness
5. Conscious Self or "I"
6. Higher Self
7. Collective Unconscious

and by their mugs:

Chapter 29 - To Infinity and Beyond: Assagioli, Jung, Ramana and the Birth of Transpersonal Psychology

I mean, have you *ever* seen Sigismund Schlomo (yes, really) crack a smile? (oops, name shame alert, my bad). He did try to crack a joke once, but it got mixed reviews. It went like this:

> "And now, it seems to me, the meaning of the evolution of culture is no longer a riddle to us.
>
> It must present to us the struggle between Eros and Death, between the instincts of life and the instincts of destruction, as it works itself out in the human species.
>
> This struggle is what all life essentially consists of and so the evolution of civilization may be simply described as the struggle of the human species for existence.
>
> And it is this battle of the Titans that our nurses and governesses try to compose with their lullaby-song of Heaven!"
>
> (Freud, 1930, Civilisation and Its Discontents, p. 103)

To his credit, Debby Downer has nothing on *him*.

But back to the iceberg and the egg. In Freud's iceberg, we have

(1) **an Id or "It"** (what we instinctually *want* to do, which for Freud was either kill people or have sex with them),

(2) **a Superego** (what we think we *should* do and *shouldn't* do, which is an internalization of cultural, subcultural or family rules, learned through reward/praise, punishment/criticism, moralizing, and other ways of conditioning infants and children to associate some things with reward (= "good") and other things with punishment (= "bad"), and

(3) **an Ego or "I"** as mediator of these, trying to satisfy the Id, which is in big time conflict with human social realities, in a realistic manner more or less acceptable to the Superego.

The battle between the Id and Superego, and the Ego's attempt to keep the peace are fought on the battlefields of the Unconscious (of which we are not aware), Conscious (of which we are aware) and Preconscious (which is kind of like a waystation between the Consciousness and the Unconscious, from which non-repressed thoughts and emotions can be accessed by conscious awareness).

In Assagioli's Egg Diagram, we similarly have an Unconscious, but it includes a

(1) **Lower Unconscious** (Freud's Unconscious),

(2) **Middle Unconscious** (Freud's Preconscious) and

(3) **Higher Unconscious** (Superconscious) with this latter corresponding with a realm overseen by the (6) Higher or Spiritual Self.

The (5) Ego is situated within the (4) Field of Consciousness (Freud's Conscious) but has a direct line to the (6) Higher or Spiritual Self. The entire Egg, or Psyche floats within Jung's Collective Unconscious (7). The dotted lines serving as borders among the various psychic components signify the potential flow of awareness among these.

Assagioli was himself a practitioner of Theosophy (an integration of various religious and mystical teachings) and was perfectly placed to himself integrate Western psychology with these Eastern meditative practices, which he did. Unfortunately it wasn't until the 1950s and 1960s that his system of psychosynthesis became more widely known internationally, and by then the field of psychology and psychiatry were dominated by a narrow focus on behavior, conscious cognition and brain chemistry, with little interest in the superconscious or how to access it (that is, outside of the field of Transpersonal Psychology, that Assagioli co-founded with Maslow):

> "Whereas Maslow explored fundamental issues in transpersonal psychology, Roberto Assagioli pioneered the practical application of these concepts in psychotherapy. Assagioli proposed a transpersonal view of personality and discussed psychotherapy in terms of the synthesis of personality at both the personal and spiritual levels. He dealt with the issue of spiritual crises and introduced many active therapeutic techniques for the development of a transcendent center of personality." (Battista, 1996, p. 52)

Both Assagioli and Jung, who were as interested in mystical consciousness practices as in the mainstream science of the day, were true to the pragmatic psychology of William James, who established the first Department of Psychology in the U.S. (James, 2022) and famously said that pragmatism

"... is completely genial. She will entertain any hypothesis, she will consider any evidence ... She will count mystical experiences if they have practical consequences ..." (James, 1907/1992, p. 53)

CARL JUNG AND RAMANA MAHARSHI

Carl Jung was well versed in the teachings of Ramana Maharshi. As Assagioli was a student of Jung, in addition to being familiar with Theosophy, which was informed by Hinduism, it is most likely not a coincidence that some of Assagioli's exercises bore such as close resemblance to Ramana's method of Self-Enquiry.

Jung could have met Ramana in 1938 but, as he explains:

"I had a chance, when I was in Madras, to see the Maharishi, but by that time I was so imbued with the overwhelming Indian atmosphere of irrelevant wisdom and with the obvious Maya of this world that I didn't care anymore if there had been twelve Maharishis on top of each other." (Jung, 1947)

Nevertheless, Jung expresses admiration for Ramana, saying

"Sri Ramana is a true son of the Indian earth. He is genuine and, in addition to that, something quite phenomenal. In India he is the whitest spot in a white space. What we find in the life and teachings of Sri Ramana is the purest of India; with its breath of world-liberated and liberating humanity, it is a chant of millenniums ... The identification of the Self with God will strike the European as shocking. It is a specifically oriental Realization, as expressed in Sri Ramana's utterances. Psychology cannot contribute anything further to it, except the remark that it lies far beyond its scope to propose such a thing. However it is clear to the Indian that the Self as spiritual Source is not different from God; and in so far as man abides in his Self, he is not only contained in God but is God Himself. Sri Ramana is clear in this respect.

The Goal of Eastern practices is the same as that of Western Mysticism: the focus is shifted from the 'I' to the Self, from Man to God. This means that the 'I' disappears in the Self, and Man in God." (Jung, 1972/1988, pp. ix-xii)

And in his Holy Men of India,

> "The goal of Eastern religious practice is the same as that of Western mysticism: the shifting of the center of gravity from the ego to the self, from man to God. This means that the ego disappears in the self, and man in God. It is evident that Shri Ramana has either really been more or less absorbed by the self, or has at least struggled earnestly all his life to extinguish his ego in it. (In Jung, 1944/1990, p. 181)

Jung went on to develop his technique of Active Imagination, a form of wakeful dreaming, a topic addressed in detail by Mary Watkins in her book Waking Dreams (1977) in which she presents diverse psychological practices aimed at maintaining awareness when accessing the unconscious. By "waking dream," Watkins (1974) refers to

> "not just an expression of dreamlike character received while awake, but an experience of the imagination undertaken with a certain quality of awareness. This conscious awareness differentiates the experience of the imagination (whether conveyed through auditory and visual imagery, or activities such as automatic writing or dancing, or less translatable experiences of imagination) from daydreams and hallucinations." (p. 33)

Watkins (1974, 1977) provides a history of the use meditative methods in psychotherapy going back to the late 19th and early 20th centuries, mostly to induce the conscious experience of unconscious imagery. For example, Alfred Binet (who developed the first I.Q. test), used a "provoked introspection" technique in which he had patients speak to images that arose. Carl Happich (1932) used muscle relaxation, passive breathing and meditation to trigger imagery in the "meditative zone," between the conscious and unconscious, in which "creations ripened in the unconscious appear in the mind's eye." Ernst Kretschmer (1951/1959) developed "meditative techniques for psychotherapy" in which he began by introducing a specific image with a goal of triggering the emergence of both personal and archetypal images into conscious awareness (Watkins, 1977, p. 55).

For the purposes of the present book, it should be noted that the use of meditation as a psychotherapeutic technique to provoke imagery that can then be experienced and effect a "cure" (in either psychoanalysis or

Chapter 29 - To Infinity and Beyond: Assagioli, Jung, Ramana and the Birth of Transpersonal Psychology

behavioral imaginal exposure therapy) is completely different from the use of meditation to train the mind to stop thinking and potentially open up consciousness to transcendental experience, or non-experience, beyond thinking. Nevertheless, the altered consciousness state of "waking dreaming" was a forerunner of the use of the lucid dreaming state for therapeutic, positive psychological and transcendent psychological purposes (corresponding with my Psychologies 2.0, 3.0 and 4.0).

Chapter 30 - *All Reality is Virtual: The Varieties of Offline Perceptual Experience (OPE)*

". . . [Unity] nearly always formatted her infos in pre-Federation 'book' style, like those that filled every wall and even some ceilings in each room of the holarchived Old New Jersey landchateau of her great great grandparents, Rimatt and Gelmar Densei, where she virted from time to time. It was, in fact, this world-renown bibliotek that was the first material chosen by the Old Parisian, Trefau Tzackaria Dinbor, A.K.A. Tzackary the Gamer, for the decade-long EarthMem Holarchive Satellite Upload Initiative that he began when the probability of the Events that would trigger the Immersion in Old Gregorian 2080 CE became too high to ignore. Even now, 31 years later, over three billion people worldwide were taking advantage of the zero income tax incentive offered to 24/7 wearers of the Dinbor Multisensory Holarchival Enviroscan Upload neurochip.

... The evening before, Unity and her best friend Nika had virted to the holarchived simcity of Old Amsterdam, where Nika's sisters had offered to show them around the places they'd frequented before the Immersion. Yem and Gem currently lived in nonsim Amsterdam's Melk Weg Onderwaterstad, which in just four years would celebrate its Centennial as the first subaquacity in the world, founded in 69 BI. They met in the Leidseplein, in the center of which an enormous crowd had gathered to listen to the melodies of some colorfully attired Old Peruvian street musicians. The square was full of people with animals of all sorts on leashes. Ever since the 'doggie virtsuit' fad had made the President's puppy Gracie the first Saint Bercockerdoodle in simuspace, pets had become commonplace on EarthMem. Some zoos and specialty shops even rented out time with domesticated virtsuit-equipped exotic animals, like the lion cub playing with Yem's shoelaces.

Chapter 30 - All Reality is Virtual: The Varieties of Offline Perceptual Experience (OPE)

... One of the things Unity enjoyed most about her quarters at the White House was that they were equipped with the latest technology. Her pod had the new SimuWear FlexiBod 3.2 Virtsuit, which was so thin and lightweight that it was barely perceptible, while at the same time providing 97 percent accurate sensorimotor simustim. Whenever she visited, she made sure to set aside several hours to enjoy a swim at one of her favorite holarchived beaches. Sometimes she went for a deep sea dive, and if she was feeling particularly energetic she asked Luc for motocross lessons. She had heard a rumor that some of the races were infected with a simsentient parasitic that deactivated the range of motion and sensory overstimulation emergency cutoff in some of the older virtgear, causing serious injury in the event of a crash. There had even been two absorptions attributed to sitic-implicated accidents. But Luc had assured her that the state-of-the-art FlexiBod was fully approved by the Simuspace Protection Agency due to its advanced JointSecure and SenStim features, and so she spent the morning training for an upcoming Old Isle de Man simmy where she was looking forward to pushing her Guzzi to the limit."

Unity's Pulse (Densei, 2008)

"'The brain's task is not to see the retinal image, but to relate signals from the retina to objects of the external world' (Gregory, 1998). On this view, establishing the identity of an object requires a match between information from the eye and a pre-existing representation of that object in the brain. Having built up a large repertoire of such representations during childhood, the brain has the task of selecting the correct one in a fraction of a second. In Richard's view we often have too little information in the image to make this identification with certainty. 'The essential problem of the brain to solve is that any given retinal image could be produced by an infinity of sizes and shapes and distances of object, yet normally we see just one stable object' (Gregory, 1998). Mistakes do occur – most of us have had the experience of misidentifying a friend in the street, only to find out that they were someone else – but such events are relatively uncommon in adulthood. A central idea in Richard's thinking is that, because of the lack of certainty, perceptions are essentially *hypotheses*: the best conclusions that can be drawn from the evidence available at the time (Gregory, 1980). Richard points out that, as in science, hypotheses are risky, as they are predictive and go beyond the sensed evidence. They are nevertheless vital, as un-interpreted images are of no use in formulating behaviour. His account is, by his own admission, derived largely from the work of Hermann von Helmholtz a century earlier (Helmholtz, 1910). In Helmholtz's view perceptions are 'inductive conclusions unconsciously formed'. Both Helmholtz and Richard pointed out the similarity of this aspect of perception to the progress of science by hypothesis and experiment."

Land & Heard

(2018; on Richard Langton Gregory. 24 July 1923 - 17 May 2010)

"The perceptual selection of sensed characteristics may create objects ... What science describes as an object may or may not correspond to what appears to the senses as an object; different instruments reveal the world as differently structured. Further, general theories change what are regarded as objects."

Richard Langton Gregory

(1980, p. 187)

"It is reasonable to suppose that a very great deal of perception is in this sense fictional: generally useful but occasionally clearly wrong, when it can be an extremely powerful deception. No doubt this holds also for science."

Richard Langton Gregory

(1980, p. 193)

Chapter 30 - All Reality is Virtual: The Varieties of Offline Perceptual Experience (OPE)

Ontogony recapitulates phylogeny. You can quote me on that. On second thought, since it's fallen out of favor scientifically (though epigenetics has begun to bring it back into favor), you can quote Ernst Haeckel (1834-1919). Who wasn't, by the way, wrong all the time – after all he did coin the term "First World War" decades before the second one happened.

The human quest to mentally trick ourselves into believing that something is what it isn't and isn't what it is (such as through art, literature and audiovisual media) has a long history and short future. Now that the holy grail of self-deception – full-body holosensory experience (virtual seeing, hearing, smelling, tasting, and bodysensing) – is almost upon us, soon the illusion will seem so real that we will live, move and breathe in it without the need for much mental trickery at all.

Ontogenetically, remember when you were a mere zygote purposely spinning around so that when you stopped it would seem like the womb was spinning?

The act of imaginal sensing/multisensing and the resulting imaginal sensory experience (visual/iconic, auditory/echoic, and tactile/haptic) is likely an individual difference on a continuum from the complete absence of sensation when there is no corresponding external input, to "eidetic" or hallucinatory-quality visual, auditory or tactile experience.

Types of eidetic imaging (EI) may be considered to include

> **Eidetic iconic imaging (eidetic vision),**
>
> **Eidetic echoic imaging (eidetic audition), and**
>
> **Eidetic haptic imaging (eidetic touch).**

Whether true or not, the example usually given for eidetic iconic imaging is Nikola Tesla, who is said to have been able to both devise and test the mechanical workings of his inventions via mental imagery prior to constructing them out of physical objects; and eidetic echoic imagery has been attributed to Mozart.

Eidetic touch is another matter. The sense of eidetic touch is an acquired skill, which can be trained by practicing imaginal movement of the body, and by training in Eastern energetic practices such as the Taoist Microcosmic

Orbit in which "energy" is mentally moved within the body. The reason that this creates sensation in the parts of the body targeted may be that focusing on a part of the body brings blood to that area, creating pressure that the mind can trick itself into thinking is the sensation of the skin touching something or something touching the skin. Alternatively, when we focus on a part of the body, we are likely, by classically conditioned association, activating the area of the sensory cortex corresponding with that part of the body, and therefore feel sensation there. Focusing attention on the lower back and then the middle of the back and then the upper back may, therefore, be sequentially activating contiguous areas of the sensory cortex governing these three areas of the back, thus creating a spaciotemporal perception of "energy" "moving" up the back.

The mind is itself Wallace Steven's "blue guitar," determining, for all practical purposes, what things "are." Communication has as its goal the creation of a representation, in the mind of another, of something (the referent, or meaning), by enacting a behavior that creates for the other the experience of something else (the symbol, in the form of one or more sounds, words, images or even bodily sensations that have acquired shared meaning). Representational art, at least as far back as cave paintings and theatrical reenactments of the hunt, progressing to literature, theatre, visual arts and music with representational motifs, seeks to create a "suspension of disbelief" in order to trick the mind into believing and enjoying temporary alternative realities. The technologies of two-dimensional photography, movies, television, and video games have now advanced to permit three-dimensional and 360-degree immersive experiences in virtual and augmented realities (VR and AR, replacing current sensation with new sensation, and adding new sensation to current sensation, respectively). While most 2020s consumer VR and AR experience is limited to vision and hearing, the next breakthrough will be the full-body "virt suit," conveying to the wearer all sensations programmed to be experienced by the virtual body in the VR environment (several days after writing the preceding and what follows, today in fact, March 22, 2021, Microsoft announced "Mesh," which may dominate computing until the arrival of the consumer virtsuit). Before the inevitable occurs and human greed and stupidity destroy Earth's atmosphere, and nature as we know it ceases to exist, hopefully some innovative soul, such as Tzackary the Gamer in Unity's Pulse (Densei, 2008), will "holarchive" the beauty, sights, sounds, smells and sensations of

Chapter 30 - All Reality is Virtual: The Varieties of Offline Perceptual Experience (OPE)

life at Earth's pre-apocalyptic surface, to be experienced thereafter in a simuspace such as EarthMem.

What prompted me to write this chapter was an experience that I had recently and a subsequent effort to understand it. I had been interested in the promise of VR since the publication of Howard Rheingold's book *Virtual Reality* back in 1991 (which, interestingly, he wrote *after* co-authoring with Stephen LaBerge the book *Exploring the World of Lucid Dreaming* in 1990, thus exploring the "organic virtual reality" of lucid dreaming prior to delving into the potentials of the machine-driven variety), but never made the time to seek out opportunities to engage in VR except once at a theme park. Until several weeks ago, I had not thought seriously of looking into consumer VR options beyond google cardboard a few years ago which hadn't taken long to outlive its novelty. Then, one evening succumbing to pandemic boredom, I googled "Oculus" and found that some pretty sophisticated equipment is now affordable. So I ordered an Oculus Quest 2 and started looking into games that were considered to provide the most realistic virtual environments without too much blood and gore. I settled on Red Matter, and then spent a few evenings standing in the middle of my living room experiencing my surroundings as being a space station on another planet. After a few days of this, sometimes I would take off the goggles and visually experience the room I was really in as itself an alternative reality, vis-a-vis the seeming reality of the space station. Then one night, when I closed my eyes to go to sleep, I began seeing three-dimensional images of things I was imagining as though I was seeing through my eyelids, which in the past had only occurred in deep states of meditation.

For several years, when teaching meditative self-enquiry (the third type of meditation, after object awareness and subject awareness) to clients with an interest in consciousness exploration, I had been using virtual reality as a metaphor for reality itself, consistent with the Hindu practice of *neti neti,* or *not this, not this* (referring to the lack of identity between "I" and the environment, including the aspects of the I's environment that we commonly self-identify with, such as body, mind, sensation, perception and thought). Here are two exercises I came up with for this purpose:

> **Exercise 1: Everything is Virtual.** Wherever you are, whatever you are doing, stop for a moment and be aware of your surroundings: what you are seeing, hearing, smelling, tasting and bodysensing. Now

imagine that this is not where you really are. Where you really are is in a neuropsychology lab in Vancouver equipped with the most cutting-edge virtual reality equipment. You are wearing a virtual reality suit, or *virt suit*, and are suspended in a spherical virtual reality pod, or *virt pod*, allowing a full range of arm and leg movement. When you move, touch something, or are touched by something in the simulation, the skin of your arms, legs and body is stimulated by sensors which simulate the pressure and temperature that would be experienced by that interaction if it were actually taking place in the environment that you perceive yourself to be in. So when you move your legs to walk on a visual simulation of a sidewalk, you feel the same sensations with your feet that you would feel if really walking on such a sidewalk. If you extend one hand to pick up a simulated coffee cup and the other to pick up a simulated grape, the sensors on your virt suit convey the same sensations as you would experience if you were really interacting with these objects. And let's go one step further. The virt pod is equipped with an organic food product which can take solid or liquid form and can be chemically altered to simulate any taste, such that when you put simulated food or drink into your mouth, you actually experience its texture and taste as you chew and swallow or drink it. Now knowing this, look around you and touch some things, pick them up, put them down, and stand up and walk around a little, interacting with objects in the room, and thinking "wow, this all seems so real, but I'm really in a virt pod in a laboratory in Vancouver." Then return and continue reading.

Exercise 2: Who Is Virting? Now comes the really interesting part. So here you are, in this virtual environment that seems really, really real, all the while knowing that you're in a virt pod, or the Matrix, or whatever. But the technology is still glitchy, and you suddenly feel a strong electrical shock to your forehead causing amnesia and you no longer remember who you are, only that your real body is in a virt pod and that you are experiencing a virtual body and environment. Back in Vancouver, the lab technicians don't dare to disconnect you from the virt suit or take you out of the virt pod, for fear of further neurological harm. They do, however, announce over the audio feed something to the effect of "How's it going in there, minor glitch, nothing to worry about, but for the next few minutes you will have no

Chapter 30 - All Reality is Virtual: The Varieties of Offline Perceptual Experience (OPE)

access to your memories of who you really are, and any memories of your life that you are currently experiencing are actually not your own but of a character in the simulation. What you need to do to regain your own memories is to ask yourself 'Who Am I? Who is seeing, hearing, smelling, tasting, bodysensing and thinking?" Now please spend the next few minutes exploring the simulation, and wondering 'Who Am I, who is the I that seems to be in this multisensory environment but is really wearing a virt suit in a virt pod in Vancouver?'"

I may be wrong, but I believe that both the Buddha and Ramana Maharshi would approve of these VR-Assisted Self-Enquiry exercises as "expedient means" for modern day self-enquiry into the illusory nature reality and the true nature of the Self.

What I realized after taking off the Oculus headset, and perceiving the reality of my living room to not necessarily seem more real than the space station where I'd just been fixing a nuclear reactor, was that the post-VR experience was a form of ASC (altered state of consciousness; Tart, 1969), as was the eidetic imagery (seeing something that is not physically present) when I closed my eyes to sleep (which was not hypnagogic imagery, as it happened immediately upon shutting my eyes and I was still, at least to my knowledge, completely alert and not yet in the slow-brainwave state typical of drifting off to sleep). Then, 2 nights ago, when I awoke in the middle of the night and thought about this further, I realized that I couldn't be the only person having these post-VR experiences and made a mental note to google "VR derealization" the next day. And since it seemed to have consciousness exploration potential, and consciousness exploration carries with it the risk of "spiritual emergency" along the path to spiritual emergence, I hypothesized that upon consulting Google, I was likely to find reports of VR-induced spiritual emergencies labeled, as they usually are, as psychiatric events, similar to the perspective of a client I once worked with who, after taking LSD and apparently having a powerful metacognitive experience (becoming hyperaware of thinking, and of himself as the observer of his thinking), just wanted to "be normal again" (identifying with cognition, rather than observing it). The next day, as expected, I found articles dating back over 20 years that have identified various VR "side effects" known as VRISE (Virtual Reality Induced Symptoms and Effects; Cobb, Nichols, Ramsey & Wilson, 1999).

VRISE can include the dissociative phenomena of depersonalization and derealization, with a reduced sense of presence in objective reality (whatever that is; Aardema et al., 2010), and symptoms similar to motion sickness, including nausea, disorientation/postural instability, and visual problems (Barrett, 2004). Part of it has to do with a mismatch between the current environment and neurological/vestibular predictions. It's like when you were a kid (or last Saturday) and the playground seemed to spin after you yourself had spun your body around for a while. Or when you've been hiking for a couple of hours and stop to look at the scenery and suddenly everything is moving away from you even though you're standing still (or moving toward you if you've been hiking backwards). Or when you're sitting on a train waiting for it to leave, and suddenly feel like it's moving when it's really the train next to it that has started to move. Your brain makes a best guess as to what's happening, and creates for you the corresponding experience that, if it isn't what is really happening, plays games with your vestibular system (though when they redesign the human body, they might want to figure out some vestibular games more fun than nausea). The redesigners would do well to take into account Rimatt Densei's (1981) "How to Safely Operate a Human Being," referring to Human 1.0, but which will likely inform the next few updated models, as well as to minimize its "defeatability proneness," an engineering term he coined for the extent to which the intended functioning of a design is capable of being thwarted, usually unintentionally, by the end user:

Chapter 30 - All Reality is Virtual: The Varieties of Offline Perceptual Experience (OPE)

The Human Factor

EXHIBIT 3.2–1

SAFETY INSTRUCTIONS | **INSTRUCCIÓNES DE SEGURIDAD**

⚠ DANGER | **⚠ PELIGRO**

HOW TO SAFELY OPERATE A HUMAN BEING
DANGER! WARNING! CAUTION!

1. Performance of this product is unreliable, unpredictable, potentially hazardous and/or self-destructive if operated for prolonged periods of time without interruption; if attention or concentration is distracted or diverted; if filled with drugs, toxic chemicals or other hazardous substances; if fatigued, worried, angered, excited or provoked. Unit may independently take risks if unrestrained, overexperienced, overconfident or complacent; may cause injury or damage to itself or other units if poorly trained; may not pay attention to or comply with inadequate warnings or instructions.

2. Unit cannot efficiently perform routine, repetitive, or very precise operations or tasks continuosly, in rapid succession, or consistently with high accuracy or precision over prolonged periods; may not respond swiftly to control signals or stimuli; cannot store and recall large amounts of information in short time frames; cannot perform complex computations rapidly with high accuracy and cannot perform many different tasks simultaneously.

3. Product is sensitive to extraneous, external factors and signals. It cannot retain operational integrity or perform satisfactory in hostile environments without extensive retrofitting. We cannot guarantee results of maintenance, reworking, or rebuilding depending upon damage sustained by product. Units are susceptible to operation under the influence of human nature and it is only a matter of *when*, rather than *whether*, error or failure will result. Failure can be partial or total, temporary or permanent.

4. Product is unique and indispensable in many applications under diverse conditions of service; unusually excellent self-reproduction capability; critical component in many control systems involving or requiring complex pattern recognition; automatic, optimum objective-seeking feature in some units; numerous self-compensating mechanisms incorporated plus creative objective-setting, decision-making and risk-taking even under

© 1981 R.M. Seiden

EXHIBIT 3.2–1 *(cont'd)*

SAFETY INSTRUCTIONS	INSTRUCCIÓNES DE SEGURIDAD
⚠ **WARNING**	⚠ **MUCHO CUIDADO**

conditions of uncertainty; creative improvisation and ability to react to unexpected low-probability events. Unit can usually profit from experience and performs to acceptable degree even when overloaded. Reasons inductively with acceptable efficiency; can function with fragmentary and indeterminate data; detects very low levels of certain energy forms and detects signals in very high noise levels. Unit can store very large amounts of data for long periods and has a random access capability. It exhibits an acceptable learning curve. Usually functions in pairs, one way or another, over much of its life cycle.

5. Unit can destroy itself, however, and other units of its class or series under variable and sometimes unpredictable conditions of service. May reject command signals based upon its internal programming. There are many built-in protective features and internal controls which increase utility, durability and economy under normal or design conditions of service. Unit is portable, compact and self-starting but may require special handling and tender, loving care. Two models are presently available but infinite variations are feasible. Major specifications cannot be altered within present state-of-the-art.

6. All series and models incorporate state-of-the-art on-board electro-optical and electro-chemical computers, electronics and telemetry, plus highly advanced signal amplification and manipulator or telechiric capabilities. However, normal wear and tear plus improper use and abuse are capable of resultant, progressive, irreversible deterioration and/or malfunction. Units should not be opened up except under compelling circumstances. Advanced internal climate-conditioning.

7. No original equipment spare parts are available from the factory. OEM (Original Equipment Manufacturer) spares can only be obtained from sound units already in the field. Such OEM spares can typically be very costly to both donor and donee. There are no assurances that donor spares will be compatible with recipient.

Chapter 30 - All Reality is Virtual: The Varieties of Offline Perceptual Experience (OPE)

The Human Factor

EXHIBIT 3.2–1 *(cont'd)*

SAFETY INSTRUCTIONS   **INSTRUCCIÓNES DE SEGURIDAD**

⚠ **CAUTION**   ⚠ **CUIDADO**

8. Delivery has historically been approximately nine (9) months. However, product is ordinarily not optimally usable for about twenty (20) years. Unfortunately, factory errors are frequently irreversible. Under no circumstances can defective units be returned for credit or refund. Customer must accept units "as is." Some parts and subsystems are replaceable by substitutes with respect to function. Salvage value can be high but scrap value is zero. However, all materials of construction can be recycled and are automatically returnable to the Home Office with special packaging usually desirable. Reworked or rebuilt units may have reduced investment value. However, rebuilt or reconditioned second-hand product is sometimes superior in performance to brand new units due to "running-in" or having been "broken in." No "trial and test" arrangements are as yet available.

9. There is nothing like it on the market. There are no competitive brands. Nor are there any acceptable or recognized substitutes. Physical replication at present impossible, even by factory. Orders can only be filled with mutual consent but are usually honored thereafter. Overall satisfactions from acquisition usually more than compensate for limitations, inherent hazards and the statistically certain occurrence of defects. Unit has very low first cost. Operating expenses are variable depending upon model and series. With proper care and use, investment returns can be unparalleled, with qualifications and limitations stated below.

10. Archival records and long applications engineering and field experience show potential to be unlimited. But be alert to incidence of early malfunctions that can permanently impair performance. Both inherent defects and adverse environmental conditions are capable of destroying or limiting utility.

11. Manufacturer has not been able to eliminate certain primitive instincts and makes no representation as to how they may affect performance under reasonably foreseeable conditions of service (C.O.S.).

12. No additional instructional, standards, parts or maintenance manuals are or will ever be available from the manufacturer. Design, de-

EXHIBIT 3.2-1 (cont'd)

SAFETY INSTRUCTIONS | **INSTRUCCIÓNES DE SEGURIDAD**

⚠ DANGER | **⚠ PELIGRO**

velopment and application of MRO (Maintenance, Repair and Operations) procedures are automatically delegated to owner-operator when delivery is made. However, such procedures are available on the basis of universal, historical experience from diverse sources. Quality, content and orientation of such sources varies widely, however, and extreme care should be exercised in their evaluation or assessment prior to application. As a matter of firm and non-negotiable policy, the manufacturer can assume no responsibility whatever for product damage or destruction due to utilization of inappropriate or improper MRO methods and procedures. Nor will the manufacturer recommend or qualify such procedures or sources of supply.

13. No guarantees or warranties have been, are or will be available. No product catalogues are available. Intentions and objectives of the manufacturer are unfathomable and inscrutable. Ordinary and reasonable care by owner will not assure risk- or error-free application or performance. Neither the manufacturer nor the factory can be held responsible for poor quality, defective features or out-of-specification performance.

14. The manufacturer reserves the right to discontinue or alter specifications, designs or material at any time without notice, in keeping with immutable natural laws, sound engineering and scientific principles and state-of-the-art practices. Longer-range strategic plans for product improvements or modifications cannot be disclosed. However, such changes will not usually alter functional capabilities relative to earlier units or models in series and are generally minor from model year to model year. Environmental factors may also generate evolutionary changes.

15. Product economic or service life approximately forty (40) to fifty (50) years. Economic obsolescence depends upon application. Only minor technological obsolescence occurs from model year to model year. Normal wear and tear will not result in perceptible physical deterioration for approximately sixty (60) years.

16. Statistically, typical product experience shows that units will presently last from sixty-eight (68) to seventy-three (73) years, depending

Chapter 30 - All Reality is Virtual: The Varieties of Offline Perceptual Experience (OPE)

EXHIBIT 3.2–1 *(cont'd)*

SAFETY INSTRUCTIONS | **INSTRUCCIÓNES DE SEGURIDAD**

⚠ **WARNING** ⚠ **MUCHO CUIDADO**

upon series and conditions of service. During last ten (10) or more years of product life cycle, units are usually relegated or downgraded to non-productive, low-level application and are generally viewed as superfluous in relation to younger "standing stock" in the field. Therefore, efforts are frequently made to restrict, confine or abandon them to reduce maintenance and operating costs, and to minimize capital investments which will not yield acceptable financial returns. Thereby, scrapping and recycling dates can sometimes be advanced by several years with significant savings in reallocable and usually scarce financial resources.

17. Product can no longer be purchased at auction but fair market value can be established through standard methods and procedures of engineering economies. Market, income and reproduction or replacement bases for appraisal should yield identical results with the qualification that, as usual, replacement applies solely to functional utility.

18. Application of cost/benefit, risk-utility, economic feasibility, cost-effectiveness or other similar analytical techniques to evaluate investment potential can yield erroneous results. Functional productivity of unit is only one of product attributes. Units capable of generating significant serendiptic and synergistic benefits when operational in Society. Many product advantages and attributes are non-quantifiable. Therefore, loss of qualitative utility and/or unrealized potential can outweigh quantifiable cost (plus imputed price) of eliminating or mitigating hazards both to and from product. A risk- or hazard-averse strategy or attitude will be found the most satisfactory owner-operator policymaking alternative with respect to product safety.

19. For further safety warnings and instructions please do not write or contact the manufacturer or the factory. However, in event of breakdown, failure, damage or other emergency consult our own local field representatives (who may frequently be readily identified by their black uni-

The Human Factor 103

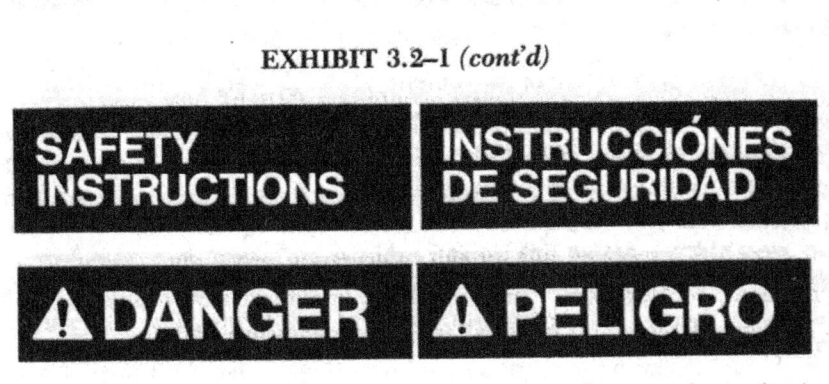

> **EXHIBIT 3.2–1** *(cont'd)*
>
> **SAFETY INSTRUCTIONS** | **INSTRUCCIÓNES DE SEGURIDAD**
>
> ⚠ **DANGER** | ⚠ **PELIGRO**
>
> forms) or authorized servicepersons (who are usually attired in white). Above all, *be careful!*
>
> 20. Failure to follow the foregoing safety warnings or instructions may result in irreparable and irreversible product failure, personal injury, property damage, economic loss, consequential damages or a combination thereof.
>
> 21. The manufacturer contemplates improving product utility and expanding production to remote corners of the Universe, conditions permitting. However, there is no assurance that present series or models will operate in such a manner that their continuance will be justified or, indeed, possible.
>
> 22. These warnings and cautionary instructions should be posted and/or affixed to the product in a conspicuous place for the benefit of owners and users.
>
> 23. These warnings and cautionary instructions are intended for your protection. Do not remove, multilate, deface, paint over, cover, or otherwise obscure their content.

VRISE can also include changes in heartrate, and in urine and salivary cortisol levels (Cobb, Nichols, Ramsey & Wilson, 1999). Aside from the depersonalization symptoms, the effects seem similar to those experienced after getting off a long speedboat ride, so are probably nothing to worry about. As for the induced depersonalization, whether this is ultimately a problem or an opportunity likely depends on one's pre-existing psychological/psychiatric stability and openness to consciousness exploration and self-discovery.

Chapter 30 - All Reality is Virtual: The Varieties of Offline Perceptual Experience (OPE)

Perhaps the first research on the effects of presenting the senses with false sensory information was that of George Stratton in Wilhelm Wundt's psychology lab in Leipzig (incidentally, the first experimental psychology lab) in the late 1800s on "vision without inversion of the retinal image" (George M. Stratton, 2021; Stratton, 1897a for days 1-6, 1897b for days 7 and 8). In normal vision, when you see something, your retina flips it upside down and from left to right, with your brain then flipping it back to correspond with the actual locations of what you are seeing (Wong, 2021). The theory of the time, in 1896 when my grandfather was born and Ramana Maharshi ran away from home to live in a cave on Arunachala, was that such inversion of the optical image is necessary for perception of objects as upright. Stratton sought to test the perceptual effects of presenting an upright image to the brain (by presenting an inverted image to the retina which would then reverse it). He first tried placing two double convex lenses in a tube extending from each eye, but as this caused "distress" he settled on doing the experiment using only one eye for vision while covering the other tube with black paper so that the other eye could stay open as well. He reported his first experiment, which has been lauded by cognitive psychology pioneer Richard Gregory (1923-2010) as "perhaps the most famous experiment in the whole of experimental psychology," at the Third International Congress for Psychology, Munich, August, 1896. In this study, Stratton wore the device for 3 days. He reported that

> "The course of experience was something as follows : All images at first appeared to be inverted; the room and all in it seemed upside down. The hands when stretched out from below into the visual field seemed to enter from above. Yet although these images were clear and definite, they did not at first seem to be real things, like the things we see in normal vision, but they seemed to be misplaced, false, or illusory images between the observer and the objects or things themselves. For the memory-images brought over from normal vision still continued to be the standard and criterion of reality. The present perceptions were for some time translated involuntarily into the language of normal vision; the present visual perceptions were used simply as signs to determine how and where the object would appear if it could be seen with restored normal vision. Things were thus seen in one way and thought of in a far different way. This held true also of my body. For the parts of my

body were felt to lie where they would have appeared had the instrument been removed; they were seen to be in another position. But the older tactual and visual localization was still the real localization.

All movements of the body at this time were awkward, uncertain, and full of surprises. Only when the movement was made regardless of visual images, by aid of touch and memory alone – as when one moves in the dark – could walking or movements of the hand be performed with reasonable security and directness. Otherwise the movement was a series of errors and attempts at correction, until the limb was finally brought into the desired position in the visual field. The reason for this seems partly to have been that the reconstruction of the visual field in terms of the normal visual experience – the translation before spoken of – was never carried out in all the details of the picture. In general, or in the main outlines, things might be referred to the positions they would have in normal vision, but the new visual field was in many of its details accepted just as found, and was acted upon without any translation whatever. So that when movements were made as if the visual signs meant just what they had meant in normal vision, the movements of course went astray. The limb usually started in the opposite direction from the one really desired. Or when I saw an object near one of my hands and wished to grasp it with that hand, the other hand was the one I moved. The mistake was then seen, and by trial, observation, and correction, the desired movement was at last brought about.

As I moved about in the room, the movement of the visual images of my hands or feet were at first not used, as in normal vision, to decide what tactual sensations were to be expected. Knocks against things in plain sight were more or less of a surprise. I felt my hand to be in a different position from that in which I saw it, and could not, except by cool deliberation, use its visual image as a sign of impending tactual experience. After a time, however, repeated experience made this use of the visual image much less strange; it began to be the common guides and means of anticipation. I wanted [*sic*] my feet in walking and saw what they were approaching, and expected visual and tactual contact to be reported perceptionally together. In this way the limbs began actually to feel in the place where the new visual

Chapter 30 - All Reality is Virtual: The Varieties of Offline Perceptual Experience (OPE)

perception reported them to be. The vivid connection of tactual and visual perceptions began to take away the overpowering force of the localization lasting over from normal vision. The seen images thus became real things just as in normal sight. I could at length feel my feet strike against the seen floor, although the floor was seen on the opposite side of the field of vision from that to which at the beginning of the experiment I had referred these tactual sensations. I could likewise at times feel that my arms lay between my head and this new position of the feet; shoulders and head, however, which under the circumstances could never be directly seen, kept the localization they had had in normal vision, in spite of the logical difficulty that the shape of the body and the localization of hands and feet just mentioned made such a localization of the shoulders absurd.

Objects lying at the moment outside the visual field (things at the side of the observer, for example) were at first mentally represented as they would have appeared in normal vision. As soon as the actual presentation vanished, the new relations gave way to the old ones brought over from the long former experience. The actual present perception remained in this way entirely isolated and out of harmony with the larger whole made up by representation. But later I found myself bringing the representation of unseen objects into harmonious relation with the present perception. They began now to be represented not as they would appear if normal vision were restored, but as they would appear if the present field of vision were widened or moved so as to include them. In this way the room began to make a whole once more, floor and walls and the prominent objects in the room getting into a constant relation to one another, so that during a movement of the head I could more or less accurately anticipate the order in which things would enter the visual field. For at first the visual search for an object out-side of the immediate sight was quite haphazard; movements were made at random until the desired object appeared in sight and was recognized. But now the various lines of visual direction and what they would lead to were more successfully held in mind. By the third day things had thus been interconnected into a whole by piecing together the parts of the ever-changing visual fields.

As to the relation of the visual field to the observer, the Feeling that the field was upside down remained in general throughout the experiment. At times, however, there were peculiar variations in this feeling according to the mental attitude of the observer toward the present scene. If the attention was directed mainly inward, and things were viewed only in indirect attention, they seemed clearly to be inverted. But when, on the other hand, full attention was given to the outer objects, these frequently seemed to be in normal position, and whatever there was of abnormality seemed to lie in myself, as if head and shoulders were inverted and I were viewing objects from that position, as boys sometimes do from between their legs. At other times the inversion seemed confined to the face or eyes alone.

On removing the glasses on the third day, there was no peculiar experience. Normal vision was restored instantaneously and without any disturbance in the natural appearance or position of objects.

The experiment was of course not carried far enough to see the final aspect the experience under these conditions would assume. But the changes which actually occurred, even the transitory feelings the observer at times had, give hints of the course a longer experiment of this kind would take. I might almost say that the main problem – that of the importance of the inversion of the retinal image for upright vision – had received from the experiment a full solution. For if the inversion of the retinal image were absolutely necessary for upright vision, as both the projection theory and the eye-movement theory hold, it is certainly difficult to understand how the scene as a whole could even temporarily have appeared upright when the retinal image was not inverted. As we said, all things which under the conditions could be seen at all repeatedly appeared to be in normal relation; that is, they seemed to be right side up." (Stratton, 1896)

In a later experiment, Stratton wore the glasses for 8 days while going about his normal daily routine. After several days, things looked normal again. However, when he took the glasses off at the end of the eight days, although up was still up and down was still down, left and right were switched for a while to the point that he would reach out to his left for things that were located on his right.

Chapter 30 - All Reality is Virtual: The Varieties of Offline Perceptual Experience (OPE)

Whereas virtual reality arguably dates back to the 1832 Wheatstone Stereoscope and the 1839 Brewster Stereoscope (Stereoscope, 2021) in which each eye saw a photograph of the same object taken from the angle of that eye, Stratton may be have been the first "augmenaut" or "augmonaut," the unsung pioneer of augmented reality, the science of which I will call "*augmonautics*" (as neither it, nor "augmenautics" currently exists as a term as per Google). Stratton's goggles would indeed qualify as an augmented reality device, as the prism presented images as being in different locations than they actually were: high was seen as low, low was high, left was right and right was left.

Stratton may also have been the first person to experience **ARISE** (the logical acronym for Augmented Reality Induced Symptoms and Effects – the augmented reality version of **VRISE**). Stratton here describes some of the less pleasant aspects of wearing the goggles for eight days (the fifth and sixth days appeared chill):

> *First Day.* – ... Whether as a result of the embarrassment under which nearly all visually guided movements were performed, or as a consequence of the swinging of the scene, described above, there were signs of a nervous disturbance, of which perhaps the most marked was a feeling of depression in the upper abdominal region, akin to mild nausea. This disappeared, however, toward evening; so that by half-past seven it was no longer perceptible.
>
> *Second Day.* – This feeling of nervous depression, just mentioned, returned the next forenoon ...
>
> *Third Day.* – I was now beginning to feel more at home in the new experience. At no time during the day did any signs of nervous distress appear ...
>
> *Fourth Day.* – By the fourth day the new experience had become even less trying. There was no sign of bodily discomfort ...
>
> *Seventh Day.* – ... On removing the glasses [to put on the sleep blindfold], my visual images relapsed into their older form [non-goggle reality], with a constant interplay and accompaniment, however, of the new.

Eighth Day. – ... When the time came for removing the glasses at the close of the experiment, I thought it best to preserve as nearly as possible the size of the visual field to which I had now grown accustomed; so that any results observed might be clearly due solely to the reversion of my visual objects and not to a sudden widening of the visual field. Instead, therefore, of removing the plaster-cast from my face, I closed my eyes and had an assistant slip out the brass tube which held the lenses, and insert in its place an empty black-lined paper tube that gave about the same range of vision. On opening my eyes, the scene had a strange familiarity. The visual arrangement was immediately recognized as the old one of pre-experimental days; yet the reversal of everything from the order to which I had grown accustomed during the past week, gave the scene a surprising, bewildering air which lasted for several hours. It was hardly the feeling, though, that things were upside down.

When I turned my body or my head, objects seemed to sweep before me as if they themselves were suddenly in motion. The 'swinging of the scene,' observed so continuously during the first days of the experiment, had thus returned with great vividness. It rapidly lost this force, however, so that at the end of an hour the motion was decidedly less marked. But it was noticeable the rest of the day, and in a slight degree even the next morning.

Movements that would have been appropriate to the visual arrangement during the experiment, were now repeatedly performed after this arrangement had been reversed. In walking toward some obstacle on the floor of the room – a chair, for instance – I turned the wrong way in trying to avoid it; so that I frequently either ran into things in the very effort to go around them, or else hesitated, for the moment, bewildered what I should do. I found myself more than once at a loss which hand I ought to use to grasp the door-handle at my side. And of two doors, side by side, leading to different rooms, I was on the point of opening the wrong one, when a difference in the metal work of the locks made me aware of my mistake. On approaching the stairs, I stepped up when I was nearly a foot too far away. And in writing my notes at this time, I continually made the wrong movement of my head in attempting to keep the centre of my visual field somewhere near the point where I was writing. I moved

Chapter 30 - All Reality is Virtual: The Varieties of Offline Perceptual Experience (OPE)

my head upward when it should have gone downward; I moved it to the left when it should have gone to the right. And this to such a degree as to be a serious disturbance. While walking, there were distinct signs of vertigo and also the depression in the upper abdominal region, noticed during the earlier days of the experiment. The feeling that the floor and other visual objects were swaying, in addition to the symptoms just mentioned, made my walking seem giddy and uncontrollable. No distinct errors in locating parts of my body occurred; I was more than once surprised, however, to see my hands enter the visual field from the old lower side.

Objects in the room, at a distance of ten or twelve feet from me, seemed to have lost their old levels and to be much higher than they were either during the experiment or before the experiment. The floor no longer seemed level, but appeared to slope up and away from me, at an angle of perhaps five degrees. The windows and other prominent objects seemed also too high. This strange aspect of things lasted (as did also the swinging of the scene, the feeling of giddiness, and certain inappropriate movements) after the plaster cast had been removed and the normal compass of the visual field was restored. In the dim light of the next morning, the upward slope of the floor and the unusual position of the windows were distinctly noticeable." (Stratton, 1897a; 1897b)

Similar research was carried out in the "Innsbruck Goggle Experiments" by Theodor Erismann, Hubert Rohracher, Ivo Kohler, Franz Schuler and Heinz Miller beginning in the 1930s. The prism-induced augmented reality experience typically consisted of three phases:

"a) Between the first and third day, the world was upside down for the participant. There were many mistakes in grabbing objects and moving. For instance, the participant held a cup upside down when it was about to be filled; or they stepped over a ceiling lamp or street sign, because they saw objects at the bottom that were actually at the top. Swift reactions (such as parrying an attack off during fencing) happened uncorrected, and thus in the wrong direction.

b) By the fifth day, the participant's clumsiness in external behavior and vision started to change. Things that had been seen upside down suddenly were upright once the participant brought their own hands in and traced the shapes they saw with their hands. Or, phrased differently: If the participant 'viewed the world using their fingers,' then it turned upright in their vision as well, an immense effort of the brain. By grasping, the perception changes.

c) From the sixth day of uninterruptedly wearing reversing spectacles, permanent upright vision ensued, and behavior was perfectly correct. For example, a participant drew a picture in a quality as if drawn without wearing reversing spectacles." (Kohler, 1951, translated by Sachse et al., 2017)

"After taking off the glasses, however, participants saw the whole world upside down, a distortion 'in the opposite direction' (negative after-effect), but the reversed vision only lasted a few minutes." (Sachse et al., 2017)

A link to an English language version of a short film about these experiments, Living in a Reversed World, is included in the references (Gibson, 2021). Additional footage is included in the references in Erismann & Kohler (2021).

Chapter 30 - All Reality is Virtual: The Varieties of Offline Perceptual Experience (OPE)

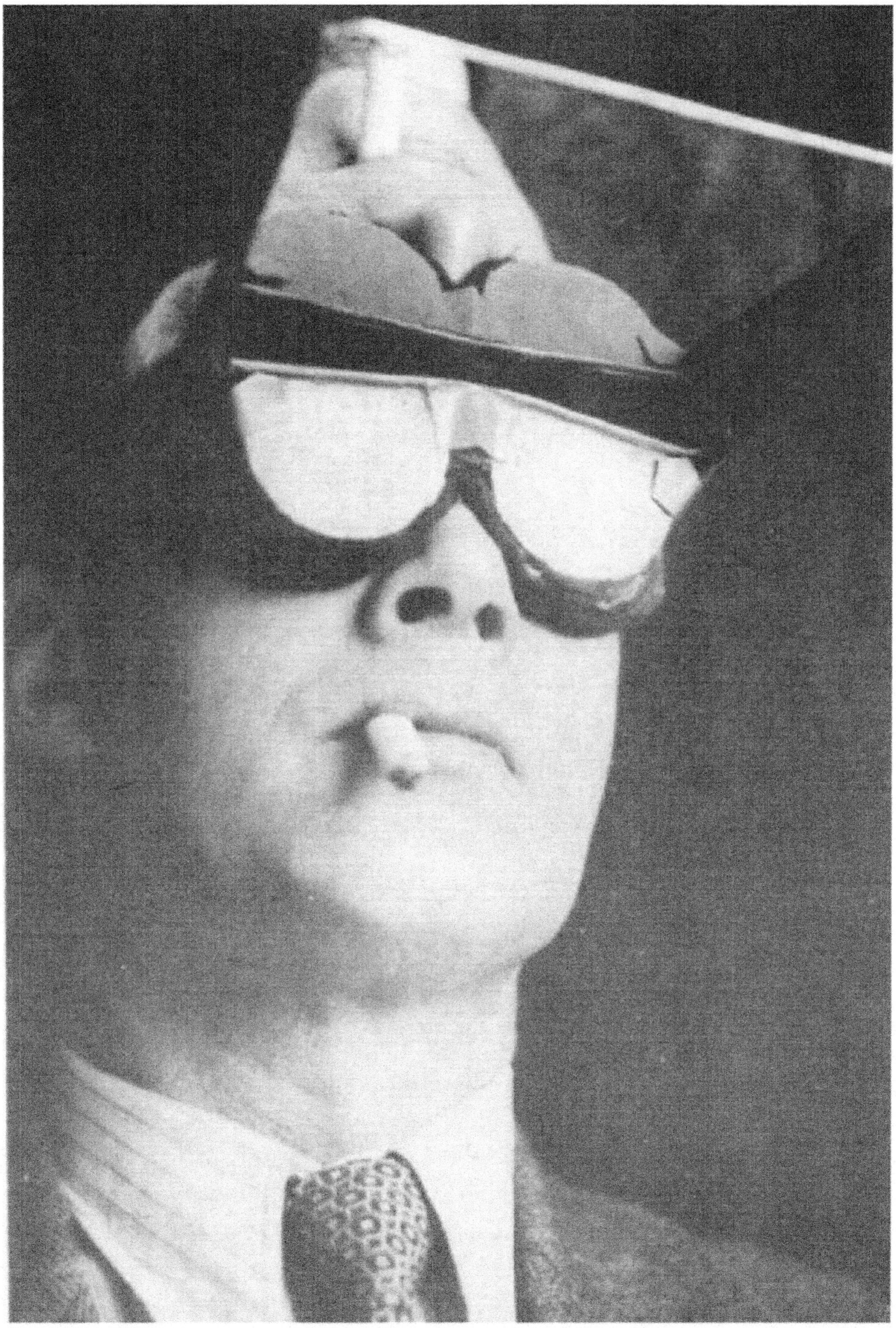

Chapter 30 - All Reality is Virtual: The Varieties of Offline Perceptual Experience (OPE)

You can get a taste of these experiences by trying to tie your shoes while looking only at your hands and shoes in a mirror. If you do it for a while, you will eventually get good at it, but you might then have difficulty tying them without a mirror. You could then remediate this by tying your shoes in the mornings by lifting your shoed feet onto the sink console if you live alone, but if you are more of a social creature, or merely care about hygiene for your own benefit, it would be best to relearn to tie them *sans* mirror. You can try this with other activities as well. And if you're really interested, you can even buy "reversing goggles" online (not "prism glasses," which are something else), though there may be some assembly required, including a need for glue, and some only invert either up and down, or left and right, at a given time (Reversing Goggles, 2021).

Recently, scientific legitimacy is being given to what is now termed "offline perception" (Fazekas, Nanay & Pearson, 2021). In a sense, this is old moonshine in a new FDA-approved bottle, the taboo moonshine being the phenomenon of "metachoric experience" coined by consciousness researchers Celia Green and Charles McCreery in their 1975 book *Apparitions*, to refer to

> "experiences in which the normal perceptual environment is entirely replaced by a hallucinatory one." (Green & McCreery, 2020)

The experiences that Green and McCreery refer to pertain to their non-FDA-approved specialty areas of lucid dreams, out of body experiences and false awakenings (there's a reason Celia refers to herself as an "exiled academic," kind of like Ram Dass who was fired from Harvard after he and Tim Leary did their LSD experiments [Leary & Alpert, 1962]; and Wilhelm Reich who died in prison after violating an injunction to cease from interstate importation of Orgone, or cosmic energy, accumulators [Franzen, 1980]).

In my own writings, I have referred to the altered state of consciousness (ASC) characterized by metachoric experiences as *metachoria*. Metachoria, an organic virtual reality characterized by full multisensory realism, has historically been known by a variety of names in accordance with culture and context. Designations include religious visions, lucid dreaming, astral projection, out of body experiences, skrying, near death experiences, pathworking, dream yoga, active imagination, vision quest, spirit walking and even alien contact experiences when considered as consciousness phenomena. Metachoria combines the insight of waking with the infinite possibilities of dreams. In the past, metachoria was thought to be the domain of the special few, such as shamans, mystics, prophets and yogis. Modern pioneers of consciousness exploration have, however, identified relatively simple techniques that can enable us all to enter this state, which is our birthright.

With the advent of virtual reality, and the technologically programmed nature of the "hallucinatory" experience that replaces our "normal perceptual environment," a new term was inevitable that allowed for the externally generated stimulation produced by VR equipment as contrasted with the content of metachoric ASCs which is hypothesized to originate at various levels of consciousness itself or be the result of contact with extra-dimensional beings or worlds.

Chapter 30 - All Reality is Virtual: The Varieties of Offline Perceptual Experience (OPE)

This new term in the literature, "offline perception," refers to

> "voluntary and spontaneous perceptual experiences without matching external stimulation." (Fazekas, Nanay & Pearson, 2021)

While the term was arguably not intended to refer to metachoric experiences pertaining to altered states of consciousness, Offline Perception can best be considered a broad category of experience that can include subcategories defined by such variables as

(1) **state of consciousness** (e.g., waking, nonlucid dreaming, dreamless sleep, and altered states such as lucid dreaming, out of body experiences, near death experiences, shared death experiences, cosmic consciousness, etc.);

(2) **stimulus type** (e.g., VR environments, mind altering chemicals, brainwave altering neurostimulation/neurofeedback, etc.); and

(3) **Degree of virtual augmentation of reality** in accordance with the definition of augmented reality as

> "an interactive experience of a real-world environment where the objects that reside in the real world are enhanced by computer-generated perceptual information, sometimes across multiple sensory modalities, including visual, auditory, haptic, somatosensory and olfactory." (Augmented Reality, 2021)

Degree of Offline Augmentation (DOA) can be quantified, on a scale of 0-100 percent, as the sensory salience of offline (environment non-matching) stimuli providing input to the senses relative to the sum of sensory saliences of environment-matching and environment-nonmatching stimuli pertaining to one or more sensory modalities. As the sum of saliences of environment-matching and environment-nonmatching stimuli is 100, DOA can be represented as:

$$\text{Degree of Offline Augmentation} = \frac{\text{Sensory Salience [0..100] of Environment Nonmatching Stimuli}}{100} \times 100$$

DOA can be calculated for a specific sensory modality (e.g., vision), or for some combination of senses (e.g., vision and audition). One hundred percent visual offline augmentation could involve conferencing technology in which you see fellow attendees, who are located elsewhere (such as in their own space stations), sitting with you around a virtual table. A lesser degree of visual offline augmentation could involve conferencing technology in which you see the room you are actually sitting in, with holograms of off-planet family members superimposed such that they appear to be sitting on furniture that is physically present in your current location. Total immersive multisensory offline augmentation could be the waking experience of a purely virtual reality in which all of your senses experience only the virtual environment, or a metachoric state such as a lucid dream or out of body experience with no relationship to what is going on around your physical body at the moment. Of course, it is unlikely that such complete offline augmentation is possible in the waking state, barring a direct hookup to the nervous system such as a headjack à la Matrix, given that we are subject to ongoing interoception (the felt sense of internal workings of the body).

Semantic precision is important in science, and an issue I have with the above definition of "offline perception" (Fazekas, Nanay & Pearson, 2021) reminds me of a similar issue that arose in 1897 when G.M. Stratton was struggling with terms to use to distinguish vision with and without prism goggles:

> "Before I attempt a narrative of the experience under the experimental conditions, a word or two as to the terminology will be necessary. One has constantly to make a distinction between the appearance of an object as seen through the reversing lenses, and either the appearance it had before the lenses were put on, or the appearance it would have if the lenses were removed and normal vision restored. This appearance just described is called in the narrative the 'older,' the 'normal,' often the 'pre-experimental' appearance of the object; while the appearance through the lenses is called its 'newer' or 'later' appearance. Similar distinguishing terms have also to be used with reference to the mere representation or idea of an object, as contrasted with its actual perception." (Stratton, 1897a, p. 343)

Breathtaking, isn't it? Mind-to-mind communication from the past. Thank God for language. Even if it is a virus (Anderson, 1986).

In a similar spirit of linguistic and semantic precision, I will therefore take the liberty of tweaking the above definition of "offline perception,"

Chapter 30 - All Reality is Virtual: The Varieties of Offline Perceptual Experience (OPE)

"voluntary and spontaneous perceptual experiences without matching external stimulation" (Fazekas, Nanay & Pearson, 2021),

to read:

"perceptual experience arising from causes other than sensory stimulation from the usual physical counterparts of the experience."

First, I've eliminated "voluntary and spontaneous" because they don't add any information. Second, I've clarified what the authors obviously mean by "matching" but which I prefer to spell out. As a result, this revised definition allows for a VR experience such as playing ping pong with a squirrel to constitute "offline perception" whereas the original definition, if one is, as I sometimes am when writing, compelled to split hairs in the name of semantic precision, does not. This is because, in the example given, "matching external stimulation" (a visual simulation of a squirrel playing ping pong with me that matches my resulting perception) is indeed being projected into my eyes by the VR headset, excluding it from being "offline perception" according to the first definition. However, as the projected image *does not* constitute "sensory stimulation from the *usual* physical counterpart of the experience" (light bouncing off an organic squirrel holding a physical ping pong paddle

$$\frac{\textit{distance of the squirrel in miles from my eyes}}{186{,}282}$$

seconds before I see it), it *does* constitute "offline perception" using the revised definition.

The following chapters will present a variety of OPEs resulting from internally-generated or non-physical stimuli (which are the main interpretations of experiences with no known physical counterparts), rather than from externally-generated physical stimuli. As there really seem to be two main categories of OPE (metachoria and virtual reality), it may be useful to create two linguistically consistent categories:

1. Internally Generated Offline Perceptual Experiences (IGOPE)

e.g., metachoric experiences "in which the normal perceptual environment is entirely replaced by a hallucinatory one" (Green & McCreery, 2020) in the form of altered states of consciousness such as lucid dreams, out of body experiences, near death experiences, shared death experiences and other experiences originating in consciousness or nonphysical realms. IGOPEs may be spontaneous or induced. Induction may be by means of psychological/meditative practices or by neural manipulation (e.g., by ingesting substances or receiving electrical stimulation).

2. Externally Generated Offline Perceptual Experiences (EGOPE)

e.g., virtual reality and augmented reality.

Chapter 31 - *To Weep, Perchance to Lucid Dream:* Lucid Dreaming and Lucid Dream Therapy

". . . if the sleeper perceives that he is asleep, and is conscious of the sleeping state during which the perception comes before his mind, it presents itself still, but something within him speaks to this effect: 'the image of Koriskos presents itself, but the real Koriskos is not present'; for often, when one is asleep, there is something in consciousness which declares that what then presents itself is but a dream."

Aristotle

(Parva Naturali, On Dreams; 350 B.C.E.)

Client: "Doctor, I finally had a lucid dream."

Me: "Tell me about it."

Client: "Well, before falling asleep, I decided that my dream sign would be a cat. Then, later that night, I was sitting with my grandmother on a couch. But I realized this was impossible, because she had died. That's when I knew I was dreaming. But I felt confused."

Me: "About what?"

Client: "Where was the cat?"

(A Client)

A lucid dream is a dream in which you know that you are dreaming. While not as common as nonlucid dreams (dreams in which you don't know that you are dreaming), 55% of adults report having had a lucid dream at least once in their life, and 23% have a lucid dream once or more per month (Saunders, 2016). Nevertheless, many people probably had not heard of lucid dreaming (despite decades of research and books on the topic) until the movie *Inception*, possibly because we don't tend to talk much about our dreams or, when we do, we assume other people experience dreaming the same way we do. That is, nonlucid dreamers may assume everyone else's dreams are nonlucid as well, and lucid dreamers may assume others' dreams are lucid. This is just a hypothesis, based on one client telling me that since childhood she had almost always been lucid (dream-aware) in her dreams, expressing surprise that others weren't.

Whereas most of us think of dreams as just something that happens when we sleep, lucid dreamers use dreams as a tool to accomplish specific goals. A study of 301 lucid dreamers found that the lucid dream applications endorsed by the highest percentages of participants were to have fun (81.4%), transform a bad dream/nightmare into a pleasant one (63.8%), solve problems (29.9%), stimulate creative ideas/insights (27.6%) and practice skills (21.3%). Whereas men tended to use lucid dreaming more frequently than women for fun, women used lucid dreaming more often than men for changing nightmares and for problem solving. Other applications mentioned by participants included self-help/self-healing; experimenting/seeking information; and meeting specific dream figures including the transitioned (Schädlich & Erlacher, 2012).

A number of years ago, I reviewed the potential therapeutic utility of altered states of consciousness in cognitive behavior therapy, including what I termed "lucid dream exposure therapy."

> "Anomalous states such as the lucid dream and out-of-body experience have therapeutic potential . . . The lucid dream, a controllable, realistic, multisensory 'bio-psychological virtual reality' (Tart, 2009, p. 223), can be used for behavioral rehearsal (LaBerge & Rheingold, 1997). Lucid Dreaming Treatment (LDT) has been employed for chronic nightmares (Spoormaker & van den Bout, 2006) and could help with this and other symptoms of Posttraumatic Stress Disorder (Gavie & Revonsuo, 2010). Lucid dream exposure

therapy for Panic Disorder with Agoraphobia, Obsessive-Compulsive Disorder and the various phobias is also worth exploring as the most vivid alternative to in-vivo procedures." (Densei & Lam, 2010, p. 105)

And yet, according to the 2019 website of the APA, there are only 4 types of exposure therapy, including: In-vivo exposure (play with spiders); imaginal exposure (imagine playing with spiders); virtual reality exposure (wear virtual reality goggles and play with virtual spiders); and interoceptive exposure (induce the sensation that makes you feel like a spider is crawling on you), with no mention of lucid dream exposure therapy (it should be noted that I am referring to the real APA, the American Psychological Association. Unfortunately, these are also the initials of the American Psychiatric Association, despite the fact that *Psychologists claimed the initials first* in 1892. The psychiatrists took a while to figure out what to call their association, which began as the Association of Medical Superintendents of American Institutions for the Insane, AMSAII, in 1844, which morphed into the American Medico-Psychological Association, AMPA, in 1893 in an obvious attempt to divert search engine queries by clients seeking psychologists. Finally, to foment mayhem and confusion, its bread and butter, AMSAII/AMPA pulled out the stops and stole its rival's initials by renaming itself the American Psychiatric Association, APA, in 1921).

In fact, there *not only* are *not only* 4 types of exposure therapy, there are at least 6. The two left out by the Real IRA, I mean the MC, I mean the APA, are:

Active Imaginal Exposure Therapy (Rentz et al., 2003), and

Lucid Dream Exposure Therapy (by various names; Abramovitch, 1995; Aurora, Zak & Auerbach et al., 2010; Brylowski, 1990; Densei & Lam, 2010; Gavie & Revonsuo, 2010; Green & McCreery, 1994; Halliday, 1988; Holzinger, Klösch & Saletu, 2015; LaBerge, 1985; LaBerge & Rheingold, 1990; Mota-Rolim & Araujo, 2016; Mota-Rolim, Erlacher, Tort, Araujo, & Ribeiro, S., 2010; Spoormaker & van den Bout, 2006; Spoormaker, van den Bout & Meijer, 2003; Tanner, 2004; Tholey, 1988[a]; Zadra & Pihl, 1997).

OK, I kind of get why APA doesn't acknowledge Active Imaginal Exposure Therapy, there being only one study on it in prehistoric times (BCS, Before the Common Smartphone). And, in truth, I also get why APA wasn't aware of lucid dream exposure therapy: because it wasn't labeled as such until my own 2010 article, and this article was in the Journal of Transpersonal Psychology, which most psychologists are about as familiar with as the Journal of Pink African Elephants (despite its 50+ year history as a branch of psychology). The fact that Lucid Dream Exposure Therapy involves the *positive* use of an altered state of consciousness (ASC), and that, with the exception of hypnosis, healthy ASCs and any research on them are some kind of taboo in mainstream psychology, probably played a role as well (though mainstream psychology has no problem doing research on ASCs related to "bad" things, such as illegal drugs and pathologies such as psychosis). Rant over.

THE VARIETIES OF EXPOSURE THERAPIES FOR CYNOPHOBIA

When I was in 6th grade, the year after a (supposed) friend threw a beer bottle over a hill and cut my hand open (I didn't find out it was him until much later in life), he and I were playing cops and robbers, cowboys and indians, or whatever that game is now called when you and your friends run around with cap guns (do they still make those?) and try to shoot one another, preferably not in the proximity of police. Things were going well until his mother, the middle school physics teacher, who apparently had not yet completed her doctorate in rocket science, walked out the front door smoking her cigar to walk her dog, who happened to be an 80-pound German shepherd. Which wouldn't have been a problem if Monster, or whatever its name was, hadn't been a *trained police dog*. You're a smart fellow, fellowette or fellowX and I can see the wheels turning and I think you know what comes next. As I had not yet completed my doctorate in rocket science either, I waved hello to her and Monster and proceeded to point my cap gun at my friend. Monster, who had not completed his doctorate in telling real from fake guns, didn't skip a beat. Person with gun pointed at Master. ATTACK! Within seconds this 6-foot thing with *very* big teeth was flying toward me. I turned around as quickly as I could, felt claws dig into my back, and ran for my life. The story ended fairly well for me, just some minor lacerations on my back and on the back of my neck (thank God I had turned around). Unfortunately, it ended worse for Monster, though he was just doing his job, as New Jersey had, and has, the death penalty for bad dogs and there is not, to my knowledge, due process or a doggy innocence project.

Chapter 31 - To Weep, Perchance to Lucid Dream: Lucid Dreaming and Lucid Dream Therapy

Although the physical wounds healed and merely left some cool scars, I had recurring dreams of being attacked by German Shepherds for the next 30 or so years, until I stumbled upon Exposure Therapy but, most importantly, *until I learned to lucid dream*. First, the Exposure therapy. On a vacation back in the mid-1980s, I frequented a beach cafe in Portugal and got to know the owner whom I'll call João (which I'm pretty sure is pronounced *Joe Wow!*, but which I never asked him about, as that wasn't his real name). One day after João closed for business and went to grab us some beers, I noticed German shepherds starting to appear, and seemingly multiply, around the shack. So I'm like (in between gasps),

> "Yo, Joe Wow! man, 'doukipudonktan'?" (Queneau, 1959 - Translation: "from whence who stinks thus so" - which was rhetorical, as it was obviously the pee in my pants), "sacrebleu, Putin de scallops, brie de merguez" (if you'll pardon my Russian and French), "what's with all the German Shepherd attack dogs?"

Though I was at the time on holiday from studying general and applied linguistics and phonetics at l'Université de Paris V René Descartes and was fairly up to speed on my French vulgarities, it wasn't until years later when I saw The Matrix Reloaded that I learned from the Merovingian that the semantically correct thing to say would have been

> "Yo, Joe Wow! man, Nom de plume de pudding de Bordeaux, de merguez, de scallop et brie de canard dans Kool Aid de la mer!" roughly translated as "the pen name of Bordeaux pudding made from sausage, scallops, and duck-flavored brie mixed with Kool Aid from sea water."

But live and learn.

Joe Wow! replied they'd been cooped up all day (12 adult German shepherds in a shack the size of a backyard shed - *that's* normal) and that he always let them out in the evening. I told him I had a touch of cynophobia (Merovingian for fear of German Shepherd police attack dogs - not to be confused with cinophobia, fear of movie theatres or sinophobia, fear of Chinese road signs - for some reason triggered by sitting in a beach chair encircled by 12 of them - did I mention there were *twelve*? - whose ability and motivation to distinguish beer bottles from guns are sometimes compromised by being *locked in 6x6 shacks*). He assured me they were friendly, and said they liked playing frisbee (like my 6th grade frienemy's attack dog liked playing cops and robbers?). Ultimately, although it would be nearly a decade before I would learn about Exposure and Response Prevention, I decided to go for it. So we began tossing the frisbee back and forth over a distance of a few hundred feet.

My worst evolving nightmare went something like this: I tossed Joe Wow! the frisbee, the 12 dogs ran toward him. He tossed it to me, the 12 dogs stopped, skidded to a halt, turned around, and ran toward me. I made sure I caught it and threw it back as quickly as possible. They skidded, turned, and ran back toward him. The 12 attack dogs mostly ran back and forth in a space between us that, as we threw and returned pretty fast, kept them just where I wanted them – far away.

Things went pretty well until one of the dogs got wise to us. Although I caught and whizzed the frisbee back in a blink of an eye and the dog was still pretty far away, when all the others slammed on the breaks and turned around, he kept running toward me. When I sensed the end was near I stopped thinking (I'd heard it worked with bears), but he continued right at me and grabbed my leg in his mouth. But it was just a light grab, quickly released, after which he looked at me with his tongue hanging out and we *came to an understanding*. He ran back toward the other dogs, and when the frisbee came flying back, I caught it and I threw it right to him. After that, the game became somewhat unsymmetrical, Joe Wow! playing frisbee with me, and I playing frisbee with smart dog (I knew which side my bread was buttered on). This unplanned E/RP treatment didn't cure the nightmares, but after German Shepherd Frisbee Day I no longer felt a rush of fear in their presence.

Over the next 20 years, the nightmares weren't frequent, but they would occur from time to time. When I learned to lucid dream (defined as knowing, when dreaming, that one is in a dream) about 20 years later, one night I dreamt that I was in a parking lot running away from 2 German Shepherds. Once I realized that I was in a dream, and that they were only dream dogs, I decided to stand and stare them down rather than continuing to run for dear life. They then began lunging toward me and I held my hands out inviting them to bite, remembering reading somewhere that it was impossible to feel pain in a dream and hoping it was true. Each time they lunged, their teeth went right through my hands. I then reached out to give

Chapter 31 - To Weep, Perchance to Lucid Dream: Lucid Dreaming and Lucid Dream Therapy

one of them a bear hug, picked it up, brought it's face up to mine (as it continued to snap at me), and kissed its snout. It then transformed into a puppy and licked my face. That was the last time I had a nightmare about dogs, and that was over 10 years ago. After that I had a few dreams about walking through a forest populated with lions (symptom substitution – from big dogs to big cats?), but interestingly there was absolutely no fear. They did their thing, I did mine.

Several years later, when teaching cognitive behavior therapy to doctoral students in clinical psychology, I did a review of the research on exposure therapy adding the keyword "lucid dreaming." I didn't find any, but did learn that while almost all of the articles were on in-vivo exposure (confronting the feared stimulus in real life) and imaginal exposure (imagining confronting it), there was one on "active" imaginal exposure (Rentz et al., 2003) that involved performing physical movements corresponding to imaginal interaction with the feared stimulus. I also found some articles on lucid dream therapy for nightmares, including Spoormaker & van den Bout (2006). This did, in effect, constitute lucid dream exposure therapy, without labeling it as such or conceptualizing it within a behavioral exposure paradigm. It rather considered such lucid dream therapy as a "cognitive-restructuring technique." While probably not their intention, this fits right in with cognitive therapy's tendency to see even behavior therapy techniques as cognitive interventions (the rationale being that behavioral exposure leads to cognitive change which contributes to a reduction in anxiety).

The Rentz study, which did not include lucid dream therapy in the comparisons, found that among the other three, the most effective was in-vivo exposure (e.g., petting a real dog), followed by *active* imaginal exposure (making hand movements as though petting a real dog with no dog present), followed by regular imaginal exposure (imagining petting a dog), which latter we might now refer to as *passive* imaginal exposure. I have for some time thought that it would be informative to conduct a study comparing in-vivo exposure, active-imaginal exposure, passive-imaginal exposure and lucid dream exposure therapy. If, Dear Reader, you happen to be a doctoral student in psychology, *this one's for you.*

Since curing my own police-dog phobia with lucid dream exposure therapy I have taught lucid dreaming to clients whom I thought could benefit, not only for nightmares, but also for social phobia, PTSD and grieving. One had already been lucid dreaming their whole life, thinking everyone does it, but didn't realize that they could program the dream in advance (similar to "incubation" rituals among the early Hebrews, Greeks, Romans and Christians) to include exposure scenarios, and change the dream from within. Others I taught to lucid dream, and used dream incubation in session and as homework to program the content to include the feared environment and how they would think and behave in it in a manner conducive to exposure therapy.

Types of lucid dream therapy (research is of course necessary but, while not holding your breath waiting for mainstream psychological research on actual effectiveness, it may not hurt to add them to a regimen of standard psychotherapy techniques) include the following:

> ***Lucid Dream Exposure Therapy*** for anyone with problems including fear, avoidance, escape or seemingly uncontrollable urges (e.g., for phobias, panic disorder, anger, OCD, PTSD, and addictions);
>
> ***Lucid Dream Grief Therapy*** for those experiencing normal or complicated grieving who want to have the *subjective experience of* communicating with their loved ones for purposes of closure or just to continue being together from time to time (whether this experience corresponds with true or imaginal communication);
>
> ***Lucid Dream Behavioral Activation*** for people suffering from depression, especially in the case of physical limitations due to illness, paralysis or aging;
>
> ***Lucid Dream Assertiveness Training*** if one has the "Disease to Please" (Braiker, 2001), and wraps him or herself into a pretzel to avoid conflict, sometimes exploding in anger due to poor communication skills when conflict actually does arise. Assertiveness involves saying what one thinks and feels, in a calm, factual manner using "I" statements rather than "you" statements; setting reasonable personal boundaries; and observing and tolerating the urge to be verbally abusive (in terms of word choice, tone or loudness) or physically aggressive, without giving in to it;

Chapter 31 - To Weep, Perchance to Lucid Dream: Lucid Dreaming and Lucid Dream Therapy

Lucid dream physical therapy for individuals who have suffered brain damage due to an injury or stroke. Although the body (except for the eyes) is paralyzed when dreaming, dreamed movements activate the same areas of the sensorimotor cortex as waking movements. Therefore, just as physical therapy moves parts of the body to stimulate the associated brain areas, moving that part of the body in a lucid dream may produce similar physical therapeutic benefits. One study found that:

> "By combining brain imaging with polysomnography and exploiting the state of lucid dreaming, we show here that a predefined motor task performed during dreaming elicits neuronal activation in the sensorimotor cortex. In lucid dreams, the subject is aware of the dreaming state and capable of performing predefined actions while all standard polysomnographic criteria of REM sleep are fulfilled . . . Using eye signals as temporal markers, neural activity measured by functional magnetic resonance imaging (Fmri) and near-infrared spectroscopy (NIRS) was related to dreamed hand movements during lucid REM sleep." (Dresler et al., 2011, p. 1833);

Lucid Dream Consciousness Exploration for those who, for purposes of self-knowledge, want to explore their unconscious; and

Lucid Dream Spirituality for people who wish to conduct their meditative, spiritual or religious practices in the lucid dream environment in order to experience a potentially deeper level of realization or connection.

PARENTAL ADVISORY: The next section contains an allusion to alcohol.

READER ADVISORY: You may want to pour yourself a stiff one before embarking on the rest of the chapter. If you're a friend of Bill, Italian and under 16, or taking certain medications, make that a double expresso.

And I am serious. The rest of this chapter is kind of heady. And it's in French (don't worry, there are translations). (Well, worry a little. I did the translations.) So join me for a moment as we enjoy the changing of the leaves (several days ago) and the first day of winter in the Berkshires (today, October 30, 2020; Year Zero of The Apocalypse). Just got off the webcam with an old friend (Saint Dominique de St. Véran of *Bear I'm Not A* fame – Full disclosure: He may not have been a 6th Century bishop – indeed, I'm fairly sure he was not a 6th Century bishop and, if he was, he never mentioned it, he is quite modest – but he has indeed been knighted for his tireless work resettling refugees in Paris). Outside his window, in the distance, was the Pompidou Center. Today France begins another big lockdown. We're all on this path together . . .

A BRIEF HISTORY OF LUCID DREAMING

There have been many books on lucid dreaming since the first, which was entitled: *Les Rêves et Les Moyens de les Diriger: Observations Pratiques* (Dreams and How to Guide Them: Practical Observations) written by the Frenchman Marie-Jean-Léon Marquis d'Hervey de Saint Denys (heretofore referred to as The Marquis), son of Alexandre Le Coq Baron d'Hervey and Mélanie Juchereau de Saint-Denys in 1867, a simpler time in which conversations continued only as long as it took for everyone to introduce

Chapter 31 - To Weep, Perchance to Lucid Dream: Lucid Dreaming and Lucid Dream Therapy

themselves and greet one another by name, after which they called it a day and went home to gargle with warm water to sooth their overtaxed uvulas and wait a day or two before continuing to practice pronouncing their own and each other's names in preparation for the next occasion.

However, despite the abundance of literature on lucid dreaming throughout the 20th century, it didn't begin its slow entry into mainstream culture until 2 doctoral students, on different sides of the pond and unbeknownst to one another, had identical strokes of genius. Keith Hearne in 1975 in the U.K. (using Alan Worsley as the dreaming subject) and Stephen LaBerge in 1978 in the U.S. (using himself as the dreaming subject) conducted strikingly similar doctoral theses on going to sleep with eye sensors on, becoming self-aware inside of a dream, and moving one's eyes in a certain way to communicate with the outside, so-called "real" world of the instruments measuring sleep stages and eye movements. These experiments inspired *psychonauts* (no, not psycho nuts, *consciousness* explorers) and oneironauts (dreamworld explorers) worldwide to collectively, and mostly as a grass roots endeavor outside of mainstream science and psychology, do their own N=1 research, with themselves as the subject (outside of mainstream psychology, due to the lack of interest or knowledge among many scientists and psychologists in anything above the Self-Actualization need at the top of Maslow's original outdated Hierarchy of Needs, prior to Maslow adding on top of that our potential for transcendence).

Just a note on that "psycho nuts" jab. I will tell you as I tell my clients: Some people feel embarrassed to see a therapist, thinking there's "something wrong" with them, or that they're "crazy." In truth, there is nothing objectively "wrong" about excessive emotions, behaving in unhelpful ways that don't meet one's goals, or even having hallucinations or thinking things that aren't believed by most other people. These are just things going on with body, brain and mind, that they have had the *insight* to recognize, the *knowledge* to realize are changeable, and the *wisdom* about which to seek the advice of someone who specializes in working with these common human experiences. Ninety-nine point nine percent of the time, my clients are some of the most "normal," reasonable, people I've ever met. But they are often surrounded by others, family members, bosses, colleagues, neighbors, people on the road and people they come across in the course of their daily lives who are certifiably *batsh#t crazy*, unfortunately in ways that are often socially acceptable and even rewarded. It is these people to whom I refer when I say things like "psycho nuts." Just wanted to clarify).

Back to the beginning. In the first book on lucid dreaming ever published, The Marquis informs the reader early on (1867/2005) that, after beginning to keep a dream journal, and learning to recall his dreams,

> "J'acquiers ensuite l'habitude de *savoir, en rêvant, que je rêve*, et j'observe dans cet état les opérations de mon esprit." (p. 11; "I then acquire the habit of *knowing, while dreaming, that I am dreaming*, and I observe in this state the functioning of my mind"; italics and translation added)

Chapter 31 - To Weep, Perchance to Lucid Dream: Lucid Dreaming and Lucid Dream Therapy

Here he discusses the evolution of his own dreams in which he knows that he is dreaming:

> "Nos occupations et nos préoccupations habituelles exercent une grande influence sur la nature de nos rêves, qui sont généralement comme un reflet de notre existence réelle." (p. 11; "Our habitual activities and our preoccupations have a strong influence on the nature of our dreams, that are generally like a reflection of our real existence"; my translation)

> "L'habitude de penser durant le jour à mes rêves, de les analyser et de les décrire eut pour résultat de faire entrer ces éléments de ma vie intellectuelle ordinaire dans l'ensemble des réminiscences qui pouvaient se présenter à mon esprit durant le sommeil. Il m'arriva donc une nuit de rêver que j'écrivais mes songes et que j'en relatais de très singuliers. Mon regret fut extrême au réveil de n'avoir pas eu conscience en dormant de cette situation exceptionnelle. Quelle belle occasion perdue! me disais-je; que de détails intéressants j'aurais pu recueillir!" (p. 11; "The habit of thinking about my dreams during the day, of analyzing and writing them down, resulted in introducing these elements of my ordinary thinking life into the collection of memories that could come to mind while sleeping. Then one night I dreamt that I wrote down my dreams and that I related some very unusual ones. Upon awakening I deeply regretted not being conscious of this exceptional situation while sleeping. What a beautiful opportunity lost! I said to myself; what interesting details I could have collected!"; my translation)

> "Cette idée me poursuivit plusieurs jours et, par cela même qu'elle assiégeait mon esprit, le même songe ne tarda guère à se reproduire, avec cette modification toutefois que, les idées accessoires ralliant désormais l'idée principale, j'eus parfaitement le sentiment que je rêvais, et je pus fixer mon attention sur les particularités qui m'intéressaient davantage, de manière à en conserver en m'éveillant un souvenir plus net et mieux arrêté. Ce nouveau mode d'observation prit peu à peu une extension très grande. Il devenait la source d'investigations précieuses, à mesure que je commençais à entrevoir dans ces études autre chose qu'un puéril passe-temps." (p. 11; "This idea pursued me for several days and, by the very fact that

it besieged my mind, the same dream didn't hesitate at all to reproduce itself, with this modification, however, that with the peripheral ideas rallying around the main idea, I perfectly knew that I was dreaming, and I was able to fix my attention on the details that most interested me, in such a way as to retain upon awakening a clearer and sharper memory. This new mode of observation, little by little, took on greater proportions. It became the source of precious investigations, as I began to see these studies as something other than a silly hobby"; my translation)

"Le premier rêve où j'eus, en dormant, ce sentiment de ma situation réelle se place à la deux cent septième nuit de mon journal ; le second, à la deux cent quatorzième. Six mois plus tard, le même fait se reproduit deux fois sur cinq nuits, en moyenne. Au bout d'un an, trois fois sur quatre. Après quinze mois, enfin, sa manifestation est presque quotidienne, et, depuis cette époque déjà si éloignée, je peux attester qu'il ne m'arrive guère de m'abandonner aux illusions d'un songe sans retrouver, du moins par intervalles, le sentiment de la réalité." (pp. 11-12; The first dream in which I had, while sleeping, the sense of my real situation happened on the two hundred seventh night of my journal; the second, on the two hundred fourteenth. Six months later, the same things happened again two out of five nights, on average. After a year, three out of four times. Finally, after fifteen months, it happened almost daily, and, since that time, already so long ago, I can attest that I hardly get lost in the illusions of a dream without, at least occasionally, regaining the sense of the reality"; my translation)

It is interesting to note that the evolution of the Marquis' ability to realize when dreaming that he was dreaming included the following elements, which are now staples of modern instructions on how to lucid dream:

(1) Keeping a dream journal;

(2) Improving dream recall;

(3) Recognition that the content of dreams mirrors the content of waking life (Freud's "day residue");

(4) "Day residue" characterized by thinking about dreams, writing them down and analyzing them, during the day;

(5) "Day residue" of wishing during the day that he would realize, when dreaming, that he was dreaming; and

(6) Finally having a dream in which he realized that he was dreaming.

WHO COINED THE TERM "LUCID DREAM"?

There is some debate in the literature as to whether it was the Marquis who coined the term "lucid dream" (in French, as *rêve lucide*) in 1867, or the Dutch Psychiatrist Frederick Van Eeden who coined it in English in 1913. From the above quotations, it is clear that the Marquis' book is about what we now call lucid dreaming. In addition, in the Marquis' original French, I counted 7 instances of the term "rêve lucide" in either its singular or plural form (Hervey de Saint Denis, 1867/2005, pp. 14, 143, 153, 159, 174, 199, 246), with the word "lucide" or "lucides" itself, singular or plural, appearing 29 times. For example, the Marquis writes:

> "Je résolus de ne point laisser échapper la première occasion qui s'en présenterait, c'est-à-dire le premier rêve lucide au milieu duquel je posséderais bien le sentiment de ma situation." (Hervey de Saint Denys, 1867/2005, p. 159; "I decided not to miss the first occasion that would present itself, that is to say the first lucid dream in which I would understand my situation"; my translation – here he is referring to setting an intention to notice a lucid dream in the future in order to do an experiment)

While it is possible that the Marquis was one of the first to place the word "rêve" (dream) *next to* the word "lucide" (lucid), he clearly was not the first person to use the word lucid to describe a dream. Moreau de Sarthe, in his work "Rêve" or "Dream," refers to Formey's use of the term "lucid" in the context of dreams as referring to awareness of having had them and remembering them.

> "Dans l'acception ordinaire, avoir des rêves, c'est donc les sentir, en conserver au moins l'impression et le souvenir. C'est là ce que Formey a justement appelé la clarté, la lucidité des songes." (De Sarthe, 1820; "In the ordinary sense, to have dreams is therefore to feel them, to preserve at least the impression and the memory. This is what Formey rightly called the clarity, the lucidity of dreams." Translated by Google Translate)

Den Blanken & Meijer point out that the Marquis' use of the word "lucid" is not limited to dreams, and considered the opinion of Morton Schatzman who

> ". . . writes in his shortened English version of Les Rêves (1982) that the author uses the expression rêve lucide (transl.: lucid dream) several times. But, according to Schatzman, we should not conclude that this expression has been used in the same manner as we use it today, i.e. for a dream in which the dreamer is aware of dreaming while dreaming. [Schatzman says the] . . . current meaning of the expression was used for the first time by the Dutch writer/psychiatrist Frederik van Eeden (1912-1913), who refers also to 'Marquis d'Herve.'" (den Blanken & Meijer, 1988)

Den Blanken and Meijer dispute this conclusion, noting that (in a translation slightly different from my own above),

> "Indeed, the author of Les Rêves uses the term 'lucid dream' as we define it today in the sentence 'aware of my true situation'. On page 287 he writes: 'C'est-à-dire le premier rêve lucide au milieu duquel je possédais bien le sentiment de ma situation' (transl.: That is to say, the first lucid dream in which I had the sensation of my situation). With the last part of this sentence, he states that he knew he was dreaming." (den Blanken & Meijer, 1988)

Let's try and put this debate to rest once and for all. The Marquis does indeed appear to use the word "lucid" in ways that don't necessarily suggest self-awareness (the bold italics below are my own, for English and French variants of "lucid" and "dream," the latter which is both "rêve" and "songe," as pointed out by the Marquis himself in a footnone (1867/2005, p. 3).

> "Ceci devant s'entendre des ***rêves lucides***, et non de ceux où l'imperfection des images tient à l'imperfection du sommeil." (1867/2005, p. 14; "This former applies to ***lucid dreams***, and not to those where the imperfection of the images is due to the imperfection of the sleep"; my translation)

> "Pour moi, j'estime en effet que toute pensée de l'homme endormi est un ***rêve*** plus ou moins ***lucide*** . . ." (1867/2005, p. 86; "As for me, I consider in effect that every thought of a sleeping man is a ***dream*** that is more or less ***lucid***"; my translation)

Chapter 31 - To Weep, Perchance to Lucid Dream: Lucid Dreaming and Lucid Dream Therapy

"En premier lieu, m'étant fait réveiller souvent à des heures différentes de la nuit, et jugeant du plus ou moins de profondeur de mon sommeil par le plus ou moins de difficulté que j'éprouvais à m'y arracher, j'ai constamment observé que plus mon rêve était vif et plus cette difficulté était grande. Quand, par un simple effort de volonté, j'ai su me réveiller moimême (ayant conservé en rêve le sentiment de ma véritable situation), j'ai toujours remarqué qu'il fallait un effort plus grand pour secouer un ***rêve*** bien ***lucide*** que pour chasser des visions incohérentes, des tableaux pâles et indécis." (1867/2005, p. 145; "In the first place, waking myself often at different hours of the night, and judging my sleep as more or less deep by whether it was more or less difficult to pull myself out of it, I constantly observed that the more vivid the dream the greater the difficulty. When, simply by trying, I was able to wake myself up [retaining in the dream the sense of my true situation], I always remarked that it took more effort to shake a very ***lucid dream*** than to chase away incoherent visions of pale and nondescript scenes"; my translation)

"Si nous parvenons à bien établir que la volonté peut conserver assez de force, durant le sommeil, pour diriger la course de l'esprit à travers le monde des illusions et des réminiscences (ainsi qu'elle dirige le corps dans la journée à travers les événements du monde réel), il nous deviendra facile de persuader qu'une certaine habitude d'exercer cette faculté, jointe à celle de posséder souvent en rêve la conscience de son véritable état, conduiront peu à peu celui qui fera des efforts suivis sur lui-même à des résultats très concluants. Non seulement, il devra reconnaître tout d'abord l'action de sa volonté réfléchie dans la direction des ***songes lucides*** et tranquilles, mais il s'apercevra bientôt de l'influence de cette même volonté sur les songes incohérents ou passionnés." (1867/2005, p. 153-154; "If we are able to establish that the will can conserve enough strength, during sleep, to direct the race of the spirit through the world of illusions and memories [the same as it directs the body during the day through the events of the real world], it will become easy to persuade ourselves that a certain habit of exercising this faculty, together with that of often possessing, while dreaming, consciousness of one's true state, will gradually lead one who works on him or herself in a sustained manner to very good results. Not only will [s/]he have to first recognize the action of his [or her] reflective will on *lucid* and tranquil *dreams*, but [s/]he will soon notice the influence of this same will on incoherent or passionate dreams"; my translation)

"Les poils de ses sourcils, une blessure qu'il semblait avoir à l'épaule, et une infinité d'autres détails offraient une précision qui permettait de ranger cette vision parmi les plus *lucides*." (1867/2005, p. 157; "The hair of (the monster's) eyebrows, a wound that it seemed to have on the shoulder, and an infinity of other details offered a precision that permitted classifying this vision among the most *lucid*"; my translation)

"Je rencontre dans la rue un jeune homme qui me paraît être de ma connaissance, je l'aborde ; nous nous serrons la main, nous nous regardons attentivement. (Mon *rêve* est très *lucide*.) 'Mais je ne vous connais pas du tout', me dit alors ce personnage, en continuant sa route. Et moi, très confus, je suis forcé de m'avouer qu'en effet je ne le connaissais nullement." (1867/2005, p. 175; "I meet a young man in the street whom I think I know, I go up to him; we shake hands, we look attentively at one another. [My *dream* is very *lucid*]. 'But I don't know you at all,' this person then says to me, continuing on his way. And I, very confused, must admit to myself that, in effect, I don't know him at all"; my translation)

"Arrêtant alors mon attention sur un plateau de porcelaine . . . Qu'arriverait-il donc si je la brisais dans mon rêve ? Comment mon imagination se représenterait-elle le plateau brisé? J'exécute aussitôt l'acte imaginaire de le mettre en pièces. J'en saisis les morceaux, je les examine attentivement; j'aperçois les cassures avec leurs arêtes vives, je distingue les figures décoratives divisées par des brisures dentelées et incomplètes en plusieurs endroits. Rarement j'avais rien *rêvé* d'aussi *lucide*." (1867/2005, pp. 178-179; "Fixing my attention on a porcelaine plate . . . What would happen if I broke it in my dream? How would my imagination represent the broken tray? I just as soon execute the imaginary act of breaking it in pieces. I take the pieces, I examine them carefully; I perceive the broken pieces with their jutting edges, I distinguish the decorative designs divided by the

Chapter 31 - To Weep, Perchance to Lucid Dream: Lucid Dreaming and Lucid Dream Therapy

> incomplete jagged cracks in certain places. Rarely have I ever **dreamed** so *lucidly*"; my translation)

In these quotations, the Marquis uses the word "lucid" and the term "lucid dream" with a variety of meanings potentially different from "awareness of my actual situation" (Hervey de Saint Denys, 1867/2016, p. 7). I would therefore suggest that in the statement at issue:

> "I decided not to miss the first occasion that would present itself, that is to say the first lucid dream in which I would understand my situation,"

the relative clause "in which I would understand my situation" is not necessarily intended as definitional of the preceding 2 words ("lucid dream"), but rather provides additional information (which is the grammatical purpose of a relative clause) about the type of dream that he decided not to miss. It's like if I were to tell you that my dog Sherwood is an aspiring actor, he finally landed the role of Lassie in the Broadway hit *Lassie Get Help*, and I won't be able to fill in for you tomorrow at work because tomorrow is Sherwood's big debut and "I decided not to miss the first Broadway show in which my dog has a starring role." Now, is it *possible* that I'm taking the existing term "Broadway show" and assigning a new meaning to it as a show in which Sherwood has a starring role? Sure, that would make Sherwood (and me, as his agent) very happy. Does it necessarily *follow* from my statement?

Think about it (unless there's a bear nearby): Why, would the Marquis wait until *page 159* to casually define a word that he has already used 3 times in either its singular or plural form? (1867/2005, pp. 14, 143, 153). What the Marquis seems to be saying is that he had dreams that varied on a continuum of visual or logical *clarity* from those characterized by "imperfection of images" and "incoherent visions of pale and nondescript scenes," to those he considers "lucid" which, by comparison, would mean having more perfect images, more coherent visions, or brighter, more defined scenes. Among these latter, there are those in which he has the "capacity . . . to know of [his] real situation" (Herve de Saint Denys, 1867/2016, p. 2; i.e., knows it's a dream) and those in which he doesn't. He is therefore deciding that on the first occasion in the future in which he is in a lucid (high quality) dream *and* realizes it is a dream, he will try his experiment.

His experiment, incidentally, involved placing himself in a situation he had never experienced in real life, in order to determine:

> " . . . if, when I would venture myself in the dream into a situation which I had never experienced in real life, my memory would be powerless in providing a picture or *corresponding* sensation, so that my imagination would be forced to surmount this impasse at [sic] its customary manner and whether this necessarily would result in an abrupt interruption in the course of the dream." (Hervey de Saint Denys, 1867/2016, p. 119)

Naturally, the situations he considered, just to make sure he had truly never done them, included

> "From five high jumping out of a window, shooting myself through the head, or cutting my throat with a razor." (1867/2016, p. 120)

About a month later, he remembered to try jumping from a building when he realized he was dreaming, only to then find himself standing in a crowd gathered around someone who had jumped off a building. He never did get himself to try cutting his own throat, as

> . . . the instinctive horror of what I was trying to simulate was greater than my considered intention." (1867/2016, p. 120)

He apparently would not have been averse to shooting himself in the head, but he could never find a gun (1867/2016, p. 120).

I believe that the single following sentence (repeated from above) written by the Marquis can put the debate to rest regarding who coined the term "lucid dream" to specifically refer to dreams in which one is self-aware:

> "Non seulement, il devra reconnaître tout d'abord l'action de sa volonté réfléchie dans la direction des ***songes lucides*** et tranquilles, mais il s'apercevra bientôt de l'influence de cette même volonté sur les songes incohérents ou passionnés." (1867/2005, p. 153-154; "Not only will [s/]he have to first recognize the action of his [or her] reflective will on ***lucid*** and tranquil ***dreams***, but [s/]he will soon notice the influence of this same will on incoherent or passionate dreams"; my translation)

Chapter 31 - To Weep, Perchance to Lucid Dream: Lucid Dreaming and Lucid Dream Therapy

Here, the Marquis specifies the quality that defines what we now refer to as dream lucidity (recognizing the action of one's reflective will, i.e., being self-aware) and how it can be applied to dreams of varying qualities: those on a continuum from lucid to incoherent, and those on a continuum from tranquil to passionate. If we can equate the Marquis' "recognizing the action of one's reflective will" with our modern notion of "self-awareness," he is then contrasting self-aware "lucid," meaning coherent, dreams with self-aware incoherent dreams, where "self-awareness" and "lucidity" are orthogonal, or non-overlapping concepts.

In my opinion, it was thus Frederick van Eeden who borrowed the Marquis' term "lucid dream," by which the Marquis simply meant a dream that possesses coherence and visually clear details, to describe dreams in which one knows one is dreaming, which the Marquis was the first to write about in detail – Aristotle having mentioned them in passing.

For van Eeden, a "lucid dream" is one of seven types of dreams, namely that in which

> ". . . the reintegration of the psychic functions is so complete that the sleeper remembers day-life and his own condition, reaches a state of perfect awareness, and is able to direct his attention, and to attempt different acts of free volition." (van Eeden, 1913)

Details are provided in his 1913 essay *A Study of Dreams*:

> "I know that Mr. Havelock Ellis and many other authors will not accept my definition, because they deny the possibility of complete recollection and free volition in a dream. They would say that what I call a dream is no dream, but a sort of trance, or hallucination, or ecstacy. The observations of the Marquis d'Herve, which were very much like mine, as related in his book, Les Reves et les moyens de les diriger, were discarded in the same way. These dreams could not be dreams, said Maury.
>
> Now this is simply a question of nomenclature. I can only say that I made my observations during normal deep and healthy sleep, and that in 352 cases I had a full recollection of my daylife, and could act voluntarily, though I was so fast asleep that no bodily sensations penetrated into my perception. If anybody refuses to call that state of mind a dream, he may suggest some other name. For my part, it was just this form of dream, which I call 'lucid dreams,' which aroused my keenest interest and which I noted down most carefully.
>
> I quite agree with Mr. Havelock Ellis, that during sleep the psychical functions enter into a condition of dissociation. My contention, however, is that it is not dissociation, but, on the contrary, reintegration, after the dissociation of sleep, that is the essential feature of dreams. The dream is a more or less complete reintegration of the psyche, a reintegration in a different sphere, in a psychical, nonspatial mode of existence. This reintegration may go so far as to effect full recollection of day-life, reflection, and voluntary action on reflection.
>
> ... The seventh type of dreams, which I call lucid dreams, seems to me the most interesting and worthy of the most careful observation and study. Of this type I experienced and wrote down 352 cases in the period between January 20, 1898, and December 26, 1912.
>
> In these lucid dreams the reintegration of the psychic functions is so complete that the sleeper remembers day-life and his own condition, reaches a state of perfect awareness, and is able to direct his attention, and to attempt different acts of free volition. Yet the sleep, as I am able confidently to state, is undisturbed, deep and refreshing.

Chapter 31 - To Weep, Perchance to Lucid Dream: Lucid Dreaming and Lucid Dream Therapy

I obtained my first glimpse of this lucidity during sleep in June, 1897, in the following way. I dreamt that I was floating through a landscape with bare trees, knowing that it was April, and I remarked that the perspective of the branches and twigs changed quite naturally. Then I made the reflection, during sleep, that my fancy would never be able to invent or to make an image as intricate as the perspective movement of little twigs seen in floating by.

Many years later, in 1907, I found a passage in a work by Prof. Ernst Mach in which the same observation is made with a little difference. Like me, Mach came to the conclusion that he was dreaming, but it was because he saw the movement of the twigs to be defective, while I had wondered at the naturalness which my fancy could never invent. Professor Mach has not pursued his observations in this direction, probably because he did not believe in their importance. I made up my mind to look out carefully for another opportunity. I prepared myself for careful observation, hoping to prolong and to intensify the lucidity.

. . . Mr. Havelock Ellis says with something of a sneer that some people 'who dabble in the occult' speak of an astral body. Yet if he had had only one of these experiences, he would feel that we can escape neither the dabbling nor the dream-body. In a lucid dream the sensation of having a body – having eyes, hands, a mouth that speaks, and so on – is perfectly distinct; yet I know at the same time that the physical body is sleeping and has quite a different position. In waking up the two sensations blend together, so to speak, and I remember as clearly the action of the dream-body as the restfulness of the physical body.

. . . On Sept. 9, 1904, I dreamt that I stood at a table before a window. On the table were different objects. I was perfectly well aware that I was dreaming and I considered what sorts of experiments I could make. I began by trying to break glass, by beating it with a stone. I put a small tablet of glass on two stones and struck it with another stone. Yet it would not break. Then I took a fine claret-glass from the table and struck it with my fist, with all my might, at the same time reflecting how dangerous it would be to do this in waking life; yet the glass remained whole. But lo! when I looked at it again after some time, it was broken.

It broke all right, but a little too late, like an actor who misses his cue. This gave me a very curious impression of being in a fake-world, cleverly imitated, but with small failures. I took the broken glass and threw it out of the window, in order to observe whether I could hear the tinkling. I heard the noise all right and I even saw two dogs run away from it quite naturally. I thought what a good imitation this comedy-world was. Then I saw a decanter with claret and tasted it, and noted with perfect clearness of mind: 'Well, we can also have voluntary impressions of taste in this dream-world; this has quite the taste of wine.'" (van Eeden, 1913)

Sigmund Freud, whom most people incorrectly consider the originator of the science of dreaming, apparently was aware of the Marquis through the works of Alfred Maury (who coined the term "hypnagogia" – the hallucinatory state of awareness that occurs as wakefulness passes into sleep, as contrasted with the term "hypnopompia" coined by Frederic Myers, founder of the Society for Psychical Research, which refers to a similar state occurring as sleep transitions back to wakefulness). (Fun fact: Notice the "a" in hypnagogia and the "o" in hypnopompia.) In his 1899 Interpretation of Dreams, Freud says that:

"A thinker like Delboeuf asserts – without, indeed, adducing proof in the face of contradictory data, and hence without real justification – 'Dans le sommeil, hormis la perception, toutes les facultes de l'esprit, intelligence, imagination, memoire, volonte, moralite, restent intactes dans leur essence; seulement, elles s'appliquent a des objets imaginaires et mobiles. Le songeur est un acteur qui joue a volonte les fous et les sages, les bourreaux et les victimes, les nains et les geants, les demons et les anges' (p. 222). The Marquis Hervey, who is flatly contradicted by Maury, and whose essay I have been unable to obtain despite all my efforts, appears emphatically to protest against the under-estimation of the psychic capacity in the dream." (Freud, 1899/1913; Translated by A. A. Brill)

To which you may justifiably respond "huh?" I guess it was above A. A.'s paygrade, when translating Freud's German into the Queen's English, to translate Freud's French citation of Of The Beef (Delboeuf) into English as

Chapter 31 - To Weep, Perchance to Lucid Dream: Lucid Dreaming and Lucid Dream Therapy

well. Like, I'll translate the German, but you're on your own with the French. It's getting a little late and my French is going offline, but luckily we have . . . Google Translate. Here is the above quotation with A. A.'s English translation of Freud combined with Google's translation of Of the Beef:

> "A thinker like Delboeuf asserts – without, indeed, adducing proof in the face of contradictory data, and hence without real justification – '*In sleep, apart from perception, all the faculties of the mind, intelligence, imagination, memory, will, morality, remain intact in their essence; only they apply to imaginary and mobile objects. The dreamer is an actor who plays the will of fools and wise men, executioners and victims, dwarves and giants, demons and angels.*' The Marquis Hervey, [35] who is flatly contradicted by Maury, and whose essay I have been unable to obtain despite all my efforts, appears emphatically to protest against the under-estimation of the psychic capacity in the dream." (Translated by A. A. Brill and *Google;* italics added)

Freud was also, apparently, unaware of the article published by Frederick van Eeden, despite the fact that they knew one another, as evidenced by a letter that Freud wrote to van Eeden on December 28th, 1914. Rooksby and Terwee (1990) considered a biography of Freud and his letter to van Eeden in historical context and concluded the following:

> "Ernest Jones writes in his biography of Freud that Dr. van Eeden was ' . . . an acquaintance of his from the old hypnosis days' and continues on to say, 'van Eeden, a Dutch psychopathologist, is now remembered more as a poet, essayist and social reformer; both Freud and I had been unsuccessful in getting him to accept psycho-analytical theories.'" (Jones, 1955, p.412, cited in Rooksby & Terwee, 1990)

> "Support for the suggestion that Freud may have known about lucid dreaming came initially from two other sources. First, van Eeden's essay, 'A Study Of Dreams,' did appear in the bibliography of the fourth German edition of Freud's The Interpretation of Dreams (1914). However, it appears that Otto Rank was responsible for bibliographical additions from the second to the eighth additions, so there can be no guarantee that Freud had read this paper, or that he even knew of it.

... The second source of support for the suggestion that Freud may have known about lucid dreaming came from references made by Freud himself to lucid-type dream experiences. Jones, in Sigmund Freud: Life and Work (Volume 1) reports that in a dream diary, Freud describes what he calls a 'sharp dream,' which we suggest has shades of lucidity to it (i.e., Freud began to question whether or not he was dreaming). Jones says this is an improvement on other reports of the 'dream within a dream' (p. 386). This questioning of the dream reality is mentioned in The Interpretation of Dreams as the 'dream within a dream' and in Freud's 1901 book, On Dreams. Whether or not these really are lucid reports, and whether or not lucid dreaming was known as the 'dream within a dream' before 1913 by Freud is a matter for further research. Up to now the investigation into Freud's knowledge of van Eeden and lucid dreaming remains elusive and speculative.

... Now as far as the general idea of lucidity in dreams goes, Freud indicates in the letter that he is basically happy with it. 'The assertion that one does not judge nor appraise in a dream, nor speak, cannot contradict your experiences...' Where he takes issue is in the interpretation of this activity and the importance that may be attached to it. Since, according to Freud, the conscious mind is the less important part of a person's total psychological activity (the bulk of which lies in constant flux in the unconscious) it is of little real importance how dreams are experienced – especially so in the context of the therapeutic process. In the final analysis, we can say that it is Freud's devaluing of the manifest dream (a point which contributed to the split with Jung) that naturally led him to 'devalue' the idea of lucid dreaming. Lucid dreaming posed no threat to his major thesis. He probably felt that he had already given it enough attention - note how he directs van Eeden back to the Interpretation of Dreams in the opening of the letter. One can't help but speculate about what might have occurred had Freud accepted van Eeden's 'lucid' term and the idea he was suggesting, but he didn't, so 'lucid dreaming' did not attract the attention of other psychoanalysts and did not become a topic of discussion earlier this century." (Rooksby & Terwee, 1990)

Chapter 31 - To Weep, Perchance to Lucid Dream: Lucid Dreaming and Lucid Dream Therapy

Now, why did I go to so much trouble, opening so many Google Chrome and Firefox windows to so many webpages, downloading version upon version of Freud's Interpretation of Dreams (as not all contain the entire manuscript), using Google Translate, copying and pasting and italicizing, and tracking down letters from 1914 just to bring you these historical tidbits on the relationships between Freud, the Marquis and van Eeden? I'll tell you why: Because these documents explain why most people have never heard of lucid dreaming (and why most people who have heard about it don't care about it, including most psychologists) and thus remain unaware of a latent potential of their own brain that could change their lives.

Let me explain. Although people have been dreaming since before they evolved into people (if evolution is true, i.e., animals dream), and although dreaming was studied way before Freud (for example by all the people he cited in his Interpretation of Dreams, including the ancient Greeks), it is probably due to Freud's theory of the unconscious and its role in dreaming (dreams being "the royal road to the unconscious") that dreams achieved a prominent place in the field of psychology through the psychoanalytic practice of dream analysis.

Freud criticizes Of the Beef for claiming without "proof" (which he would have found in both the Marquis' book and van Eeden's article) that when we dream we have access to the same mental faculties as when we are awake, only we use them to interact with things that are imaginary. This failure of Freud to obtain the first book on lucid dreaming, as well as either not obtaining, not reading or not considering as important the first scientific article on lucid dreaming, set the stage for a science of dreaming in which patients told therapists what they remembered from their dreams and then the therapists interpreted what the dreams meant using Freud's theories (mainly regarding repressed sex and aggression) as guidelines. In other words, dreams were (and mostly continue to be) studied from a distance thrice removed (the dreamer's questionable memory of the dream, with this memory then interpreted by someone else using still another person's theories). Contrast this with a science of dreaming in which the dreamer *wakes up inside of* his or her *own* dream and *asks the dream itself* what it means (a practice among lucid dreamsters).

If only Freud had been able to go to Amazon.com and download the Marquis' book onto his Kindle Paperwhite (or his iPhone - which he might today call his EgoHandy – since his father, whom he hated and wanted to kill when he was a baby, spoke Latin, and his mother, whom he loved and wanted to marry when he was a baby, followed the modern German practice of inserting English words unknown to English speakers into her native language), we wouldn't have had to wait for the movie Inception for most people to learn about lucid dreaming. If Freud had, back in 1899, been able to get a copy of the Marquis' 1867 book on lucid dreaming, or had both read and realized the full import of van Eeden's article, he might have taught his own patients how to lucid dream. Lucid dreaming would have been a part of the popular culture for the last 120 years, and we probably would all have been taught to lucid dream as children.

But alas, dear millennial readers, back in the 1800s when the internet still used dial up connections and email was in its infancy, Freud was unable to procure a copy of the Marquis' book that would have proven to him that Of The Beef was correct (that we can have access to all of our mental faculties inside of a dream). And in 1913, though email had become more reliable, van Eeden's article may very well have wound up in Freud's spam box. So it probably wasn't until you saw the movie Inception in 2010 that you learned about lucid dreaming, the only problem being that Inception made it seem like you need a drug to have lucid dreams, which is not true, though certain over the counter and prescription substances that increase the availability of acetylcholine in the brain can be off assistance, as discussed later in this chapter.

A FOX, A GOLEM AND AN IMMORTAL FOETUS

WALK INTO A BAR . . .

Oliver Fox (1)

Oliver Fox (the pen name of Hugh George Callaway) was a writer, electrical engineer and actor who dabbled in the occult sciences in the early 1900s.

In 1920, he published an article in the Occult Review entitled *The Pineal Doorway: A Record of Research*, which he describes as "a very condensed account of my practical researches into the little-known realms of dream-consciousness, astral traveling, and self-induced trance . . ." (p. 190). He states from the outset that there are two standpoints from which such phenomena can be viewed:

Chapter 31 - To Weep, Perchance to Lucid Dream: Lucid Dreaming and Lucid Dream Therapy

"(a) *Scientific*: It is merely a new brain state, the produce of self-induced trance, and the seeming external experiences all originate within the mind of the investigator – a third level of consciousness, differing from both waking life and ordinary dream, and far more vivid.

(b) *Occult*: The spirit actually leaves the entranced physical vehicle and functions – perfectly aware of doing so – apart from it upon the astral plane, the transition from normal waking life being achieved without any break in consciousness." (Fox, 1920, p. 190)

This distinction is important to remember, both when interpreting the writings of consciousness explorers and interpreting your own experiences. There is also a third possibility, in which some altered states are merely brain phenomena, and others involve the "spirit" or the nonphysical. For example, despite my own openness to interpreting some of my lucid dreams and out-of-body experiences as having involved contact of my disembodied consciousness with nonphysical realms, I have also had lucid dreams and out-of-body experiences that I consider merely the chaotic workings of a sleepy brain. I should point out that Fox's definition of the "occult" standpoint especially applies to the subjective experience of wake-initiated lucid dreams (WILDs, discussed below) and out-of-body experiences (OBEs, discussed in additional detail in the next chapter) in which there is a distinct sense of continuity between waking consciousness and the onset of the lucid dream or out-of-body state. Whereas such continuity is definitional of WILDs and the norm for OBEs, other types of lucid dreams (dream-initiated lucid dreams or DILDs, nondreaming sleep-initiated lucid dreams or ND-SILDs) and some out-of-body experiences are characterized by a discontinuity between waking consciousness and the insight that one is in a dream or out-of-body state.

While lucid dreaming terminology distinguishes between the states preceding lucidity (i.e., WILD versus DILD), no such distinction is common in the literature on out-of-body experiences. I therefore propose that under the umbrella term of out-of-body experiences (OBEs) there are 8 possibilities as represented below. As these states implicate, in various combinations, both lucid dreams and OBEs, they will be presented here rather than in the following chapter on OBEs.

Chapter 31 - To Weep, Perchance to Lucid Dream: Lucid Dreaming and Lucid Dream Therapy

8 Types of Out-Of-Body Experiences
By Previous State of Consciousness and Perceived Continuity

	Continuous (Aware during transition)	*Discontinuous* (Unaware during transition)
Formerly Awake	WICOBE (Wake-Initiated Continuous)	WIDOBE (Wake-Initiated Discontinuous)
Formerly in Nondreaming Sleep	ND-SICOBE (Nondreaming Sleep Initiated Continuous)	ND-SIDOBE (Nondreaming Sleep Initiated Discontinuous)
Formerly Non-Lucid Dreaming	NL-DICOBE (Non-Lucid Dream Initiated Continuous)	NL-DIDOBE (Non-Lucid Dream Initiated Discontinuous)
Formerly Lucid Dreaming	L-DICOBE (Lucid Dream Initiated Continuous)	L-DIDOBE (Lucid Dream Initiated Discontinuous)

I have categorized the varieties of OBEs in terms of the state of consciousness preceding separation or perceived separation from the body and the perceived continuity of the transition (this notwithstanding some reports of people seeing the nonphysical bodies of others who are currently in an out-of-body state that the OBEers themselves are unaware of). Please note that the validity of the concept of "perceived continuity of the transition" or "awareness during the transition" may be questionable for transitions from a nonlucid, non-self-aware state (such as from a nonlucid dream or from nonlucid nondreaming sleep – as differentiated from the clear light nondreaming sleep of the Tibetan dream yogis) to the lucid, self-aware state of consciousness characterizing OBEs.

The 8 categories in the chart are generated from 3 root categories of OBEs, with those preceded by a dream being differentiated by whether the dream was lucid or nonlucid.

WIOBEs: Wake-initiated out-of-body experiences, characterized by a transition from the waking state to subsequent awareness of being (or believing oneself to be) out of the body;

DIOBEs: Dream-initiated out-of-body experiences, characterized by a transition from the dreaming state to subsequent awareness of being (or believing oneself to be) out of the body;

This category includes:

> **NL-DIOBEs** if the initial dream state was non-lucid, and
>
> **L-DIOBEs** if the initial dream state was lucid.

ND-SIOBEs: Nondreaming sleep-initiated out-of-body experiences, characterized by a transition from the nondreaming sleep state to awareness of being (or believing oneself to be) out of the body. Theoretically these could be preceded by lucidity versus nonlucidity in the nondreaming sleep state, such as the clear light nondreaming state of the Tibetan dream yogis, but the acronyms here would get out of control (NL-ND-SIOBE versus L-ND-SIOBE), so let's not go there.

These 3 root categories may be further specified in terms of continuity of the transition and, if the preceding state was a dream, whether it was lucid or

Chapter 31 - To Weep, Perchance to Lucid Dream: Lucid Dreaming and Lucid Dream Therapy

nonlucid. I have placed asterisks before the categories that constitute the final 8 types of OBE presented in the chart.

COBEs: Continuous out-of-body experiences, when one experiences, or has the sensation of experiencing, a transition between the previous consciousness state and the out-of-body (or perceived out-of-body) state. These can be specified as:

>   ***WICOBEs:** Wake-initiated continuous out-of-body experiences, when one experiences, or has the sensation of experiencing, a transition between a waking state and the out-of-body (or perceived out-of-body) state;

>   ***ND-SICOBEs:** Nondreaming sleep initiated continuous out-of-body experiences, when one experiences, or has the sensation of experiencing, a transition between nondreaming sleep and the out-of-body (or perceived out-of-body) state. It should be noted that this type of experience requires conscious awareness during nondreaming sleep (such as "clear light sleep" in Tibetan dream yoga) in order to experience the transition from this to the out-of-body state; and

>   **DICOBEs:** Dream-initiated continuous out-of-body experiences, when one experiences, or has the sensation of experiencing, a transition between a dream state and the out-of-body (or perceived out-of-body) state. These can be further specified as including

>> ***NL-DICOBEs** if the initial dream state was non-lucid, and

>> ***L-DICOBEs** if the initial dream state was lucid.

DOBEs: Discontinuous out-of-body experiences, when one becomes aware of being (or believes oneself to be) out of the body, without having experienced (or had the sensation of) the process of separation itself. These can be specified as:

>   ***WIDOBEs:** Wake-initiated discontinuous out-of-body experiences, characterized by a discontinuity between the waking state and conscious awareness of being outside of the body (or perceiving oneself to be outside of the body), without awareness of the process of leaving the body (or perceiving oneself to be leaving the body);

*ND-SIDOBEs: Nondreaming sleep-initiated discontinuous out-of-body experiences, when one does not experience, or does not have the sensation of experiencing, a transition between nondreaming sleep and the out-of-body (or perceived out-of-body) state. Here, one suddenly finds oneself in the out-of-body state, having previously been sleeping in the absence of conscious dreaming. As an example from my own experience just came to mind, I'll add it here. One may sometimes have the sense of being in an OBE rather than in a lucid dream due to the familiarity of the surroundings (e.g., suddenly experiencing oneself as floating above one's body in one's present environment) even without having experienced a perceived moment of separation. As a case in point, I once "awoke" to find myself looking down upon my sleeping body. At first, I wondered whom I was looking at. Then I realized it was me in desperate need of a shave. I was, in effect, seeing my physical body from the viewpoint of my nonphysical *doppelgänger* or "double." Kind of like when you hear an audio recording of yourself for the first time and cringe in disbelief. I then heard myself in my floating body giving myself in my sleeping body a word of much needed advice.

DIDOBEs: Dream-initiated discontinuous out-of-body experiences, when one does not experience, or does not have the sensation of experiencing, a transition between a dream state and the out-of-body (or perceived out-of-body) state. These can be further specified as including

> ***NL-DIDOBEs** if the initial dream state was non-lucid, and

> ***L-DIDOBEs** if the initial dream state was lucid.

Don't worry about memorizing these (I just made them up on the basis of some of my own experiences that I found no names for in the literature, and they don't exactly roll off my tongue either). Simply realize that there are subtleties to lucid dreams and OBEs and, *when* you have one (I just hypnotized you), the above table may come in useful for understanding and communicating your experience to others. I have intentionally limited the terms to acronyms of the variables at play (waking v. nondreaming sleep v. dreaming; continuous v discontinuous; lucid versus nonlucid). Could less cumbersome names be thought up for each of these? Certainly. Just like NaCL is typically known as "salt" (or halen if you're Welsh). But at the current level of ignorance regarding these states, I think it better to remain boring and descriptive in order to clarify the basics.

Oliver Fox (2)

Fox dates his first lucid dream to 1902:

> "THE FIRST STEP.
>
> *To acquire, by observing some incongruity or anachronism, the knowledge that one is dreaming.*
>
> Eighteen years ago, when I was a student at a technical college, a dream impelled me to start my research. I dreamed simply that I was standing outside my home. Looking down, I discovered that the paving-stones had mysteriously changed their position – the long sides were now parallel to the curb instead of perpendicular to it. Then the solution flashed upon me: though that glorious summer morning seemed as real as real could be, I was *dreaming*!
>
> Instantly the vividness of life increased a hundredfold. Never had sea and sky and trees shone with such glamorous beauty; even the commonplace houses seemed alive and mystically beautiful. Never had I felt so absolutely well, so clear-brained, so divinely powerful. Verily the world had become my oyster. The sensation was exquisite beyond words; but it lasted only a few moments, and I awoke. As I was to learn later, my mental control had been overwhelmed by my emotions; so the tiresome body asserted its claim and pulled me back. And now I had a (for me) wonderful new idea: Was it possible to regain at will the glory of the dream? Could I *prolong* my dreams?
>
> I have italicized the heading to this section. It sounds simple; but in practice I found it one of the most difficult things imaginable. A hundred times I would pass the most glaring incongruities, and then at last some inconsistency would tell me that I was dreaming; and always this knowledge brought the change I have described. I found that I was then able to do little tricks at will, levitate, pass through seemingly solid walls, mould matter into new forms, etc.; but in these early experiments I could stay out of my body for only a very short time, and this dream consciousness could be acquired only at intervals of several weeks." (pp. 190-191)

He also notes some pain associated with his technique:

> "The mental effort of prolonging the dream produced a pain in the region of the pineal gland – dull at first, but rapidly increasing in intensity – and I knew instinctively that this was a warning to me to resist no longer the call of my body." (p. 191)

In addition,

> "In the last moments of prolonging the dream, and while I was subject to the above pain, I experienced a sense of dual consciousness. I could feel myself standing in the dream and see the scenery; but at the same time I could feel myself lying in bed and see my bedroom." (p. 191)

I would like to here interject that although Fox is describing an experience that clearly corresponds with what every writer on lucid dreams considers the defining aspect of a lucid dream, and which he himself even specifies as "knowledge that one is dreaming," he then refers to it as "staying out of my body," which would classify it as an OBE. I sympathize, as to this day I cannot clearly classify one of my two most important experiences (The Park) as one or the other (more on this two chapters down the road), as there was no awareness or belief regarding separation from the body (to my best recollection, it was an **ND-SIDOBE**, Nondreaming sleep-initiated discontinuous out-of-body experience as, having fallen asleep, I suddenly found myself standing in a park).

Let's see how Fox's story unfolds (this is exciting for me as well, as only this morning I located the website with this entire archive of these old articles, preserved by **IAPSOP** – The International Association for the Preservation of Spiritualist and Occult Periodicals). Fox goes on to detail, in a Reefer Madness sort of way, the dangers of such experiments, cautioning that

> "Any one who, without being under the guidance of an Adept or Master, investigates on my lines exposes himself to the following grave risks – at least, so I believe:
>
> (1) Heart failure, or insanity, arising from shock. This dream world is very lovely, but it has its horrors also.
>
> (2) Premature burial.

Chapter 31 - To Weep, Perchance to Lucid Dream: Lucid Dreaming and Lucid Dream Therapy

(3) Obsession.

(4) Severance of cord.

(5) Repercussion effects upon the physical vehicle, caused by injuries to the astral." (p. 193)

To which one might reply "Chill out dude." Fox's fears are clearly due to his own interpretation of his experiences through the filter of his occult readings.

This said, similar warnings are voiced in the course of instructions on how to leave the body in more mainstream traditions such as mystical Judaism and Taoist Internal Alchemy. For example:

Golems

Gershom Scholem (1965) provides a history of mystical judaic "instructions for golem-making" (p. 184). A golem is "a man created by magical art" (p. 159; see also Meyerink, 1928, 1986). He cites Rabbi Eleazar of Worms (1176-1238) commentary on the Sefer Yezirah, in which you

> "'take some virginal mountain earth' and 'knead it in running water,' you 'recite the combinations of the alphabet' but carefully, because 'One prescribed order of the alphabet produces a male being, another female; a reversal of these orders turns the golem back to dust.'" (p. 186)

Scholem also cites someone named Pseudo-Saadya, who him or herself, but probably himself (as people didn't used to cite women) cited a certain "R.I.B.E.," who Pseudo thinks was Rabbi Ishmael ben Elisha, who was teaching his students how to make golems by walking in circles and reciting the alphabet, walking around the circle forward and reciting the alphabet forward to enliven it, and walking backwards around the circle and saying the alphabet backwards in order to kill it (suddenly making a 48 hour binge involving Heisenberg Kush and Cyberpunk 2077 sound like a productive use of one's time). As it turned out, in a Richard Alpert (Ram Dass, R.I.P.) and Timothy Leary getting fired from Harvard for conducting LSD experiments moment, Rabbi Ishmael's students, "who busied themselves with the *Book Yetsirah,"*

> ". . . by mistake went around backward, until they themselves by the power of the letters sank into the earth up to their navels. They were

unable to escape and cried out. Their teacher heard them and said: Recite the letters of the alphabets and walk forward, instead of going backward as you have been doing. They did so and were released." (Scholem, 1965, pp. 187-188)

Whew. Close call.

The relevance of golems to lucid dreaming, and to Fox's cautions regarding "staying out of my body," (I inserted the commas out of compassion for those of you reading this either under the influence of Heisenberg Kush, or during breaks from Cyberpunk 2077, so as not to disturb the resonance of multitasking brain cells) relates to the debate within Judaism as to whether golems are actual physical beings or mystical thought forms (and, if they are of the latter persuasion, where Rabbi Ishmael was getting his kush):

> ". . . an important but anonymous Spanish author of the early fourteenth century explains that the process is not corporeal, but a 'creation of thought,' *yetsirah mahshavtith.*
>
> . . . And a disparaging remark of Abulafia himself, the leading representative of an ecstatic Kabbalah in the thirteenth century, seems to imply a similar view of golem-making as a purely mystical process. He ridicules the 'folly of those who study the Book of Yetsirah in order to make a calf; for those who do so are themselves calves.'" (Scholem, 1965, p. 188)

Either way, Scholem echoes Fox in cautioning that

> "Golem-making is dangerous;"

Duh.

> "like all major creation it endangers the life of the creator – the source of danger, however, is not the golem or the forces emanating from him, but the man himself. The danger is not that the golem, become autonomous, will develop overwhelming powers; it lies in the tension which the creative process arouses in the creator himself. Mistakes in carrying out the directions do not impair the golem; they destroy its creator." (Scholem, 1965, pp. 190-191)

Chapter 31 - To Weep, Perchance to Lucid Dream: Lucid Dreaming and Lucid Dream Therapy

Moving Right Along to Taoism and Immortal Foetuses

And while we're on the subject of *golems*, in Taoist Internal Alchemy, which Charles Luk (Lu K'uan Yü), scholar of Chinese meditation and Zen, calls *Taoist Yoga* (1984/1970), Microcosmic Orbit meditation is used to create the "immortal foetus" (p. 149). Luk's book *Taoist Yoga* is "a translation (with introduction and notes) of The *Secrets of Cultivating Essential Nature and Eternal life* (*Hsin Ming Fa Chueh Ming Chik*) by the Taoist Master Chao Pi Ch'en, born in 1860." Unfortunately for many alchemists throughout history who thought that turning lead into gold actually involved metals, which they experimented with to our benefit (creating the science of chemistry) and ingested to their detriment (eating metal does not usually lead to good things), alchemy is really about transforming (or *transmuting*) physiological energy into altered states of consciousness with various real (or imagined) results.

Below on the left is a simplified image of the Microcosmic Orbit, in which vital energy is breathed in, up the back of the body, and breathed out, down the front of the body. On the right is a drawing of the same from Taoist Master Chao Pi Ch'en's The Secrets of Cultivating Essential Nature and Eternal Life (Chao, in Luk, 1984/1970, p. 91):

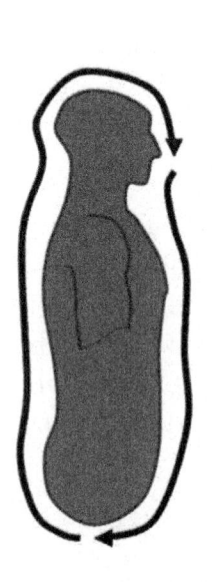

According to Master Chao (1860+; in Luk, 1984/1970),

> "This immortal foetus is formed by the union of two prenatal vitalities: prenatal true nature-vitality in (essential) nature whose light is like moonlight and prenatal true life-vitality in (eternal) life whose light is golden.
>
> When this stage is reached the practiser should not dwell in the inactive (wu wei) state, but should direct the (active) inner (vital) breath to reach and enter the prenatal true vitality in order to invigorate and help it form and nurture the immortal foetus.
>
> . . . This latter should be quickly lifted to the ni wan or brain. This is ascent to the upper tan t'ien where the union of (positive) with (negative) spirit and return to the brain will produce one uniform prenatal positive spirit." (pp. 155-156)
>
> ". . . At this stage breath will not (be felt to) enter or leave (the body), the serenity experienced is full of bliss, and the six senses are blotted out to reveal one essential nature which is perfect and radiant with the shining and pervading light of vitality." (p. 156)
>
> ". . . Only when this foetus has been nurtured by vitality, and is full and mature can flowers be seen falling from the sky before the eyes, which shows the time is ripe for leaving the foetus which should be done immediately. Dancing snow reveals full development of the immortal foetus.
>
> The patriarch Hua Yang commenting on the Hui Ming Ching said 'This is the time to come out of serenity. If the practiser does not leave this state he will get bogged down in the spiritual body, will be tied up by serenity and will not achieve the transcendental powers which enable him to appear in myriad transformational bodies. When snow and flowers are seen, spirit should leave the mortal body *stirred by thought* of entering the great emptiness [the aim of alchemy]." (p. 157)

I would like here to point two things. First, something very similar to how earlier in this book we proposed that thinking can be stopped by favoring awareness of, or filling awareness with, other senses. Here, Master Chao just told us that:

Chapter 31 - To Weep, Perchance to Lucid Dream: Lucid Dreaming and Lucid Dream Therapy

> " ... the six senses are blotted out to reveal one essential nature which is perfect and radiant with the shining and pervading light of vitality." (p. 156)

This is pointing to what occurs when awareness becomes so full of something beyond the six senses (of seeing, hearing, smelling, tasting, bodysensing and thinking), that not only do we stop thinking, we stop all semblance of experiencing things in the only ways we have ever experienced them (through the six senses) and are initiated into a *new way of being* which is, according to every mystical tradition, our True Self, which was there all along but to which we were blinded to by our learned habit of filling awareness with the six senses rather than attending to *The One Who Is Attending*.

Second, how Master Chao's warning not to get "tied up by serenity" (p. 157), is similar to Ramana's caution that "The moment one experiences this, one must revive consciousness and enquire within as to who it is who experiences this stillness (in Swarnagiri, 1981, pp. 25-27; cited in Godman, 1985 pp. 63-64).

Now, this is where things get interesting, and Master Chao echoes Fox's and Scholem's "better safe than sorry" advice:

> "When spirit manifests for the first time it should only be allowed to leave the body in fine weather and it should be well looked after, like a baby just born. Its egress should on no account take place when there is thick fog, heavy rain, gale, lightning and thunder.
>
> When for the first time positive spirit comes out it should (be made to) return to the body at once. During the first three months it should be pulled out once a week. After this it will gradually develop perception and knowledge and is very sensitive to fear and awe which should be avoided at all costs.
>
> Its egress and return to the body should be orderly and at regular intervals. Each coming out should be immediately followed by re-entry until the practiser is familiar with the exercise. It should take place in the day but never at night.
>
> After six months positive spirit can be let out once every three days; and after a year once a day. During these exercises it should always

be kept close to the body and not allowed to stray. In the case of fright and awe it should be quickly returned to the body. These instructions should be carried out carefully.

After two years of exercise the egress can take place either in the full day or at night and the number of times can be increased gradually. The positive spirit can now leave the body to wander inside or outside the grotto (place of meditation) and then return to the body to [draw nourishment from the body].

After three years of exercise the practiser can send the positive spirit to distant places. If it meets men and animals it should return swiftly to the body. From now on it can cover a distance of half a mile or a mile and return quickly.

. . . Now is the time for a course of training which will enable this immortal to dwell in the state of serenity for nine years in order to return to the great emptiness thereby transforming his physical body into that of a golden immortal (chin hsien)." (Luk, 1984/1970, pp. 165-166)

If you are like I used to be, and like most people are, of course, all of this sounds really, really crazy. So I don't expect you to understand why anybody would take it seriously, even if they did find it interesting in the way one might enjoy reading Lord of the Rings. However, if one day you have an out-of-body experience or near-death-experience, it will all start to make senses, and you may find yourself re-reading portions of this book no longer out of cognitive dissonance (I bought it, so I should read the whole thing, the good, the bad and the bonkers) but in a desperate search to make sense of a life-changing experience. And then, depending on the nature of your particular experience, old Master Chao may not sound so nutty anymore.

If you are interested in understanding Taoist Internal Alchemy, Luk's (1970) translation of Master Chao Pi Ch'en is one of the most literal (i.e., least metaphorical) English instruction manuals I've found. On a practical level, however, it's a little complicated. To learn microcosmic orbit meditation, I would suggest familiarizing yourself with free online instructions by Robert Peng (2019), and possibly purchasing his audio or that of Sharon Smith (2019). Both Robert and Sharon also offer personal training in use of the microcosmic orbit. A word of caution: I either read or was told that one

Chapter 31 - To Weep, Perchance to Lucid Dream: Lucid Dreaming and Lucid Dream Therapy

should not practice the microcosmic orbit when pregnant. Also, the direction of the movement of the energy is different according to different authors, sometimes involving breathing the energy up the back of the body and down the front, and sometimes vice versa. In addition, sometimes this depends on whether you are male or female. These are things that perhaps Robert or Sharon could clarify if you wish to explore further. An additional resource is Kohn & Wang's (2009) book *Internal Alchemy*.

Oliver Fox (3)

But back to Oliver Fox and lucid dreaming or astral projection or whatever he was really doing. Where were we? Right-O. Debby Downer, heart failure, premature burial. In order to distinguish them from ordinary dreams, Fox referred to dreams with "knowledge that one is dreaming" as "Dreams of Knowledge" (1920, p. 193). He then discovered that these "were often followed by a false awakening" (p. 193) characterized by bodily semi-rigidity, seeing through the eyelids, hallucinations and fear (p. 194). He labeled it "the Trance Condition," which we now call sleep paralysis (Hurd, 2011). He wondered "Can the Trance Condition be a prelude to a Dream of Knowledge as well as an after-effect? Time showed that the answer was, Yes" (p. 194).

His sequence of experience would appear to be from a (1) nonlucid dream to a (2) lucid dream, then involuntarily to a (3) "false awakening" or "Trance Condition" (which sounds like sleep paralysis, and could be either waking sleep paralysis with the eyes actually open, or a dream of sleep paralysis, dreaming of seeing the room one is sleeping in through one's eyelids), from which he then intentionally entered, without perceiving the transition, into (4) another lucid dream.

He says that at this point he couldn't enter the Trance Condition at will, and "did not yet realize that it was possible to pass from the Trance Condition into the Dream of Knowledge *without any break in consciousness*" as "always there was a break in consciousness before I found myself enjoying the glorious emancipation of the Dream of Knowledge" (p. 194). In modern parlance, he was still having only dream-initiated lucid dreams (DILDS) or in my system dream-initiated discontinuous out-of-body experiences (DIDOBEs) and not wake-initiated lucid dreams (WILDS) or in my system wake-initiated out-of-body experiences (WIOBEs)(Unless we consider his trance, or sleep paralysis, a waking state). This is when he discovered something truly bizarre:

> "In the ordinary way I could not step out of my body when in the Trance condition. Before this was possible a mysterious something had to happen – and in those earlier experiments it probably occurred during the break in consciousness. And at last it flashed upon me what this something was: I had to force my incorporeal self through the doorway of the pineal gland, so that it clicked behind me. Then a further stage – a stage beyond the Trance Condition with its terrifying sensations: shapes and sounds – was reached. Then, and only then, could I step out of my physical body (now invisible), experience the dual consciousness, and be in the Dream of Knowledge (or a traveller on the astral plane) without any previous break in consciousness. It was done, when in the Trance Condition, simply by concentrating upon the pineal gland and willing to ascend through it." (Fox, 1920, p. 195)

He thus learned to have a DICOBE (dream-induced continuous out-of-body experience) if the Trance is seen as a dream state or WICOBE (wake-induced continuous out-of-body experience) if the Trance is seen as a waking state.

Does any of this make any sense? In fact, it does.

The Pineal Gland

Descartes considered the pineal gland the seat of the soul. Functionally, the pineal gland produces melatonin (necessary for sleep), and is activated by darkness and deactivated by light. Mantak Chia (2019), a Master of Taoist Internal Alchemy, for this reason conducts 7- and 14-day "Dark Room Retreats" in a "cave of darkness . . . with all the conveniences of modern technology." Fourteen Days!? you wonder. How about the Kogi of the Sierra Nevada de Santa Marta, in Columbia (who were interviewed by the BBC for "The Heart of the World: Elder Brother's Warning"), where male children who are selected to become *Mamos* (priests) are put in a dark cave at birth to live in darkness for *9 years* as they are trained to tune in to Aluna (The Great Mother – You'd probably tune in to Aluna too after *9 years* in a dark cave) (Kogi People, 2019).

Chapter 31 - To Weep, Perchance to Lucid Dream: Lucid Dreaming and Lucid Dream Therapy

As it turns out, the secret of pineal gland activation (and thus altered consciousness states, and perhaps their true transcendent effects) via exposure to prolonged darkness is a tradition among the Tibetan Buddhists (AKA our Dream Yoga elders), as well as

> The ancient Egyptians (in pyramids);
>
> The ancient Europeans (in tunnels);
>
> The ancient Greeks (in incubation sanctuaries);
>
> The ancient Romans (in catacombs);
>
> The Israeli Essenes (in caves); and
>
> The Daoists (in caves).
>
> (Dark Retreat, 2019)

Coincidentally, in addition to melatonin, the pineal gland, at least of rodents, has been found to contain the hallucinogen DMT (Barker, Borjigin, Lomnicka, & Strassman, 2013). Fox's own hypothesis of pineal stimulation as the trigger for his Dreams of Knowledge no doubt was inspired by his readings in Theosophy, founded by Madame Blavatsky who considered the pineal gland the "Third Eye" or eye of the Spirit. Here's Madame Blavatsky:

Incidentally, her old house in Philadelphia is now a restaurant (The White Dog Cafe) and has this picture on the wall. Try the Autumn Squash Soup.

But think about it: If the pineal gland isn't an eye, how does it know to turn melatonin production on and off on the basis of ambient light or darkness? Well,

> "The primary function of the pineal gland is to produce melatonin. Melatonin has various functions in the central nervous system, the most important of which is to help modulate sleep patterns. Melatonin production is stimulated by darkness and inhibited by light ... Light sensitive nerve cells in the retina detect light and send this signal to the suprachiasmatic nucleus (SCN), synchronizing the SCN to the day-night cycle. Nerve fibers then relay the daylight information from the SCN to the paraventricular nuclei (PVN), then to the spinal cord and via the sympathetic system to superior cervical ganglia (SCG), and from there into the pineal gland." (Pineal Gland, 2019)

So although the pineal gland isn't *technically* an eye, it's primary function is to detect light (which sounds quite eyeish). It happens to do so in a tortuous way (it's certainly torturous to read about), but does so nonetheless. Further support for Madame Blavatsky (and Oliver Fox, by association) is that

> "From the point of view of biological evolution, the pineal gland represents a kind of atrophied photoreceptor. In the epithalamus of some species of amphibians and reptiles, it is linked to a light-sensing organ, known as the parietal eye, which is also called the pineal eye or third eye." (Pineal Gland, 2019)

Regarding the pineal gland as a parietal or third eye,

> "Until the 1950s, scientists regarded the human pineal gland as a single, probably vestigial organ. Comparative anatomical studies had shown that this gland had the same embryological origin as the parietal ('third') eye in other, less evolved vertebrates. Several lizards, for example, have a parietal eye seated in an opening at the top of their skulls. This 'third eye' consists of a cornea, a lens, and a retina and is connected to the brain by a pedicle that is comparable to the optic nerve. In amphibians, birds, and mammals, this parietal opening has closed, so the pineal gland remains inside the skull. It

Chapter 31 - To Weep, Perchance to Lucid Dream: Lucid Dreaming and Lucid Dream Therapy

has thus of course lost its visual function, but continues to exert a highly significant influence on the rest of the body through the secretion of melatonin. Histological studies have subsequently shown that the pineal gland is not really a single organ but a dual one whose two hemispheres have nearly fused." (Dubuc, 2019)

Finally, the ancient Egyptians held the pineal gland in high esteem. Here is a drawing of a cross-section of the brain, and next to it the Egyptian *Eye of Horus* which represents the cortical area containing the pineal gland (Adapted from TokenRock.com, 2021, public domain), and below it an actual cross section of a brain revealing the pineal gland, along with another drawing of the Eye of Horus:

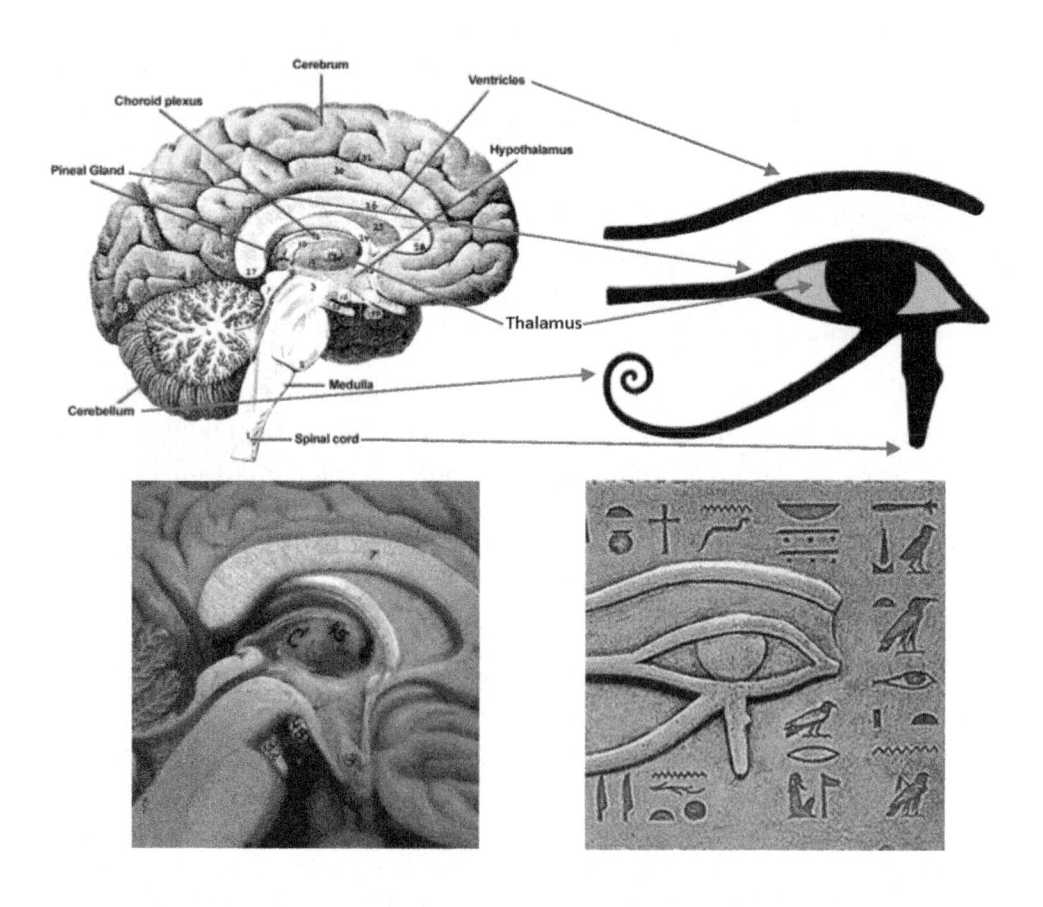

The pineal gland is shaped like a pine cone, thus its name, derived from the Latin "pinea." Interestingly, the Egyptian Staff of Osiris (the god of the afterlife), has two snakes winding up a rod, calling to mind the Hindu image of the kundalini energy ascending the spine, and culminates in a pine cone. The pineal gland on the Staff of Osiris has a parallel in the wings at the top of the Caduceus, or Rod of Hermes (who was conductor of souls into the afterlife), which also consists of a rod ascended by two snakes.

In sum, whether or not the human pineal gland still functions as an eye, as in our less evolved co-sentients, or functions as a "doorway" to the astral (during lifetime OBEs or at the time of death) there do seem to be some ancient and modern, spiritual and scientific smoking guns.

Now, if the pineal gland *is* an eye of sorts, why can't we see out of it? Tap water and toothpaste, apparently. It turns out that fluoride causes pineal calcification. But there may be bigger problems with calcifying your pineal gland than loss of its potential spiritual third eye properties. Melatonin deficiency, caused by a malfunctioning pineal gland, has been associated with depression, peptic ulcers and sexual dysfunction (Maurizi, 1984). The link with depression may be related to the fact that serotonin, the precursor of melatonin, is synthesized in the pineal gland. This may be why research has linked decreased pineal gland activity with suicide (Kurtulus et al., 2018). Also, due to the influence of the pineal gland on pituitary gland functioning, pineal dysfunction can affect pituitary secretion of sex hormones, follicle-stimulating hormone and luteinizing hormone (Motta, Fraschini & Marini, 1967). Finally, calcification of the pineal gland disrupts one's sense of direction, ". . . perhaps by altering the intrinsic intracranial electromagnetic environment and thus affecting the magnetite response mechanism" (Bayliss, Bishop & Folwer, 1985). Recent research confirms that magnetite in the human brain helps orient to the environment in a manner similar to its role in the homing response in animals (Wang et al., 2019).

So, why is fluoride added to the water supply when it calcifies our pineal gland and can lead to ulcers, sexual dysfunction, depression, suicide and getting lost on the way back from the corner grocery store? Good question. While some say that "fluoride is as American as pumpkin pie on Thanksgiving" and is necessary to strengthen our teeth (ILikeMyTeeth.org, 2019), others retort that

Chapter 31 - To Weep, Perchance to Lucid Dream: Lucid Dreaming and Lucid Dream Therapy

> "It is now well established that fluoride is not an essential nutrient. This means that no human disease – including tooth decay – will result from a 'deficiency' of fluoride. Fluoridating water supplies is therefore different than adding iodine to salt. Unlike fluoride, iodine is an essential nutrient (the body needs iodine to ensure the proper functioning of the thyroid gland). No such necessity exists for fluoride." (FluorideAlert.org, 2021a)

There are even claims that its presence in the water supply has nefarious origins and motivations:

> "Around 1945, local water treatment facilities began to add sodium fluoride to our water supply.
>
> The first thing you should know is that the fluoride they put in our drinking water is not a pharmaceutical grade additive.
>
> It is an industrial waste byproduct.
>
> As aluminum production increased in the first half of the twentieth century, it became necessary to find somewhere to put the fluoride. Manufacturers could no longer dump it into rivers or landfills, because it was poisoning crops and making livestock sick. Francis Frary, chief scientist for ALCOA, had an idea. He commissioned Gerald Cox at the Mellon Institute, to conduct research regarding the benefits of adding fluoride to the water supply. The Mellon Institute was frequently hired by big business to produce research that supported their industries, and for several decades they produced research showing that asbestos was safe and did not cause cancer. Hmmm.
>
> They also produced reports assuring everyone that fluoride was not toxic and would be beneficial to add to our drinking water for healthy teeth.
>
> Another proponent of the safety of fluoride at that time was scientist Harold Hodge, who was later revealed to have been part of the Human Radiation Experiment; injecting test subjects with plutonium and uranium in 1945-46. This was documented by Pulitzer Prize winning reporter Eileen Welsonne in The Plutonium Files.

Hodge was also chief toxicologist of The Manhattan Project and fluoride was a key component in the production of the atom bomb. His studies were conducted with a bias toward proving fluoride safe, which would protect the government and industry from lawsuits.

The 'research science' done to support water fluoridation was underwritten by these massive companies:

Aluminum Company of America (ALCOA)
Aluminum Company of Canada
American Petroleum Institute
Dupont
Kaiser Aluminum
Reynolds Steel
US Steel
National Institute of Dental Research

Convincing the general public that we need to add fluoride to our water supply was one of the most sophisticated cons of all time. It created a multi-billion dollar industry and enabled manufacturers to sell this worthless toxic byproduct of aluminum to local municipalities for a profit." (Wark, 2019)

It turns out that, perhaps for the above reasons,

"Most developed nations in the world have rejected fluoridation, including 97% of western Europe. The United States, which fluoridates more than 70% of its water supplies, is an exception to this rule. According to the British Fluoridation Society, there are more people drinking artificially fluoridated water in the United States than all other countries combined." (FluorideAlert.org, 2021b)

It does make you wonder. Whether it makes you wonder enough to stop drinking tap water and brushing your teeth with fluoride-containing toothpastes is another issue that I'll leave to you and Google.

Oliver Fox (4)

Fox, likely unaware in 1920 of pineal psychoneuroendoctrinology and unlikely in possession of neurstimulation technology, no doubt attempted to

Chapter 31 - To Weep, Perchance to Lucid Dream: Lucid Dreaming and Lucid Dream Therapy

stimulate his pineal gland by doing something that created a sensation in his head in the general area in which he imagined his pineal gland to be. He may have tensed his eye muscles or other muscles of his face, neck or head, or brought awareness (and thus increased blood flow) to various regions of his head. This may be why he got headaches. However, it is also possible that by moving the eyes and manipulating cerebrovascular blood flow via awareness, he did indeed activate the pineal gland. For present purposes, I will focus on the techniques that Fox used to trigger lucid dreams, rather than to his neurophysiological hypotheses (which even Freud, an actual neurologist, deferred to generations 100 years in his future. Oh, that's us. Time to apply for another 100 year deferral).

According to Fox,

> "The sensation was as follows: my incorporeal self rushed to a point in the pineal gland and hurled itself against the imaginary trap-door, while the golden light increased in brilliancy, so that it seemed the whole room burst into flame." (Fox, 1920, p. 195)

He then, however, finds himself back in his body and needs two to three tries before "the little door had clicked behind me" and

> "I enjoyed a mental clarity far surpassing that of the earth-life. And the fear was gone. With a few exceptions, I have never felt afraid once I had got clear of my body; it was the Trance Condition, before and after, that I dreaded." (p. 195)

To his credit, he writes

> "The reader is warned not to take my statements on the pineal gland too seriously." (p. 195)

(You mean like spending 6 hours this afternoon googling all of the relevant research?)

He continues,

> "The result I obtained is beyond all question; but my explanation of the actual process involved may be more symbolical than accurate." (p. 196)

Fox then focuses on the one remaining thing needed, "to be able to pass at will into the preliminary Trance Condition" (p. 196). He notes that 9 times out of 10 the trance was broken by "the slightest disturbance," and at other times he "would suddenly lose consciousness and find myself, after an unremembered gap, free to move as I would upon the astral plane" (p. 196).

At this point, Fox has no trouble (1) inducing a DILD (dream initiated lucid dream), as from the dream state he has developed the skill of realizing he is dreaming or, (2) from the Trance following the lucid dream, effecting a discontinuous transition into an OBE (a DIDOBE; dream initiated discontinuous out-of-body experience). But what he really strives for is a WILD (wake initiated lucid dream), and specifically a WICOBE (wake initiated continuous out-of-body experience) in which he can, when he has a spare moment, put himself into his Trance state and then, from there, focus on his pineal gland and leave his body. Don't we all! (That's rhetorical, both as a Big NOooooo! for most people, but as a Big YESssssss! for those of us who have had the fortune of having OBEs.)

While not as consistent as he would have preferred, Fox did sometimes succeed "as many as six times in one night, without a single break in the continuity of the experience" (p. 196). Here is the technique he settled on:

> "To induce the trance I would lie down, with muscles relaxed, turning my consciousness inward upon the pineal door and excluding all other thoughts;"

(Must have had a high IPA-Q, or drunk a strong IPA.)

> ". . . the body was passive, but the mind positive in its concentration upon this inner point. My eyelids were closed; but I believe the eyes were rolled upwards and slightly squinting – that was the sensation."

AHA!!! I *knew* he was messing with his eyes. Here, we (or at least I) are/am reminded of the importance assigned by the Taoist masters to movement of the eyes when performing the Microcosmic Orbit.

Back to the Immortal Foetus

The following diagrams (Chao, 1860+ in Luk, 1984/1970, pp. 13, 124) illustrate points at the base of the spine (bottom), in the spine (right), at the top of the head (top) and in in the front of the body (left).

Chapter 31 - To Weep, Perchance to Lucid Dream: Lucid Dreaming and Lucid Dream Therapy

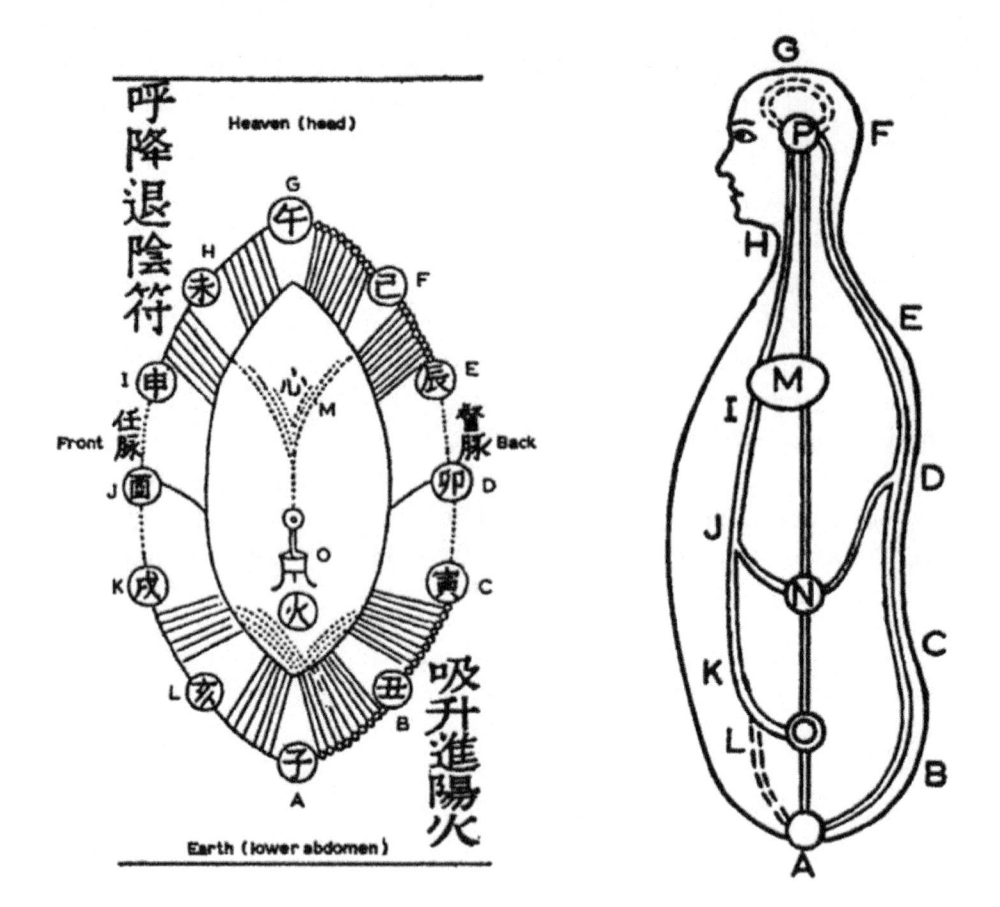

"When breathing in, the heart, spirit and thought should rise together from the base of the spine at the cardinal point A . . . to the intermediate points B and C before reaching D where they are held up for a short pause for cleansing, and thence to the cardinal point G (the top of the head); this involves six phases of rise (A, B, C, D, E, F) in the channel of control (tu mo in the spine) and is called the ascent of the positive fire.

When breathing out, the heart, spirit and thought should together go down from the brain at the cardinal point G to the intermediate points H and I before reaching J where they pause a little for purification, and thence to A; this involves six negative phases of descent in the channel of function (jen mo) to return vitality to the source and is called the descent of negative fire.

So these positive ascents and negative descents are caused by in and out breathing.

When the generative and vital forces start vibrating (in the lower tan t'ien cavity under the navel) you should breathe in – this is to close (ho) the respiratory mechanism (so that the air goes down to exert pressure on the lower abdomen); and at the same time by rolling your eyes up you should follow the ascent of generative force and vitality from the bottom to the top of the head . . .

When you breathe out, you should open (p'i) the respiratory mechanism so that the air goes out of the body (to relax pressure on the lower abdomen); at the same time your eyes should follow the descent of generative force and vitality from the top to the bottom . . .

So to complete an orbit you should roll your eyes right around thus . . .

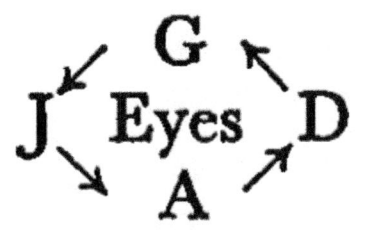

```
        G
      ↙   ↖
   J   Eyes   D
      ↘   ↗
        A
```

All this is generally called the ascent of positive and descent of negative fire; while *inhalation, shutting, ascent* and *opening, exhalation, descent* are the phases of the alchemical process." (Chao, 1860+ in Luk, 1984/1970, pp. 35-36; italics added)

Please note, and it took me some time to realize this, that in the above diagram, D represents the back of the body and J represents the front of the body, corresponding with the two diagrams just preceding it. So the eyes are not making a counterclockwise circle from the bottom to the right to the top to the left and to the bottom. What is really happening is that you begin by looking down (with your eyes closed) when you are sensing the energy at the base of the spine, imagining that you are looking directly down through your

Chapter 31 - To Weep, Perchance to Lucid Dream: Lucid Dreaming and Lucid Dream Therapy

body to the base of your spine (point A). You then slowly move your eyes as though you were looking up, *imagining* them rolling backwards and continuing up until *imagining* your pupils are then facing the middle of your back (point D). Then imagine the eyes continuing to roll up towards the back of your head until you imagine your pupils are pointing directly upwards toward the crown of your head (point G). You then move your eyes down so they are facing directly in front of you (imagining facing the middle of the front of your body, point J), and then repeat the movement of your eyes down until you imagine they are looking at the base of your spine again (point A). You then repeat, up to point D, etc. Again, the actual movement of your eyes is just up and down, as though you were looking at the floor, then directly in front of you, then at the ceiling, then directly in front of you, then at the floor again. It's only in your imagination that the eyes are rotating down, backwards, up, forward and down.

More challenging is learning to create and perceive the actual physical sensation of energy at a given place in your body, and then moving that energy (or imagining moving the energy), in this case around the Microcosmic Orbit. What you will eventually feel has been labeled Chi in Taoism and Prana in Hinduism. I assure you that you can learn to perceive it and move it, and later in the book I will tell you about a lifechanging experience that I had when I did so. I will not assure you of what it actually is or whether the experiences you may have correspond with anything more than your imagination. Maybe it's chi or prana, or maybe it's just a sensation you've learned to create by paying attention to a part of your body, and learned to move by moving your attention to other parts of the body. You'll decide that for yourself, preferably on the basis of your own experience.

Regarding the relation of Taoist *eye movements* to alterations in consciousness, it is possible that this too is related to pineal gland activation. The pineal gland is located in the midbrain and surrounded by the two superior colliculi (known in non-mammalian vertebrates as the optic tectum, or tectum). The superficial layers of the superior colliculi receive input from the retina (Wallace, Meredith & Stein, 1998) and the deeper layers can activate eye movements (Gandhi & Katani, 2011). The superior colliculi surrounding the pineal gland

> "get a direct site-specific projection from the retina in all vertebrates. This retinotopic map is distributed over the surface of the tectum,

and aligned with this sensory map, there is a motor map with tectal efferents that, when activated, will produce eye or orienting/evasive movements." (Robertson et al., 2014)

As movements of the eyes, and visual stimuli resulting from moving the eyes, implicate stimulation of the superior colliculi surrounding the pineal gland, it is possible that the pineal gland in turn is stimulated by the superior colliculi. In addition, as the pineal gland's main function involves detecting visual stimuli (at least changes in light intensity), it is possible that visual stimuli caused by movements of the eyes would also activate the pineal gland.

Oliver Fox (5), In Which Oliver Learns to Have a WICOBE

Rolling the eyes upward as Fox reported doing is a well-known way of inducing alpha brainwaves, associated with deep relaxation (which I first learned in 1975 at age 13 in a Silva Mind Control course).

> "The first symptom was the effect of seeing through my eyelids the room full of the golden light. Then came the numbness, beginning at the feet and extending upwards." (p. 196)

(The sensations of seeing images through my eyelids and numbness were precisely my own first experiences of the meditative state in my teens, occasioned by the same technique of lying perfectly still for about 30 minutes.)

> "When the trance was deep this became quite painful, especially in the muscles of the jaw; there was also a sense of enormous pressure in the brain." (p. 196)

(STOP SQUINTING OLIVER! This is like an advertisement for Why You Need A Teacher.)

> "This, then, was the climax of my research. I could now pass from ordinary waking life to this new state of consciousness (or from life to 'death') and return, without any mental break. It is easily written but it took fourteen years to accomplish." (p. 196)

Funny, that's what I was thinking today about this book. I wrote about 300 Word for Windows pages (equals about 600 book pages, I think) in the course of 3 weeks of PTO (one in February, 2019, and two in March, 2019), but I've been gathering the bulk of this material since beginning a consistent

Chapter 31 - To Weep, Perchance to Lucid Dream: Lucid Dreaming and Lucid Dream Therapy

meditation practice in 2004 (of course, with the requisite lapses, short and extended).

Oliver Fox (6), In Which Oliver Forgets How to Have a WICOBE

(Debby Downer Alert)

Fox ends "with a brief account of how I lost this power I had so painfully acquired" (p. 197):

> "In April, 1916, when out of the body, I attempted to get back into a past incarnation which had been described to me by a lady who was an unprofessional trance medium . . ."

(Now really, *why* would someone go and do that? Bad judgement Oliver. Bad judgement.)

> "Now, if I had willed to travel to India, I should have immediately rushed off with enormous velocity; but I willed to get back into my past life, and no motion occurred. Suddenly a gap appeared in the astral scenery (as though a round hole were made in a picture) and I saw very, very far away the open door of a temple, and beyond this a gleaming statue. This scene was blurred and had the appearance of being at the other end of a very long and narrow tunnel. I willed to pass through this tunnel, but found myself swept violently away, in a lateral direction, to some other astral locality. I willed once more; again the tunnel and the temple appeared; and again I tried to travel to it. This time, however, I was hurled back to my body, and with such force that the trance was broken.
>
> The next time I tried to induce the Trance Condition, I found that always before my inner eyes was the vision of a black *crux ansata;* . . ." (p. 197)

That sounds scary, especially with the italics, but I have no idea what it is. Let's see what Google thinks. Well, I don't think he's referring to H.G. Wells' book "Crux Ansata: An Indictment of the Roman Catholic Church" which was written in 1943. Let's see what else came up. Looks like he's referring to the *ankh*, "an ancient Egyptian symbol of life" OR the Gnostic Ankh, from the Gospel of Judas, this latter Ankh associated with "Ritual magick" with a "k" (SymbolDictionary.net).

> "and now my magic would not work, the trap-door *would not open . . .*"

(Is anyone else getting the impression that in the intervening years he may have been tappin' the Theosophy – or the Heisenberg Kush – a bit too much?)

> "The *crux ansata* could not be dispelled. When I closed my eyes and turned to the light, the symbol showed clear-cut, as though painted in black on the red field of my eyelids. With my eyes open, in dim light, I could still see it as though it were projected in front of me. And try as I might I could no longer pass the pineal door." (p. 197)

After this, he began studying with a "direct voice medium, who had, however, the rather unenviable reputation of being a black magician." (OLIVER!!!!) He could no longer leave his body at will, but would find himself in the astral plane with the magician and some spiritual beings whose teachings seemed "high" though he didn't know whether their teachings were "white" or "black."

> "They told me they had sealed my door, because I was becoming attuned to psychic forces, which might sweep me away before my work on earth was done. I do not know. *Some* things I have proved to myself; but each little advance we make serves only to emphasize the depths of our abysmal ignorance . . . The visionary symbol still remains before my inner eyes, but it is now very faint and difficult to see. Perhaps when it has faded altogether my pineal door will open once again. I do not attempt to explain these happenings, but I have written a true account of them." (pp. 198-199)

Fox concludes with a note regarding Freud (for context, this was 1920, the year that Freud first proposed his "dual drive" theory of sex and aggression, and came up with the theory of the Id, Ego and Superego. He had published the Interpretation in Dreams much earlier, in 1899).

> "Psycho-analysis is not exactly a new discovery, but lately it has penetrated into the penny populars. Mention dreams, and you are met with a triumphant 'But Freud says ---'! I think that some of my friends believed that if I read Freud I should die broken-hearted. Well, I have read Professor Siegmund Freud's great and admirable work – 'The Interpretation of Dreams' – and it has not disturbed my

Chapter 31 - To Weep, Perchance to Lucid Dream: Lucid Dreaming and Lucid Dream Therapy

equanimity. I think there is much truth in it, and I have applied his methods quite satisfactorily to interpret some of my ordinary dreams – especially the nonsensical kind. But there are dreams and *dreams*! I am convinced that the psycho-analytic theories will not explain all of them. I believe the Vienna doctor to be a kindly man with a mighty intellect, but even he does not know everything. For instance, I do not think he would admit that astrology 'works'; but I know it does." (p. 198)

Chapter 32 - *How To Lucid Dream and Not Get Eaten by a Golem*

> "Today a young man on acid realized that all matter is merely energy condensed to a slow vibration, that we are all one consciousness experiencing itself subjectively, there is no such thing as death, life is only a dream, and we are the imagination of ourselves.
> Here's Tom with the Weather."
>
> **Bill Hicks (1989)**

Well, that Fox is a hard act to follow, but I'll try. In addition to the techniques that he found useful and thankfully discarding the squinting and jaw clenching, the sciences of lucid dreaming and OBEs have progressed in leaps and bounds (or at least hops and jumps) in the 100 years since Fox's article about (and Freud's ignorance of) them.

Now, the problem with run-of-the-mill dreaming is you're being chased by a golum because you just read a book about not getting eaten by a bear, then the golum changes into a bear and you come to the edge of a cliff, scream, and wake up sweating. That's no fun, is it? Enter the lucid dream: You're being chased by a golum because you just read a book about not getting eaten by a bear, then the golum changes into a bear and you come to the edge of a cliff, realize "there's no such thing as a golum, I must be dreaming, and this bear must be a dream bear." You look at the bear, make him smaller, put him in your pocket, float up into the air, fly to a nearby beach, manifest and settle into a big leather reclining chair, take the bear out of your pocket, enlarge him, and tell him to fetch you a margarita while you watch the psychedelic dolphins play water volleyball.

Lucid dreaming can also be used to create virtual environments conducive to *other* activities and purposes corresponding with whichever of the Four Psychologies are at issue. For example, one might wish to

1. *Prevent* (Psy 1.0) a mishap by practicing for an upcoming activity or performance such as a sporting event or public speech;

2. *Cure* or *treat* (Psy 2.0) an existing problem such as a phobic reaction to driving across bridges;

3. Produce a *positive* (Psy 3.0) creative product, such as a musical piece; or

4. Continue one's *transcendent* (Psy 4.0) daytime spiritual practice while asleep, such as by meditating in dreams.

Below I will list a number of lucid dream induction techniques. While research has been conducted on which techniques work best (Aspy, 2020), which techniques will work best *for you* will be a matter of trial and error.

Tholey's Techniques to Trigger the Lucid Dream State

German psychologist Paul Tholey first thought of becoming aware in dreams in 1959, writing:

> "If one develops a critical frame of mind towards the state of consciousness during the waking state, by asking oneself whether one is dreaming or awake, this attitude will be transferred to the dreaming state. It is then possible through the occurrence of unusual experiences to recognize that one is dreaming. One month after beginning with this method, I had my first lucid dream." (Tholey, 1988b)

In 1983, he published a paper entitled *Techniques for Inducing and Manipulating Lucid Dreams* in the journal *Perceptual and Motor Skills*. This is the same journal that in 1980 published psychophysiologist Stephen LaBerge's doctoral dissertation sleep lab results as *Lucid Dreaming as a Learnable Skill: A Case Study*, and in 1982 published British psychologist Keith Hearne's 1978 doctoral dissertation sleep lab results as *Effects of Performing Certain Set Tasks in the Lucid Dream State*.

Tholey's (1983) "Reflection Technique" involves taking a "critical-reflective attitude" about one's consciousness during the day while awake. Specifically, one asks oneself, or nonverbally wonders during various daytime activities "Am I dreaming?" This is reminiscent of the Tibetan Dream Yoga daytime practice of reminding oneself that "This is a dream." Similar techniques do not, however, imply similar goals, as clarified by the Editor of Namkhai Norbu's *Dream Yoga and the Practice of the Natural Light*:

> "Another technique discussed by various dream researchers, including Paul Tholey, involves state testing. This term refers to the practice of asking oneself if one is dreaming at frequent intervals during the day, while concurrently analyzing the situation to attempt to be sure of the answer. The 'critical state testing' [LaBerge & Rheingold, 1990, p. 59] in many cases subsequently leads to a similar testing process within the dream, and then to lucidity.
>
> These techniques that attempt to induce lucidity contrast with the practice of natural light found within the Buddhist, Bonpo and Dzogchen traditions as discussed by Norbu Rinpoche, which does not particularly focus on developing lucidity but considers lucidity a natural by-product of the development of awareness and presence." (Katz, in Norbu, 1992, pp. 32-3)

I think that Katz is here distinguishing Western lucid dreamchasers' cultivation of awareness with a goal of triggering lucid dreams, from Tibetan cultivation of awareness, which incidentally results in lucidity both in the dreaming and waking state, for purposes of enlightenment. Once developed, the Tibetans use this lucidity as a spiritual practice to further clarify the nature of reality, whereas Westerners mostly use lucidity to fly around and have dream sex (not that there's anything wrong with that).

If you think about it, asking yourself during the day whether you are dreaming, in order to later become lucid in a nighttime dream, makes a lot of sense. When we are dreaming, we often find ourselves in an environment pretty worldy and we behave there much like we do in our waking world. For example, we see a staircase and we walk up it. Now, since it is our dream, we could just as easily fly up it. But we don't. We have a glass of water in our hand and we drink it. Does our dream body really need to stay hydrated? We walk up dream stairs and drink dream water because we don't realize we are in a dream. We are thinking the way that we think in waking life. See staircase, walk up staircase. See water, drink water. Similarly, we're in a dream and we're driving. But why drive? It's our dream and we could just as easily wiggle our nose like Samantha Stevens (she actually wiggled her mouth, not her nose) or blink like Jeannie (no, her arms didn't need to be crossed) to get where we want to go. But we *don't*. In dreams we do what we would do in real life *because we don't realize it's a dream.*

There is only one thing that we can do in real life, one transformative *cognitive behavior,* that if we then do in a dream awakens us from our ignorance. Unfortunately, this is not something we are taught to do, and if for some reason we do it and tell someone we did it, we will likely be institutionalized. And that behavior is, you guessed it, asking ourselves if we are dreaming (or, in Tibetan style, telling ourselves we are dreaming). Just as the habit of climbing stairs in waking life becomes the habit of climbing stairs in dreams, developing a habit of asking yourself "am I dreaming" in waking life will become a habit of asking yourself "am I dreaming?" in dreams. But by contrast with climbing dream stairs, which won't buy you lucidity, asking "am I dreaming?" *will* buy you lucidity. That is, unless you are really good at *rationalizing* (or *confabulating,* as we say in the biz), making up reasons for things you don't understand, like flying elephants, as in "Oh, I must be on the set of Dumbo."

Tholey recommends that you ask the "critical question" ("Am I dreaming or not") frequently (5 to 10 times per day), close to the moment of falling asleep, and in situations that resemble those encountered in dreams. In addition, as things may not be particularly bizarre at the point in the dream when you remember to ask the question, during the daytime practice you should remember events of the day leading up to the present moment. Then, when you ask the question in the dream, even though at that moment in the dream you are waiting on line at MacDonald's for the all-day breakfast and things seem pretty standard issue, searching your memory you may recall that earlier in the day you escaped from an alien spaceship piloted by your second grade teacher who used to yell at you a lot ("pay attention! focus! concentrate!), and then realize "wait, when did s/he learn to fly a spaceship – this must be a dream!"

To maximize success, Tholey found it useful to follow up the question by wondering "How do I know?" (Waggoner, 2016). In order to find out, one can do reality tests or, as I prefer to call them, "unreality tests." LaBerge and Rheingold (1990) adapted Tholey's reflection technique into a *Critical State Testing Technique,* that includes reality tests such as

"Look around for any oddities or inconsistencies that might indicate you are dreaming. Think back to the events of the last several minutes. Do you have any trouble remembering what just happened? If so, you may be dreaming." (p. 62)

LaBerge and Rheingold (1990, p. 64) suggested that you use the same state test each time. They give some examples, including (here paraphrased):

- Look at some writing, look away, and look back at it. Did it change?

- If you're wearing a digital watch in the dream, look at it, look away, and look again. Did it change?

- Look around you. Is anything changing right before your eyes?

The authors suggest that eventually you will recognize that any time that you actually wonder whether you are dreaming, and any time that you feel a need to test reality, *this means you are dreaming*.

Over time, you will develop your own reality tests to do during the day and then in your dreams. My favorite is trying to float. So I could have used the Critical State Testing Technique the first day I saw egg McMuffins *and* hash browns being offered *all day* with free coffee refills. I would have first asked myself "Am I dreaming," and then tried to float. Not succeeding at floating, I would have concluded that I was not dreaming.

Now you try it. Right now, wherever you are, ask yourself "Am I dreaming?" Look around to see if anything seems odd. Maybe you're dreaming. Think back to what you were just doing and earlier events of the day. Can't remember? Sounds to me like you're dreaming. Now, try to float. Floating? Then you're definitely dreaming (unless you're reading this in a bathtub or swimming pool, in which case you should try to float *above* the water. Are you floating yet? By the way, if you are dreaming, you didn't really have to pay for this book. Then again, it was only dream money. And if you are floating, don't stop there, fly somewhere warm for the dream winter. Another unreality test I like is to make things appear or disappear (with your mind) such as a flower. Again, if you can do it, you're probably dreaming

LaBerge and Rheingold (1990) further developed Tholey's technique into what they termed the *Reflection-Intention Technique*,

"1. Plan when you intend to test your state;

2. Test your state;

3. Imagine yourself dreaming;

4. Imagine doing what you intend to do in your lucid dream."

(cited in Paulsson & Parker, 2006, p. 3)

Tholey's Techniques to Program Lucid Dream Content

Tholey (1983, pp. 86-90) proposes a number of techniques to program the *content* of lucid dreams once one has realized one is in a dream. This is similar to an ancient practice known as *dream incubation* for programming the content of dreams in general, the difference being that dream incubation is typically used *prior* to falling asleep and has historically been used to shape the content of regular, or nonlucid, dreams.

(1) Manipulation by Wishing: Here one alters the dream once already inside of it, for example "altering a dream scenery by simply wishing it so." For example ". . . to change the environment of the dream or even their own person, as well as being able to transport themselves to other locations in space or time" (p. 86). Tholey says that it is, however, easier to make things happen if they don't require "miracles." Thus, if one wants to meet a certain friend in the dream, it is more effective to call them (or, I presume, call their name, if no dream phone is available) than to just wish they were there.

(2) Manipulation by Inner State: Here, one exercises cognitive and emotional self-control in the dream, for example by deciding that since it is a dream, one has nothing to fear, and then confronting the phobic stimulus with confidence (as I confronted the dogs both in my lucid dream and in reality on the beach). In the dream, my confidence and benevolence towards one of the attack dogs turned it into a puppy (the other one just kind of disappeared).

(3) Manipulation by Means of Looking: Tholey says that "Fixation on a stationary point in the dream environment causes the dreamer to awaken after 4 to 12 seconds. In this process the fixation point begins to blur, and the entire dream scenery commences to dissolve . . . Reestablishing the dream by means of rapid eye movements can prevent awakening" (p. 87). In other words, if you don't like the dream you're in, you can either stare at something in order to wake up, or you can stare at something until the

dream begins to dissolve, and then rapidly move your eyes to solidify the environment again (possibly using the above "manipulation by wishing" to create a new environment more to your liking, or more in line with your psychological purpose). This use of rapid eye movements to prevent the dream from dissolving can be especially useful if you are spending time in the dream with a transitioned loved one. The tendency here is to gaze at their face while speaking with them, but as Tholey points out (which I can verify from personal experience), they then start to melt or disintegrate, on top of which you are now awake, all of which, when taken together, is an enormous bummer, as you might imagine.

(4) Manipulation by Means of Verbal Utterances: Here, you can learn about others, as well as learn about yourself, by speaking to people, or even objects in the dream. For example, you can ask who they are, or who you are, or what they (the person or object) symbolize. You can also manipulate the environment by commanding it to do what you want such as, if it is too dark to see, shouting "Lights!"

(5) Manipulation with Certain Actions: Though different people find different techniques to do certain things such as fly or time travel, Tholey proposes that certain things seem to work for most people, such as initiating flying or floating by leaping from a great height.

(6) Manipulation with Assistance of Other Dream Figures: Tholey gives the example of a woman taught to fly by a ghost.

(7) Limitations of Manipulation: Tholey and Hearne both agreed that you can't create a sudden increase in brightness in a lucid dream, for example by turning on a dream light switch, but that a gradual brightening can be effected by "using a flashlight with variable intensity or by slowly approaching a distant light source." Tholey makes this claim on the basis of research with "8 normal subjects." I will have to respectfully disagree, once having brightened my flight path quickly by simply shouting "Light!" Then again, this was in an OBE and not in a lucid dream, so perhaps they are correct. But seriously, who carries around a "flashlight with variable intensity" in a dream? I don't even have one in real life.

LaBerge's Mnemonic Induction of Lucid Dreams (MILD)

LaBerge developed the MILD technique (LaBerge, 1980; LaBerge & Rheingold, 1990) as a way of having lucid dreams at will in order to carry out his doctoral dissertation (which he completed in the physical world, not in a dream, as far as I know, unless I've been living in his dream). He reports that prior to devising this technique, he would have lucid dreams less than once per month. Then, merely telling himself before bed each night "Tonight, I will have a lucid dream," he increased lucidity to an average of 5 per month, with a range of 1 to 13. Gradually, he identified the *intention* to remember to recognize he was dreaming as a key factor, and eventually he perfected the method and had up to 4 lucid dreams per night.

MILD is designed to increase *prospective memory*, or remembering to do something later, like remembering to bring your tall coffee mug with you when you go away for a week to write a book so you don't need to rely on those tiny little white mugs at the cabin (needless to say, I forgot, and I haven't been having any lucid dreams lately – I need this chapter as much as you).

> "First of all, if you can't reliably remember to carry out future intentions while you are *awake*, there is little chance that you will remember to do anything while *asleep*." (LaBerge & Rheingold, 1990, p. 75)

Touché. I usually write reminders on my hand and scatter pieces of paper here and there that say "Look at your hand!" which I guess won't help when I am in my dreambody. Luckily Dr. LaBerge was one step ahead of me and provided an "Exercise: Prospective Memory Training" in which each day I am to memorize 4 targets. Today is over, but tomorrow is Wednesday, so my targets will be, as he suggests: "The next time I turn on a television or radio . . . see a vegetable . . . see a red car . . . money," do a state test ("Am I dreaming?"), with success defined as remembering to do it the first time it occurs, with no credit for remembering to do it on later occurrences that day (pp. 76-77).

Once I can remember things during the day, I (and you) are ready for MILD. OR, we can live dangerously and go right to MILD.

You may be wondering what's going on, with me sounding like I'm learning this stuff at the same time that I'm teaching it to you. Truth be told, over the last 15 years or so, I've read and skimmed countless books on lucid dreaming, learned things, forgotten things, succeeded, failed, and for the past few years have been personally neglecting my own dreamworld in favor of heightened activity in consensual reality. I guess I've been taking a more organic approach to it, figuring if I go lucid I go lucid, if I go comatose, I go comatose. So it's pretty much been coma after coma most nights for a while, with the exception of the night after a recent meditation retreat when, after spending several days practicing daytime awareness of awareness, I retained pure and stable awareness in the dream state as well. From a lucid dreaming perspective, the problem is that unless you are lucidly gifted (i.e., you are one of those people who has been self-aware in dreams for your whole life, like my client with PTSD who was able to create lucid dream exposure environments at will) or have attained a persistent heightened state of meditative self-awareness, if you ain't motivated, you ain't going lucid.

So, here are the MILD steps:

>(a) Before bedtime, decide that you will wake up after each dream and remember it.

>(b) When you awaken from a dream, try to remember as many details of the dream as possible.

>(c) As you return to sleep, set the intention "Next time I'm dreaming, I want to remember I'm dreaming."

>(d) At the same time, imagine being in the dream that you just recalled, recognizing something that makes you realize it's a dream (a "dreamsign"), and then doing things that you would do if you were actually in that dream and knew it was a dream (e.g., fly somewhere). (Adapted from LaBerge & Rheingold, 1990, p. 78)

I use my own mnemonic to remember the steps of LaBerge's mnemonic. Before falling asleep, or when you wake up in the night, as you go back to sleep, do these 4 steps, represented by:

>(a) M for Memorize (Call to memory a previous dream, or imagine a desired dream),

>(b) I for Intend (Set an intention to have a lucid dream, saying "Next time I'm in a dream I'll know that I'm' dreaming"),

>(c) L for Lucidify (Imagine becoming lucid in the memorized or desired dream, realizing it's a dream and doing what you would intend to do in the dream) and

(d) D for Drill (Repeat these steps several times).

It will be noted that my mnemonic either begins after awakening from a dream and corresponds with Laberge's 2nd, 3rd and 4th steps of **MILD**, or can be done before bedtime either with a remembered dream from the past or a desired dream. This is because I have found LaBerge's **MILD** technique, which is a modern variant on the ancient practice of "dream incubation" mentioned above (with the addition of lucidity-related imagery and intention), to be effective in programming lucid dreams that possess the requisite environment for a given person's lucid dream exposure therapy (Densei & Lam, 2010). For example (I here change a few details for the sake of confidentiality), I have worked with clients who have developed **PTSD** after being threatened with guns. In addition to imaginal exposure (imaginal multisensory re-experiencing of the moment of the crime) and in-vivo exposure (eventually spending time in the currently avoided environment where the crime occurred, as it was normally a safe environment), I used guided lucid dream incubation via **MILD** in the session, assigning homework to practice **MILD** incubation each day. In one case, this resulted in the client having lucid dreams of re-experiencing the moment of the crime, remaining frightened and passive in the initial dreams but gradually coming to confront the aggressor in later dreams. Over time the dreams were characterized by both a reduction in fear, an increase in confidence and even humor and positive outcomes (for example, the weapon turning into a flower and the aggressor fleeing).

Wake-Initiated Lucid Dreaming (WILD)

Wake-initiated lucid dreaming, which LaBerge refers to as "falling asleep consciously," was taught to him in 1970 as a Tibetan Dream Yoga technique by Tarthang Tulku, followed by LaBerge's first lucid dreams as an adult (though he recalled having had lucid dreams as a child; LaBerge and Rheingold, 1990). Tholey (1983) refers to this as a "hypnagogic lucid dream," in which rather than realizing that one is already dreaming, one retains awareness of consciousness as one passes from waking into sleeping, and therefore is self-aware during the intervening hypnagogic state. Hypnagogia has been written about in encyclopedic detail by Andre Mavromatis (1987). Clare Johnson (2017) distinguishes between a variety of hypnagogic states in a very comprehensive book on lucid dreaming, that also includes material on meditative approaches to lucid dreaming, therapeutic lucid dreaming, neurostimulation research, out-of-body experiences (OBEs) and near-death experiences (NDEs).

Experientially, WILDS and some OBEs overlap. What distinguishes them is that WILDs are defined by perceived continuity between the waking state and the dream state, whereas WICOBEs (wake induced continuous out-of-body experiences) involve perceived continuity between being in the physical body and transitioning into the dream (or spirit) body. The potential overlap occurs when the conscious transition from waking to dreaming (definitional of a WILD) is accompanied by perceived separation of the dream body from the physical body (definitional of an OBE). It is of course possible that OBEs are merely lucid dreams, but it is also possible that lucid dreams are really OBEs.

Sleep Interruption or the Wake Back To Bed (WBTB) Technique

Laberge, Phillips and Levitan (1994) reviewed some studies involving interrupting sleep for lucidity induction practices. They found that participants had lucid dreams on average once every 1.6 nights when they adhered to the following procedure: (a) go to bed at your regular time; (b) awaken 1 hour before your regular rising time; (c) read about lucid dreaming for 1 hour; (d) set an alarm for 90 minutes and go back to sleep practicing a modified MILD procedure for at least 10 minutes before falling asleep.

More recently, LaBerge, LaMarca & Baird (2018) have recommended beginning the WBTB period 4.5 hours after bedtime, and then staying awake for not less than 30 minutes, as 30 minutes provides superior results to shorter periods, and not more than 30 minutes, as longer periods do not increase its effectiveness.

The reason that WBTB is best used during the second half of the night is that by then you have gotten most of your deep sleep and periods of REM dreaming sleep are becoming more frequent and of longer duration. By waking up and staying up for a while, you are strategically and temporarily depriving the brain of REM sleep, so that when you then fall back asleep you have what is called an "REM rebound." REM may then set in more quickly upon falling asleep, and the proximity to the waking state that you were just in may promote the paradoxical "mind awake body asleep" state of lucidity.

I have personally found WBTB very effective. If you use this technique on a work night, you might want to go to sleep 45 to 60 minutes earlier than usual in order to recoup the 30-minute WBTB period and allow some additional time to fall back asleep. Also, if you read on an e-book reader or tablet with blue light this could interfere with falling back asleep, so books made from trees would, unfortunately, be advisable, preferably used or library books out of love for our slower metabolic, still, silent, exo-lungs (marginally fun fact: did you know that without trees we would have no air to breathe and we would all die within 3 minutes, and the only beings left on earth would be viruses, single-celled microbes and multicellular Mediterranean ocean floor oocytes?).

Rapid Eye Movement (REM) Neurofeedback Eye Mask

Dream masks operate on the same principle as state testing. In Tholey's (1983) Reflection Technique, reviewed above, you develop habits during the day of (1) asking yourself whether you are dreaming and (2) conducting tests that would provide you with an affirmative answer to the question if you were asleep and dreaming (e.g., if when you try to float you succeed, either gravity is broken and we're all in a lot of trouble, or you're dreaming). Again, it especially helps to ask yourself if you are dreaming when something seems odd (e.g., you are looking out of your kitchen window at the French Alps when you're pretty sure you live in Hoboken).

Thanks to dream masks, you no longer need to wait until something odd happens in the dream to remember to ask yourself if you're dreaming. The dream mask *makes* something odd happen, and not coincidentally makes it happen while you are in a dream. It does this by using infrared sensors to detect when your eyes are moving, meaning that you are in the sleep phase of Rapid Eye Movement which is the phase in which we usually dream. It then flashes lights at you, based on research of Stephen LaBerge that showed that external (real world) visual stimuli can be perceived in dreams without causing awakening. Then, by developing the habit during the day of doing state testing when we see lights, this habit carries over into the dream. When the dream mask detects that we are dreaming, it flashes, we see flashing lights in the dream, we ask ourselves if we are dreaming, realize we are, and KABOOM, we realize we're in a dream and can take it from there. Ideally, since we can do *anything we want*, we will choose things more fun or productive than our friend Marie-Jean-Léon Marquis d'Hervey de Saint Denys (remember him? "Hmm, it's my dream and I can do anything I want.

I know! How about *jumping off a building, cutting my throat or shooting myself?*'). Good Grief, Charlie Manson ...

REM-based dream masks are a form of neurofeedback, with neurofeedback defined as some sort of feedback contingent upon neurological events. They involve feedback (flashing lights) triggered by an indicator (rapid eye movement) of a distinct neurological state (dreaming). The first REM-based dream mask came into being as a result of experiments that Stephen LaBerge and his students were doing on the introduction of sensory stimulation as dream cues during REM phase sleep. Research participants slept in the laboratory, hooked up to equipment that monitored brainwaves and eye movements. When they showed signs of being in REM sleep, one or another stimulus was introduced. In the initial experiment, when REM began, a tape-recorded message ("This is a dream!") was played. In another, a tactile stimulus (vibration through a mattress) was used, combined with a daytime practice of wearing vibrating ankle devices controlled by a timer. During the day, when the timers were activated, participants conducted state testing and set an intention to later remember they were dreaming whenever they felt a vibration in a dream (which they then did, due to sleeping on a mattress through which a vibration was administered). The next studies used flashing red lights when the sleep lab equipment detected REM. These studies were reported in research journals between 1981 and 1988, each showing that sensory cues during REM sleep can induce lucid dreams (LaBerge, 1991, pp. 83-86).

Sometimes, however, the cues woke up the dreamer or were integrated into the dreams in a manner that did not lead to lucidity (Ibid., p. 84). This was my own experience on one occasion when I used an REM-based dream mask. I was climbing up a mountain to get to a castle at the top. The side of the mountain was strewn with boulders, and I was jumping from one boulder to another to proceed upwards. Then I saw flashing lights and it became hard to gauge how far to jump from one boulder to the next. So it occurred to me, not to wonder whether I was dreaming, but to time my jumps to occur with the "on" flashes of the light. I didn't become lucid. I also don't recall making it up to the castle (*you* try jumping from boulder to boulder up a mountain to a castle with glaring lights flashing on and off blinding you so you can't even see the stones!).

Chapter 32 - How To Lucid Dream and Not Get Eaten by a Golem

The first dream mask, the DreamLight, was conceived when in 1985 Darrel Dixon, an engineer, having read LaBerge's first book *Lucid Dreaming* where LaBerge pondered creation of a "lucid dream induction device," wrote to LaBerge and proposed developing one together. Research on the DreamLight showed that it was as effective as MILD in inducing lucidity, and that use of both together was the best induction method tested (LaBerge, 1991). LaBerge & Levitan (1995) found that when participants wore the DreamLight and weren't told that it was only delivering REM-contingent light cues every other night, 11 subjects had 22 lucid dreams on nights with cues and only 10 on nights without cues.

Continued research by LaBerge's Lucidity Institute led from the DreamLight to the 1994 Nova Dreamer, which then went out of production in 2004. The Nova Dreamer 2 has been awaited for years, but meanwhile other dream masks have hit the market, such as the REM Dreamer, produced by Pawel Herchel in Warsaw, Poland, and it's newer 2020 version, called SmartLucider, which rather than being a full eye mask only covers the lower middle area of the forehead and the bridge of the nose (SmartLucider.com).

REM-Triggered Neurostimulation

At least one dream mask is in development that uses neuro*stimulation* in addition to neurofeedback as opposed to the above dream masks that use uniquely a neurofeedback procedure. REM-triggered neurostimulation is a promising model for lucid dream induction, as it is based on findings that synchronous 25 to 40 Hz electrical stimulation (corresponding with the frequencies of low gamma brainwaves) of the fronto-temporal region of the brain can trigger dream lucidity (Voss et al., 2014).

Neurostimulation differs from neurofeedback, which latter involves a device detecting brain activity and then providing feedback regarding this activity. Neurofeedback uses passive sensors, without introducing electrical current into the brain. Neurostimulation, by contrast, does electrically stimulate the brain. I have not personally tried transcranial alternating current stimulation (tACS), but have experimented on myself with transcranial direct current stimulation (tDCS) to the dismay of my forehead which took a while to heal from the mild burns and may have some permanent discoloration (or maybe that's from my motorcycle helmet, or frying myself in the sun until I turned dark brown during most of my youth). Granted, as tDCS is generally considered safe, maybe I just used too much current or have sensitive skin, but I have seen Google images of burn marks on others due to tDCS, and an Open Access (free downloadable PDF) 2017 review in the journal Clinical Neurophysiology Practice (Matsumoto & Ugawa; Volume 2, pp. 19-25) confirms "skin lesions similar to burns, which can arise in healthy subjects, and mania or hypomania in patients with depression" (p. 19). By contrast, the article says that in tACS "no persistent adverse events have been reported, but considerably fewer reports are available on the safety of tACS than on the safety of tDCS" and "Further safety investigations are required."

The way I see it, and this is just a personal opinion (though shared by Les Fehmi, my neurofeedback mentor who was a pioneer in Neurofeedback, with whom I discussed the issue),

Feedback: Good.

Possibly frying your brain: Bad.

So until I see some longitudinal research in which users of neuro*stimulation* don't have fried eggs for brains at some point down the road, I and my clients will respectfully sit this fad out until further notice. It's kind of like the difference between a blood pressure monitor, that *measures* your blood pressure, versus an *injection* of blood into your body. I'm sure that my opinion will be criticized by those researchers and clinicians out there who use tDCS and tACS with their patients, and by people who use it on themselves without incident, and all I can say is "My burn lesions, My choice." I realize it is just the experience of 1 person and I have no desire to impose it on anyone else, but I won't recommend to my readers something that may have burnt me (again, this regards tDCS, not tACS, the latter which I haven't tried).

Neurofeedback

For several years I spent considerable time making tables of areas of the brain and brainwaves implicated in lucid dreaming in studies. Holzinger, LaBerge and Levitan (2006) found that, in lucid dreaming, Beta 13-19 Hz was increased in both parietal regions as compared with nonlucid dreaming, with the frontal to parietal Beta 13-19 Hz ratio being 1 : 1.16 in nonlucid dreams and 1 : 1.77 in lucid dreams. Voss et al. (2009) found that during lucid dreaming, Gamma 40 Hz was strongest frontally and frontolaterally, and that there was increased Delta and Theta coherence, especially frontally and frontolaterally, and lower alpha coherence than in the waking state. Voss (2014) used these findings to successfully trigger lucid dreams through 25-40 Hz frontotemporal neurostimulation.

Based on the above findings, I developed corresponding protocols in an attempt to increase those brainwaves, in those areas, using feedback rather than stimulation methods, not during nighttime sleep but during the daytime utilizing my own God-given ability to fall asleep anytime, anywhere, anyplace (with the exception, sometimes, of nighttime after an over-caffeinated evening at the office). This is still a work in progress, but I have not thus far succeeded in triggering lucidity during neurofeedback-based napping. I once asked Siegfried Othmer, a pioneer in clinical neurofeedback, his take on this, and he warned me that he knew at least one person who had spent years trying to induce altered states using neurofeedback to no avail. This said, Elmer and Alyce Green did find that Theta brainwave training, combined with a periodic sound to awaken participants if they fell asleep, induced a "reverie" state of "voluntary hypnagogic imagery" which they felt "will eventually become 'the royal road to the unconscious,' rather than dreams or hypnosis" (Green & Green, 1986, p. 201). A comprehensive, if somewhat dated, overview of physiological correlates of lucid dreaming is provided by LaBerge (1990), upon whose early work he himself and the above researchers continue to build. A more recent review of the research on lucid dreaming neurobiology is provided by Baird, Mota-Rolim and Dressler (2019).

Organic Neuorstim: Senses Initiated Lucid Dream Technique (SSILD):

I just learned about this technique today (2/24/21), while revisiting this chapter and stumbling upon Aspy's (2020) International Lucid Dream Induction Study (ILDIS). Truth be told, for some time I've avoided reading about new techniques that have been developed, maybe having fallen victim to some kind of satiation-induced burnout regarding grassroots proliferation of new LD techniques and acronyms. However, in the interest of providing you with the most up-do-date information, I did some exposure therapy ("Just Do It!" despite my aversion) and behavioral activation ("Just Do It!" despite not feeling like it) on myself, and asked Google what was new in the LD induction world. When I read the abstract and saw that after comparing some of the most effective techniques there was a tie between MILD and SSILD, an acronym I'd never heard of, my first reaction was "good grief, do

I really now need to actually read this article and figure out what that is," followed by "and why does it have two S's?" So again, I administered a mild dose of exposure and behavioral activation to calm my urge to move on to other sections of the book, and looked for the section on SSILD.

I learned that this is a technique developed by Gary Zhang in 2011 to teach lucid dreaming on a Chinese forum. It combines sequential monosensory meditation with the WBTB technique. As such, it is a combined technique, integrating sensory awareness with meditation and WBTB, all three of which have been shown by research to increase the frequency of lucid dreaming. You may note, as I just did, that the exercise is a lucid dream induction version of my Seehearbody exercise, which itself resembles an Ericksonian hypnosis technique in which one sequentially attends to seeing, hearing and the bodysense (my term, not Erickson's).

I will here paraphrase the steps from Aspy's instructions in the link provided in the reference section for Zhang (2011; which is Cosmic Iron, 2013). I will replace his instruction to "focus" with the instruction to "be aware of."

1. Go to bed early, before 11 p.m. and set the alarm to awaken 4-5 hours later (this may be a way of compensating for the time spent doing the exercise during the WBTB period).

2. Get out of bed for 5-10 minutes and walk around, trying not to become too awake.

3. Get back in bed and find a comfortable position different from the one you usually sleep in.

4. Perform the following cycle 4-6 times, doing each step for only a few seconds:

> a. With eyes closed, be aware of sight, which will be the light or darkness of the back of the eyelids. Keep the eyes relaxed. There is no need to move them around.
>
> b. Be aware of sound.
>
> c. Be aware of bodily sensations.
>
> Be sure not to "try" to see, hear or feel, just passively see, hear or feel whatever the natural experience is of seeing, hearing and feeling.

5. Perform the same cycle slowly 3-4 times, being aware of each sense for at least 30 seconds. If you find yourself distracted by thoughts, or realize you have briefly fallen asleep, as sometimes happens in meditation, this is fine. Gently bring yourself back to the exercise, beginning again with seeing.

6. Get back into your sleeping position, and go back to sleep.

In the research that validated this technique (Aspy, 2020), participants were instructed to do 4 fast cycles for 2-3 seconds on each sense; 4-6 slow cycles, spending about 20 seconds on each sense; not to count the number of seconds; and to then fall asleep as normal after the slow cycles.

A few moments ago (it's now 2/27/21, 7:56 A.M.), I was in bed practicing this technique (I still haven't tried it out at night, due to a current reluctance to disrupt my sleep with WBTB), when I noticed my mind stop for a moment, from the vantage point of then noticing it start again, as happens from time to time as I am going to sleep using my usual sleep induction strategy of monsensory meditation on seeing. Then my mind started analyzing why SSILD induces lucid dreams. What I came up with is that the act of sequentially attending to different single senses is doing a number of things. Getting back to the findings of a doctoral dissertation (Downar, 2002) I found yesterday and included in the glossary at the beginning of this book (in the Attention and Awareness entry), awareness increases when something is perceived as important:

> "Sensory stimuli must be at the focus of attention to reach conscious awareness. Attention may serve as a mechanism for identifying salient (i.e., potentially behaviorally relevant) features of the sensory environment. Neuroimaging studies have identified a frontal-parietal-cingulate network of regions involved in attentional control and conscious sensation. The present work was designed to test the hypothesis that these regions represent the salience of sensory stimuli. Brain regions sensitive to stimulus salience across multiple sensory modalities were identified in four studies using event-related functional magnetic resonance imaging. *A right-lateralized network of frontal, parietal, cingulate, and insular cortical areas responded to salient changes in visual, auditory, and tactile stimuli ... They responded more strongly to changes in visual or auditory stimuli when the stimuli were task-relevant rather than task-irrelevant.*" (Downar, 2002, pp. ii-iii).

It occurs to me that it is possible that the areas of the brain stimulated by intentional prolonged monosensory attention and awareness (monosensory mindfulness) may be the same areas that lucid dream researchers have found implicated in the onset of awareness in dreams, which I'll repeat here:

> Holzinger, LaBerge and Levitan (2006) found increased 13-19 Hz in both parietal regions, with the frontal to parietal Beta 13-19 Hz ratio being 1:1.16 in nonlucid dreams and 1:1.77 in lucid dreams.
>
> Voss et al. (2009) found
>
>> Strong frontal and frontolateral Gamma;
>>
>> Increased frontal and frontolateral Delta and Theta coherence;
>>
>> Reduced alpha coherence.
>
> Voss (2014) used these findings to successfully trigger lucid dreams through 25-40 Hz frontotemporal neurostimulation.

Where I'm going with this is that intentional attention to sensory information increases neuronal firing in regions of the brain involved in sensory awareness. There's an old adage "Neurons that wire together fire together" (Reeves, 2018 and, as consciousness researcher Dan Siegel has suggested, "Where attention goes, neural firing flows and neural connection grows"; Siegel, 2017). If the areas of the brain activated by sensory attention/awareness are the same regions involved in the onset of self-awareness when dreaming, SSLD is employing intentional sensory awareness as a form of organic, or endogenous, neurostimulation targeting regions of the brain implicated in lucid dreaming. A comparison of brain scans from Downar's (2002) study and the results of the Holzinger, Laberge & Levitan (2006) and Voss (2014) studies could be informative. Specifically, are the attention and awareness areas identified by Downar similar to the areas found by the latter studies to be activated in lucid dreams or capable of triggering lucid dreams when externally stimulated? And is it possible that the brainwave patterns activated by SSILD are 25-40 hz, similar to the neurostimulation frequencies in the Voss (2014) study (frequencies associated with wakefulness, as are likely implicated in SSILD which is performed when awake)?

Chapter 32 - How To Lucid Dream and Not Get Eaten by a Golem

I have a related theory regarding why the Taoist meditational practice known as the Microcosmic Orbit triggers out-of-body experiences (see the chapter on out-of-body experiences) which I began formulating when I saw some diagrams in Itzhak Bentov's (1988) book *Stalking the Wild Pendulum: On the Mechanics of Consciousness* in his section on Kundalini, in which he notes that the Kundalini experience involves a polarization of gray matter in the sensory cortex. What I think is happening is that moving attention up the back of the body and down the front of the body – don't try this if you are pregnant, as it may not be safe, and the direction may be different for men and women in general – is creating a corresponding pattern of neuronal firing from the top center of the brain, extending down both sides of the sensory cortex simultaneously – the left side sensing the right side of the body and the right side sensing the left side of the body – and then rising back up both sides of the cortex simultaneously to the top (as the sensory cortex rises from one side of the brain, over the top, and down the other). As the different parts of the body are represented in different parts of the sensory cortex, beginning with the toes in the top center of the cortex and rising to the head at the sides of the cortex, moving awareness up and down the body is, in effect, creating an energetic wave of neuronal firing back and forth from the top of the brain, down the sides, and then back up again. The surge of energy experienced during a "kundalini awakening," and the corresponding perception of consciousness rising from the base of the spine upward, in my case induced an *experience*, whether real or hallucinated, of propelling my consciousness through the crown of the head, through a spinning tunnel and into the cosmos on October 8-9, 2007. As Bentov (1988) writes:

> "This model, which we may call the 'physio-kundalini' since it deals only with the physiological part of the kundalini, describes the kundalini as a stimulus spreading along the sensory cortex of the two hemispheres, starting from the bottom of the cleft between the two hemispheres of the brain. The layout of points on the sensory or motor cortices corresponds to the points in the body, so that when a point on the cortex, representing, for example, the knee, is electrically or mechanically stimulated, the person feels the stimulus in his knee. He has no way of knowing that the stimulus is caused by his brain being artificially stimulated ... I am trying to show that the layout of points on both the sensory and the motor cortices

> corresponds closely to the path the kundalini takes in the body. The path is described in esoteric literature ...
>
> To cause such a stimulus to move along the cortex, acoustical standing waves in the cerebral ventricles are postulated ... These vibrations will stimulate and eventually 'polarize' the cortex in such a way that it will tend to conduct a signal along the homunculus [the 'little man' superimposed over the sensorimotor cortex corresponding with the parts of the body governed by individual sections of the cortex], starting from the toes and up."

It should be noted that in my experience the kundalini rose from the base of the spine rather than from the toes, so experiences obviously differ. Bentov continues:

> "The states of bliss described by those whose kundalini symptoms have completed the full loop along the hemispheres may be explained as self-stimulation of the pleasure centers of the brain, caused by the circulation of a 'current' along the sensory cortex.
>
> When the kundalini has finally completed its circuit, it can be said that the human nervous system has achieved what is analogous to the state of puberty in the body in the sense that it can start functioning more fully on ever higher levels of consciousness.
>
> I hope you still remember what was said ... about the rudimentary consciousness of the planet and the higher consciousness, which uses the planet as a place to hang its hat on, so to speak. Once a person's nervous system has developed to this point, energies provided by these high consciousnesses begin to flow automatically into the nervous system of the recipient due to a state of resonance with the above beings. This will cause further evolution of the nervous system, and eventually these consciousnesses may make themselves known in ways that are individually matched to each person's needs and abilities. Later, an unfolding of knowledge occurs that opens up broader and broader vistas about the workings of Nature, so that a person starts feeling that he is very much a part, and indeed a very active part, of Nature and the universe.
>
> ... Presently still in the conceptual stage, the so-called 'holistic medical centers' will be staffed by physicians and psychotherapists

> who have themselves experienced the symptoms described above or have been trained to understand them ...
>
> ... Such holistic medical centers will be able to deal not only with the medical aspects of a health situation but also with its spiritual component ..." (pp. 178-184)

Bentov was clearly on to something. Tragically, the man who escaped from a Prague deathcamp and without a university degree designed Israel's first rocket and invented the first flexible heart catheter, not to mention diet spaghetti (yes, really), died on Flight 191 in 1979 (Green, 2015). May his memory be a blessing, and may his work be an inspiration for our continued investigation into how we may evolve our consciousness individually and as a species through continued research on kundalini and other phenomena still P.O.E.T.ically exiled from the scientific mainstream (for being politically, ontologically, epistemologically or theologically incorrect)(Densei & Lam, 2010).

Nutritional Supplements and Cholinergic Enhancement

The most comprehensive reference on the use of nutritional supplements to facilitate lucid dreaming is Thomas Yuschak's 2006 cult classic *Advanced Lucid Dreaming: The Power of Supplements: How to Induce High Level Lucid Dreams and Out of Body Experiences.* The most reliable chemical method of inducing lucid dreaming (if Inception didn't totally scare you off) appears to be cholinergic enhancement by means of galantamine. This is an alkaloid that can be extracted from bulbs and flowers such as the red spider lily, as well as produced synthetically. It is marketed legally as a nutritional supplement, as the FDA is not allowed to regulate (i.e., monopolize access and cost) of nutritional supplements. However, since it is also marketed on a prescription basis as the Alzheimer's and memory impairment medications *Razadyne* and *Reminyl,* pharmacies don't sell it over the counter. To get the nutritional supplement version (which is the same thing in a container saying "nutritional supplement"), you therefore need to buy it online (you can easily find it on Amazon.com). Cholinergic enhancement is also targeted by donepezil, marketed as the Alzheimer's medication *Aricept.*

A number of studies have shown that cholinergic enhancement dramatically increases the probability of lucid dreaming (LaBerge, 2001; LaBerge,

LaMarca & Baird 2018; Sparrow, Carlson, Hurd & Molina, 2018). Laberge, LaMarca and Baird (2018) used a procedure involving

1. awakening 4.5 hours after bedtime (the Wake Back to Bed or WBTB procedure);

2. each participant then taking a placebo or 4 mg or 8 mg of galantamine on any given night of the three nights during which the study was conducted;

3. then reading about lucid dreaming or recording/reviewing their dreams for 30 minutes; and finally

4. practicing MILD for at least 10 minutes before falling back asleep.

As compared with a baseline of 4% of participants experiencing a lucid dream on a given night during the preceding 6 months, 14% had at least 1 lucid dream on the night they used WBTB plus MILD plus placebo pill; 27% had a lucid dream on the night they used WBTB plus MILD plus 4 mg of galantamine; and 42% had a lucid dream on the night they used WBTB plus MILD plus 8 mg of galantamine. In total, 67% of the group had a lucid dream on one of the 2 nights they used WBTB plus MILD plus one or another dose of galantamine. It should be noted that 94 of the 121 participants decided to wear REM biofeedback masks on all three nights of the study, and no data was provided comparing the effects of the other interventions for maskers versus non-maskers so, not to be a downer here as it's otherwise a fantastic study, but the results may be specific to individuals who are wearing REM neurofeedback masks.

Now, before going online and ordering over the counter galantamine, please realize that in LaBerge, LaMarca & Baird's 2018 study, participants were screened for asthma, beta-blockers, severe mental illness or cardiac arrhythmias. If any of these were present, they were not accepted as participants due to potential health risks. In addition, even without these risk factors, the warning labels on medications containing galantamine or donepezil for cognitive enhancement in dementia contain long lists of potential side effects, drug interactions and medical counter-indications. Twelve percent of the study participants reported side effects including mild gastrointestinal upset, insomnia and next-day fatigue. So, before taking galantamine as an over the counter lucid dream enhancer, you should really check with a physician to make sure that there are no medical reasons for you not to take it. The catch-22 here is that I'm pretty sure no medical

Chapter 32 - How To Lucid Dream and Not Get Eaten by a Golem

doctor will clear you to take what s/he knows only as a medication for dementia unless they feel that for medical reasons you could benefit from cognitive enhancement. So, let's put it this way: ask your physician whether it would be *harmful* for you to take it. If they say yes, then of course you shouldn't take it. If they say no, then it's really up to you to weigh the potential benefits of lucid dreaming against potential side effects of ingesting the supplements in question.

Regarding their mechanism of action, galantamine and donepezil do not themselves alter consciousness, but are acetylcholinesterase inhibitors, meaning that they inhibit the inhibitor (eraser) of acetylcholine, thereby making acetylcholine - which both increases Rapid Eye Movement (REM) dreaming sleep (Riemann et al., 1994) and promotes awareness, thought and memory - more available for use by the brain. If you were to take either of them during the day, you might feel more alert, you might feel sick from side effects, but you would not feel "high" or start dreaming or hallucinating (remember, they are prescribed to *improve* cognition in dementia). The reason that they are useful for inducing lucid dreaming is that if acetylcholine is enhanced when you are asleep, it wakes up your brain without waking up your body, creating a state that Robert Monroe, a pioneer in the induction of out-of-body experiences, termed "mind awake - body asleep," and which Gackenbach and Laberge (1988) call "conscious mind - sleeping brain." This state is conducive to lucid dreams and out-of-body (and possibly near-death) experiences. The mind becomes self-aware due to the increased availability of acetylcholine, which has not been reduced by its own acetylcholinesterase, due to the latter being inhibited by the galantamine or donepezil. You might wonder why, then, aren't all of the people taking these for dementia having lucid dreams every night. I sure do. I can only guess that (a) maybe they are - has anyone ever asked them?; (b) maybe rather than increasing acetylcholine to lucid dreaming levels as it does in individuals without dementia, when someone has dementia galantamine and donepezil merely bring acetylcholine levels up to "normal" but not lucid dreaming levels; or (c) maybe they are having lucid dreams but aren't remembering them. Duh. Remembering dreams is already something that many of us are not skilled at, and the whole reason that people with dementia are being treated with acetylcholinesterase inhibitors is that they are having challenges regarding memory.

I experimented with the over-the-counter version of galantamine combined with choline bitartrate (the latter which helps the brain produce acetylcholine rather than just stopping the brain from inhibiting it) myself about 10 times a number of years ago, with a 90% success rate at inducing lucid dreams and with no side effects other than rapid heartbeat on one occasion and sometimes achiness and sluggishness the next day (the latter which may have been due to using the sleep interruption technique, without making up for the sleep by going to sleep earlier or waking up later, rather than due to the galantamine). Having gone online and read the information on the warning labels, I personally prefer using psychological rather than these chemical techniques, but that's just me.

If you are already a nicotine afficionado, which is unhealthy but according to research not as unhealthy as not exercising (Mandsager et al, 2018), and while I'm not recommending it, nicotine on a WBTB basis may also stimulate the brain and trigger the mind awake, body asleep state and thus lucid dreaming. Pipe tobacco, which isn't inhaled, has been said to work quite well, and it can be dry vaped rather than smoked which may be less dangerous to one's health. If you are using nicotine patches to stop smoking, you may find yourself awake in your dreams for the same reason. On a side note, regarding the dangers of tobacco, in 2006, at age 83, Kurt Vonnegut threatened to sue the makers of Pall Mall, which he had been smoking since the age of 12, for false advertising. "And do you know why? Because I'm 83 years old. The lying bastards! On the package Brown & Williamson promised to kill me." He died the next year from a fall (Grossman, 2007).

Virtual Reality Induced Lucid Dreaming (VRILD)

Virtual reality may be considered a halfway point between waking perception in the absence of VR equipment, and lucid dreaming. Experience of realistic sensation and perception in virtual environments gives one a new perspective on neurosensory constructionism, so to speak, the role of neurology and sensory processes and limitations in determining experience. Just as learning a second language creates a metalinguistic framework from which emerges a greater understanding of one's own language, learning to function in a second virtual reality (the VR environment) changes the way that one relates to one's primary virtual reality, this being the *experience* constructed by one's brain in response to one's non-virtual physical and social environment. Note that I am calling the *experience* of one's day to day reality virtual, and not the reality itself, which must be considered real if the word "real" is to have any meaning whatsoever.

As virtual reality has the potential to help induce lucid dreams as well as to program their content for specific purposes (e.g., lucid dream skills practice or exposure therapy) and enhance their quality (e.g., vividness, stability/length and control), it is not surprising that research on VR-assisted lucid dreaming has now begun (Gott et al., 2021; Kitson, DiPaola & Riecke, 2019) Gott et al. (2021) compared (1) a treatment group participating in four weeks of a combined protocol (twelve 45-minute VR sessions in surreal environments simulating things that happen in dreams, plus lucid dream training in critical state testing consisting of asking oneself "Am I dreaming" 5-10 times per day combined with reality checks); (2) an active control group which only did the critical state testing; and (3) a passive control group that received no VR or lucid dream training. Likely due to the lack of statistical power resulting from insufficient sample size, the results indicated superiority of Combined VR and critical state testing to no training, but no statistically significant difference between critical state testing and the passive control, or between VR and critical state testing. However, statistical significance aside, twice as many participants in the VR group had lucid dreams than in the critical state testing group, and the passive control group had no lucid dreams. The authors hypothesize that VR may facilitate lucid dreaming for a variety of reasons. First, it may increase metacognition (stepping back from one's cognitive experience and observing it rather than fully identifying with it); second, the surreal VR content may have been incorporated into participants' dreams and reminded them of the goal to become lucid; and finally, the post-VR experience of dissociation from one's natural environment, one type of VRISE (Virtual Reality Induced Symptoms and Effects; Cobb, Nichols, Ramsey & Wilson, 1999, as termed in the literature, may have enhanced the effects of critical state testing which has as its goal to alert one to any unusual perceptions (after which one does a reality test which, if one is dreaming, indicates that one is indeed dreaming).

Biofeedback-Based Virtual Reality-Induced Lucid Dreaming (BB-VRILD)

Another research group (Kitson, DiPaola & Riecke, 2019) has done some serious cross-subdisciplinary consciousness exploration research on inducing a lucid dream-like virtual reality experience, which they call "Lucid Loop," consisting of visuals "based on Deep Convolutional Neural Networks

(DCNNs)," with the visual and auditory environment determined by biofeedback/neurofeedback from patterns of respiration, heart rate and brainwaves. The virtual visual and auditory environment becomes more lucid/clear when these physiological measures are indicative of focused attention. Specifically, the positive reinforcement of clearer audiovisual stimuli is delivered when high frequency Beta and Gamma brainwaves increase, low frequency Theta and Alpha brainwaves decrease, and respiration, heart rate and skin potential indicate higher autonomic nervous system arousal. The authors base this protocol on findings from lucid dream research indicating that lucid dreaming, as compared with REM sleep, involves increased power of parietal Beta waves and frontal Gamma waves, citing the work of Holzinger, LaBerge and Levitan (2006) and Voss and colleagues (2009, 2014). Whether the Lucid Loop VR bio/neurofeedback protocol actually facilitates lucid dreaming when used for training during sustained wakefulness, or even with the instruction to allow oneself to become sleepy and drift into sleep while wearing it (with eyes closed there would still be auditory feedback), will have to await research.

Mystical Weeping

"Falling asleep weeping ... seems part of the sequence: visiting a cemetery – weeping – revelatory dream." (Idel, 1990, p. 77).

"If you will only cry for God with a tenth of the fervour with which you cry for your spouse and children, you will see God in no time." (Ramakrishna Paramahamsa, in Saranagati, June, 2021, p. 4)

"If you can cry tears for not finding God, he will not be able to hide himself." (Bhagavan Sri Ramana Maharshi, in Saranagati, June, 2021, p. 4)

I'm inserting this section 2 years after beginning this book, having discovered something new (with such new discoveries having something to do with how long it's taking to get to the part where the butler, or Corky Coben, does it, or even to what *it* is). I was sitting here watching Schitt's Creek, when one of the character's expressions during a happy event reminded me of a question a client posed recently regarding why he tears up when listening to music. So I googled "why do people cry when they are happy" (google doesn't require question marks). It turns out that when strong emotions occur, positive *or* negative, which both involve activation of the amygdala and hypothalamus, the corresponding activation of the autonomic nervous system takes one of two forms: sympathetic arousal (fight or flight) or parasympathetic arousal (relaxation). Whereas the main neurotransmitter that activates the autonomic nervous system (fight or flight – so you don't have to look back at the preceding sentence) is norepinephrine, the parasympathetic nervous system activation (the relaxation response) is primarily triggered by acetylcholine (Matoba, 2020), which also happens to activate the tear ducts (Lewis, 2013) AND, as learned earlier in this chapter, facilitates lucid dreaming. To the extent that the same neurological processes implicated in lucid dreaming may be involved in out-of-body experiences (OBEs), near death experiences (NDEs) and other experiences sometimes interpreted as being of a "mystical" nature, my train of thought during Schitt's Creek may very well have shed some light on the cholinergic mechanism by which the heightened emotional state corresponding with "mystical weeping" (Alter, 1989; Idel, 1990) is related to subsequent altered states of consciousness.

Maintaining Lucidity

Becoming lucid in your dream is only half the battle, albeit the most important half. The other half is *staying* lucid. I can't tell you how many lucid dreams I've had that were going beautifully, such as when I was sitting and chatting with my transitioned father or grandparents, or when I was in a meditation circle in a tent in Tibet with the Master finally arriving at my place and leaning down to whisper my True Name in my ear, when POOF, I was back in my bed.

Some techniques that have been proposed for staying lucid in a dream environment that is still intact include Carlos Castaneda's (1972) "look at your hands" technique, moving them back and forth (Tholey, 1983), or spinning. But maybe most importantly is: Don't stare. Not only is it not polite, but staring at something in a lucid dream is kind of like shooting it with a ray gun. It melts. So if you want to stay in the dream rather than find yourself back in your bed, keep your eyes moving around a little, and maybe keep your body at least in slight motion as well. There is no doubt some neurological basis for this, but we can leave that to the neuroscientists. If you find yourself back in bed, the best way to re-enter the lucid dream is to stay perfectly still and fall back asleep vividly imagining yourself in the exact same dream scene that you just left (that is, unless you were being attacked by monsters, in which case you could imagine returning and giving them big hugs so they'll turn into puppies, or a more pleasant scene such as a beach if you'd rather skip the monsters altogether).

So Which One(s) to Try First?

As I mentioned, there has been some research on the comparative effectiveness of various techniques. Aspy's (2020) International Lucid Dream Induction Study (ILDIS) compared Reality Testing (RT), Wake Back to Bed (WBTB), the Mnemonic Induction of Lucid Dreams (MILD) technique (which was always paired with the WBTB technique), the Senses Initiated Lucid Dream (SSILD) technique (which includes the WBTB technique and has an apparently intentional addition of the second S so I'll reluctantly leave it there – maybe it's magic or something), and a combined MILD and SSILD hybrid. The winners were MILD and SSILD with no advantage of the hybrid over either MILD or SSILD alone. Nevertheless, LaBerge (1991) found that wearing a REM biofeedback mask combined with MILD was better than either one by itself. Laberge, LaMarca and Baird (2018) seem to have settled on WBTB plus MILD as the techniques of choice to compare with and without galantamine (though an REM biofeedback mask appears to be one of their go-tos as well); and the Australian Lucid Dream Induction Study indicated the superiority of RT plus WBTB plus MILD (Aspy, 2017). My recommendation is to expend the additional effort to combine as many of these approaches as you feel motivated to practice and here is what I would suggest for starters without getting fancy by spending money on a mask or ingesting red spider lily extract (galantamine):

1. Pick up a book on lucid dreaming. There are lots of them out there, differing in the proportional time spent on theory, research, anecdotes and techniques. Go to Amazon, sign in, and use the "look inside" feature to peruse the table of contents and read a few pages to see which one appeals to you.

2. Get in the habit of doing critical state testing (asking yourself, silently, "am I dreaming") and reality testing (e.g., try to float) 5-10 times per day. If you are around other people, there should be nothing in your behavior that alerts them to the fact that you are trying to float. It's a purely mental effort. Please DO NOT try to float by stepping off or out of something such that if you are *not* dreaming you will fall to your death.

Chapter 32 - How To Lucid Dream and Not Get Eaten by a Golem

3. Add a half hour to the time you usually insert between going to sleep at night and getting out of bed in the morning, as preparation for the **WBTB** technique. Set your alarm for 4.5 hours after you predict you will fall asleep. When you awaken, do one of the following:

> a. read about lucid dreaming for 30 minutes or write down memories of past dreams. Then practice the **MILD** technique for at least 10 minutes before falling asleep; or

> b. do the **SSILD** exercise and then go back to sleep.

4. Establish a daily meditation and mindfulness practice, or play video games. As meditation and mindfulness enhance meta-awareness (awareness of awareness), and as lucid dreaming is all about meta-awareness, meditation and mindfulness logically, and according to the research (Baird et al., 2019; Stumbrys & Erlacher, 2017; Stumbrys, Erlacher & Malinowski, 2015) increase your likelihood of becoming aware that you are in a dream. Importantly, however, while a sitting meditation practice is correlated with increased lucid dream frequency, and mindfulness is as well, it is not clear from the research whether mindfulness in activity alone, without a sitting meditation practice, does so (Baird et al., 2019). If you don't feel like meditating or practicing mindfulness, no problem, just play video games. Research indicates that video gaming increases both the frequency and ability to control the content of lucid dreams (Stumbreys & Erlacher, 2017). I suspect that this may be due to developing, through gaming, a habit of interacting with a virtual environment.

5. If after about 1 month of practicing the foregoing you have still not had a lucid dream, it may be time to invest in an **REM** neurofeedback mask. I would recommend SmartLucider, at SmartLucider.com, which is sold by Pawel Herchel in Warsaw, Poland and costs 70 Euros (US$85). They are of good quality, and I have had both the original and newer model for years and have never had any technical problems with them. I have noticed that it takes quite a while to arrive in the US from Poland, so it might be worth it to pay extra for expedited shipping. In case you are wondering, I have no business relationship with Mr. Herchel and do not receive any profits from his sale of the masks.

6. If, after about 1 month of practicing all of the above you *still* have not had a lucid dream, consider the galantamine option, with the cautions noted above.

Chapter 33 - *Up, Up and Away:* Out-of-Body Experiences (OBEs)

"Golly, gee, Toto, this can't be Kansas!"

"There is a point twixt sleep and waking

Where thou shalt be alert without shaking.

Enter the new world where forms so hideous pass;

They are passing – endure, do not be taken by the dross.

Then the pulls and the pushes about the throttle,

All those shalt thou tolerate.

Close all ingress and egress,

Yawnings there may be;

Shed tears – crave – implore, but thou will not prostrate.

A thrill passes – and that goes down to the bottom;

It riseth, may it bloom forth, that is Bliss.

Blessed Being! Blessed Being!

O greetings be to Thee!"

Swami Lakshmanjoo Brahmachari

(2003, p. 115)

"The life principal is not in the body. Rather, the life principal is an electronic pattern, or circuit, descending and ascending. And the body is its expression. *It* contains the body. And this is the first degree of liberation. Because, when it is realized, truly, stably, with mastery, the individual no longer identifies with the gross physical life, no longer identifies with the fixed pattern that appears, but knows it as an extension of the energies that enclose and permeate the manifest life ... One can, while alive, by manipulating certain functions in consciousness, have the experience of going into planes beyond this gross one, of leaving the body, of even moving around in this gross world outside of the physical body."

Bubba Free John / Adi Da Samraj (1975)

Chapter 33 - Up, Up and Away: Out-of-Body Experiences (OBEs)

> "The inner mind appears to be a quiet river
> until that curled-up and shining portion of us
> meets the luminous, immaterial, and boundless nonlocal light –
> that oceanic intelligence our genius calls God."

Edward Bruce Bynum

(2012, p. 2; in Dark Light Consciousness: Melanin, Serpent Power, and the Luminous Matrix of Reality. "Summary: How to awaken the Ureaus – the serpent power of spiritual transcendence within each of us – and connect to the superconscious of the universe -- Provided by publisher" [of Bynum, 2012]; Copyright Page)

"I think it not improbable that man, like the grub that prepares a chamber for the winged thing it never has seen but is to be – that man may have cosmic destinies that he does not understand. And so, beyond the vision of battling races and an impoverished earth I catch a dreaming glimpse of peace."

Justice Oliver Wendell Holmes Jr.

(1913/1934, p. 103)

I've always been a psychonaut (with an *a,* thank you – an explorer of inner space, though I always was fascinated by jumping beans). When I was 13, after learning electronics and Morse code and getting a ham radio license, I and, as I later learned, my friend Pope John Paul George Ringo – whose great grandfather, by the way, invented aspirin – enrolled in the Silva Mind Control course at a local Holiday Inn. It was there that I had my first exposure to meditation and neural (brainwave) entrainment (in this case, audio induction of alpha waves). Throughout my teen years, I would practice a technique that I had somehow discovered, involving lying on my back, arms straight down at my sides, perfectly still, without moving a muscle (and observing and tolerating any discomfort or urge to do so) for 30 minutes to an hour. Eventually the sense of having a body would dissolve into disembodied awareness, which at the time I had no name for as I hadn't read books on the matter.

I used to go to the bookstore B. Dalton (later acquired by Barnes and Noble) at the mall and gravitate toward the section that we would now call New Age. I'd flip through books on magic, hypnosis, ESP, telepathy and astral projection. I'll never forget my first attempts at inducing an out-of-body experience: I lay on the bed, as described above, and imagined being in a barrel, with the inside of the barrel spinning past my face in order to trick myself into thinking that I myself were spinning (much as, when on a train, if the train on the next track starts moving before you do, you think you are moving). Suddenly I felt myself beginning to spin upwards, out of my head, and into the air. I am not saying that my consciousness really was outside of my body, as theories vary and the jury's still out, but the *experience,* which seemed as real to the senses as my current experience of sitting at a table typing, was of spinning up, up, and away. For some reason, maybe I had read it in some book, I then had the fear "what if I keep spinning away, and then can't come back?" At that moment, I snapped back into my body, and didn't have another out-of-body experience for another 30 years (which were spent on marginally more productive things than spinning out of one's head), again as a result of employing a variety of techniques with that specific intention. I do recall, however, having two wisdom teeth pulled in the old days when dentists had spinning psychedelic lights on the ceiling and gave you headphones playing Pink Floyd while you drifted into la-la land as the nitrous took effect. On that occasion (which I don't really count as an OBE, because it involved a chemically induced altered state of consciousness)(or ASC; Aberdeen Evening Express, 1892; Tart, 1969) I had the experience (if not the reality) of being outside of my body in a spinning vortex of numbers, and having the Pythagorean insight that "music is numbers," in between screaming at the dental assistant to duck so the train wouldn't hit us. Pythagoras, I just realized, has thus been implicated in two of my OBEs – the other involving the "music of the spheres." More on that to come.

Regarding "mind altering substances," it is important to remember that when the mind is altered by a substance, even though things seem different, the only thing different is the mind:

> "Two monks were arguing about a flag.
>
> One said: 'The flag is moving.'
>
> The other said: 'The wind is moving.'

Chapter 33 - Up, Up and Away: Out-of-Body Experiences (OBEs)

> The sixth patriarch happened to be passing by.
>
> He told them:
>
> 'Not the wind, not the flag;
>
> mind is moving.'"
>
> **Ekai, The Gateless Gate #29**

External reality, though seemingly more alive, intricate, engaging and profound when molecularly enhanced, is as it always has been. It should therefore be possible to learn to experience things in the altered, enhanced way without the benefit of chemical brain hacking and to, so to speak, ride the brain bareback. And this is what the meditative traditions do, which uniformly counsel against the use of mind altering substances other than attention and awareness.

In high school I began reading books with Eastern philosophical themes, such as those by Herman Hesse (*Siddhartha, The Glass Bead Game*) and Aldous Huxley, including an enormous biography of the latter. At some point I stumbled upon *The Psychology of Man's Possible Evolution* (1947), by Ouspensky and *The Wisdom of the Overself*, by Paul Brunton (1943). I probably read the former, as it is very thin, and never got myself to read more than a word or two of the latter. However, the titles themselves inspired and continue to inspire me.

I took a course in psychology in 11th grade, and then decided to major in psychology in college. Unfortunately, Western academic psychology at the time (and, for the most part, at present, as well) had no knowledge of or interest in consciousness exploration or what are now called "anomalous experiences" (e.g., lucid dreams, out-of-body experiences, pure awareness) and I was trained in experimental psychology, mostly involving how to conduct research on sensation, perception, cognitive *content* and behavior, sometimes sacrificing small animals to the psychological Gods.

After college, in the 1980s, I sought out knowledge on altered states of consciousness, for a time studying the works and visiting U.S. and European schools of Rudolf Steiner (1910/1904), who developed the field of Anthroposophy and created the Waldorf system of education.

At this time I also became acquainted with the mindfulness teachings of Thich Nhat Hanh (1974), introduced to me by a friend in France who had escaped Vietnam, and of Chogyam Trungpa Rinpoche (1988), whom I learned about in a walk through a French mountain forest with someone familiar with his teachings (which discussion triggered, during the walk, one of those openings, or expansions of consciousness familiar to those who practice meditation). In the 1990s, I returned to graduate school to study clinical psychology, which, like experimental psychology, had no knowledge or interest whatsoever in consciousness exploration or anomalous experiences. But there I learned the geography of pathological states of consciousness and how to treat them, which can be a valuable prerequisite to navigating the "farther reaches of human nature," as Maslow would say, in a psychologically healthy way (Part 2 of the present book). As a famous jazzman once said, "you gotta learn to play far in before you can play far out" (or something like that).

After graduate school, in the 2000s, my father got sick and, after a year of chronic illness, various non-diagnoses and misdiagnoses (including "depression" which was erroneously used to explain the weight loss), my father received his final misdiagnosis of lung cancer at a cancer hospital that should have known better. When he was finally given the proper tests (or when the proper tests were read correctly) it turned out to be lymphoma, morphing into leukemia. Coincidentally, or maybe not, this period corresponded with what I now look back upon as a mid-life crisis, and the beginning of an exploration of meditative traditions including Tibetan Buddhism (Trungpa, 1988) and Dream Yoga (Norbu, 1992); Zen (Hanh, 1974; Suzuki, 2003/1970); *Advaita Vedanta* (Hindu nondualism, especially through the writings of Bhagavan Sri Ramana Maharshi [1988], and Nisargadatta Maharaj [1999/1973], but also through inspiration from Paramahansa Yogananda [1946] and his teacher Swami Sri Yukteswar Giri [1894]); Kashmir Shaivism (Lakshmanjoo, 2003); Jewish Kabbalah (Kaplan, 1995; Pinson, 2004); Christian esotericism (Ashcroft-Nowicki, 1990); and Sufism (Khan, 1982). And of course, (what would a mid-life crisis be without it), a 1998 Triumph Thunderbird 900 motorbike. Simultaneously, I educated myself in transpersonal psychology (the psychology that not a single professor or textbook mentioned during my ten years studying for my BA, MA or PhD in psychology), including the experience and sciences of lucid dreaming, out-of-body experiences (OBEs), and near-death experiences (NDEs), with a focus on how to induce the first two while avoiding the latter.

COSMIC CONSCIOUSNESS

"Master Lu Tzu said: That which exists through itself is called Meaning (*Tao*) . . . To-day I will be your guide and will first reveal to you the secret of the Golden Flower of the Great *One* . . . The

Golden Flower is the Light. What colour has the Light? One uses the Golden Flower as an image. It is the true power of the transcendent Great *One* . . . Therefore you only have to make the Light circulate: that is the deepest and most wonderful secret. The Light is easy to move, but difficulty to fix. If it is allowed to go long enough in a circle, then it crystallizes itself: that is the natural spirit-body. This crystallized spirit is formed beyond the nine Heavens. It is the condition of which it is said in the Book of the Seal of the Heart: Silently in the morning thou fliest upward."

Master Lu Tzu

(in Wilhelm, 1950, pp. 23-25)

"After having gathered the macrocosmic alchemical agent and circulated it through the three gates of the backbone, all psychic centers (and channels) are cleared of obstructions so that the two vitalities (of nature and life) which have now developed fully, can move freely by themselves, ascending and descending endlessly; this is how the two vitalities help produce the (immortal) foetus."

Taoist Master Chao Pi Ch'en

(in Luk, 1984/1970, p. 149)

"The individual consciousness is specially related to the body. The organs of the body are in some degree its organs. But the whole body is only as one organ of the Cosmic Consciousness. To attain this latter one must have the power of knowing one's self separate from the body – of passing into a state of ecstasy, in fact. Without this the Cosmic Consciousness cannot be experienced."

Edward Carpenter

(1892, p. 153; in Bucke, 2009/1901, p. 243)

Monday, October 8, 2007, probably started out like any other day (sunrise, coffee, etc.) and proceeded in kind. That evening I went out to a movie, and caught a bite to eat at Panera. I had a mozzarella and tomato sandwich. My partner in crime, who knew that I had been meditating pretty regularly, asked me what my goal was, and I might have said something silly like "enlightenment." Then they asked how long I thought that would take. I had never really thought about it in those terms, but I realized it would take as long as it would take and, to be on the conservative side, I said maybe 30 more years. I think we saw an action movie.

That night, at around midnight, I decided to meditate in bed before sleep. The previous week, a client (who is now a Tai Chi master) with whom sessions had come to integrate CBT and meditation in what I was then calling "Psychotherapy-Meditation Integration" had taught me the Taoist Microcosmic Orbit (M.O.). I lay perfectly still on my back, and began doing the M.O., feeling the vital energy travel back to the base of the spine on the inhale and, still on the inhale moving up the spine to the back of the head and up to the crown. Then on the exhale, I moved the energy down the chakras on the front of the head and body, including the spleen which isn't usually used but of which I was aware from a book by Leadbeater (The Chakras). I continued for about 30 minutes, nothing happened, and I went to sleep.

I unintentionally awoke at 5:00, decided to try again, and again began the M.O., but this time I was determined. In effect, I was frustrated with what I saw as a lack of "progress" after three years of fairly intensive Zen meditation practice and, though it had been nearly a year, I began feeling a wave of grief over my father's death. I decided to "throw in everything but the kitchen sink" during this meditation. So again, I lay perfectly still on my back, and while circulating the energy (chi, prana), I also mentally used the Ham Sa mantra, mentally saying Ham on the inhale and Sa on the exhale as I imagined the breath leaving the body through the nose with the breath then extending to about 12 inches outside of the body, as per either Swami Lakshmanjoo or Paramahansa Yogananda – the teachings and memories merge into each other after a while. But I also at times contemplated my koans, "Who Am I," "What Am I," "What is the Object Corresponding with I," given to me by my Zen Master, with my memory of that Dokusan meeting including our flying around the room in Dharma Battle. But, as a good patriot (the kitchen sink analogy goes back to contributing all kitchen metals to the war effort – sinks at the time were made of porcelaine), I also did some self-enquiry as instructed by Ramana Maharshi (modifying it, which is not recommended by Ramana Maharshi, to correspond with the rhythm of the microcosmic breath, contemplating "I" on the inhale and "Am" on the exhale, or vice versa). Finally, as I was feeling pretty desperate, I cried out to God, pleading to just let me have a glimpse of Reality, as I knew there was more to see and I was going to persist until it was shown to me, so why not NOW? I continued this makeshift meditation for about a half an hour, once again acknowledged that nothing was happening, and turned my head to the right side, cheek on the pillow, to go to sleep continuing to keep the rest of my body perfectly still. I cleared my mind and allowed a small amount of awareness to remain observant of consciousness as it transitioned from wakefulness to sleep.

Suddenly, I felt a strong sensation at the base of my spine, heard a roaring noise, and felt an enormous energy rising upwards through the spine. There was a sense that this rising energy was my own consciousness. "I" rose up the spine, to the back of the head, then shot down to the area of the heart, and then rose to the top of the head. Then I was spinning up through a dark grayish tunnel, or the tunnel was spinning around me as I rose, still hearing the thunderous noise. I recalled the out-of-body experience I had begun to have as a teenager, when fear caused me to return, and this time I told myself to remain calm and continue flying upward.

I continued rising through the spinning vortex until, again suddenly, everything became still and silent and I was suspended in space, surrounded by its blackness speckled with stars, at a distance, all around me. Then I heard what sounded like music, but it was more of a continuous multitonal harmony, seemingly emanating from the stars. I noticed that in front of me at a short distance was what I sensed to be a woman in a white gown, with her back to me. I somehow telepathically communicated with her, asking if I could fly. I sensed permission, and so I flew through space, at times diving down to the earth, looking carefully at the works of nature, such as a blade of grass. At one point I dove down through my head into my own body, descending to the base of the spine and rising back up and back into space, this time with no thundering or fear. I asked the gowned lady if I could fly to Jupiter, sensed permission, and tried to do so, however giving up when I realized that I didn't really know what Jupiter looked like. I asked if I could see Jesus, but didn't find him either. Then I found myself entering a grayish cloud, sensed that it was evil, and turned around deciding I wasn't strong enough to confront it. After a while, I decided I had had enough, and decided to return. I then felt myself melting down into my head, like liquid metal, opened my eyes and I was back in the bedroom. The clock said it was 7:30. I had been "gone" for 2 hours.

Chapter 33 - Up, Up and Away: Out-of-Body Experiences (OBEs)

It took me a moment to get my bearings, after which I got out of bed and walked around a little wondering "what was that? Was that 'It'?" I picked up the last book I had been reading, *Kashmir Shaivism: The Secret Supreme*" by Swami Lakshmanjoo, and opened to where I had left off, which apparently had been the poem with which I began this chapter. This poem was at the end of a chapter entitled *The Seven States of Turya* (the "Fourth" state, after waking, dreaming and dreamless sleep). Lakshmanjoo (2003) explains that:

> "The practical theory of the seven states of *turya*, also known as the seven states of *ananda* (bliss), which I will now explain to you, was taught to the great Saivite philosopher Abhinavagupta by his master Sambhunatha.
>
> Between the three states of the individual subjective body, waking, dreaming, and deep sleep, there is a gap. This gap is the junction between the waking and dreaming state . . . This junction is actually the fourth state, *turya*. This *turya*, however, cannot be experienced by focusing on it because, whenever you gaze on this junction, waiting for it to happen, it will never happen. You will remain waiting in the waking state. It is when you fall asleep and enter into the dreaming state that you will find it. And yet ordinarily you remain absolutely unaware of the experience of this junction.
>
> The only way to experience this junction is to concentrate on any center of the heart while breathing, while talking, or while moving about. You must concentrate on the center. You should watch the center of any two movements, any two breaths. Concentrate on that junction. After some time, whenever you go to bed to rest, you will automatically enter the dreaming state through that junction. In this case though, you will not enter into the dreaming state. Instead, you will be aware at that point, at that junction. This junction is only a gate, the entrance to *turya*. Your awareness of this junction occurs only by the grace of your previous practice of centering your mind between any two movements or any two breaths. This is the first state of *turya*, called *nijananda* which means 'the bliss of your own Self.'" (pp. 107-108)

Swami Lakshmanjoo then details the progression to the second state of *turya*, called *nirananda* or "devoid of limited bliss," where you enter into the gap and "hear hideous sounds" and see "furious forms" (p. 109) which must be tolerated. This begins the movement "from individuality to universality" (p. 110). This is followed by the state of *parananda* or "the *ananda* [bliss] of breathing" (p. 110). "Here your breathing becomes full of bliss and joy, even though you are experiencing terrible forms and sounds or the reality that your breath is about to stop" (pp. 111-112). Then there is the experience that the "breath is moving round and round" which is the state of *bhrahmananda,* or "that bliss which is all pervading" (p. 111).

> "The only thing the *yogi* must do here is to shed tears of devotion. He must pray for the experience of universal 'I.' After a few moments, when the whirling state of breath becomes very fast, moving ever more quickly, you must stop your breath at once. You must not be afraid. If your master is there, he will tell you at that moment to just stop your breath. When there is the whirling of breath, then there is the possibility that you may start breathing again. At this point, it is in your hand to stop it or to let it go. When it has come to the extreme intensity of whirling, then you should and must stop it at once!
>
> When you stop your breathing, then what happens next is that your breath immediately rushes down the central vein. Your breath is 'sipped' down and you actually hear the sound of sipping. The gate of the central vein (*madhyanadi*) opens at once and your breath reaches down to that place called muladhara, which is near the rectum. This state of *turya* is called *mahananda* which means 'the great bliss.'
>
> After *mahananda,* no effort is required by the aspirant. From this point on, everything is automatic . . .
>
> . . . From the Saiva point of view, from mahananda onwards, you must adopt *bhramavega. Bhramavega* means 'the unknowing force.' Here you have to put your force of devotion, without knowing what is to happen next . . .
>
> . . . Here, breathing takes the form of force (*vega*). It is this *vega* which pierces and penetrates the *muladhara cakra* so that you pass through it.

Chapter 33 - Up, Up and Away: Out-of-Body Experiences (OBEs)

When the penetration of the *muladhara cakra* is complete, then this force rises in another way. It is transformed and becomes full of bliss, full of ecstasy, and full of consciousness. It is divine. You feel what you are actually. This is the rising of *cit kundalini*, which rises from *muladhara cakra* to that place at the top of the skull known as *bhrahmarandhra*. It occupies the whole channel and is just like the blooming of a flower. This state, which is the sixth state of *turya*, is called *cidananda*, which means, 'the bliss of consciousness.'

This force then presses the passage of the skull (*brahmarandhra*), piercing the skull to move from the body out into the universe. This takes place automatically; it is not to be 'done.' And when this brahmarandhra is pierced, then at once you begin to breathe out. You breathe out once for only a second, exhaling from the nostrils. After exhaling, everything is over and you are again in *cidananda* and you again experience and feel the joy of rising, which was already present. This lasts only for a moment and then you breathe out again. When you breathe out, your eyes are open and for a moment you feel that you are outside. You experience the objective world, but in a particular way. Then once again your breathing is finished and your eyes are closed and you feel that you are inside. Then again your eyes are open for a moment, then they close for a moment, and then they are again open for a moment. This is the state of *krama mudra*, where transcendental 'I' consciousness is beginning to be experienced as one with the experience of the objective world.

The establishment of *krama mudra* is called jagadananda, which means universal bliss. This is the seventh and last state of turya. In this state, the experience of Universal Transcendental Being is never lost and the whole of the universe is experienced as one with your own Transcendental 'I' Consciousness.

All of the states of *turya* from *nijananda* to *cidananda* comprise the various phases of *nimilana samadhi*. *Nimilana samadhi* is internal subjective *samadhi*. In your moving through these six states of *turya*, this *samadhi* becomes ever more firm. With the occurrence of *krama mudra, nimilana samadhi* is transformed into *unmilana samadhi*, which then becomes predominant. This is that state of extroverted *samadhi*, where you are experiencing the objective world.

And when *unmilana samadhi* becomes fixed and permanent, this is the state of *jagadananda*." (pp. 111-115)

I believe that this chapter by Swami Lakshmanjoo goes a long way toward explaining what I experienced in the early morning of October 9, 2007. I will once again quote his poem that I placed at the beginning of this chapter as an example of how the poetic language of mystics and sages is actually much more literal than it seems in the absence of personal experience:

"There is a point twixt sleep and waking

Where thou shalt be alert without shaking.

Enter the new world where forms so hideous pass;

They are passing – endure, do not be taken by the dross.

Then the pulls and the pushes about the throttle,

All those shalt thou tolerate.

Close all ingress and egress,

Yawnings there may be;

Shed tears – crave – implore, but thou will not prostrate.

A thrill passes – and that goes down to the bottom;

It riseth, may it bloom forth, that is Bliss.

Blessed Being! Blessed Being!

O greetings be to Thee!"

Swami Lakshmanjoo Brahmachari

(2003, p. 115)

Chapter 33 - Up, Up and Away: Out-of-Body Experiences (OBEs)

From Left: Swami Lakshmanjoo Brahmachari, Eleanor Pauline Noye, and Bhagavan Sri Ramana Maharshi

With regard to the above photograph, on May 26, 2018, I was in Grey Matter bookstore in Hadley, Massachusetts looking for works on Ramana Maharshi's teachings. Thanks to a habit of sorting through piles of old books without legible titles on their spines (I see it as some kind of Cosmic game of "no pain no gain" that God plays with bibliophiles), I stumbled upon a 1948, 4th edition, of the book "Spiritual Instruction: Being Original Instruction of Bhagavan Sri Ramana Maharshi," originally published in 1939 (Ramana Maharshi, 1939/1948).

How To Stop Thinking and Not Get Eaten By A Bear

Chapter 33 - Up, Up and Away: Out-of-Body Experiences (OBEs)

First Edition —1939
Second Edition —1940
Third Edition —1944
Fourth Edition —1948

The Jupiter Press Ltd., Madras.

Bhagavan Sri Ramana Maharshi

From the Compiler's Preface to the Tamil Original

Worshipping in thought, word and deed the Sacred Lotus-Feet of BHAGAVAN SRI RAMANA MAHARSHI, the very Embodiment of the Universal, Eternal *Sat - Chit - Ananda*, I have gathered together this Bunch of Flowers for the benefit of the Foremost among those who seek Liberation and are eagerly sought by even the learned, that they may enjoy the Bliss of their Fragrance and attain Salvation.

Leafing through the book, on the inside of the back cover, I noticed the name plate of a woman who sounded very familiar.

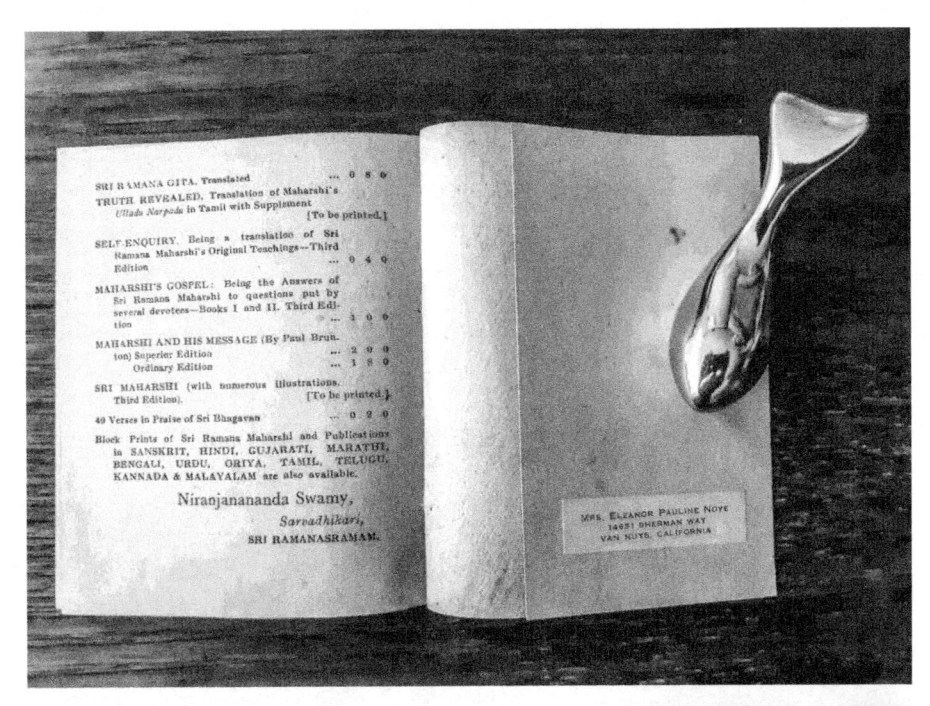

Chapter 33 - Up, Up and Away: Out-of-Body Experiences (OBEs)

I googled her and realized, with some degree of amazement, that she was the woman sitting between Bhagavan Sri Ramana Maharshi and Swami Lakshmanjoo in the above and below photos taken in 1939 or 1940. As I had always been intrigued by these images, often wondering who the Western woman seated between my two spiritual teachers at a spacetime distance was, it was quite surreal to suddenly have a book from her library in my hands.

According to Swami Lakshmanjoo,

> "When I was in my twenties, someone told me of Bhagavan Sri Ramana Maharshi. Then and there I left Kashmir and went to South India. From Madras I took another train for Tiruvannamalai. There I took a cart and reached the blessed Sri Ramanasramam.
>
> As I entered the Hall I saw Bhagavan seated on a sofa with his legs stretched out. I was thrilled with joy on having darshan of Bhagavan, who asked me to sit in front of him. I sat and gazed on the Feet of Bhagavan and entered the blissful state of samadhi.
>
> I felt those golden days were indeed divine. I used to walk on Arunachala Hill with Bhagavan. Bhagavan used to sit on a rock and I would be seated at his Feet. One day I was overjoyed by the nearness of Bhagavan and composed these slokas to offer them to Bhagavan:
>
> 'There are four kinds of body: the gross (sthula), the subtle (sukshma), the causal (karna) and the void (sunya). For Sages (achalanam, lit. those who are motionless) as well (there are four kinds of body). Transcending these (four kinds of body) is the great Hill Arunachala, which is praised as the form of the all-knowing Supreme (lit. the form of the supreme Knower). We worship Sri Ramana, who blissfully abides in His own true nature (swarupa), which is named Arunachala, the foremost among the foremost of hills.'
>
> When these slokas were placed before Bhagavan, He was so pleased that he explained them to the devotees who were seated in the Hall. Some of his devotees took a camera to take a picture of Bhagavan on Arunachala Hill. At that time Bhagavan addressed me: 'Lakshman Joo! Lakshman Joo! Sit here by my side. This man is going to take a picture of us.' I cannot express how Divine were those days of my stay at Sri Ramanasramam and how kind was Bhagavan to me! I have received the copies of 'The Mountain Path' and also the issue of April, 1983 (p.105), in which I am seated at the Divine Feet of Bhagavan Ramana.
>
> Eleanor Pauline Noye, who is seen in the picture of Bhagavan's group, shed tears of joy when I was seated in front of Bhagavan.

Those were golden days for me when I was near Bhagavan, my Divine Lord!" (Lakshmanjoo, 1985, pp. 107-108)

In the words of Ms. Noye, in the Spring of 1940, ten months after visiting India for the first time and meeting Bhagavan,

"I had been planning to leave the Ashram for five months, but each time I thought I was going, something unforeseen presented itself. It was not his will that I should go. Bhagavan says, 'Your plans are of no avail.' I did not want to go but felt I should. My twin sister wrote several times and said there were matters which needed my attention. And she was very ill, although I did not know it at the time, somehow I sensed it. That was probably the reason why I felt I should leave ... I knew this time I would really go. It had been eight months since I returned to the Ashram for the second time! Those last days I spent with the Master were blissful. He was so kind and tender, and when he smiled at me, tears would fill my eyes. I wondered how I could ever leave the place. When the day of parting came, I could not stop crying. In the morning, I walked on the Hill with Bhagavan and some other devotees. Then again in the afternoon when we had our pictures taken with him. As I walked down the Hill with him for the last time, he alone knew what was in my heart. Little monkeys lined up on either side of the hill path. Bhagavan told them to come and say goodbye to me. When we reached the hall, Bhagavan read a few comforting passages from Psalm 139: 7-10. He invited me to have supper with him, even though ladies are not allowed in the dining hall at night. It was blessed joy to have that last meal with him. I shall never forget it. Just before I left, I went to him for his blessing and wept at his feet, as my heart overflowed with adoration and love. He is dearer to me than life itself. May I consecrate my life to him! Then I said good-bye to the devotees in the Ashram, who were invariably kind to me." (Noye, 1946)

Ms. Noye visited Ramanasramam from 1939-1940 (first for 2 months, then leaving to tour India for a short time, and subsequently returning to the Ashram for another 8 months), and traveled there again in 1950. It is possible that it was on the occasion of her 1950 visit that she obtained the 1948 edition of *Spiritual Instruction* that at some point made it from her library in Van Nuys, California, to Hadley, Massachusetts. During her 1950 stay at the Ashram, Bhagavan Sri Ramana Maharshi attained Mahasamadhi (transition), upon which Ms. Noye reflected in 1953:

> "Words cannot express the infinite love and tenderness we experienced during those last days beside him. He seemed to clasp us to his bosom as a mother clasps her child. As we beheld his utter submission, one could not help but think of Lord Jesus before the crucifixion. Sri Bhagavan treated his body as something apart from him. As the body grew weaker his face became more radiant, his eyes shone like two stars. He was ever abiding in the Self, the Sun of Pure Consciousness. He made this remark a few days before he passed away. 'They say I am dying, but I shall be more alive than before.' Now he is all-pervading ... Sri Bhagavan never asked anything for himself but was always looking after the comforts of his devotees, and he did this to the day he passed away. He insisted upon giving darshan twice daily and thousands walked past the room where he lay. A brilliant meteor moved slowly across the sky and disappeared over Arunachala, just as Bhagavan was released from his physical form at 8 47 p.m. on the 14th of April 1950 (Tamil month of Chitrai, Krishna Trayodasi), but it was not the end. He has no beginning or end. As the devotees chanted 'Arunachala Siva', the curtain was drawn on one of the greatest souls that ever trod this earth. Sri Bhagavan is indeed a blessing to all mankind. But what tribute can a candle pay to the sun? 'What we best conceive, we fail to speak.' [From the Koran] Needless to say this was the most blessed experience of my life, my stay at the feet of Bhagavan Sri Ramana Maharshi, the Lord of Love and Compassion. May I be worthy of the many blessings and the great Love he has so graciously bestowed upon me!" (Noye, in The Call Divine, August 1953 p. 48, cited in Saranagati, June, 2021, Vol. 15, No. 6, p. 8)

Nearly twelve years after my 2007 experience, while reading Guru Vachaka Kovai (The Garland of the Guru's Sayings), verses crystallizing Ramana Maharshi's teachings written by his devotee Muruganar who would present each verse to Ramana for verification and any necessary editing, I found Ramana's clarification of the paradoxical experiential (dualistic) nature of the cosmic consciousness following the ascent of the kundalini energy:

Chapter 33 - Up, Up and Away: Out-of-Body Experiences (OBEs)

> "The transcendental *turiya* firmament surges as fullness, as if it is a new experience, in the serene and focused minds of devotees who belong wholly and solely to God. You should know that this *turiya* firmament is alone the rarely attained *loka* which flourishes as the light of *swarupa*." (Muruganar/Ramana, 2008, p. 95, Verse 196)

Ramana however clarifies that the apparent dualistic nature of both the method and result are illusory:

> "The yogi may be definitely aiming at rousing the *kundalini* and sending it up the *sushumna*. The *jnani* may not be having this as his object. But both achieve the same result, that of sending the Life-force up the *sushumna* and severing the *chit-jada-granthi*. *Kundalini* is only another name for *atma* or Self or *sakti*. We talk of it as being inside the body, because we conceive ourselves as limited by this body. But it is in reality both inside and outside, being no other than the Self or the *sakti* of Self . . . Though the *yogi* may have his methods of breath-control, *pranayama*, *mudras*, etc., for this object, the *jnani's* method is only that of enquiry. When by this method the mind is merged in the Self, the Self, its *sakti* or *kundalini*, rises automatically." (Ramana Maharshi, September 14th, 1945; in Mudaliar, 1952/2006, p. 17)

My efforts, non-efforts, karma, grace, etc., may have taken me to the point of *cidananda*. That I did not progress to *jagadananda* was no fault of the teachings, but of my own lack of persistence in following them more rigorously after this one brief glimpse of (what I interpret as) this higher level of Being.

Some things that I learned from this experience are that:

> (1) Meditative techniques can lead to very powerful altered states of consciousness;

> (2) Descriptions in the spiritual literature of out-of-this-world sounding experiences are literal, not figurative;

> (3) Kundalini as an energy and Kundalini rising and "awakenings" are real physiological/energetic or at least subtle physiological/energetic phenomena; and

(4) Altered states of consciousness, including Cosmic Consciousness do not imply "Enlightenment" or "Self-Realization."

I want to emphasize this latter, because a lot of people out there, including myself at times, have practiced meditation with a goal of "enlightenment" or Self-Realization in this lifetime (Jivanmukti). My experience (and the experiences of many others, no doubt) proves that, through the proper attitude and techniques, a person can have a conscious cosmic experience (beyond the one we are all always having, being in and part of the cosmos), temporarily removing at least one layer of the veil that keeps us from higher knowledge and wisdom, *without becoming enlightened*. Because, I assure you me (and I am at no loss for family, friends and acquaintances who will vouch for me), I ain't "Enlightened." I did glow in the dark once (though I'm pretty sure beans and a match may have been involved), and I have been known to put a cup over a spider and bring it outside rather than smooshing it (if it behaves), but that's about as far as it goes.

Over the years, I have mentioned the experience to a number of meditation teachers. My own Zen master assured me that it was merely a hallucination. However as in Buddhism *everything* is a hallucination, I took that to mean that he wasn't necessarily doubting that I flew through the cosmos, but saw it as no more real or unreal than washing the car. I asked some other meditation teachers about it, but again didn't come away with any additional understanding. At one point in my googling, I discovered that in 2007, the Islamic "Night of Power," *Lailatul-Qadr*, fell on October 8th:

> "The night is not comparable to any others in view of Muslims ... and according to a tradition, the blessings due to the acts of worship during this night cannot be equaled even by worshipping throughout an entire lifetime. The reward of acts of worship done in this one single night is more than the reward of a thousand months of worship ..." (Quadr Night, 2022)

The most informative interpretation and advice regarding the incident was from John White, an expert on the kundalini phenomenon, who in 1972 worked with Apollo 14 astronaut Edgar Mitchell (who I think most of us can agree *did* fly through the cosmos) to begin the Institute of Noetic Sciences, "a research organization founded by Dr. Mitchell to study the human potential for personal and planetary transformation."

Chapter 33 - Up, Up and Away: Out-of-Body Experiences (OBEs)

(Photo courtesy of your tax dollars at work at https://history.nasa.gov/alsj/a14/AS14-64-9088HR.jpg ; My detailing of photo to reveal Dome City, a little known lunar getaway for those in the know, hidden for decades right under our noses by the inexplicably overexposed version of this photo of Ed that we all grew up with.)

Dr. Mitchell related his own cosmic consciousness experience as follows:

> "You develop an instant global consciousness, a people orientation, an intense dissatisfaction with the state of the world, and a compulsion to do something about it. From out there on the moon, international politics look so petty. You want to grab a politician by the scruff of the neck and drag him a quarter of a million miles out and say, 'Look at that, you son of a b!#@$'" (Mitchell, 2022. My censorship).

John's 1979 book *Kundalini, Evolution and Enlightenment* includes essays by experts in the phenomenon regarding what Kundalini is, relevant scientific research, and its relationship to the occult. John explained that my experience of floating in the cosmos was that of "consciousness without a form," corresponding to the state of "Nirvikalpa samadhi." He said that this is a sixth-stage phenomena, higher than fifth-stage "Savikalpa samadhi" (samadhi with form) and lower than seventh-stage "Sahaja samadhi" (open-eyes samadhi, knowing "I Am That" while fully engaged in bodily pursuits – which, as an aside, appears to correspond with the 10th oxherding picture, the healed healer healing – my interpretation – see Johnson, 1982). He felt that the task at the sixth stage is learning to function in the body, while realizing that neither the body nor the physical universe are Ultimate, whereas the seventh-stage conclusion to the Kundalini process is awareness of the "pre-luminous void," a state in which God is resting before deciding to emanate part of [Itself] to create the universe. He suggested that a wise course of action once back in normal consciousness after the profound realization of one's divine state in Nirvikalpa samadhi may well be to move back down a level and clean up one's act. Accordingly, the mantra that he teaches is "Thy will be done, show me the way," shortened to "thine" mentally voiced on the outbreath. John is currently working on a book entitled *Enlightenment 101: A Guide to God-Realization and Higher Human Culture* (the Introduction has been published as White, 2015). He believes

> "We often think that the enlightened ones are somehow special, different from us, with a state of mind that is unattainable to an ordinary person. And yet, each human being has an equal opportunity to attain wisdom, happiness, and enlightenment by cultivating a correct motivation—a sincere aspiration to benefit all sentient beings—and engaging in diligent practice." (White, 2021)

When I looked further into the three states of consciousness that he distinguished, I found an explanation by Sri Chinmoy:

> "There are three types of samadhi: Savikalpa samadhi, Nirvikalpa samadhi and Sahaja samadhi. In Savikalpa samadhi there can be thoughts inside the trance, but the trance will not be disturbed or perturbed. The thoughts are like children playing in a room when the father is deeply absorbed in his studies. The children are playing, but they do not disturb him. So in Savikalpa samadhi there can be a

Chapter 33 - Up, Up and Away: Out-of-Body Experiences (OBEs)

turbulence of thoughts and ideas, but the divine trance that the seeker is enjoying will not be affected.

In Nirvikalpa samadhi there is no thought, no idea, nothing whatsoever. All is tranquility, or you can say tranquility's flood. Here nature's dance comes to an end. The restless activity of human nature cannot play its role. There is no thought, no idea, no form, only the transcendental Silence and boundless Peace, Light and Delight. In this expanse of infinite Peace, Light and Delight, there exist only the seeker and his Beloved Supreme, who have become one.

Then comes a samadhi known as Sahaja samadhi. In this samadhi, after having attained the highest realm of consciousness, one can remain on earth and enter into multifarious activities while maintaining his highest realisation. It is as if one is sitting quietly inside a jet plane which is flying at a speed of seven-hundred miles per hour, but one does not notice any motion at all. In Sahaja samadhi one maintains the highest transcendental consciousness within and, at the same time, throws himself into the world's activities in order to transform humanity and free humanity from ignorance. This samadhi is for those who have reached the Highest and whom the Highest Absolute Supreme wants to manifest Himself in and through." (Chinmoy, 1975)

It is of course possible that, in my own unenlightened state, not only did appearing in space have nothing to do with enlightenment, but that the whole experience was merely a wake-initiated lucid dream (WILD), out-of-body experience (OBE) or even near-death experience (NDE), with content borrowed by unconscious memories of the chapter by Lakshmanjoo which I had probably read a day or two prior to the experience. However, the Buddhists and Hindus say the same thing about our *current* waking experience, that it is merely a dream. And yet it seems pretty real, doesn't it? So what is it – are our current experiences and my OBE "real"? Are our current experiences and my OBE "dreams," "hallucinations"? It is a fact that my self-aware, conscious experience of leaving my body, being in the cosmos and melting back into my body were just as *subjectively* real as my experience of typing these words. Could this mean that people such as myself who have taught ourselves to have OBEs have made ourselves psychotic? As a psychologist who has researched the distinctions between hallucinations in psychosis and subjective experiences in lucid dreams, OBEs, and NDEs, I can assure you that psychosis is as hard to turn *off* as these altered states of consciousness are to turn *on* (at least using psychological and spiritual means. I imagine that people who take hallucinogenic drugs may have similar experiences with less preparation, but even there, I don't think they can just decide "I'm going to stop hallucinating now" until the chemical effect has run its course).

The explanation that makes the most sense (from a scientific materialist perspective) is that whether we are awake, dreaming or in the midst of an OBE or NDE, we are experiencing a virtual model of realty constructed by the brain. When we are awake, this model corresponds, in part, with ongoing information received from the environment in the form of sensory stimuli. For example, a pen is on the table, light bounces off the pen and enters my eye, and a series of electrochemical events occur by which my brain neuropsychologically creates and projects to my awareness the image of a pen which then combines with memories of similar looking things associated with the word and meaning of "pen." At that point I see a pen. Although there *is* a pen out there in the "real" world, I am not really experiencing *that* pen, I am experiencing the pen in my brain. In a sense, "I" am seeing my brain. And in a more profound sense, since "seeing" is also a function of *my* brain, which in a scientific materialistic sense is also "I," then whatever I am perceiving, and whatever I am doing, is really "I" "Iing" "I." And in the *most* profound sense of God's omnipresence, in which God is in everything and everything is in God, whatever we do, and whatever anything does, is really God God-ing God, consistent with Rabbi David Cooper's (1997) teaching that "God is a Verb." When we are dreaming (lucid or not) or having an OBE or NDE, this virtual model is similarly constructed from memories of past sensory information. Furthermore, when we are *lucid* dreaming, awake, OBEing or NDEing, we are *self-aware* and immersed in a brain-generated environment characterized by *multisensory realism*.

Now, psychosis also involves a brain-generated environment characterized by self-awareness and multisensory realism. The differences between psychosis and the waking, lucid dream, OBE and NDE states are that, by contrast with these other four states, in psychosis,

(1) there is no *control* over when multisensory realism corresponds with and doesn't correspond with current external reality (other than intentionally *not* taking medications that reduce involuntary non-referential multisensory realism, clinically known as "hallucinations"), and

(2) there is little to no *insight* into whether multisensory realism corresponds with current external reality.

For example, someone with psychosis may see somebody sitting at the dinner table who isn't really there, think they are really there (lack of insight), and not be able to stop seeing them (lack of control). By contrast, someone whose body is asleep in bed may be having an OBE and seeing someone sitting at a dinner table who isn't really there (as even "there" isn't really there), but they *know* (have *insight* into the fact that) their body is sleeping, that they are in an OBE, that "there is no there there" (Stein, 1937), and that neither the person nor the environment are physically present. They not only will easily be able to wake up or simply make the person disappear (*control*), but will need to be quite skilled at employing various devices to keep the experience stable for risk of suddenly waking up in their bed. Show me someone with "psychosis" who knows their hallucinations are distinct from consensual reality (reality as agreed upon by others), and can stop them at any time, and I'll show you someone who is *not psychotic*.

One may argue that not all psychosis involves nonconsensual multisensory realism (hallucinations), that incorrect beliefs (delusions) too constitute psychosis, and that believing one's experiences in dreams, OBEs or NDEs to correspond with realities beyond the imagination is delusional and thus psychotic. I would only suggest that a lot of people believe in things with which they have had way less realistic multisensory experience (e.g., the Big Guy in the Sky) than lucid dreamers, OBEers and NDEers who believe their experiences to be more than dreams; and further, although in most areas of life who is *considered* delusional (when there is difference of opinion) is usually settled by a show of hands or which TV network has the most obnoxious and self-righteous anchors, Truth cannot be gerrymandered.

SOME OBE HISTORY

There is a lot of literature out there on OBE history, theory, research and practice. Brazilian parapsychologist, physician and dentist Waldo Vieira's 1248 page *Projectiology* (2002)(Yes, I found Waldo) is probably the best single historical reference. Alvarado (1989) presents a history of the study of OBEs in the 19th and 20th centuries, beginning in the mid-1800s with the concept of "projection" of a "'double' or subtle body" (p. 28).

Our old friend G.M. Stratton, in addition to designing the first augmented reality device in 1896 and using it to conduct "perhaps the most famous experiment in the whole of experimental psychology" in the words of cognitive psychologist Richard Gregory, also constructed the first device for the experimental induction of out of body experiences in the waking state. His rationale for the experiment was that

> "The more recent investigating concerning touch and sight seems to indicate that the place in which any part of the body is persistently seen influences the localisation of the dermal and kindred sensations arising from that part. If one were to see his feet, for instance, in some direction different from their present visual position, he would in the end refer thither their kinaesthetic impressions also. This much, it seems to me, was implied in the results of my experiments on inverted vision, reported not long ago." (Stratton, 1899)

He wore a horizontal mirror over his head that reflected the image of his body as seen from above into a diagonal mirror in front of his face. He then wore the contraption for 3 days to see what would happen.

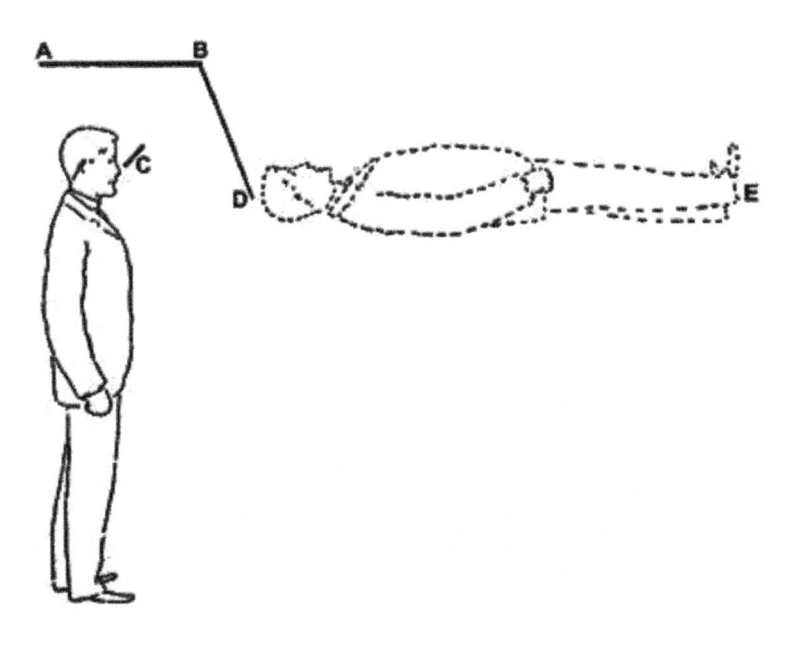

Chapter 33 - Up, Up and Away: Out-of-Body Experiences (OBEs)

What happened was that

> "He found the senses adapted in a similar way over three days. His interpretation was that we build up an association between sight and touch by associational learning over a period of time (Wade, 2000). During certain periods, the disconnect between vision and touch made him feel as if his body was not where his touch and proprioceptive feeling told him it was. This out-of-body experience, caused by an altered but normal sensory perception, vanished when he attended to the issue critically, focusing on the disconnect (Wade, 2009)." (George M. Stratton, 2021)

It should be noted that while Stratton perceived himself as being outside of his physical body, his was in fact an augmented reality experience rather than an out-of-body experience in the sense in which the term is usually used. A true out-of-body experience is an Internally Generated Offline Perceptual Experience (IGOPE), a metachoric state, that is, an altered state of consciousness in which one perceives oneself in an organic virtual environment created entirely by one's brain without immediate spaciotemporal stimulation from the body's physical environment. By contrast, Stratton had induced an Externally Generated Offline Perceptual Experience (EGOPE), with the perceived environment being an alteration of the body's immediate temporospatial environment constructed on the basis of simultaneous stimulation from that environment (thus its categorization as augmented reality).

SYLVAN MULDOON

An early book of a "How to Leave Your Body" nature (and you thought "How to Stop Thinking" was *out there*) was written by Sylvan Muldoon along with Hereward Carrington (they sure don't make names like they used to . . .) in 1929 and entitled *The Projection of the Astral Body*.

Chapter 33 - Up, Up and Away: Out-of-Body Experiences (OBEs)

Muldoon writes:

"When my first out-of-body experience occurred I was but twelve – so young and immature in mind that I did not realize the magnitude. The occurrences came about involuntarily and repeated themselves frequently, until I became so accustomed to them that, as a matter of fact, I soon regarded them as nothing extraordinary and seldom mentioned them even to members of my own family, to say nothing of keeping a record of them, although I had been urged to do so by many interested persons.

I had been told, by persons professing to know, that conscious projection of the astral body was nothing unusual, and that many psychics could produce it at will. I, too, wanted to be able to produce it at will, and I admit that I was envious of those who (I had heard) could do so. So I began a search for some one who could produce the phenomenon voluntarily. But my search proved fruitless, and eventually I concluded that I could not find that 'some one.' Thus I began to experiment with the phenomenon myself, and in this book you will find the results of my experiments.

Although we are living in the twentieth century we still have with us the intolerance of the Middle Ages, and I am not optimistic enough to believe that a great many will read without prejudice what I have to say. I have written this work with the idea of giving the results of my findings to other students of the occult. Unfortunately many occultists are of the belief that what is claimed to be conscious astral projection is nothing more nor less than a dream.

I am well aware of the fact that one must first experience conscious astral projection before he can believe in it, and I confess that I should not accept it as true myself, perhaps, had I not experienced it and *know* it to be true. The sceptic says, 'I want the proof, the objective proof, then I will believe it!'

And the projector replies, 'You cannot have objective proof. You must *experience* it, then you will have the proof.'" (1929, p. v)

Robert Monroe (2001/1971), who also began having OBEs spontaneously, albeit as an adult, and went on to conduct personal experiments, places a similar emphasis on the importance of personal experience:

> "Throughout this writing, I have made many references to one evident fact: the only possible way for an individual to appreciate the reality of this Second Body and existence within it is to experience it himself. Obviously, if this were an easy task, it would now be commonplace. I suspect that only an innate curiosity will enable people to overcome the obstacles in the path of this achievement. Although there are many cases of existence experienced apart from the physical body, they have for the most part - at least in the Western world - been of a spontaneous, onetime nature, occurring during moments of stress or physical disability. We are speaking of something entirely different, which can be objectively investigated. The experimenter will want to proceed in a manner that will produce consistent results, perhaps not every time, but often enough to validate the evidence to his own satisfaction. I believe that anyone can experience existence in a Second Body if the desire is great enough. Whether or not anyone should is beyond the scope of my judgment." (p. 203)

Monroe eventually founded an institute for the study and teaching of OBEs using various patterns of auditory binaural beats (playing a different tone, or combination of tones, in each ear) to trigger brainwave patterns that his research found conducive to inducing OBEs with various content. His institute has also done work with the government on the military use of remote viewing (no goats were harmed in the making of the preceding sentence. Though some may have been puzzled).

THERAPEUTIC OBE-ING

Just as lucid dreams can provide a virtual environment for behavioral exposure therapy, OBEs also have therapeutic potential (you knew this was coming didn't you: Out of Body Exposure Therapy, OBET. You heard it here first). One possible limitation is that, at least in my own experience (personal, not clinical), environments in OBEs are less subject to both waking incubation (via imaginal rehearsal during the day or during wakeful moments in bed) and conscious manipulation than those of lucid dreams. However, OBEs, like dream yoga, have been proposed as a way of preparing oneself for life after death:

> "The out-of-body experience, in which consciousness is perceived as existing independently of the physical body, may lead to more

positive attitudes regarding death (Alvarado, 2000) and therefore has special relevance for work with hospice patients. An intervention that bridges the three or four functional psychologies is the Going Home program (Monroe Products, 2005) created by Elisabeth Kubler-Ross, Charles T. Tart and Robert A. Monroe for individuals with terminal illness and their families. Here, portable audio-administered brainwave manipulation technology (binaural beats and guided imagery listened to with headphones) is used to induce OBEs during which the individual can get acquainted in advance with the after-death environment (or that which is perceived as such), thereby reducing fear of dying and instilling hope. The effects of this program and other OBE-induction strategies on optimizing the cognitive, emotional, behavioral and physiological adaptation of this important population could be studied and compared with standard hospice care." (Densei & Lam, 2010, p. 105)

WILD AND OBE INDUCTION TECHNIQUES

As mentioned previously, WILDs (wake-initiated lucid dreams) are similar to WIOBES, or Wake-Initiated OBEs, as both are entered into from the waking state. As such, techniques for inducing WILDs may have relevance for the induction of OBEs.

LaBerge's "Falling Asleep Consciously"

LaBerge (1990) defines WILDS as "falling asleep consciously" (p. 94):

> "The basic idea has many variations. While falling asleep, you can focus on hypnagogic (sleep onset) imagery, deliberate visualizations, your breath or heartbeat, the sensations in your body, your sense of self, and so on. If you keep the mind sufficiently active while the tendency to enter REM sleep is strong, you feel your body fall asleep, but *you*, that is to say, your consciousness, remains awake. The next thing you know, you will find yourself in the dream world, fully lucid." (pp. 94-95)

LaBerge has found that WILDs are less frequent than DILDs, and that WILDs happen later in the sleep cycle when "the tendency to enter REM sleep is strong" (p. 95). Use of the WBTB technique mentioned in the previous chapter can promote WILDs due to the REM rebound effect (depriving oneself of REM sleep for 30 minutes creates "REM pressure," causing one to enter quickly into REM sleep at the end of the sleep interruption interval).

LaBerge (1990) presents detailed WILD induction techniques involving attention to hypnagogic imagery, the "Dream Lotus and Flame Technique" taught to him by Tibetan Master Tarthang Tulku in 1970, attention on mental tasks such as counting yourself to sleep, and attention on either the sense of having a body, or of not having a body. He notes that

> "If you focus on your body while falling asleep, you will sometimes notice a condition in which it seems to undergo extreme distortions, or begins to shake with mysterious vibrations, or becomes completely paralyzed. All of these unusual bodily states are related to the process of sleep onset and particularly REM sleep onset." (p. 108)

Now, I find this really interesting, and so might you if you were paying attention to what Swami Lakshmanjoo said about what one experiences prior to a kundalini awakening:

> "There is a point twixt sleep and waking
>
> Where thou shalt be alert without shaking.
>
> Enter the new world where forms so hideous pass;
>
> They are passing – endure, do not be taken by the dross.
>
> Then the pulls and the pushes about the throttle,
>
> All those shalt thou tolerate.
>
> Close all ingress and egress,
>
> Yawnings there may be;
>
> Shed tears – crave – implore, but thou will not prostrate.
>
> A thrill passes – and that goes down to the bottom;
>
> It riseth, may it bloom forth, that is Bliss.
>
> Blessed Being! Blessed Being!
>
> O greetings be to Thee!"
>
> **Swami Lakshmanjoo Brahmachari (2003, p. 115)**

Chapter 33 - Up, Up and Away: Out-of-Body Experiences (OBEs)

Swami Lakshmanjoo doesn't use the term "vibration" here, but he may be alluding to such when he speaks of "the pulls and the pushes about the throttle." In fact, the "vibratory" or "vibrational" state is usually the precursor of OBEs, and holds a central place in the OBE-induction teachings of Robert Monroe (of the Monroe Institute) and Waldo Vieira (of the International Academy of Consciousness; IAC), both which run prominent OBE research and training programs.

You may be wondering why, if vibrations and sleep paralysis precede REM, you have never (or rarely) experienced them. This is because by the time they usually happen, you have already lost self-awareness and are asleep. Even if you've experienced a DILD, you become self-aware *after* the dream has already commenced, and thus *after* the termination of the vibrational state. Though your physical body is in a state of sleep paralysis during a DILD, you don't notice it because you are at that point aware of your dream body and not of your physical body.

It is not really accurate to say that the vibrational state *causes* WILDS or OBEs, but rather that maintaining self-awareness as the brain transitions from waking to REM provides the opportunity *both* to be aware of the vibrational state that precedes REM *and* to carry this self-awareness into the subsequent dream state.

Through personal experience consistent with instruction that I have received both from Monroe Institute readings and products and from instruction at the IACs New York office, I can confidently state that the single most important determinant of entering the vibrational state is *staying perfectly still* throughout whatever induction practice you perform, and remaining still until you perceive yourself separating from the body. Interestingly, "Don't Move!" is also something you grow accustomed to hearing on the cushion during Zen sits.

Tholey's "Techniques for Retaining Lucidity"

Tholey (1983) presents three types of "techniques for retaining lucidity" as methods of retaining self-awareness (lucidity) during the waking to dreaming transition, including "falling asleep on hypnagogic images, the body, or merely the thinking ego" (p. 83). He presents a number of techniques focusing on the body, including

"The Dual-Body Technique": Here, one

> "imagine[s] intensively that one has a second, moveable body with which one can float out of, fall out of (through the bed), twist out of, or in some other fashion detach oneself from the immobile body. After separation from the immobile body, the second body, which is initially 'airy' or 'etherial,' solidifies until it appears to be completely identical to the usual waking body." (p. 84)

Tholey considers this technique "comparable to so-called astral projection" as by using it "it is possible to produce a variety of out-of-the-body experiences" (p. 83). Clear in his opinion on the matter,

> "In contrast to esoterical views we should emphasize that we are discussing dream-like experiences and not real processes. Contrary to the assumptions of the occultists, it is impossible to detach oneself from the physical organism." (pp. 83-84)

It surprises me that someone as apparently open minded as Tholey would take such a firm stance on the absence of evidence being evidence of absence, but to each his own. It's one thing to have a personal belief that is *completely unsupported by any evidence whatsoever*, but to state it as a *fact* seems either delusional or unethical (thus my affinity for words like *seems, maybe, might, possible, potentially,* etc. It's called *comfortable* with *uncertainty*, though I suppose it could also be criticized as a *discomfort* with *certainty*).

"The One Body Technique": Consistent with his belief that there is not really a second body, in this technique

> "one merely makes the immobile body (appear to be) moveable again. The subject attempts to imagine that he is in a different situation or in a different place from the physical body, which is sleeping in bed. It is relatively easy to bring about this experience because one receives in this state hardly any sensory information concerning the physical world." (p. 84)

It will be noted that the reason that one doesn't receive sensory information here is because one is remaining so still that the brain habituates to the monotony of whatever sensations are being received from the immobile body.

"The Image Body Technique": Here, one concentrates both on the body and on visual images, imagining that "his own body is light and can move freely." At that point "It seems to glide into the dream scenery or even to drive or ride into it, if an appropriate vehicle is imagined" (p. 84). This can be facilitated by imagining scenery in which things are moving in a uniform manner, such as a herd of animals or flock of birds, which movement can then be transferred to the perceived dream body.

Tholey's next two techniques really amount to "no body" techniques, realizing that there is not really a body in the dream but merely a point of awareness that itself can see things from differing perspectives.

"The Ego-Point Technique": Here,

> "it is necessary to concentrate while falling asleep on the thought that the body will soon no longer be perceived. As soon as this state is reached, it is possible to float freely as an ego-point in space which seems to be identical with the room in which one went to sleep." (p. 85)

"The Image-Ego-Point-Technique":

> "This technique differs from the preceding one only in that the subject also concentrates on the images seen while falling asleep. If a visual dream scenery has become established, then it is possible to travel into this scenery. The ego-point can under certain circumstances enter into the body of another dream figure and take over its 'motor system.'" (p. 85)

Robert Monroe's Binaural Beats

Over the years, the Monroe Institute has developed a variety of programs for learning to have OBEs. These include residential programs lasting a weekend or longer, online programs, and audio sets using binaural beats to trigger brainwave patterns conducive to OBEs in specific nonphysical environments. Binaural beats (Dove, 1839; Oster, 1973) involve playing a tone of one frequency in one ear (e.g., 100 Hz), and a tone of another frequency in the other ear (e.g., 104 Hz) in order to induce an increase in the power of brainwaves corresponding with the *difference* between the two frequencies. In this example, the resultant frequency would be 4 Hz, which corresponds with a brainwave in the Theta range, associated with a trance-like state. Multiple pairs can be layered on top of one another, to strengthen more than one brainwave frequency simultaneously, and combinations of frequencies can be phased in and out to gradually reduce one or a combination of frequencies while strengthening others, and vice versa. If you're of the nerdic temperament, you can create and experiment with your own sophisticated binaural beat audios using DIY software such as SBaGeN (2019), but unless you really know what you are doing I would stick to the audios created professionally, and based on OBE research, such as those offered by The Monroe Institute (MonroeInstitute.org).

Robert Bruce's Astral Dynamics

Bruce is an Australian mystic who has developed a variety of techniques for inducing OBEs, with an emphasis on chakras, energy work and awakening the Kundalini. His approach, like Robert Monroe's, assumes the reality of the beings and environments encountered in lucid dreams and OBEs. In his book *Astral Dynamics* (Bruce, 2009), he presents preliminary techniques to increase awareness of the "energy body" or "pure-energetic aspect of the etheric body" (p. 107). He emphasizes "nonvisual imaging" which he describes as "tactile imaging, based on the active use of the sense of touch and feel and body awareness" (p. 109), and "mobile body awareness . . . the ability to focus body awareness on any specific part of the body" (p. 114). These are similar to the manner in which energy is circulated around the microcosmic orbit in Taoist meditation.

From a neurological perspective, both the microcosmic orbit and Bruce's method involve tactile imaginal sensorimotoric behavior without motoric movement of the *physical body*, but which according to subtle energy theory involves movement of the etheric body. To get a feeling for what this involves, you could close your eyes and imagine moving your arms as though you were swimming. But don't just visualize it; try to actually feel your imaginary arms making the movements. If you can't feel anything at first, you will, eventually, with practice. The greater the extent to which you feel your imaginary arms moving when you imagine them moving, the greater the sensorimotor cortex is being stimulated. It is possible that cultivating waking awareness of sensorimotor cortex activation in the absence of movement increases the likelihood of such awareness being triggered in dreams when the sensorimotor cortex is likewise stimulated without movement.

Chapter 33 - Up, Up and Away: Out-of-Body Experiences (OBEs)

Bruce's techniques for projecting the etheric body outside of the physical body begin with "relaxation, trance induction and energy-stimulation techniques" (p. 270) followed by various tactile imaging strategies, all done without actually moving the body. These include such exercises as bouncing awareness off the wall, increasing and decreasing body size on the in and out breath, spinning inside of the body, floating away from the body, pulling oneself out of the body by climbing an imaginary rope, using a ladder to climb out of the body, making various movements with the hands or rolling out of the body. You can also use the "point shift" technique in which you use tactile imagination to leave the body and then imagine seeing the room from the perspective of your etheric body now floating or standing at arm's reach from your physical body. You then feel yourself distancing from the physical body.

Bruce advises not to tense up when doing the tactile imagery, remembering that "these are all imaginative body-awareness actions." The goal is always to "trigger the projection reflex" (p. 271). This advice reminds me of an instruction regarding "breathing into the hara" or into the "lower dan tien" in Japanese Zen and Chinese Qigong, respectively, stating that you don't mess with your breathing to try to make it *physically* descend to and arise from the area 2 inches under and behind the navel (as that is not where the lungs are, and would be absurd), but rather to breath normally but diaphragmatically and *imagine* the air descending to and rising back out of that area. Similarly, when one does the microcosmic orbit, although the instruction often states to breathe up the back and down the front of the body, an alternative instruction is to breathe normally and simultaneously guide the chi (or sensation being labeled and interpreted as chi or qi) around the orbit at whatever pace the energy seems to be amenable to moving.

For beginners it may take time to feel the energy at all, and to make your in-breath twiddle its thumbs while you try to feel the energy move all the way up from the base of the spine to the top of the head would not be kind, sustainable or, ultimately, healthy. So maybe on the first in-breath you are able to imagine and feel the energy go from the base of the spine halfway up to the middle of the back. Then you could continue breathing normally as you move the energy further up the back with each in-breath, arriving at the top of the head perhaps after 3 or 4 breaths. Then when it reaches the top of the head, you imagine and feel the energy descending down the front of the face and body, reaching wherever it reaches at the end of each out-breath and continuing down from that point on the next out-breath, and so forth, until it eventually reaches the perineum and then moves back to the base of the spine to begin another ascent and circulation on the next in-breath.

I have a hunch that the operative element of any technique that triggers lucid dreams and OBEs is the extent to which it keeps the sensorimotor cortex stimulated simultaneously with the onset of dreaming, thus triggering the state of "mind awake, body asleep." Bruce's tactile imaging and mobile body awareness are theoretically consistent with this neurological hypothesis.

The Microcosmic Orbit and Kundalini Yoga

If you are interested in cultivating OBEs within a traditional spiritual tradition, instruction in the Microcosmic Orbit is offered by a number of Taoist meditation practitioners such as Mantak Chia, Sharon Smith and Robert Peng. Kundalini Yoga is taught in many yoga studios.

Chapter 34 - *Am I Dead Yet?: Near-Death Experiences (NDEs) and Shared-Death Experiences (SDEs)*

". . . this life is but the childhood of our immortality."

Denis Johnson

(In Tree of Smoke, 2007, p. 394.

Not said by Goethe, despite Internet fake news)

"4. Now, when he is diseased and about to die, those around him enquire, 'Do you recognise me? do you recognise me?' He recognises them as long as he does not depart from his body.

5. When he quits his body he rises upwards with the aid of the rays aforesaid, resounding *Om*. When his mind ceases to act he attains the sun. That is the way to the region *above*. It is open to the learned, but closed to the ignorant.

6. Thereof is the verse: 'There are a hundred and one arteries issuing from the heart; one of them penetrates the crown of the head. The man, who departs this life through that artery secures immortality. The rest *of the arteries* lead to *various* transitions, – they lead to *various* transitions."

Chhándogya Upanishad

(in Mitra, 1862, pp. 137-138)

"William James was one of the strongest exponents of the transmission theory. He described in his book *Human Immortality* (1898) the idea that beyond the 'veil of reality' in this world, and particularly beyond the brain, there is a transcendent reality in which the soul may live. He argued that it is the brain which transmits through it and modifies the beam of consciousness. He pointed out that there is no specific test which will allow us to determine whether the brain creates consciousness or whether it transmits, through its functioning, the beam of consciousness . . . The attraction of transmission theories is that they allow for the concept of survival and personal identity after death."

Fenwick & Fenwick

(1977, pp. 376-377)

"My thesis now is this: that, when we think of the law that thought is a function of the brain, we are not required to think of productive function only; *we are entitled also to consider permissive or transmissive function.* And this the ordinary psycho-physiologist leaves out of his account." (James, 1898, p. 32)

"The brain would be the independent variable, the mind would vary dependently on it. But such dependence on the brain for this natural life would in no wise make immortal life impossible, – it might be quite compatible with supernatural life behind the veil hereafter." (pp. 38-39)

"The theory of production is therefore not a jot more simple or credible in itself than any other conceivable theory. It is only a little more popular. All that one need do, therefore, if the ordinary materialist should challenge one to explain how the brain can be an organ for limiting and determining to a certain form a consciousness elsewhere produced, is to retort with a *tu quoque*, asking him in turn to explain how it can be an organ for producing consciousness out of whole cloth. For polemic purposes, the two theories are thus exactly on a par." (pp. 45-46)

Chapter 34 - Am I Dead Yet?: Near-Death Experiences (NDEs) and Shared-Death Experiences (SDEs)

"In the great orthodox philosophic tradition, the body is treated as an essential condition to the soul's life in this world of sense; but after death, it is said, the soul is set free, and becomes a purely intellectual and non-appetitive being. Kant expresses this idea in terms that come singularly close to those of our transmission-theory. 'The death of the body,' he says, 'may indeed be the end of the sensational use of our mind, but only the beginning of the intellectual use. The body,' he continues, 'would thus not be the cause of our thinking, but merely a condition restrictive thereof, and, although essential to our sensuous and animal consciousness, it may be regarded as an impeder of our spiritual life.'" (pp. 56-57, citing Kant, 1787)

William James
(1898; Human Immortality)

"If, therefore, having assumed (in some non-speculative connection) the nature of the soul to be immaterial and not subject to any corporeal change, we are met by the difficulty that nevertheless experience seems to prove that the exaltation and the derangement of our mental powers are alike in being merely diverse modifications of our organs, we can weaken the force of this proof by postulating that our body may be nothing more than a fundamental appearance which in this our present state (in this life) serves as a condition of our whole faculty of sensibility, and therewith of all our thought, and that separation from the body may therefore be regarded as the end of this sensible employment of our faculty of knowledge and the beginning of its intellectual employment. Thus regarded, the body would not be the cause of thought, but merely a restrictive condition of it, and therefore, while indeed furthering the sensible and animal life, it would because of this very fact have to be considered a hindrance to the pure and spiritual life . . .

. . . we can propound a transcendental hypothesis, namely, that all life is, strictly speaking, intelligible only, is not subject to changes of time, and neither begins in birth nor ends in death; that this life is an appearance only, that is, a sensible representation of the purely spiritual life, and that the whole sensible world is a mere picture which in our present mode of knowledge hovers before us, and like a dream has in itself no objective reality; that if we could intuit ourselves and things as they are we should see ourselves in a world of spiritual beings, our sole and true community with which has not begun through birth and will not cease through bodily death—both birth and death being mere appearances."

Immanuel Kant

(1787, pp. 618-619)

My last moments with my father before he died were surreal. Ever since I had read of the last moments of Zen Master Shunryu Suzuki's death, when he called his chief disciple to his room and they touched foreheads at the moment when Suzuki left the body, I had vowed to do the same if the cancer ever got the best of Dad. However, I underestimated the chaos that ensues when one dies in a hospital. After speaking to him for the last time, as we waited for him to be put under in order to have a breathing tube inserted, shortly after the tube was inserted he stopped breathing and the small room was quickly swarmed by more doctors than I have ever seen in one place at one time. I was pushed further and further back and away from the bedside by the intervening wave of white cloaks and realized that either some serious healthcare or some serious CYA (most likely both) was going on. I tugged on one of the cloaks and asked if I could move up to the bedside, and was told that I couldn't. I asked who could, and he said "only doctors, priests and rabbis." Without thinking, I shouted "I'm a Buddhist priest, let me through" (I wasn't wearing a yarmulke and didn't know at the time that it was spelled with an "r" and an "l," being from New Jersey where we pronounce it "yahmahkah," so I couldn't pretend to be a rabbi, most of whom probably know how to spell yarmulke, even if they're from New Jersey, but I had recently shaved my head in solidarity with my father's Zen hairdo of non-hairdo so I figured I could pass for the Buddhist version), at which point the sea of cloaks parted and I placed my forehead on my father's until his transition was complete and the wave of doctors receded.

Several days later, I had either the most vivid dream of my life or a DOBE (discontinuous OBE). The multisensory realism was palpable, and as

Chapter 34 - Am I Dead Yet?: Near-Death Experiences (NDEs) and Shared-Death Experiences (SDEs)

compared with many subsequent lucid dreams and OBEs, its stability was of an OBE quality, rivaled only by my Kundalini awakening into the cosmos the following year. I was standing in a clearing in a park on a sunny day when I saw what looked like a large white rectangular wing, high up and at a distance. It approached a heavily forested area at the other end of the park, and I realized that it was carrying my father, whose body was underneath it, parallel with the ground and pressed up against the wing along the axis of its flight (i.e., flying head first). It was as though he was hang-gliding on his back. I feared that he didn't know how to land and would crash into the trees (he was a smart guy, but to my knowledge he had never learned to hang-glide on his back), and I telepathically communicated to him to fly toward me to land in the clearing. The wing changed course, flew toward me, and then slowly descended, gently laying my father on the ground, the white wing covering him.

I lifted the wing, which was now a white sheet, and helped my father to his feet. He appeared dazed and stood unsteadily. I saw a group of people in the distance, at what I sensed was a cocktail party attended by his parents and other transitioned relatives. Placing my hands on his shoulders, I turned him in their direction, and he began walking toward them, still somewhat unsteadily. I intuitively remained behind as his form grew smaller in the distance. Then I awoke.

WHAT WAS THAT?

In the car ride to the funeral, I recounted this dream to our family's Cantor, and he told me a story. He said that back in the 1940s or 50s, before the term Near-Death Experience entered popular culture and before everyone knew about "the tunnel" from paperback bestsellers, movies and talk shows, his mother had a medical event and told him that she entered a tunnel similar to those that he now knew of from the media. He emphasized that it was extremely unlikely that his mother could have possibly learned about such a thing from others.

I was already familiar with Moody's (2015/1975) book Life After Life, in which he coined the term "Near-Death Experience" to describe the accounts of 150 interviewees who had been close to death for one reason or another. Moody distilled common features of their reports, "about fifteen separate elements which recur again and again in the mass of narratives that I have collected," with the caveat that no two persons' experiences are likely to be identical. He also presented an "'ideal' or 'complete' experience which embodies all of the common elements, in the order in which it is typical for them to occur" (p. 11):

> "A man is dying and, as he reaches the point of greatest physical distress, he hears himself pronounced dead by his doctor. He begins to hear an uncomfortable noise, a loud ringing or buzzing, and at the same time feels himself moving very rapidly through a long dark tunnel. After this, he suddenly finds himself outside of his own physical body, but still in the immediate physical environment, and he sees his own body from a distance, as though he is a spectator. He watches the resuscitation attempt from this unusual vantage point and is in a state of emotional upheaval.
>
> After a while, he collects himself and becomes more accustomed to his odd condition. He notices that he still has a 'body,' but one of a very different nature and with very different powers from the physical body he has left behind. Soon other things begin to happen. Others come to meet and help him. He glimpses the spirits of relatives and friends who have already died, and a loving, warm spirit of a kind he has never encountered before – a being of light – appears before him. This being asks him a question, nonverbally, to make him evaluate his life and helps him along by showing him a panoramic, instantaneous playback of the major events of his life. At some point he finds himself approaching some sort of barrier or border, apparently representing the limit between earthly life and the next life. Yet, he finds that he must go back to the earth, that the time for his death has not yet come. At this point he resists, for by now he is taken up with his experiences in the afterlife and does not want to return. He is overwhelmed by intense feelings of joy, love, and peace. Despite his attitude, though, he somehow reunites with his physical body and lives.
>
> Later he tries to tell others, but he has trouble doing so. In the first place, he can find no human words adequate to describe these unearthly episodes. He also finds that others scoff, so he stops telling other people. Still, the experience affects his life profoundly, especially his views about death and its relationship to life." (pp. 11-13)

Chapter 34 - Am I Dead Yet?: Near-Death Experiences (NDEs) and Shared-Death Experiences (SDEs)

Both my own Kundalini awakening in the previous chapter and my dream of greeting my father in the Park bore similarities to the above. My OBE shared the elements of noise, a dark tunnel, finding myself out of my body, meeting a being of light (the woman in the white gown) and confronting a barrier (in the form of the grey cloud). That the being did not conduct a life review may have had something to do with my not having died yet and having traveled there voluntarily on a mission of self-knowledge.

The Park dream contained the NDE elements of glimpsing the spirits of relatives who had already died, and intuitively respecting an invisible barrier separating where my father was heading and where I remained standing. Over the years, trying to make sense of it, I came to think of it as a "Vicarious Death Experience." Interestingly, when I tell others about it, they don't scoff, at least not outwardly, and my self-disclosure often prompts them to tell me of their own, or a family member's, anomalous experiences.

ON THE WINGS OF GOD

In the Bible, the image of a wing with pinions (feathers) appears numerous times, sometimes symbolizing the Shekinah, a term that does not appear in the Bible itself but is employed in the Rabbinic literature to signify God or the Divine Presence (Dan, 2006, p. 46). It literally, means "the dwelling" (Kohler & Blau, 2019), and God's feminine attributes (Ginsburgh, 1999). With the exception of the below verses from Deuteronomy and the Hashkiveinu prayer for protection during sleep, these biblical references to wings do indeed refer to the transition between life and death.

In Devarim, Deuteronomy, Chapter 32:

> "10. He found them in a desert land, and in a desolate, howling wasteland. He encompassed them and bestowed understanding upon them; He protected them as the pupil of His eye.
>
> 11. As an eagle awakens its nest, hovering over its fledglings, *it spreads its wings, taking them and carrying them on its pinions.*
>
> 12. [So] the Lord guided them alone, and there was no alien deity with Him."
>
> (Devarim – Deuteronomy - Chapter 32, 2019; italics added)

In the morning prayer for donning the tallis, one hopes that this act, in This World, has effects in the Next:

> "Just as I cover myself with the tallis in This World, so may I merit the rabbinical garb and a beautiful cloak in the World to Come in the Garden of Eden. Through the commandment of tzitzis may my life-force, spirit, soul and prayer be rescued from the external forces. *May the tallis spread its wings over them and rescue them like an eagle rousing his nest, fluttering over his eaglets.*"
>
> (Deuteronomy 32:11, in Schacter & Weinberger, 2003, p. 3; italics added)

And before sleep, "the little death," The Hashkiveinu prayer (Hashkiveinu, n.d.) for protection in the bedtime Shema includes:

> ". . . Cause us to lie down, O God, Lord, in peace and raise us up again, O our King, in life.
>
> O spread thy pavilion of peace over us, and direct us with good counsel from Thy presence, and save us for the sake of Thy name.
>
> O shield us, and remove far from us the foe, pestilence, sword, famine, and sorrow, and *shelter us under the shadow of Thy wings*; for Thou art a merciful and gracious Lord and King, and guard our going forth and coming into life and peace from now and for evermore."
>
> (Night Prayers, 1872, p. 253)

In a Jewish burial,

> "The casket is carried from the hearse to the gravesite by Jewish men, usually by the Chevra Kaddisha, with the decedent's feet facing the front. It is customary that direct descendants of the deceased do not touch or carry the casket.
>
> During the procession, Psalm 91 is recited seven times. Beginning from a short distance from the grave (approximately thirty feet), it is customary to halt the procession every few feet and repeat the Psalm, pausing at certain words in the final verse and reciting again from the top." (Goldstein, 2019a)

Chapter 34 - Am I Dead Yet?: Near-Death Experiences (NDEs) and Shared-Death Experiences (SDEs)

Psalm 91 contains this passage:

> "You who dwell in the shelter of the Most High, who abides in the shadow of the Omnipotent,
>
> I say [to you] of the Lord who is my refuge and my stronghold, my G-d in Whom I trust,
>
> that He will save you from the ensnaring trap, from the destructive pestilence.
>
> *He will cover you with His pinions and you will find refuge under His wings*; His truth is a shield and an armor.
>
> You will not fear the terror of the night, nor the arrow that flies by day,
>
> the pestilence that prowls in the darkness, nor the destruction that ravages at noon.
>
> A thousand may fall, at your [left] side, and ten thousand at your right, but it shall not reach you.
>
> You need only look with your eyes, and you will see the retribution of the wicked.
>
> Because you [have said,] 'The Lord is my shelter,' and you have made the Most High your haven,
>
> no evil will befall you, no plague will come near your tent.
>
> . . . For He will instruct His angels in your behalf, to guard you in all your ways."
>
> (Goldstein, 2019a; italics added)

In the Kel Maleh Rachamim, the Prayer for the Soul of the Departed, one entrusts the care of their loved one to God, with these words:

> "O G-d, full of compassion, Who dwells on high, *grant true rest upon the wings of the Shechinah* (*Divine Presence*) in the exalted spheres of the holy and pure, who shine as the resplendence of the firmament, to the soul of
>
> (mention his Hebrew name and that of his father)

who has gone to his [supernal] world, for charity has been donated in remembrance of his soul; may his place of rest be in Gan Eden. Therefore, *may the All-Merciful One shelter him with the cover of His wings forever,* and bind his soul in the bond of life. The Lord is his heritage; may he rest in his resting-place in peace; and let us say: Amen."

(Goldstein, 2019b; italics added)

And in the Prayer for Mourners, the following is recited:

"O how great is Thy goodness which Thou hast wrought for them that trust in Thee before the sons of man. How excellent is Thy loving kindness, O God! and *the children of men shall find protection under the shadow of thy wings.* They shall be abundantly satisfied with the fatness of Thy house, and Thou shalt make them drink of the river of Thy pleasures. Let the saints be joyful in glory; let them sing aloud upon their resting place.

. . . May the Supreme King of Kings, in His abundant mercy have compassion, and be gracious unto them; *may He shelter them under the shadow of His wings* and in the secret of His tabernacle, that they may behold the beauty of the Lord and inquire in His temple. May peace be with them, peace in their resting place; as it is said: 'Peace shall come, they shall rest on their couches; those who walked in uprightness.' May it be granted unto them, and unto all the departed of Israel, and in the grace of God. Amen."

(Prayer for Mourners, 1872, pp. 267-269; italics added)

I have presented the above citations from Judaic texts to point out the potential significance of the fact that in my OBE to "the Park," my father, who had died several days earlier, was being carried by a wing. On the one hand, the presence in my dream of the wing could be taken as "evidence" or the literal truth of the above texts. On the other hand, one might think it logical that such a symbol, associated with protection both in life and death in Judaism, would enter the dream of a person such as myself raised in the Jewish tradition. However, before concluding thus, I should say that prior to the dream, I was not familiar, at least consciously, with any of these texts, which I have only just identified by doing a google search for terms such as "wing," "death," etc. Might I have read or heard them in temple at some point in my life? Sure, and so maybe they still existed in some hidden recess of my unconscious. And I was reading certain liturgical prayers including one of the above during the days between my father's death and the dream, and now that I recall, did read the one for donning the tallis. All said and done, whatever the reason the wing was in the dream, in retrospect it certainly did belong there.

SHARED-DEATH EXPERIENCES (SDE)

Reviewing the NDE literature more thoroughly for this book in order to see if others had had what seemed like what I was calling "vicarious NDEs" without themselves being near death, I learned that shortly after identifying the NDE as a scientific reality (in the sense of a discreet human subjective experience with reliably observed characteristics), Moody did indeed investigate another type of death experience, which he called the "Shared-Death Experience (SDE)." He first came upon this when he was in medical school, which would have been sometime prior to 1976 when he received his M.D. He later variously referred to these as "Empathic NDEs," "Conjoint NDEs" and "Mutual NDEs" (Moody, 1999, cited in Howarth & Kellehear, 2001, p. 72) and wrote about SDEs in detail in his 2010 book with Paul Perry, *Glimpses of Eternity: Sharing a Loved One's Passage from This Life to the Next*.

Peter and Elizabeth Fenwick included some shared death experiences in their book *The Truth in the Light: An Investigation of Over 300 Near-Death Experiences* (1995). As an aside, I had the pleasure of dining with the Fenwicks at an NDE conference some years ago, along with their fellow NDE researchers Pim Van Lommel, who wrote *Consciousness Beyond Life: The Science of Near Death Experiences* (2010), and Erlendur Haraldsson, who wrote about deathbed encounters (Osis & Haraldsson, *At the Hour of Death: The Results of Research on Over 1000 Afterlife Experiences*, 1977) and children's experiences of reincarnation (Haraldsson, 2017). As I googled these references, I sadly (for we the living) learned that Erlendur transitioned in 2020. If anyone knew what to expect in his new adventure, I imagine it was he.

From left to right, me, Jeffery Martin, Kelly Larson, Pim van Lommel, Peter Fenwick, Erlendur Haraldsson, Gino Yu, and Marcus Anthony

Moody relates that he first heard of an SDE from a Dr. Jamieson, a physician on the faculty of the medical school where he was a student. Her mother had just died, and she told him that "something had happened during her death that she had not seen in [his] research nor heard from anyone else." Following her mother's cardiac arrest, her own attempt at resuscitating her, and her conclusion that her mother had died,

> "Suddenly, Dr. Jamieson felt herself lift out of her body. She realized that she was above her own body and the now-deceased body of her mother, looking down on the whole scene as though she were on a balcony.
>
> 'Being out-of-body took me aback,' she said. 'As I was trying to get my bearings I suddenly became aware that my mother was now hovering with me in spirit form. She was right next to me!'

Chapter 34 - Am I Dead Yet?: Near-Death Experiences (NDEs) and Shared-Death Experiences (SDEs)

Dr. Jamieson calmly said goodbye to her mother, who was now smiling and quite happy, a stark contrast to the corpse down below. Then Dr. Jamieson saw something else that surprised her.

'I looked in the corner of the room and became aware of a breach in the universe that was pouring light like water coming from a broken pipe. Out of that light came people I had known for years, deceased friends of my mother. But there were other people there as well, people I didn't recognize but I assume they were friends of my mother's whom I didn't know.'

As Dr. Jamieson watched, her mother drifted off into the light. The last Dr. Jamieson saw of her mother, she said, was her having a very tender reunion with all of her friends. 'Then the tube closed down in an almost spiral fashion, like a camera lens, and the light was gone,' she said.

How long this all lasted Dr. Jamieson didn't know. But when it ended she found herself back in her body, standing next to her deceased mother, totally puzzled about what had just happened.

'What do you make of that story?' she asked.

I could only shrug. At this point I had heard dozens of regular near-death experiences, and was hearing new ones each week. But there was little about Dr. Jamieson's experience that I could comment on, since this was the first of this kind I had ever encountered.

'I said, what do you make of the story?' she asked again.

'It's empathic,' I said, using the word that means the ability to share another's feelings. 'It is a shared death experience.'

'Have you heard of many of these?' she asked, clearly excited at the notion that I had.

'No, Dr. Jamieson, I haven't,' I said. 'I am afraid that yours is the first I have ever heard.'"

(Moody & Perry, 2010, pp. 5-7)

Moody goes on to recount his own SDE in 1994, when his own mother died. At the moment before her death,

> "We all held hands around the bed – my two sisters, their husbands, Cheryl and I – and waited for the inevitable moment of death.
>
> And as we waited, it happened to us: a shared death experience. As we held hands around the bed, the room seemed to change shape and four of the six of us felt as though we were being lifted off the ground.
>
> . . . 'Look,' said my sister, pointing to a spot at the end of the bed. 'Dad's here! He's come back to get her!'
>
> . . . Everyone there reported later that the light in the room changed to a soft and fuzzy texture.
>
> . . . It was as though the fabric of the universe had torn and for just a moment we felt the energy of that place called heaven.
>
> . . . What should have been one of life's least happy moments was suddenly cause for elation. We had gone partway to heaven with our mother. We had personally seen her off to heaven." (pp. 43-44)

Moody identified seven common elements of SDEs:

> "Change of geometry" (of the room)
>
> "Mystical light"
>
> "Out-of-Body experience"
>
> "Co-living a life review"
>
> "Encountering unworldly or 'heavenly' realms"
>
> "Mist at death"
>
> "A different world." (pp. 73-95)

He adds, however, that "I have yet to find a person who reports all seven. Likewise, no case study includes just one element. Usually a person reports several of the seven elements in their experience. He also adds that there is a very common report of ineffability: "Nearly everyone who contributed their

Chapter 34 - Am I Dead Yet?: Near-Death Experiences (NDEs) and Shared-Death Experiences (SDEs)

story to my study says that the experience is very difficult to explain in words" (p. 95).

Moody proposes that SDEs challenge the materialist view of NDEs as brain phenomena:

> "One of the arguments of the skeptics of the near-death experience is that they are 'fear-death' experiences made up in the mind of a person who is facing death. I think that shared death experiences could possibly prove that the light and all of the good things that come from it originate *outside* of the dying person's brain, where others can share them. This phenomenon, known as *non-local memory*, involves personal information that resides outside of an individual's brain." (Moody & Perry, 2010, p. 38)

Looking over Moody's list of SDE criteria, it is not clear whether my Park experience was a typical SDE. I did encounter a "different world" that had qualities of a "'heavenly' realm." Whether it was an out-of-body experience rather than a lucid dream is debatable. It emerged from sleep and not from a dream, and there was no continuity of separation from the physical body, so if it was a lucid dream, it was an **ND-SILD** (nondreaming sleep-initiated lucid dream). However, as it was more stable than any lucid dream I'd ever had, similar to my Kundalini Awaking/Cosmic Consciousness OBE, I would tend to classify it as an **ND-SIDOBE** (Nondreaming sleep initiated discontinuous out-of-body experience).

THE PARK REVISITED

In the OBE literature, Robert Monroe reports on his and others' disembodied voyages to a place that he calls . . . "the Park." I should mention here that I was not aware of the writings of Robert Monroe or of the Park until after my own SDE when I began researching OBEs. He describes this as a "Reception Center" that can be accessed by going into the state of consciousness that he labels "Focus 27." Monroe defines the Park as

> ". . . an artificial synthesis created by human minds, a way station designed to ease the trauma and shock of the transition out of physical reality. It takes on the form of various earth environments in order to be acceptable to the enormously wide variety of newcomers." (Monroe, 2000, p. 249)

He relates a conversation he had in the Park during an OBE:

> "I turned to George. 'How did you get here?'
>
> 'Well, I was sitting in the Park, and Fred here came up and sat beside me, and then . . . What's the matter? Are you all right?'
>
> He must have seen the shock on my face as the wave of memory flowed into me. The Park! Years ago, I had arrived at the Park. But how or why I got there I could not recall. There had been a welcoming group of ten or twelve men and women, who greeted me warmly and explained where I was. It was a place to calm down in after the trauma of physical death—a way station, for relaxation and decision as to what to do next. The Park!" (Monroe, 2000, p. 237)

In Monroe's experience, the Park is actually a human creation;

> "'This place, then . . . ?'
>
>> 'Is a creation that is here and will be here whatever your beliefs. It will not disappear if you don't believe it exists.'
>
> 'Who made it?'
>
>> 'A human civilization many thousands of years ago. They have been gone long since. Is there anything more you need to know?'
>
> 'What about those who simply want—or need—to return to what I have called their I-There? I'm sure you understand what I mean.'
>
>> 'I do. That is the destination of most who depart from here.'
>
> 'So, when we bring people here, you calm them down and give them the opportunity to consider what they want to do next.'
>
>> 'That is so. We show them what opportunities do exist. The Park is but a starting point. You will be astounded when you see all of the little individual places that residents have created.'" (Monroe, 2000, p. 242)

Chapter 34 - Am I Dead Yet?: Near-Death Experiences (NDEs) and Shared-Death Experiences (SDEs)

The Monroe Institute has a training program, called, Lifeline, which is described as a

> ". . . 5-day/6-night journey of exploration into the afterlife state. Over the course of your time with us, you will experience being of service to those still in embodiment as well as to others who have transitioned and desire assistance.
>
> Lifeline is a unique and powerful program that takes you into profound states of consciousness using Hemi-Sync audio guidance technology. Explore Focus Levels 23 - 27, specific states of awareness associated with the afterlife state. Discover how to enter into these states of consciousness, comfortably make contact with people who have passed over, perform 'rescues and retrievals,' and return at will. In addition, discover techniques to direct healing energies to those still embodied." (Lifeline, 2019)

The Lifeline program is advertised as providing opportunities for:

> "Contacting people who have departed;
> Performing 'rescues and retrievals' on souls unable to move on;
> Visiting 'The Park,' an afterlife reception center;
> Connecting with new guides and/or systems of guides;
> Reuniting with friends and relatives who have transitioned;
> Sending healing energy to those still embodied;
> Retrieving lost parts or fragments of oneself." (Monroe Institute, 2019)

The first Lifeline program

> ". . . took place at the Institute during the week beginning June 22, 1991. In the following fourteen months, some two hundred people participated in the six-day intensive learning process. Among those attending were physicians, psychologists, engineers, researchers, business executives, psychiatrists, writers, attorneys, educators, therapists, musicians, and artists. All were graduates of at least one previous Institute program, as this was a prerequisite for attendance at Lifeline. Apart from that, they represented widely divergent backgrounds, interests, lifestyles, and previous experiences with the exploration of consciousness. Yet at the end of each program almost all attested to their ability to visit the Reception Center—the Park—

and many also acknowledged that they now knew for certain that they would survive the physical death process." (Monroe, 2000, p. 246)

While many SDEs occur when the experiencer is with a loved one at the moment of death, others, like my own, can happen at a distance of time or space. Here is an example of a "co-lived life review" at a distance:

> "'One weekend my brother went to another state for a high-school football game and I stayed here at home. He drove there with friends, and on the day he was returning, I was lying on the couch watching sports when I suddenly had the sensation of leaving my body and moving toward a bright light. As this happened I flashed back on events that had taken place with my brother. I relived several events from our childhood, including some things that were so insignificant that I had forgotten them. These were all memory images, but none of them were daydreams or the same as sleeping dreams. They were so vivid that I really thought I was reliving them.'
>
> The young man had no idea how long the episode lasted, but when it was over he found himself back in his body and deeply disturbed . . . About an hour later, he said, his mother received a telephone call from the police in the other state that her son had been killed in an automobile accident." (Moody & Perry, 2010)

WHERE TO GO FROM HERE

Whereas friends and clients over the years have told me stories of how they or someone else somehow "knew" from a distance when a loved one had died, until researching this book I was unaware of the lucid or out-of-body vicarious death experiences of anyone but myself. As they say, you learn something new every day. Just today (6/12/22), while proofreading this book and googling a little here and there, I found out that in 2011, William Peters, a licensed psychotherapist who provides end of life care, founded the Shared Crossing Project. He was inspired by an SDE that he had when reading aloud to a hospice patient, and

> ". . . suddenly felt himself floating in midair, completely out of his body. The patient, who was also aloft, looked at him and smiled. The next moment, Peters felt himself return to his body . . . but the

Chapter 34 - Am I Dead Yet?: Near-Death Experiences (NDEs) and Shared-Death Experiences (SDEs)

patient never regained consciousness and died." (Shared Crossing Project, 2022)

The mission of the Shared Crossing Project is "to positively transform relationships to death and dying through education and raising awareness about shared crossings and their healing benefits. We aim to bring people together in community to support open exploration and discussion of this important topic in a safe place" (Shared Crossing Project, 2022). Peters has written a recent book on SDEs (Peters, 2022), and the website SharedCrossing.com posts videos where SDEers recount their own experiences.

Chapter 35 - *Why Antimatter Matters*

"As a matter of psychological fact, mystical states of a well pronounced and emphatic sort *are* usually authoritative over those who have them. They have been 'there' and know. It is vain for rationalism to grumble about this. If the mystical truth that comes to a man proves to be a force that he can live by, what mandate have we of the majority to order him to live in another way? We can throw him into a prison or a madhouse, but we cannot change his mind – we commonly attach it only the more stubbornly to its beliefs. It mocks our utmost efforts, as a matter of fact, and in point of logic it absolutely escapes our jurisdiction. Our own more 'rational' beliefs are based on evidence exactly similar in nature to that which the mystics quote for theirs. Our senses, namely, have assured us of certain states of fact; but mystical experiences are as direct perceptions of fact for those who have them as any sensations ever were for us. The records show that even though the five senses be in abeyance in them, they are absolutely sensational in their epistemological quality, if I may be pardoned the barbarous expression – that is, they are face to face presentations of what seems immediately to exist.

The mystic is, in short, *invulnerable* and must be left, whether we relish it or not, in undisturbed enjoyment of his creed. Faith, says Tolstoy, is that by which men live. And faith-state and mystic state are practically convertible terms."

William James

(1902/1928, pp. 423-424)

Chapter 35 - Why Antimatter Matters

> "Absence of evidence
> is not evidence of absence"
>
> **Carl Sagan**
>
> **(1997, p. 223. Also known as Rummy's Razor)**

Some of the things written about in the last few chapters may seem pretty far out, *because they are*. But the truth is that *the truth isn't always what sounds like the truth*. And yet, as the Buddha cautions, while

> "things are not as they are seen, nor are they otherwise" (Buddha, Lankavatara Sutra, in Suzuki, 1932, LXV: 36, p. 156), "*even the misconception of a reality is the reality of a misconception*" (Grandma Densei, 1922).

For example, you're sitting here reading a book on How to Stop Thinking because it's something you want to learn and the title of the book (as well as some of your own experiences while reading it, I hope) suggests that thinking is a problem and stopping it is possible. But most people would be at a loss to figure out on their own why someone would want to do such a thing which, in any event, they assume can't be done. Why would anyone want to stop thinking! Thinking is important! More, Bigger, Better, Faster! Pay attention! Focus! Concentrate!

In Part 1, we learned that the way to stop thinking isn't to tell yourself to stop thinking, as logical as this might sound, but rather to be aware of something else. In Part 2, the key to CBT for depression, anxiety, anger and their variants was discovered to be "think of what you feel like doing or not doing, and do the opposite." Here in Part 3, the solution to existential despair might very well be: If you think you're going to die, *realize that you won't*, or at least that what dies *isn't you.*

The fact is that *most* humans believe that although their body dies, they don't die. In other words, they believe in *immortality*. Not in the persistence of the body, but of the self, consciousness, or awareness, in one form or another. Even scientists who will dispute immortality tooth and nail at their day job often pray in their spare time, somehow seeing no inconsistency in this double life they are living. As Einstein said,

> "Science without religion is lame,
> religion without science is blind." (1956, p. 26)

So why can't we all just get along, and agree to disagree, except on the one fact that we can all agree on, at least in our heart of hearts, that *we're all full of it and have no idea what we're talking about or dealing with.*

We have looked at a number of altered states of consciousness (WILDs, DILDs, ND-SILDs, WICOBEs, WIDOBEs, ND-SICOBEs, ND-SIDOBEs, NL-DICOBEs, NL-DIDOBEs, L-DICOBEs, L-DIDOBEs, NDEs, SDEs), each of which involves perceived personal identity (who or what we think we are), environmental content (where and when we seem to be and what seems to be happening there), a continuum of self-awareness (lucidity), a continuum of multisensory experience and realism (seeing, hearing, smelling, tasting, and bodysensing) and a continuum of volition (the extent to which we can do what we intend to do). We have also distinguished between 10 states of sleeping, dreaming and waking consciousness in terms of whether the perceived content is referentially "real" or "true," and whether we have insight into this referential truth or falsehood (in which case we are lucid) or remain clueless (in which case we are nonlucid).

In each of these states, we are likely to find ourselves in environments and situations that we probably shouldn't mention Monday morning at work.

> "What did *you* do this weekend?"

> "Oh, nothing much, I found this French soldier who had been standing on a battlefield since 1918 thinking he was still alive. But no worries, I set him straight and took him to the Park to get oriented. George is bringing him up to speed, and I'll check in on him later tonight."

But let's say you really *did* spend time (or perceive spending time) in the Park over the weekend. Was it "just a dream" or was it "real"?

This is where *scientism* (believing things are necessarily false because we have no evidence that they are true) comes into play, despite the fact that we pick and choose what we are going to be scientismic about. Scientism tends

Chapter 35 - Why Antimatter Matters

to take a hands-off approach to mainstream religious *beliefs* regarding things we have had absolutely no experience with other than being told they are true by people, books and institutions that we trust (it knows which side its bread is funded on). Meanwhile, it loves to condemn any shred of belief in physical and mental *experiences* of otherworldy places, beings and events in our altered states that often correspond with the experiences of others at various geographical and historical distances.

Scientism would assure me that what I am believing to be an SDE merely borrowed content from my daytime experiences, as Freud suggested. The Flying wing could have been borrowed from the passage in the prayer book about the Shekhina and morphed into a white hospital sheet for obvious reasons. The Park could have been from some movie I saw about Heaven (I had not yet read books by Robert Monroe). The cocktail party of transitioned loved ones in the distance could have been from an unconscious memory of something I read in Moody's book years before. I obviously had memories of spending time with my father. So there we were.

But anything can be explained away as "just a dream" (especially if it happened when we were asleep), including your and my experience right now, according to some of the religions. Bottom line: When all is said and done, we each believe what we believe. I'm going to believe that I helped my father get oriented into the afterlife, and someone else is going to believe I'm nuts (while retaining their own nutty beliefs about the afterlife). Because *most* people believe in *some* form of non-physical reality. Even 32% percent of *Atheists and Agnostics* have acknowledged thinking that there is "life, or some sort of conscious existence, after death" (Shermer, 2018).

So why does antimatter matter? For two reasons: (1) Because *bananas* produce antimatter (specifically, 1 positron, the antimatter equivalent of an electron, every 75 minutes), and (2) Bananas produce enough antimatter to power a house. Bananas are also radioactive organic clones, but this is beside the point, which is: I *believe* that bananas produce enough antimatter to power a house.

Why do I believe this? Because *I've seen the math* (Allain, 2013).

Oh, you'd like to see it? Ok, be careful what you wish for:

$$E = (m_{e+} + m_{e-})c^2 = (2)(9.11 \times 10^{-31} \text{ kg})(3.0 \times 10^8 \text{ m/s})^2 = 1.64 \times 10^{-13} \text{ J}$$

$$P_{banana} = \frac{E}{\Delta t} = \frac{(.5)(.5)(1.64 \times 10^{-13} \text{ J})}{(75 \text{ min})(60 \text{ s/min})} = 9.11 \times 10^{-18} \text{ Watts}$$

Now, technically, it would take *a lot* of bananas to power a house:

$$P = 2000 \text{ Watts} = nP_{banana}$$

$$n = \frac{2000 \text{ Watts}}{P_{banana}} = \frac{2000 \text{ Watts}}{9.11 \times 10^{-18} \text{ Watts}} = 2.2 \times 10^{20} \text{ bananas}$$

And if you wanted to put the banana generator somewhere that didn't smell and arrange it into a really cool, modern looking sphere it would be *really* big and a little blurry:

$$V = \frac{m}{\rho} = \frac{3.3 \times 10^{19} \text{ kg}}{1000 \text{ kg/m}^3} = 3.3 \times 10^{16} \text{ m}^3$$

$$V = \frac{4}{3}\pi r^3$$

$$r = \left(\frac{3V}{4\pi}\right)^{1/3}$$

with a radius of 2 x 10.5 meters (Allain, 2013).

From a practical perspective, this means I would need like 220,000,000,000,000,000,000 bananas arranged into a pretty big sphere. Let's just say that if you looked at it from space you would see the earth and something that looks like a second moon, but yellow (see the photo in Allain, 2013). And realistically, the zoning board would never approve it.

The point is that I *believe* the whole spherical banana-based antimatter power generator thing *even though* I don't know what the hell antimatter is, and neither do scientists, but some really smart guy did the math and published it in Wired Magazine. In other words, it's been *quantified and agreed* upon by scientists (or at least by a guy who writes for a science magazine and his editor).

How do I know that the formulas are correct? I *don't*, and that's the beauty of quantification. It turns your brain into horse grass and relinquishes control to whomever made up the numbers. On the other hand, even though I have *personally experienced* spinning out of my body into the cosmos, *seeing* the white gowned lady with my own (nonphysical) eyes, *standing* in the Park, *helping* my father get up from under the Shekinah, if my life depended on it I don't know whether I'd vote yea or nay on whether all this was real or *just* a dream.

But I'd probably vote yea. You know why? Because I *have to* believe it. Just like you do or will choose to when your time comes, which hopefully won't involve a certain big furry mammal. Because antimatter keeps the universe together, and faith in immortality, that *this isn't all there is,* at some point in our lives may be all we can hang on to in order to give life meaning, or at least keep it from losing meaning.

As Jung said regarding immortality:

> "For reasons of psychic hygiene, it would be better not to forget these original and universal ideas; and wherever they have disappeared, from neglect or intellectual bigotry, we should reconstruct them as quickly as we can regardless of 'philosophical' proofs for or against (which are impossible anyway)." (1970/1950, p. 4)

But we don't have to stop at "ideas." We can cultivate our human psychological potential to "know thyself" *experientially* in our potentially nonphysical form. This is the promise of naturally induced altered states. And conducting such experiments on ourselves is a valid form of science, namely *state-specific science* (Tart, 1972), in which the experimenter him or herself, or others, enter into a state of consciousness in order to study it. Charles Tart, who popularized the term "altered state of consciousness" in 1969 and has conducted studies on OBEs, published the following in the journal *Science*, which is the journal of the American Association for the Advancement of Science (AAAS) and a gold-standard among international academic journals:

> "I now propose the creation of various state-specific sciences. If such sciences could be created, we would have a group of highly skilled, dedicated, and trained practitioners able to achieve certain SoCs [states of consciousness] and able to agree with one another that they have attained a common state. While in that SoC, they might then investigate other areas of interest, whether these be totally internal phenomena of that given state, the interaction of that state with external, physical reality, or people in other SoC's.
>
> The fact that the experimenter should be able to function skillfully in the SoC itself for a state-specific science does not necessarily mean that he would always be the subject. While he might often be the subject, observer, and experimenter simultaneously, it would be quite possible for him to collect data from experimental manipulations of other subjects in the SoC, and either be in that SoC himself at the time of data collection or be in that SoC himself for data reduction and theorizing." (Tart, 1972)

By conducting state-dependent science on ourselves, for example by stopping thinking in order to make awareness available to our Assagiolian superconscious True Self, or even by simply keeping an open mind when we read the reports of others who have, we can reconnect with mankind's perennial heritage of communing with "lost" realities that tend, when found right where we left them ("just behind the tree"), to bring great meaning and joy to human life. Happy Trails!

Chapter 36 - *Love Everybody, Yes, Everybody:* The Bodysnatching Exercise

"Love Everybody."

Ram Dass

(Psychologist Richard Alpert)

"Why are you unhappy?

Because 99.9 percent

Of everything you think,

And of everything you do,

Is for yourself –

And there isn't one."

Wei Wu Wei (2002)

"Love your neighbor as yourself.

Unless they're an axe murderer.

Then love them from afar."

Grandma Densei (1922)

> "Love your neighbor as yourself.
>
> Unless *you're* an axe murderer.
>
> Then love them from afar."
>
> **A Client Who One-Upped Grandma Densei (2022)**

Every world religion teaches the "Golden Rule," which is to treat others as you would be treated, or to *not* treat others as you would *not* want to be treated. In his notes, Norman Rockwell listed out various religions' versions of the Golden Rule:

"**BUDDHISM**. Hurt not others with that which pains yourself. *Udanavarga.*

CHRISTIANITY. All things whatsoever ye would that men should do to you, do ye even so to them: for this is the law and the prophets. *Bible, St. Matthew.*

HEBRAISM. What is hurtful to yourself do not to your fellow man. That is the whole of the Torah and the remainder is but commentary. Go learn it. *Talmud.*

HINDUISM. This is the sum of duty: do naught to others which if done to thee, would cause thee pain. *Mahabarata.*

ISLAM. No one of you is a believer until he loves for his brother what he loves for himself. *Traditions.*

JAINISM. In happiness and suffering, in joy and grief, we should regard all creatures as we regard our own self, and should therefore refrain from inflicting upon others such injury as would appear undesirable to us if inflicted upon ourselves. *Yogashastra.*

SIKHISM. As thou deemest thyself so deem others. Then shalt thou become a partner in heaven. *Kabir.*

TAOISM. Regard your neighbor's gain as your own gain: and regard your neighbor's loss as your own loss. *T'ai Shang Kan Ying P'ien.*

Chapter 36 - Love Everybody, Yes, Everybody: The Bodysnatching Exercise

> **ZOROASTRIANISM.** That nature is only good when it shall not do unto another whatever is not good for its own self. *Dadistan-i-dinik.*"
>
> (Rockwell, 2021)

It will be noted that some religions go a step further than merely teaching the Golden Rule: They state that this teaching represents the *totality* of the religion's instructions. For example:

> "That which is hateful to you do not do to another;
>
> that is the entire Torah, and the rest is its interpretation. Go study."
>
> **Hillel**
>
> **(Shabbat 31a, composed in Babylon c.450 – c.550 C.E.)**

> "Do not to others what ye do not wish done to yourself...
>
> This is the whole Dharma, heed it well."
>
> **The Mahabarata**
>
> **(cited in Das, 1955, p. 398, cited in Ethics, 2021)**

> "So in everything, do to others what you would have them do to you,
>
> for this sums up the Law and the Prophets."
>
> **Matthew 7:12**

The Golden Rule is similar, but not identical, to the "categorical imperative" in philosophy (Categorical Imperative, 2021; Kant, 1785) which is to (1) behave as you would want all others to behave, and (2) treat yourself and others not as means to an end, but as the end itself.

You might notice, as do I as I am writing and Googling (as I have only a rough idea of what I will write before sitting down to write and only while simultaneously writing and researching does the chapter come together) that while one is fully capable, theoretically, of following the Golden Rule *behaviorally* (I say "theoretically" as, face it, none of us really behaves toward others as we would want others to behave toward us: how many couches at home have you, or I, offered to the homeless?), actually *loving* our neighbor (which really amounts to Ram Dass' "love everybody"), is not necessarily something we can do at will. So, assuming that we did have as a goal to "love everybody," how would we go about it?

To love another being is to *identify* with them. In a talk on "loving everybody," Ram Dass (former Harvard psychologist Richard Alpert) points out the relationship between a sense of oneness and a feeling of compassion:

> "Two levels of consciousness. One level, here we are in Maui. And another level, where we are all One. Now, I, you, your question is my question. My answer is your answer. I'm talking to myself, at that level. And I'm playing a game on another level, that we are One, testing our wisdom. Our wisdom. Through your question and my answer. Now, as you go on two levels, you gravitate towards the One. Until you see all as the One. You see all of these manifestations of the One. Including this (pointing to his body). Including this. And that's the place that true compassion comes from, 'cause compassion is 'with.' Somebody has suffering, and it's your suffering. And you go to fix that suffering like you fix a splinter on your hand. It's not like you're doing something for somebody else. You're doing something to yourself." (Ram Dass, 2021b)

As love involves an enhanced sense of identification with another, it's possible that love can be cultivated by enhancing such identification. In a sense, the goal is to transform the other from a Buberian "it" into a "thou" or, better yet, into an "I." From an *object* of awareness into the *person* they really are. To love someone is to experience them from their own perspective, as an "I" rather than as a "s/he" (or, if they don't love themself, indicating that they are objectifying themself, then from the perspective they would have if they did – which again reminds me of something Adyashanti said on a 9-day silent retreat a few years ago – yes, talking is permitted on silent retreats under certain circumstances, such as during question and answer sessions with the teacher – "Imagine if you treated yourself like you were someone you actually cared about").

To this end, I sometimes lead clients through an exercise that I have developed to enhance a sense of connectedness with people in their life whom they love but feel that they may not be fully appreciating. I believe that this exercise might also help us in our efforts to practice the Golden Rule. I

Chapter 36 - Love Everybody, Yes, Everybody: The Bodysnatching Exercise

sometimes call it the "Imaginal Somatosensory Identification Exercise," but it just occurred to me that there is a better name: The Bodysnatching Exercise. Hmm. Just googled it and might should give it a rethink. The term "bodysnatching" came to mind as the exercise involves imagining inhabiting the body of the other person and experiencing things through their senses, which of course reminded me of the film "Invasion of the Body Snatchers." But Google for some reason is obsessed with body snatching as "secretly removing corpses from burial sites," which apparently is more common than one would hope (Body Snatching, 2021). It says here, OMG, New Jersey! Did you know that ... never mind. Moving right along, it's a perfectly good name for the exercise, Jon Kabat-Zinn has his "Raisin Exercise," and I want an exercise too, so here it is:

The Bodysnatching Exercise

1. Find a comfortable position. How should I know where you put it, where did you see it last? It's probably right under your nose. There it is.

2. Close your eyes and breathe normally through your nose, being aware of the feeling of the air as it enters and leaves the nose (if your nose is stuffy or runny, breathe through your mouth, and if you are a fish breathe through your gills).

3. Now imagine that rather than being in *your* body, you are in the body of the person whom you want to increase your connection with. Imagine that you look like them and are wearing clothes you've seen them wear. Imagine seeing their body under your head rather than your own.

4. Be aware of the physical sensations of your/their body, continuing to imagine that it is their body that you are in. Feel your/their feet on the floor, your/their legs, torso, arms, head.

5. Now be aware of your senses, each for about 30 seconds, while continuing to feel the overall tactile bodysense of being in their body.

> **Seeing:** Be aware of seeing whatever you are seeing, possibly the color created by the light going through your eyelids. Imagine now that you are the other person, inhabiting their body, and you/they are seeing the light coming through your/their eyelids.
>
> **Hearing:** Be aware of any sounds that you/they are hearing.

Smelling: Be aware of any smells that you/they are smelling.

Tasting: Be aware of any tastes that you/they are tasting.

Bodysensing: Be aware once again of the feeling of your/their feet, legs, torso, arms, head.

Thinking: Be aware of what you/they are thinking. You might even conjure up an image of *you* in your/their mind.

6. Repeat Step 5 as many times as necessary in order to really feel like you are inhabiting their body, seeing and thinking about things from their perspective.

7. When you are ready, open your eyes and stay still for 2 or 3 minutes to readjust to being in your own body. You might want to then, or at another time, try the exercise with your eyes open.

Buddhist lovingkindness exercises may begin by wishing oneself well, then expanding these wishes to others. For example, the Buddhist teacher and psychologist Jack Kornfield suggests that after wishing oneself lovingkindness, safety, wellness and ease, you then do the same for someone who has cared for you, and then

> ". . . you can include others: ... a wider circle of friends ... community members, neighbors, people everywhere, animals, all beings, the whole earth.
>
> Finally, include the difficult people in your life, even your enemies, wishing that they too may be filled with lovingkindness and peace. This will take practice. But as your heart opens, first to loved ones and friends, you will find that in the end you won't want to close it anymore." (Kornfield, 2021)

Similarly, the Bodysnatching Exercise can be done to feel more connected with not only loved ones but friends, colleagues, and strangers; people you've been or are in conflict with; pets and other animals; plants and trees; the earth or other planets; the sun; and even the infinite space of the universe, which has just provided the name for a second exercise: *Bodysnatching the Universe*, to which I will devote the next chapter rather than include it in this chapter mostly because it would make such a great chapter title. But before we get there, the format of lovingkindness exercises,

Chapter 36 - Love Everybody, Yes, Everybody: The Bodysnatching Exercise

in which the same formula may be applied to the self, close others and distant others in the course of the same session, suggests that we might do the same with the Bodysnatching Exercise.

For example, Steps 3, 4 and 5 could be done once for a family member (shortening the awareness of each sense in Step 5 to maybe 10 seconds instead of 30 seconds), then repeated for other family members, friends, acquaintances and strangers.

Chapter 37 - *Supersize It:*
Bodysnatching the Universe

"Going for the one"

Jon Anderson (1977)

What brought to mind the title of this exercise was the combination of Jack Kornfield's suggestion that we send lovingkindness to the Universe; the insight that love is directly proportional to identity; and the memory of how my 2007 kundalini awakening into the cosmos was preceded, in part, by meditating the night before on how my physical presence in the space that I inhabited at that moment would resonate at that same location for eternity, though the location would continuously move from where the initial presence occurred, as we are constantly moving at about 429,126 mph, given the speeds of earth's rotation, earth's orbit around the sun, and the sun's orbit around the galaxy (Scudder, 2016), which doesn't even take into account our galaxy's orbit around the center of our galaxy group, the group's orbit around the center of its cluster, and its cluster's orbit around the center of its supercluster. Not to mention the increasing speed at which the Universe is expanding (about 166,320 miles per second per megaparsec – a megaparsec is roughly 3 million light-years; Moskowitz, 2012). In other words, our bioenergy is at each moment blazing a course through space and time at inconceivable speeds over inconceivable distances. Ponder that for a megaparsec.

Just as imaginal somatosensory identification with or "bodysnatching" people can facilitate identity with and ultimately love for individuals and humanity as a whole, imaginal somatosensory identification with the Universe can facilitate identity with It, and you know what that's called, don't you ...

Chapter 37 - Supersize It: Bodysnatching the Universe

Oneness with the Universe! I hope you realize that we're moving WAY beyond raisins here people, so hold on to your hats.

The Bodysnatching the Universe Exercise

1. Find a comfortable position.

2. Close your eyes and breathe normally through your nose, being aware of the feeling of the air as it enters and leaves the nose.

3. Now imagine that rather than being in your body, you *are* the entirety of the space of the whole Universe. Imagine that you look like the Universe and are wearing the stars that you've seen it wear (ok, I'm cutting and pasting a little here). Imagine seeing stars and planets and lots and lots and lots and lots of space under your head rather than a human body.

4. Be aware of the physical sensations of being the Universe, the physical feeling of being space and interstellar gases (mostly hydrogen and helium) and suns and planets of rock and water and organic life forms.

5. Now be aware of your senses, each for about 30 seconds, while continuing to feel the overall tactile bodysense of being space itself as well as being the Universe and every object and life form in it. We will assume for the purpose of this exercise that the Universe has eyes, ears, a nose, taste buds, touch and a mind because ... it DOES. It isn't like *here* we are and *there's* the Universe. We *are* the Universe.

> **Seeing:** Be aware of seeing whatever you the Universe are seeing, as you move your awareness to different places in the Universe, from space to the insides of stars, to the surfaces of planets, to living environments of civilizations on earth and other planets, to the bodies of humans and alien beings.
>
> **Hearing:** Be aware of any sounds that you the Universe are hearing. as you move your awareness to different places in the Universe, from space to the insides of stars, to the surfaces of planets, to living environments of civilizations on

earth and other planets, to the bodies of humans and alien beings.

Smelling: Be aware of any smells that you the Universe are smelling as you move your awareness to different places in the Universe, from space to the insides of stars, to the surfaces of planets, to living environments of civilizations on earth and other planets, to the bodies of humans and alien beings.

Tasting: Be aware of any tastes that you the Universe are tasting as you move your awareness to different places in the Universe, from space to the insides of stars, to the surfaces of planets, to living environments of civilizations on earth and other planets, to the bodies of humans and alien beings.

Bodysensing: Be aware once again of the feeling of the physical sensations of being the Universe, the physical feeling of being space and interstellar gases (mostly hydrogen and helium) and suns and planets of rock and water and organic life forms.

Thinking: Be aware of what you the Universe are thinking, the thoughts that come to mind as you move your awareness to different places in the Universe, from space to the insides of stars, to the surfaces of planets, to living environments of civilizations on earth and other planets, to the bodies of humans and alien beings.

6. Repeat Step 5 as many times as necessary in order to really feel like you are the Universe, perceiving and thinking about things from Its perspective.

7. When you are ready, open your eyes and stay still for 2 or 3 minutes to readjust to being just a little part of the Universe rather than the *whole shebang*.

I should say here that as I was making up the above exercise, the names of several Tibetan books came to mind, such as Time, Space and Knowledge by Tarthang Tulku (1977) which, if I remember correctly, has exercises in which one imagines oneself as space, and You Are the Eyes of the World by

Chapter 37 - Supersize It: Bodysnatching the Universe

Longchenpa (2000), a Tibetan Buddhist who lived in the 14th century. I suspect that Tibetan Buddhism has developed *Bodysnatching the Universe* into a science and if you are interested in realizing your identity with the Universe (which you already, of course, Are), these two books might be a nice place to begin. Then, once you have become proficient in bodysnatching the Universe, you can move on to bodysnatching the *Multiverse.*

Some time after writing the above, I realized that I had failed to mention anywhere in this book one of my favorite authors, Douglas Harding, who himself developed numerous exercises to help people to personally experience his own realizations resulting from a combination of years of self-enquiry and some amount of dumb luck. But this will require a momentary detour into the world of art.

"A true self-portrait has no face."

Grandma Densei (1922)

Usually, by which for most of us I mean *all the time*, when we think of a self-portrait we imagine a drawing, painting or photo, possibly a sculpture, of a face, most likely attached to a head, and maybe to a portion of a body beneath the head. Take for example this self-portrait by young Rembrandt on a bad hair day in 1630:

Or Van Gogh's self-portraits smoking a pipe before (1887) and after (1889) accidentally cutting off his ear shaving and buying a Russian hat:

Chapter 37 - Supersize It: Bodysnatching the Universe

The artistic tradition of representing oneself as having a face and a head of some sort has continued uninterruptedly until the present day with a notable exception in 1870 when Austrian physicist-philosopher Ernst Mach (not to be confused with painter Max Ernst, a mistake that occasionally leads me on wild goose chases in search of the drawing on the internet) realized that

> "My body differs from other human bodies – beyond the fact that every intense motor idea is immediately expressed by a movement of it, and that, if it is touched, more striking changes are determined than if other bodies are touched – by the circumstance, that it is only seen piecemeal, and, especially, *is seen without a head*." (Mach, 1870/1914, pp. 18-19; italics added)

Mach proceeded to draw a self-portrait of himself *from the inside looking out*, as seen through his left eye (known as "View from the Left Eye," with one version appearing in Mach, 1870/1914, p. 19, and another in Pearson, 1892/1900, p. 64 after Mach had acquired paper on which to better make use of his pencil);

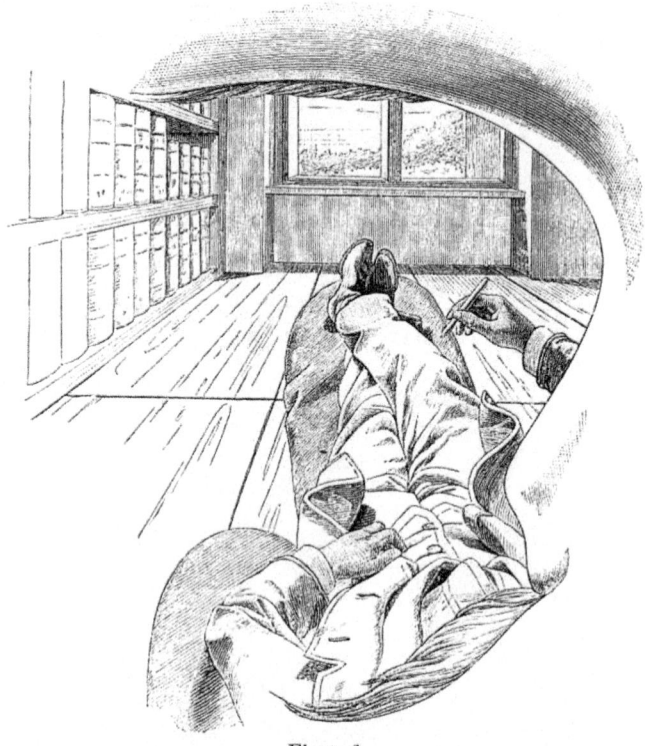

Figur 1.

He relates that:

> "It was about 1870 that the idea of this drawing was suggested to me by an amusing chance. A certain Mr. L., now long dead, whose many eccentricities were redeemed by his truly amiable character, compelled me to read one of C.F. Krause's writings, in which the following occurs: –
>
> 'Problem: To carry out the self-inspection of the Ego.
>
> Solution: It is carried out immediately.'

In order to illustrate in a humorous manner this philosophical 'much ado about nothing,' and at the same time to shew [*sic*] off how the

Chapter 37 - Supersize It: Bodysnatching the Universe

self-inspection of the Ego could really be 'carried out,' I embarked on the above drawing. Mr. L's society was most instructive and stimulating to me, owing to the naivety with which he gave utterance to philosophical notions that are apt to be carefully passed over in silence or involved in obscurity." (Mach, 1870/1914, p. 20)

Mach also at some point sketched a self-portrait in which he is smoking and drinking coffee (presumably with his left eye, a logical if awkward choice when one lacks a mouth) rather than drawing (Ernst Mach Papers, 1865-1918, p. 231):

Flash forward to 1943, when British architect-philosopher Douglas Harding "happened to be in the Himalayas" and

> "There [pointing up] were the wonderful Himalayas. I looked down from the sky and the mountains, and in the nearer valleys I could see some grass. Closer still I saw Douglas's feet and Douglas's tummy. But I found I just stopped here at my chest. Above my chest was Everest. I stopped here as Douglas, and I was replaced by the scene. I simply noticed that I had no head. Crazy, isn't it? Well, it's not quite accurate because I should say I didn't have a head Here. Of course I had a head, but I kept it about a meter away in the bathroom mirror. Here, I didn't have a head, and instead of my head I had Kitchunjunga and Everest . . .
>
> When I was very little I was like this. I was busted wide open for the world. Then when I grew up, I did a naughty, stupid, and ill-mannered thing. In order to join the human club, I took that little Douglas in the mirror and enlarged him, turned him around, and put him on my shoulders, which of course I can't do, and I walked about in the world as though there were a meatball Here to keep the world out with. If I had a friend in front of me, I said silently, 'Keep out! I've got one!' But I haven't got one. I find absolutely nothing Here whatever." (Harding, 2000)

Harding recalls that when he realized he had no head, thinking ceased:

> "What actually happened was something absurdly simple and unspectacular: just for that moment I stopped thinking. Reason and imagination and all the mental chatter died down. For once, words really failed me. I forgot my name, my humanness, my thingness, all that could be called me or mine. Past and future dropped away. It was as if I had been born that instant, brand new, mindless, innocent of all memories. There existed only the Now, that present moment and what was clearly given in it. To look was enough. And what I found was khaki trouserlegs terminating downwards in a pair of brown shoes, khaki sleeves terminating sideways in a pair of pink hands, and a khaki shirtfront terminating upwards in – absolutely nothing whatever! Certainly not in a head." (Harding, 1961/1986, p. 2)

Chapter 37 - Supersize It: Bodysnatching the Universe

Harding's 1943 experience was in fact preceded by years of inquiry into the nature of the Self. In the early 1930s, influenced philosophically by the Theory of Relativity, he sensed that

> "... his identity depended on the range of the observer – from several metres he was human, but at closer ranges he was cells, molecules, atoms, particles ... and from further away he was absorbed into the rest of society, life, the planet, the star, the galaxy ... Like an onion he had many layers. Clearly he needed every one of these layers to exist. But what was at the centre of all these layers? Who was he really?" (Headless.org, 2022)

Then in the mid-30s, he moved to India and one day stumbled upon the self-portrait by Mach.

> "When Harding saw this self-portrait the penny dropped. Until this moment he had been investigating his identity from various distances. He was trying to get to his centre by peeling away the layers. Here however was a self-portrait from the point of view of the centre itself. The obvious thing about this portrait is that you don't see the artist's head. For most people this fact is interesting or

amusing, but nothing more. For Harding this was the key that opened the door to seeing his innermost identity, for he noticed he was in a similar condition – his own head was missing too. At the centre of his world was no head, no appearance – nothing at all. And this 'nothing' was a very special 'nothing' for it was both awake to itself and full of the whole world. Many years later Harding wrote about the first time he saw his headlessness:

'I don't think there was a 'first time'. Or, if there was, it was simply a becoming more aware of what one had all along been dimly aware of. How could there be a 'first-time' seeing into the Timeless, anyway? One occasion I do remember most distinctly – of very clear in-seeing. It had 3 parts. (1) I discovered in Karl Pearson's Grammar of Science, a copy of Ernst Mach's drawing of himself as a headless figure lying on his bed. (2) I noted that he – and I – were looking out at that body and the world, from the Core of the onion of our appearances. (3) It was clear that the Hierarchy, which I was then in the early stages of, had to begin with headlessness, and that this had to be the thread on which the whole of it had to be hung.'" (Headless.org, 2022)

Harding spent the rest of his long life (he transitioned in 2007 at the age of 97) writing and lecturing about his discovery. His first book, *The Hierarchy of Heaven and Earth* (1952), was recognized by C.S. Lewis as "a work of the highest genius." In 1961 he published *On Having No Head*, an introduction to "The Headless Way" for a popular audience. Then in the late 1960s and 1970s he developed

> "the experiments – awareness exercises designed to make it easy to see one's headlessness and to explore its meaning and implications in everyday life." (Headless.org, 2022; nicely presented by David Lang, who edited various of Harding's workshops in *Face to Face*, 2000)

Personally I have found Harding's exercises to be effective in immediately shifting the sense of self from separation to inclusiveness. When the usual identification of "I" as *only* this body/head/face and its thoughts/emotions/sensations/personality is replaced by the *experiential content* of the *space* where the head and face are no longer imagined (the new content being all that is seen at the moment, including the world and other people), one senses a merging with, being at one with, or even *Being* these as the formerly assumed embodied self disappears from awareness as a separate entity.

Chapter 38 – *If You Can't Beat'm, Join'm: The God Exercise*

"God is a Verb."

Rabbi David Cooper (1997)

"Okay, Houston, we've got some **good** news and some **bad** news.
On the **up**side, there **is** a God and she **doesn't** play **dice**.
On the **down**side, she **does** play . . . . Houston?"

Chapter 38 – If You Can't Beat'm, Join'm: The God Exercise

Well, why stop at being the universe … In order to find out what aspects of your life are fostering or creating barriers to your happiness, it can be useful, mentally, to completely deconstruct your world and then reconstruct it piece by piece in a way that you think would be ideal (the logical extreme of Glasser's [1998] "Quality World"; and what you would focus on manifesting if bringing thinking in line with the Law of Attraction [Hicks & Hicks, 2004]). Unless you have a really, really good memory for instructions, you might want to record the following guided meditation so that you can listen to it with your eyes closed.

1. Sit comfortably, close your eyes, take a few deep breaths and relax your body.

2. Sit quietly for the next minute, just breathing normally, bringing your awareness to the feeling of the air entering and leaving your nose, mouth or gills, the coolness of the breath on the inhale and the gentle passing of the air through your nose, mouth or gills on the exhale (if recording, let 1 minute pass before reading the next instruction).

3. Imagine that everything around you has suddenly disappeared, and you are floating in space surrounded by a soft white light in all directions for as far as you can see (let 1 minute pass in silence).

4. Remain suspended in space, enjoying the peace and silence emanating from the soft white light (let another minute pass in silence).

5. Now imagine that you can populate a new world with whatever and whomever you want, including yourself in the same or different form.

6. Think about who or what is the first being or thing that you would like to appear, and make them or it appear (let 30 seconds pass in silence).

7. Think about who or what is the next being or thing that you would like to appear. This could be a person or persons (living, transitioned or imaginary), a natural environment, an artificial environment, or other life forms or objects. Make them or it appear (let 30 seconds pass in silence).

8. Repeat 7 as many times as you would like, until your world is fully populated with only the people and things that you would like to have in your life (let 2 minutes pass in silence).

9. Compare the world you have created with the world you currently live in, the people, places and activities that make up your life. Be aware of what elements are the same and what elements are different. Be aware of any new elements, and any old elements that are no longer there (let 1 minute pass in silence).

10. Consider whether any of the new people or things could be introduced into your current or future life experience. Consider whether any of the old people or things that are no longer there could be taken away from your current or future life experience (let 1 minute pass in silence).

11. Open your eyes, and write down any actions that you could take to implement item 10 above. Needless to say, but I'll say it anyway, this should not involve impinging in any way on the rights of others.

Chapter 39 – *Near-GEBAB-Experiences (NGEs): Four Case Studies*

"Try to pose for yourself this task: not to think of a polar bear, and that cursed thing will come to mind every minute."

Fyodor Dostoevsky

(1863, in Зимние заметки о летних впечатлениях Zimniye zametki o letnikh vpechatleniyakh)

"Guns don't eat people,

Bears eat people."

Grandma Densei (1922)

Ever notice that whenever you have an idea that you think you must be the first person ever to have thunk, it always turns out that others either beat you to it or had the idea after you but beat you to *doing* something about it? Stereo ear buds, for example. Back in the early 1970s when I was 10 or so, I used to take two single portable radio earphones, each with a single wire to its plug, and use a wire cutter and electrical tape to merge them into stereo earphones so I could listen to the radio in both ears using its single jack. Of course, the effect was monophonic, but cool enough that by 1979 everyone had a Walkman with real stereo headphones. Apparently it was also cool enough that over 100 years ago, by 1903, everyone had an electrophone, "a sort-of upside-down pair of headphones that fine Victorian ladies and gentlemen would hold under their chins," so I guess those Victorians beat both me and the Walkman.

The mystery of how to listen to the radio in stereo that I encountered in the early 1970s would not of course be solved until about 40 years earlier, in 1931, by Alan Dower Blumlein who, according to his grandson Alan,

> ". . . wasn't very good at school ... was a poor reader and a poor writer, but he loved trains and cranes ... He had an incredible mind, but I think it was probably quite cluttered ... So he and his wife went to the cinema and the ballet as a form of relief – but even while he was relaxing, he was thinking he couldn't understand why the sound didn't follow the actor, and he thought he could fix that." (Trenholm, 2015)

Chapter 39 – Near-GEBAB-Experiences (NGEs): Four Case Studies

Alan Dower Blumlein, the man who invented stereo

EMI Group Archive Trust

Nevertheless, he invented binaural sound, now known as stereophonic sound or "stereo" as well as some knickknacks including television and radar. My guess is that he owes his success to doing something useful with his mind in school (like looking out the window at trains and cranes) rather than listening to his teachers.

What I'm getting at here is that while I thought the notion of protecting oneself from getting eaten by a bear by stopping thinking was an insight for which I might win a Nobel Prize (or at least a Darwin Award, for "'a great idea' gone veddy, veddy wrong"; DarwinAwards.com), apparently there have already been reports in the literature of a consciousness phenomenon that, because of its overlap with Near Death Experiences (NDEs), has all but been overlooked by the scientific community. I am referring here to the Near-GEBAB-Experience (with or without hyphens), in which one *almost* gets eaten by a bear whether spontaneously (e.g., when hiking through the woods) or intentionally (e.g., when hiking through the woods – I mean, not to *blame the victim*, but seriously, *who would do that* when they could be home safely playing Animal Crossing on their phone?).

Therefore, as a service to you, Dear Reader, I have spent countless sunny days scouring the non-fiction collection relegated to the Lenox Library dungeon, far from the radiance gracing the countless tomes of false news and alternative facts (euphemistically glorified as *fiction*),

without nevertheless venturing to discover the purpose of the pressurized solitary confinement cells (they looked kind of scary so I minded my own business). I've also spent countless sleepless nights turning the internet inside down and upside out in search of accounts by **NGE** survivors. And I am pleased to report that I have finally accumulated enough data to identify a pattern of behavior that determines whether an encounter with a bear culminates in an **NGE** for the human, or a Near-**GSBAH**-Experience for the

Chapter 39 – Near-GEBAB-Experiences (NGEs): Four Case Studies

bear (Near Got-Shot-By-A-Human Experience; also abbreviated NGE, kind of like both the American Psychological Association and the American Psychiatric Association, as mentioned earlier, abbreviating themselves as APA, though we psychologists, the *Real* APA – got there first while our plagiaristic drug-pushing, electro-shocking, lobotomizing – not that there's anything wrong with that – counterparts were still calling themselves the *Association of Medical Superintendents of American Institutions for the Insane*). Which NGE, by the way, Private Wojtek, the soldier bear, is said to have had recurring nightmares about during his retirement. Oh, you think I'm joking? Well, the *Internet* says otherwise:

> "Wojtek (1942 – 2 December 1963; Polish pronunciation: [ˈvɔjtɛk]; in English, sometimes spelled Voytek and pronounced as such) was a Syrian brown bear ... (Ursus arctos syriacus) bought, as a young cub, at a railway station in Hamadan, Iran, by Polish II Corps soldiers who had been evacuated from the Soviet Union. In order to provide for his rations and transportation, he was eventually enlisted officially as a soldier with the rank of private, and was subsequently promoted to corporal ... He accompanied the bulk of the II Corps to Italy, serving with the 22nd Artillery Supply Company. During the Battle of Monte Cassino, in Italy in 1944, Wojtek helped move crates of ammunition and became a celebrity with visiting Allied generals and statesmen. After the war, mustered out of the Polish Army, he was billeted and lived out the rest of his life at the Edinburgh Zoo in Scotland." (Wojtek [bear], 2022)

I can just imagine the face of the Scottish telegraph operator who received the message:

> "Polish soldiers evacuated from Russia to Iran arrive in Edinburgh from Italy with Syrian bear."

As they say, "Have bear will travel."

Happily, Corporal Wojtek (bear) became close in later years with the families of some former army buddies who from time to time would take him on picnics.

Chapter 39 – Near-GEBAB-Experiences (NGEs): Four Case Studies

But getting back to the topic at hand (NGEs). As it turns out, and contrary to received opinion such as all those national park signs that say things like:

> "Scare That Bear! Normally bears are shy around humans and avoid them as much as possible. It is important to reinforce this fear by scaring bears away so that conflicts are reduced. If you see a bear in your yard or around your home ... place yourself in a secure area so the bear has a clear escape path. Make a lot of noise by yelling, honking a car horn or banging pots and pans . . . Talk to the bear or start shouting if it doesn't leave." (Wisconsin Department of Natural Resources, 2022),

the pattern emerging from my research on NGEs (of both varieties) is that the best predictor of who will have the NGE, you or the bear (or if you're a bear reading this, you or the human) is . . . (drum roll) . . .

Who meditates better.

As four cases in point, I would like to present four case studies, including two Near-GEBAB-Experiences while meditating and two Partial-GEBAB-Experiences (PGEs) while yelling at bears (go figure).

Messenger (2016) reports that a camper, as fate would have it, was in his tent meditating, when he became aware of a bear watching him through the tent window. Upon seeing the bear, he shifted from classic meditation (meditative inactivity) to mindfulness (meditation in activity), probably thinking or nonthinking to himself something like one of the *gathas* that never made it into Thich Nhat Hanh's books:

> "Breathing in I see the big hungry bear looking into my tent window, breathing out I see the big hungry bear looking into my tent window, *F@*#!!!!!*"

At this point, he sprang into action and wished the bear "Good Morning." He then proceeded to speak softly to the bear until they (most bears' preferred pronoun) eventually scratched their head, wondering why they were unable to read the camper's mind to find out where he hid the food (never before having encountered a human with the ability to stop thinking). As nature and bears abhor a vacuum (*Natura et ursas abhorret vacuum*; loose translation of Rabelais, after Aristotle's *horror vacui*), the bear then waved goodbye and decided to leave. Or so it seemed, until they came back and tried to open the tent door. However, as bear paws were not designed for opening tiny zippers (thank heavens for big favors), and growing bored of the continued emptiness of the camper's mind *cultivated through countless eons of meditation*, the bear eventually yawned and left. The lucky camper walked away from the NGE uneaten and generously posted a video of the encounter on his YouTube channel (Weale, 2016).

A more recent case of nonthinking-induced survival of a bear encounter occurred not far from where I have been writing this book, in the Berkshires region of Massachusetts:

> "Micah Mortal of Pittsfield has come across a few bears over the years while mountain biking around the Berkshires. One encounter, in October 2007, will stick with him forever, he said. While biking in Kennedy Park in Lenox, Mortal got off and decided to meditate under an oak tree. A few minutes into his meditation, he heard a twig snap directly behind him, he said. 'I really slowly turned to look behind my shoulder, and there was a really big black bear. I could literally reach back and touch it,' he said. 'I didn't want to frighten this bear by doing anything sudden.' Resisting his 'fight or flight' response, Mortal said he decided to stay put and hoped that the bear wouldn't be disturbed. 'It walked around and kind of sat down right next to me,' he said. 'It was there for about a minute, and we just sat.' Then the bear got up and lumbered over a hill and out of sight, Mortal said." (Orecchio-Egresitz, 2018)

By contrast with these rather peaceful NGEs owing to skill at stopping thinking in the presence of a bear, recently a Wisconsin couple saw a bear on the porch outside their kitchen window, didn't meditate, didn't stop thinking, and instead followed the Wisconsin Department of Natural Resources advice, opening a window "to yell at it to go away."

> "But instead of scaring the bear off, the couple said the animal charged at the home and broke through the window. Inside the home, the bear immediately attacked the couple, who suffered 'numerous bites and injuries,' the sheriff's office said." (Sorace, 2022)

While they themselves ended up only partially GEBAB, the bear wound up fully GSBAH. I can't bring myself to reproduce here the photo of the bear in its post-GSBAH state, being, despite appearances to the contrarywise, a

Chapter 39 – Near-GEBAB-Experiences (NGEs): Four Case Studies

big softy for bears that are just minding their own business stealing birdseed to bring back to their cubs so they won't *starve*, (kind of like Wolverine in Les Mis) and get *scared* when people yell at them.

The "Scare That Bear!" technique similarly failed for a woman in Maryland who

> " . . . was walking her two dogs, Kylie and Bones, when they came across a large bear. Kylie lunged at the bear and tried to fight it — and that's when the bear locked eyes with Levow. The 55-year-old said she did what she was always told to do when encountering a bear in the wild: Be loud and act big. However, this move backfired — as the bear now came at her. Levow recalled the scary experience as the bear attacked her all over her body, she said. 'After a few seconds, he swatted me down and then bit my left leg twice just above my knee, and then he tossed me to the side and continued to bite me,' she said." (Kasko, 2022)

On the basis of these four case studies, while further investigation is warranted, it seems likely that trying to scare bears by banging things and yelling at them may lead to unpredictable results. Instead, it might be wise to immediately *stop thinking*. Conversely, if you are a bear in Wisconsin, rather than stopping thinking maybe you should *think twice* before smashing through people's kitchen windows even if they are rude to you when you steal their birdseed. You might also want to consider taking an ANGSBAH Management class offered twice a year as a free service for angry bears by the Wisconsin Department of Natural Resources.

Chapter 40 – To A Caged Bear *at the Brighton Aquarium*

"If taking one step forward two steps back

is distancing you from your goal,

turn around."

Grandma Densei

Remember that 1906 Punch cartoon in Chapter 7 ("WELL, MUM, SOMETIMES I SITS AND THINKS; AND THEN AGAIN I JUST SITS.")? It took some effort to locate the original when I started to switch out some of the lower quality images in the book for ones with more pixels and such (Thanks Vinnie!), and when I did (you caught me – I waited until February, 2023 to proofread the already-published manuscript), out of curiosity (yes, I know what it did to the cat, but they would have been just *fine* if they had just STAYED IN THE BOX where they weren't technically alive, but were both dead *and* alive. I suppose they figured that if they tried to get out of the box they would at least have a 50-50 chance of being *only* alive and not simultaneously dead, which latter even a cat knows is not entirely *copasetic* [Bacheller, 1919, pp. 69, 287; Wilton, 2021]. Funny thing, nobody ever considers things from the *cat's* perspective. It's always, like, "if we don't open the box, it's both alive and dead, har har har!" A lot of good that does the *cat* from whose point of view "if someone doesn't open this dang box soon, asphyxiation and starvation aside, I'm going to be simultaneously alive and *bored* to death.")

(Then *again*, until the cat is *determined* to be simply alive and not simultaneously dead – though I'd wager the cat itself is pretty determined to be simply alive – maybe they're in some kind of suspended state in which they can't think, much less feel bored. Not to mention that until someone opens the box, from the cat's point of view - does quantum physics discriminate among observers? - the *humans* are both alive and dead and have been of uncertain existence ever since they closed the box and became, from the cat's perspective, themselves uncertain. Somewhat of a Catch-22. The people outside the box won't know whether the cat is simply alive or simply dead until they open the box, but until the cat can see - or hear or smell or scratch, I suppose - what's outside of the box, the people who put them in the box are neither simply alive nor simply dead either. The real question here clearly hinges upon whether the uncertainty of one's human or feline existence must be resolved prior to the opening or closing of boxes.) (Which is probably why the Buddha, in his infinite wisdom accumulated over countless eons of experiences, no doubt including being simultaneously alive and dead while imprisoned by quantum physicists - when they ran out of cats - in as many boxes as there are grains of sand in my sneakers, counselled Ananda to

JUST THROW THE BOX AWAY!!!)

(Luk, 1966/1999, p. 67; Italics and screaming added - The Buddha was known to speak in bold so that's on him.)

Apologies, my parentheticalitis (not to be confused with parentheticolitis, a related condition apparently affecting some of my readers, which should probably be added to the "bear ingestion" rider on my malpractice insurance seeing as much of the tangential content is ursine in nature) seems to be acting up again. (By the way, did you know that in the days preceding the extinction of the typewriter it was customary to tap the spacebar twice after a period? This isn't necessary nowadays as word processors do it automatically.) Where were we? Right, when I located the original of the 1906 cartoon, proving for all intents and purposes, or at least for one or two intents and purposes, that it wasn't Pooh Bear who originated the expression "Sometimes I sits and thinks and sometimes I just sits" - Winnie was born in 1926 - I noticed that right under that Punch cartoon was the continuation of a poem entitled "To a Caged Bear at the Brighton Aquarium" by a fellow, fellowette or fellowX named *Algol*. Ignoring for the moment the wisdom of housing a bear in an aquarium, the poem seems to involve said *Algol* having a one-sided conversation with said *bear* who, along with their (the bear's) brother James or Jim, was orphaned, when they (Algol) realize that they (Algol) are hungry and that they (the bear) are asleep (or *pretending* to be asleep so Algol will leave them alone – can't they [Algol] read the sign that they [Algol] themself wrote about in the poem that instructed aquarium visitors "Please not to irritate the bear"?) – prompting them (Algol) to give them (the bear) a "slice of currant cake as token of my deep regard" since they (bears) can sleep and eat at the same time, especially when *underwater* in their *aquariums*. That's about what I got from it. Here it is for your perusal:

Chapter 40 – To A Caged Bear at the Brighton Aquarium

THE CONSPIRACY OF 1906.

On Wednesday, the 17th day of October, before *Mr. Punch* at his Court in Bouverie Street, Mr. HOOPER, and Messrs. MOBERLY BELL, POULTEN, BYLES, and HALL CAINE were charged with conspiring together with intent to cause a breach of the peace of the breakfast-table. A gentleman who gave his name as R 17623/284975 was charged with aiding and abetting them. Mr. HOOPER failed to put in an appearance, but the Court decided to take the case without him.

JOHN SMITH was called first, and gave evidence that the peace and harmony of his breakfast-table had been completely spoiled by the accused. After reading their letters to each other he felt quite ill, and was unable to digest properly. Some letters, of course, were worse than others. It was an interview with Mr. BYLES, for instance, that gave him that stab in the back.

Mr. Punch said he thought witness must be thinking of something else.

Witness admitted that this might be so, but said that in any case the nuisance was an intolerable one. He simply dared not open his paper at the breakfast-table now.

Messrs. BROWN, JONES, and ROBINSON having given similar evidence, the counsel for the prosecution intimated that that was his case.

The prisoners elected to give evidence on their own behalf, whereupon Mr. POULTEN went into the witness-box and said: I am Secretary to the Publishers' Association. I write those pretty letters that appear in the papers every day. I write them all myself. Nobody helps me.

Cross-examined.—He wrote them in the mornings. He could not say how he spent his afternoons, but generally he would be resting. It was not true that he derived great benefit from the *Encyclopædia Britannica* in the composition of his letters. He had already given his opinion of that work, and he would repeat it here. On second thoughts he wouldn't, but it was true all the same. He had never conspired with the other prisoners. Some of them he had never heard of. He had heard of HALL CAINE, of course. He had never seen Mr. HOOPER.

Re-examined.—He was not Mr. HOOPER.

Mr. BYLES said: I am a publisher. I have been interviewed nine times, and have written eighteen letters on the matter. I had no reasons for doing this, save love of Literature. I have nothing at all to gain; on the contrary I have spent one and sixpence in stamps. I have never conspired with anybody. I have seen Mr. HOOPER. (Sensation.)

Cross-examined.—When he said he had seen Mr. HOOPER he meant that he had seen a gentleman who gave his name as HOOPER. He (Mr. BYLES) did not belong to the Publishers' Association. He could not say that too often. So far he had said it twenty-seven times. Though he did not belong to the Association he admired Mr. POULTEN's style. It was true his firm was a rising one, but he has never told his interviewers so. He had no idea how these things got in the paper.

Re-examined.—He was not Mr. HOOPER.

Mr. MOBERLY BELL said: I am Manager of *The Times*. I have written very few letters to the papers. My speciality is interviews. I am interviewed every day. In my interviews I always say I am quite happy and that the War is over. As a matter of fact it has only been a sort of war.

Cross-examined.—He had heard of Lord HALSBURY and Mr. CHAMBERLAIN. They were members of the Book Club, but he didn't quite see the connection. The war really *was* over. He was very busy just now, but that was only because he had to be interviewed so many times. He had never conspired with anybody. It was the other way round. He had heard of America, of course. COLUMBUS discovered it.

Re-examined.—That was in the *Encyclopædia Britannica*, Ninth Edition.

Cross-examined.—He would swear to that. He did not understand what counsel insinuated by "Stop - Press News." It was in the main article on America. There was no American Syndicate that controlled *The Times*. Mr. HOOPER wrote some of the advertisements, that was all. He had frequently seen Mr. HOOPER, and had given him orders. He could not swear that Mr. HOOPER was not an American. He had never asked him. He really could not be bothered with the private history of all his subordinates.

Re-examined.—He was not Mr. HOOPER.

Mr. HALL CAINE said : I am a novelist and a dramatist. I am about to publish a perfectly new work of fiction at half-a-crown.

Cross-examined.—It was called *The Bondman*. It was not an old work. He admitted that he had written a book called *The Bondman* many years ago, and that a dramatised version was now being played at Drury Lane, but this was neither of those. This was the play turned back into a story again, and was therefore quite different. Also it was to contain a photograph of himself. He would not swear that he had never been photographed before. Many people denied that this would be a test of the dearness of novels, but he himself was quite self-satisfied.

Re-examined.—Quite satisfied, he meant, of course. He was not Mr. HOOPER.

Cross-examined.—He believed the advertisement rates of *The Daily Mail* were very high. He had never heard of the expression "Self-advertisement rates."

R 17623/284975 said: I am a member of the T.B.C.

Cross-examined.—He had written to *The Times* to say how grateful he was. He had not signed it. He hated self-advertisement. He was not "Author of Forty Years Standing," nor was he "Book Lover." He was just R 17623/284975. M.O.2846 was another gentleman.

Before witness could be re-examined *Mr. Punch* interposed, saying that he had heard enough. The prisoners were found guilty, and Messrs. BELL, BYLES, POULTEN and CAINE would be condemned to read each other's letters. Mr. HOOPER and R 17623/284975 would come up for judgment together when called upon.

TO A CAGED BEAR AT THE BRIGHTON AQUARIUM.

EPHRIM—for such the trivial name
  Thy race familiarly was dealt,
What time 'Old Jake's' unerring aim
  Probed thine invaluable pelt;

What time, inspired by MANVILLE FENN,
  I stalked thee in my dreams and slew
The beetling moose, or, one to ten,
  Outclassed the hair-compelling Sioux;

Most pensive Bruin, I descry
  Thy presence with profound regret,
This bosom weeps for thee, this eye
  Is sympathetically wet.

Pent in yon dark Cimmerian den
  Thou liest in enforced repose;
A barren wall obscures thy ken,
  Odours of fish assail thy nose.

The crowd moves by, but thou art banned,
  An object of delight to none;
No smiles encourage thee, no hand
  Confers the unexpected bun.

And lo! as though to point the jest,
  A board confronts the empty air,
Bearing the humorous request
  "Please not to irritate the bear!"

Oh I have seen in many lands
  Bears of all sorts and divers hues :
Bears that performed with gipsy bands,
  And some immured in alien Zoos.

Some crawled up mercenary poles,
  While others stood upon their head;
All seemed profoundly cheerful souls,
  And not a few were overfed.

Thou only, friendless and apart,
  Sitting disconsolate dost brood
Alike on man's unfeeling heart,
  And the prevailing dearth of food.

CHANGE OF OCCUPATION.

Vicar's Wife (sympathisingly). "Now that you can't get about, and are not able to read, how do you manage to occupy the time?"

Old Man. "Well, Mum, sometimes I sits and thinks; and then again I just sits."

And many a dream-born vision racks
  Thine uncommunicative breast
With thoughts of old frequented tracks
  Down the dim cañons of the West.

Out yonder where the setting sun
  Leaves Tallac's rugged slopes aglow,
Painting with silver, grey and dun,
  The shadowed deeps of Lake Tahoe,

Thou and a brother ball of fur
  Roamed through the woods in cubsome glee,
Watched with maternal care by her
  Whose family you chanced to be;

Chased the white-footed mouse among
  The Autumn leaves, or in the quest
Of toothsome eatables got stung
  By the ferocious bee his nest;

Fished in the shallow streams for trout,
  With eager paws, or from the ground
Extracted with unerring snout
  Roots of a succulence profound.

Then came the fatal day when fired
  By pickled pork and hunger's thrall
Thine unsuspecting Ma expired
  Beneath the log-trap's deadly fall.

And monsters seized on thee and him,
  Thy brother JAMES, and full of care
Thou wast to exile sent, but JIM
  Fosters the growth of backward hair.

Bruin, farewell! I fain would stay
  And o'er thy wrongs conjointly weep,
But hunger bids me haste away:
  I note besides that thou 'rt asleep.

Yet may it still be mine to make
  Thy tedious lot a shade less hard:
Accept this slice of currant cake
  As token of my deep regard!
                        ALGOL.

The Wonders of Nature.

"FOR SALE, 2 Trees Eating Pears."
                      Gloucester Citizen.

"The Shaver's Calendar."

Mr. Punch begs to recommend this original calendar, compiled by Mr. F. SIDGWICK and published by A. H. BULLEN, to all to whom it may appeal at eight o'clock in the morning or thereabouts. He is tempted to quote the mottoes for four February days. "I'll shave you as well as I can" (*Ben Jonson*). "Upon this promise did he raise his chin" (*Venus and Adonis*). "The bright death quivered at the victim's throat, touch'd, and ——" (*Tennyson*). "There remains some scar of it" (*As you Like It*). "O cursed be the hand that made these holes" (*Richard III.*), and "'E lifted up my 'ead, An' 'e plugged me where I bled" (*Kipling*) will bring back memories of cheap barbers to most of his readers. It is, however, a pity (for obvious reasons) that each quotation has not a page to itself; but none the less Mr. SIDGWICK is to be congratulated upon the very successful result of what must have been a labour of love and much laughter.

TO A CAGED BEAR AT THE BRIGHTON AQUARIUM

"EPHRIM – for such the trivial name
      Thy race familiarly was dealt,
What time 'Old Jakes' unerring aim
      Probed thine invaluable pelt ;

What time, inspired by MANVILLE FENN,
      I stalked thee in my dreams and slew
The beetling moose, or, one to ten
      Outclassed the hair-compelling Sioux ;

Most pensive Bruin, I descry
      Thy presence with profound regret,
This bosom weeps for thee, this eye
      Is sympathetically wet.

Pent in you dark Cimmerian den
      Thou liest in enforced repose ;
A barren wall obscures thy ken,
      Odours of fish assail thy nose.

The crowd moves by, but thou art banned,
      An object of delight to none ;
No smiles encourage thee, no hand
      Confers the unexpected bun.

How To Stop Thinking and Not Get Eaten By A Bear

And lo ! as though to point the jest,
    A board confronts the empty air,
Bearing the humorous request
    'Please not to irritate the bear !'

Oh I have seen in many lands
    Bears of all sorts and divers hues :
Bears that performed with gipsy bands,
    And some immured in alien Zoos.

Some crawled up mercenary poles,
    While others stood upon their head ;
All seemed profoundly cheerful souls,
    And not a few were overfed.

Thou only, friendless and apart,
    Sitting disconsolate dost brood
Alike on man's unfeeling heart,
    And the prevailing dearth of food.

And many a dream-born vision racks
    Thine uncommunicative breast
With thoughts of old frequented tracks
    Down the dim cañons of the West.

Chapter 40 – To A Caged Bear at the Brighton Aquarium

Out yonder where the setting sun
      Leaves Tallac's rugged slopes aglow,
Painting with silver, grey and dun,
      The shadowed deeps of Lake Tahoe,

Thou and a brother ball of fur
      Roamed through the woods in cubsome glee.
Watched with maternal care by her
      Whose family you chanced to be ;

Chased the white-footed mouse among
      The Autumn leaves, or in the quest
Of toothsome eatables got stung
      By the ferocious bee his nest ;

Fished in the shallow streams for trout
      With eager paws, or from the ground
Extracted with unerring snout
      Roots of a succulence profound.

Then came the fatal day when fired
      By pickled pork and hunger's thrall
Thine unsuspecting Ma expired
      Beneath the log-trap's deadly fall.

And monsters seized on thee and him,

    Thy brother JAMES, and full of care

Thou wast to exile sent, but JIM

    Fosters the growth of backward hair.

Bruin, farewell! I fain would stay

    And o'er thy wrongs conjointly weep,

But hunger bids me haste away:

    I note besides that thou 'rt asleep.

Yet may it still be mine to make

    Thy tedious lot a shade less hard:

Accept this slice of currant cake

    As token of my deep regard!"

                  ALGOL (1906, pp. 296-297)

Epilogue

WARNING: This chapter can expose you to facts that are known to the state of Massachusetts to be more than 99% alternative.

"... and how much more falsity is still necessary to me that I may therewith always reassure myself regarding the luxury of my truth."

(Nietzsche, 1878/1908)

Friedrich Nietzsche by Edvard Munch. 1906.

Captain's log, stardate 3012.4. The Merovingians have been contained, promising not to speak French for the next 2000 years at penalty of terraformation of their planet into a domed buckyball arena.

Oops, wrong book.

Two Merovingian stars walk into a bar on Hollywood Boulevard, continuing their conversation:

"You can't be serious!"

"Do I look like a binary?"

"Actually, you do. By the way, sorry to hear about your twin. They say he collapsed."

"He'll be fine. He just ran out of steam."

(The Merovingian Book of Science Jokes Not-To-Be-Published-Or-Told-In-French)

"In the newly discovered manuscript, written by Gregory of Tours in the sixth century and described in an article in the Nov. 7 issue of the British journal Nature, Sirius was referred to as 'Rubeola' or 'Robeola' – the 'red' or 'rusty' star. This Merovingian text, preserved in a West German library, was designed to help monastaries [*sic*] to determine when the constellations were properly aligned for nocturnal divine services. Sirius is also referred to as 'Stella Splendida,' implying that then, as now, it was the brightest star.

. . . Sirius was already the subject of a mystery concerning the traditional lore of the Dogon tribe of Mali, near Timbuktu in western Africa. According to this lore, confided to French anthropologists who observed the tribe from 1931 to 1979, Sirius has a small invisible companion of extreme density and the two bodies circle each other every 50 years.

The existence of such a companion star had been deduced in 1836 by the German astronomer Friedrich Bessel, based on his observation that the motion of Sirius through space was irregular because of the gravitational influence of an object circling it. But the

Epilogue

> Dogon lore was thought by some to have originated centuries before that discovery, and a number of writers have expressed amazement that the secret lore of the Dogon priests should include such knowledge of Sirius as well as the existence of Jupiter's four inner moons, the rings of Saturn and the fact that all the planets including Earth fly elliptical orbits around the Sun.
>
> . . . By the 1920's it had been deduced that this companion star, Sirius B, was a "white dwarf," a small, extremely dense remnant of a star that has exhausted its nuclear fuel and collapsed because it no longer generates the heat needed to support its gaseous envelope. The stage of a star's life cycle that precedes such a collapse is typically that of a huge 'red giant.'"

W. Sullivan (11/18/1985; New York Times)

And while we're on the topic of famous companions, my cousin Paul is a trivia buff, and one day while we were walking along the Ocean Beach boardwalk in New London, he told me that one of the best kept secrets in Hollywood of the 1930s was that Abbott and Costello, of comedic fame, were practicing Hindus. Bud Abbott, born Budhjan Chakraborty, and Lou Costello, born Loukik Chaudhari, met when they were studying accounting at the Indian Institute of Technology. To earn extra money they would perform comedy skits at local Delhi venues. After an American exchange student whose family had Hollywood connections saw one of their skits, a local audio crew was commissioned to record a short dialogue which was broadcast on The Kate Smith Hour on February 3, 1938, under the condition that they anglicize their names.

As Chakraborty remembered it in an interview with Jack Linkletter on December 7, 1962,

> "It was 1938 and we were putting on shows for the Punjab prisoners, as Gandhi implored them to end their hunger strike. We were all fired up for independence and were proud of our heritage. To now go on American radio as Bud Abbott and Lou Costello seemed a betrayal of our country. But Loukik felt that once we got famous we could use our real names. Unfortunately, that's not how Hollywood

works, and when we tried it the lawyers pointed out the small print in our original contract."

Chakraborty and Chaudhari came up with one of their most famous skits when they were visiting their childhood friend, Venkataraman Iyer, by that time known as The Maharshi, the Sage of Arunachala, at his ashram in Tiruvannamali. The Maharshi took them to a new restaurant where at one point the following conversation ensued:

Waitress: Welcome to Cafe Fiji. What's the special of the day.

Maharshi: Who wants to know?

Waitress: Who already knows. Who's the cook.

Costello: I don't know.

Waitress: At your service. My friends call me Ida.

Costello: You're the cook?

Waitress: I'm the waitress. Who's the cook.

Costello: Who?

Waitress: Yes.

Costello: That's what I'm asking you.

Waitress: That's what I'm telling you.

(Abbott returns from the men's room)

Abbott: What's for dinner?

Waitress: And very tasty, I might add.

Costello: What?

Waitress: Yes. Should I make that 3 specials?

Maharshi: Who wants to know?

Waitress: Of course, he's a cook, not a mind reader.

Costello: A-bbott!!!!!!!!!!!!!!!!!!!!!!!!!

Epilogue

(Excerpted from

Abbott, Costello and the Maharshi Meet the Cannibals)

Afterward - *In Which the Author Finally Understands* the Meaning of His Own Book's Title

"How do you get to Wonderland?

Over the hill or underland,

or just behind the tree?"

Alice in Wonderland

(Bob Hilliard, 1951)

And so one journey ends, and another begins. I have finally set in words what I try to impart to each of my clients during their first session (I talk fast). Those of you whom I haven't met (at least not across the faux oriental rug) finally know, hopefully, how to stop thinking, how to cope a little better with various forms of distress, how to enter some really cool altered states of consciousness, and maybe a tiny bit about how to not get eaten by a bear.

So where to go from here when there's no *there* there? In one sense, if you lived here you'd be home by now, and you do, and you are. You can't go anywhere from here, because, even if you do, you'll still be here.

As my favorite psychologist, Ram Dass said, "Be Here Now." He later reminded us that "I'm Still Here." I imagine now if he was asked for some words of wisdom, he might respond "Been There, Done That." Another one of my favorite psychologists, Adyashanti, isn't actually a psychologist, but if you heard him responding to retreatants' questions about their life struggles, you'd swear he was. (In a good way.) Several years ago I had the

Afterward - In Which the Author Finally Understands the Meaning of His Own Book's Title

good fortune to webcam with Ram Dass and chat about psychology and some personal issues, when he was still in Hawaii (and in a body) and I was still in Hong Kong (and in a body - which I'm still hopefully in as you read this book, but if not, *c'est la mort*). I'm sure he's busy enlightening beings in other realms as we speak.

In the words of Jon Kabat Zinn (who was the first mindfulness teacher I met in a healthcare environment, during my postdoc): "Wherever you go, there you are." Every time I hear this I think it should rather be "Wherever you go, here you are" but maybe it's an MIT quantum physics thing.

In any case, here, there, "It is one event" (Nisargadatta, 1999/1973, p. 138).

So, where to go? Here, I guess.

A Koan

Ever since I was a child, I've had a special relationship with bears. There was (and is, in a drawer somewhere) Teddy, the furry hand puppet; Gentle Ben, who had a pull string and said stuff ("Most bears are clumsy, but I'm not. You can depend on me, 'cause I'm your friend. Oh, I think it's time for my long winter's nap. Watch me climb up and get some honey")(I found it on YouTube), and of course, my favorite bear of all time, Pooh, my first meditation teacher ("Sometimes I sits and thinks, and sometimes I just sits") - wink wink. Never was big on Yogi or Smokey, for some reason. Probably because Smokey was a big liar (*I'm* the only one who can prevent forest fires? Yeah, right).

Among my childhood phobias, right up there with (1) getting bitten by Dracula (the first time I ever did exposure therapy on myself was upon realizing that in the summer it was too hot to sleep with the blanket all the way up to the bottom of my chin and that it was time to "get over it"), and (2) being turned into a werewolf (after seeing The Werewolf Of London and Abbott and Costello Meet the Werewolf), was (3) getting my leg stuck in a bear trap. Not that I often had playdates in those Manhattan neighborhoods frequented by bears or lived with anyone who didn't keep their bear traps in a securely locked bear trap cabinet when they weren't using them (well maybe Denis), but because bears were *good* and bear traps were *bad*. I may not have had much of a memory for important dates in history, but I had my priorities straight.

As I grew older, I developed a healthy respect for bears, at a distance, and never turned into one of those morons who gets out of the car in Yellowstone to get closer to the "cute little bear" for a selfie. The nearest I ever got to a real bear, without intervening motes, bars or plexiglass was when that kid on the camping trip hung a piece of raw meat on the clothesline and in the middle of the night a shadow appeared on the wall of the tent that was way too big to be a camper or counselor (and no, we hadn't ordered pizza).

In full self-disclosure, Fate has never called upon me to make that important and ultimate call between Brown, Black, White and Lie Down, Fight Back, Say Goodnight. And I hope that I, and you, never will. But if you do, that might be a good time to ask the Critical Question: "Am I dreaming" and try to float. If you can float, then try giving the bear a big hug and a kiss on the snout and maybe s/he'll turn into Pooh or your favorite movie star. If you can't float but you bop him in the nose with this book, you'll have a one in three chance of reading my next bestseller, "How To Decide From Whom To Take Advice About Encounters with Bears."

One day, after the first draft of this book was pretty much finished in March, 2019 – don't ask me why I'm still adding stuff in June, 2022, against the counsel of my friend Frank, also a psychologist, to STOP IT AND FINISH THE DANG BOOK – As an aside, Frank thinks he's writing a musical that doesn't involve bears but, as we all know that music soothes the savage beast, I think I might be able to convince Dave at the Appalachian Mini Mart to stock a few CDs of the musical next to this book and the bear spray in aisle 2. Here's Frank at his Pandemic office where there's a wood burning stove inside that confuses the virus:

the suspense builds . . .

Afterward - In Which the Author Finally Understands the Meaning of His Own Book's Title

And, fast-forwarding a bit to December, 2022, Frank is a generally thoughtful fellow, but apparently oblivious to even the most rudimentary etiquette regarding how to respond to a friend who has just informed you, with relief, that he has finally sent his book on *how to not get eaten by a bear* off to the printer. No sooner had I conveyed to him the latter than Frank started telling me new bear stories that, honestly, he'd had ample, and frankly (npi) more appropriate, opportunity to mention during the *four years* prior while I was writing the book and perhaps even in *the fifty-four years* prior since we'd met in Indian Guides. I'll forgive him this time, as the top-secret title and content of this monstrosity was unknown even to him until more recently, but let this be a lesson to us all:

> **Friends don't tell friends *new* bear stories *after* their friends finish their bear story books.**

Nevertheless, *here we are,* and it turns out that Frank may very well be *the only psychologist ever to have walked the earth* who has had to grapple with how to protect his therapy clients (and himself) from getting eaten by bears *during therapy*, warranting yet another "correction" to this First Edition.

For better or for worse, just as necessity is the mother of invention, the latter is oft prone to beget new necessities themselves in need of further inventiveness. In the present case,

(1) the first *necessity* in question was that of continuing to provide therapy during a pandemic.

(2) Frank solved this by *inventing* a new way (at least new for him) of providing therapy, namely in the open air while hiking or sitting in the woods. The only problem was that the woods in question were *infested with BEARS* (he told me that he had himself seen bears on 20 to 30 occasions where he lives in Northern New Jersey, including in his own backyard and garage, walking past him as he sat on his deck or looking in a window).

(3) Thus, the new *necessity* of keeping bears at bay while conducting therapy.

(4) Luckily both he and his clients were up to the task. One day, a bear approached during hiking therapy and the client, *unperturbed*, clapped his hands and scared it away. Another day, a bear approached as Frank and a client sat therapizing and Frank himself, having learned from the first client, clapped and sent it back from whence it came (that client apparently *was* perturbed – go figure).

Here, in sum, necessity (how to continue providing therapy during a pandemic) led to invention (providing therapy outdoors) which, as the outdoors contained **BEARS**, led to necessity (figuring out how not to get eaten by a bear during therapy), which itself led to further invention (clapping). One must needs wonder, of course, whether, upon spotting a bear approaching during therapy, the *elegant solution* might not have been simply to have *stopped thinking* or, perhaps, to have sung the *Bear I'm Not A* song rather than clapping, which obviously risked being mistaken by the bear for applause and *approval* of its uninvited, and likely, HIPAA-violating intrusion on the privacy of a healthcare procedure. But the fact is, the clapping worked, everyone left the therapy session with all of their limbs intact, *if it ain't broke don't fix it*, and so clapping may provisionally be added to stopping thinking and singing as ways to not get eaten by a bear, at least during therapy, and again, remember the *don't quote me* rule.

Afterward - In Which the Author Finally Understands the Meaning of His Own Book's Title

But back to the koan. One day in 2019, I decided after a meeting uptown to go back downtown to The Strand Bookstore (*5 million miles of books*), and browse through the Self-Help section to get some insight into the types of book covers and formatting of various bestsellers. After all, if I'm gonna spend my vacation weeks and weekends sitting at a table for 12 hours a day drinking leftover MacDonald's coffee because the cabin coffee maker is kaput, why not make a few bucks? As it turned out, the most interesting events of the day ended up not happening in the bookstore itself, but on the subway rides there and back.

First, on the subway from Port Authority to Union Square, I had a Kabatzinnesque "Wherever You Go, There You Are" moment. My mind was racing with this problem and that after oversleeping, running late and rushing to Park & Ride when I remembered "Hold on a sec, aren't I writing a book on How to Stop Thinking? Oh yeah. Why don't I try that Seahearbody exercise I made up a few weeks ago?" So, standing on the train, I closed my eyes (which *isn't* necessary), saw the light through my eyelids, heard the speeding train and voices, and felt my whole bodysense. I suddenly realized (nonverbally) that "this is no different from sitting in silent stillness," except of course for the standing in noisy movement part. But fundamentally, there was the sense of "I AM," and the (nonverbal) sense that the path to I AM is seahearbody, passing through "Who" seahearbodies (which of course is "I"), and finally all the way back to Who is this I?

Then, on the subway back from The Strand, something very strange happened, but a little bit of back story is necessary. I originally thought of calling this book *How To Stop Thinking and Other Tricks of the Trade*. For some reason, about half way through the book, I got on the topic of bears, probably related to seeing a sign at my lodging about bears that triggered a memory from a bear safety brochure I once read. It had suggested surviving a bear attack by "giving it a good bop to the nose," with the qualifier that this should be done only to a black bear and not to a brown bear with whom it would be mega counterproductive, and the additional qualifier that black bears can be brown and some brown bears are "almost black." Thanks a lot. Anyway, I must have got to thinking that *other tricks of the trade* sounded kind of dorky, but had *How to Stop Worrying and Start Living* in mind as a prototype 2-part title ("OVER SIX MILLION COPIES SOLD!"), and if I was going to scrap *other tricks of the trade* I would need to replace it with something along the lines of *and Start Living*. And what better way to start living (or at least to keep living) than to *not get eaten by a bear*? That's probably when the light bulb went off (on?). If actual *national park safety brochures* were giving advice like the above, how much worse could *I* possibly do?

Further confirmation of the low bar set for bear safety advice by the so-called experts is provided by this declassified National Park Service Twitter feed of February 28th, 2023 (I really can't stop editing this book. It's getting like the DSM. Or Leaves of Grass. Or Finnegan's Wake. Lassie, I mean Sherwood, get help! I dove back in to correct some typos and thinkos, but when I saw this Twitter feed, well, I think you'll agree that if it belongs anywhere other than Twitter, it's here):

> "If you come across a bear, never push a slower friend down ... even if you feel the friendship has run its course." (National Park Services @ NatlParkService)

>> "What if you're the slower friend?" (Doug Jones @ BPrtch)

> "Check in on the friendship before you head to the woods" (National Park Services @ NatlParkService)

>> "OK, but what if the bear looks really hungry? Don't they deserve a lil snack as a treat?" (Jeff Brown @ jeffmeister777)

> "Do you consider yourself the faster or slower friend?" (National Park Services @ NatlParkService)

>> "What if they consider me a friend but I just consider them an acquaintance? Then is it OK to push them in front of said bear? Asking for an acquaintance . . ." (Madlabscientist @ blueandgold90)

> "Friendships are special, but they don't happen by chance. It takes effort and trust to build a lasting friendship. Good luck." (National Park Services @ NatlParkService)

> (National Park Service, 2023)

Now, this is where, if you're a psychologist, or have read this book rather than just skipped to the Afterward (Corky Coben's butler did it. Actually, Corky would have done it herself, but she was busy umping little league that

Afterward - In Which the Author Finally Understands the Meaning of His Own Book's Title

day. On a similar note, I always did appreciate Harlan sending Myron Bolitar into harms way to save my own mother from Art Teacher and Ascot Bite, though I often do wonder whether they might not have abducted her in the first place had Myron run for cover into a different old friend's childhood house; Coben, 2006), you might be thinking "but of *course*" - or if you're French, "but of *ourse*" - as "ourse" is French for female bear, with "ourses" being French for more than one female bear, though the "s" is silent so like *what's the point* - yes, if you're a psychologist or have read this book you might be thinking that I obviously wrote about bears in a book about stopping thinking because "don't think of a white bear" is a psychology (and Russian novelist) joke. But I assure you, though I would like to assure you otherwise in order to maintain my aura of infallibility (or ineffability)(or one of those ibilities or abilities that we are all challenged with), that prior to writing this book, and prior to adding the bear thing, *I had never heard the "try not to think of a white bear" joke.* In fact, I had always thought the joke was *"try not to think of a pink elephant."* Lucky for me I was wrong, because "How To Stop Thinking and Not Get Eaten By A Pink Elephant" would have scared even fewer people into buying a self-help book with instructions on how to leave your body, and good luck getting a plug from Dave at the Appalachian Mini Mart for a book with *that* title. I mean, "Aisle 2 on the left next to the pink elephant spray" doesn't sound convincing even to *me*.

Getting back to this afternoon, I was on the train heading back to Port Authority and I thought "how about if I put a picture of a bear and a meditator on the cover?" So I google-imaged "bear and meditator" and, in addition to some really funny images from BearmageddonNews.com by Ethan Nicolle, the author of the book *Bears Want to Kill You*, was dumbstruck to see the cover of a new book by Ajahn Brahm (2017), a Buddhist monk, whom I meditated with about 10 years ago in the mountains of Hong Kong. And then it hit me like a ton of bricks, the "meaning of" and "answer" to the title of my book, as though it were a Zen koan. I will leave you with it as I bid you adieu with gratitude for accompanying me on this journey:

Q: How do you stop thinking and not get eaten by a bear?

A: Bare Awareness!

Afterthought 1 - *A Bear Walks Into Bill Barr*

A bear walks into Bill Barr and says "You really should, ummm, watch where you're going."

"But you walked into me!" says Barr.

"Fake, ummm, News!" says the Bear.

"How did you get past security anyway, and what's with the long pauses?" asks Barr.

"I ate them, and what's with the, ummm, bad grammar?" says the bear.

Just then a tiger walks into Bill Barr.

Bill Barr eats the tiger, the bear eats Bill Barr and then spits out a big pair of glasses (Bill Barr's. Tigers don't wear glasses).

President Trump walks out, sees the mess in the hall and says "Hey, you can't just leave that, uh, lyin' there."

"It's a, ummm, tiger" responds the bear, "and I need a pardon for eating your, ummm, Attorney General."

"Granted" says Trump, "but what's with the, uh, long pauses?"

The bear answers "Haven't you people, ummm, ever seen a bear before? And what's with the *short* pauses?"

To which Trump replies: "I guess I was just born that way."

(My translation from the Belarusian. Heard on the Minsk metro somewhere between Pervomayskaya and Kuntsevshchina or maybe on the Slutskiy Gostinets line, I forget. If you are thinking of visiting Minsk, Wikitravel.org assures us that "Minsk is a very safe and clean city. Unlike most Eastern

European cities, there are very few homeless and drunkards wandering the streets. Although locals might insist otherwise, Minsk is a city where you really must go out of your way to find trouble, even at night." But if you *want* to find trouble at night, you could [not that you *should*, but you *could*] walk up to someone in uniform and scream "Святлана Георгіеўна Ціханоўская!" [Sviatlana Heorhiyeuna Tsikhanouskaya!]. Alternatively, if spending the night in Следственный изолятор КГБ Республики Беларусь, СИЗО КГБ, SIZO KGB [Pre-Trial Detention Centre of the KGB of Belarus – also informally called Amerikanka] doesn't appeal to you, but you still fashion a walk on the Wild Side, you could just look for someone with a badass tat or two and greet them with "Абадай цябе халера," which a friend once told me meant "cool tat" but really means "May you get ill with cholera.")

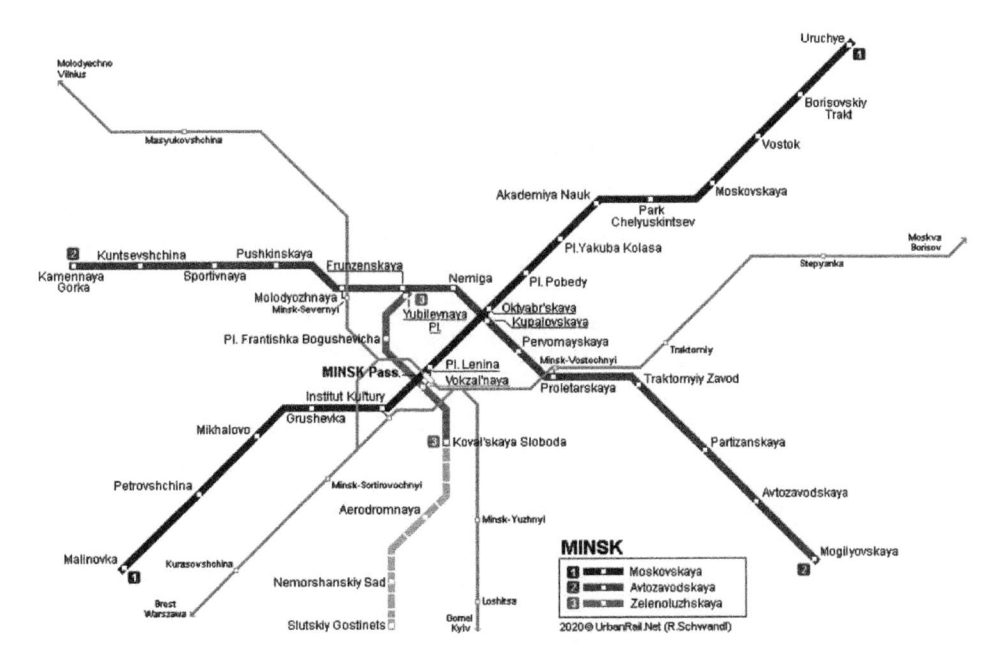

Afterthought 2 - *Do Computers Have Near-Crash-Experiences (NCEs)?*

Heck if I know. Ask Siri. The more important question may be where they *go* when they crash. Probably not to the "good" place, if their former user has any say. Or maybe the more important question is: Are *humans* computers, in which case Near-Death-Experiences are themselves Near-Crash-Experiences. And what if we *are* computers, and where we and our metal brothers and sisters go when our wetware/dryware goes kerplotz is *itself* a simulation. What if when Neo finally "wakes up" in Zion, it is a simulation (as suggested at the end of the incomprehensible-to-mere-mortals-like-me Matrix Revolutions)? While there are good arguments against Zion being a simulation (JonTherkildsen, 2019), and against the heavens and hells of world religions being simulations, there are good internally-logical arguments for all sorts of things that are, ultimately, not true. As Einstein said: "We cannot solve our problems with the same thinking we used when we created them." Similarly, we cannot understand a simulation from within the simulation. The best we can do is *reduce* the incorrect thinking, the logical extreme which is, of course, to *stop thinking*. But how? Who wants to know ...

Afterthought 3 - *Noise: A Poem*

1.

Noise.

2.

Hearing noise, I remember noise and think noise.

Thinking noise, I say noise.

Saying noise, others hear noise, remember noise, think noise, and say noise.

3.

Hearing more noise, I remember more noise and think more noise.

Until I stop thinking noise.

4.

Hearing noise, I remember noise but don't think noise.

Not thinking noise, I don't say noise.

Not saying noise, others don't hear noise, don't remember noise, don't think noise and don't say noise.

5.

Not hearing noise, I don't remember noise, don't think noise, and don't say noise.

6.

Not hearing noise, others don't remember noise, don't think noise and don't say noise.

7.

 No noise.

Afterthought 4 - *The Internet Just Makes Shift Up* to Futz With Your Head

> "The fox has many tricks.
>
> The hedgehog has but one.
>
> But that is the best of all."

Erroneously Attributed on the Internet to Erasmus and Emerson

In 1953, philosopher Isaiah Berlin published an essay entitled *The Hedgehog and the Fox*, with reference to Archilochus' saying "The fox knows many things, but the hedgehog knows one big thing."

Berlin sought to distinguish between "hedgehogs,"

> who "relate everything to a single central vision ... a single, universal, organizing principle in terms of which alone all that they are and say has significance"

and "foxes,"

> who "pursue many ends, often unrelated and even contradictory, connected, if at all, only in some defacto way, for some psychological or physiological cause, related by no moral or aesthetic principle."

He gave as examples:

> **Hedgehogs:** Dante, Plato, Lucretius, Pascal, Hegel, Dostoevsky, Nietzsche, Ibsen & Proust;

Afterthought 4 - The Internet Just Makes Shift Up to Futz With Your Head

Foxes: Shakespeare, Herodotus, Aristotle, Montaigne, Erasmus, Molière, Goethe, Pushkin, Balzac & Joyce.

And then there was Tolstoy who, according to Berlin, "was by nature a fox, but believed in being a hedgehog" (Berlin, 1953).

Wikipedia (The Hedgehog and the Fox, 2022) says Berlin included Fernand Braudel as a hedgehog and Philip Warren Anderson, who won the 1977 Nobel Prize in Physics for research leading to computer memory (Philip Warren Anderson, 2022), as a fox, but I couldn't find reference to either in Berlin (1953). Maybe he added them later. *Or maybe not.*

I know all of this not because I have read much written by the above (though as a pseudointellectual, I've heard all the names, except Philip's, and probably have a bunch of their books in a box somewhere), but because in the writing of this book, I stumbled upon a saying attributed to Emerson and wrote it down without noting the citation:

"The fox has many tricks.

The hedgehog has but one.

But that is the best of all."

And then, when it was time to be a good citizen and verify my sources, I googled the above, and what did I find? A book on Amazon.com entitled "The fox has many tricks. The hedgehog has but one. But that is the best of all" by ... Desiderius Erasmus (Amazon.com, 2022). That's what the cover said. The book was just full of blank lines. It was out of stock. "Makes a wonderful gift for a graduate - sister - aunt - friend - cousin - teammate - bridesmaid - mom - or anyone who could use a motivational-inspirational boost." I added it to my *Wish List.*

Anyway, I'm sitting there thinking: "*Huh? Didn't Emerson say it? Let's google it again.*" This time it did have my man Waldo as the author on BrainyQuote.com (2022) *and* "InspirationalStories.com (2022).

Three out of four is as good a truth criterion as anything when dealing with "facts" in cyberspace, but I googled it again *again* just to be sure (uh oh, "again" is doing that thing were it doesn't look like a real word. Give me a moment). *Now* it was written by some guy named Archilochus, and there was even a citation of a book by an author with Spelling Indecision Disorder (SID): "Archilochus, Carmina Archilochi: The Fragments of Archilochos" (GoodReads.com, 2022).

As this is the type of thing that, if it wasn't becoming so common in alleged "reality," would be worthy of prompting a lucid dream unreality test, I asked myself "Is this a dream? Any discrepancies *besides* facts changing every time I google something? Try to float ... Nope, still sitting."

Afterthought 4 - The Internet Just Makes Shift Up to Futz With Your Head

Since the only actual citations of primary sources I'd found thus far were for Archilochus (or Archiloci or Archilocos or whatever) and Erasmus, I then start googling "Archilochus fox" to verify. The top result was for a Wikipedia entry entitled "The Hedgehog and the Fox" (2022).

Here it read:

"πόλλ' οἶδ' ἀλώπηξ, ἀλλ' ἐχῖνος ἓν μέγα

Multa novit vulpes, verum echinus unum magnum

The fox knows many things, but the hedgehog knows one big thing."

This was different from the quotation variously attributed to Erasmus and Emerson but the entry did mention Erasmus, and it was written in Greek or mathematical symbols or something so it probably wasn't made up by some social media influencer (though it might have been made up by Philip Warren Anderson who predicted the existence of the Higgs Boson and claimed to be the 5th best Go player in Japan)(Coleman, 2020; Philip Warren Anderson, 2022).

Since I was now in an information-verification mode and dabble in Go, I probed Philip's claim a little further and learned that

> "In addition to his work in physics, Anderson also played Go, which he had picked up while living in Japan. He could be mischievous about it, as Arthur remembers.
>
> 'I said, 'Oh, are you any good at Go?' Phil shrugs his shoulders. 'Yes. I suppose.' I said 'How good?' Typical Phil, you have to pump all this out of him. And Phil says 'Well, there are four people in Japan who can beat me.' And there's dead silence. Half a minute later, we're all just sitting open-mouthed, staring at Phil. And then Phil says, 'But they meditate.' As if that was cheating,' Arthur said.
>
> Anderson was, in fact, a master. In 2007, he was conferred a lifetime achievement award from the Nihon-Ki-in, the Japanese professional Go association." (In Garisto, 2020)

It should be noted, however, that when I asked online Go tournament director DrQuantum about this (after I'd played J15 to his H17 in a game in which you can probably guess the outcome – word to the wise: if you're risk-averse, don't even *think* of entering a Go tournament populated by quantum physics professors) he said that as far as he knew, Philip made it to 1 *Dan*. This means there were closer to 4999 people in Japan who could beat him. Still, no small feat in a country of 126,476,461 at last count in which infants are exposed to Go (or at least the muffled sounds of stones clacking) in the womb.

Afterthought 4 - The Internet Just Makes Shift Up to Futz With Your Head

Now I was at an *inflection* point (it used to be called a *decision* point, but I guess some "thought leader" – whatever the h-e-double-hockey-sticks that is, don't get me started – got bored and took a word that *nobody knew* and started using it instead). It was dinner time and I was hungry, but I had to get the list of citations together for a meeting in 2 days with some people who advertised that they would help obtain copyright permissions and I still didn't know who said the thing, or things, about the Hedgehog and the Fox. I was beginning to forget why I had even quoted it in the first place.

In any event, I was now in too deep to abandon the quest. So I tolerated the hunger and strategized. I thought first I'll google "Archilochus Adagia" on the lead from Wikipedia, and then "Archilochus, Carmina Archilochi: The Fragments of Archilochos" cited by GoodReads.com, then I'll find the full texts online and search them for foxes and hedgehogs.

The search results contained an essay by Paul Saffo, in which he wrote:

> "'The fox has many tricks; the hedgehog only one great trick.' This proverb credited to the 7th century B.C.E soldier-poet, Archilochus was immortalized by Dutch Humanist Desiderius Erasmus in the publication of his Adagia in Paris in 1500, and it has been invoked anew by every generation since. Fifty years ago, historian Isaiah Berlin borrowed Archilochus's parable as the title of his gem of an essay, 'The Hedgehog and the Fox.' Berlin's nominal topic was Tolstoy's view of history, but the essay speaks eloquently about two very different worldviews. As Berlin observed, hedgehogs believe in one thing, one truth, to the exclusion of all else. Foxes are the opposite, comfortable juggling many competing and contradictory truths. Hedgehogs are monists; foxes are pluralists. The fox is agile; the hedgehog doughty and immovable." (Sapho, 2006)

Now that I was dealing with an actual person, with a long list of academic credentials and a really cool green thing that he looks through in his bio,

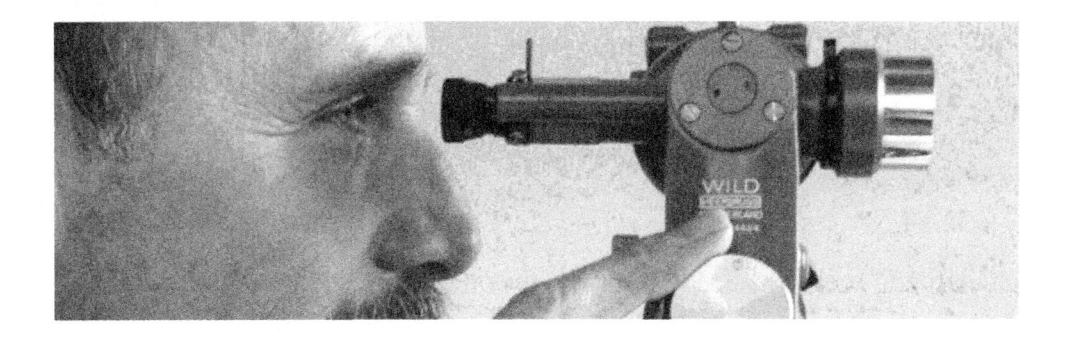

I figured this is probably how it went down:

1. Archilochus, most likely sometime between 680 and 645 BC (because that's when he was alive) said

πόλλ' οἶδ' ἀλώπηξ, ἀλλ' ἐχῖνος ἓν μέγα

I hesitate to put quotation marks around it, as they might appear to be parts of the letters. Though I suppose anyone who knows how to read Greek wouldn't confuse them with the letters and for anyone who doesn't know how to read Greek it really doesn't matter whether they confuse them with the letters or not as either way they have no idea what they are reading. Now, whether Archilochus was the first person to say this or was merely repeating something he'd heard at the *agora* seems to be a matter of contention on the internet. For example, Dmitry Pruss (aka MOCKBA) said on December 26, 2014 at 1:58 pm:

> "the modern educated opinion seems to be certain that Archilochus wasn't *original* (perhaps borrowing from [a pseudo-?] Homer, according to Zenob), or possibly from Hermogenes)."[sic for that final hanging parenthesis] (LanguageHat, 2014)

2. Then, in 1500, Erasmus, who famously said

> "When I get a little money I buy books;
>
> and if any is left I buy food and clothes,"

must have "got a little money," come across a book by Archilochus at a nudist bookstore cafe, and translated it into Latin as:

"Multa novit vulpes,

verum echinus

unum magnum"

(Erasmus, 1536/2010),

which made sense because he was from Rotterdam and spoke Dutch.

Erasmus was very serious about his work as a translator, complaining that

> ". . . one thing the facts cry out, and it can be clear, as they say, even to a blind man, that often through the translator's clumsiness or inattention the Greek has been wrongly rendered; often the true and genuine reading has been corrupted by ignorant scribes, which we see happen every day, or altered by scribes who are half-taught and half-asleep." (Erasmus, Epistle 337)

He nevertheless believed in a certain amount of *wiggle-room* in the accuracy of his own translations, as evidenced by his attempts to improve upon *the Bible*, for

> "It is only fair that Paul should address the Romans in somewhat better Latin" (Erasmus, Epistle 695),

and was not averse to coining new expressions by mistranslating the Greek into Latin, such as changing "to call a bowl a bowl" into "to call a spade a spade" (Spade, n.1) and morphing "Pandora's storage jar" into a box (Erasmus, 1508), perhaps judging a jar insufficiently spacious to house all the evils of the world.

Afterthought 4 - The Internet Just Makes Shift Up to Futz With Your Head

Pandora by John William Waterhouse (1849-1917)

3. Emerson, who probably said a lot of smart stuff and that's why we remember his name, nonetheless never said anything, or at least never wrote anything, about a hedgehog and a fox. He may never have even said anything about *either* a hedgehog *or* a fox (I searched a pdf of his complete works and found *nada*). As a result, I'm afraid that in the absence of a verified citation of Emerson, we must conclude as follows:

4. Someone on the internet was simply in a pissy mood one day and decided to futz with our heads and assign famous quotes to famous people who didn't write them.

This said, adding the extra line was a nice touch, so nice in fact that it deserves to be quoted and cited in some form or another. How about:

> "'The fox has many tricks.
>
> The hedgehog has but one'
>
> SAID ARCHILOCHUS
>
> 'But that is the best of all'
>
> SAID SOMEONE WHO WASN'T
>
> ARCHILOCHUS, ERASMUS OR EMERSON."

Postscript: After this chapter was written, further investigation revealed that an individual going by the name of "rebar," writing to Jen Betton, author/illustrator of *Hedgehog Needs a Hug*, whose original post must have read "This Emerson quote just seemed perfect for my book," agrees with our conclusion:

"A friend just sent me HEDGEHOG NEEDS A HUG and it's so lovely!! but I have to tell you...this isn't an Emerson quote." (rebar, 2018)

Afterthought 4 - The Internet Just Makes Shift Up to Futz With Your Head

Post-Postscript: And wouldn't you know it, as I proofread this chapter for the umpteenth time, it occurred to me "Why don't I find Archilochus' original text and get it from the horse's mouth?" So I did, and looky here:

> "Fox knows many,
>
> Hedgehog one solid trick"

and

> "Fox knows
>
> Eleventythree
>
> Tricks and still
>
> Gets caught.
>
> Hedgehog knows
>
> One but it
>
> Always works."
>
> (Archilochos, 1964, p. 64)

I must admit, the end of this latter translation ("but it always works") sounds *a lot* like the last line of the quotation misattributed to Erasmus and Emerson ("but that is the best of all") which, with allowances for translational poetic license, actually *does* now seem to have kind of been said by Archilochus. My bad.

Pre-Postscript - *Who Would Buy Such A Book?*

> "The palm at the end of the mind,
> Beyond the last thought, rises
> In the bronze decor ...
>
> ... You know then that it is not the reason
> That makes us happy or unhappy.
> The bird sings. Its feathers shine."
>
> **Wallace Stevens**
> **(1990; Excerpt from "Of Mere Being")**

It is now October, 2020, about one and a half years since I finished writing the foregoing. (Well, now it's May, 2022, about one and a half years since I finished writing the foregoing about the fore-foregoing.) (And now it's December, 2022, *yikes.*) Yes my real name is Wallace Stevens (just kidding, for those of you who don't know who Wallace Stevens was). I am calling this a *pre*-postscript because the book isn't technically finished and I may write a real postscript when done, probably inserting it in the environs of an afterward and epilogue, though possibly at the beginning of the book as a postdated ante-preface. Also to note, that while this may be a pre-postscript with respect to the book's postscript, it's a post-postscript with respect to some prior chapters' postscripts. But who's counting.

So, I was about to go find a place in the woods to do my morning stretching and Tai Chi and I suddenly had another thought about the "bear thing," maybe triggered by a new sign I saw downstairs about what to do if you see a bear. I didn't read the whole thing, but did notice that it said to "make a lot of noise." Understandably, as this book has not yet been published and become required reading for people writing notices on how not to **GEBAB**, it did not say anything about stopping thinking. And just as I was again getting in the mindset to go outside, I realized something that had never occurred to me: The title of the book (How to Stop Thinking and Not Get Eaten By a Bear) is not only really weird, it is also ambiguous. I will here enumerate *some* of the things it could mean, though of course it will mean as many things as there are eyes that set upon it divided by 2 (assuming intact corpus callosi), or as there are fingers that set upon it divided by however many fingers one uses to read braille, or as there are ears that hear it divided by 2 or perhaps multiplied by 3 if listening in Dolby (powerful stuff) or 10 if listening in Sensurround (developed in 1974 for the film earthquake, but unlikely as most movie theatres are still locked down). Of course, the eye, ear and finger multiples and divisors could be affected by the **IQ** or creativity of the reader/hearer/feeler, and this still ignores the issue of whether the perceiver is literate, human or both. For example, if a bear were to find this book in the garbage at a campsite and the cover had come in contact with mustard that left some of the letters in the title visible to impinge on its brain albeit as random shapes, and assuming bears like mustard, the title could be interpreted as **FOOD**.

As a working model then, assuming the reader is human or literate, here are some of the things the title could mean along with the assumptions or premises suggesting the meaning.

1. Thinking can cause **GEBAB**, and this book will teach you how to stop and not.

2. Stopping thinking can cause **GEBAB**, but there is a way to stop thinking and yet **NGEBAB** and this book will show you how.

3. Bears have telepathy and so, when you stop thinking, they don't know what your next move will be or that you're only pretending to know karate (by fighting back), be dead (by lying down), or that it is time for their bedtime (by saying "good night"), and so they will decide to eat your acquaintance, whom you've just unfriended mid-hike and poured honey on, as per National Park Service etiquette and Madlabscientist's workaround regarding not pushing "a slower *friend* down" if you come across a bear (National Park Service, 2023; italics added).

4. This is one of those two-for-the-price-of-one books, with the first book being "How to Stop Thinking" and the second book being "How to Not Get Eaten by a Bear" (assuming one reads both books, the alternative being to just read the first one and remain at risk of GEBAB, or to just read the second one and remain neurotic but at least do it next to the bear rather than inside the bear where it's too dark to read).

Which brings me to another thing I realized after realizing the first thing, namely, that I might owe different apologies to different readers depending on what they thought the title meant when they bought (or stole or borrowed but invested time in reading or eating) the book. Accordingly, here are my apologies, *respectively, vis-à-vis* the number of the meaning above (I hope the typesetter isn't charging me extra for italics – I considered un-italicking the commas and hyphens, but it got complicated)(apologies as well if un-italicking isn't a word, doesn't contain a hyphen, or is spelled without a *k*).

1. This meaning is false, thinking won't cause you to GEBAB (unless you think there isn't a hungry bear when there is and don't take *real* precautions proven in multi-campsite randomized clinical trials to cause NGEBAB) and even if it did there are probably other factors involved beyond the scope of this treatise.

2. This meaning is false too, *not* thinking won't cause you to be eaten by a bear and, even if it did, see apology number 1 regarding alternative causation.

3. This meaning may or may not be false, but we are very unlikely to ever know the truth about bear telepathy as it's hard enough to get scientists interested in studying human telepathy.

4. This meaning may or may not be false as well, depending on whether you have opened the box to feed or bury the cat. If the cat was in a bag rather than a box (bags protect cats from quantum uncertainty, like they protect open beer bottles in public places from getting you arrested) whether or not this meaning is false will depend upon whether during the editing process I add a bonus one-chapter book on how to *really* not GEBAB, but I have either *not* yet decided *or* have decided *not* to let the cat out of the bag (my typesetter just texted me that italics are free, so I figured I'd get my money's worth. Heck, maybe I'll just hit *select all* and do the whole book in italics, randomly unitalicking for effect. What do you *think*? Good call! That's

exactly the type of wasteful thinking you now know how to stop. Me, on the other foot . . . [intentional absence of closed parentheses for effect]

Postscript - *Walking Meditation*

As a postscript, how about a practice rather than more information. Walking meditation is a perfect practice for learning to stop thinking, because it embodies first replacing of our usual way of thinking with its opposite and then *going beyond thinking* to *being*. Of course, we are always being, but usually with our awareness filled with thinking. What I mean by "being" is attending to awareness of being itself, which is facilitated by first moving attention away from thinking to multi-sensing, thereby emptying awareness of thinking and filling it with sensation, which eventually drops away due to its lack of meaning, leaving awareness empty of anything other than awareness of being aware, and eventually empty even of that.

Thich Nhat Hanh offers a rationale for walking meditation and then a practice:

> "The Zen master Ling Chi said that the miracle is not to walk on burning charcoal or in the thin air or on the water; the miracle is just to walk on earth. You breathe in. You become aware of the fact that you are alive. You are still alive and you are walking on this beautiful planet. That is already performing a miracle . . . I would like to propose to you a short poem that you might like to use for walking meditation:

> *I have arrived. I am home.*
> *In the here. In the now.*
> *I am solid. I am free.*
> *In the ultimate I dwell.*

Postscript - Walking Meditation

You might like to take two steps and breathe in and say, I have arrived, I have arrived. And when you breathe out, you take another two steps and say silently, I am home, I am home. Our true home is really in the here and in the now.

Because only in the here and the now can we touch life."

Thich Nhat Hanh (2021)

You can practice walking meditation anywhere, either when already walking indoors or outdoors by bringing more awareness to the sense experience of walking itself, or by taking some time, even just a few minutes, to walk in a meditative way indoors or outdoors.

Here is a brief guided walking meditation. You might record it on your phone and then listen to it the first few times you practice until you get the hang of it:

1. Stand still and be aware of the feeling of your body and of your feet on the floor.

2. Ran out of ink. Continue 1 as Standing Meditation until your legs get tired. Then sit down, go to Amazon or AbeBooks and order Thich Nhat Hahn's "How to Walk."

Appendix 1 - *The 12 Existential Distortions*

The 12 Existential Cognitive Distortions

Existential Cognitive Distortion	How Would It Affect Your Life If This Were True	How Would It Affect Your Life If This Were False
1. I AM THIS BODY		
2. I AM THIS MIND		
3. OTHERS ARE THEIR BODIES		
4. OTHERS ARE THEIR MINDS		
5. I AM MORTAL		
6. OTHERS ARE MORTAL		
7. THE UNIVERSE IS PHYSICAL		
8. TIME IS UNIDIRECTIONAL		
9. SPACE IS UNIDIMENSIONAL		
10. CAUSE AND EFFECT ONLY OPERATE IN PHYSICAL SPACETIME		
11. EVENTS ARE RANDOM AND WITHOUT A HIGHER PURPOSE		
12. THINGS ARE WHAT THEY SEEM		

Copyright © 2022 By Dogu Densei, How To Stop Thinking And Not Get Eaten By A Bear: The New Cognitive Behavioral Mind Training

Appendix 2 - Cognitive Behavioral Mind Training Plan

Cognitive Behavioral Mind Training (CBMT) Plan

Identify Target Problems (on the Left)

and Use √'d CBMT Skills (Along the Top)

SKILL → PROBLEM ↓	Cognitive Disputation	Behavioral Activation	Multisensory Awareness In Activity ("Mindfulness")	Multisensory Awareness in Silent Stillness ("Sitting Meditation")	Exposure and Response Prevention
Depressive Thinking Not Happy Sad Depressed	√	√	√	√	
Worry/Obsessing/ Anxiety/Panic (and related Insomnia)	√		√	√	√
Angry Thinking/ Irritability/ Anger	√		√	√	√
Escape/ Avoidance (As in Panic/Phobia/PTSD/ OCD)	√		√	√	√
Compulsions/ Tourette's/Tics/ Trichotillomania/ Addictions	√		√	√	√
ADD: Inattention/ Poor Concentration	√		√	√	√
ADHD: Inattention with Hyperactivity/ Impulsivity components	√		√	√	√

Copyright © 2022 By Dogu Densei, How To Stop Thinking And Not Get Eaten By A Bear

Appendix 3 - *The Serenity Prayer Thought Record*

Serenity Prayer Thought Record

THE PROBLEM				THE SOLUTION			
1. SITUATION/ EVENT (S)	2. AUTOMATIC THOUGHTS (AT)	3. DOWN THE RABBIT HOLE THOUGHTS (RH)	4. EMOTIONS (EMO)	5. EVIDENCE THAT THE THOUGHTS ARE TRUE (EV+)	6. EVIDENCE THAT THE THOUGHTS AREN'T TRUE (EV-)	7. ALTERNATIVE RATIONAL THOUGHTS (RT)	8. SERENITY PRAYER (WHAT TO DO/CHANGE OR ACCEPT) (SP)

Copyright © 2022 by Dogu Densei. In How To Stop Thinking And Not Get Eaten By A Bear: The New Cognitive Behavioral Mind Training. NY: Caduxeus Press

Questions to Ask Yourself While Doing A Serenity Prayer Thought Record:

1. SITUATION/EVENT: What is the objective situation or event that you are bothered about, without any interpretations or judgements?

2. AUTOMATIC THOUGHTS: What thoughts come immediately to mind regarding the situation/event? If a thought is a *question*, convert it into a *statement* of the answer you don't like.

3. DOWN THE RABBIT HOLE THOUGHTS: If the Automatic Thoughts are literally true, why is this BAD? What does it mean about you, others, the world or the future? Repeat this process for each of the Rabbit Hole Thoughts (i.e., if this RHT is true, why is it BAD? What does it mean about you, others, the world or the future?).

4. EMOTIONS: Which emotions were/are triggered by the thoughts? (Happy, Sad, Anxious, Fearful, Angry)

5. EVIDENCE THAT THE THOUGHTS ARE TRUE: Pick one or two ATs or RHTs that bother you the most as "hot thoughts." If you were trying to convince your best friend to bet $1000 that they are true, what evidence would you present?

6. EVIDENCE THAT THE THOUGHTS AREN'T OR *MIGHT NOT* BE TRUE: For the same "hot thoughts," if you were trying to convince your best friend to bet $1,000 that they are NOT true, what evidence would you present?

7. ALTERNATIVE RATIONAL THOUGHS/INTERPRETATIONS: On the basis of the Evidence in columns 5 and 6, what would be more rational thoughts, a more evidence-based interpretation of the Situation? What *literal* interpretation would you encourage your friend to bet $1000 on?

8. SERENITY PRAYER: On the basis of the Alternative Rational Thoughts or Interpretation in Column 7, what *changeable* things might it be helpful for you to try to do or change, and what *unchangeable* things might it be helpful for you to try to accept, or at least acknowledge are real and unchangeable.

Appendix 4 - *How to Do a Thought Record* and *NGEBAB in Ate Acts*

Me: Jack, how's my skiing?

Jack: "Dogu-baby, you see that guy dressed in red whizzing through that mogul field?"

Me: "Yeah?"

Jack: "That ain't you."

Tzack's father on the chairlift at Stratton

(circa 1977)

Caregiver Advisory: Contains suicide, sexual ambiguity, 4-letter words, Democrats, 5-letter words, nudity (the bears), Republicans, masked snouts (the people), social distancing (the bears), antisocial proximity (the people), Shakespearian affectation and an attempt at flying-pig denial.

SYNOPSIS

How to Do A Thought Record and NGEBAB, set primarily in Scotland, mixes witchcraft, prophecy and murder. Three "Queïr Sisters" appear to Joe and his comrade Jimmy after a battle and prophesy that Joe will be king and that the descendants of Jimmy will also reign. When Joe arrives at his castle, he and Lady Joe plot to assassinate the Thing King, soon to be their guest, so that Joe can become king.

After Joe murders the Thing King, the king's two sons flee, and Joe is crowned. Fearing that Jimmy's descendants will, according to the Queïr Sisters' predictions, take over the kingdom, Joe has Jimmy killed. At a royal banquet that evening, Joe sees Jimmy's ghost appear covered in blood. Joe determines to consult the Queïr Sisters again. They comfort him with ambiguous promises.

Another nobleman, Macmuffin, rides to England to join Thing King's older son, Adolph Blaine Charles David Earl Frederick Gerald Hubert Irvin John Kenneth Lloyd Martin Nero Oliver Paul Quincy Randolph Sherman Thomas Uncas Victor William Xerxes Yancy Zeus Wolfeschlegel-steinhausen-bergerdorff-welche-vor-altern-waren-gewissenhaft-schafers-wessen-schafe-waren-wohl-gepflege-und-sorgfaltigkeit-beschutzen-vor-angreifen-durch-ihr-raubgierig-feinde-welche-vor-altern-zwolfhundert-tausend-jahres-voran-die-erscheinen-von-der-erste-erdemensch-der-raumschiff-genacht-mit-tungstein-und-sieben-iridium-elektrisch-motors-gebrauch-licht-als-sein-ursprung-von-kraft-gestart-sein-lange-fahrt-hinzwischen-sternartig-raum-auf-der-suchen-nachbarschaft-der-stern-welche-gehabt-bewohnbar-planeten-kreise-drehen-sich-und-wohin-der-neue-rasse-von-verstandig-menschlichkeit-konnte-fortpflanzen-und-sich-erfreuen-an-lebenslanglich-freude-und-ruhe-mit-nicht-ein-furcht-vor-angreifen-vor-anderer-intelligent-geschopfs-von-hinzwischen-sternartig-raum Sr., known to his friends as "Wolfy" (Wolfy, n.d.).

Hubert Blaine
Wolfeschlegelsteinhausenbergerdorff
Sr.

613

Appendix 4 - How to Do a Thought Record and NGEBAB in Ate Acts

Joe has Macmuffin's wife and children murdered.

Wolfy and Macmuffin lead an army against Joe, as Lady Joe goes mad and commits suicide. Joe confronts Wolfy's army, trusting in the Queïr Sisters' comforting promises. He learns that the promises are tricks, but continues to fight. Macmuffin kills Joe, and Wolfy becomes Scotland's king.

Oops, wrong play in 8 acts. My bad.

SYNOPSIS

A bear walks into a bar.

Everyone stops thinking.

The bear eats them anyway.

SYNOPSIS

(third times a charm)

Wolfy logs in for his 3rd teletherapy session after paying Dr. Densei through PayPal as Dr. Densei is not in the Celtic Cross Celtic Shield provider network. Dr. Densei guides him through the use of the Thought Record to challenge his gebabophobia. Wolfy feels better.

Act 1

The Situation

Me: Good morning, Mr. Wolfeschlegel-steinhausen-bergerdorff-welche-vor-altern-waren-gewissenhaft-schafers-wessen-schafe-waren-wohl-gepflege-und-sorgfaltigkeit-beschutzen-vor-angreifen-durch-ihr-raubgierig-feinde-welche-vor-altern-zwolfhundert-tausend-jahres-voran-die-erscheinen-von-der-erste-erdemensch-der-raumschiff-genacht-mit-tungstein-und-sieben-iridium-elektrisch-motors-gebrauch-licht-als-sein-ursprung-von-kraft-gestart-sein-lange-fahrt-hinzwischen-sternartig-raum-auf-der-suchen-nachbarschaft-der-stern-welche-gehabt-bewohnbar-planeten-kreise-drehen-sich-und-wohin-der-neue-rasse-von-verstandig-menschlichkeit-konnte-fortpflanzen-und-sich-erfreuen-an-lebenslanglich-freude-und-ruhe-mit-nicht-ein-furcht-vor-angreifen-vor-anderer-intelligent-geschopfs-von-hinzwischen-sternartig-raum Sr., how are you feeling today.

    Mr. Wolfeschlegelsteinhausenbergerdorff: My friends call me Wolfy.

Me: I appreciate that. I should make clear that the therapist-client relationship is a little different from a friendship as it is, by its nature, very one-way in terms of self-disclosure, with the client revealing many personal aspects of their lives and thoughts, but with the therapist remaining mostly quiet about personal issues unless there seems to be a reason that discussing these would in some way help with the treatment. That said, I will be VERY happy to call you Wolfy. By the way, your name really is unique. If you don't mind me asking, is there a history?

> Wolfy: In fact there is. You see, as my great-grandfather explained to me when I was three, there was this "wolf-killer, a resident of a stonehouse in a village, whose ancestors were conscientious shepherds whose sheep were well fed and carefully guarded against attack by ferocious enemies and whose ancestors 1,200,000 years before the first earth man, in a space ship made with tungsten and seven iridium motors and using light as a source of power, started a long journey across interstellar space, searching for a star around which was an inhabitable planet where they could establish a new race of intelligent mankind and where they would live long, happy lives and be free from attack by other intelligentsia from the outer space from whence they came." (Wolfy, n.d.)

Me: Interesting. So Wolfy, how you been feeling this week.

> Wolfy: Not bad, not bad.

Me: How's Macmuffin doing.

> Wolfy: He's having a hard time of it.

Me: It was a real tragedy.

> Wolfy: Yes it was.

Me: Wolfy, did you have a chance to do that Thought Record I emailed you last week?

> Wolfy: Sure did.

Me: If I recall correctly, your main worry lately has been that you'll get eaten by a bear.

> Wolfy: You've got quite the memory, Doc.

Appendix 4 - How to Do a Thought Record and NGEBAB in Ate Acts

Me: Hard thing to forget, a King in a castle in a country with no bears outside of captivity who's afraid of bears, but I'll take the compliment.

> Wolfy: Regarding your timeline, I believe that it is currently the year 1040 environs, and Scottish bears won't be extinct for another 500 or so years, unfortunately for me. I tried doing the Thought Record on my fear but had a little trouble when it got to the Evidence sections. Then I got hard on myself, telling myself to "Dispute it like a man," but then I heard your voice in my head telling me that I can only do my best.

Me: Well, how about if we put the Thought Record on today's Agenda. Anything else you would like to cover today?

> Wolfy: Well, I would like to decide which U.S. presidential candidate's campaign to hack into to protect Scotland's interests.

Me: Wolfy, we've already discussed that. It's the 11th century and there is no U.S. And even if there were, I'm not allowed to discuss politics with clients. Getting back to the Thought Record, what did you put as the Situation?

> Wolfy: Well, I was Googling "bears" again and came across these 2 books on Amazon entitled *Bears Want to Kill You: The Authoritative Guide to Survival in the War Between Man and Bear* (Nicolle, 2019) and *Bears of the Apocalypse* (Nicolle, 2016), and suddenly my heart started racing and my hands got tingly.

Me: Excellent. You stayed descriptive in the Situation column, without interpretation. Now, just as an aside, remember what we discussed about Exposure and Response Prevention, feeling the anxiety and discomfort and resisting the urge to google "bears"?

> Wolfy: I sure do. And I did pretty well, I only googled bears one evening after allowing myself to feel it all day, when the urge was just too powerful to resist. That's the least I've googled bears since ordering all those bear traps on Etsy to clear our path to the castle to take it back from Joe after he murdered my dad.

Me: Again, very sorry for your loss.

> Wolfy: I thank you Doctor.

Me: He was a good King.

Wolfy: The best.

Act 2

Automatic Thoughts

Me: Now, after writing down the situation, what did you put for Automatic Thoughts?

Wolfy: I wrote "There a bears everywhere and they want to kill me. This is war. I need to tell Macmuffin to get the army ready for battle. I miss Young Siward. We were going to get married and he was to become Lady Wolfeschlegel-steinhausen-bergerdorff-welche-vor-altern-waren-gewissenhaft-schafers-wessen-schafe-waren-wohl-gepflege-und-sorgfaltigkeit-beschutzen-vor-angreifen-durch-ihr-raubgierig-feinde-welche-vor-altern-zwolfhundert-tausend-jahres-voran-die-erscheinen-von-der-erste-erdemensch-der-raumschiff-genacht-mit-tungstein-und-sieben-iridium-elektrisch-motors-gebrauch-licht-als-sein-ursprung-von-kraft-gestart-sein-lange-fahrt-hinzwischen-sternartig-raum-auf-der-suchen-nachbarschaft-der-stern-welche-gehabt-bewohnbar-planeten-kreise-drehen-sich-und-wohin-der-neue-rasse-von-verstandig-menschlichkeit-konnte-fortpflanzen-und-sich-erfreuen-an-lebenslanglich-freude-und-ruhe-mit-nicht-ein-furcht-vor-angreifen-vor-anderer-intelligent-geschopfs-von-hinzwischen-sternartig-raum"

Me: You actually wrote that? I mean, I can't even imagine what you are going through, losing your betrothed and your father on the same day.

Wolfy: It's very hard.

Act 3

Downward Arrow / Rabbit Hole / Turtles All The Way Down / Black Hole / Vortex

Me: Now, which of the Automatic Thoughts is the one that made you the most anxious?

Wolfy: That would have to be "There are bears everywhere and they want to kill me."

Appendix 4 - How to Do a Thought Record and NGEBAB in Ate Acts

Me: Naturally. OK, let's consider that the "Hot Thought." And did you do the Downward Arrow, or as I like to call it, the "Rabbit Hole" column?

> Wolfy: Sure did.

Me: And what did you come up with?

> Wolfy: Well, I did what you said, I took my Automatic Thought "There are bears everywhere and they want to kill me" and asked myself: "If this were true, what would it mean about me, others, the world or the future, and why would it be bad?"

Me: And how did you answer?

> Wolfy: How do you think I answered? It would mean a bear could get into the castle.

Me: And continuing the downward arrow, if *that* were true, what would *that* mean about you, others, the world or the future and why would *that* be bad.

> Wolfy: It would mean the bear could eat me and Scotland would be without a King.

Me: And then, if that were true? Why would that be bad?

> Wolfy: I guess it wouldn't. I'd go to Heaven and Donalbain would get to be King. He would have made a better King than me anyway, but when I went to England he went to Ireland because I figured we'd both be safer if we went separate ways, though wherever we went, men would smile at us while hiding daggers and our closest relatives would be the ones most likely to murder us. Anyway, last time we spoke, Donnie told me that some time ago in Ireland he took a stroll on the old long walk of a day-I-ay-I-ay, and he met a little girl and they stopped to talk of a fine soft day-I-ay. And he hasn't been back to the castle since. If I got eaten by a bear, and Donnie and his Gallstone girl took up residence here at Castle Forres, that might just be the thing to unite the Isles.

Me: Well, let's not go to our happy place just yet, there may be time for that in one of the later columns. For the moment, since we're still in the Rabbit Hole column, could things get any worse if you are eaten by a bear and Scotland is without a King?

Wolfy: Well, I guess if there is no Heaven, or I go to Hell or something.

Me: Are these actually concerns?

Wolfy: No, I know there's a Heaven, and one day Young Siward and I will be reunited.

Me: OK, so, let's finish the Rabbit Hole column with you getting eaten by a bear and Scotland having no King, as these are your real concerns.

Act 4

Emotions

Me: Now, when the Automatic Thoughts popped up in response to seeing the two book titles, what emotions were triggered? Remember, here we are only talking about the basic emotions, happy, sad, angry, anxious or fearful.

Wolfy: Well I sure as heck didn't feel happy. I would say fearful.

Act 5

Evidence that the Thoughts are True

Me: You mentioned that you had some difficulty with the Evidence columns. First, looking at all of the thoughts in both the Automatic Thoughts and Rabbit Hole columns did you identify one or a few that you thought contributed the most to your fear?

Wolfy: Bears are everywhere, they want to kill me and I'll get eaten by a bear.

Me: And did you generate any evidence in support of these?

Wolfy: I did. First of all, my castle guards are big jessies, and if they saw a bear heading for my chambers they would most certainly run and hide.

Me: Big jessies?

Wolfy: I think you Yanks call them "wusses."

Me: Yanks?

Appendix 4 - How to Do a Thought Record and NGEBAB in Ate Acts

>Wolfy: Sorry, I forgot, Yanks won't exist for another 7 centuries. That's what we'll call you blokes.

Me: I see. Any other evidence that you could get eaten by a bear?

>Wolfy: Well, they're everywhere and they want to kill me.

Me: That was actually one of the Automatic thoughts. Usually in the "Evidence that the Thoughts are True" column, we put information that supports the Automatic Thought. In this case, rather than use another Automatic Thought to support the "hot" thought, maybe we could look at any evidence that the one you want to use as evidence is true. What evidence can we generate regarding the truth of the thought that bears are everywhere and they want to kill you?

>Wolfy: Well, I keep imagining them roaming the castle fields, swimming across the moat, climbing the walls and running all through the castle until they find someone to eat. Like me!

Me: Actually, Castle Forres doesn't have a moat. But how does imagining all those things make you feel?

>Wolfy: *Actually*, the original Castle Forres, where Castle Hill Gardens now stands, did have a moat. And the thoughts make me scared.

Me: Understandably. And since they are popping up by themselves, they could go in the Automatic Thoughts column, where we can also put images. But what we need to be careful of is assuming that thinking something is evidence for its existence. For example, take a moment and think of a white bear.

>Wolfy: Why would I want to do that?

Me: Sorry, that's exposure therapy. We'll get to that in another session. For now, think of a pink elephant. Tell me when you have a clear image of a pink elephant in your mind.

>Wolfy: I do right now.

Me: So you're thinking of a pink elephant. Does that mean pink elephants are real?

> Wolfy: Well, I saw a photo in the Journal of African Elephants of an elephant born with albinism.

Me. Of course you did.

> Wolfy: They're called "white elephants" but they're actually pink, kind of like many "white" people, especially when they are on safaris and see pink elephants.

Me: Good point. OK, Wolfy, you got me. Let's try this another way. Take a moment and think of a flying pig.

> Wolfy: Dr. Densei, I *am* impressed. You certainly are up to snuff on your Scottish adynatons! And I mean that in a good way.

Me: Well thank you. In fact I wrote the *definition* of cross-cultural behavior therapy (Densei, 1999). What's an adynaton? Are they like adenoids? Never mind. Are you thinking of a flying pig?

> Wolfy: Yes I am.

Me: OK., Now, does the fact that you are thinking of a flying pig mean there are really flying pigs?

> Wolfy: In point of fact, a pig finally flew on 4th November 1909, when John Moore-Brabazon, 1st Baron Brabazon of Tara took a small pig with him on board an aeroplane (Flying Pig, n.d.).

Me: Wolfy, you're killin' me here. Let's tweak it a little. Imagine for a moment a pig with wings.

> Wolfy: OK, I see it.

Me: Now, does the presence in your mind of a pig with wings mean that pigs with wings are real?

> Wolfy: Of course not, silly!

Me: BINGO! So is the presence in your mind of bears invading your castle evidence of bears invading your castle?

> Wolfy: I see where you're going with this. But as my buddy across the pond Rummy will say in a little short of a thousand years, absence of evidence is not evidence of absence.

Me: Carl Sagan said it first, but very true. Now is absence of evidence evidence of *presence*?

> Wolfy: I feel ya. No, of course not.

Me: So should we put your thoughts of bears roaming the castle fields, swimming across the moat, climbing the walls and running all through the castle until they find someone to eat, like you, as evidence that you will get eaten by a bear?

> Wolfy: I guess not.

Me: Now, can you come up with any more evidence that you will get eaten by a bear other than *if* a bear were to enter the castle your guards are big wusses and would probably hide?

> Wolfy: No, that's about it.

Act 6

Evidence that the Thoughts May Be False

Me: Moving right alone, in column 6, did you generate any evidence that maybe it *isn't* true that bears are everywhere, want to kill you and that you will get eaten by a bear?

> Wolfy: This is where I had some difficulty.

Me: Well, you're doing great so far. This is a new way of thinking about things. Usually we encounter a situation, have thoughts about it, these trigger emotions, and then we keep cycling back and forth between the thoughts and the emotions. In cognitive therapy, we break out of this cycle and look at the thoughts critically, and that is what you are already getting the hang of, realizing that just because you *think* something doesn't mean it's *true*.

> Wolfy: Actually, when I was time traveling to the country you don't think exists yet last weekend, I did see a bumper sticker that said "Don't believe everything you think." Are you sure you aren't a Traveler too?

Me: OK, Wolfy, you caught me. but please keep it on the DL. To self-disclose a little, right now I'm webcamming with you from 20th century Massachusetts.

> Wolfy: I knew that already. I was just wondering when you would fess up.

Me: But getting back to our Thought Record, did you come up with any evidence against your fear thoughts?

> Wolfy: I did try Googling "evidence that it may not be true that bears are everywhere, want to kill me and that I will get eaten by a bear."

Me: And what did you find?

> Wolfy: The first result was "Dispelling Myths About Bears," on BearSmart.com. It said "The best thing people can do for bears is replace misconceptions with facts." It pissed me off a little that the people at BearSmart.com seem more interested in what *we* can do for *bears* rather than keeping *bears* from eating *us*, but then I took a cold shower and felt better.

Me: Maybe you could do another thought record on that anger as homework. Did you just say you took a cold shower?

> Wolfy: That's what my previous therapist said to do if I get angry or anxious.

Me: Was your previous therapist your grandmother?

> Wolfy: In fact it was.

Me: Did the shower work?

> Wolfy: Yes, she had it fixed last week. You need the name of a good plumber?

Me: No, I mean ... never mind. So you searched for evidence in the form of facts from the internet. A little risky, but I'll take it.

> Wolfy: But then I saw the next result, which was "Six Terrifying Bear Attack Stories" on FieldAndStream.com. I started reading and got really scared when it got to the point where it said "John was screaming, trying to get the bear's attention. He thought she was going to kill me ... I could feel blood running down my legs ..."

Me: Wolfy?

Appendix 4 - How to Do a Thought Record and NGEBAB in Ate Acts

>Wolfy: . . . and then there was another story where the guy wrote "Now we were face-to-face . . . That's when the bear opened its mouth to bite me . . ."

Me: Wolfy?

>Wolfy: But the worst was the one where a guy wrote "I threw up my hands to protect my face, and the bear latched onto my arms with his teeth and claws . . ."

Me: WOLFY?!

>Wolfy: Sorry Doc, I get carried away.

Me: That's OK, I just noticed the sweat forming on your forehead as it turned purple and thought it might be more useful to finish working on the Thought Record than continue terrifying yourself. It's up to you though, what do you prefer?

>Wolfy: Let's go with the Thought Record.

Me: Good choice. To continue with the Evidence Against column, let's look for a moment at that article you were just citing. Where were these people when they encountered the bears?

>Wolfy: North America.

Me: And how many bears are there in 21st century North America?

>Wolfy: There are 600,000 black bears and 55,000 brown bears.

Me: And how many bears are there in Scotland?

>Wolfy: As far as I know, "In the 21st century, Blair Drummond Safari Park has European brown bears, the Highland Wildlife Park has two male polar bears while Edinburgh Zoo has giant pandas and sun bears" (Bear Necessities, 2013). Truth be told, that's one of the reasons I moved back to the 10th century, to get away from the bears. It's a virtual Scottish bear invasion is what it is up there in the 21st. Then I got here and met Young Siward, and things were looking up. But when I lost Siward and Joe killed my dad, the gebabophobia came back.

Me: Stress and negative emotions often trigger thoughts associated with past stress and negative emotions. We call this "state-dependent cognition." These thoughts then trigger anew the negative emotions associated with them from the past. Continuing with the Thought Record, it looks like there are 655,000 bears in 21st America. Now that you are in 11th century Scotland, where you said you went to get away from bears, I wonder if information about the bear population there might serve as evidence for or against your fearful thoughts. How many bears are there in 11th century Scotland?

> Wolfy: I don't know precisely, but they did become extinct around 500 C.E., so I guess that means there aren't any. But what if there are? What if someone sends them here from the 21st?

Me: Why would someone do that?

> Wolfy: I don't know. But people are strange when you're a stranger.

Me: True. And one useful way of looking at the Evidence columns in the Thought Record is to think of them as two lawyers presenting their case to a jury. The defendant is the hot automatic or rabbit hole thought or collection of thoughts. The Evidence that the Thought Is True column is then filled with arguments made by the defense attorney that the thought is true, or innocent. The Evidence that the Thought Might Not Be True column is then filled with arguments by the prosecuting attorney that the thought is false, or guilty. The verdict of the jury, after weighing the evidence, goes in the Rational Alternative Interpretation column. Another strategy is to imagine that you have to convince someone to bet money that the thought is or isn't true, and write the evidence for and against the thoughts in the Evidence columns. Right now we are in the Evidence That the Thoughts Might Not Be True column, so if you were a lawyer prosecuting the thoughts that there are bears everywhere, they want to kill you, and you will get eaten, or were trying to convince someone to bet $1,000 that these thoughts are not true, what would you come up with?

> Wolfy: Well, for one, I've never seen a bear in Scotland other than the giant panda in the Edinburgh Zoo nearly 1000 years in the future. And looking down from the top of Castle Forres in what one day will be Castle Hill Gardens, I can see pretty far out and have never seen a bear.

Me: Has anyone you've known in 11th century Scotland ever been attacked by a bear?

>Wolfy: Heavens no!

Me: If a bear did manage to swim across your moat, what is the likelihood that it could climb the castle wall?

>Wolfy: Don't be ridiculous.

Me: Great. You are accumulating a good deal of evidence against those scary thoughts.

>Wolfy: I sure am.

Me: So, what have we got so far there?

>Wolfy: I've never seen a bear in Scotland, probably because they are extinct, nobody I know has ever gotten attacked, probably because I don't know anybody but also probably because they are extinct, and even if there were a non-extinct bear and it made it across the moat it could never climb the castle wall.

Me: Excellent! Anything else we should add there?

>Wolfy: No, that would seem enough for the moment. I'm feeling better already.

Me: Good to hear.

Act 7

Rational Alternative Thoughts

Me: Now let's see what the jury has to say. Looking at the evidence supporting and not supporting that there are bears everywhere that want to kill you and that they will eat you, what verdict do you think the jury would reach regarding the innocence or guilt of your scary thoughts? Would the jury conclude that they are more likely innocent (true) or guilty (false).

>Wolfy: Definitely guilty.

Me: So whereas upon encountering those two books on Amazon the original thoughts making you anxious were that there are bears everywhere, they want to kill you, and they will eat you, what is a more rational alternative interpretation based on the situation?

> Wolfy: Bears are extinct in 11th century Scotland, and even if some were to swim across the Channel or be time-traveled here by some sicko, and even if they were able to swim across the moat, they wouldn't be able to climb the castle wall.

Me: And how do you feel when you think that?

> Wolfy: Pretty good.

Act 8

Serenity Prayer: What I Can Change and What I Can Accept

Me: Now, the thing about cognitive therapy is that it is not the same as "positive thinking." Sometimes what we arrive at as Rational Alternative Thoughts will not be what we would, ideally, like to be our reality. For example, is what you arrived at in Column 7, the most ideal situation you can imagine?

> Wolfy: I see what you mean. Even if they couldn't get into the castle, they could still wait outside the castle until I leave and then eat me.

Me: Exactly. So while your Rational Alternative Thoughts are clearly less scary than your Automatic Thoughts and Rabbit Hole, they are still not 100% positive.

> Wolfy: Right. For example, someone could timetravel them and set the geotarget to my bedroom and I could GEBAB while I'm asleep.

Me: That's right. But you don't seem anxious as you say that.

> Wolfy: Hey, look at that. I think this Thought Record thing has flipped a switch or something. I mean, what's the likelihood of someone doing that, right?

Me: Wolfy, you're really getting the hang of it now. So in this final column, we remind ourselves of the Serenity Prayer Short Form, to change what we can change and accept what we can't change. Can you think of what you can change and what you can accept, with respect to the whole bear thing?

>Wolfy: Well, I can change how I think when I notice myself getting anxious, and I can accept that if there is some sicko with a time machine out to get me by assassinating me with a bear from the future then I'll just have to cross that drawbridge when I come to it, we all gotta go sometimes, Donalbain and the Gallstone Girl will get to try their hands at governing, and Young Siward and I will be reunited in the afterlife and be able to start where we left off.

Me: Sounds like a plan. It looks like our time is almost up for today. Now in terms of homework for the coming week, how about if you do a thought record on that anger you felt when you saw that thing on BearSmart.com about what people can do for bears.

>Wolfy: Will do.

Me: Did you find the session helpful?

>Wolfy: I did.

Me: Is there anything that we didn't cover that we should make sure to get to next time?

>Wolfy: Besides hacking the election?

Me: Yes, besides that.

>Wolfy: I don't think so.

Me: Have a good week then.

>Wolfy: You too, doc.

Appendix 5 - *The Magic Cross Decision-Making Worksheet*

Magic Cross Decision-Making Worksheet

Option 1:			
Potential Advantages	How Good 0 to 100 (100 is best)	Potential Disadvantages	How Bad 0 to 100 (100 is worst)
1. 2. 3. 4. 5. 6. 7. 8. 9. 10.	1. 2. 3. 4. 5. 6. 7. 8. 9. 10. *Average Score A:	1. 2. 3. 4. 5. 6. 7. 8. 9. 10.	1. 2. 3. 4. 5. 6. 7. 8. 9. 10. *Average Score B:
Average Score A – B = SCORE FOR OPTION 1 =			

Option 2:			
Potential Advantages	How Good 0 to 100 (100 is Best)	Potential Disadvantages	How Bad 0 to 100 (100 is Worst)
1. 2. 3. 4. 5. 6. 7. 8. 9. 10.	1. 2. 3. 4. 5. 6. 7. 8. 9. 10. *Average Score C:	1. 2. 3. 4. 5. 6. 7. 8. 9. 10	1. 2. 3. 4. 5. 6. 7. 8. 9. 10. *Average Score D:
Average Score C – D = SCORE FOR OPTION 2 =			

Copyright © 2022 By Dogu Densei, How To Stop Thinking And Not Get Eaten By A Bear: The New Cognitive Behavioral Mind Training

*To get each Average Score A, B, C and D, add all of the scores in that quadrant and divide by the number of scores added. If the top left quadrant scores are 50, 10, 100, and 20, Average Score A would be 180 / 4 scores = 45.

Appendix 6 - *The Intersessionary Papers*

"*Cuernavaca, June 1958-Sept. 1959.* I'm reading Kierkegaard's Journals and have recently finished Ruth Benedict's Journal set & am thinking of the advantages of keeping one myself. Also, the system I've been using is getting to the point of breaking down, what with carbon copies & cross-indexing and numberless headings under which to file. I have file cabinets full – so full & big that things get lost in them. I've always had the custom of thinking & writing simultaneously on 30 or 40 topics at the same time anyway, but now there are even more – must be 100 or so – & also I can see that it's all falling together & interlocking into a single big job, a philosophy of human nature. Everything I write seems to be related & connected with everything else I'm writing, so that often I'm tempted to make 6 carbons for cross-indexing – & it could as easily be 12 carbons. Also I don't have enough typing help ever. A journal system should help on this score. I can have typed out of it whatever seems useful at its second stage of development. Often for me the first stage is almost free association, not necessary to type . . . I think I'll continue to use my present system of organizing my thinking and writing – 3x5 cards and 8 ½ by 11 sheets, topically filed – whenever the topic is clear enough and well enough developed to be singled out & separated for future developing & perfecting . . ."

Abraham Maslow

(In Maslow, 1982, p. 1)

Checking the dates of the file names for this book as it evolved, it was begun in February through May, 2019, as that's when I was able to take several 1-week periods to hole up in the Berkshires which is the only place I am able to write, with activities pretty much limited to writing, drinking coffee, eating egg McMuffins and chocolate munchkins, and sleeping, in roughly that order.

Other vacations weeks were saved for less solitary pursuits, like pre-Apocalypse international travel, and unfortunately I saved 5 weeks in 2020-21 for post-apocalyptic travel but then switched jobs and learned that employers can change their policies on paying out unused PTO *WITHOUT TELLING YOU* (putting them, by the way, at high risk of **GEBAB**, as bear telepathy is particularly sensitive to trickery, deception, deceitfulness, duplicity, dishonesty, unscrupulousness, underhandedness, subterfuge, fraudulence, legerdemain, sophistry, sharp practice, skulduggery, swindling, cheating, duping, hoodwinking, deviousness, guile, palace intrigue, craftiness, slyness, wiles, misleading talk, crookedness, monkey business, funny business, hanky-panky, shenanigans, flimflam, jiggery-pokery, monkeyshines, codology, knavery, and **ESPECIALLY CHICANERY** which smells like fowl [Skulduggery, 2022]. And yet, my sincere hope is that this book may in some way help my former ethically-challenged employer too to **NGEBAB**, mostly out of lovingkindness for bears who, as tasty as they find chicanery, have difficulty chewing it and end up with a tummy ache).

In between May, 2019, and the present (October, 2020)(now, May, 2022)(ok, full disclosure, it's now June, 2022)(July 2022)(and yes, you win, Frank, it's not even Tuesday and I've made another revision)(well, 2 or 3)(maybe 4 or 5)(it's the end of August now but I'm only staying here a moment to fix a typo above) my mind was nevertheless (despite the title of this book) not idle. In-between sessions and at other times (though technically all "other times" were in-between sessions, just as all sessions were in-between "other times") I would write insights on scraps of paper or skin, whichever was closest, that I thought might have a place in the book (the insights, not the skin, this is not that kind of book, though I almost got a tattoo once, which could have provided fodder for a chapter on good or bad decisions). The book correspondingly expanded, notably from October, 2020, through March, 2021, and then again from May onward in 2022.

Appendix 6 - The Intersessionary Papers

A more organized (and less dermatographic) person would have used a notebook for such musings, but we all have our AOAIs (Areas of Acknowledged Incompetence – mine are any knowledge whatsoever of what's going on in professional sports, ice skating without my ankles buckling, and using organizational skills for anything outside of my day job) and so I relied mostly on scraps of whatever was within reach and looked vulnerable to the markings of a pen. At a certain point, this got a little out of control (we're talking a pile of scrap paper a year and half high here) when, suddenly, a lightbulb went off (on?) and I looked under the printer table and was reminded of that marvelous invention known as a "folder." Here it is, for those of you who may not be tech-savvy, with a box of chocolate-covered expresso beans to give an indication of size. In case you are reading, or perceiving, this book in black and white, the folder is yellow, but I believe that the technology has, in some sectors, advanced to the point of other colors being available upon proof of concept or some other annoying business cliché.

It is the contents of this folder that provided material for the present Appendix. The original plan had been to integrate it, and whatever coffee beans would fit, into the body of the book, but it just seemed so much *easier* to put it all in one place. So here it is. I will number these thoughts in the order in which they were randomly placed in the folder, for purposes of pseudoscientific illusory quantification (you know, "Treatment Goal: The patient's anxiety score on the Physicians Health Questionnaire Anxiety Module will be less than 5 out of 21, unless he's getting eaten by a bear in which case it will be less than 9, unless the bear has no teeth in which case it will be less than 7, unless the bear has really sharp claws in which case it will be less than 8").

February 21, 2021: Change of Plan. Anxious avoidance of the aforesaid pile grew to the point that 2 days ago, back up in the Berkshires for another marathon writing week, it occurred to me to categorize the ideas and maybe insert them at relevant places in the book rather than throwing them into the current appendix. Ended up with 51 piles of mostly orthogonal (independent) categories, which caused its own difficulties, as most surfaces sufficiently elevated, hard and accessible by chair for activities such as eating were now spoken for.

Appendix 6 - The Intersessionary Papers

That's when I realized that if I were to put each pile into its own makeshift paper folder, I could then stack the folders and reclaim eating space.

And if I were then to number the folders and list the categories, I could organize them and decide where to insert them into existing chapters or come up with new chapters for categories not yet addressed.

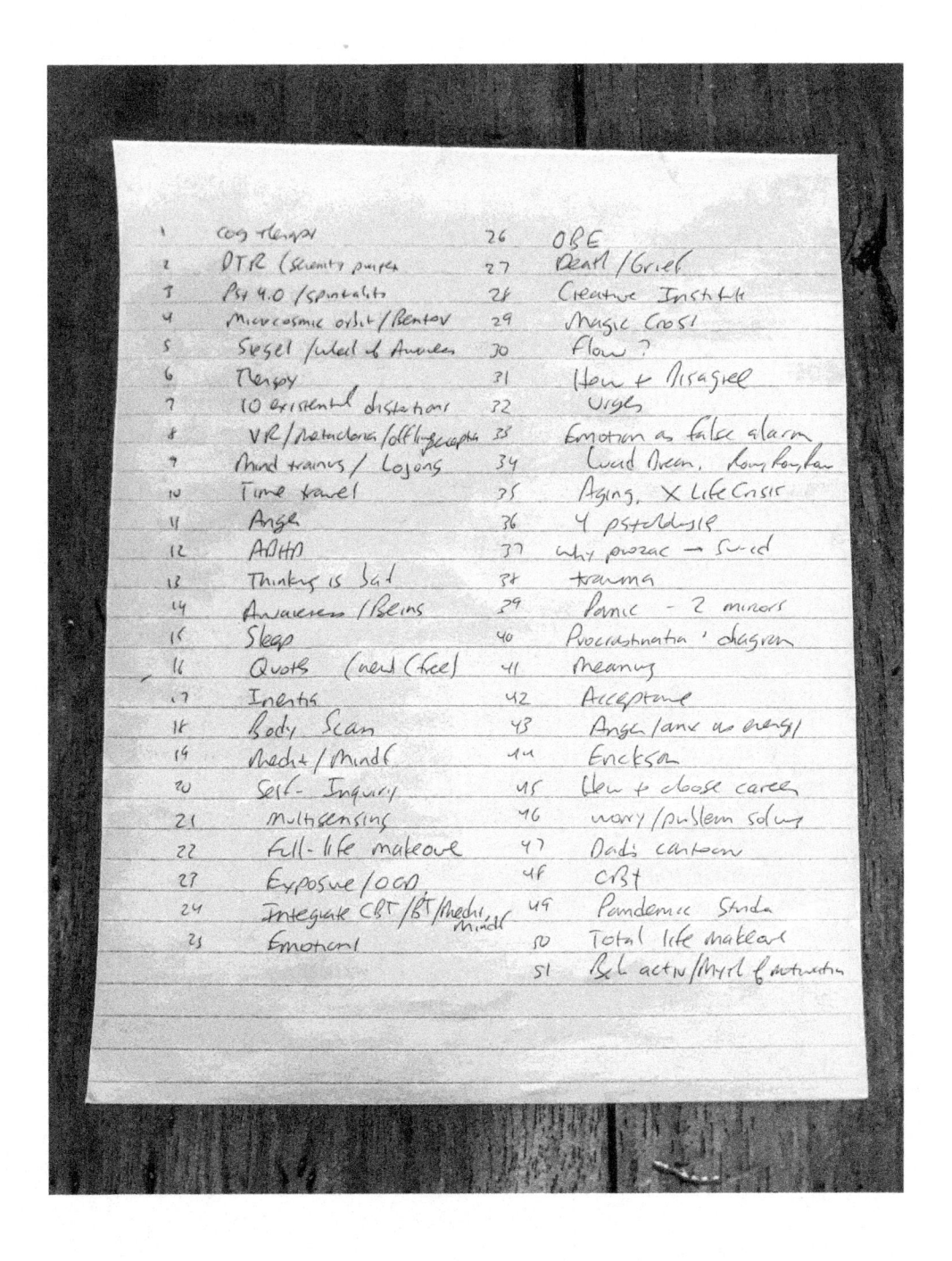

Appendix 6 - The Intersessionary Papers

Because, let's face it, that idea of an appendix consisting of a list of about 1000 ideas in no logical order was pretty much a nonstarter from the get-go.

Appendix 7 - *The Riddle of 12*

The Riddle of Twelve

By

Rimatt Densei AKA Matt Hazard

If one asks the question, "What is the meaning of The Old Testament?" or "What is it about?" it can be answered by saying that it is a beautiful riddle in twelve parts:

Part 1 - If the Bible is about God, then it is about godliness.

Part 2 - If the Bible is about godliness, then it can be said to be about conscience, for good conscience can be said to be godliness.

Part 3 - If, in a word, the Bible is about conscience, then it can be said that conscience is the spiritual or moral driving force or soul rather than a human invention, construct or contrivance.

Part 4 - If conscience can be said to be wedded to the soul, then it can be said that the Bible is about the journey of conscience-soul through life.

Part 5 - If the Bible is about the journey of the conscience-soul throughout life, then though man's conscience goes with him to the grave, it is only half his conscience-soul.

Part 6 - But it can be said that Man's soul dwells in the collective conscience-soul of Mankind and does not end with the grave but moves on in the journey of Mankind's collective life, whose conscience soul is infinite, perpetual and eternal.

Part 7 – If the collective conscience-soul of Mankind is everlasting, then it must be an absolute, timeless, omnipotent force that transcends the capacity of Mankind to comprehend it but is universal in its influence and its power to be perceived by Mankind, though inscrutable.

Part 8 – If Mankind has any awareness at all of his conscience-soul, if but a shadow, ephemeral and fleeting, and conscience is part of Mankind's collective conscience-soul, then conscience-soul can be likened to a good and great Life Force.

Part 9 – If the collective conscience-soul of Mankind can be said to be the Great Life Force, Force of Nature or essence of Mankind, then it also can be said to be the essence of eternal and everlasting God.

Part 10 – If God likened to the Great Life Force and conscience-soul of Mankind resides in each of us, then the great riddle of the Bible lies in the mystery surrounding the omnipresence and endless journey of Mankind's conscience-soul or Life Force, Force of Nature or, in its essence, God everlasting.

Part 11 – It must follow that a human being whose days are lived lacking conscience already has one foot in the grave and is a dead man walking, though his soul will live on and dwell in the collective conscience-soul of all Mankind.

Part 12 – A Human Being without conscience in life is redeemed in death when his soul is reunited with conscience in the realm of the everlasting conscience-soul of Mankind.

Thus, the Old Testament can be said to be a story about conscience and the journey of the conscience-soul as the manifestation of godliness and the nature-essence of God.

rms

Appendix 8 – *My First Guru*

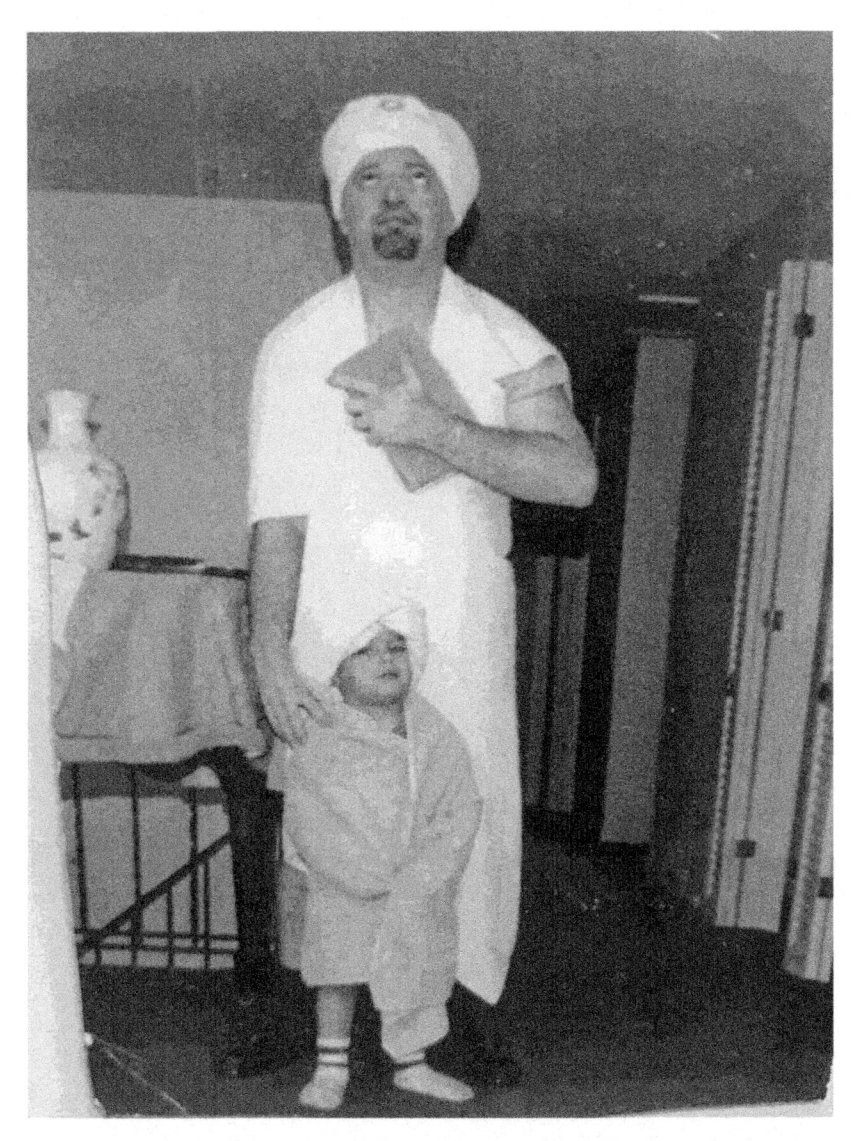

EVEN GURUS GET THE MEASLES

Appendix 8 – My First Guru

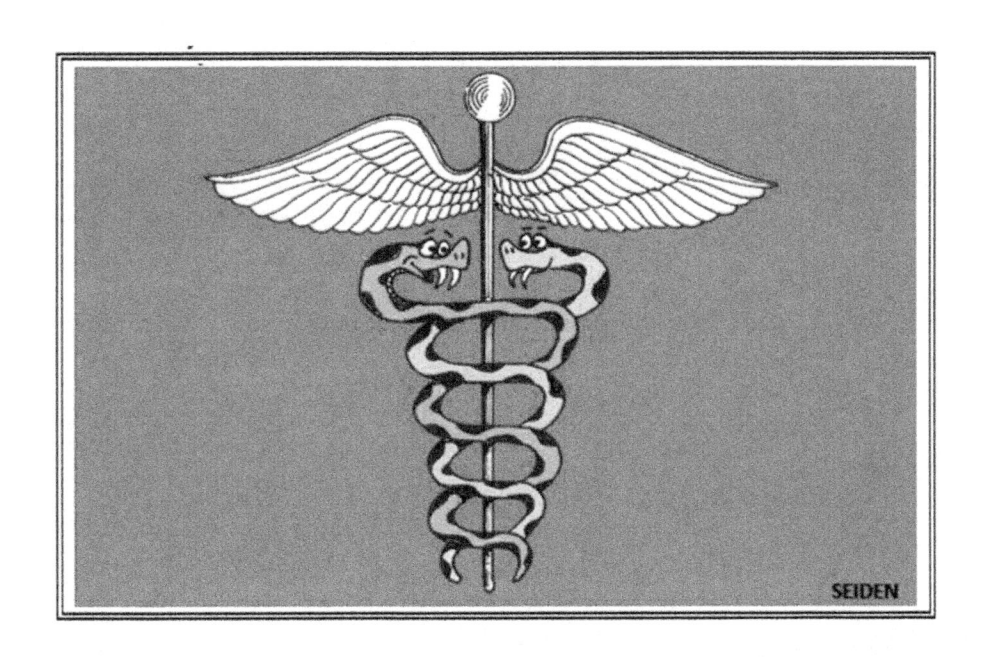

THE END.

(Of *this* page. One never knows what's lurking on the *next*...)

UH, WAIT ...

"Evolution and Creation
Are not *at-odds* at-all
God evolves things in Her Mind
Then creates them for y'all."
Grandma Densei (1922)

Grandpa Densei:

"Who the H-E-double-hockey-sticks is Todd?"

Grandma Densei:

"Go back to sleep."

God On Trial *by Rimatt Densei*

I.D.

"Now, Mr. Serpent... do you really expect the ladies and gentlemen of this jury to believe that you were just slithering along, minding your own business, when Ms. Eve, being so hungry, came up to you and begged you to get her an apple from the tree because she couldn't reach it?"

I.D.

"Now, then, Ms. Eve... do you really expect us to believe that some big bad snake approached you, held up a shiny apple, and you were so hungry that you took a bite out of it?"

How To Stop Thinking and Not Get Eaten By A Bear

I.D.

"Counselor, may I reasonably presume that your expert witness will favor us with his professional opinion as soon as he finishes his banana?"

God On Trial by Rimatt Densei

I.D.

"Now then, Sir, with all due respect, isn't it true that your so-called 'Intelligent Design' procedure incorporates a number of product design defects including the glaring character weakness of Ms. Eve? What do you say to that!"

How To Stop Thinking and Not Get Eaten By A Bear

Copyright Acknowledgements

Every effort has been made by the publisher to contact the sources of the selections in this book. Grateful acknowledgement is made for permission to reprint excerpts from the following:

Berakhot, 32b and Mishnah Berakhot 5:

Reprinted with permission from The Toby Press LLC, www.tobypress.com and Koren Publishers Jerusalem, www.korenpub.com, Distributors of Koren Publishers Jerusalem, Steinsaltz, Ofeq, Toby Press, Maggid, and Menorah Books.

CenteringPrayer.com (2019):

Reprinted with permission of Contemplative Outreach and Fr Thomas, www.ContemplativeOutreach.org , West Milford, New Jersey.

Daido Loori (2000, Summer):

Reprinted with permission of Zen Mountain Monastery. www.Dharma.net www.zmm.org

Densei, Rimatt (1997-2006):

All cartoons, whether signed or not, except those cited from specific newspapers or magazines are the artwork of Rimatt Densei, AKA Matt Hazard, copyright © 1997-2006 by Rimatt Densei and 2006-2022 by Dogu Densei and the Estate of Rimatt Densei. How to Safely Operate a Human Being: DANGER! WARNING! CAUTION! copyright © By Rimatt Densei 1981 and 2006-2022 by Dogu Densei and the Estate of Rimatt Densei.

Durrell, L. (1957; Bitter Lemons):

For USA: Reproduced with permission of Curtis Brown Group Ltd, London on behalf of the Beneficiaries of the Estate of Lawrence Durrell. Copyright © Lawrence Durrell 1957.

For World excluding USA: Reproduced with permission of Faber and Faber Ltd.

Durrell, L. (1957; Justine):

For USA, Phillippines and Open Market (incl. European Union):

Excerpt(s) from JUSTINE by Lawrence Durrell, copyright © 1957, renewed © 1985 by Lawrence George Durrell. Used by permission of Dutton, an imprint of Penguin Publishing Group, a division of Penguin Random House LLC. All rights reserved.

For World excluding USA: Reproduced with permission of Faber and Faber Ltd.

Fox, O. (Photo):

Oliver_Fox.jpg licensed under the Attribution-Share Alike 3.0 Unported (CC BY-SA 3.0) license. Retrieved from https://handwiki.org/wiki/File:Oliver_Fox.jpg

Hilliard (1951):

Alice in Wonderland
from ALICE IN WONDERLAND
Words by Bob Hilliard
Music by Sammy Fain
© 1951 Walt Disney Music Company
Copyright Renewed.
All Rights Reserved. Used by Permission.
Reprinted by Permission of Hal Leonard LLC

Huxley (1954):

Photo. Public Domain, as published in the United States between 1927 and 1963, and although there may or may not have been a copyright notice, the copyright was not renewed. From: A Case For ESP, PK and PSI. *Life*

Magazine, 11 January, 1954. Retrieved on 7/29/2022 from https://commons.wikimedia.org/wiki/File:Aldous_Huxley_psychical_researcher.png#filehistory

Kaplan, A. (1985):

Excerpt(s) from JEWISH MEDITATION by Aryeh Kaplan, translation copyright © 1985 by Schocken Boos. Used by permission of Schocken Books, an imprint of the Knopf Doubleday Publishing Group, a division of Penguin Random House, LLC. All rights reserved.

Lovecraft, H.P. (1928):

First page of The Call of the Cthulhu, In *Weird Tales*, Vol. XI, 2, pp. 159-176. Indianapolis: Popular Fiction Publishing Company. Retrieved on 5/19/22 from https://commons.wikimedia.org/wiki/File:Weirdtales-1928-02-thecallofcthulhu.jpg reproduced from https://archive.org/details/WeirdTalesV11N02192802/page/n15/mode/2up

As per Wiki, "the author died in 1956, so this work is in the public domain in its country of origin and other countries and areas where the copyright term is the author's life plus 60 years or fewer.

This work is in the public domain because it was published in the United States between 1928 and 1963 and although there may or may not have been a copyright notice, the copyright was not renewed."

Papaji (n.d., https://www.inner-quest.org/Poonja_Words.htm):

Reprinted by permission of Inner-quest.org to use Papaji's quotes from their website, for which use they received permission from Papaji.

Papaji (H.W.L. Poonja)(2000):

Material excerpted from **The Truth Is** by Sri H.W.L. Poonja, Compiled and edited by Prashanti de Jager, Copyright © 1995, 1998, 2000 Prashanti de Jager and Yudhishtara. Red Wheel/Weister, LLC. Newburyport, MA. www.redwheelweiser.com

Ram Dass (2021):

Reprinted by permission of the Love Serve Remember Foundation, www.ramdass.org

Ramana Maharshi quotations and photograph:

© Ramanasramam. Reprinted by permission of Sri Venkat S. Ramanan, President, Sri Ramanasramam, Tiruvannamalai, Tamil Nadu, India.

Ramana Maharshi (n.d., possibly in the 1920s). (M. James, Transl):

Reprinted with permission of Michael James, www.HappinessOfBeing.com

Red Pine (1989):

Excerpt from THE ZEN TEACHINGS OF BODHIDHARMA translated by Red Pine. Translation copyright © 1987 by Red Pine. Reprinted by permission of North Point Press, a division of Farrar, Straus and Giroux. All Rights Reserved.

Sachse, P., Beermann, U., Martini, M., Maran, T., Domeier, M. & Furtner, M. R. (2017):

3 photos reprinted with permission of Pierre Sachse.

Skinner, B.F. photograph:

Photograph by Steven Stone. Reprinted with permission of Steven Stone.

Sørensen, K. (2019):

Reprinted with permission of Kenneth Sørensen, www.kennethsorensen.dk

Stevens, W. (1954/2015):

For the USA:

"The Latest Freed Man" from THE COLLECTED POEMS OF WALLACE STEVENS by Wallace Stevens, copyright © 1954 by Wallace Stevens and copyright renewed 1982 by Holly Stevens. Used by permission of Alfred A. Knopf, an imprint of the Knopf Doubleday Publishing Group, a division of Penguin Random House, LLC. All rights reserved.

For the UK and British Commonwealth excluding Canada for Print:

Reproduced with permission of Faber and Faber Ltd.

Copyright Acknowledgements

Stevens, W. (1967/1990):

For the USA:

"Of Mere Being" from THE PALM AT THE END OF THE MIND: SELECTED POEMS AND A PLAY by Wallace Stevens, copyright © 1967, 1969, 1971 by Holly Stevens. Used by permission of Alfred A. Knopf, an imprint of the Knopf Doubleday Publishing Group, a division of Penguin Random House, LLC. All rights reserved.

For the UK and British Commonwealth excluding Canada for Print:

Reproduced with permission of Faber and Faber Ltd.

Wachowski, L., & Wachowski, L. (1999):

Reproduced with permission of Warner Bros. Entertainment Inc.

We'll Be Right Back:

Graphic. Public Domain. Retrieved on 7/30/2022 from https://commons.wikimedia.org/wiki/File:Content_intermission.svg

Bibliography

"I went to the mountains

to learn how to live a new type of existence,

an existence without time, without thought,

without the emotions, feelings, and energies of the self . . .

While the discoveries were numerous

and I have much to say about this adventure,

I think I can sum it up in one phrase by saying:

until I went to the mountains I had never truly lived."

Bernadette Roberts

(Former Catholic Nun; 1982, p. 33)

Aardema, F., O'Connor, K., Côté, S & Taillon, A. (2010). Virtual reality induces dissociation and lowers sense of presence in objective reality. *Cyberpsychology, Behavior, and Social Networking, 13*(4), 429-435. http://doi.org/10.1089/cyber.2009.0164

Aberdeen Evening Express (1892, December 14). *An Aberdeen doctor on hypnotism.* [Occurrence 3/4 down page, 3rd column, adjacent to article spacing rule in 2nd column. "The faculties of reason and judgement, the elaborate and regulative faculties, in this *altered state of consciousness*, are obviously dependent on sense perceptions, and vary accordingly as they do"; italics added]

Abraham Maslow (2019). *Abraham Maslow.* Retrieved on 3/5/19 from https://en.wikipedia.org/wiki/Abraham_Maslow

Bibliography

Abramovitch, H. (1995). The nightmare of returning home: a case of acute onset nightmare disorder treated by lucid dreaming. *Israel Journal of Psychiatry and Related Sciences, 32*(2), 140-5.

Abramowitz, J. S., Deacon, B. J., & Whiteside, S. P. H. (2012). *Exposure therapy for anxiety: principles and practice.* NY: The Guilford Press.

Acting Wise King of Westeros (2022). *Edict.* Sorry, the rest of this reference was eaten by the bear that ate the Acting Wise King. Try googling "better ways to spend time than checking references to imaginary Edicts by imaginary Acting Kings of imaginary places eaten by imaginary bears."

Adamatzky, A. (2022). Language of fungi derived from their electrical spiking activity. *Royal Society of Open Science, 9*: 211926. Retrieved on 6/18/22 from https://royalsocietypublishing.org/doi/epdf/10.1098/rsos.211926

Adams, D. (1982). *Life, the universe and everything.* New York: Harmony Books.

Adi Da Samraj (1975). *The paradox of realization.* Retrieved on 3/26/2021 from https://youtu.be/0Ex5TG4lv-g

Agathon, M. (1976). Les therapies comportementales en France. *Revue de Psychologie Appliquee, 26,* 75-94.

Agathon, M. (1982). Behavior therapy in France, 1976-1981. *Journal of Behavior Therapy and Experimental Psychiatry, 13,* 271-277.

Albert Ellis (2022). Wikipedia. Retrieved on 7/29/2022 from https://en.wikipedia.org/wiki/Albert_Ellis

Alexander, J. (1915). *The cure for self-consciousness.* Newcastle-upon-Tyne: Andrew Reid & Co.

Alexander, J. (1928). *Thought-control in everyday life.* New York: Funk & Wagnalls Company.

Alexander Bain (2022). Wikipedia. Retrieved on 5/21/2022 from https://en.wikipedia.org/wiki/Alexander_Bain_(philosopher)

Algol (1906). To a caged bear at the Brighton aquarium. In *Punch, Or the London Charivari,* p. 297. London. Retrieved on 3/13/23 from https://ia800300.us.archive.org/BookReader/BookReaderImages.php?zip=/28/items/punchvol130a131lemouoft/punchvol130a131lemouoft_jp2.zip&file=punchvol130a131lemouoft_jp2/punchvol130a131lemouoft_0810.jp2&id=punchvol130a131lemouoft&scale=4&rotate=0

Allain, R. (2013). Could you build a banana powered generator? *Wired: Dot Physics.* Retrieved on 3/9/2019 from https://www.wired.com/2013/02/could-you-build-a-banana-powered-generator/

Alter, R. (September, 1989). Jewish mysticism in dispute. *Commentary Magazine.* Retrieved on 2/7/21 from https://www.commentarymagazine.com/articles/robert-alter-2/jewish-mysticism-in-dispute/

Alvarado, C. S. (1989). Trends in the study of out-of-body experiences: An overview of developments since the nineteenth century. *Journal of Scientific Exploration, 3* (1), 27-42.

Alvarado, C. S. (2000). Out-of-body experiences. In E. Cardena, S. J. Lynn, & S. Krippner (Eds.), *Varieties of anomalous experience: Examining the scientific evidence* (pp. 183–218). Washington, DC: American Psychological Association.

Amazon.com (2022). *The fox has many tricks. The hedgehog has but one. But that is the best of all: Desiderius Erasmus – Place for writing thoughts.* Cyberspace: SpotNotebooks. Retrieved on 6/22/22 from https://www.amazon.sg/many-tricks-hedgehog-one-that/dp/B085HLYTD8 ISBN-13: 979-8621467890

Anderson, J. (1977). *Going for the one.* WB Music Corp.

Anderson, J., & Foster, D. (1970). *Time and a word.* WB Music Corp.

Anderson, L. (1986). Language is a virus from outer space. *Home of the brave.* Warner Records Inc.

Anderson, P. W. (1972). More is different. *Science, New Series, 177*(4047). (Aug. 4, 1972), pp., 393-396. Retrieved on 8/4/22 from https://cse-robotics.engr.tamu.edu/dshell/cs689/papers/anderson72more_is_different.pdf

Andriana.Marine (2022). Stunning shark encounter video reveals how to avoid attacks. *CNN Travel.* Retrieved on 8/26/22 from https://www.cnn.com/videos/travel/2022/08/26/shark-diver-video-tips-tiktok-orig-jk.cnn

Apollinaire, G. (1913). Le Pont Mirabeau. *Alcools – poèmes 1898-1913.* NRF, troisième édition, 1920. Retrieved on 1/9/21 from https://fr.wikisource.org/wiki/Alcools

Archilochos (1964). *Carmina: The fragments of Archilochos.* Berkeley: The University of California Press. Translated from the Greek by Guy Davenport. Retrieved on 6/23/22 from https://archive.org/details/carminafragments0000arch/page/64/mode/2up?q=hedgehog

Aristotle (350 B. C. E.). On dreams. In Parva Naturalia. Translated by J.I. Beare & G. R. T. Ross (1908), *The Parva Naturalia.* Oxford: Clarendon Press. Retrieved on 2/22/21 from http://classics.mit.edu/Aristotle/dreams.html

Arntz, A., & Jacob, G. (2013). *Schema therapy in practice: An introductory guide to the schema mode approach.* Chichester, West Sussex: John Wiley & Sons.

Ashcroft-Nowicki, D. (1990). *Inner landscapes: A Journey into awareness by pathworking.* London: Harper Collins.

Aspy D. J. (2020). Findings from the International Lucid Dream Induction Study. *Frontiers in Psychology, 11*(1746). https://www.ncbi.nlm.nih.gov/pmc/articles/PMC7379166/pdf/fpsyg-11-01746.pdf

Aspy, D. J., Delfabbro, P., Proeve, M., & Mohr, P. (2017). Reality testing and the mnemonic induction of lucid dreams: Findings from the national Australian lucid dream induction Study. *Dreaming, 27,* 206-231.

Assagioli, R. (n.d.). *Psychosynthesis egg diagram.* Retrieved 1/9/21 from https://commons.wikimedia.org/wiki/File:Psychosynthesis-egg-diagram.png

Assagioli, R. (1927). *A new method of healing: Psychosynthesis.* Lecture delivered at the English Speaking Union in Rome, on May 1st, 1927. Rome, Italy: Institute of Psychosynthesis (Applied Psychology and Psychotherapy: Know thyself. Possess thyself. Transform thyself). London: L.N. Fowler and Co.; New York, NY: Lucis Publishing Co. Retrieved on 7/3/22 from https://kennethsorensen.dk/en/a-new-method-of-healing-psychosynthesis/

Assagioli, R. (1933, Oct.). *Practical contributions to a modern Yoga.* The Beacon, Vol. 12. Retrieved on 7/3/22 from https://kennethsorensen.dk/en/practical-contributions-to-a-modern-yoga/

Assagioli, R. (1965). *Psychosynthesis: A manual of principles and techniques.* Oxford, England: Hobbs, Dorman & Co., Inc.

Assagioli, R. (2012). *Psychosynthesis: A collection of basic writings.* Amherst, MA: The Synthesis Center.

Augmented Reality (2021). Retrieved on 2/23/21 from https://en.wikipedia.org/wiki/Augmented_reality

Aurora, R. N., Zak, R. S., & Auerbach, S. H., et al. (2010). Best practice guide for the treatment of nightmare disorder in adults. *Journal of Clinical Sleep Medicine, 6*(4), 389-401.

Bacheller, I. (1919). *A man for the ages.* New York: Grosset & Dunlap. Retrieved on 12/2/22 from https://babel.hathitrust.org/cgi/pt?id=hvd.hxdgu7&view=1up&seq=9

Bain, A. (1868). *The senses and the intellect.* 3rd ed. London: Longman's, Green, and Co.

Bain, A. (1887). On 'association'-controversies. *Mind, 12*(46), 161-182.

Baird, B., Mota-Rolim, S. A., & Dresler, M. (2019). The cognitive neuroscience of lucid dreaming. *Neuroscience and Biobehavioral Reviews, 100,* 305-323.

https://www.ncbi.nlm.nih.gov/pmc/articles/PMC6451677/pdf/nihms-1525230.pdf

Baird, B., Riedner, B. A., Boly, M., Davidson, R. J., & Tononi, G. (2019). Increased lucid dream frequency in long-term meditators but not following mindfulness-based stress reduction training. *Psychology of Consciousness: Theory, Research, and Practice, 6*(1), 40-54.

Barker S. A., Borjigin, J., Lomnicka, I., Strassman, R. (July 2013). LC/MS/MS analysis of the endogenous dimethyltryptamine hallucinogens, their precursors, and major metabolites in rat pineal gland microdialysate. *Biomedical Chromatography, 27*(12): 1690-1700.

Barlow, D. H., Farchione, T. J., Fairholme, C. P., Ellard, K. K., Boisseau, C., Allen, L. B., & Ehrenreich-May, J. T. (2011). *Unified protocol for transdiagnostic treatment of emotional disorders: Therapist guide.* New York: Oxford University Press.

Barrett. J. (2004). *Side effects of virtual environments: A review of the literature.* Edinburgh, S. Australia: DSTO Information Sciences Laboratory.

Battista, J. (1996). Abraham Maslow and Roberto Assagioli: Pioneers of transpersonal psychology. In B. Scotten, A. Chinnen & J. Battista (Eds.), *Textbook of transpersonal psychiatry and psychology* (pp. 52-61). New York, NY: Basic Books.

Bayliss, C. R., Bishop, N. L., & Fowler, R. C. (1985). Pineal gland calcification and defective sense of direction. *British Medical Journal, 291*, 21-28. Retrieved on 6/20/22 from https://www.bmj.com/content/bmj/291/6511/1758.full.pdf

Bear Necessities (2013). *Bear necessities: 10 Scottish facts about bears.* Retrieved 10/28/2020 from https://www.bbc.com/news/uk-scotland-highlands-islands-24725156

Béarn, P. (1951). *Couleurs d'usine* [Factory colors]. Paris: P. Seghers. Retrieved 3/26/2019 from https://en.wiktionary.org/wiki/métro,_boulot,_dodo

BearSmart.com (2021). *Dispelling myths about bears.* Retrieved on 1/10/21 from http://www.bearsmart.com/about-bears/dispelling-myths/

Beck, A. T. (1963). Thinking and depression: I. Idiosyncratic content and cognitive distortions. *Archives of General Psychiatry, 9,* 324-333.

Beck, A. T. (1964). Thinking and depression: II. Theory and therapy. *Archives of General Psychiatry, 10,* 561-571.

Beck, A. T. (1970a). The core problem in depression: The cognitive triad. *Science and Psychoanalysis, 17,* 47-55.

Beck, A. T. (1970b). Cognitive therapy: Nature and relation to behavior therapy. *Behavior Therapy, 1,* 184-200.

Beck, A. T., Rush, A. J., Shaw, B. F., & Emery, G. (1979). *Cognitive Therapy of Depression.* New York: Guilford Press.

Berakhot 32b. English from The William Davidson digital edition of *The Noé Edition of the Koren Talmud Bavli,* with commentary by Rabbi Adin Even-Israel Steinsaltz. Jerusalem: Koren Publishers. Retrieved 10/27/2020 from https://www.sefaria.org/Berakhot.32b.20?lang=bi

Berlin, I. (1953). *The hedgehog and the fox.* London: Weidenfeld & Nicolson. Retrieved on 6/22/22 from https://silo.pub/the-hedgehog-and-the-fox.html

Bharati, Swami J. (2022). *Maslow's needs hierarchy and advanced yoga psychology.* Retrieved on 6/25/22 from https://www.swamij.com/maslow-yoga.htm.

Blom, J. D. (2010). *A dictionary of hallucinations.* New York: Springer.

Body Snatching (2021). Retrieved on 2/25/21 from https://en.wikipedia.org/wiki/Body_snatching#United_States_2

Brahm, A. (2016). *Bear awareness: Questions and answers on taming your wild mind.* Somerville, MA: Wisdom Publications.

BrainyQuote.com (2022). *Ralph Waldo Emerson quotes.* Retrieved on 6/22/22 from https://www.brainyquote.com/quotes/ralph_waldo_emerson_120404

Braiker, H. B. (2001). *The disease to please.* New York: McGraw Hill.

Bridgman, T., Cummings, S., & Ballard, J. (2019). Who built maslow's pyramid? A history of the creation of management studies' most famous symbol and its implications for management education. *Academy of Management Learning and Education, 18*(1), 81-98. Retrieved on 6/25/22 from https://journals.aom.org/doi/10.5465/amle.2017.0351

Brown, J., & Frey, G. (1972). *Take it easy.* New York: Downtown Music Publishing.

Bruce, R. (2009). *Astral dynamics: The complete book of out-of-body experiences.* Charlottesville, VA: Hampton Roads Publishing.

Brunton, P. (1943). *The wisdom of the overself.* London: Rider.

Brunton, P., & Venkataramiah, M. (1983). *Conscious immortality: Conversations with Sri Ramana Maharshi recorded by Paul Brunton and Mungala S. Veskataramiah.* Tamil Nadu: Sri Ramanasramam.

Brylowski A. (1990). Nightmare in crisis: clinical applications of lucid dreaming techniques. *Psychiatric Journal of the University of Ottowa, 15*(2), 79-84.

Bucke, R. M. (2009/1901). *Cosmic consciousness: A study in the evolution of the human mind.* New York: Dover Publications Inc. Originally published in 1929 by E.P. Dutton & Co., New York.

Burns, D. D. (2020). *Feeling great: The revolutionary new treatment for depression and anxiety.* Eau Claire, WI: PESI.

Bynum, E. B. (2012). *Dark light consciousness: Melanin, serpent power, and the luminous matrix of reality.* Rochester, VT: Inner Traditions.

Carnegie, D. (1948/1990). *How to stop worrying and start living.* New York: Pocket Books.

Carpenter, E. (1892). *From Adam's Peak to Elephanta.* London: Swann Sonnenschein & Co.

Castaneda, C. (1972). *Journey to Ixtlan: The lessons of Don Juan.* New York: Simon & Schuster.

Categorical Imperative (2021). Retrieved on 2/25/21 from https://en.wikipedia.org/wiki/Categorical_imperative

Cautela, J. R., & Wisocki, P. A (1977). The thought stopping procedure: Description, application, and learning theory interpretations. *The Psychological Record, 2,* 255-264.

CenteringPrayer.com (2019). *Centering prayer.* Retrieved on 3/28/2019 from http://www.centeringprayer.com/

Chia, M. (2019). *Dark room retreat schedule and daily program.* Retrieved on 3/29/2019 from https://www.universal-tao.com/dark_room/schedule.html

Chimnoy (1975). *Earth-bound journey and Heaven-bound journey.* Retrieved on 5/28/2022 from https://www.yogaofsrichinmoy.com/the-higher-worlds/samadhi-fld/samadhi/ and https://www.srichinmoylibrary.com/ebj

Chinen, A. B. (1996). The emergence of transpersonal psychiatry. In Scotton, B. W., Chinen, A. B., & Battista, J. R. (Eds.). *Textbook of Transpersonal Psychiatry and Psychology.* New York: Basic Books.

Chris (2019). How to not get eaten by a bear. In *Global shenanigans: The adventure specialist,* January 14, 2019. Retrieved on 7/14/22 from https://global-shenanigans.com/how-not-to-get-eaten-by-a-bear/

Cobb, S. V. G., Nichols, S., Ramsey, A., & Wilson, J. R. (1999). Virtual reality-induced symptoms and effects (VRISE). *Presence, 8*(2), 169-186. https://www.mitpressjournals.org/doi/pdf/10.1162/105474699566152

Coben, H. (2006). *Promise me* (Myron Bolitar Mysteries). New York: Dutton.

Cole, N. K., & ahbez, e. (1948). *Nature boy. Vocal popular sheet Music Collection.* Score 2037. https://digitalcommons.library.umaine.edu/mmb-vp-copyright/2037

Coleman, P. (2020). Obituary. Philip W. Anderson (1923-2020): Nobel prize winner who transformed condensed-matter and particle physics. *Nature, 581* (May 7, 2020), 29. Retrieved on 6/23/22 from https://www.nature.com/articles/d41586-020-01318-4

Collard, J., & O'Kelly, M. (2011). Rational emotive behaviour therapy: A positive perspective. *Journal of Rational-Emotive & Cognitive-Behavior Therapy, 29,* 248-256.

ContemplativeOutreach.org (2021). *History of centering prayer.* Retrieved on 1/18/2021 from https://www.contemplativeoutreach.org/history-of-centering-prayer/

Cooper, D. (1997). *God is a verb: Kabbalah and the practice of mystical Judaism.* New York: Riverhead.

Cooper, D. (2000). *The handbook of Jewish meditation practices: A guide for enriching the Sabbath and other days of your life.* Woodstock, NY: Jewish Lights Publishing.

Cosmic Iron (2013). Senses initiated lucid dream (SSILD) Official Tutorial. *Cosmic Iron's blog on senses initiated lucid dream (SSILD) and other lucid dreaming related topics.* Retrieved on 5/20/2022 from https://cosmiciron.blogspot.com/2013/01/senses-initiated-lucid-dream-ssild_16.html

Cottraux, J. (1979). *Les thérapies comportementales.* Paris: Masson.

Cottraux, J. (1990). *Les thérapies comportementales et cognitives.* Paris: Masson.

Coué, E. (1920/1989). *La maîtrise de soi-même par l'autosuggestion consciente.* [Self Mastery Through Conscious Autosuggestion]. Paris: Renaudot et Cie.

Crystal, D. (2006). *The fight for English: How language pundits ate, shot and left.* Oxford: Oxford University Press.

Csikszentmihalyi, M. (1975). *Beyond boredom and anxiety: Experiencing flow in work and play.* San Francisco: Jossey-Bass.

Dacey, M. (2022). Associationism in the philosophy of mind. *In Internet encyclopedia of philosophy: A peer reviewed academic resource.* Retrieved on 5/21/22 from https://iep.utm.edu/associationism-in-philosophy-of-mind/

Daido Loori, J. (2000, Summer). *Mountain record: The Zen practitioner's journal.* Mt. Tremper, NY: Dharma Communications, Inc.

Dan, J. (2006). *Kabbalah: A very short introduction.* Oxford University Press.

Dark Retreat (2019). *Dark retreat.* Retrieved 3/29/2019 from htttps://en.wikipedia.org/wiki/Dark_retreat

De Sarthe, M. (1820). Rêve. Extrait du *Dictionnaire des sciences médicales Panckoucke*, tome quarante-huit, RES-RHU, pp. 245-300. Retrieved on 5/20/22 from http://www.histoiredelafolie.fr/psychiatrie-neurologie/moreau-de-la-sarthe-reve-extrait-du-dictionnaire-des-sciences-medicales-panckoucke-paris-tome-quarante-huit-res-rhu-1820-pp-245-300-1-tableau-depliant

De Silva, P. (2000). Buddhism and psychotherapy: The Role of Self-Control Strategies. *Hsi Lai Journal of Humanistic Buddhism, V.1.*, 169-182.

Deikman, A. J. (1982). *The observing self: Mysticism and psychotherapy.* Boston: Beacon Press.

den Blanken, C. M., & Meijer, E. J. G. (1988). A historical view of dreams and the ways to direct them; practical observations by Marie-Jean-Léon-Lecoq, le Marquis d'Hervey-Saint-Denys. *Lucidity Letter, 7*(2), 67-78, retrieved on 3/7/19 from http://members.casema.nl/carolusdenblanken/Downloads/Historical%20Saint-Denys.PDF

Densei, D. (1994) Behavior and cognitive therapies in France: An oral history. *Journal of Behavior Therapy and Experimental Psychiatry, 25* (2), 105-112.

Densei, D. (1999). Cross-cultural behavior therapy. In J. S. Mio, J. E. Trimble, P. A. Arredondo, H. E. Cheatham, & D. Sue (Eds.), *Key words in multicultural interventions: A dictionary* (pp. 55-56). Westport, CT: Greenwood Press.

Densei, D. (2008). *Unity's pulse: A psi-co-logical out-of-body pre-cognitive trans-personal post-2012 psi-fi e-novella.* New York: Caduxeus Press.

Densei, D., & Lam, K. (2010). From Moses and monotheism to Buddha and behaviorism: Cognitive Behavior Therapy's Transpersonal Crisis. *The Journal of Transpersonal Psychology, 42* (1), 89-113.

Bibliography

Densei, D. (2022). *HOW TO STOP THINKING and not get eaten by a bear: The New Cognitive Behavioral Mind Training*. Tralfamadore: Caduxeus Press.

Densei, G. (1922). *The Wit and Wisdom Teeth of Grandma Densei*. Originally published as #@$ %^#$# $#%^@# !!!!!! $$$$$$ %^#&@*^%. Tralfamadore: Caduxeus Press. Translated from the Trantorian *What Hari Seldon Forgot to Tell Us*. (1923; Translator unknown. Trantor: Streeling University Press).

Densei, R. (1981). *How to Safely Operate a Human Being: DANGER! WARNING! CAUTION!* New Jersey: The Densei Group. Also reprinted with commentary in R. M. Densei (1984), Product Safety Engineering for Managers: A Practical Handbook and Guide (pp. 98-103). Englewood Cliffs, NJ: Prentice Hall.

Devarim – Deuteronomy – Chapter 32 (2019). Retrieved on 3/28/2019 from https://www.chabad.org/library/bible_cdo/aid/9996/jewish/Chapter-32.htm#v11

Dimidjian, S., Barrera, M., Jr., Martell, C., Muñoz, R. F., & Lewinsohn, P. M. (2011). The origins and current status of behavioral activation treatments for depression. *Annual Review of Clinical Psychology, 7*, 1–38. http://dx.doi.org/10.1146/annurev-clinpsy-032210-104535

Dimidjian, S. et al. (2006). Randomized trial of behavioral activation, cognitive therapy, and antidepressant medication in the acute treatment of adults with major depression. *Journal of Consulting and Clinical Psychology, 74*(4), 658-670.

Donovan (1967). *There is a mountain*. On Mellow Yellow. Epic Records.

Dostoevsky, F. (1863). In Зимние заметки о летних впечатлениях Zimniye zametki o letnikh vpechatleniyakh.

Douglas, K. (2003, May 16). Opinion: My first cigarette, and my last. *New York Times*.

Dove, H. W. (1839). *Repertorium der Physik*, III, p. 494.

Downar, J. (2002). *neuroimaging evidence for the representation of salience in the neural correlates of attention and awareness of the human brain. Doctoral thesis.* Graduate Department of the Institute of Medical Science and Collaborative Program in Neuroscience, University of Toronto.

Dresler, M., Koch, S. P., Wehrle, R., Spoormaker, V. I., Holsboer, F., Steiger, A., Sämann, P. G., Obrig, H., & Czisch, M. (2011). Dreamed movement elicits activation in the sensorimotor cortex. *Current Biology, 21,* 1833-1837. Retrieved 3/28/2019 from https://doi.org/10.1016/j.cub.2011.09.029

Dubuc, B. (2019). *The suprachiasmatic nuclei and the pineal gland.* Retrieved 3/29/2019 from http://thebrain.mcgill.ca/flash/d/d_11/d_11_cr/d_11_cr_hor/d_11_cr_hor.html

Durant, W. (1926). *The story of civilization.* New York: Simon and Schuster.

Durrell, L. (1957). *Bitter lemons.* London: Faber and Faber Ltd.

Durrell, L. (1957). *Justine.* London: Faber and Faber Ltd.

Earle, S. (2000). Galway girl. On *Transcendental blues.* E-Squared Records.

Easwaren, E. (1977/2009). *The mantram handbook: A practical guide to choosing your mantram and calming your mind.* Tomales, CA: Nilgiri Press.

Easwaren, E. (1978/2016). *Passage meditation: A complete spiritual practice.* Tomales, CA: Nilgiri Press.

Ebel, R. L. (1974). And still the dryads linger. *American Psychologist, 29*(7), 485-492.

eden ahbez (n.d.). Retrieved on 10/27/2020 from https://en.wikipedia.org/wiki/Eden_ahbez

Egenes, T. (2010). *Maharishi Patanjali Yoga Sutra.* Fairfield, Iowa: 1st World Publishing.

Eighth (2022). Retrieved on 7/3/22 from https://www.etymonline.com/word/eighth

Einstein, A. (1956). *Ideas and opinions.* New York: Citadel Press.

Ekai, called Mu-mon (1934)(N. Senzaki & P. Reps, Transl). *The gateless gate.* Retrieved on 10/31/2020 from https://www.sacred-texts.com/bud/zen/mumonkan.htm

Ellis, A. (1955). New approaches to psychotherapy techniques. *Journal of Clinical Psychology, Monograph Supplement, 11*, 1-53.

Ellis, A. (1958). Rational psychotherapy. *Journal of General Psychology, 59*, 35-49.

Ellis, A., & Harper, R. A. (1962). *A guide to rational living.* Englewood Cliffs, NJ: Prentice Hall.

Epictetus (1890)(George Long, trans.). *The Discourses with the Encheiridion and Fragments.* London: George Bell and Sons.

Epictetus (2007)(S. Lebell, trans.). *Art of Living: The classical manual on virtue, happiness, and effectiveness.* New York: HarperCollins.

Erasmus (Epistle 337) in Collected works of Erasmus Vol. 3, 134. Retrieved on 6/23/22 from https://en.wikipedia.org/wiki/Erasmus#cite_note-48

Erasmus (Epistle 695) in Collected works of Erasmus Vol. 5: Letters 594 to 841, 1517-1518 (tr. R. A. B. Mynors and D. F. S. Thomson; annotated by James K. McConica; Toronto: University of Toronto Press, 1976), 172. Retrieved on 6/23/22 from https://en.wikipedia.org/wiki/Erasmus#cite_note-45

Erasmus (1508). Adagia. Cited in Pandora's box in Greek mythology. Retrieved on 6/23/2022 from https://www.greeklegendsandmyths.com/pandoras-box.html

Erasmus (1536/2010). In *Les adages d'Érasme*, présentés par les Belles Lettres et le GRAC (UMR 5037), 418. I, V, 18 (p. 406). Retrieved on 6/23/22 from https://web.archive.org/web/20120114123112/http://sites.univ-lyon2.fr/lesmondeshumanistes/wp-content/uploads/Adages.pdf

Erismann, T., & Kohler, I. (2021). *Erismann and Kohler inversion "upside-down" goggles – Film 1*: https://youtu.be/JQJ5SFnytfo *Film 2*: https://youtu.be/z1HYcN7f9N4

Ernst Mach Papers (1865-1918). *Smithsonian libraries*. Retrieved on 8/25/2022 from https://archive.org/details/ErnstMachpapers00Mach/page/n230/mode/1up?q=231

Ethics (2021). Ethics. Chapter 9. *Kantian theory: The categorical imperative. Not the Golden Rule*. Retrieved on 2/25/21 from https://www.qcc.cuny.edu/SocialSciences/ppecorino/ETHICS_TEXT/Chapter_8_Kantian_Theory/Not_Golden.htm

Fagen, D., & Becker, W. (1972). *Do it again*. ABC Records.

Fazekas, P., Nanay, B., & Pearson, J. (2021). Offline perception: An introduction. *Philosophical Transactions of the Royal Society B*. 376: 20190686. https://www.ncbi.nlm.nih.gov/pmc/articles/PMC7741075/pdf/rstb20190686.pdf

Fazekas P, Nemeth G, Overgaard M. (2020). Perceptual representations and the vividness of stimulus-triggered and stimulus-independent experiences. *Perspectives on Psychological Science, 15,* 1200–1213.

Fehmi, L, & Fehmi, S. S. (2021). *The open focus life: Practices to develop attention and awareness for optimal well-being*. Boulder: Shambhala.

Fehmi, L., & Robbins, J. (2007). *The open focus brain: Harnessing the power of attention to heal the mind and body*. Boston: Trumpeter Books.

Fehmi, L., & Robbins, J. (2010). *Dissolving pain: Simple brain-training exercises for overcoming chronic pain*. Boston and London: Trumpeter.

Fenwick, P., and Fenwick, E. (1995). *The truth in the light: An investigation of over 300 near-death experiences*. London, England: Headline.

Ferrigno, T. (2018). *An oasis in the wilderness.* Bloomington, IN: LifeRich Publishing.

Ferster, C. B. (1973). A functional analysis of depression. *American Psychologist, 28*, 857-870.

FieldAndStream.com (2019). *Six terrifying bear attack stories.* Retrieved on 1/10/21 from https://www.fieldandstream.com/against-all-odds-attacked-by-bears-and-living-to-tell-story/

Fight (2022). Retrieved on 7/3/22 from https://www.etymonline.com/word/fight?ref=etymonline_crossreference#etymonline_v_5926

Fischer, R. (1971). A cartography of the ecstatic and meditative states. *Science, 174*(4012), 897-904, retrieved on 6/17/2022 from https://wisebrain.org/papers/MapofMedEcstaticStates.pdf

Fischer, R. (1980). A cartography of the ecstatic and meditative states. In *Understanding Mysticism*, ed., Richard Woods. Garden City, NY: Image Books, 270-285.

FluorideAlert.org (2021a). *Do we need fluoride?* Retrieved on 1/10/21 from https://fluoridealert.org/faq/

FluorideAlert.org (2021b). *What countries fluoridate their water?* Retrieved on 1/10/21 from http://fluoridealert.org/faq/what-countries-fluoridate-their-water/

Flying Pig (n.d.). *When pigs fly.* Retrieved on 10/28/2020 from https://en.wikipedia.org/wiki/When_pigs_fly

Forman, K. C. (1999). *Mysticism, mind, consciousness.* Albany, NY: State University of New York Press.

Fox, O. (1920). The pineal doorway: A record of research. *Occult Review, XXXI*(4), 190-198. Retrieved from http://iapsop.com/archive/materials/occult_review/occult_review_v31_n4_apr_1920_uk_nc_nw.pdf

Frankl, V. (1984). *Man's search for meaning.* New York: Simon and Schuster. Originally published in German in 1946.

Franzen, D. (1980, January). American inquisition: The FDA's persecution of Wilhelm Reich. *Reason*. Retrieved on 5/20/22 from https://reason.com/1980/01/01/american-inquisition-the-fdas/

Free Euripides (2021). *Hippolytus*. Retrieved on 1/5/21 from http://classics.mit.edu/Euripides/hippolytus.html

Freeman, T. (1977). *Bringing Heaven down to Earth: 365 Meditations on the Wisdom of the Rebbe Rabbi M.M. Schneerson*. Vancouver, BC: Class One Press.

Freud. S. (n.d.). Structural iceberg diagram. Retrieved 1/9/21 from https://commons.wikimedia.org/wiki/File:Structural-Iceberg.svg#/media/File:Structural-Iceberg.svg

Freud, S. (1899/1913). *The interpretation of dreams*. Translated by A. A. Brill (1913). New York: Macmillan. Retrieved on 1/9/21 from https://psychclassics.yorku.ca/Freud/Dreams/dreams1b.htm

Freud, S. (1915). Letter to Dr. Frederik van Eeden. *The standard edition of the complete psychological works of Sigmund Freud, Volume XIV (1914-1916): On the History of the Psycho-Analytic Movement, Papers on Metapsychology and Other Works*, 301-302.

Freud, S. (1922). Sigmund Freud Papers: *Oversize, 1859-1985; Writings; 1922; "Dream and telepathy" [a], typewritten English translation by Wilson Vance with corrections not in Freud's hand but signed by him and holograph comments by Freud*. Retrieved on 10/31/2020 from https://www.loc.gov/resource/mss39990.OV0804/?st=gallery

Freud, S. (1930). *Civilization and its discontents*. Joan Riviere (Trans.). London: Hogarth Press. Retrieved on 6/12/22 from https://archive.org/details/in.ernet.dli.2015.95747/page/n7/mode/2up

Freud, S., & Breuer, J (1895/2004). (N. Luckhurst, Transl). *Studies in hysteria*. NY: Penguin Books.

Gackenbach, J., & LaBerge, S. (Eds.), (1988). *Conscious mind, sleeping brain: Perspectives on lucid Dreaming*. New York: Plenum.

Gandhi, N. J., Katani, H. A. (2011). Motor functions of the superior colliculus. *Annual Review of Neuroscience, 34*, 205–231

Garisto, D. (2020). In memorium: Philip Anderson. *Santa Fe Institute: Home/News.* Retrieved on 2/28/2023 from https://santafe.edu/news-center/news/memoriam-philip-anderson

Gavie, J., & Revonsuo, A. (2010). The future of lucid dreaming treatment: Commentary on "The neurobiology of consciousness: Lucid dreaming wakes up" by J. Allan Hobson. *International Journal of Dream Research, 3*(1), 13–15.

George M. Stratton (2021). Retrieved on 2/24/21 from https://en.wikipedia.org/wiki/George_M._Stratton#Wundt's_lab_and_the_inverted-glasses_experiments

Gibson, J. (2021). *Living in a reversed world.* English version of Erismann, T., Kohler, I., & Scheffler, P. (1954). Verkehrte Welten [Living in a reversed world]. Wien: Firma Pacher & Co. Retrieved on 2/24/21 from https://youtu.be/C-Opnrb6l9A

Ginsburgh, Y. (1999). *The mystery of marriage.* Rechovot, Israel: Gal Einai.

Glasser, W. (1998). *Choice theory: A new psychology of personal freedom.* New York: HarperCollins.

Godman, D. (1985). *Be as you are: The teachings of Sri Ramana Maharshi.* London: Arkana.

Goldstein, K. (1939). *The organism, A holistic approach to biology derived from pathological data in man.* New York: American Book Co. Retrieved on 6/26/22 from https://archive.org/details/organismholistic00gold/page/198/mode/2up?q=actualization

Goldstein, Z. (2019a). *The Jewish burial.* Retrieved on 3/28/2019 from https://www.chabad.org/library/article_cdo/aid/368092/jewish/The-Jewish-Burial.htm

Goldstein, Z. (2019b). *Kel Maleh Rachamim – Prayer for the soul of the departed.* Retrieved 3/28/2019 from https://www.chabad.org/library/article_cdo/aid/367837/jewish/Kel-Maleh-Rachamim.htm

Goleman, D. (2004). *Destructive emotions: A scientific dialogue with the Dalai Lama.* NY: Bantam Dell.

GoodReads.com (2022). Archilochos > Quote > Quotable Quote. Retrieved on 6/22/22 from https://www.goodreads.com/quotes/247249-the-fox-has-many-tricks-the-hedgehog-has-but-one

Gorman, G. (2022). George Gorman, New York State Parks Regional Director for Long Island, Interviewed by Glen Schuck. Aired at 11:02:59 am to 11:03:40, on 7/15/22, on 1010 WINS, *Newsline with Brigitte Quinn,* 11:00 am – 12:00 pm. Retrieved on 7/15/22 at 2:15 pm from https://www.audacy.com/1010wins/podcasts

Gott J. et al. (2021). Virtual reality training of lucid dreaming. *Philosophical Transactions of the Royal Society, 376*: 20190697. http://dx.doi.org/10.1098/rstb.2019.0697

Green, C., & McCreery, C. (1994). *Lucid dreaming: The paradox of consciousness during sleep.* London: Routledge.

Green, C., & McCreery, C. (2020, August 15). Metachoric experiences. In Green, C., *Notes from an exiled academic.* Retrieved on 2/23/21 from https://celiagreen.blogspot.com/2020/08/metachoric-experiences.html

Green, E. E., & Green, A. M. (1986). Biofeedback and states of consciousness. In *Handbook of States of Consciousness* (B. B. Wolman & M. Ullman, eds.). New York: Van Nostrand Rheinhold.

Greenwald, J (2001/2017). *Who are you? An interview with H.W.L. Poonja: Papaji explains how to get an immediate glimpse of enlightenment.* Retrieved 2/10/2019 from https://realization.org/p/h-w-l-poonja/who-are-you/who-are-you.3.html

Gregory, R. L. (1980). Perceptions as hypotheses. *Philosophical Transactions of the Royal Society of London, B*(290), 181-197. Retrieved on 2/24/21 from https://royalsocietypublishing.org/doi/pdf/10.1098/rstb.1980.0090

Gregory, R. L. (1998)(5th Ed.). *Eye and brain.* Oxford: Oxford University Press.

Grof, S., & Grof, C. (1989). Spiritual emergency: Understanding evolutionary crisis. In S. Grof & C. Grof (Eds.). *Spiritual emergency: When personal transformation becomes a crisis*, pp. 1-26. New York: Jeremy P. Tarcher/Putnam.

Grossman, L. (April 12, 2007). Kurt Vonnegut, 1922–2007. *Time Magazine.*

Halliday, G. (1988). Lucid dreaming: Using nightmares and sleep-wake confusion. In J. Gackenbach, & S. LaBerge (Eds.), *Conscious Mind, Sleeping Brain* (pp. 305-307). New York: Plenum.

Hanh, T. N. (1974). *Zen keys.* NY: Anchor Books.

Hanh, T. N. (2021). *Resting in the river.* Retrieved on 1/29/2021 from https://dhammatalks.net/Books2/Thich_Nhat_Hanh_Resting_in_the_River.htm

Haraldsson, E., & Matlock, J. (2017). *I saw a light and came here: Children's experiences of reincarnation.* Hove, UK: White Crow Books.

Harding, D. (1961/1986). *On having no head. Zen and the rediscovery of the obvious.* London: Arkana.

Harding, D. (2000). (D. Lang, Ed). *Face to face. Rediscovering our original nature.* Dialogues with Douglas E. Harding. Agoura Hills, CA: Inner Directons.

Harner, M. (1990). *The way of the shaman.* New York: HarperCollins.

Hashkiveinu (n.d.). *Hashkiveinu.* Retrieved on 3/9/2019 from https://en.wikipedia.org/wiki/Hashkiveinu

Hastings, A. (1999). Transpersonal psychology: The fourth force. In D. Moss (Ed.), *Humanistic and transpersonal psychology: A historical and biographical sourcebook* (pp. 192-208). Westport, CT, US: Greenwood Press/Greenwood Publishing Group.

Hayes, S. (1984). Making sense of spirituality. *Behaviorism, 12*(2), 99-110.

Hayes, S. C. (1988). Contextualism and the next wave of behavioral psychology. *Behavior Analysis, 23*, 7-23.

Hayes, S. C. (2004). Acceptance and commitment therapy, relational frame theory, and the third wave of behavioral and cognitive therapies. *Behavior Therapy, 35*, 639-665.

Hayes, S. C., & Hofmann, S. (2017, Oct.). The third wave of cognitive behavioral therapy and the rise of process-based care. *World Psychiatry, 16*(3), 245-246.

Hayes, S. C., Nelson, R. O., & Jarrett, R. B. (1987). The treatment utility of assessment. A functional approach to evaluating assessment quality. *American Psychologist, 42*(11), 963-974.

Hayes, S. C., Strosahl, K. D., & Wilson, K. G. (2016). *Acceptance and commitment therapy: The process and practice of mindful change.* New York: Guilford.

Haynes, S. N., & O'Brien, W. H. (1990). Functional analysis in behavioral therapy. *Clinical Psychology Review, 10*, 649–668.

Hearne, K. M. T. (1982). Effects of performing certain set tasks in the lucid-dream state. *Perceptual and Motor Skills, 54*, 259-262.

Heidbreder, E. (1933). *Seven psychologies.* New York: Appleton.

Hervey de Saint Denys (1867/2005). *Les rêves et les moyens de les diriger.* Geneve: Arbre d'or. Free PDF offered by publisher. Retrieved on 3/7/19 from https://arbredor.com/collections/sante-et-bien-etre/168-les-reves-et-les-moyens-de-les-diriger Note that the wrong book cover is shown. Click below the description where it says "TÉLÉCHARGEZ PDF" to download the book.

Hervey de Saint Denys (1867/2016). *Dreams and the ways to direct them: Practical observations.* C. den Blanken & E. Meijer (Eds.). Free PDF offered by publisher. Retrieved on 3/7/19 from http://members.casema.nl/carolusdenblanken/Downloads/Hervey%20de%20Saint-Denys%20-%20Dreams%20and%20The%20Ways%20to%20Direct%20Them;%20Practical%20Observations.pdf

Hicks, B. (1989). *Sane man.* Studio City, CA: Sacred Cow Productions.

Hicks, E., & Hicks, J. (2004). *Ask and it is given: Learning to manifest your desires.* New York: Hay House.

Hilliard, B. (1951). *Alice in wonderland.* Walt Disney Music Company.

Hoffman, D. (2019). *The case against reality.* New York: W.W. Norton and Company.

Hollon S. D., & Garber, J. (1990). Cognitive therapy for depression: a social cognitive perspective. *Personality and Social Psychology Bulletin, 16,* 58–73

Holmes, O. W. Jr. (1913, February 15). Law and the court. Speech at a dinner of the Harvard Law School Association of NY, New York. In *Speeches by Oliver Wendell Holmes.* Boston: Little Brown, 1934; Clark, NJ: The Lawbook Exchange, LTD, 2006, pp. 98-103. Retrieved 3/8/2019 from https://books.google.com/books?id=QYG0XLtIf30C

Holmes, O. W. Sr. (1858, September). The autocrat of the breakfast table: Every man his own Boswell. *Atlantic Monthly, 2* (11), pp. 496-506. Retrieved on 3/8/2019 from https://books.google.com/books?id=BoQ3AQAAMAAJ&dq

Holzinger, B., Klösch, G., & Saletu, B. (2015). Studies with lucid dreaming as an add-on therapy to Gestalt therapy. *Acta Neurologica Scandinavica, 131*(6), 355-363.

Holzinger, B., LaBerge, S., & Levitan., L. (2006). Psychophysiological correlates of lucid dreaming. *Dreaming, 16*(2), 88.

Howarth, G., & Kellehear, A. (2001). Shared near-death and related illness experiences: Steps on an unscheduled journey. *Journal of Near Death Studies, 20*(2), pp. 71-85.

Huber, D., Rev. (2009 October 10). Matter of faith: Sometimes you have to 'just sits' by Leader-Telegram, p. D3, column 1. Eau Claire, Wisconsin. Cited in https://quoteinvestigator.com/2018/08/29/sit/ *Sometimes I Sits and Thinks, and Sometimes I Just Sits. A. A. Milne?*

Satchel Paige? William Gunning King? Lucy Maud Montgomery? Alice G. Young? Woodrow Wilson? Anonymous?

Hurd, R. (2011). *Sleep paralysis: A guide to hypnagogic visions and visitors of the night.* Los Altos, CA: Hyena Press.

Hutchinson, H. G. (1911). A saga of the 'Sunbeam.' London: Longmans, Green and Co. Cited in https://quoteinvestigator.com/2018/08/29/sit/ *Sometimes I sits and thinks, and sometimes i just sits. A. A. Milne? Satchel Paige? William Gunning King? Lucy Maud Montgomery? Alice G. Young? Woodrow Wilson? Anonymous?*

Huxley, A. (1932). *Brave new world.* New York: Harper and Brothers.

Huxley, A. (1945). The perennial philosophy. New York: Harper & Brothers.

Huxley, A. (1954). A case for ESP, PK and Psi: Famous writer argues that evidence proves the mind is capable of telepathy, can foresee events and even exert influence over matter. *Life,* January 11, 1954, 20 cents, pp. 97-108. Retrieved on 7/31/22 from https://books.google.com/books?id=vkgEAAAAMBAJ&lpg=PP1&pg=PP1#v=onepage&q&f=false

IAPSOP (1999). *The International Association for the Preservation of Spiritualist and Occult Periodicals.* Retrieved on 3/29/2019 from http://www.iapsop.com/archive/materials/index.html

Idel, M. (1990). *Kabbalah: New perspectives.* New Haven: Yale University Press.

Illahi, S., & Illahi, T. B. (2019). *Physiology, pineal gland.* Treasure Island, FL: StatPearls Publishing. Retrieved on 3/29/2019 from https://www.ncbi.nlm.nih.gov/books/NBK525955/

InspirationalStories.com (2022). Retrieved on 6/22/22 from https://www.inspirationalstories.com/quotes/the-fox-has-many-tricks-the-hedgehog-of-ralph-waldo-emerson-quote/

Iyengar, B. K. S. (1979). *Light on Yoga: Yoga Dipika.* New York: Schocken Books.

Iyengar, B. K. S. (1993). *Light on the Yoga sutras of Patanjali.* San Francisco: Thorsons.

Jacobson N. S., Dobson K. S., Truax, P. A., Addis, M. E., & Koerner K., et al. (1996). A component analysis of cognitive-behavioral treatment for depression. *Journal of Consulting and Clinical Psychology, 64,* 295–304

James, M. (2021a). Nāṉ Ār? (Who Am I?)Retrieved on 1/18/2021 from https://www.happinessofbeing.com/nan_yar-5#translation

James, M. (2021b). Introduction to Ramana Maharshi's Nāṉ Ār? (Who Am I?)   https://www.happinessofbeing.com/nan_yar-5#introduction

James, W. (1890/1950). *The principles of psychology, Vol. 1.* Henry Holt and Company.

James, W. (1898). *Human immortality: Two supposed objections to the doctrine.* Westminster: Archibald Constable & Co. Retrieved on 6/12/2022 from https://archive.org/details/in.ernet.dli.2015.272137/mode/2up

James, W. (1902/1928). *The varieties of religious experience: A study in human nature. Being the Gifford lectures on natural religion. Delivered At Edinburgh in 1901-1902.* New York: Longmans, Green and Co.

James, W. (1907/1992). What pragmatism means. In D. Olin (Ed. .), William James: *Pragmatism, In Focus* (pp. 38–53). London: Routledge.

James, W. (1912). *The will to believe and other essays in popular philosophy.* New York: Longmans, Green, and Co. Retrieved on 2/24/2021 from https://www.gutenberg.org/files/26659/26659-h/26659-h.htm#P1

James, W. (2022). *William James.* Retrieved from the Harvard University Department of Psychology website on 5/20/22 from https://psychology.fas.harvard.edu/people/william-james

James Haggerty. Retrieved on 1/5/21 from https://en.wikipedia.org/wiki/James_Hagerty

Jeffers, S. (1987). *Feel the fear and do it anyway.* New York: MJF Books.

Johnson, C. (2017). *The complete book of lucid dreaming.* Woodbury, MN: Llewellyn Publications.

Johnson, D. (2007). *Tree of smoke.* New York: Farrar, Straus and Giroux.

Johnson, W. (1982). *Riding the ox home.* Boston: Beacon Press.

Jonathan (n.d.). *When and how rabbits sleep: In-depth guide.* Retrieved on 10/29/20 from https://newrabbitowner.com/when-and-how-rabbits-sleep/

Jones, E. (1953-57). *Sigmund Freud: Life and work* (3 vols.). London: The Hogarth Press.

JonTherkildsen (2019, April 11). FAQ: THE MATRIX – Why Zion is NOT a simulation. Retrieved 1/19/2021 from https://moviesandscience.com/blog/movies/the-matrix/faq-zion

Jung, C. (1944/1990). Holy men of India. In Jung, C. (1990), *Psychology and the East.* Princeton: Princeton University Press. Extracted from Volume 11, The Collected Works of C.G. Jung, Psychology of Religion, West and East, copyright © 1958, 1969, Princeton University Press. Originally published as an Introduction to Heinrich Zimmer, Der Weg zum Selbst: Lehre und Leben des indischen Heiligen Shri Ramana Maharshi aus Tiruvannamalai (Zurich, 1944), edited by C. G. Jung, retrieved 1/9/21 from https://realization.org/p/misc/jung.holy-men-of-india.html

Jung, C. (1947, Sept. 15). *Letter to Gualthernus H. Mees.* Retrieved on 3/4/2019 from https://carljungdepthpsychologysite.blog/2018/04/12/carl-jung-and-ramana-maharshi/#.XH3l6ChKg2w

Jung, C. (1972/1988). Sri Ramana and his message to modern man. In *The Spiritual Teachings of Ramana Maharshi.* Boston, MA: Shambhala.

Jung, C. G. (1950/1977). Foreword to Jung: Phénomènes occultes. In *Psychology and the Occult,* pp. 3-5. Extracted from Volume 18, The Symbolic Life, copyright 1950 by Princeton, N.J.: Princeton University Press. Preface originally written in 1938.

Kabat-Zinn, J. (2005). *Wherever you go, there you are – Mindfulness meditation in everyday life.* New York: Hyperion.

Kaliman, P., Álvarez-López, M. J., Cosín-Tomás, M., Rosenkranz, M. A., Lutz, A., & Davidson, R. J. (2014, February). Rapid changes in histone deacetylases and inflammatory gene expression in expert meditators. *Psychoneuroendocrinology, 40,* 96-107.

Kalweit, H. (1992/1987). *Shamans, healers, and medicine* Men. Boston: Shambhala.

Kant, I. (1785)(Trans., T. K. Abbott). Fundamental principles of the metaphysics of morals. London: Longmans, Green & Co. Retrieved on 2/25/21 from https://www.gutenberg.org/ebooks/5682

Kant, I. (1787). Kritik der reinen Vernunft (Critique of Pure Reason), second edition. Riga: Johann Friedrich Hartknoch. https://archive.org/details/in.ernet.dli.2015.149681/page/n1/mode/2up

Kaplan, A. (1985). *Jewish meditation: A practical guide.* New York: Schocken Books.

Kassinove, H. (1995). *Anger disorders: Definition, diagnosis, and treatment (Series in clinical and community psychology.* New York: Taylor and Francis.

Kasko, B. (November 1, 2022). Bear attacks woman who's walking her dogs, she plays dead even with 'crunched' skull. *Fox News.* Retrieved on 11/9/2022 from https://www.foxnews.com/lifestyle/bear-attacks-woman-walking-dogs-plays-dead-crunched-skull

Kaufman, S. B. (2020). *Transcend: The new science of self-actualization.* New York: TarcherPerigee.

Kazdin, A. E. (1978). *History of behavior modification: Experimental foundations of contemporary research.* Baltimore: University Park Press.

Keen, S. (1974, December). The golden mean of Roberto Assagioli. *Psychology Today, 8,* 97-107.

Kel Maleh Rachamim. Retrieved on 3/9/2019 from https://www.chabad.org/library/article_cdo/aid/367837/jewish/Kel-Maleh-Rachamim.htm

Khan, P. V. I. (1982). *Introducing spirituality into counseling and therapy.* NY: Omega Press.

King, W. G. (Oct. 24, 1906). Change of occupation (cartoon). In *Punch, Or the London Charivari,* p. 297. London. Cited in https://quoteinvestigator.com/2018/08/29/sit/ *Sometimes I sits and thinks, and sometimes i just sits. A. A. Milne? Satchel Paige? William Gunning King? Lucy Maud Montgomery? Alice G. Young? Woodrow Wilson? Anonymous?* Original cartoon retrieved from https://ia800300.us.archive.org/BookReader/BookReaderImages.php?zip=/28/items/punchvol130a131lemouoft/punchvol130a131lemouoft_jp2.zip&file=punchvol130a131lemouoft_jp2/punchvol130a131lemouoft_0811.jp2&id=punchvol130a131lemouoft&scale=4&rotate=0

KJV (2022). King James Bible online, 1611 King James Version, 2 Kings, Chapter 2, Verses 22-25. Retrieved on 11/18/22 from https://www.kingjamesbibleonline.org/1611_2-Kings-Chapter-2/

Kogi People (2019). *Kogi people.* Retrieved on 3/29/2019 from https://en.wikipedia.org/wiki/Kogi_people

Kohler, I. (1951). Warum sehen wir aufrecht e obwohl die Bilder im Inneren des Auges verkehrt stehen? *Die Pyramide,* 28-33. Excerpts translated in P. Sachse, U. Beermann, M. Martini, T. Maran, M. Domeier & M. R. Furtner (2017). "The world is upside down" – The Innsbruck Goggle Experiments of Theodor Erismann (1883-1961) and Ivo Kohler (1915-1985). *Cortex, 92,* 222-232. Retrieved on 2/24/21 from http://www.allgemeine-psychologie.info/cms/images/stories/allgpsy_pub/Cortex%20The%20world%20is%20upside%20down.pdf

Kohler, K., & Blau, L. (2019). *Shekinah.* Retrieved on 3/28/2019 from http://www.jewishencyclopedia.com/articles/13537-shekinah

Koltko-Rivera, M. E. (2006). Rediscovering the later version of maslow's hierarchy of needs: Self-transcendence and opportunities for theory, research and unification. *Review of General Psychology, 10*(4), 302-317.

Kopp, S. (1972). *If you meet the Buddha on the road, kill him!: The pilgrimage of psychotherapy patients.* New York: Bantam Books. Science and Behavior Edition.

Kornfield (2000). *After the ecstasy the laundry: How the heart grows wise on the spiritual path.* New York: Bantam Books.

Kornfield, J. (2021). Meditation on lovingkindness. Retrieved on 2/25/21 from https://jackkornfield.com/meditation-on-lovingkindness/

Korzybski, A. (1933/1993). S*cience and sanity: An introduction to non-aristotelian systems and general semantics.* With Preface by Robert P. Pula. Brooklyn, NY: Institute of General Semantics. Retrieved on 6/19/22 from https://holybooks.com/science-and-sanity-by-alfred-korzybski/

Kretschmer, W. Jr. (1951). Die Meditative Verfahren in der Psychotherapie. *Zeitschrift fur Psychotherapie*, I, Heft 3.

Kretschmer, W. Jr. (1959)(W. Swartley, Trans.). *Meditative techniques in psychotherapy.* New York, Psychosynthesis Res. Found.

Krishnamurti, J. (1970). *Think on these things.* New York: HarperPerennial.

Krishnamurti, U. G. (1988).(T. Newland, Ed.). *Mind is a myth: Disquieting conversations with the man called U.G.* Goa, India: Dinesh Publications.

Kuper, P. (2007). *Stop forgetting to remember: The autobiography of Walter Kurtz.* New York: Crown Publishers.

Kurtulus, D. A., Demırci, G. N., Dodurga, Y., Özbal, S., Cankurt, U., Boz, B, Adiguzel E., & Acar, K. (2018, Oct.). Evaluation of human pineal gland acetylserotonin O-methyltransferase immunoreactivity in suicide: A preliminary study. *Medicine, Science, and the Law, 58*(4), 233-238.

LaBerge, S. (1980). Lucid dreaming as a learnable skill: A case study. *Perceptual and Motor Skills, 51,* 1039-1042.

LaBerge, S. (1985). *Lucid dreaming: The power of being awake & aware in your dreams.* New York: Ballantine Books.

LaBerge, S. (1990). Lucid dreaming: Psychophysiological studies of consciousness during REM sleep. In R. R. Bootsen, J. F. Kihlstrom & D. L. Schacter (Eds.), *Sleep and Cognition.* Washington, D.C.: APA Press (pp. 109-126). http://www.lucidity.com/LaBerge1990-Lucid_Dreaming=Psychophysiological_Studies_of_Consciousness_during_REM_Sleep.pdf

LaBerge S. (2001). *The paradox and promise of lucid dreaming: Research update: Cholinergic stimulation of lucid dreaming; voluntary control of auditory perception during REM lucid dreams.* Berkeley, CA: International Association for the Study of Dreams.

LaBerge, S., LaMarca, K., & Baird, B. (2018) Pre-sleep treatment with galantamine stimulates lucid dreaming: A double-blind, placebo-controlled, crossover study. *PLoS ONE 13*(8): e0201246. https://doi.org/10.1371/journal.pone.0201246

LaBerge, S., & Levitan, L. (1995). Validity established of DreamLight cues for eliciting lucid dreaming. *Dreaming, 5*(3), 159-168.

LaBerge, S., & Rheingold, H. (1990). *Exploring the world of lucid dreaming.* New York: Ballantine.

Lakshman Joo (1985, April). Letter from a holy man. *The Mountain Path, Vol. 22, No. 2,* pp. 107-108. Retrieved on 7/6/22 from http://www.sriramana.org/ramanafiles/mountainpath/1985%20II%20April.pdf

Lakshmanjoo, Swami (2003). *Kashmir Shaivism: The Secret Supreme.* Universal Shaiva Fellowship.

Land, M. F., & Heard, P. (March, 28, 2018). Richard Langton Gregory. 24 July 1923 – 17 May 2010. Biographical memoirs of the fellows of the Royal Society. Retrieved on 2/24/21 from https://royalsocietypublishing.org/doi/10.1098/rsbm.2017.0034#RSBM20170034C19-19R

LanguageHat (2014). The hedgehog and the fox. Retrieved on 1/10/21 from http://languagehat.com/the-hedgehog-and-the-fox/

Bibliography

Lasseter, J. (1995). *Toy story.* Buena Vista Pictures.

Law, W. (1749). *The spirit of prayer. Chapter 2: Discovering the true way of turning to God, and of finding the Kingdom of Heaven, the riches of Eternity in our souls.* Retrieved on 1/4/2021 from https://www.ccel.org/ccel/law/prayer/files/prayer2.htm

Le Beau, E. (2006, November 28). Not enough 'me time.' Special to the Tribune, Section 5: KidNews. Chicago Tribune, p. 12, column 2. Chicago, Illinois. Cited in https://quoteinvestigator.com/2018/08/29/sit/ *Sometimes I Sits and Thinks, and Sometimes I Just Sits. A. A. Milne? Satchel Paige? William Gunning King? Lucy Maud Montgomery? Alice G. Young? Woodrow Wilson? Anonymous?*

Leary, T., & Alpert, R. (1962). Letter from Alpert, Leary. *The Harvard Crimson*, December 13. Retrieved on 5/20/22 from https://www.thecrimson.com/article/1962/12/13/letter-from-alpert-leary-pfollowing-is/

Lejuez, C. W., Hopko, D. R., & Hopko, S. D. (2001). A brief behavioral activation treatment for depression. *Behavior Modification, 25,* 255-86.

Lenon, J., & McCartney, P. (1970). *Get back.* New York: Sony/ATV Music Publishing LLC.

Lesser, M. (2013). *Know yourself, forget yourself: Five truths to transform your work, relationships and everyday life.* Novato, CA: New World Library

Lewinsohn, P. M.; Biglan, A., & Zeiss, A. S. (1976). Behavioral treatment of depression. In P. O. Davidson (Ed.), The behavioral management of anxiety, depression and pain, (pp. 91-146). New York: Brunner/Mazel.

Lewinsohn, P. M., & Libet, J. (1972). Pleasant events, activity schedules and depression. *Journal of Abnormal Psychology, 79,* 291-295.

Lewis, J. G. (2013). Why do we cry when we're happy? *Psychology Today.* Retrieved on 2/7/21 from https://www.psychologytoday.com/us/blog/brain-babble/201308/why-do-we-cry-when-were-happy

Linehan, M. (2015). *DBT skills training manual*. 2nd Ed. New York: Guilford Press.

Linick, E. F. (1969). *Computer*. The World Book Encyclopedia, Volume 4: Ci to Cz (pp. 740-745). Chicago: Field Enterprises Educational Corporation. Retrieved on 3/1/21 from a wooden bookshelf with books made of paper.

Lojong (2021). Retrieved on 2/24/21 from https://en.wikipedia.org/wiki/Lojong

Longchenpa (2000)(Translators: K. Lipman & M. Peterson). *You Are the Eyes of the World*. Ithaca, NY: Snow Lion.

Lovecraft, H. P. (1928, February). The call of the Cthulhu. In *Weird Tales*, Vol. XI, 2, pp. 159-176. Indianapolis: Popular Fiction Publishing Company. Retrieved on 5/19/22 from https://commons.wikimedia.org/wiki/File:Weirdtales-1928-02-thecallofcthulhu.jpg reproduced from https://archive.org/details/WeirdTalesV11N02192802/page/n15/mode/2up

Low, A. A. (1950). *Mental health through will training: A System of Self-Help in Psychotherapy As Practiced by Recovery, Incorporated.* West Hanover, MA: The Christopher Publishing House.

Loyola Press (2019). *Peace prayer of Saint Francis.* Retrieved 3/28/2019 from https://www.loyolapress.com/our-catholic-faith/prayer/traditional-catholic-prayers/saints-prayers/peace-prayer-of-saint-francis

Luk, C. (Lu K'uan Yu)(1966/1999). *Surangama Sutra (Leng Yen Ching).* London: Rider (1966). New York: Penguin Random House (1999).

Luk, C. (Lu K'uan Yu)(1984/1970). *Taoist Yoga: Alchemy & immortality.* A translation, with introduction and notes, of *The Secrets of Cultivating Essential Nature and Eternal Life* (Hsin Ming Fa Chueh Ming Chih) by the Taoist Master Chao Pi Ch'en, born 1860. York Beach, Maine: Samuel Weiser. First published in England by Rider & Co., 1970.

Mach, E. (1870/1914). *The analysis of sensations.* Chicago: The Open Court Publishing Company. Retrieved on 8/25/2022 from https://archive.org/details/analysisofsensat00mach/page/18/mode/2up?view=theater
Clean Image retrieved on 8/25/2022 from https://publicdomainreview.org/collection/self-portrait-by-ernst-mach-1886

MacPhillamy, D. J., & Lewinsohn, P. M. (1982). The pleasant events schedules: studies in reliability, validity, and scale intercorrelation. *Journal of Consulting and Clinical Psychology, 50,* 363-380.

Madhavatirtha, S. (1981). Conversations with Bhagavan. *The Mountain Path, 18,* pp. 154-155.

Maier, S. F., & Seligman, M. E. P. (1976). Learned helplessness: theory and evidence. *Journal of Experimental Psychology: General, 105,* 03-46.

Maltz, M. (1960/1969). *Psycho-cybernetics: A new way to get more living out of life.* New York: Pocket Books.

Mandsager K, Harb S, Cremer P, Phelan D, Nissen SE, Jaber W. (2018, Oct 5). Association of cardiorespiratory fitness with long-term mortality among adults undergoing exercise treadmill testing. *Journal of the*

American Medical Association Network Open, 1(6): e183605. doi: 10.1001/jamanetworkopen.2018.3605

Martin, J. A. (2019). *The finders.* Jackson, WY: Integration Press.

Martin, J. A. (2020). Clusters of individuals [sic?] experiences form a continuum of persistent non-symbolic experiences in adults. *CONSCIOUSNESS: Ideas and Research for the Twenty-First Century. Vol. 8*: Iss. 8, Article 1. Available at: https://digitalcommons.ciis.edu/conscjournal/vol8/iss8/1 Retrieved on 7/6/22 from https://digitalcommons.ciis.edu/cgi/viewcontent.cgi?article=1031&context=conscjournal

Maslow, A. H. (1943). A theory of motivation. *Psychological Review, 50,* 370-396.

Maslow, A. H. (1962). *Toward a psychology of being.* New York: Van Nostrand Company.

Maslow, A. H. (1969). Theory Z. *Journal of Transpersonal Psychology, 1*(2), 31-47.

Maslow, A. H. (1969/1967). The farthest reaches of human nature. *Journal of Transpersonal Psychology (1)*1, 1-9. Edited by Dr. James Fadimen from the tape of a lecture given at the First Unitarian Church, San Francisco (under the auspices of the Esalen Institute), September 14, 1967. A footnote on p. 1 states that "This lecture is the first public presentation of the emergence of Transpersonal psychology (fourth force)." Retrieved on 6/25/22 from https://atpweb.org/jtparchive/trps-01-69-01-001.pdf

Maslow, A. H. (1969-1970). Chapter 2 – *The possibilities for human nature.* Maslow Paper, Folder: Mostly Tapes "Rough" – Prop, Box M 4483, Archives of the History of American Psychology, Cummings Center for the History of Psychology, University of Akron, Akron, OH.

Maslow, A. H. (1971). *The farther reaches of human nature.* New York: The Viking Press.

Maslow, A. H. (1979). *The journals of A. H. Maslow* (R. J. Lowry, Ed.; Vols. 1-2). Monterey, CA: Brooks/Cole.

Maslow, A. H. (1982). *The journals of Abraham Maslow* (1-vol. ed.; R. J. Lowry, Ed., & J. Freedman, Abridger). Brattleboro, VT: Lewis.

Matoba, B (2020). *Understanding the sympathetic and parasympathetic nervous systems.* Retrieved on 2/7/21 from https://www.ems1.com/ems-products/training-tools/articles/understanding-the-sympathetic-and-parasympathetic-nervous-systems-qOLHBDeIfMiauKoO/

Maurizi, C. P. (1984). Disorder of the pineal gland associated with depression, peptic ulcers, and sexual dysfunction. *Southern Medical Journal, 77(2),* 1516-1518.

Mavromatis, A. (1987). *Hypnagogia: The unique state of consciousness between wakefulness and sleep.* London: Routledge Kegan & Paul.

McDermid, C. D. (1960). How money motivates men. *Business Horizons, 3*(4), 94.

McKay, M., Wood, J. C., & Brantley, J. (2007). *The dialectical behavior therapy skills workbook: practical dbt exercises for learning mindfulness, interpersonal effectiveness, emotion regulation & distress Tolerance.* Oakland, CA: New Harbinger Publications.

McMarsin, F. (2004). *Blokette.* Retrieved 10/26/20 from https://www.urbandictionary.com/define.php?term=blockette

Meriam-Webster (n.d. 1) *Complex.* In *Merriam-Webster.com Dictionary*, Merriam-Webster, Retrieved 10/27/20, from https://www.merriam-webster.com/dictionary/complex.

Meriam-Webster (n.d. 2) *Define.* In *Merriam-Webster.com Dictionary*, Merriam-Webster, Retrieved 10/27/20, from https://www.merriam-webster.com/dictionary/define

Merriam-Webster (n.d. 3). *Inertia.* In *Merriam-Webster.com dictionary.* Retrieved 5/26/22, from https://www.merriam-webster.com/dictionary/inertia

Merriam-Webster (n.d. 4). *Mind*. In *Merriam-Webster.com dictionary*. Retrieved 10/27/20, from https://www.merriam-webster.com/dictionary/mind

Merriam-Webster (n.d. 5). *Realize*. In *Merriam-Webster.com dictionary*. Retrieved on 6/26/22 from https://www.merriam-webster.com/dictionary/realize

Merriam-Webster (n.d. 6). *Thinking*. In *Merriam-Webster.com dictionary*. Retrieved 10/27/20, from https://www.merriam-webster.com/dictionary/thinking

Merriam-Webster (n.d. 7). *Thought*. In *Merriam-Webster.com dictionary*. Retrieved 5/21/2022, from https://www.merriam-webster.com/dictionary/thought

Merton, T. (1969/2019). *Climate of monastic prayer*. Collegeville Minnesota: Liturgical Press.

Messenger, S. (2016). Guy meditating in the woods stays calm as bear destroys his tent. *The Dodo, August 12*. Retrieved on 5/21/22 from https://www.thedodo.com/guy-meditating-bear-tent-video-1970641227.html

Meyerink, G. (1928).(Transl. by Madge Pemberton). *The Golem*. New York: Houghton Mifflin Co.

Meyerink, G. (1986). (Trans. by Madge Pemberton). *The Golom*. New York: Dover.

Millman, D. (1980/2000). *The way of the peaceful warrior*. Novato, CA: H.J. Kramer.

Milne, A. A. (1926). *Winnie the Pooh*. New York: E.P. Dutton.

Mishnah Berakhot 5. English from The William Davidson digital edition of *The Noé Edition of the Koren Talmud Bavli*, with commentary by Rabbi Adin Even-Israel Steinsaltz. Jerusalem: Korem Publishers. Retrieved on 1/18/2021 from https://www.sefaria.org/Mishnah_Berakhot.5?lang=bi

Mitchell, E. D. (2022). *Edgar Mitchell*. Retrieved on 5/28/2022 from https://en.wikipedia.org/wiki/Edgar_Mitchell#cite_note-21

Bibliography

Mitra, Rájendralála (Translator)(1862). *The Chhándogya Upanishad of the Sáma Veda.* Calcutta: C.B Lewis, Baptist Mission Press. Retrieved 4/15/2019 from https://books.google.com/books?id=IGAmAQAAIAAJ&pg

Monroe, R. (2000/1994). *Ultimate journey.* New York: Broadway Books. First Published in 1994 by Doubleday.

Monroe, R. (2001/1971). *Journeys out of the body.* New York: Broadway Books. Originally published in 1971 by Doubleday.

Monroe Institute (2019). *Lifeline program.* Retrieved on 3/9/2019 from https://www.monroeinstitute.org/Lifeline

Monroe Products. (2005). *Going home.* Lovington, VA: Monroe Products.

Moody, R. A. Jr. (2015). *Life after life.* New York: HarperCollins. Originally published in 1975 by MBB Inc.

Moody, R. A. Jr., & Perry, P. (2016/2010). *Glimpses of eternity: Sharing a loved one's passage from this life to the next.* Paradise Valley, AZ: Sakkara Publishing. Originally published in 2010 by Guideposts.

More Than A Thousand (2010). A sharp tongue can cut your own throat. On album: *Vol 4 Make Friends and Enemies.* Paul Leavitt: Portugal.

Morey, S. (1980). Living life backwards. On *The Tonight Show*, 1/10/80. Retrieved from http://youtube.com/watch?v=KXshYoUonN8 (Morey made 2 appearances that year, also appearing on 11/19/80, but on the show on which he did the skit, Johnny said it was Morey's first appearance on TV).

Morgan, C. W., & Mogenson, G. J. (1966). Preference of water-deprived rats for stimulation of the lateral hypothalamus rather than water. *Psychonomic Science, 6,* 337-338.

Moskowitz, C. (October 3, 2012). *Speed of the universe's expansion measured better than ever.* Space.com Retrieved on 2/25/21 from https://www.space.com/17884-universe-expansion-speed-hubble-constant.html

Mota-Rolim, S. A., & Araujo, J. F. (2016). Neurobiology and clinical implications of lucid dreaming. *Medical Hypotheses, 81*(2013), 751-756.

Mota-Rolim, S. A., Erlacher, D., Tort, A. B. L., Araujo, J. F., & Ribeiro, S. (2010). Different kinds of subjective experience during lucid dreaming may have different neural substrates: Commentary on "The neurobiology of consciousness: Lucid dreaming wakes up" by J. Allan Hobson. *International Journal of Dream Research, 3*(1), 33-35.

Motta, M., Fraschini, F., Martini, L. (1967). Endocrine effects of pineal gland and of melatonin. *Experimental Biology and Medicine, 126* (2), 431-435.

Mudaliar, A. D. (1952/2006). *Day By day With Bhagavan: From the diary of A. Devaraja Mudaliar.* Tiruvannamalai: Sri Ramanasramam.

Mudaliar, A. D. (1965). *Gems from Bhagavan.* Tiruvannamalai, S. India: T.N. Venkataraman.

Muldoon, S., & Carrington, H. (1929). *The projection of the astral body.* London: Rider.

Muruganar/Ramana (2008). (D. Godman, Ed.). *Guru Vachaka Kovai [The garland of Guru's sayings] by Muruganar.* Translated by Dr. T.V. Venkatasubramanian, Robert Butler and David Godman. Boulder, CO: Avadhuta Foundation.

Nagamma, S. (1970/1985).(D.S. Sastri, Transl). *Letters from Sri Ramanasramam.* Tiruvannamalai: Sri Ramanasramam.

Nanay, B. (2018). Multimodal mental imagery. *Cortex, 105*(1). https://www.ncbi.nlm.nih.gov/pmc/articles/PMC6079145/?report=reader#__ffn_sectitle

NASA (2013). *Taken under the "wing" of the small Magellanic cloud.* Retrieved on 1/4/21 from https://www.nasa.gov/mission_pages/spitzer/multimedia/pia16884.html Image credit: NASA/CXC/JPL-Caltech/STScI

NASA (2022). *Taken under the "wing" of the small Magellanic cloud.* Retrieved on 5/15/22 from https://www.jpl.nasa.gov/images/pia16884-taken-under-the-wing-of-the-small-magellanic-cloud Image credit: NASA/CXC/JPL-Caltech/STScI

Natanananda, S. (2002)(D. Godman, Ed.). *Sri Ramana Darsanam.* Tiruvannamalai: V.S. Ramanan, Sri Ramanasramam.

National Park Service (2023, February 28). "If you come across a bear . . ." Retrieved on 2/28/23 from https://twitter.com/NatlParkService/status/1630653487825526786

Newcombe, R. (2008). Ketamine case study: The Phenomenology of a ketamine experience. *Addiction Research & Theory 16* (3), 209-215.

Newhart, B. (2019/2001). *Stop it!* Retrieved 3/28/2019 from https://www.youtube.com/watch?v=Ow0lr63y4Mw Originally aired on MadTV, Season 6, 2001.

Nicolle, E. (2016). *Dickinson Killdeer's guide to bears of the Apocalypse: Ursine abominations of the end times and how to defeat them.* EthanNicolle.com: AxeBear.

Nicolle, E. (2019). *Bears want to kill you: The authoritative guide to survival in the war between man and bear.* Bearmageddon.com: Bearmageddon.

Nietzsche, F. W. (1878/1908). 1878 in German: *Menschliches, allzumenschliches: Ein buch für freie geister.* Chemnitz: Ernst Schmeitzner. 1908 in English: *Human, all too human: A book for free spirits.* Translated by A. Harvey. Chicago: Charles H. Kerr & Co.; 1910 English translation by Helen Zimmern, published by T.N. Foulis (Edinburgh), retrieved on 8/4/22 from https://digitalassets.lib.berkeley.edu/main/b20790001_v_1_B000773557.pdf

Nietzsche, F. W. (1879/1913). 1879 in German: *Vermischte meinungen und sprüche* [Assorted opinions and maxims]. 1913 in English: *Human all-too-human: A Book for Free Spirits. Part II.* Translated by Paul V. Cohn. New York: The MacMillan Company. Retrieved on 8/4/22 from https://www.gutenberg.org/files/37841/37841-h/37841-h.html

Night Prayers (1872). In The daily prayers for American Israelites, Revised in Conference. Cincinnati: Block & Co., p. 253. Retrieved on 3/28/2019 from https://books.google.com/books?id=i4gMAAAAIAAJ&pg=PP1#v=onepage&q&f=false

Nine Ninety-Nine Euripides (2017). *Hippolytus: Silence is true wisdom's best reply.* Scribe Publishing. Retrieved on 1/5/2021 from https://www.amazon.com/Euripides-Hippolytus-Silence-wisdoms-reply/dp/1787371492. Note that the subtitle "Silence is True Wisdom's Best Reply" is apparently the publisher's invention and was NOT said by Euripides here or anywhere else.

Nisargadatta Maharaj (1999/1973). *I Am That: Talks with Sri Nisargadatta Maharaj.* Durham, NC: The Acorn Press. Originally published by Chetana Pvt. Ltd., Bombay, in 1973.

Norbu, N. (1992). *Dream Yoga and the practice of natural light.* Ithaca, NY: Snow Lion.

Norbu, N. (1996). *The mirror: Advice on the presence of awareness.* Translated from Tibetan into Italian and edited by Adriano Clemente. Translated from Italian by Andrew Lukianowicz. Barrytown, NY: Station Hill Openings.

Norbu, N. (2000)(Compiled and Edited by J. Shane). *The crystal and the way of light: Sutra, tantra and Dzogchen.* Ithaca: Snow Lion Publications.

Noye, E. P. (1946). My Pilgrimage to Sri Ramanasraman, Part II. In *The Maharshi, Sept/Oct 2005, Vol. 15,* No. 5. Retrieved on 7/6/22 from https://archive.arunachala.org/newsletters/2005/sep-oct#article.1

[Regarding Eleanor Pauline Noye, See also:

*Noye, E. P. (1983, April). How I came to Sri Bhagavan. In *The Mountain Path, Vol. 20, No. 2*, pp. 103-106. Retrieved on 7/7/22 from https://www.sriramana.org/ramanafiles/mountainpath/1983%20II%20April.pdf

*Introducing: Mrs. Eleanor Pauline Noye. In *The Mountain Path, April, 1972, Vol. 9*, No. 2, pp. 156-157. Retrieved on 7/7/22 from https://www.sriramana.org/ramanafiles/mountainpath/1972%20II%20April.pdf

*My Pilgrimage to Sri Ramanasraman, Part I. In *The Maharshi,*

July/August 2005, Vol. 15, No. 4. Retrieved on 7/6/22 from https://archive.arunachala.org/newsletters/2005/jul-aug#article.1

*In Profile: Eleanor Pauline Noye, Part I. In *Saranagati, May, 2021, Vol. 15*, No. 5, pp. 3-8. Retrieved on 7/6/22 from https://www.sriramanamaharshi.org/saranagati/Saranagathi_eNewsletter_May_2021.pdf

*In Profile: Eleanor Pauline Noye, Part II. In *Saranagati, June 2021, Vol. 15*, No. 6, pp. 3-8. Retrieved on 7/6/22 from https://www.sriramanamaharshi.org/saranagati/Saranagathi_eNewsletter_June_2021.pdf]

O'Neill, M. L., & Whittal, M. L. (2002). Thought stopping. In M. Herson & W. Sledge (Eds.). *Encyclopedia of Psychotherapy, Volume 2*, 803-806.

Orecchio-Egresitz (June 9, 2018). Experts warn: 'If you're living in the Berkshires, you're living in bear country.' The Berkshire Eagle. Retrieved on 11/9/2022 from https://www.berkshireeagle.com/archives/experts-warn-if-youre-living-in-the-berkshires-youre-living-in-bear-country/article_640f563f-67b5-595f-a22f-1b317e2d3ba2.html

Osborne, A. (1962). *True happiness: The teachings of Ramana Maharshi*. Charlottesville, VA: Hampton Roads.

Osborne, A. (1962/2010). *The teachings of Ramana Maharshi in His own words*. Tiruvannamalai: Sri Ramanasramam.

Oster, G. (1973, October). Auditory beats in the brain. *Scientific American, 229* (4), 94-102.

Osborne, A. (1997). *The collected works of Ramana Maharshi*. York Beach, ME: Samuel Weiser, Inc.

Ouspensky, P. (1945/1950). *The psychology of man's possible evolution*. Oxford: The HedgeHog Press.

Packer. T. (1990/2007). *The work of this moment*. Boston: Shambhala.

Packer, T. (2002). *The wonder of presence and the way of meditative inquiry.* Boulder: Shambhala.

Packer, T. (2007). *The silent question: Meditating in the stillness of not knowing.* Boulder: Shambhala.

Papaji (Sri H. W. L. Poonja)(n.d.). Retrieved from https://www.inner-quest.org/Poonja_Words.htm

Papaji (Sri H. W. L. Poonja)(2000). *The Truth Is.* Compiled and edited by Prashanti de Jager. Newburyport, MA: Red Wheel/Weiser.

Paulsson, T., & Parker, A. (2006). The effects of a two-week reflection-intention training program on lucid dream recall. *Dreaming, 16*(1), 22-35.

Pearson, K. (1892/1900). *The grammar of science.* London: Adam and Charles Black. Retrieved on 8/25/2022 from https://archive.org/details/grammarofscience00pearuoft/page/64/mode/2up?q=Mach

Pedersen, P. (1990). The multicultural perspective as a fourth force in counseling. *Journal of Mental Health Counseling, 12*(1), 93-95.

Peng, R. (2019). *Small heavenly circuit: The Qigong way to immortality.* Retrieved on 3/29/2019 from http://www.robertpeng.com/shc/

Pennington, M. B. (2001). *An invitation to centering prayer.* Liguori, MO: Liguori Publications.

Perlis, M. L., Smith, M. T., Andrews, P. J., Orff, H., & Giles, D. (2001). Beta/Gamma EEG activity in patients with primary and secondary insomnia and good sleeper controls. *SLEEP, 24*(1), 110-117.

Peters, W. (2022). *At Heaven's door.* New York: Simon and Schuster.

Phelps, W. L. (1939). *Autobiography, with letters.* New York: Oxford University Press.

Philip Warren Anderson (2022). Retrieved on 6/22/22 from https://en.wikipedia.org/wiki/Philip_W._Anderson

Phonemic Orthography (2022). Retrieved on 7/3/22 from https://en.wikipedia.org/wiki/Phonemic_orthography

Pichot, P. (1989). The historical roots of behavior therapy. *Journal of Behavior Therapy and Experimental Psychiatry, 20,* 107-I 14.

Pine, F. (1988). The four psychologies of psychoanalysis and their place in clinical work. *Journal of the American Psychoanalytic Association, 36*(3), 571-596.

Pineal Gland (2019). Retrieved on 3/29/2019 from https://en.wikipedia.org/wiki/Pineal_gland

Pinson, D. (2004). *Meditation and Judaism: Exploring the Jewish meditative path.* Lanham, MD: Jason Aronson, Inc.

Poonja, H. W. L. (n.d.). *H.W.L. Poonja: Words.* Paris: InnerQuest. Retrieved on 1/16/21 from https://www.inner-quest.org/Poonja_Words.htm

Poonja, Sri H. W. L. (2000). *The Truth Is.* Compiled and edited by Prashanti de Jager. Newburyport, MA: Red Wheel/Weiser/LLC. www.redwheelweiser.com

Prabhavananda & Isherwood, C. (1952/1981). *How to know God: The Yoga Aphorisms of Patanjali.* Hollywood, CA: Vedanta Press.

Preston, B., & Fisher, B. C. (1974). *Nothing From nothing.* Universal Music Publishing Group.

Prayer for Mourners (1872). In *The daily prayers for American Israelites,* Revised in Conference. Cincinnati: Block & Co., pp. 267-269. Retrieved on 3/28/2019 from https://books.google.com/books?id=i4gMAAAAIAAJ&pg=PP1#v=onepage&q&f=false

Progoff, I. (1957). *The cloud of unknowing (Introductory commentary and translation).* New York: Dell.

Psychonautics (2019). Retrieved on 3/8/2019 from https://psychonautwiki.org/wiki/Psychonautics

Purohit (1938/1975). *Bhagwan Shree Patanjali: Aphorisms of Yoga.* With an introduction by W.B. Yeats. London: Faber and Faber.

Qadr Night (2022). Retrieved on 5/22/2022 from https://en.wikipedia.org/wiki/Qadr_Night

QuoteInvestigator.com (2010). *Outside of a dog, a book is man's best friend. Inside of a dog, it's too dark to read.* Retrieved on 5/16/22 from https://quoteinvestigator.com/2010/09/08/dog/

QuoteInvestigator.com (2014) *Relativity: A hot stove and a pretty girl.* Retrieved 10/27/2020 from https://quoteinvestigator.com/2014/11/24/hot-stove/#note-10163-2.

Ram Dass (2021a). *The practice of Self Inquiry: "Who Am I?"* Retrieved on 1/22/2021 from https://www.ramdass.org/practice-self-inquiry/

Ram Dass (2021b). *Ram Dass, Love Everybody.* Retrieved on 2/25/21 from https://youtu.be/5lTNcmQVb_o

Ramana Maharshi (n.d., possibly in the 1920s). (M. James, Transl). Nāṉ Ār? (Who Am I?). Retrieved on 1/18/2021 from https://www.happinessofbeing.com/nan_yar-5#translation

Ramana Maharshi (1901)(T. M. P. Mahadevan, Transl., 1982). *Who Am I? (Nan Yar?).* Tiruvannamalai, S. India: Sri Ramanasramam.

Ramana Maharshi (1930/1994). *Self-Enquiry (Vicharasangraham).* Tiruvannamalai: Ramanasramam. Retrieved on 6/26/22 from https://www.sriramanamaharshi.org/wp-content/uploads/Downloadable/English/self_enquiry.pdf

Ramana Maharshi (1939/1948). *Spiritual Instruction: Being Original Instruction of Bhagavan Sri Ramana Maharshi.* Madras: The Jupiter Press Ltd.

Ramana Maharshi (1955/2006). *Talks with Sri Ramana Maharshi.* Tiruvannamalai: Sri Ramanasramam.

Ramana Maharshi (1988). *The Spiritual Teachings of Ramana Maharshi.* Boston: Shambhala.

Ramana Maharshi (1997). *The Collected Works of Ramana Maharshi.* A. Osborne (Ed.). York Beach, ME: Samuel Weiser, Inc.

rebar (2018). Retrieved on 6/22/22 from http://jenbetton.blogspot.com/2018/07/this-emerson-quote-just-seemed-perfect.html

Red Pine (1989)(Translator). *The Zen teaching of Bodhidharma.* New York: North Point Press, a Division of Farrar, Straus and Giroux. ISBN 978-0865473997

Reeves, C. (2018). *Neurons that fire together wire together.* Retrieved on 2/27/21 from https://themindisthemap.com/neurons-that-fire-together-wire-together/

Rembrandt (1630). Public domain, via *Wikimedia Commons.* Retrieved on 8/25/2022 from https://commons.wikimedia.org/wiki/File:Rembrandt_-_Self-Portrait,_Staring_-_WGA19083.jpg

Rentz, T. O.; Powers, M. B.; Smits, J. A. J.; Cougle, J. R.; Telch, M. J. (2013), *Active-imaginal exposure: Examination of a new behavioral treatment for cynophobia (dog phobia).* Retrieved from https://habricentral.org/resources/25313.

Reversing Goggles (2021). Retrieved on 2/24/21 from https://www.grand-illusions.com/reversing-goggles-c2x21140037

Richet, C. (1906). The future of psychology. *Annals of Psychical Science, 4*, 201–216.

Riemann D., Gann H., Dressing H., Mueller, W. E., & Aldenhoff, J. B. (1994). Influence of the cholinesterase inhibitor galanthamine hydrobromide on normal sleep. *Psychiatry Research, 51*(3), 253–67.

Roach, M., & McNally, C. (2005). *The Essential Yoga Sutra: Ancient Wisdom for Your Yoga.* New York: Three Leaves Press/Doubleday.

Roberts, B. (1982). *The Experience of No-Self: A Contemplative Journey.* Boston and London: Shambhala.

Roberts, C. (2021). *The Matrix: Yoga's Matrix.* Retrieved on 2/28/21 from https://celiaroberts.com.au/the-matrix/

Robertson, B. (2014). Chapter 16: The lamprey blueprint of the mammalian nervous system. *Progress in Brain Research, 212*, 337-349.

Rockwell, N. (2021). *The Golden Rule is common to all religions.* Retrieved on 2/25/21 from https://www.nrm.org/2018/03/golden-rule-common-religions/

Rooksby, B., & Terwee, S. (1990). Freud, van Eeden and Lucid Dreaming. *Lucidity Letter, 9* (2). Retrieved on 1/10/21 from https://journals.macewan.ca/lucidity/article/download/657/573/

Routtenberg A, & Lindy J. (1965). Effects of the availability of rewarding septal and hypothalamic stimulation on bar pressing for food under conditions of deprivation. *Journal of Comparative and Physiological Psychology, 60*(2), 158-61.

Sachse, P., Beermann, U., Martini, M., Maran, T., Domeier, M. & Furtner, M. R. (2017). "The world is upside down" – The Innsbruck Goggle Experiments of Theodor Erismann (1883-1961) and Ivo Kohler (1915-1985). *Cortex, 92,* 222-232. Retrieved on 2/24/21 from http://www.allgemeine-psychologie.info/cms/images/stories/allgpsy_pub/Cortex%20The%20world%20is%20upside%20down.pdf

Sagan, C. (1997). *The demon-haunted world: Science as a candle in the dark.* New York: Ballantine Books.

Saint John of the Cross (1542-1591). I came into the unknown. In *The poems of St. John of the Cross,* English Version and Introduction by Willis Barnstone. Pages 60 (Spanish) and 61 (English). New York: New Directions.

Saint-Véran (2022). Retrieved on 12/2/22 from https://en.wikipedia.org/wiki/Saint-V%C3%A9ran Accompanying image of Saint-Véran in the public domain and retrieved on 12/2/22 from https://en.wikipedia.org/wiki/Veranus_of_Cavaillon#/media/File:V%C3%A9ran_de_Cavaillon_(cropped).jpg

Salter, A. (1949). *Conditioned reflex therapy.* New York: Creative Age Press.

Sapho, P. (2006). *Of foxes and hedgehogs.* Sapho.com. Retrieved on 1/10/21 from https://www.saffo.com/02006/09/10/of-foxes-and-hedgehogs/

Saranagati (2021, June). In Profile: Eleanor Pauline Noye, Part II. *Saranagati, Vol. 15*, No. 6, pp. 3-8. Retrieved on 7/6/22 from https://www.sriramanamaharshi.org/saranagati/Saranagathi_eNewsletter_June_2021.pdf

Satchidananda (1978/1999). *The Yoga Sutras of Patanjali: Translation and Commentary.* Yogaville, Virginia: Integral Yoga Publications

SBaGen (2019). Retrieved on 3/9/2019 from https://uazu.net/sbagen/

Schacter, J. J., & Weinberger, D. (2003). *The complete service for the period of bereavement.* The Union of Orthodox Jewish Congregations of America. Siddur adapted from The Complete ArtScroll Siddur by Rabbi Nosson Scherman, Brooklyn, NY: Mesorah Publications. Siddur Nechamas Yisrael / The Complete Service for the Time of Bereavement, Nusach Ashkenaz, Copyright 1995 by Mesorah Publications.

Schädlich, M., & Erlacher, D. (2012). Applications of lucid dreams: An online study. *International Journal of Dream Research, 5*(2), 134-138.

Schindler, J. A. (1954/2003). *How to live 365 days a year: 12 principles to make your life richer.* Philadelphia: Running Press Book Publishers. Original Edition by Prentice Hall.

Scholem, G. (1965). The idea of the Golem. In *On the Kabbalah and Its Symbolism*, pp. 158-204. New York: Schocken. Retrieved 5/20/22 from https://archive.org/stream/OnTheKabbalahAndItsSymbolismGershomScholem/OnTheKabbalahAndItsSymbolismGershomScholem_djvu.txt

Schopenhauer, A. (1891).(R. B. Haldane & J. Kemp, Trans.). *The world as will and idea.* London: Kegan Paul, Trench, Trübner, & Co., Ltd. Retrieve on 10/31/2020 from https://books.google.com/books/about/The_World_as_Will_and_Idea.html?id=6L1aAAAAYAAJ&printsec=frontcover&source=kp_read_button&newbks=1&newbks_redir=1

Scotton, B. W., Chinen, A. B. and Battista, J. R. (1996). (Eds.). *Textbook of transpersonal psychiatry and psychology.* New York: Basic Books.

Scudder, J. (April 27, 2016). How fast are you moving through space? *Forbes.* Retrieved on 2/25/21 from https://www.forbes.com/sites/jillianscudder/2016/04/27/astroquizzical-how-fast-moving-space/?sh=373f247e21c8

Segal Z. V., Williams J. M. G., & Teasdale J. D. (2002). *Mindfulness-based cognitive therapy for depression: A new approach to preventing relapse.* New York: Guilford.

Seligman, M. E. P., & Maier, S. F. (1967). Failure to escape traumatic shock. *Journal of Experimental Psychology, 74,* 01-09.

Shabbat 31a. English from The William Davidson digital edition of *The Noé Edition of the Koren Talmud Bavli,* with commentary by Rabbi Adin Even-Israel Steinsaltz. Jerusalem: Korem Publishers. Retrieved on 2/25/21 from https://www.sefaria.org/Shabbat.31a.6?lang=bi&with=all&lang2=en

Shakespeare, W. (Circa 1600). *The tragedie of Hamlet, Prince of Denmarke.* Retrieved on 5/21/2022 from https://www.gutenberg.org/files/1524/1524-h/1524-h.htm

Shared Crossing Project (2022). Retrieved on 6/12/22 from https://www.sharedcrossing.com/

Shermer, N. (2018). The number of Americans with no religious affiliation is rising: The rise of Atheists. *Scientific American,* Retrieved on 3/9/2019 from https://www.scientificamerican.com/article/the-number-of-americans-with-no-religious-affiliation-is-rising/ Originally published with the title "Silent No More" in *Scientific American 318*(4), 77 (April 2018).

Siegel, D. (2017). *Mind: A journey to the heart of being human.* New York: W. W. Norton & Company, Inc. Retrieved from D. Siegel (2021). Dr. Dan Siegel on neuroplasticity: An excerpt from Mind. Retrieved on 2/21/21 from https://www.psychalive.org/dr-daniel-siegel-neuroplasticity/

Silva, J., & Miele, P. (1977). *The Silva mind control method.* New York: Pocket Books.

Silver, F., Conn, I. (1923). *Yes! We have no bananas.* Shapiro, Bernstein & Co., Inc.

Bibliography

Sivananda, Swami (2019). *Essence of the Mandukyopanishad.* Retrieved on 4/15/2019 from http://sivanandaonline.org/public_html/?cmd=displaysection&section_id=585

Skinner B. F. (1937). Two types of conditioned reflex: a reply to Konorski and Miller. *Journal of General Psychology, 16,* 272–279.

Skinner, B. F. (1953/2014). *Science and human behavior.* New York: Macmillan. Retrieved on 7/25/2022 from https://www.bfskinner.org/newtestsite/wp-content/uploads/2014/02/ScienceHumanBehavior.pdf

Skinner, B. F. (1975, January). The steep and thorny way to a science of behavior. *American Psychologist, 30*(1), 42–49.

Skulduggery (2022). Retrieved from https://wordhippo.com/what-is/another-word-for/skulduggery.html

Smart, N. (1965). Interpretation and mystical Experiences. *Religious Studies 1,* 75-87.

Smith, H. (1976). *Forgotten truth: The common vision of the world's religions.* New York, NY: HarperCollins.

Smith, S. (2019). *Inner smile / Microcosmic orbit meditation.* Retrieved on 3/29/2019 from https://www.taosharon.com/store/#!/Downloadable-Files-Inner-Smile-Microcosmic-Orbit-Meditation/p/18662960/category=4379296

SoberRecovery.com (2008). *What's the source of quote on "act our way to right thinking"?* Reply by 1Cor13, 2/25/2008, 12:27 pm. Retrieved on 7/17/22 from https://www.soberrecovery.com/forums/alcoholism-12-step-support/144611-whats-source-quote-act-our-way-right-thinking.html#post1686131

Sorace, S. (2022). *Wisconsin couple stabs, fatally shoots black bear that attacked them in their home.* Retrieved on 5/23/2022 from https://www.foxnews.com/us/wisconsin-couple-stabs-shoots-black-bear

Sørensen, K. (2019). *Roberto Assagioli, his life and work: A biography* (Book review). Retrieved on 3/6/19 from https://kennethsorensen.dk/en/roberto-assagioli-his-life-and-work/

Spade (n.1). Etymonline, retrieved on 6/23/22 from https://www.etymonline.com/word/spade

Sparrow, G., Carlson, R., Hurd, R., Molina, A. (2018, August), Exploring the effects of galantamine paired with meditation and dream reliving on recalled dreams: Toward an integrated protocol for lucid dream induction and nightmare resolution. *Consciousness and Cognition, 63,* 74-88.

Spelling Reform (2022). Retrieved on 7/3/22 from https://en.wikipedia.org/wiki/Spelling_reform

Spoormaker, V. I., & Van Den Bout, J. (2006). Lucid dreaming treatment for nightmares: A pilot study. *Psychotherapy and psychosomatics, 75*(6), 389-394.

Spoormaker, V. I., van den Bout, J., & Meijer, E. J. (2003). Lucid dreaming treatment for nightmares: a series of cases. *Dreaming, 13,* 181-186.

Stein, G. (1937). *Everybody's autobiography.* New York: Random House.

Steiner, R. (1910/1904). *Theosophy: An introduction to the supersensible knowledge of the world and the destination of man.* New York: Rand McNally and Co.

Stevens, W. (1954/2015). The latest freed man. In *The Collected poems of Wallace Stevens.* Second Vintage Books Edition, 2015, p. 217. Originally published by Alfred A. Knopf in 1954. New York: Vintage Books, A Division of Penguin Random House. ISBN: 978-0-307079187-0

Stevens, W. (1967/1990). Of mere Being. In *The palm at the end of the mind: Selected poems and a play,* p. 387. New York: Vintage Books, A Division of Penguin Random House. ISBN: 978-0-679-72445-2

Stewart, M. A. (1961). Psychotherapy by reciprocal inhibition. *American Journal of Psychiatry, 188,* 175-177.

Stratton, G. M. (1896). Some preliminary experiments on vision without inversion of the retinal image. *Psychological Review, 3*(6), 611-617. Read at the Third International Congress for Psychology, Munich, August, 1896. Retrieved on 2/24/21 from http://www.cns.nyu.edu/~nava/courses/psych_and_brain/pdfs/Stratton_1896.pdf

Stratton, G. M. (1897a). Vision without inversion of the retinal image. *Psychological Review, 4,* 341–360. [Days 1-6 of the experiment]. Retrieved on 2/24/21 from https://commons.wikimedia.org/w/index.php?title=File:Stratton.1897a.pdf&page=1

Stratton, G. M. (1897b). Vision without inversion of the retinal image. [Days 7-8 of the experiment]. *Psychological Review, 4,* 463-481. https://commons.wikimedia.org/w/index.php?title=File:Stratton.1897b.pdf&page=1

Stratton, G. M. (1899). The spatial harmony of touch and sight. *Mind, 8,* 492-493. Retrieved on 2/24/21 from https://www.jstor.org/stable/2247990?seq=1

Stumbrys, T., & Erlacher, D. (2017). Mindfulness and lucid dream frequency predicts the ability to control lucid dreams. *Imagination, Cognition and Personality, 36*(3), 229-239.

Stumbrys, T., Erlacher, D., & Malinowski, P. (2015). Meta-awareness during day and night: The relationship between mindfulness and lucid dreaming. *Imagination, Cognition and Personality, 34*(4), 415–433.

Styron, C. W. (2005). Positive psychology: Awakening to the fullness of life. In Germer, C. K., Siegel, R. D., & Fulton, P. R. (Eds.). *Mindfulness and Psychotherapy.* New York: The Guilford Press.

Sullivan, W. (1985, November 18). 6th century manuscript adds to mystery of star. *New York Times,* p. A17. Retrieved on 3/30/2019 from https://www.nytimes.com/1985/11/18/us/6th-century-manuscript-adds-to-mystery-of-star.html

Suzuki, D. T. (1932). *The Lankavatara Sutra: A Mahayana text.* London: George Routledge and Sons. Retrieved on 6/19/22 from https://holybooks-lichtenbergpress.netdna-ssl.com/wp-content/uploads/The-Lankavatara-Sutra-A-Mahayana-Text.pdf

Suzuki, S. (1970/2006). *Zen mind, beginner's mind: Informal talks on Zen meditation and practice.* Boston: Shambhala.

Swarnagiri, R. (1981). *Crumbs from His table.* Tiruvannamalai: Sri Ramanasramam.

SymbolDictionary.net (2019). *Ankh.* Retrieved on 3/29/2019 from http://symboldictionary.net/?p=641

Tafrate, R. C., & Kassinove, H. (1998). Anger control in men: Barb exposure with rational, irrational, and irrelevant self-statements. *Journal of Cognitive Psychotherapy, 12*(3), 187-211.

Tanner, B. A. (2004). Multimodal behavioral treatment of nonrepetitive, treatment resistant nightmares: a case report. *Perceptual and Motor Skills, 99*(3), 1139-1146.

Tart, C. T. (1969). *Altered states of consciousness: A book of readings.* New York: John Wiley & Sons.

Tart, C. T. (1972). *States of consciousness and state-specific sciences. Science, 176,* 1203-1210.

Tart, C. T. (2009). *The end of materialism: How evidence of the paranormal is bringing science and spirit together.* Oakland, CA: New Harbinger Publications.

Taylor, J. G. (1955). Cited in Wolpe (1958), *Psychotherapy by reciprocal inhibition,* p. 230, as a Personal Communication. Retrieved on 6/12/22 from https://archive.org/details/psychotherapybyr0000wolp/page/230/mode/2up?q=taylor

The Hedgehog and the Fox (2022). Retrieved on 6/22/22 from https://en.wikipedia.org/wiki/The_Hedgehog_and_the_Fox

Tholey, P. (1983). Techniques for inducing and manipulating lucid dreams. *Perceptual and Motor Skills, 57,* 79-90.

Tholey, P. (1988a). A model for lucidity training as a means of self-healing and psychological growth. In J. Gackenbach, & S. LaBerge (Eds.), *Conscious Mind, Sleeping Brain* (pp. 263-287). New York: Plenum

Tholey (1988b). Overview of the German research in the field of lucid dreaming. Proceedings of the European Symposium on Lucid Dream Research. *Lucidity Letter, 7*(1). Retrieved on 1/10/21 from https://journals.macewan.ca/lucidity/article/download/804/745

Thompson, J. J., Blair, M. R., & Henrey, A. J. (2014). Over the hill at 24: Persistent age-related cognitive-motor decline in reaction times in an ecologically valid video game task begins in early adulthood. *PLoS ONE 9*(4): e94215. https://doi.org/10.1371/journal.pone.0094215

Thurber, J. (1937/2021). *Let your mind alone.* Victoria, B.C., Canada: Rare Treasures.

Tokenrock.com (2021). *Similarities between the cross section of the brain showing the Pineal Gland and "Eye of Ra."* Retrieved from https://www.tokenrock.com/stock/pg-tokenrock.jpg

Torrey, E. F. (1986). *Witchdoctors and psychiatrists: The common roots of psychotherapy and its future.* Revised Edition of *The Mind Game.* New York: HarperCollins.

Travers, P. L. (1935/1997). *Mary Poppins comes back.* New York: Houghton Mifflin Harcourt Publishing.

Trenholm, R. (2015). *The fascinating story of the man who invented stereo (and pioneered TV and radar too).* CNET.com. Retrieved on 5/21/2022 from https://www.cnet.com/science/meet-alan-blumlein-the-man-who-invented-stereo/

Trungpa, C. (1988). *The myth of freedom and the way of meditation.* Boston: Shambhala. Berkeley, CA: Dharma Publishing.

Tulku, R. (2007). *Mind training. Ithaca,* NY: Snow Lion Publications.

Tulku, T. (1977). *Time, space, and knowledge: A New Vision of Reality.* Emeryville, CA: Dharma Publishing.

Tulku Urgyen Rinpoche, *As It Is, Volume 2.* Hong Kong: Rangjung Yeshe Publications.

van Eeden, F. (1913). A study of dreams. *Proceedings of the Society for Psychical Research, Vol. 26.* Retrieved on 7/4/22 from http://www.lucidity.com/vanEeden.html

Van Gogh (1887). Vincent van Gogh, Public domain, via *Wikimedia Commons.* Retrieved on 8/25/2022 from https://commons.wikimedia.org/wiki/File:Zelfportret_met_pijp_en_strohoed_-_s0163V1962_-_Van_Gogh_Museum.jpg

Van Gogh (1889). Vincent van Gogh, Public domain, via *Wikimedia Commons.* Retrieved on 8/25/2022 from https://commons.wikimedia.org/wiki/File:Van_Gogh_-_Selbstbildnis_mit_verbundenem_Ohr_und_Pfeife.jpeg

Van Lommel, Pim (2011). *Consciousness beyond life: The Science of Near-Death Experience.* New York: Harper-Collins Publishers.

Vanhuffel, H., Rey, M., Lambert, I., Da Fonseca, D., & Bat-Pitault, F. (2018). Apport de la pleine conscience dans les thérapies cognitives et comportementales de l'insomnie. [Contribution of mindfulness meditation in cognitive behavioral therapy for insomnia]. *Ensephale, 44*(2), 134-140.

Varela, F. J. (1997). *Sleeping, dreaming and dying: An Exploration of Consciousness with the Dalai Lama.* Somerville, MA: Wisdom Publications

Vieira, W. (2002). *Projectiology: A panorama of experiences of the consciousness outside the human body.* International Institute of Projectiology and Conscientiology

Voss, U., Holzmann, R., Hobson, A., Paulus, W., Koppehele-Gossel, J., Klimke, A., & Nitsche, M. A. (2014). Induction of self awareness in dreams through frontal low current stimulation of gamma activity. *Nature Neuroscience, 17*(6), 810-812.

Voss, U., Holzmann, R., Tuin, I., & Hobson, A. J. (2009). Lucid dreaming: a state of consciousness with features of both waking and non-lucid dreaming. *Sleep 32*(9), 1191–1200.

Wachowski, L., & Wachowski, L. (1999). *The Matrix*. Warner Bros.

Wade, N. J. (2000). An upright man. *Perception. 29* (3): 253-57.

Wade, N. J. (2009). Beyond body experiences: Phantom limbs, pain and the locus of sensation. *Cortex, 45* (2): 243-55

Waggoner, R. (2016). *The lucid dreaming pack: Gateway to the inner self.* New York: Chartwell Books.

Wallace, M. T,, Meredith, M. A., Stein, B. E. (1998). Multisensory integration in the superior colliculus of the alert cat. *Journal of Neurophysiology, 80* (2), 1006-1010.

Wang, C. X., et al. (2019). Transduction of the geomagnetic field as evidenced from alpha-band activity in the human brain. *eNeuro, 2019 Apr 26; 6*(2).

Wark, C. (2019). *Fluoride: How A toxic poison ended up in our water supply.* Retrieved on 3/31/2019 from https://www.chrisbeatcancer.com/fluoride-is-poison/

Watkins, E. R. (2016). *Rumination-focused cognitive-behavioral therapy for depression.* New York: Guilford Press.

Watkins, M. (1974). The waking dream in European psychotherapy. *Spring*, 33-58.

Watkins, M. (1977). *Waking dreams*. NY: Harper Colophon Books.

Watts, A. (2018). *Alan Watts (June 1, 2018) - Why nothing Is as It seems*. Retrieved on 6/19/2022 from https://youtu.be/JL70y2sA-I

Weale, D. (2016, August 9). the scariest thing I've ever woken up to. *The David Weale Show.* Retrieved on 5/21/2022 from https://youtu.be/WAQZK5qjlOc

Wegner, D. M., Schneider, D. J., Carter, S., III & White, T. (1987). Paradoxical effects of thought suppression. *Journal of Personality and Social Psychology, 53*, 5-13.

Wegner, D. M. (1994). *White bears and other unwanted thoughts: suppression, obsession, and the psychology of mental control.* New York: The Guilford Press.

Wehr, T. A. (1991). The durations of human melatonin secretion and sleep respond to changes in daylength (photoperiod). *Journal of Clinical Endocrinology and Metabolism, 13*, 1276-1280

Wehr, T. A. (1992). In short photoperiods, human sleep is biphasic. *Journal of Sleep Research, 1*, 103-107.

Wei Wu Wei (2002). *Ask the awakened: The negative way.* Boulder, CO: Sentient Publications.

Wellmuth, J. (1944). *The nature and origins of scientism.* Milwaukee, WI: Marquette University Press.

White, J. (1979)(Ed.). *Kundalini, evolution and enlightenment.* Garden City, NY: Anchor Press.

White, J. (2015). *Introduction to ENLIGHTENMENT 101: A guide to God-Realization and higher human culture.* CreateSpace Independent Publishing Platform.

White, J. (2021, February 3). *Toward Homo Noeticus.* Retrieved on 5/28/2022 from https://noetic.org/blog/toward-homo-noeticus/

Wilhelm, R. (1950, Translator). *The secret of the golden flower: A Chinese Book of Life.* London: Routledge & Kegan Paul, LTD.

Wilton, D. (2021, January 13), *Copacetic,* Retrieved on 12/2/22 from https://www.wordorigins.org/big-list-entries/copacetic

Wisconsin Department of Natural Resources (2022). *Living With Black Bears In Wisconsin.* Retrieved on 5/23/2022 from https://p.widencdn.net/io8myi/bearpractice

Wojtek (Bear)(2022). Retrieved on 5/29/2022 from https://en.wikipedia.org/wiki/Wojtek_(bear)

Wolfy (n.d.). *Hubert Blaine Wolfeschlegelsteinhausenbergerdorff Sr.* Retrieved on 1/10/21 from https://en.wikipedia.org/wiki/Hubert_Blaine_Wolfeschlegelsteinhausenbergerdorff_Sr.#cite_note-goldstein-1 Retrieved on 10/28/2020 from https://en.wikipedia.org/wiki/Hubert_Blaine_Wolfeschlegelsteinhausenbergerdorff_Sr.

Wolpe, J. (1958) *Psychotherapy by reciprocal inhibition.* Stanford: Stanford University Press. Retrieved on 6/12/22 from https://archive.org/details/psychotherapybyr0000wolp

Wolpe, J., & Theriault, N. (1971). Franfois Leuret: A progenitor of behavior therapy. *Journal of Behavior Therapy and Experimental Psychiatry, 2,* 19-21.

Wong, R. V. (2021). *Your retina sees backwards.* Retrieved on 2/24/21 from https://retinaeyedoctor.com/2010/03/eye-images-reversed-on-retina/

WorldAtlas.com (2022). *What animals live at the North Pole?* Retrieved on 6/18/22 from https://www.worldatlas.com/articles/what-animals-live-in-the-north-pole.html

Yerkes R. M., & Dodson, J. D. (1908). The relation of strength of stimulus to rapidity of habit-formation. *Journal of Comparative Neurology and Psychology, 18*(5), 459–482. Creative Commons image retrieved on 1/5/21 from https://en.wikipedia.org/wiki/Yerkes%E2%80%93Dodson_law#/media/File:OriginalYerkesDodson.svg

Yogananda, P. (1946). *Autobiography of a Yogi.* NY: Philosophical Library.

Yogananda, p. (1980). *Sayings of Paramahansa Yogananda (1893-1952).* Los Angeles: Self-Realization Fellowship. Retrieved on 6/26/22 from https://archive.org/details/sayingsofparamha00yoga/page/34/mode/2up?q=realization

Young, J. E., & Klosko, J. S. (2003). *Schema therapy: A practitioner's guide.* New York: Guilford.

Young, J. E., Klosko, J. S., & Weishaar, M. E. (2007). *Schema therapy: A practitioner's guide.* New York: Guilford

Young, S. (2011). *Natural pain relief: How to soothe and dissolve physical pain with mindfulness.* Boulder CO: Sounds True.

Yukteswar Giri, Swami Sri (1894/1949). *The holy science.* Yogoda Satsanga Society of India.

Yuschak, T. (2006). *Advanced lucid dreaming: The power of supplements. How to induce high level lucid dreams and out of body experiences.* Raleigh, NC: LULU Enterprises.

Zadra, A. L., & Pihl, R. O. (1997). Lucid dreaming as a treatment for recurrent nightmares. *Psychotherapy and Psychosomatics, 66*, 50-55.

Zen Studies Society (2021). *Heart Sutra.* Retrieved on 1/18/2021 from https://zenstudies.org/wp-content/uploads/2019/04/Daily-Sutras-New.pdf

Zhang, G. X.-L. (2013). *Senses initiated lucid dream (SSILD) Official Tutorial.* Retrieved on 2/24/21 from https://cosmiciron.blogspot.com/2013/01/senses-initiated-lucid-dream-ssild_16.html

The Index of No Index

*"When there is no thought,
the mind experiences happiness."*

(Bhagavan Sri Ramana Maharshi
in *Who Am I*, 1901/1982)

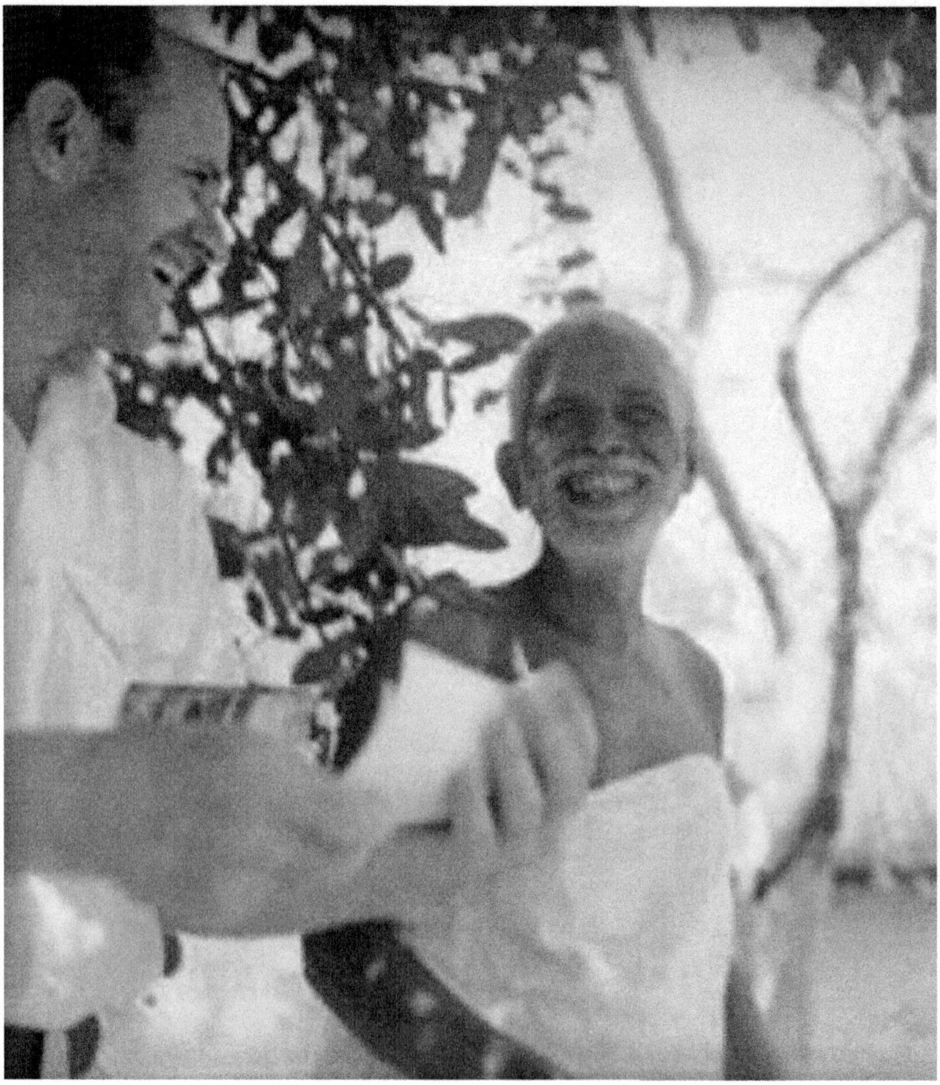

Don't Forget YOUR UMBRELLA

GRANDMA DENSEI, PLACE DE LA CONCORDE

PAGE
UNINTENTIONALLY
LEFT
BLANK

Printed in Great Britain
by Amazon